UNNATURAL MURDER

UNNATURAL MURDER

Poison at the Court of James I

ANNE SOMERSET

Weidenfeld & Nicolson
LONDON

Published in Great Britain in 1997 by
Weidenfeld & Nicolson

The Orion Publishing Group Ltd
Orion House
5 Upper Saint Martin's Lane
London WC2H 9EA

ISBN 0 297 81310 2

A catalogue record for this book is available
from the British Library

Filmset by Selwood Systems, Midsomer Norton
Printed in Great Britain by Butler & Tanner Ltd
Frome and London

In memory of my mother, with love

CONTENTS

ILLUSTRATIONS

Portrait of Thomas Howard, Earl of Suffolk, probably by John Belkamp (From the collection of Lord Sackville at Knole; photo, Courtauld Institute of Art, London)

Engraving of Simon Forman by Godfrey (By courtesy of the National Portrait Gallery, London)

Engraving of Dr Theodore Turquet de Mayerne (By courtesy of the National Portrait Gallery, London)

Sir Edward Coke. Engraving by M. van der Gucht (By courtesy of the National Portrait Gallery, London)

Woodcut of Sir Gervase Elwes (By courtesy of the National Portrait Gallery, London)

Woodcut of Mrs Anne Turner (By courtesy of the National Portrait Gallery, London)

Portrait of George Villiers by William Larkin (By courtesy of the National Portrait Gallery, London)

Letter sent by the Countess of Essex to Sir Gervase Elwes (Public Record Office, London)

AUTHOR'S NOTE

The most famous portrait of Frances, Countess of Somerset is attributed to William Larkin and hangs in London's National Portrait Gallery. Some people have commented that the lady's faint smirk, bold stare and exposed breasts make it easy to believe that she was a murderess steeped in depravity. It should be noted, however, that such low-cut necklines were commonplace at the Jacobean court, and that matrons of unimpeachable virtue were painted revealing a comparable expanse of bosom. Furthermore, it is not absolutely certain that the sitter is the Countess of Somerset. There is an almost identical picture at Woburn Abbey, which is believed to be a portrait of Frances's sister, Catherine, Countess of Salisbury.

King James I's generosity with titles creates difficulties for historians of his reign, as the names of leading court figures alter with bewildering frequency. The main protagonists of this book each changed names three times. Robert Carr was created Viscount Rochester in 1611 and Earl of Somerset in 1613. Lady Frances Howard became Countess of Essex in 1606 and then Countess of Somerset on her remarriage at the end of 1613. Throughout the successive stages of this book I have in general tried to refer to each character by their correct title, but it has not always been possible to adhere to this. For instance, until Chapter Five, I sometimes refer to 'Rochester's trial' when in fact he had become Earl of Somerset by the time he was brought to trial. I hope that readers will understand that I have done this in the hope of avoiding confusion.

Throughout the book I frequently quote financial figures. Obviously, any sum mentioned would have been much larger in today's values. Although this cannot be more than a guideline, it should be noted that the Bank of England estimate that £1 in 1610 would have been worth £80.47 in May 1996.

In Jacobean England, the calendar year was held to start on 25 March. However, I have taken it to begin on 1 January, in accordance with modern usage. In the interests of clarity I have also modernised Jacobean spelling.

I should like to thank the following people for assistance they gave me while writing this book: Dr Harry Boothby, who gave medical advice regarding the death of Overbury; my father-in-law, Sir Raymond Carr, with whom I much enjoyed discussing the Overbury case and whose comments after reading the typescript were extremely helpful; Eddy Chancellor; Dr Neil Cuddy of Toronto University whose expertise on the workings of the Jacobean court was invaluable, and who took immense trouble commenting in detail on the typescript; Professor D.J. Gee, a Fellow of the Royal College of Pathologists who read Chapter Four of this work and who answered numerous enquiries about poisons and other possible causes of the death of Sir Thomas Overbury; Professor Michael A. Green; the Hon. Justice W.M.C. Gummow; Marianne Hinton; Greville and Corty Howard who showed me the Earl of Northampton's almshouses at Castle Rising; Allegra Huston; Peter James, who translated relevant sections from the works of Thomas Aquinas and Canon Law from Latin into English; Douglas Matthews, who compiled the index; Michelle Minto of the Wellcome Institute for the History of Medicine; Roberto Petz, who translated Anna Maria Crino's article from the Italian; Margaret Phillips of Ed Victor Ltd; Patrick Trevor-Roper; Ed Victor, my agent, who, as ever, was unfailingly supportive; Dr Diana Wetherill; Mr Wildman of Trinity Hospital, Greenwich, who showed me the tomb of the Earl of Northampton; my editor, Rebecca Wilson.

I should also like to thank the staff of the following libraries: the Bodleian, Oxford; the British Library; Cambridge University Library; Chester City Record Office; the Folger Shakespeare Library; the Heinz Archive of the National Portrait Gallery; the Huntington Library, California; Lambeth Palace Library; the London Library; the Public Record Office; West Yorkshire Archive Service, Leeds.

Lastly, I should like to thank my husband, Matthew Carr, whose reading of the typescript was just one of many ways he helped me while writing this book.

PROLOGUE

O n 24 May 1616 Frances, Countess of Somerset was put on trial for her life in Westminster Hall. At the age of twenty-five, the Countess was already an infamous figure. The previous January she had been formally indicted as an accessory before the fact to the murder of Sir Thomas Overbury, who in September 1613 had died in agony in the Tower of London. At the time his death had been ascribed to natural causes, but it was now recognised as murder. In the autumn of 1615 a man named Richard Weston had been found guilty of killing Overbury, and he had been hanged shortly afterwards. At Weston's trial the Prosecution had contended that Weston had fed Overbury poisoned tarts and jellies which had been prepared on the Countess of Somerset's directions. When this had failed to kill Sir Thomas, the Countess had allegedly bribed an apothecary's boy to administer Overbury an enema of mercury sublimate, causing death within twenty-four hours.

Other people had also faced capital charges in connection with Overbury's murder. At their trials the Countess's name had been further blackened by a mass of sordid revelations, which had exposed her not only as a poisoner, but as an adulteress who dabbled in black magic. So far three men and one woman had been executed for their part in the conspiracy, but few people doubted that these individuals had merely acted as the agents of the Countess and her husband, whom the Prosecution had described as 'the principal movers' of this 'work of darkness'. For a time there had been fears that these two powerful figures would escape prosecution, and that the authorities would be content to 'make a net to catch little birds and let the great ones go'.[1] Now, however, it appeared that all were to be brought to justice. Like his wife, the Earl of Somerset stood indicted as an accessory to Overbury's murder, and his trial was scheduled to take place the day after hers finished.

The case had excited intense public interest. Prior to the hearing, numerous scaffolds had been erected in Westminster Hall to accommodate the anticipated hordes of spectators. Despite the hall's imposing size, space was at a premium: one man had paid £10 to secure admittance for his wife and himself, and it had cost £50 to reserve 'a corner that could hardly contain a dozen'.[2]

Among the audience was Frances's first husband, Robert, Earl of Essex. He and Frances had married in their early teens, but Essex had found it impossible to consummate the union. In 1613 the marriage had been dissolved amid bitter recriminations, freeing Frances to marry her lover, the Earl of Somerset. Now the woman who had inflicted such humiliation on Essex faced nemesis, and he was savouring the opportunity of seeing her humbled.

The proceedings opened with the utmost solemnity. The Lord Chancellor, who was to preside over the hearing, was conducted to his seat by six sergeants-at-arms, bearing maces. To his left and right sat a row of judges, robed in scarlet. Behind them, the twenty-two noblemen who were to try the Countess had already taken their places. As their names were called in turn, each peer rose to signify his willingness to act as juror, doffing his hat as he did so. Only once these preliminaries had been completed was the prisoner led in to face her accusers. Having taken her place at the bar, she slowly performed three curtsies, first to the Lord Chancellor, who sat opposite her, and then to the peers and judges who were ranged on either side of him.[3]

The Countess was renowned for being one of the most beautiful women in England. One man later wrote of her, 'Those that saw her face might challenge nature of too much hypocrisy for harbouring so wicked a heart under so sweet and bewitching a countenance.' Even now she looked undeniably lovely, despite the fact that in place of the sumptuous, low-cut costumes that had been her customary attire, she was clothed austerely in a black 'gown of ordinary stuff', trimmed with a ruff and cuffs of finest cotton. Looking at her, many of the spectators were moved to pity, but others recalled the words of one miscreant who had gone to the gallows for complicity in Overbury's murder, and who had remarked bitterly of the Countess, 'She was able to bewitch any man.'[4]

When ordered to do so, the Countess held up her right hand for the reading of the indictment. As the charge against her was formally recited, she 'stood, looking pale, trembled, and shed some few tears', shielding her face with her fan when Richard Weston's name was mentioned. When he had finished, the Clerk of the Crown demanded, 'Frances, Countess of Somerset, what sayest thou? Art thou guilty of

this felony and murder, or not guilty?' Making another obeisance to
the Lord Chancellor, the Countess uttered a single word in 'a low
voice ... wondrous fearful': 'Guilty'.[5]

CHAPTER ONE

O n 5 January 1606 a very grand wedding took place in the Chapel Royal, Whitehall. The bride was an extraordinarily beautiful girl of fifteen,[1] named Lady Frances Howard. She was the younger daughter of Thomas Howard, Earl of Suffolk, one of the highest-ranking officials at the court of King James I of England. The groom was Robert Devereux, third Earl of Essex. He was still a few days short of his fifteenth birthday, but he conducted himself so 'gravely and gracefully' that he appeared much older. It was a union between two of the most aristocratic and influential dynasties in England, and the celebrations that marked the occasion reflected this. Not only was the marriage solemnised in the chapel of the King's principal London residence, Whitehall, but King James gave away the bride himself. In attendance were leading members of the nobility and all the most important court dignitaries, and the wedding presents they bestowed on the young couple were unusually lavish. It was afterwards reported that Frances and her husband had received silver plate with a cumulative value of £3,000, as well as jewels, money and a miscellany of other gifts worth £1,000.[2]

The highlight of the festivities that evening was an elaborate masque entitled *Hymenaei*, staged in the Banqueting House, Whitehall. The masque was a traditional form of courtly entertainment, combining music, poetry and dance. Since James I's accession the modest presentations of Queen Elizabeth's days had evolved into much more extravagant spectacles, with vast budgets for costumes and sets. The production put on that night, and paid for by the bride and groom's families and friends, was particularly splendid. The script was written by the playwright Ben Jonson, author of the *Masque of Blackness*, which had been well received when staged at court exactly a year earlier. Jonson's verse was declaimed by professional actors, but the interludes of dancing, to music written by court composer Alfonso Ferrabosco, and choreographed by Thomas Giles, were performed by ladies and gentlemen of the court. What excited the greatest admiration, however, were the costumes, scenery and special effects designed by Inigo Jones. The male dancers were clothed in mantles of different coloured silks, and the ladies in flowing garments of white and silver inspired by statues from classical antiquity. They wore headdresses of herons' feathers embellished with pearls and jewels borrowed from courtiers and wealthy London citizens. So opulent was the effect that 'the Spanish ambassador seemed but poor to the meanest of them'.[3]

Jones's set provided more visual excitement. At the forefront of the stage was a matrimonial altar, and behind that a globe of the earth, with the seas picked out in silver. Vast golden figures were placed on either side of the stage, respectively identified as Atlas and Hercules. On their shoulders these giants supported a region of clouds, and in the midst of this a group of musicians was ensconced.

Taking its theme from the day's events, the masque opened with the re-enactment of the rites of marriage as performed in ancient Rome. Then, after the god of marriage, Hymen, had delivered a speech

> In honour of that blest estate
> Which all good minds should celebrate,

the audience were entranced when the globe swivelled on a hidden pivot and eight gentlemen, representing the humours and affections, were displayed seated in the concave interior. These issued forth, and to the accompaniment of 'contentious music' they performed a menacing dance, apparently intent on disrupting the proceedings over which Hymen benignly presided. At this, however, another superhuman entity, Reason, materialised. She rebuked these obstreperous beings and, duly chastened, they withdrew.

At their departure from the stage the clouds which were held aloft by the great golden statues parted to reveal a still more breathtaking tableau. In the centre of the heavens sat Juno, divine patroness of matrimony, flanked by two of her sacred birds, the peacock. Four female attendants were ranged on either side of her, and these were now lowered gently to the ground, where they in turn performed a graceful display of dancing. The mechanism by which their descent was effected remains unknown, but in some way an optical illusion was created which gave the impression that the statues were bending down to deposit their burdens on the earth, a device received 'with some rapture of the beholders'.[4]

It was fortunate that the audience could not know that Reason would have less success in subduing the 'wild affections' and unruly forces that would undermine the marital harmony of young Lord and Lady Essex. The masque met with widespread acclaim, not merely on account of its uplifting message but also – according to Ben Jonson – because it lacked nothing 'either in richness, or strangeness of the habits [costumes], delicacy of dances or divine rapture of music'.[5]

There was, however, one way in which it was clear that Jonson's paean of praise to matrimony was inapplicable to the ceremony which had preceded it. Although it was asserted in the course of the entertainment that the altar before which the couple had made their vows was

> ... but a sign
> Of one more soft and more divine,
> The genial bed where Hymen keeps
> The solemn orgies, void of sleeps,

it was in fact never intended that the marriage between Frances and Essex should be consummated that night. In early seventeenth-century England the age of consent was twelve for a girl and fourteen for a boy. Nevertheless, although it was legal to marry once those ages had been attained, many people felt that it was inadvisable to do so. In particular, it was widely held that premature sexual activity was dangerously debilitating for young people. Thus when the Earl of Clare was urged that his sixteen-year-old son should be permitted to sleep with his young wife, he expressed fears that this 'unripe marriage' would 'hinder his corporeal growth or proficiency in learning'. Nor was it only young males who were thought to be at risk: in a crusading pamphlet issued in 1620 a clergyman named Alex Niccholes declared that though 'forward virgins' frequently desired to follow their mothers' examples and marry at fourteen or even thirteen, such precipitancy could only result in 'dangerous births, diminution of stature, brevity of life and such like'.[6]

It was largely because of these fears that early marriage was ceasing to be fashionable among the English aristocracy. Whereas in the latter half of the sixteenth century over a fifth of peers' sons were married by the age of seventeen, at the accession of James I in 1603 only about twelve per cent of them had acquired wives when so young.[7]

Nevertheless, the Earl of Suffolk, 'a man never endued with much patience', remained among the minority who thought it desirable that his children should marry at a very early age. As befitted a man who was responsible for the upkeep of seven sons and four daughters ('the youngest and best beloved' of whom died three years after Frances married Essex), he was businesslike about such matters. Fat and genial, and renowned for being 'every way a kind father to his children',[8] he was not so indulgent that he was prepared to let them choose their own partners. Like most men of his class, he thought that marriage was too important a matter to be determined by frivolous considerations like physical attraction or romantic love. At the highest levels of society marriage was expected to bring with it solid advantage, and the wealth and status of prospective partners was of crucial significance when assessing whether or not a match was desirable.

Suffolk's attitude was doubtless conditioned by the fact that he himself had benefited from marrying well. While still in his teens he had fulfilled his father's dying wish by marrying his stepsister Mary Dacre, a wealthy heiress. Five years after Mary's death in 1578 he had married Katherine Knyvet, daughter of Sir Henry Knyvet of Charlton, Wiltshire, whose share in her father's estate was valued at £2,000 a year.[9] Unfortunately Suffolk and his wife both had expensive tastes and consistently overspent, which may well have sharpened his anxiety to procure rich matches for his children.

Few of Suffolk's contemporaries would have criticised him for having the wrong priorities. Although it was a standard theme of preachers that money should not be a primary concern when marriage was contemplated, such exhortations were invariably dismissed as impossibly idealistic. Furthermore, Suffolk's assumption that it was entirely up to him to decide whom his children should marry would not have seemed unduly authoritarian at a time when parental rights extended very far. One seventeenth-century pamphleteer declared that 'Children are so much the goods, the possessions of their parent that they cannot, without a kind of theft, give away themselves without the allowance of those that have the right in them.'[10]

However, although it was frequently reiterated that children should defer to their parents' wishes regarding marriage, in practice young people at the Jacobean court enjoyed a greater degree of independence than had been the case a generation before. In Queen Elizabeth's day severe sanctions were applied if young people eloped. Dismissal from court was automatic and in several cases one or both parties suffered terms of imprisonment. Since the Queen's death in 1603 a more liberal attitude had prevailed. In October 1604 Lady Susan Vere's family were displeased when she announced her engagement to Sir Philip Herbert without consulting them. Nevertheless, they dropped their objections after 'the King, taking the whole matter on himself, made peace on all sides', and the marriage was celebrated with much fanfare ten weeks later. A few years afterwards Sir Thomas Smith's son married Lady Isabella Rich in defiance of his father's wishes. Despite this, the wedding was attended by the Countess of Bedford and 'divers other ladies and persons of account' and the bride was given away by the Earl of Pembroke. A shocked observer commented that it was 'thought a strange thing that so great a man and a counsellor should give countenance to such an action as the robbing a man of his only child ... Sure I have seen the time when such a matter would not have been so carried.' Much as traditionalists deplored these developments, the trend was irreversible, and the fact that on occasion the King took a sentimental pleasure in smoothing the path of young love only accelerated the erosion of parental authority. Wise fathers took heed of the saying 'Marry thy daughters in time lest they marry themselves',[11] and it was perhaps Suffolk's fear that Frances might develop some unsuitable preference of her own that accounted for his urgency about finding her a partner.

Nevertheless, because of the warnings regarding the damage that early sexual intercourse could do to unformed minds and bodies, it was agreed that Frances and her new husband should live apart for some years following their marriage, and that they should delay sleeping together until after their eighteenth birthdays. The arrangement seemed so satisfactory to the Earl of Suffolk that he did likewise when concluding alliances for several of Frances's siblings. In December 1608 her younger sister Katherine was married to Lord Cranborne, eldest son of Lord Salisbury, but the bridegroom departed for a tour of Europe immediately after the wedding. In 1606 Suffolk's eldest son Theophilus married the heiress daughter of the Scots Lord Dunbar, but it was only in 1612, when they had been 'a good while wedded', that the union was consummated. Even then, it seems, the couple were brought together only because the King urged it.[12]

Suffolk evidently considered that he had found the ideal way of upholding his paternal authority without endangering his children's welfare. Unfortunately the system was not without disadvantages. As one contemporary later remarked, at the time of their marriage Frances and her husband were 'too young to consider but old enough to consent'. The years when they were separated were crucial ones in the development of their characters, and it was only when they were reunited that their incompatibility became evident. With hindsight the King, who had been so conspicuous on Frances's wedding day, came to regret his part in the business, and 'fell to inveighing these marryings of young couples before they be acquainted with one another'.[13]

It is not clear whether Frances was consulted at all before arrangements were finalised, but some consideration was given to Essex's feelings. It was later said that Essex had originally been intended for the Suffolks' third daughter, Katherine. In the opinion of at least one person, she would have been 'much the fitter spouse for him', but there was a change of plan after he expressed a preference for her elder sister. The story seems plausible in view of the fact that Frances was a few months older than her husband, and hence not an obvious bride for him. Furthermore, in April 1605 there was gossip at court that Essex and Katherine would be betrothed, and this reportedly occasioned 'great contentment' to Essex's aged grandmother, Lady Leicester. As for Frances, at the time she was expected to marry Lord Roos, and it may well have been at Essex's request that this project was abandoned. At any rate, it was hardly surprising if at this stage he found Frances so appealing. One friend of her family later declared that 'having known her from infancy, he had ever observed her to be of the best nature and the sweetest disposition of all her father's children, exceeding them also in the delicacy and comeliness of her person'.[14] It was only later that Essex would have cause to regret that he had not settled for her sister.

With a pedigree that dated back to Norman times, Essex was sufficiently nobly born to satisfy the requirements of the Howards, who took a fierce pride in the antiquity of their lineage. Nevertheless, while such considerations were far from immaterial to the Lord Chamberlain, his motivation in pursuing the match with Essex was primarily political. It was done, in fact, to help and strengthen Suffolk's most trusted associate, Robert Cecil, Earl of Salisbury, who wished to protect himself from the consequences of actions committed some years earlier.

Towards the end of the reign of King James's predecessor, Queen Elizabeth I, court rivalries had become more bitter and destructive. A struggle for power had developed between the second Earl of Essex – father of the man whom Frances married – and Robert Cecil, the puny and deformed son of England's foremost elder statesman, Lord Treasurer Baron Burghley. Essex was attractive and charming, and the Queen found him delightful company, but she was determined that the court would not be dominated by him. Much as she relished the way he treated her as a romantic icon, she regularly rebuffed his attempts to place protégés of his own in key positions, or to block the advancement of men affiliated with the Cecils. In 1596 Robert Cecil was appointed Principal Secretary of State, dashing Essex's hopes that one of his followers would secure the office. With every failure, Essex grew more frustrated and resentful, convinced that his rivals were using unfair means to circumvent him. In 1599 he volunteered to lead an army to Ireland, but having failed to crush an insurrection there, he deserted his post and came home in the hope of justifying his actions. Having crossed the Irish Sea, he rode at a furious pace to court, arriving mud-stained and bespattered at Nonsuch Palace. Hearing that the Queen had not yet emerged from her bedchamber, he burst in uninvited, surprising her as she was dressing.

After that day, Essex never saw the Queen again. For a time he was placed in confinement and, even when his freedom was restored, he was not permitted to return to court. Denied the financial benefits that access to the Queen had secured him in the past, he feared being bankrupted by his creditors. In these desperate circumstances Essex's behaviour became increasingly wild and irrational. At length, in February 1601, he broke into rebellion. From the start the rising was a fiasco, attracting little support and collapsing within hours. Essex was captured and, after a speedy trial, he was executed on 25 February 1601.

To the public, Essex had always been a hero. Since they blamed Robert Cecil for his downfall (Lord Burghley had died in 1598), the Secretary became an object of hatred throughout the land. Shortly after Essex's return from Ireland, Cecil's unpopularity was such that he had to be accompanied by a bodyguard when he ventured out. Following Essex's execution, he was more widely reviled than ever. Yet, despite the public's profound dislike of him, at court Cecil's position was unassailable. Now that his rival had been eliminated, there was no one to challenge the Secretary's pre-eminence with the Queen, and his hold over policy and patronage became absolute.

Those who remained loyal to Essex's memory could only wait for the day when the childless Elizabeth died, at which time it was confidently expected that her cousin, King James VI of Scotland, would succeed her. Since James had been an admirer of Essex, it was assumed that on his accession he would avenge the late Earl by ousting Cecil from power. Yet to a man like Cecil, who from his earliest youth had been 'nourished with the milk of policy',[15] the situation was not irretrievable. After Essex's execution he entered into secret communication with King James. He earned the King's gratitude by advising him on his dealings with Queen Elizabeth and undertook that, when the time came, he would see that the transference of power went smoothly. When Elizabeth died, in March 1603, Cecil had performed all that he had promised. James was so delighted at the efficient way that England's sovereignty had been vested in him that there was no longer any question of his discarding Cecil.

Having been confirmed in his position of Principal Secretary of State, on 13 May 1603 Cecil was created Baron Cecil of Essenden. The following year, in August, the title of Viscount Cranborne was conferred on him. Nine months later he was raised still higher in the peerage when he was created Earl of Salisbury. Finally, on 6 May 1608 he became Lord Treasurer of England. The King not only appreciated Salisbury's shrewd grasp of policy and untiring industry, but he enjoyed his company, for the Lord Treasurer had a sly sense of humour and knew how to amuse his master. In 1609 James paid him the supreme tribute of declaring, 'I believe not a King in the world has such a Secretary as I have, both for earnest matter and great affairs and also for jest.'[16]

Salisbury's continued dominance of the political scene naturally disappointed the adherents of the second Earl of Essex. It was true that, following his accession, King James had taken steps to vindicate the executed man. On his journey south from Scotland the King gave a warm welcome to Essex's twelve-year-old son. He 'kissed him openly ... loudly declaring him the son of the most noble knight that English land has ever begotten'. In the hope that the boy would become 'the eternal companion' of his own eldest son, he decreed that henceforth they should be brought up together. The following July the King restored young Essex's titles and the property which had been alienated to the Crown on his father's conviction for treason. Yet this was scant consolation for the late Earl's former followers. Chief among these was the Earl of Southampton, who had only narrowly escaped execution for his part in the rising of 1601. James freed him from the Tower, but he did not give him a seat on the Privy Council. In years to come Southampton and others associated with him remained firmly excluded from power.[17]

Salisbury could justly congratulate himself on the way he had weathered the difficult transitional period. Nevertheless, he was aware that his future was far from secure. He feared that when the young Earl of Essex reached adulthood, he would harbour a grudge against him for his father's execution. Once Essex attained his majority he would be the natural figurehead for all those who resented Salisbury's pre-eminence, and with these men behind him he might turn into a formidable political opponent. Anxious to prevent this destructive factional feud from perpetuating itself into the next generation, Salisbury decided that some means must be found of making Essex identify himself with the party in power.

His solution was to promote the marriage between Essex and Lady

Frances Howard. The bride's father was on the closest possible terms with Salisbury: in his will Salisbury went so far as to declare that he thought it 'the felicity of his life to exchange his dearest thoughts with him whenever he had cause to use and trust a friend'.[18] Salisbury calculated that if Essex became the son-in-law of this devoted colleague, the young man would automatically be drawn into his own political circle, and hence would cease to constitute a threat. Suffolk was all in favour of the scheme, particularly when it emerged that the King himself warmly approved.

The Earl of Suffolk had at least one thing in common with his future son-in-law. In 1572, when he had been eleven years old, his father, the fourth Duke of Norfolk, had been beheaded for treason by Queen Elizabeth. At the time it had seemed that the prospects of the then Lord Thomas Howard had been permanently blighted. Admittedly he had not forfeited his entire inheritance, as happened to the offspring of most men convicted of treason. Though the Duke of Norfolk's own lands were all seized by the Crown, his son was allowed to retain his estate at Audley End in Essex which had been bequeathed to him by his mother. However, he had to work hard to obliterate the memory of his father's disloyalty. On attaining his majority Howard had sought to commend himself to Elizabeth by serving in the navy. In 1588 he had distinguished himself in the fight against the Armada, and three years later he was made commander of the squadron which attempted to waylay the Spanish treasure fleet at the Azores. The venture ended in failure, but the Queen was evidently not one of those who held Howard responsible, for on his return she made him a Knight of the Garter. In 1596 and 1597 Howard served on two more overseas expeditions, and Elizabeth signalled her gratitude to the man she now called 'Good Thomas' by cautiously releasing to him small portions of the lands confiscated from his father. In 1597 he was permitted to take a seat in the House of Lords under the title Lord Howard de Walden, and towards the end of Elizabeth's reign Howard was also granted the right to collect the customs imposed on gold and silver thread imported into England. But though at the Queen's death one of Howard's friends congratulated him on having 'felt her sweet bounties in full source and good favour', in some respects his position remained far from enviable. Whenever he had participated in naval expeditions it had cost him a great deal of money, and he had never managed to recoup these investments. Such losses, combined with his extravagant lifestyle and the necessity of supporting a large family, meant that he had become so deeply in debt that he had to sell off some of his lands to survive.[19]

It was James I's accession to the throne that brought about a
transformation in Howard's circumstances. When Thomas and his
brother were first presented to the King by their uncle, James exclaimed
effusively, 'Here be two of your nephews, both Howards. I love the
whole house of them.'[20] On 6 April 1603, less than a fortnight after
James's accession, Howard was appointed Lord Chamberlain, and thus
became one of the most senior officers at court. The King's carvers,
cupbearers, Grooms of the Privy Chamber and Gentlemen Pensioners
were just some of the royal servants who came under the jurisdiction of
the Lord Chamberlain, and he also bore ultimate responsibility for the
organisation of the royal progresses and the provision of entertainment
for the monarch. It was a position that carried with it enormous prestige,
and was valued not merely on this account but also because the Lord
Chamberlain's duties brought him into frequent contact with the King.
He was hence extremely well placed to prefer suits to James, both on
behalf of himself and others. In May 1603 Howard became a member
of the Privy Council, the advisory body that played a key part in both
the formulation and execution of royal policy. Three months later he
received a further mark of royal esteem when he was created Earl of
Suffolk.

The King also conferred material benefits on Suffolk. Not only was
the Earl permitted to retain his revenues deriving from gold and silver
thread, but in 1604 he was granted the profits arising from customs
duties levied on imported currants. After paying his rent to the Crown,
this brought him £678 a year. More significant still was the restitution
of family property in East Anglia and Shropshire seized by the Crown
from the Duke of Norfolk. This was a great coup for Suffolk for, as his
father's second son, he had never stood to inherit much of this. In the
normal course of events the land would have passed to Suffolk's nephew,
the Earl of Arundel, but now these extensive holdings were divided
between Suffolk and his uncle. On learning that the King was thinking
of granting him these estates Suffolk had declared, 'My meaning is not
to prejudice my nephew in anything, but happily to help myself a little
without his harm.'[21] Understandably, however, Arundel was annoyed at
the way his claims had been overlooked.

A few years before, Suffolk had only narrowly averted having his
mortgaged properties seized by creditors; now he felt confident enough
to acquire new estates. Between 1604 and 1608 he purchased land worth
£13,000, but this was by no means his most extravagant commitment.
Around 1605 he started work on a colossal building project at his Essex
estate, Audley End. There Suffolk constructed a stupendous new

residence, its design inspired by engravings of the French Château de Verneuil. It was originally intended that the house should be built around a single courtyard, but while work was in progress Suffolk's conception became more grandiose and an outer court, with an impressive arcaded loggia, was added. When completed, Audley End was easily England's largest house in private hands. It occupied a total of five acres and was furnished with treasures such as the specially commissioned series of tapestries of Hannibal and Scipio, woven by Francis Spiering of Delft. In anticipation of royal visits it was equipped with matching suites of state rooms so that separate accommodation could be provided for the King and Queen. Suffolk allegedly declared that in all he spent £200,000 on Audley End. While this seems to have been something of an exaggeration, the house and its contents probably did cost him at least £80,000. Despite Suffolk's enlarged income, this was a sum beyond his means. It was chiefly to pay for this excessive undertaking that the man whom the King once delighted to call 'honest big Suffolk' would ultimately be driven into massive fraud.[22]

In the years following his accession King James sometimes joked that England was now ruled by 'a trinity of knaves', by which he meant Salisbury, Suffolk, and Suffolk's uncle, Henry Howard. The third member of this triumvirate was a complex and intriguing figure, infinitely cleverer than Suffolk, who in comparison to his uncle was 'a spirit of more grosser temper'. By the time James came to the throne Howard was already in his early sixties, but the advancing years had not softened his appearance, which remained so strikingly saturnine that the King described him as being 'tall, black and coal-faced'. Like so many of his family, Howard had endured periods of great adversity, and this had shaped his personality in strange ways. When young Henry was only six, his father had been executed by Henry VIII. His grandfather, the third Duke of Norfolk, had been incarcerated in the Tower but, on the accession of Mary Tudor, the family was rehabilitated. When the old Duke died, Henry Howard's elder brother succeeded him as fourth Duke of Norfolk. The Howards remained in favour when Queen Elizabeth ascended the throne. It was the Queen who paid for Lord Henry Howard's studies when he read civil law at King's College, Cambridge. There Howard proved himself a brilliant scholar, emerging fluent in Latin, Greek, Spanish, French and Italian, and with a wide knowledge of history, theology and philosophy. Having taken his degree, Howard became the only nobleman in England to pursue an academic career, accepting a place as a Reader in Rhetoric at the university. Although one disgruntled contemporary remarked that his learning 'rendered him no less tedious to the wise than unintelligible to the ignorant', there was no denying its profundity.[23]

Then, in 1572 the fortunes of the Howards were one again reversed. Lord Henry's brother, the Duke of Norfolk, was convicted of treason after becoming involved in a conspiracy in support of the imprisoned Mary, Queen of Scots, and in June he was executed. Some people believed that it was Lord Henry who had persuaded his brother to participate in the misguided venture, and that Norfolk would never have met a traitor's death had it not been for Howard's 'practising and double undoing'. Certainly Howard was known to be one of Queen Mary's sympathisers, and even after his brother's execution he maintained illicit contacts with her. His activities aroused the suspicions of the authorities, and on five separate occasions he was arrested and questioned about his links with Mary Stuart. While formal charges were never preferred, he suffered the indignity of being imprisoned for short periods.[24]

Although Howard's behaviour was scarcely calculated to endear him to those in power, he was deeply resentful at being kept from what he called 'the place by birth my due'. Believing passionately that he was entitled to high office both by virtue of his aristocratic descent and his undoubted abilities, he argued that nothing had ever been proved against him which could act as a bar to future advancement. He sought to ingratiate himself with Elizabeth by writing slavish propaganda pieces, but these nauseating productions accorded ill with his record as an intriguer, and merely increased his reputation for being disingenuous and untrustworthy. To his disgust he remained as far from royal favour 'as others are distant from America', obliged to endure 'contempt, oblivion and secret nips'. Much later he would indignantly recall that 'I was branded with the mark of reprobation ... I was esteemed, and termed, a man dangerous', and the humiliations and privations he experienced during these years left him permanently twisted and embittered. With his exaggerated sense of hierarchy he found it intolerable that a member of a ducal family like himself should be reduced to eking out a miserable existence in a garret, living on charity doled out sparingly by his sister, Lady Berkeley. Yet he realised that it was only by dissembling his fury that he could have any hope of ameliorating his lot, and 'this unsuitable condition, to a mind to its own apprehension capable of the highest employment, acquainted him with a subtle kind of stalking towards all, though but in small or trivial things, as rendered what he did suspected of design'. Subterfuge and deception became an indelible habit, and the behaviour patterns he acquired in this way left him of 'so venomous and cankered a disposition that indeed he hated all men of noble parts, nor loved any but flatterers like himself'.[25]

About 1597 Howard's dispiriting existence was suddenly transformed. Declaring that the treatment meted out to him because of his suspected links with Mary Stuart had been 'too mean and too heavy for a man that had so clearly freed himself from imputation in all', Queen Elizabeth invited him to kiss her hand. As Howard later recalled, she assured him that 'as my misfortunes had sprung wholly from the spleens of others, so my satisfaction should grow from her self', and certainly from that day forwards the Queen manifested a marked fondness for him. Her own impressive education meant that she appreciated Howard's great learning, and she enjoyed exchanging scholarly badinage with him.

Howard now had endless opportunities to deliver the inflated compliments which were his trademark, all overlaid with an erudite gloss which prevented the flattery from seeming too crude. Elizabeth became so devoted to him that when she visited her hunting lodge at Oatlands during the wet autumn of 1600, she would not hear of Howard spending the night in a tent in the garden – the only accommodation on offer for the majority of the court – but instead 'commanded his bed should be set up in the Council Chamber'. Two years later Lord Henry wrote complacently, 'Queen Elizabeth never used me in my life so well as she doth now, making a poor use of my aptness for her humour of recreation and jollity, for which I am only fit, being otherwise unable to sound the deeps of her capacity.'[26]

Things were obviously going much better for Lord Henry, but he was still irked that real power continued to elude him. Determined that in future he should have a role with genuine substance, he initiated a secret correspondence with James VI of Scotland, signing himself '3' in order to keep his identity secret if the letters fell into the wrong hands. His letters were well received. James was 'a great lover of subtle conceits' and, though at times even he found his correspondent's tortuous style excessively 'Asiatic', he relished Lord Henry's malicious humour, and the way his prose was heavily larded with biblical allusions and apt quotations from the classics.[27]

By the time that Sir Robert Cecil started cultivating the King on his own account, James had already formed a high opinion of Lord Henry. Since it was obviously difficult for a man in Cecil's position to maintain frequent contact with the sovereign of a foreign country, James suggested that Howard should act as an intermediary, and to this Cecil gladly assented. In many ways Lord Henry was the perfect instrument for his purposes, for Cecil not only wished to establish himself on good terms with his future ruler, but also to undermine the men he feared would otherwise become his political rivals once James was King of England. Although Cecil affected a becoming reluctance to denigrate colleagues who were ostensibly friends of his, he knew that Lord Henry would be only too happy to do the job for him, for beneath Howard's abject and fawning manner there lurked a seldom-equalled talent for vilification. On Cecil's instructions, vicious attacks on Sir Walter Ralegh, Lord Cobham and the Earl of Northumberland became standard features of Lord Henry's letters to King James. All the bile he had accumulated from the degradations and disappointments of his career to date now came flooding out in a stream of invective. He warned James that this 'damned crew' – a favourite phrase to describe enemies and one which he would use again on numerous occasions – were intriguing to prevent his accession to the throne. What was even more insidious, however, was the way he employed repellent imagery calculated to inspire James with a physical abhorrence of the unfortunate trio. He wrote with loathing of 'Cobham and Ralegh and their complices, who hover in the air for an advantage, as kites do for carrion', and claimed that the meetings of 'this diabolical triplicity' had aroused alarmed conjecture regarding 'what chickens they could hatch out of these cockatrice eggs that were daily and nightly sitten on'.[28]

When James ascended the throne, the power of Howard's vindictive pen became plain. The King immediately dismissed Sir Walter Ralegh from his post of Captain of the Guard, deprived him of his main sources of income, and evicted him from Durham House, which Sir Walter rented from the Crown. In July 1603 Ralegh and Lord Cobham were arrested on suspicion of treason and, despite the paucity of evidence against them, the following November they were found guilty and condemned to death. The sentence was not carried out as scheduled, but the two men remained in the Tower. For a time Northumberland fared better, being made a Privy Councillor and Captain of the Gentlemen Pensioners, but in November 1605 he too was sent to the Tower after being tenuously linked with the Gunpowder Plot.

In contrast with his luckless victims, Lord Henry prospered as never before. Within a year of James's accession he had been made a Privy Councillor, awarded the lucrative post of Warden of the Cinque Ports and raised to the peerage as Earl of Northampton. Having attained the power he craved, he revealed many statesmanlike qualities, and worked hard to uphold what he conceived to be the King's best interests. And yet, mindful of the vicissitudes he had experienced in the past, he could not believe that merit alone would suffice to keep him in a position of such eminence. Terrified that he would once again revert to being a despised outcast, he guarded against this obsessively, using the weapons he had already deployed to such devastating effect, namely, sycophancy and underhand attacks. He became 'famous for secret insinuation and fortuning flatteries, and by reason of those qualities became a fit man for the condition of these times'.[29]

Determined to prevent himself being superseded, he took every opportunity to weaken potential rivals, while nevertheless eschewing direct confrontations. His letters were full of wicked innuendoes and snide attacks on colleagues and though, taken individually, these did not seem of great significance, the cumulative effect was undoubtedly pernicious. A favourite trick was to loosen the ties of obligation that connected court grandees to lesser men. For example, Northampton particularly disliked the Lord Admiral of England, the Earl of Nottingham. He made no allowances for the fact that they were cousins, for he once remarked that it was 'very seldom in this age for kinship and friendship to concur'. In 1605 Northampton wrote sorrowfully to the English ambassador in Spain, Sir Charles Cornwallis, deploring Nottingham's conduct. He explained that, despite Nottingham's promises to try to secure Cornwallis a higher rate of pay, the Lord Admiral 'never stroke one stroke since that time (which is too long), though others that used not so many words have fought more manfully. I have begun the motion . . .' Several years later he acted to prevent Nottingham from appointing his eldest son Vice-Admiral of the navy. Northampton commented that the navy was already run very inefficiently, for Nottingham's experience was not matched by 'integrity or understanding'. Spitefully he added that Nottingham's son, 'that wants all three', would make things immeasurably worse. Northampton might maintain that in making such observations he had his country's welfare at heart, but those who knew him believed that his motivation was personal, and that he acted out of 'spleen'.[30]

Northampton's relations with Salisbury were ambivalent. He resented the fact that the Lord Treasurer reserved the choicest offices in the court and administration for his own friends. Occasionally he tried to overturn Salisbury's arrangements, as in 1611, when he attempted to oust the men the latter had chosen to run the customs with a nominee of his own. Nevertheless, when Salisbury reacted sharply to this, Northampton hastily retreated, for the Lord Treasurer was too powerful to risk permanently antagonising. He once disarmingly assured Salisbury that, although many people would be pleased if they fell out, a mutual 'affection to our master, regard of our own duty, love to the public ... hath drawn both of us to that ... fastness in affection and correspondent love which shuts up the gate to the Trojan horse'. Salisbury knew better than to take this seriously: he was so wary of Northampton that, when absent from court, he employed men to keep him informed of the Earl's activities. He hoped that in this way he would find out if Northampton was intriguing against him and, thus forewarned, would be able to take pre-emptive action.[31]

The wisdom of such precautions was demonstrated when Salisbury died in May 1612. At last Northampton was free to voice his real feelings without fear of retribution. He wrote with glee to inform an associate of 'the death of the little man, for which so many rejoice, and so few do so much as seem to be sorry'. Now that the Lord Treasurer could no longer defend himself, Northampton was happy to accuse him of a variety of failings, including corruption.[32]

Towards the King, Northampton – who once had the gall to describe himself as 'one that will die before he flatter' – displayed almost limitless obsequiousness. On one occasion he fulsomely thanked the King for writing to him, asking in wonder, 'How can a lowly vassal expect so great a favour from a prince so potent, or a prince so potent cast down his eyes so low upon so poor a vassal?' Grovellingly he continued, 'Your Majesty ... may be confident that when you stroke my head with favour I kiss your hand, when you strike me on the head I kiss the rod, and whether you stroke or strike I learn of the lowly camel to receive my load with bended knee.'[33]

King James was highly susceptible to such an approach. It was true that when in Scotland he had advised his eldest son always to pick servants 'free of that filthy vice of flattery, the pest of all princes and wreck of republics', but he failed to keep his own injunction. Perhaps one reason why he found flattery so irresistible was that his Scots subjects – whom James variously described as 'barbarous and stiff-necked' and 'men not of the best temper' – were less prone to sycophancy than their English counterparts. For the King, therefore, receiving such mannered tributes was an agreeably novel experience. A mere three months after James inherited his new throne one English observer was sufficiently concerned by the way the King revelled in the adulation accorded him that he noted, 'I pray unfeignedly that ... the painted flattery of the court [does not] cause him to forget himself.'[34]

His prayer went unanswered. Far from growing immune to flattery, James grew to expect flamboyant praise from those who surrounded him, and his courtiers adapted their conduct accordingly. The Earl of Suffolk, who as Lord Chamberlain was well placed to observe the phenomenon, secretly counselled an old friend that if he wished to extract favours from James, he must be ready to deliver extravagant eulogies on all things in which the King took pride. In particular, he urged him to extol the good qualities of the King's new horse, a roan jennet with which he was very pleased. Suffolk explained that when a nobleman who had failed to observe such preliminaries had recently presented a petition to the King, it was unceremoniously rejected. 'Will you say the moon shineth all summer?' Suffolk asked wryly. 'That the roan jennet surpasses Bucephalus and is worthy to be bestridden by Alexander? That his eyes are fire, his tail is Berenice's locks, and a few more such fancies worthy your noticing?'[35]

When it came to idolatry of the King, no one surpassed the Earl of Northampton. James himself could not but be aware that there were times when the Earl laid it on very thick: he once genially admitted, 'Set another leg as well made beside mine, I warrant you 3 [Northampton] will swear the King's sweet leg is far the finest.' And yet he still found Northampton's blandishments irresistible. On one occasion Northampton was present when the King gave an audience to Sir Thomas Smith, who was about to take up a post as English ambassador in Russia. James remarked, 'It seems Sir Thomas goes from the sun,' whereupon Northampton seized upon the commonplace observation to declare, 'He must needs go from the sun, departing from your resplendent Majesty.' An observer reported that James was visibly pleased by the interruption.[36]

Many people considered that Northampton was guilty of a far worse sin than mere sycophancy. In the past he had rightly been suspected of being a crypto-Catholic but, in the indignant words of a contemporary, 'To keep himself capable of honours and preferments at court (of which he was the most liquorish man living ...) he dissembled the contrary.' Before conferring high office on the then Lord Henry Howard, James had required him to take the Oath of Supremacy, disavowing papal authority. This may perhaps have caused Howard momentary disquiet, but he had swiftly overcome his scruples. He even capitalised on his crisis of conscience to ingratiate himself further with James, declaring winningly that his decision to conform owed more to 'the example of the king ... than the disputes of theologians'. However, having gained what he wanted, Northampton scarcely troubled to conceal that his conversion had been purely superficial. Once, when requesting a favour from the Countess of Shrewsbury, he declared slyly that such an overture came naturally to him for, 'being very much accustomed in old time to crave our Lady's intercession to our Lord, I have much ado to discontinue this superstitious custom yet, notwithstanding all the learned preachers I have heard speak before the King'.[37]

Northampton's religious inclinations naturally predisposed him towards drawing closer to Spain, the most strongly Catholic of the continental great powers. In 1604 he was among the commissioners who negotiated peace with Spain, bringing to an end a conflict which had lasted almost twenty years. Thereafter he always reacted furiously if there was talk of renewing a war which, even in the late Queen's day, had proved an appalling drain on national resources. Yet, though Northampton was correct in arguing that peace was desirable, it was also in his own interests to support such a policy. Following the conclusion of the treaty Northampton had been awarded an annual pension by the Spanish, which he pocketed without embarrassment.

It is only fair to set Northampton's behaviour in context. He was by no means the only influential figure at the Jacobean court to take money from Spain. The Earl of Salisbury himself received an annual payment which, at £1,500, was slightly larger than that given to Northampton. The Spaniards' expectations of their pensioners were very modest: the grant to Salisbury, who was far from well disposed towards them, was justified on the fatalistic grounds that he would be still more hostile if deprived of it. Northampton, it is true, was more friendly towards the Spanish. He had frequent dealings with their ambassador, who always referred to him in his despatches by the codename of 'El Cid'. Nevertheless, his helpful attitude should not be ascribed solely to the fact that he was in the pay of the Spaniards. His pension was frequently in arrears, but this does not seem to have bothered him unduly, and his attempts to improve relations with Spain doubtless stemmed from a genuine conviction that this was in the best interest of his country.

Although Northampton never informed the King of his financial links with the Spaniards, James had a relaxed attitude about such matters. In December 1613 the King learned through his ambassador in Madrid that prominent members of his court were in receipt of Spanish pensions. He took no action against those named, apparently believing that their acceptance of the money did not create a conflict of interests. He was probably correct: one of the Spanish ambassadors who dispensed the cash told his masters that it was an entirely futile exercise, and that the money would be better spent building up the Spanish navy.[38]

Not everyone was so tolerant as King James. However closely Northampton guarded his secret that he was in the pay of Spain, the fact that he favoured friendly relations with that country was sufficient to damn him in the eyes of some people. To militant English Protestants Spain remained the national enemy, and Northampton's attitude convinced them that he was not a loyal patriot. Men such as these looked on it as an abomination that the King allowed such power to a man whose adherence to the Church of England was, at best, ambivalent. It was even alleged that after Northampton had presided at the trials of the gunpowder plotters, he had apologised to the Vatican, claiming he had acted under duress. There were also persistent rumours that he used his position as Warden of the Cinque Ports to let Catholic priests slip undetected into the country. Northampton took vigorous action through the courts to quash these claims – which were, in fact, baseless – but his recourse to law had the unfortunate consequence of giving them further publicity. Certainly the Archbishop of Canterbury, Richard Bancroft, was unimpressed by Northampton's attempts to vindicate himself. In 1610 he was so enraged by reports that the Earl was urging the King to moderate the persecution of English Catholics that he burst out to James 'that he should not trust some councillors since they were never seen to assist at the communion supper', naming Northampton as one of the guilty parties.[39]

The Earl of Suffolk much respected his uncle's intellect, and doubtless consulted him before proceeding with his daughter's marriage. Northampton undoubtedly had great hopes of the benefits it would bring. While discussions between the young couple's families were still in progress, he prophesied that it would heal the divisions that had split the court in the past. In Northampton's words, 'Now the roots being very likely to unite, the branches must accord.'

Others were equally excited at the prospect of the impending reconciliation. When the first moves were made, one of those who had been aligned with Essex in Queen Elizabeth's day wrote joyfully, 'I begin to observe some kindness ... where much strangeness was before. I trust God will unite us together, this time of union [between Scotland and England] is fitting for it.'

Negotiations took several months as such matters as the size of the bride's dowry (which was eventually fixed at £6,000), and the income that would be settled on her if she was widowed, had to be agreed.[40] Nevertheless, by October 1605 these matters had been arranged, and the wedding was delayed until the following January only to enable the King to attend.

It had been decided in advance that for some years after the wedding,

Frances and her husband should live apart. It is not clear exactly how Essex occupied himself in the eighteen months following his marriage. He had already attended Eton and Oxford, gaining a Master's degree from Merton College in 1605. Presumably he took this opportunity to pursue his studies further. Then, in the summer of 1607, when he was aged sixteen, he set out on a grand tour of Europe, and during the next year and a half he visited the Netherlands, Germany and France. In Paris he was received by the French King, Henry IV, who had fond memories of the late Earl of Essex from the days when both had been involved in the war against Spain. In the Netherlands he met with Maurice of Nassau, another great military leader who had campaigned alongside his father. Elsewhere, diplomats and merchants exerted themselves to entertain the young peer.

While abroad Essex sent the King's eldest son Prince Henry several letters, whose dutiful but dull contents suggest that, despite the fact they had spent so much time together, they had never become close. He also politely sent his father-in-law a gift of wild boar meat from Flushing, but if he wrote to Frances, the text has not survived. We know, however, that while on his travels he sent her a valuable ring, for Frances would subsequently put this to sinister use.

Meanwhile, as befitted her status as a married woman (albeit one whose marriage was as yet in name only), Frances assumed her place at court. She was chaperoned by her mother, Katherine, Countess of Suffolk, by no means a person ideally fitted to supervise an impressionable young girl. It is true that Lady Suffolk seems to have had the knack of making life enjoyable for the young. In 1606 the Earl of Salisbury's daughter, Lady Frances Cecil, wrote entreating her father for permission to spend more time with the Countess of Suffolk and her children, 'for there is no place I desire so much to be in as with her and my Lady Katherine [Howard] and the rest'. But, while Lady Suffolk could teach her daughter a great deal about the pursuit of pleasure, her moral sense was not so highly developed. A French diplomat who encountered her wrote in his memoirs that she was an assertive woman who dominated her husband, describing her as 'witty, scheming, ambitious and indiscreet'. She was also financially rapacious and, though it is not clear whether at this time she was already enriching herself by exploiting her husband's proximity to the King, she certainly did so at a later stage in her career.

In 1614 Suffolk was appointed Lord Treasurer, but four years later he was dismissed and he and his wife were charged with embezzlement. When the case was heard in the autumn of 1619 it emerged that it was

Lady Suffolk who had instigated various corrupt transactions, including misappropriating funds destined for the army in Ireland and extorting money from England's leading trading company, the Merchant Adventurers. Furthermore, when creditors of the Crown had applied to the exchequer for payment, they had been told by Lady Suffolk that no money would be forthcoming unless they offered her a substantial bribe. Extracts from Lady Suffolk's letters, described as 'impious in style and odious in matter', were read out in court but, despite the wealth of evidence against her, she refused to admit her guilt. Instead, as the Prosecution put it, 'If she yielded in anything brought against her, it was but as the mouse would do, being in the cat's mouth.'[41] At the end of the trial, she and her husband were found guilty and sentenced to pay large fines. Of course, when Frances first came to court these events were still far in the future, but a brief acquaintance with Lady Suffolk's methods of business does help to explain the sort of woman she was.

According to Sir Anthony Weldon, an exceptionally malicious authority, the Countess of Suffolk was the Earl of Salisbury's mistress. Certainly they were very close: early in James's reign she was described as one of his 'great favourites'. She was also believed to have great influence over him, so much so, indeed, that in 1610 the Spanish ambassador could declare, 'She is the one who manages Salisbury.' On the other hand it does seem hard to credit that Salisbury could have an affair with the wife of a man for whom he professed the deepest affection. Towards the end of his life Salisbury wrote that in his dealings with Suffolk, 'this heart of mine did never offend in thought since my first contract of friendship with him', and such a solemn declaration would hardly have been consistent with cuckolding him on a long-term basis. However, in his memoirs the French diplomat the Comte de Tillières claimed that Suffolk was a *mari complaisant*, and that Lady Suffolk 'managed things in such a way that her husband shared her contentment'. There are signs that the King had heard of the connection, and that the contemplation of this cosy triangle afforded him sly pleasure. In 1604 he sent Cecil a somewhat obscure letter in which he teased him for being 'wanton and wifeless' and then added, 'I know Suffolk is married and hath also his hands full now in harbouring that great little proud man that comes in his chair.' In French, 'chair' means 'flesh', so James may well have been making a bawdy pun at the expense of the Lord Chamberlain.[42]

According to a person familiar with her habits, the Countess of Suffolk 'never received the communion', and in this her daughter Frances emulated her. Lady Suffolk herself told the Spanish ambassador that she was not happy in the Church of England, and promised that she would die a Catholic;[43] it seems more likely that she was not a deeply spiritual person. As with the Earl of Northampton, Lady Suffolk's lack of enthusiasm for Anglicanism was coupled with leanings towards Spain. She was one of the most valued informants of successive Spanish ambassadors, who referred to her in their despatches under the codename 'Roldan'.

It must be stressed that, though the Spaniards felt they benefited from the connection, these activities of hers were often far from detrimental to England. She urged the Spaniards to grant English merchants the right to trade in their New World colonies, she protested about the Spanish Inquisition's victimisation of English sailors, and she objected to the colleges set up in Spain to train missionaries to send to England. Yet it would be misguided to suggest she acted out of idealism for, as she herself admitted, her motives were primarily venal. Over the years she did very well out of her connection with the Spaniards, who were prepared to pay large sums in return for her cooperation. In 1606 a Spanish ambassador wrote home, 'The sauce for Roldan is money, as she told me. We have to proceed according to "Give me" and she takes it.' After the conclusion of the peace treaty of 1604 Lady Suffolk received slightly less than £4,500 in cash from the Spaniards, plus jewels worth nearly £4,000. Anxious to milk them of even more, she put forward a proposal that her paymasters should hand over an additional sum approaching £48,000. She proposed to use this to alleviate the sufferings of the English Catholics by paying the fines imposed on them. The Spaniards initially showed interest, but at least one of Philip III's councillors was fearful that Lady Suffolk would not really spend the money on the Catholics, but would simply appropriate it for herself. In view of these reservations it was perhaps not surprising that the scheme ultimately came to nothing.[44]

The Earl of Suffolk did not receive direct payments from the Spaniards, preferring that such matters should be handled by his wife. In 1605 he even declared himself 'infinitely wronged' when he heard it was being said that 'we Howards should be principal means about his Majesty to draw him ... to incline to Spaniards'. While conceding that other members of his family should be left 'to answer for their own affections', he vowed 'before God, I have no inclination to the Spaniard more than the necessity of my mere service draws me to'. Lamenting his 'ill hap' in being 'made much Spanish in opinion', he added, 'This is a burthen that I would fain throw off,' but since he could hardly have failed to be aware of the rewards received by his wife for services to Spain, the injury done him was not so monstrous as it seemed to him.[45]

With her mother as a mentor, Frances would scarcely have been encouraged to place a premium on qualities such as self-restraint and piety. After Frances was dead moralists would also argue that her character was inevitably adversely affected because she spent her formative years in the corrupting environment of the court. It was a commonplace that courts were pernicious places where honour and integrity were unknown, and only the most unscrupulous individuals flourished. In Queen Elizabeth's day the court was described as 'a glittering misery', 'full of malice and spite'; one weary inhabitant declared that those who were lured there by 'ambition's puffball' soon found that nothing lay beneath the meretricious glamour other than 'empty words, grinning scoff, watching nights and fawning days'. The poet John Donne was particularly scathing of the iniquities of the late-Elizabethan court. He wrote wistfully to a friend that during visits to it, 'because I must do some evil, I envy your being in the country', and then added that his own faults were minuscule in comparison with other people he encountered there, 'for they live at a far greater rate and expense of wickedness'. In 1598 he gave vent to his feelings in verse, writing savagely,

> Here no one is from the extremity
> Of vice, by any other reason free,
> But that the next to him, still, is worse than he.

A generation later another, anonymous poet produced a still more devastating indictment of the institution it was by now almost obligatory to lampoon:

> The court is fraught with bribery, with hate,
> With envy, lust, ambition and debate,
> With fawnings, with fantastic imitation,
> With shameful sloth and base dissimulation.
> True virtue's almost quite exiled there.[46]

It was universally agreed that the archetypal courtier was a despicable figure who, beneath his polished exterior, was malevolent, selfish and false. Sir John Harington, an irreverent wit familiar with the establishments maintained by both King James and his predecessor, reminded the Bishop of Bath and Wells that 'He that thriveth in a court must put half his honesty under his bonnet, and many do we know that never part with that commodity at all, and sleep with it all in a bag.' Superficially a courtier might seem the most agreeable of men, always ready with glib offers of assistance, but only the naive believed such utterances were anything other than empty. The Earl of Derby sombrely warned his son, 'Court friendship is a cable that in storms is ever cut,' and the perfidious tendencies of many at court gave rise to the saying that, 'Among courtiers, enmity is holden for perfect amity.' It was proverbial, too, that courtiers cared only for their own advancement: in May 1611 Sir Henry Wotton wrote to a friend from Greenwich Palace, 'Here I am tied about mine own business, which I have told you like a true courtier; for right courtiers indeed have no other business but themselves.' The courtier bore such a 'reprobate name' that it occasioned real shock when one failed to conform to the stereotype. Describing Lord Hay's efforts to secure him preferment, John Donne confided to a friend, 'He promised so roundly, so abundantly, so profusely, as I suspected him, but performed whatever he undertook ... so readily and truly that ... having spoke like a courtier, did like a friend.'[47]

Critics of the court deplored that it was the repository of such unworthy values, arguing that courtiers were not just odious in themselves, but that they contaminated the entire kingdom. They undermined standards of public conduct, and sapped the morale of genuine patriots, whose services often went unrecognised. Ultimately they even brought the monarchy into disrepute, for it was hard to respect a ruler who countenanced their activities.

In theory King James would not have disagreed that it was essential that courtiers conformed to high standards of conduct. In an admonitory tract he wrote for his eldest son in 1599 he urged him, 'Make your court ... to be a pattern of godliness and all honest virtues to all the rest of the people. Maintain peace in your court, banish envy, cherish modesty, banish debauched insolence, foster humility and repress pride ... that when strangers shall visit your court they ... admire your wisdom in the glory of your house and comely order among your servants.'[48] Sadly, James never came close to filling his own high-minded prescription. Far from purging his court of undesirables, he presided over an establishment with a reputation still more depraved than had been the case in Queen Elizabeth's day.

According to the Puritan Lucy Hutchinson, the Jacobean court was 'a nursery of lust and intemperance ... The honour, wealth and glory of the nation ... were soon prodigally wasted, ... the nobility of the land utterly debased by setting honours to public sale, and conferring them on persons that had neither blood nor merit fit to wear ... their titles, but were fain to invent projects to pill[age] the people, and pick their purses for the maintenance of vice and lewdness.' Another

anonymous tract charted the country's perilous moral decline, fulmi-
nating against the way that in grand circles, 'The holy state of matrimony
[was] most perfidiously broken, and amongst many made but a may-
game ... Bad houses in abundance tolerated, and even great persons
prostituting their bodies to the intent to satisfy and consume their
substance in lascivious appetites of all sorts.'[49]

Such wholesale denunciations by unidentified sources should of course
be treated with caution, but comments gleaned from the private papers
and correspondence of observers do tend to confirm that immorality
was on the increase. Soon after James's accession the heiress Lady Anne
Clifford noted in her diary 'how all the ladies about the court had gotten
such ill names that it was grown a scandalous place'. At the time, Lady
Anne was an innocent young girl who might have been easily shocked,
but even a man of the world like Sir John Harington was disturbed by
the growing laxity. In 1604 he confided to a friend, 'I ne'er did see such
lack of good order, discretion and sobriety as I have now done ... We
are going on, hereabouts, as if the devil was contriving every man should
blow up himself by wild riot, excess and devastation of time and
temperance.' His concern was shared by Samuel Calvert, who wrote to
a diplomat stationed overseas, 'The court has become debauched and
no one cares for anything. We may expect better, but we cannot hope
for it.'[50]

Admittedly, while there is no shortage of generalised allegations
concerning the Jacobean court's degeneracy, it is less easy to prove the
point by citing individual cases. Arthur Wilson wrote a scurrilous history
of James I's reign some years after being discharged from his post in
the exchequer, in which he claimed that a characteristic of the age
was 'licentiousness raised up to a stupendous and excessive height'.
Nevertheless, he declined to be more precise: having alleged
that 'many young gentlewomen (whom their parents' debaucheries
drive to necessities) made their beauties their fortunes, coming to
London to put them to sale', he added mysteriously, 'Although I name
the vices I shall spare the persons, out of respect to their posterity.'
We know that James I's first Lord Treasurer, the Earl of Dorset, was
'much given to women and corruption in the general opinion', so his
nickname of 'Lord Fillsack' can be said to have been apt in more
than one sense. His successor, Salisbury, was said to be guilty of
'unparalleled lust and hunting after strange flesh', allegedly numbering
the Countess of Pembroke among his conquests, as well as Lady
Suffolk. Some people were shocked when the King's wife, Anne of
Denmark, made a confidante of Lady Rich, notorious for producing

several illegitimate children by her lover.

The younger members of Queen Anne's household also had a poor reputation. Towards the end of 1613 the Queen announced that she would celebrate the forthcoming wedding of her lady-in-waiting Jane Drummond by putting on 'a masque of maids', but cynics prophesied that she would have difficulty finding a sufficient number of virgins for the performance. The audience, however, may not have been much better: one person claimed that masques staged at court were nothing other than 'incentives to lust', and that the courtiers invited citizens' wives to the show 'on purpose to defile them'. Certainly during the performance of the *Masque of Blackness* at Whitehall in 1605, 'One woman among the rest lost her honesty, for which she was carried to the porter's lodge, being surprised at her business at the top of the terrace.'[51]

In 1619 a report that Lady Roos had committed incest with her brother Sir Arthur Lake caused a sensation at court, although sympathy for Sir Arthur's late wife declined when it was discovered that she had left behind her an illegitimate child of uncertain paternity. Over the years various other figures on the fringes of the court featured in a succession of unsavoury scandals. In April 1616 Sir Michael Stanhope's wife was suspected of producing a bastard by Sir Eustace Hart. Five years earlier, 'a young minion of Sir Pexall Brocas ... whom he had entertained and abused since she was twelve years old', was obliged to atone for her misdemeanours by standing in a white sheet in St Paul's churchyard.

For the purposes of this study it is perhaps more to the point that several members of Frances Howard's immediate family were touched with scandal. Apart from Lady Suffolk, several of Frances's brothers and sisters were believed to have committed adultery. Theophilus, Lord Howard de Walden, had a mistress known as 'Mistress Clare', and his sister Elizabeth produced two sons who were presumed to be fathered by her lover Lord Vaux rather than her husband, William Knollys.[52] In the reign of Charles I Frances's younger brother, Robert Howard, had a passionate affair with Viscountess Purbeck. It was also rumoured (though never proved) that Frances's sister, the Countess of Salisbury, was the Duke of Buckingham's lover.

To cite all this as proof that the Jacobean court was riddled with vice is perhaps somewhat tendentious. However, in the very nature of things, fornication and infidelity are rarely fully documented, and the absence of detailed information should not necessarily lead one to assume that the descriptions which survive of a society in a terminal state of moral decay are wholly misleading. While the condemnation of James's court may at times have been excessive, the climate there was undoubtedly louche.

If it is impossible to be specific about levels of promiscuity in Jacobean England, there is firmer evidence for dissipation of another sort. King James was a heavy drinker, and though he had a strong head for alcohol he took more of it than was good for him. His personal physician noted of his alcohol consumption that the King 'errs as to quality, quantity, frequency, time and order. He promiscuously drinks beer, ale, Spanish wine, sweet French wine ... muscatelle and sometimes alicante wine. He does not care whether the wine be strong or not, so [long as] it is sweet.' It would be uncharitable to take the word of Sir Anthony Weldon (who was embittered by having been dismissed from office on the King's orders) that James slobbered when he drank but, though he may not have made a spectacle of himself every time, there undoubtedly were occasions when his dignity suffered. In January 1607 he wrote jovially to the Earl of Salisbury, describing a riotous feast he had attended, 'wherein I assure you it chanced well that the Act of Parliament against drunkenness is not yet passed, otherwise the Justice of Peace had much work ado here at that time'. He had not been on the throne very long before his subjects began to display a similar lack of moderation. At a 'solemn feast' held by the Privy Council in 1604 the numerous toasts which were proposed and drunk were taken as a sign that 'the good fashion of drinking will again come in request'. Confirmation was supplied by figures which showed that, whereas before, rations of the expensive fortified wine known as sack had been issued only occasionally to high-ranking officers at court – and then only for medicinal purposes – by 1604 it was 'used as a common drink and served at meals as an ordinary to every mean officer, ... using it rather for wantonness and surfeiting than for necessity'.[53]

In the summer of 1606 the visit to England of Queen Anne's brother, King Christian IV of Denmark, was the signal for the entire court to embark upon a stupendous drinking bout. Sir John Harington reported in disgust that, under the influence of the Danes, even noblemen who hitherto had been reluctant 'to taste good liquor now follow the fashion and wallow in beastly delights. The ladies abandon their sobriety and are seen to roll about in intoxication.' He penned a grotesque account of a masque that followed a banquet given in honour of the King by the Earl of Salisbury. The lady chosen to play the main role of the Queen of Sheba was so inebriated that when the moment came for her to present King Christian with rich offerings, she fell on top of him, spilling her gifts in his lap. King Christian himself proved incapable of staying upright and had to be led to a bedroom, where he collapsed in an alcoholic stupor. The masque continued in his absence, but the remainder of the cast were in a scarcely better state, for some had been rendered speechless by drink, others were 'sick and spewing', and at least one became involved in an unseemly brawl.[54] Even making some allowance for hyperbole on Harington's part, it was a scene of utter degradation which did no credit to any of the participants.

Another disturbing trend was the reckless extravagance that was a feature of life at court. In the rueful words of Bishop Godfrey Goodman, 'Being a time of peace, we fell to luxury and riot.' Maintenance of status became dependent on the ostentatious parading of wealth, and even those whose finances could not stand it squandered vast sums without compunction. In the words of one chronicler of the time, 'To what an immense riches did the merchandise of England rise to above former ages! What buildings, what sumptuousness! What feastings, what gorgeous attire, what massy plate and jewels! What prodigal marriage portions were grown in fashion among the nobility and gentry, as if the skies had rained plenty.' Gambling stakes became enormous: in 1605 the Earl of Salisbury lost £1,000 dicing with the King and, at a Twelfth Night party three years later, no one was permitted to take their place at the royal gaming table unless they were ready to wager a minimum of £300. Court masques not only were costly to stage, but provided the audience with an opportunity to strut about in exorbitant finery. At the performance of the *Masque of Beauty* in 1608 one lady was loaded with jewels estimated to be worth over £100,000. Two years later, those who attended the investiture of the Prince of Wales dazzled onlookers with the magnificence of their attire. One man who had been present declared, 'To speak generally of the court, I must truly confess unto you that in all my life I have not seen so much riches in bravery as at this time. Embroidered suits were so common as the richest lace which was to be gotten seemed but a mean grace to the wearer.' Nevertheless, the peak of prodigality had not yet been reached, for the outfits worn to the wedding of James's only daughter in 1613 were of unparalleled splendour. Lady Wotton wore an embroidered gown made of material that had cost £50 a yard, while Lord Montague spent £1,500 on dresses for his daughters. The male guests were no less gorgeous, with the Earl of Dorset, Viscount Rochester and Lords Dingwall and Hay standing out above the others.[55]

The clothes on which such huge amounts were lavished were opulent rather than tasteful, for the fashions of the time were crudely exhibitionist. To achieve the fantastic silhouettes that were then considered modish, vast quantities of stiffening, padding and underwiring were used when constructing dresses. Ladies' necklines were cut provocatively low, 'the paps embossed, laid forth to men's views', and ruffs were so large that, despite being heavily starched, they would have collapsed if not held up by wiry frames, or 'supportasses'. Skirts, too, had swelled to monstrous proportions, distended by whalebone farthingales which could be conical or drum-shaped. Men's fashions were scarcely less exaggerated. As a middle-aged man the Earl of Carlisle recalled that, in his dancing days at James I's court, 'The mode was to appear very small in the waist. I remember I was drawn up from the ground by both hands, whilst the tailor with all his strength buttoned on my doublet.'[56] The complexions of court ladies were noted for their unnatural pallor, achieved by heavy application of cosmetics, and the favoured hairstyle was a frizzy halo of tightly crimped curls, frequently whitened with powder.

These 'inordinate attires' provoked outrage among moralists. One puritanical tract maintained fiercely that 'It was never a good world since starching and steeling, busks, whalebones and supporters and rebaters, cart wheels and carter's hoops, painting and dyeing ... came to be in use.' The author explicitly linked these contrivances to the moral decline of the country, for 'since these came in, covetousness, oppression and deceit have increased'. Even King James had moments when he felt the exigencies of fashion had become intolerable. In February 1611 it was reported that James intended 'to reform excess of apparel, both in court and elsewhere, by his own example and by proclamation'. Nothing was done at this point, but two years later James did actually issue a proclamation banning farthingales as 'this impertinent garment took up all the room in the court'. The prohibition proved completely ineffectual, for the size of skirts 'rather increased than diminished'.[57]

Serious-minded people deplored this sartorial exuberance not simply because the styles were so immodest, but because 'this extreme cost and riches makes us all poor'. Courtiers were able to sustain their prodigal way of life only by persuading the King to award them large chunks of his revenue, leaving the royal coffers dangerously depleted. It was acknowledged to be a princely duty to reward loyal servants but, while Queen Elizabeth's parsimony in such matters had been criticised, James was felt to be altogether too munificent. The largest pension granted by Elizabeth was £300 *per annum*, but James was so much more generous that when he offered Lord Sheffield an annuity of £1,000, the peer complained that this was insultingly meagre. The cost to the Crown of fees and annuities rose steadily, from £27,279 12s. 1d. in 1603, to

£63,287 10s. 4d. in 1612. The figures for outright grants of cash made by the Crown were equally alarming, mounting from £11,741 in 1603 to £78,791 19s. 11d. eight years later. James could enrich courtiers in a variety of other ways, such as licensing them to collect sums of money which were owed to the Crown, or granting them the sole right to manufacture or market a commodity. Both devices were unpopular, as those called upon to settle unpaid debts were naturally resentful, while monopolies drove up prices for the consumer. Nor could the King afford to alienate such sums. Despite the fact that the war with Spain had ended, the Crown grew progressively deeper in debt. Not only was James too soft-hearted about dispensing largesse, but royal expenditure had risen in other areas.

From time to time, James tried vainly to economise. In 1607, anxious to 'stay this continual haemorrage of outletting', he asked that in future the Council scrutinise any grants he made, and veto those considered excessive. The measure signally failed to lessen his expenses. Subjects faced with tax demands to pay for the King's liberality were incensed at the way that 'court cormorants' exploited James's good nature. In 1610 one MP said it was 'unfit and dishonourable that those should waste the treasure of the state who take no pains to live of their own, but spend all in excess and riot, depending wholly upon the bounty of their prince'. Some years later another angrily branded this voracious breed 'spaniels to the King, and wolves to the people'.[58]

The court of James I was probably not so iniquitous a place as its detractors alleged. One must bear in mind that some of the Jacobean regime's harshest critics were men such as Arthur Wilson and Anthony Weldon, whose testimony is suspect because they wished to gain revenge for having lost jobs in the administration. James suffered, too, because his reign was sandwiched between the supposedly glorious days of Queen Elizabeth and the great cataclysm of the English Revolution. As one apologist for James remarked, 'It was no novelty then to applaud the former times and vilify the present.'[59] Conversely, under the Cromwellian commonwealth it became axiomatic that it was in the reign of James I that a process of estrangement between subject and sovereign had started, but this perception owed a great deal to hindsight. Nevertheless, even with these qualifications it is hard to deny that the Jacobean court was decadent, materialistic and shallow, and that the lives of too many of its denizens revolved exclusively around frivolity and sensual pleasure.

Significantly, two people hanged for their part in the murder of Sir Thomas Overbury implied that they had been corrupted by contact with the court, and that it was this which had caused their downfall. Sir Gervase Elwes, the former Lieutenant of the Tower of London who was condemned as an accessory to murder, recalled on the scaffold that his father had 'charged him on his blessing, that he should not follow the court nor live about London, which he promised to perform ... and yet ambition and worldly vain deceit made him neglect his father's charge ... wherein now in this bloody fact he findeth he greatly offended Almighty God and his own conscience'. Mrs Anne Turner, who was also found guilty of being an accessory, told the Sheriff of London as she awaited execution, 'O, the court, the court! God bless the King and send him better servants about him, for there is no religion in the most of them, but malice, pride, whoredom, swearing and rejoicing in the fall of others. It is so wicked a place as I wonder the earth did not open and swallow it up. Mr Sheriff, put none of your children thither.'[60]

In the seventeenth-century accounts of the Overbury murder Frances Howard was invariably depicted as being very much the product of a culture whose whole ethos was contemptible. As Arthur Wilson put it, 'The court was her nest, her father being Lord Chamberlain; and she was hatched up by her mother, whom the sour breath of that age (how justly I know not) had already tainted; from whom the young lady might take such tincture that ease, greatness and court glories would more distrain and impress on her, than any way wear out and diminish.' In fact, while her husband was away, Frances may have spent less time at court than has previously been imagined. In the autumn of 1606 she is named as having been present at a convivial evening's dancing in the Queen's Presence Chamber at Hampton Court. Thereafter she disappears from view, and the next mention of her is not until February 1609, when she was one of the ladies who featured in Ben Jonson's *Masque of Queens*. By that time her husband may have already returned from the continent. It could be that in the meantime she had led a fairly quiet existence. Certainly her sister Katherine voluntarily withdrew from society during her husband's travels. Her father-in-law the Earl of Salisbury wrote approvingly to his son that she was 'refusing to come to court or London as places she will take no pleasure in during the time of her virginal widowhood'. We do not know if Frances emulated her in this, but it is at least a possibility.[61]

On one point all sources are unanimous: by the time her husband returned from abroad, there were few women at court who could rival Frances in appearance. We are told that she was considered 'a beauty of the greatest magnitude in that horizon' and that 'every tongue grew an orator at that shrine'. Another account refers to the 'devastation the beauty of the Countess caused in the hopes, hearts, estates and understandings' of all those who laid eyes on her. We do not know which role she took in the *Masque of Queens*, in which the noble performers each represented a legendary female ruler. In the light of subsequent events it would perhaps have been most appropriate if Ben Jonson had cast her as Valasca, Queen of Bohemia, 'that to redeem herself and her sex from the tyranny of men that they lived in ... led on the women to the slaughter of their barbarous husbands and lords'. At any rate, as this strikingly lovely young woman paraded about the stage in a triumphal chariot designed by Inigo Jones and drawn by eagles, griffins and lions, she cannot have failed to create a great sensation.[62]

When Essex returned in early 1609 to reclaim his bride, he was doubtless one of the most envied men at court. He himself had been looking forward to setting up home with his wife, even if he did not display the same eagerness as Frances's brother-in-law, Lord Cranborne, who in 1610, 'carried away ... upon wings of earnest desire', cut short his own European tour in order 'to gather the first fruits of his fair young lady'. As Frances soon discovered, such romantic gestures were not in Essex's style. Essex subsequently testified on oath that 'When I came out of France, I loved her,' but these ardent feelings proved short-lived. Arthur Wilson, who in 1614 became the Earl of Essex's steward, and thereafter proved a vehement defender of his employer, claimed that this was Frances's fault. Essex, he wrote, hurried home, 'sick with absence from her whom his desires longed after', only to find 'that beauty which he had left so innocent, so farded and sophisticated with some court drug ... that he became the greatest stranger at home'.[63]

Sadly, it is not hard to think of reasons why Frances found her husband unappealing. Essex's father had been a legendarily attractive man, who had made innumerable sexual conquests, but his son had inherited none of his charm. In looks the young Earl resembled his maternal grandfather, Queen Elizabeth's grim and forbidding spymaster, Sir Francis Walsingham. As a conversationalist he was inept: in 1613 the Archbishop of Canterbury described him as 'generally much reserved in talk', and even the loyal Wilson conceded, 'Nature had not given him eloquence.' That this was so was perhaps not surprising in view of the traumas he had experienced in earliest youth. He had been aged ten at the time of his father's execution, which had stripped him of his titles and inheritance, and left his mother struggling to bring up her children 'without one penny for their education and maintenance'.[64] More hurtful still was the fact that, even as the end approached, the second Earl of

Essex had displayed a chilling indifference to his son's welfare. He neglected to write the affectionate letters that condemned aristocrats customarily sent their families from the Tower, and failed to mention them in his speech from the scaffold. Denied even the consolation of knowing that his father had died thinking of him, it is understandable that the third Earl of Essex developed into a morose and incommunicative adult. Equally, however, it was hard for Frances being yoked to someone so dour and inarticulate.

Essex was never a gregarious man, but he may have felt particularly ill at ease with women. According to one authority, 'He was always observed to avoid the company of ladies, and so much to neglect his own that to wish a maid into mischief was to commend her to grumbling Essex.' The suggestion that Essex had a preference for masculine company is in part corroborated by the glimpses one gains of him elsewhere. While staying with her husband in the country Frances wrote to a friend that her husband was 'merry, and drinketh with his men'. On a different occasion he is described as entertaining 'five or six captains and gentlemen of worth in his chamber'. In the autumn of 1609 there was another gathering in his lodgings, at which no women appear to have been present. Two of the guests fell out over a card game, and 'came to blows with daggers'. Those present managed to part the combatants, but the following morning they duelled, and both were killed.[65]

On that occasion Essex had not been involved in any violence, but he clearly had a fiery temper. In August 1610 he quarrelled with the Earl of Montgomery while out hunting, and the dispute was resolved only with the utmost difficulty. After he parted from Frances there were various other times when Essex showed himself eager to fight with his contemporaries. Sometimes the initial trouble arose because he was understandably touchy if mocked about the failure of his marriage, but this was by no means the invariable cause.[66]

Bearing in mind that Essex had what the Earl of Clarendon described as a 'rough, proud nature', it is easy to believe John Chamberlain's account of how Frances and her husband first became estranged. Chamberlain (whose knowledgeable and entertaining newsletters are an indispensable source for all students of the Jacobean age) heard that when the young couple were first reunited, Essex found Frances difficult and unresponsive. At this, instead of trying to win her over, 'He grew to that impatience that he prayed God to damn him if ever he offered her any such kindness till she called for it, and she in like heat wished to be damned if ever she did.'[67]

Allied to their temperamental differences, the young couple were
sexually unsuited. In 1613 Essex would depose to a divorce commission
that during the first year he and Frances cohabited, he 'divers times
attempted' to consummate their marriage, but always without success.
He implied that Frances was partly responsible for his failure, for
though on some occasions 'when he was willing to have carnal knowledge
of her body, she showed herself ready thereunto ... some other times
she refused it'. In contrast, Frances maintained that she had done
everything possible to help her husband overcome his difficulties.
Lawyers acting for her claimed that 'desirous to be made a mother ...
[she] again and again yielded herself to his power, and, as much as lay
in her [power], offered herself and her body to be known, and earnestly
desired conjunction and copulation'. Despite this, Essex was 'not able
to penetrate into her womb, nor enjoy her'. Essex admitted that, after
a year of futile attempts, he lost interest altogether. He continued to
share a bed with his wife for another two years, 'and yet did find no
motion or provocation in himself to have any carnal copulation with
her, by which means he did not attempt in that time carnally to know
her'.[68]

We cannot know why Essex failed to have sexual relations with
Frances. Shortly after they started living together he contracted small-
pox, and for the next few weeks he was so dangerously ill that there
was no question of him even attempting intercourse. However, at the
end of that time he made a full recovery (though his face was permanently
pock-marked) and thereafter his health presented no problems. Essex
always insisted that he would have been capable of coition with another
woman, and that it was only Frances who rendered him frigid. As we
shall see, Frances herself does not seem to have believed that he was
completely impotent. Once she had decided that she did not want their
relationship to be consummated, she employed various remedies to
prevent her husband from enjoying his marital rights, which suggests
that she assumed his problem was not congenital. It may well be,
however, that she could have spared herself the trouble. Certainly the
circumstances in which Essex's second marriage collapsed were taken as
confirmation by some of his contemporaries of 'his insufficiency to
content a wife'.

After the breakdown of his first marriage Essex 'had taken that
prejudice against woman' that he remained single for seventeen years.
However, in 1630 he married Elizabeth Paulet. Six years later he
became convinced she had been unfaithful to him, and he decided
to separate from her. Elizabeth then announced that she was pregnant,

whereupon Essex declared that he would only recognise the child as his own if it was born by 5 November. The baby was in fact delivered on that date, whereupon Essex acknowledged him as his heir. A month later the little boy died, and Essex reverted to his intention of leaving the mother.[69] While it would appear from this that Essex had managed to consummate his second marriage, the indications are that he and his wife had intercourse infrequently. This warrants the conclusion that the Earl was seriously undersexed, even if not totally impotent.

As time went by, the fact that Frances and Essex were completely incompatible only became more apparent. As an expert rider, who was capable of covering scores of miles on horseback in the course of a single day, Essex was by nature a countryman who could never 'close with the court'. To Frances, however, its gaieties were central to her existence. Arthur Wilson stated, 'To be carried by him into the country out of her element ... were to close (as she thought) with an insufferable torment.'[70]

For some time she managed to avoid the ordeal of living in rural exile with her husband. As a daughter of the Lord Chamberlain, Frances was allocated lodgings when the King was in residence at Greenwich Palace, Hampton Court and Whitehall, which Essex shared with her. At other times they stayed with relations. These included Essex's grandmothers, Lady Leicester and Lady Walsingham, and Frances's brother-in-law, Lord Knollys, who also happened to be an uncle of Essex. In June 1610 Frances was at Whitehall for the investiture of the Prince of Wales, and on 5 June she appeared in Samuel Daniel's masque, *Tethys Festival*, in which the performers impersonated the principal rivers of England. Dressed in a costume draped with shells and festoons of seaweed, Frances played the nymph of the River Lee, whose banks bordered the county of Essex. Shortly after this the court dispersed when the King went on his summer progress. Instead of travelling to Chartley, her husband's estate in Staffordshire, Frances decided to spend the remainder of the summer with her parents at Audley End in Essex. Her husband could not be with her all of the time, although he paid several visits, 'and stayed sometimes a week and sometimes a fortnight'. At such times he and Frances always slept together 'in naked bed', but, as usual, nothing happened.[71]

It was towards the end of July 1610 that an extraordinary rumour gained currency. Samuel Calvert informed the diplomat William Trumbull that Frances's brother-in-law, Lord Cranborne, was reported to be on bad terms with his wife, and 'so hath my Lord of Essex cause, for they say plots have been laid by his to poison him'.[72] There are no other contemporaneous references to suspicions of this sort against Frances and, since Calvert did not elaborate, we have no way of knowing what lay behind this. Years later, when Frances was arrested in connection with the poisoning of Sir Thomas Overbury, it was never suggested that she had earlier contemplated murdering Essex. The episode therefore remains a mystery. At the time the matter was not pursued further, so whatever it was that had given rise to the report in the first place, it was clearly insufficient to concern the authorities.

It may be that by this time there was another cause of friction between Frances and her husband. After Frances died there were persistent stories that she had had an affair with the King's eldest son, Henry, Prince of Wales. Born in 1594, the Prince was a young man of immense promise. To his admirers he embodied every kingly quality. He had a manly bearing, an affable manner (which nevertheless did not encourage over-familiarity), was athletic, dignified and brave, as well as being 'most religious and Christian'. His premature death in 1612 plunged the nation into paroxysms of grief and, in years to come, he was mourned as England's lost saviour, who would have averted the slide into civil war. It might seem to be an inherent contradiction that those panegyrists who hailed Prince Henry as the incarnation of knightly virtue should at the same time believe him capable of committing adultery with the wife of a man he had known since boyhood. Those who recounted the tale of his liaison with Lady Essex nevertheless attributed the lapse to a combination of Frances's feminine wiles and the machinations of her family, thus absolving Prince Henry of responsibility. In his autobiography the antiquarian Sir Simonds d'Ewes wrote that Frances 'was so delicate in her youth as, notwithstanding the inestimable Prince Henry's initiation into the ways of godliness, she, being set on by the Earl of Northampton, her father's uncle, first taught his eye and heart, and afterwards prostituted herself to him, who reaped the first fruits'. Another anonymous account referred to the 'common report' that Prince Henry was 'captivated by her eyes, which then found no match but themselves'. The author of this piece even alleged that the Howards were wildly excited by the situation, flattering themselves that the Prince was their 'prisoner of love, and not likely to be changed', but the claim that the Earl of Suffolk actually hoped to pressure the Prince into marrying his daughter is risible.[73]

Whether there was any truth in the rumours linking Frances and Prince Henry is impossible to say. It may well have simply been an extension of the black legend which grew up around Frances after her conviction. There is no mention in contemporary gossip of any affair between Frances and Prince Henry. In August 1612 the Venetian ambassador did disclose that the King and Queen were anxious to find Henry a suitable wife, because 'His Highness has begun to show a leaning to a certain lady of the court', but by that time Frances was involved elsewhere, so the report was either out of date or concerned another woman. Those who wrote memoirs of the Prince after his death praised him for having avoided sins of the flesh. Francis Bacon noted, 'With regard to that of love, there was a wonderful silence considering his age, so that he passed that dangerous time of his youth ... without any remarkable imputation of gallantry.' Another biographer, Sir Charles Cornwallis, also stressed his hero's chastity. He described banquets at which court ladies vied to win Prince Henry's attention, but could 'neither then discover by his behaviour, his eye or his countenance any show of singular or special fancy to any'. On the other hand Prince Henry is supposed at some unspecified time to have quarrelled violently with Essex during a game of tennis. He is said to have called Essex 'son of a traitor' and struck him 'so shrewdly' with his racquet that he drew blood, and the King had to intervene to make peace between them. It is just conceivable that the incident was caused by tension over the Prince's attentions to Frances.[74]

Frances and Prince Henry could never have had more than a brief relationship. Simonds d'Ewes claimed that the affair was peremptorily ended by Henry because, 'those sparks of grace, which even then began to show their lustre in him, with those more heroic innate qualities derived from virtue ... soon raised him out of the slumber of that distemper, and taught him to reject her following temptations with indignation and superciliousness'. In contrast, Arthur Wilson heard that the Prince abandoned Frances after realising that he was sharing her favours with a rival. He recounted that one day Frances accidentally dropped a glove while dancing at a court ball. An onlooker picked it up and, thinking to please the Prince of Wales, presented it to him. The Prince haughtily spurned the offering, 'saying publicly, he would not have it, it is stretched by another'.[75] One thing, at least, is beyond dispute: if Frances did have a romance with the Prince of Wales, it was insignificant in comparison to the passion which subsequently engulfed her for another man, and which was unquestionably the love of her life. Exactly when we do not know, but at some stage Frances became deeply enamoured of a Scot named Robert Carr, who was the King's current favourite.

CHAPTER TWO

King James had been aged thirteen when he had fallen in love with a man for the first time. Until then his childhood had been bleak. In July 1567, when he was one year old, he had been crowned King of Scotland after his father had been murdered and his mother imprisoned and forced to abdicate. He never saw his mother again. The infant monarch was entrusted to the care of the Countess of Mar, a forbidding woman who 'held the King in great awe'. His tutor, George Buchanan, educated James to a very high standard, but he had a terrifying temper and subjected his pupil to regular beatings. The Regents who ruled Scotland in the young King's name were also callous men who thought it inappropriate to indulge James or to show him affection.

Then, in September 1579, Esme Stuart, Seigneur d'Aubigny, arrived from France to visit his distant cousin the King. For James it was a revelation. Stuart was his senior by more than twenty years, and in the eyes of the impressionable young King he exuded sophistication and glamour. He introduced James to 'many French fashions and toys', and treated the King with a deference and charm that James found irresistible. Very soon after Stuart's arrival it was noted that the King was 'so much affected to him that he delights only in his company'.[1] James swiftly raised Stuart to the Scots peerage, creating him first Earl and then Duke of Lennox. He also showered him with lands and offices, appointing him Lord Great Chamberlain and First Gentleman of the Bedchamber in October 1580.

Lennox's rise was viewed with great hostility in certain circles. The Scottish clergy were particularly antagonistic towards him because he was a Catholic, and they feared he might undermine James's attachment to the national church. Even after Lennox converted to Protestantism in June 1580 these worries were not allayed, for some held that he had changed faith out of pure expediency. But the clergy also attacked Lennox on moral grounds, alleging that he 'went about to draw the

King to carnal lust'. James's decision to confer the revenues of the Archbishopric of Glasgow on Lennox provoked a clash with senior churchmen, who harangued James at a specially convened meeting. They told him, 'We pray God to remove evil company from about you. The welfare of the Kirk is your welfare; the more sharply vice is rebuked, the better for you.' On another occasion the minister John Durie publicly reproved James in a sermon, urging him to avoid popish contamination, and to keep his body unpolluted. In dismay James protested that they were wrong to doubt his purity.[2]

The suspicion that James and Lennox's relationship had a sexual dimension was understandable in view of the fact that James showed his affection for his favourite in a highly demonstrative manner. In 1581 it was reported that James was 'in such love with him as in the open sight of the people, oftentimes he will clasp him about the arms and kiss him'. Years later, however, James will tell his son that the churchmen's censure of him had been unjustified. He claimed that their real motive for attacking him had been political, for they had wished to circumscribe royal power. According to him, 'I was oft-times calumniated in their popular sermons, not for any evil or vice in me, but because I was a King, which they thought the highest evil. And because they were ashamed to profess this quarrel, they were busy to look narrowly in all my actions.'[3] It is difficult to assess whether or not this was an honest interpretation.

In August 1582 the sixteen-year-old James was wrenched away from Lennox when a group of nobles seized the King and ousted the favourite from power. On pain of death Lennox was forced to leave Scotland, 'without sight or good night of the King; neither was the King anyways permitted to see him'. The following May Lennox died in France, leaving directions that his heart should be embalmed and sent to James.[4]

For a time James was inconsolable. For more than twenty years no other favourite meant as much to him as Lennox had done. Nevertheless, until his marriage in 1589, he evinced so little interest in the opposite sex that one observer reported that he 'never regards the company of any woman, not so much in any dalliance'. Instead he continued to be drawn towards members of his own sex, to an extent which some people considered regrettable. In 1589, for example, an English spy reported, 'It is thought this King is too much carried by young men that lie in his chamber and are his minions.'[5]

In 1585 James had opened negotiations for the hand of the King of Denmark's younger daughter, Anne. The marriage was celebrated by proxy in Copenhagen in August 1589. Soon afterwards Anne embarked for Scotland, but when her ship was driven back by storms, James impetuously set sail to claim her in person. Having spent the autumn and winter in Scandinavia with Anne and her family, he returned to Scotland with his wife in May 1590. Initially James appeared delighted by his bride. Anne was not yet sixteen, with blonde hair and a pale complexion that was considered very becoming, and James described himself as a 'happy monarch' to be married to her. In reality, however, he and Anne were far from ideally suited. Anne grew into a shallow and frivolous woman whose delight for infantile amusements soon palled on her husband. Although amiable enough when things were going her way, she became petulant and sulky when crossed, and proved surprisingly effective at making things uncomfortable for those she held responsible. Despite her limited intellect and natural indolence, she resented the way that James resolutely excluded her from state affairs. In Scotland she strove to cause trouble for him on several occasions by engaging in feuds with leading politicians.

Because he was uneasily aware that he was not the most loving of husbands, James strived to placate Anne in other ways, allowing her to spend excessive amounts on jewels, clothes and household expenses. Wanting to remain on good terms with Anne, but finding her company irritating, James evolved a system whereby they spent much of the year living apart. When the couple moved to England in 1603 he encouraged her to set up a separate London residence at Somerset House, and Anne rarely accompanied her husband when he left the capital for extended trips to his hunting lodges at Newmarket and Royston. During their early years in England the King and Queen still occasionally slept together. While in Scotland Anne had presented her husband with two sons and a daughter and, after James inherited the English throne, she produced two more children. Mary, who was born in April 1605, died two years later, and Sophia died the day after she was born in June 1606. It is likely that shortly after this Anne and James ceased to have sexual relations, and it was from this point that James's male favourites became overwhelmingly important to him.

It had not taken James's new subjects very long to realise that he was not interested in women, but that handsome courtiers excited his undisguised admiration. Young men who appealed to him were in constant attendance on him and, because James had weak legs, he was in the habit of putting an arm around their shoulders to support him while walking. In his descriptive sketch of the King, Anthony Weldon supplied the additional malicious detail: 'his fingers ever in that walk fiddling about his codpiece'.[6]

The first favourite of the reign was a Scot called James Hay. Hay had started his career in France, where he was a member of the French King's Scotch Guard. Returning home shortly before James's accession to the English throne, Hay was presented to the King by the French ambassador to Scotland. James at once took to this 'comely handsome gentleman' who was 'indeed made for a courtier'. In 1603 Hay was invited to accompany him to England and in June Hay was appointed a Gentleman of the King's Bedchamber. By the following winter James's fondness for him was attracting comment. The King showed his liking for Hay by bestowing a series of endowments and gifts on him. These including granting him the right to export cloth worth £1,500, paying Hay's debts in 1606, and giving him permission the following year to collect £10,000 of debts owed to the Crown. In June 1606 Hay was created Baron Hay, albeit with a proviso that, as a Scot, he could not take a seat in the English House of Lords. Envious people naturally begrudged Hay his good fortune but, in comparison to later favourites, the King's feelings for him were not particularly ardent. One person commented that though Hay was always 'under the comfortable aspect of King James his favour', he was never 'in his bosom, a place reserved for younger men and of more endearing countenances'.[7]

The next young man to catch the King's eye was Philip Herbert, younger brother of the Earl of Pembroke. His appeal for James was two-fold, for he not only had a beautiful face, but he was also extremely knowledgeable about hunting and country pursuits, in which James took an obsessive interest. In December 1604 Herbert married the Lord Treasurer's niece Lady Susan Vere, but the King did not seem to mind. He gave the young couple a most generous wedding present, conferring on Herbert lands worth £1,200, and contributing an additional £500 worth of property for the bride's jointure. The couple spent their wedding night at Whitehall, and the following morning the King, 'in shirt and nightgown', came to chat to them. Finding them not yet up, he 'spent a good time in or upon the bed' with them. Thereafter Herbert remained in high favour. In May 1605 James created him Earl of Montgomery. As with Hay, at the end of 1606 James undertook to settle Montgomery's outstanding debts. He stipulated that this was the last time he would intervene in this way and that in future they must 'shift for themselves' but, in fact, the following year he awarded Montgomery £10,000 deriving from recusancy fines.[8]

Montgomery had done very well out of the King, but in some ways he was ill-suited to the role of royal favourite. Despite his angelic features his temper was 'intolerable choleric and offensive' and, while he was never discourteous to James, he found it something of a strain constantly to have to subordinate his own desires to those of his master. Lacking the pliancy and servile instincts of the true courtier, he was quite relieved when the King's interest was aroused in another young man, leaving Montgomery with more leisure.[9]

The young man's name was Robert Carr. He was a Scot, being the fourth and youngest son of Sir Thomas Ker of Ferniehurst, near Edinburgh. Sir Thomas had died in 1586, and Robert was born either shortly before or just after that date. Sir Thomas had been an adherent of James's first favourite, the Duke of Lennox. After James had been seized by nobles opposed to Lennox, Ker had attempted to capture Edinburgh on behalf of the King and Lennox. He had failed, but James did not forget the way Ker had tried to help him. His son Robert was subsequently to remind James, 'I was even the son of a father whose services are registered in the first honours and impressions I took of your Majesty's favour.'[10] It may indeed have been in the hope of conferring some form of posthumous recognition on Sir Thomas that in 1601 James took his youngest son Robert (who previously had been in the service of the Earl of Dunbar) into his household as a page.

Carr came to England with James in 1603. Years later it was claimed that initially he fared badly there and that, along with several other of the King's Scots pages, he was 'dismissed the court' soon after James's accession. This, however, was false. Although it was true that several pages from Scotland were demoted following James's arrival in England, Carr had a powerful protector in the shape of his former employer, the Earl of Dunbar. Dunbar was appointed to the influential post of Groom of the Stole, the chief officer in the royal Bedchamber, and it was probably he who secured for Carr a post as Groom of the Bedchamber. As such Carr's responsibilities would have included making the King's bed and caring for his bedlinen.[11] These duties might seem menial, but the job brought its occupants into close proximity to the King, and was regarded as supremely desirable.

However, it was not until the spring of 1607, when Carr was aged about twenty, that people began to think that James had an especial fondness for him. By that time Carr had developed into a strikingly attractive, if slightly androgynous, young man. He was light haired with a 'fair complexion, equally sharing the beauty of both sexes'. He also had a handsome physique, being described as 'straight-limbed, well-favoured, strong-shouldered and smooth-faced'. The fact that he was beardless was particularly significant for, at the time, men with homosexual inclinations were meant to find this highly appealing. In his memoirs the French diplomat Tillières claimed that one reason why the King discarded James Hay as his favourite was that the latter lost his beauty after growing a luxuriant beard. Years after King James was dead his son Charles put on a masque at Whitehall which alluded in allegorical terms to Charles's efforts to bring about moral regeneration at court. One character, Momus, read out a list of desirable reforms, including the decree, 'Ganymede is forbidden the bedchamber, and must only minister in public. The gods must keep no pages nor grooms of their chamber under the age of twenty-five, and those provided of a competent stock of beard.'[12]

In early 1607 Carr was invited by either Lord Hay or Lord Dingwall (accounts differ on this point) to serve as a shieldbearer in the tournament held annually on 24 March, the anniversary of James's accession. The shieldbearer's task was to ride into the tilting arena and then dismount and present the King with a painted shield, known as an *impresa*, while uttering a few verses which explained the meaning of the symbols pictured on it. On this occasion, as Carr was dismounting, his horse reared and he fell awkwardly, breaking his leg. At once the King lost all interest in the jousting, instead concerning himself solely with the welfare of the injured young man. Carr was removed to a nearby house, where the King sent his own physicians to tend him. Before the afternoon was out he came to visit, fussing solicitously about the best diet to be given the patient. In the ensuing weeks he saw Carr as often as possible, 'sometimes an hour or more discoursing with him'. It became evident that once Carr had recovered, a promising future lay ahead of him. One disgruntled onlooker sneered, 'If any mischance be to be wished, 'tis breaking a leg in the King's presence, for this fellow owes all his favour to that.'[13] In fact, as James had already had ample opportunity to notice Carr, the tiltyard episode probably represented less of a *coup de foudre* for the King than some at court imagined. The significance of Carr's accident was not so much that it resulted in James's being suddenly smitten by the young man's charms, as that it first made other people aware of James's interest.

As predicted, once Carr was fit enough to resume his place at court, his career flourished. A flow of gifts from the King soon came his way. Within months of his accident, the King arranged that a Catholic whose property was to be sequestered should surrender two-thirds of his land to Carr. In December 1607 Carr was awarded for the term of fifteen years an annual fee of £600, to be paid to him by four men who collected rent arrears on the Crown's behalf. Then, on 23 December, he was knighted and promoted to Gentleman of the Bedchamber, a significant rise in status. Not only did the Gentlemen of the Bedchamber dress James every morning but, at night, they took it in turns to sleep on a pallet bed in the room where James was sleeping. This meant that they were constantly 'in the eye and ear' of their master. James was noted for being 'very familiar with his domestics and Gentlemen of the Chamber' and their access to him at all hours gave them unparalleled opportunities to secure favours from him, both on their own account and for third parties. In theory, those who had suits to present to James were supposed to proceed through the Master of Requests, but anyone who had decent contacts at court invariably found it more effective to approach the King through a Bedchamber man. Whereas in the reign of Elizabeth it had usually been government officers, such as the Principal Secretaries of State, who procured the royal signature on warrants authorising disbursements, now this role was performed more frequently by Gentlemen of the Bedchamber.[14] There was a tacit understanding that those whose aspirations were met as a result of such intercessions would give suitable recompense to the individual responsible.

Robert Carr soon established himself as the foremost Gentleman of the Bedchamber. Soon after his appointment, James's apartments at his hunting lodge at Royston were remodelled, so that at night Carr could sleep nearer the King. In February 1608 Sir Robert was described as 'the especially graced man', and at some time during that year the King conferred a pension on him worth £800 per annum.[15]

This was merely the preliminary to a more substantial endowment that the King arranged in early 1609. For some time James had been anxious to make generous provision for Carr, but he had been inhibited by the knowledge that the Crown was already badly encumbered with debt, and it was therefore inadvisable to alienate any of the royal estates to the favourite. However, towards the end of 1608, James hit on the alternative of transferring to Carr Sir Walter Ralegh's house and estate in Somerset, Sherborne. The year before his trial for treason, Ralegh had settled this property on his eldest son, but it subsequently transpired that the document recording the transaction was invalid. As a result, Sherborne still technically belonged to Ralegh and, because he was a condemned man, was liable to be forfeited. Ralegh had initially understood that James was prepared to waive his rights over Sherborne but, at Salisbury's suggestion, the King now thought better of this.

Once it had become clear that James intended to bestow the property on Robert Carr, Ralegh sent a letter to the favourite, imploring him not to deprive his family of their rightful inheritance. Lady Ralegh came to court on a similar mission, falling on her knees before the King in supplication. Though plainly embarrassed, James refused to reconsider. 'I maun have the land, I maun have it for Carr,' he muttered in his broad Scots accent. On 9 January 1609 Sherborne was formally granted to Carr. James did compensate Ralegh's family for their loss, paying Lady Ralegh a lump sum of £8,000, with an undertaking to pay an additional £400 a year during her own and her eldest son's lifetime. This seemed a satisfactory settlement at the time, but it appeared less generous when, in April 1610, the King repossessed Sherborne (he subsequently handed it to Prince Henry), and paid Carr £20,000 in exchange for it.[16]

Carr showed his gratitude to the King in the most assiduous fashion. In contrast to Montgomery, who was 'given more to his own pleasures than to observe the King', Carr was unfailingly attentive to James. Having been in the King's service from his boyhood he knew 'his taste, and what pleaseth', submitting himself 'so entirely to the whims of his master that it seemed he wished for nothing else but to second his every desire'.[17] Although the accident in the tiltyard suggests that Carr was not the most accomplished of horsemen, he was a good enough rider to keep up with James on the hunting field, a vital qualification in view of the King's passionate attachment to bloodsports. James liked absenting himself from court for weeks on end in order to sequester himself in the country with a small group of attendants known as his 'hunting crew', and Carr was always with him on these occasions.

When at court Carr was invariably dressed in the height of fashion, knowing that the King liked to see him expensively adorned. In 1598 James had urged his eldest son to avoid clothes which 'by their painted preened fashion serve for baits for filthy lechery ... Especially eschew to be effeminate in your clothes.' Yet, though James dressed fairly conservatively himself, he liked his favourites to have 'good looks and handsome accoutrements', and Carr accordingly was always elaborately costumed and bejewelled. One witness disdainfully related, 'This young man doth much study all art and device; he hath changed his tailors and tiremen many times, and all to please the Prince.' Carr wore his hair tightly frizzled, as fashion dictated, leading hostile observers to condemn his appearance as positively unmanly.[18]

Carr did not object when the King displayed his affection in the most fulsome manner. James was so besotted that, if Carr was in the room, he could hardly bear to take his eyes off him even when he was talking to another. Many of James's subjects were taken aback by the undignified way he showed his feelings. The governor of the Isle of Wight, Sir John Oglander, declared, 'I never yet saw any fond husband make so much or so great dalliance over his beautiful spouse as I have seen King James over his favourites.' One of James's harshest critics, Roger Coke, venomously recorded that 'The King had a loathsome way of lolling his arms about his favourites' necks and kissing them,' while even the more charitable Bishop Godfrey Goodman admitted, 'I never knew any man who had ... so great an affection and such a violent passion of love as he had.'[19]

There were men at the Jacobean court who could not have borne such treatment. It was said that James had once taken a fancy to a young courtier named Henry Rich, but the latter spurned him, losing 'that opportunity his curious face and complexion afforded him, by turning aside and spitting after the King had slabbered his mouth'. In contrast, Carr appeared not to mind when James pawed at him, making no protest when the King 'leaneth on his arm, pinches his cheek, smooths his ruffled garment'. One hostile source alleged that, on the contrary, he encouraged the King with 'whoreish looks and wanton gestures'.[20]

As James was so uninhibited in public it was inevitable that people suspected that he went further in private. One of James's subjects subsequently wrote of the royal favourites, 'The King's kissing them after so lascivious a mode in public and upon the theatre, as it were, of the world, prompted many to imagine some things done in the tiring house that exceed my expressions no less than they do my experience, and therefore left floating upon the waves of conjecture, which hath in my hearing tossed them from one side to another.' The priggish antiquarian Sir Simonds d'Ewes was one of those who speculated on the matter. In August 1622 he and a friend had a discussion lamenting the prevalence of sodomy in London. They agreed that this could only result in divine retribution, 'especially it being, as we had probable cause to fear, a sin in the prince as well as the people, which God is for the most part the chastiser of himself, because no man else indeed dare reprove or tell them of their faults'.[21]

It is impossible to say for certain if d'Ewes was correct in thinking that the King was an active homosexual. Certainly, as a Gentleman of the Bedchamber, Carr would have slept in the same room as the King fairly regularly. James evidently valued the service Carr provided on such occasions and, it seems, expected that the practice would continue even after 1614, when Carr was promoted to the position of Lord Chamberlain. In 1615 when James was becoming disenchanted with Carr, he wrote to him stating that one of the things that had most displeased him was Carr's 'long creeping back and withdrawing yourself from lying in my chamber, notwithstanding my many hundred times earnest soliciting you to the contrary'. However, in view of the fact that it was fairly standard practice for servants to sleep on truckle beds in the bedrooms of their employers, it would be wrong to make too much of this. On the other hand a letter written to the King by George Villiers, the man who succeeded Carr as royal favourite, does suggest that on at least one occasion when he and James shared a room, some form of physical intimacy took place. James's nickname for Villiers was 'dog' and, some years after he had first engaged the King's affections, Villiers wrote to him, musing 'whether you loved me now ... better than at the time I shall never forget at Farnham, where the bed's head could not be found between the master and his dog'.[22]

It is possible that the King also wrote a compromising letter to Carr, which would have gravely embarrassed him if it had been made public. At the time of his arrest in 1615 a great deal of correspondence belonging to Carr (who by that time had been created Earl of Somerset) was seized by Lord Chief Justice Edward Coke. This cache of papers included several letters which the King had written to his favourite. They were subsequently returned to the King but not, it would seem, before Coke had read them. Simonds d'Ewes appears to have heard that Coke was very shocked by what he saw in at least one of the documents: during the conversation referred to above on the King's sexual proclivities, d'Ewes cited a mysterious 'letter in Somerset's casket found by my Lord Coke'. The letter was never produced at Somerset's trial, so we cannot know if d'Ewes had an accurate idea of its contents (or, indeed, if it ever existed), but d'Ewes maintained that James never forgave Coke for having uncovered such sensitive material, and that this was the reason for Coke's subsequent disgrace.[23]

If James did engage in homosexual activities the implications were serious for, by a statute dating from the reign of Henry VIII, sodomy was a felony, punishable by hanging. Admittedly, the purpose of that act had been as much political as moral. It was passed, not because Henry felt concerned by a supposed upsurge in homosexuality, but because he wished to reduce the power of the church courts, which hitherto had had jurisdiction over such cases. The law proved particularly useful during the dissolution of the monasteries, for government agents found that the threat of bringing prosecutions for buggery was an effective way of cowing monastic communities into submission.[24]

Henry's statute did not define what was meant by sodomy. Some people assumed that it applied to all forms of homosexual activity, including mutual male masturbation. Others, however, were clear that anal intercourse was involved. In his pioneering legal textbook, *The Institutes of the Law of England*, the eminent jurist Sir Edward Coke took the view that no one could be convicted of the crime unless penetration had taken place. In other respects, however, his definition remained a broad one, for he stated, 'Buggery is a detestable and abominable sin, among Christians not to be named, committed by carnal knowledge against the ordinance of the creator and order of nature by mankind with mankind, or with brute beast, or by womankind with brute beast.' Coke affirmed that women had been included in the Henrician legislation because, shortly before the act in question was passed, 'a great lady had committed buggery with a baboon and conceived by it'.[25]

Though Coke equated buggery with bestiality, the law as applied distinguished between these offences. The records for the Home County assizes during the years 1553–1602 show that prosecutions for bestiality were six times more common than those brought for sodomy. It was in fact extremely rare for accusations of buggery to come before the courts and, even then, juries seem to have been particularly reluctant to return convictions. In the reign of Henry VIII at least two men were executed for buggery, but thereafter prosecutions were highly unusual. In the period 1559–1602 there were only six recorded indictments for buggery in the home counties, and in only one case was the defendant found guilty. He was Roland Dyer, who in 1569 was sentenced to hang after being convicted of sodomy with five-year-old Barnaby Wright. Of the other five cases all but one indictment states that the charge relates to sodomy with a minor, the ages of three of the boys in question being given as three, eight and ten. In other words, these cases relate to homosexual rape of children, offences which would be viewed as serious crimes today. It was not until the reign of Charles I that the Earl of Castlehaven was executed for committing sodomy with an adult male, and the case against him was compounded by the fact that he had been involved in other forms of gross licentiousness, including abetting a rape on his Countess, and presiding over the debauching of his daughter. Interestingly, Castlehaven sought to defend himself by claiming that witnesses could verify that, though there had been an emission of semen, penetration had not occurred, but the officiating judge still ruled that he was guilty.[26]

In theory, James I approved of the laws against sodomy. Before he came to the English throne he told his son, 'There are some horrible crimes ye are bound in conscience never to forgive,' and he numbered sodomy among them. In July 1610 he specifically ordered Salisbury that sodomy should be among the offences omitted from a general pardon that was to be issued at the end of the present session of Parliament. Possibly, however, James thought of sodomy in terms of forcible anal intercourse with minors, and took a more lenient view of other forms of homosexual activity. Alternatively, this may have been one of the many instances in which James's theoretical principles differed from his practice. Furthermore, even in cases involving homosexual child molestation, he may have been reluctant for the law to take its course. Simonds d'Ewes alleged that James once exerted pressure on the Lord Chief Justice to secure an acquittal of a Frenchman who had been brought to trial at the Guildhall for buggering the son of an English knight.[27]

In Jacobean England homosexuality does not seem to have acted as a bar to advancement in public life. Sir John Holles was shocked by the fact that the King created Sir Philip Stanhope a baron, despite the fact that Stanhope had twice been indicted for buggery. The case had been dismissed on both occasions, but Holles (whose views, it is true, were probably coloured by his long-standing feud with the Stanhope family) claimed this was because Stanhope had bribed the judge, and that his subsequent elevation to the peerage meant 'as it were, all his ill countenanced'.[28]

Far more prominent than Stanhope, however, was Francis Bacon, who in James's reign became successively Solicitor-General, Attorney-General, Lord Keeper and finally Lord Chancellor. Bacon was a married man, but he was widely believed to have homosexual relations with the serving boys he employed in his household. Bacon's conduct was considered particularly provocative because of the indiscreet way he undermined the hierarchical nature of society by lavishly rewarding the 'young, prodigal and expensive youths' in whose company he delighted. Even so, while he occupied high legal office, few people dared voice criticisms of him. In 1619, when Bacon was Lord Chancellor, a Canon of St Paul's who had been annoyed by an adverse decision in Chancery did attack Bacon in a sermon, railing 'somewhat scandalously at him and his catamites'. Bacon promptly committed the man to prison. In 1621, however, Bacon was charged in Parliament with having accepted payments from litigants in Chancery, and thereupon he became vulnerable to attack on other grounds. At first Bacon implied that he would vigorously fight the allegations of corruption, but then, unexpectedly, he suddenly acknowledged himself guilty and craved mercy of Parliament. At the time some people believed that he did so because he feared that if he contested the charges, he would be tried for sodomy.[29]

After he had been dismissed from office, Bacon continued to flaunt his sexual preferences. In his autobiography Simonds d'Ewes (who seems to have had somewhat of an obsession on this subject) noted that, despite the Lord Chancellor's humiliation, 'yet would he not relinquish the practice of his most horrible and secret sin of sodomy, keeping still one Godrick, a very effeminate faced youth, to be his catamite and bedfellow'. D'Ewes considered this the more outrageous, 'because men generally after his fall began to discourse of that his unnatural crime which he had practised many years, deserting the bed of his lady, which he accounted, as the Italians and Turks do, a poor and mean pleasure in respect of the other'. On one occasion the following scurrilous couplet was tacked up on Bacon's door:

> Within this sty a hog doth lie
> That must be hanged for sodomy.

The reference to a hog, according to d'Ewes, was both a pun on Bacon's surname and an allusion to 'that swinish abominable sin' which he committed. However, although there continued to be rumours that Bacon would be prosecuted, and that he would pay for having broken 'the law most severe against that horrible villainy with the price of his blood', legal proceedings were never in fact instigated against him.[30]

In comparison to continental countries, where burning was still the prescribed punishment for sodomy, the English can be said to have treated homosexuality fairly leniently at this time. It is, however, difficult to tell whether this relatively tolerant attitude derived from enlightenment, ignorance or incompetence on the part of the authorities. It is probable that only a few Englishmen believed, as d'Ewes obviously did, that sodomy between consenting adults deserved a death sentence, but this did not mean that such activities were widely condoned. More common reactions were bewilderment and distaste, and the absence of punitive action may well have owed more to a reluctance to confront the issue than to genuine liberalism. The notion that a man could be 'a homosexual' was at that time a completely alien concept; indeed, the very term 'homosexual' did not exist. Instead, sodomy was viewed, not as a way of life, but as one of a number of perversions which would appeal to men who were exceptionally depraved. Like other forms of lust it was deplored as a degrading and soulless activity, which reduced participants to the level of beasts. But the repugnance which sodomy theoretically inspired was coupled with a degree of naivety, for many considered it unthinkable that they could encounter this particular species of vice in someone who was not otherwise an out-and-out debauchee. In the case of the King, cultural conditioning did much to mute criticism of his attachments to young men. In an age of instinctive deference to royalty most people found it easiest not to ponder too deeply about the exact nature of these relationships. Nevertheless, even in the most sophisticated circles, there was unease at the depth of his infatuations and, despite the determination of all at court to make allowances for him, the demeaning way he conducted himself did insidiously undermine respect for him.

Although no one risked attacking the King's dealings with his favourites on moral grounds, public indignation at the profligate way James lavished money and property on these young men was not so easily contained. In the Parliament of 1610 members plainly showed their resentment of the King's excessive generosity. During a debate on the royal finances Thomas Wentworth said fiercely that it was pointless for Parliament to devise ways of replenishing the depleted exchequer unless the King undertook that in future he would show more restraint. ' "For," says he, "To what purpose is it for us to draw a silver stream out of the country into the royal cistern, if it shall daily run out thence by private cocks?" ' Presumably, Wentworth's choice of metaphor was deliberate, and he hoped his listeners would appreciate the sly *double entendre*.[31]

Because he was a Scot, Carr's enrichment aroused particular hostility, for the English felt he was depriving them of what was rightfully theirs. It was hardly to be expected that when James became King of England as well as Scotland, the ancient enmity that had existed for centuries between the two kingdoms would dissolve without trace. Realising that some friction was inevitable, James had promised he would handle the issue with sensitivity: he gave an assurance to Robert Cecil that he would 'never be that greedy of Scottishmen's preferment as to prefer any by whom occasion might be given of the least discontentment to the people here'. In some ways James kept this undertaking for, with the exception of the positions of Master of the Rolls and Chancellor of the Exchequer, all the great offices of state remained in English hands.

James's household, however, was a different matter: by 1607 Scots outnumbered English Gentlemen of the Bedchamber eight to one.

Since the Gentlemen of the Bedchamber had such a stranglehold over patronage, the English considered this a real grievance. Sir John Holles even prepared a remonstrance on the subject, which he hoped to bring to James's attention during the Parliament of 1610. Mournfully Holles lamented, 'The Scottish monopolise his princely person, standing like mountains betwixt the beams of his grace and us and, though it becomes us not to appoint particulars about him, yet we most humbly beseech his Majesty his Bedchamber may be shared as well to those of our nation as to them.'[32] It is not clear if this petition was ever presented, but certainly the situation did not improve for some time.

Above all, however, the English begrudged any financial benefits which accrued to the Scots. At the start of James's reign the English could at least console themselves that he was dispensing money with such a prodigal hand that courtiers of both nations were doing very well. However, once the King's economic position worsened, he could not afford to continue as before and, thereafter, awards to the Scots were subject to more unfriendly scrutiny. For example, when Sir Henry Neville informed Ralph Winwood in June 1606 that James had recently given land worth £1,000 a year to the Scots Gentleman of the Bed-chamber Sir John Ramsay, he added sourly, 'so the King's land, enclosed to all other, is only open to them'.[33]

James maintained that the English had no cause for complaint, asserting stoutly that they 'have tasted as much and more of my liberality than the Scots have done'. But, though it was true that, throughout his reign, numerically more English than Scots received financial benefits from the Crown, a small number of Scots were given disproportionately large amounts. This created a serious imbalance. In 1611, for instance, thirty-one people divided between them royal grants worth £90,688. Eleven of this group were Scots, and it was they who received over three-quarters of the total amount.[34] In the circumstances it was not surprising that the English became jealous and, since Carr was such a notable beneficiary of James's largesse, he was a natural focus for hostility.

Carr was aware that many Englishmen were prejudiced against him on account of his nationality, and he did his best to mitigate this. Instead of surrounding himself with Scots and commending to James the claims of his compatriots, he did all he could to distance himself from his origins. As Bishop Goodman recalled, 'He did utterly mislike the bold carriage and importunity of the Scots; he knew there was nothing to be gained from them ... He did desire to ingratiate himself with the English.' Anthony Weldon confirmed this, stating that Carr was 'naturally more addicted to the English than the Scotch, insomuch as he endeavoured to forget his native country and his father's house, having none about him but English'.[35]

It is debatable whether Carr was wise to cut himself off from his roots in this way. It is true that initially some Englishmen were so relieved at his lack of partisanship towards his own countrymen that they 'magnified and loved him for this his natural disposition to our nation'. Nevertheless, although Carr did everything he could to be accepted (including adopting the anglicised spelling of his surname), in the eyes of most people he remained very much an outsider. Even in 1615 his Scots accent remained so strong that one Englishwoman of his acquaintance declared, 'He spoke so broad Scottish as she understood him not.' However much Carr strived to integrate himself into his adoptive country, the English never looked on him as one of their own, damning him for the fact that 'to the ever odious name of a minion, his birth had unhappily added that of a Scot'.[36] As for the Scots, they were naturally infuriated by the way that Carr sought to disown them. This did not matter while he was in his heyday but, when he encountered troubles in 1615, he soon found that he was dangerously isolated. At that time an English observer noted, 'His countrymen now bring forth a long ulcerous dislike against him for that he disclaimed from their blood ... [and] conversed more inwardly with ours.'[37] The English, on the other hand, showed no gratitude for the way he had courted them, and this left him peculiarly vulnerable.

It was in keeping with Carr's policy 'to please the English by entertaining them his domestics' that his closest friend and adviser should be an Englishman, Thomas Overbury. Overbury was the son of Sir Nicholas Overbury, of Bourton-on-the-Hill, Gloucestershire, and he was about four or five years older than Carr. He was intelligent and well educated, having attained a Bachelor's degree from Queen's College, Oxford, in 1598. After that he had become a student at the Middle Temple, one of the Inns of Court in London, which were known colloquially as England's third university. It was a common practice for young gentlemen to attend one of these even if they had no intention of taking a place at the Bar, which normally required eight years' training. Overbury decided against following his father into the legal profession, staying at the Middle Temple only long enough to acquire a basic grounding in the law. By 1601, aged twenty, he had completed his studies, and then rounded off his education with a little foreign travel. He journeyed to Scotland on 'a voyage of pleasure' and, while there, he looked up William Cornwallis, an acquaintance from Oxford.

It was Cornwallis who introduced him to Robert Carr, who at that time was aged about sixteen and serving as a page to the Earl of Dunbar. When Carr came to England in 1603 he and Overbury were reunited, although it seems it was not until the following year that they became truly devoted. In a letter written to Carr in 1613 Overbury speaks of there having been to date 'nine years' love' between them.[38]

In many ways Overbury was a promising young man. He was attractive-looking: when Queen Anne was first introduced to him she remarked, "tis a pretty young fellow'. He 'had an able body, either to run, play at foils or such like exercise', and this kept him fit and trim. He was so studious that, after his death, one of his servants recalled that Overbury's health had sometimes suffered 'in respect of his much sitting at his books'. A tract written some years after that was full of praise for his application, noting that when Overbury travelled on the continent in 1609 he 'spent not his time, as most do, to loss, but furnished himself with things fitting a statesman by experience in foreign government, knowledge of the language, passages of employment'. This may have somewhat exaggerated Overbury's diligence, for in 1613 he himself claimed that he could speak no foreign languages. However, following his visits to France and the Netherlands in 1609 he wrote a series of 'observations' on these countries, comprising assessments of their trade, military strength, industry, raw materials and population.[39] While not particularly enthralling, these works are indicative of an alert mind, and were clearly written by a man who hoped to make his mark in politics.

Overbury also had literary pretensions, and assiduously cultivated his modest talent. His most celebrated poem was *The Wife*, in which he set out in verse the qualities he considered desirable in a spouse. For him the main requisites in a partner were piety and virtue, which he sententiously declared to be more important than birth and beauty. He would, he claimed,

> Rather in her alive one virtue see,
> Than all the rest dead in her pedigree.

In addition, while allowing that

> Some knowledge on her side will all my life
> More scope of conversation impart,

he cautioned against marriage with a highly educated female. In his view, 'learning and pregnant wit in womankind' was unseemly, for such erudition could only distract from the domestic duties which were a woman's natural province. Above all, however, Overbury insisted that his wife must be discreet, and so obviously pure that no man would even contemplate attempting to seduce her. He considered that it reflected badly on a woman if she allowed herself to be put in such a position, and that

> ... in part to blame is she,
> Which hath without consent been only tried,
> He comes too near that comes to be denied.[40]

The poem was never printed in Overbury's lifetime, but after his death it became very popular. It was first licensed for publication in December 1613, and went through five editions in the ensuing twelve months. Ben Jonson claimed that Overbury had written it in order to impress the Countess of Rutland, whom he desired, but the content of the poem was hardly calculated to make a married woman look favourably on his advances. More plausible is the statement of Overbury's father that he wrote it in hopes of deterring Robert Carr from marrying the Countess of Essex.[41]

Overbury also fancied himself as a writer of prose. He penned a series of descriptive sketches, collectively known as 'characters'. This literary genre, which Overbury pioneered, enjoyed a great vogue immediately after his death, and was widely copied. In 1614 Overbury's *Characters* was published, together with similar offerings written by various emulators, who sought to pass off their work as Overbury's. The collection was a runaway success, and was reprinted several times before his murder came to light and gave his name an added celebrity.

Today it is a little difficult to understand why they were so highly regarded. The pen portraits of the characters whom Overbury despised are the ones which have best retained their immediacy, for they are full of sardonic wit and sharp-edged detail. Overbury's description of 'The Courtier' conveys a vivid impression of an effete type with which he was undoubtedly familiar: 'He knows no man that is not generally known. His wit, like the marigold, openeth with the sun, and therefore he riseth not before ten of the clock ... He follows nothing but inconstancy, admires nothing but beauty, honours nothing but fortune. Loves nothing ... He is not, if he be out of court, but fish-like breathes destruction, if out of his own element.' The 'Affectate Traveller' is another good example of his humour: 'He censures all things by countenances, and shrugs, and speaks his own language with shame and lisping; he will choke rather than count beer good drink, and his pick-tooth is a main part of his behaviour. He chooseth rather to be counted a spy, than not a politician; and maintains his reputation by naming great men familiarly ... His discourse sounds big, but means nothing.'[42]

Overbury is less successful when he depicts archetypes whom he holds up as ideals, for then he becomes embarrassingly mawkish. He writes approvingly of 'The Virtuous Widow' who, in contrast to most women in her position, does not think of remarrying. 'She is like the purest gold only employed for princes' medals, she never receives but one man's impression ... To change her name were (she thinks) to commit a sin should make her ashamed of her husband's calling. She thinks she hath travelled all the world in one man; the rest of her time therefore she directs to Heaven.'

Worse still is his depiction of 'A Fair and Happy Milkmaid', in which he glorifies a rustic way of life that bore little resemblance to the hard existence of most seventeenth-century farmhands. 'The lining of her apparel (which is her self) is far better than the outsides of tissue; for though she be not arrayed in the spoil of the silkworm, she is decked in innocency, a far better wearing. She doth not with lying long abed spoil both her complexion and her conditions; nature hath taught her, too immoderate sleep is rust to the soul; she rises therefore with Chaunticleer, her dame's cock, and at night makes the lamb her curfew.'[43]

From his writings Overbury would seem to have been a repository of homespun values, who viewed with contemptuous detachment the follies of his contemporaries. The impression could not be more misleading. As Simonds d'Ewes remarked, Overbury himself spent his life 'vainly enough, according to the court garb'[44] and, despite his censoriousness of others, his own conduct could not always have withstood close scrutiny. He was consumed by worldly ambition, and was as anxious as anyone to exploit any opportunities for jobbery and corruption which offered themselves to him. Ironically, his ultimate downfall was brought about by his refusal to absent himself from the court which he so mercilessly satirised and, despite his professed admiration for loyalty, sweetness and simplicity, it is manifest that these were qualities con-spicuously lacking in him.

Contemporaries attested that Overbury's worst fault was a breath-taking arrogance that came close to negating his undoubted gifts. As Anthony Weldon put it, he was 'a man of excellent parts, but those made him proud', prone to 'over-valuing himself and under-valuing others'. He was, says Weldon, 'infected with a kind of insolency', and this is corroborated by others. Bishop Goodman described Overbury as 'a very witty gentleman, but truly very insolent', while Francis Bacon would sum him up as 'a man of unbounded and impudent spirit'. Writing about fifty years after Overbury's death, John Aubrey recorded, 'It was a great question who was the proudest, Sir Walter [Ralegh] or Sir Thomas Overbury, but the difference that was, was judged on Sir Thomas's side.' Another person reminisced, 'Though Overbury was of excellent parts, the prodigiousness of his pride was the greater miracle.' He added the detail that when Carr left his coach at the palace gate, Overbury habitually availed himself of this luxurious means of transport, leaving the hapless Carr to shift for himself.[45]

A good example of Overbury's arrogance is afforded by a letter sent from Francis Rous to William Trumbull in May 1609, which has a postscript by Overbury. Trumbull was an experienced diplomat: having formerly been secretary to Sir Thomas Edmondes, the English ambassador in the Spanish Netherlands, he stayed behind as chargé d'affaires when Sir Thomas was recalled from Brussels in 1609. In his letter Rous expresses himself with the utmost diffidence, even though it appears that Trumbull had invited him to keep in touch. Apologetically he wrote, 'I might make excuses for venturing so much upon a friendship whereto I had no right but by the kind and free offer of itself.'

Overbury's postscript, in contrast, is peremptory in the extreme. It is not clear whether Overbury had ever met Trumbull, but he treated him as an underling and, considering that at this stage Overbury had never held an official position, his tone was nothing short of offensive. Briskly he informed Trumbull that, during his recent trip to the Netherlands, he had visited the State House at Antwerp and there 'saw the names of the Dukes of Burgundy being writ by their pictures, down to this present Archduke. Being straitened in time I did not write them out: I ask you to take the pains to send an entire note of them as they are there in Mr Rous his next letter from you.'[46] The fact that Trumbull was not even stationed at Antwerp, and that it would have necessitated a journey there in order to fulfil this errand, only makes Overbury's effrontery the more outrageous.

Four years later Overbury sent another curt missive to the unfortunate Trumbull, who was still resident in Brussels. By that time Robert Carr had become one of the most powerful men in the country, and although Overbury had never been given an administrative post, the fact that Carr relied on him for advice and assistance had conferred on him a certain amount of prestige. Even so, his standing in the country was scarcely such as to justify the air of superiority with which he now addressed Trumbull. Uninvited, he lectured his correspondent on the history of Ireland, proposing simplistic solutions for the notoriously

complex problems that bedevilled that island. Patronisingly he concluded, 'You might do well to send for Sir John Davies's story of
Ireland, lately written.'[47]

Reading these letters, it is not hard to understand why Overbury was
widely disliked. Since he was also exceptionally contentious, such
friendships as he did make tended not to last. For a time Ben Jonson
was greatly taken with Overbury, hailing him as a rising literary talent.
He even wrote an enthusiastic epigram in his honour:

> So Phoebus make me worthy of his bays,
> As but to speak thee, Overbury's, praise.
> So where thou li'st, thou mak'st life understood
> Where, what makes others great, doth keep thee good!
> I think, the fate of court thy coming crav'd,
> That the wit and manners might be sav'd;
> For since, what ignorance, what pride is fled!
> And letters and humanity in the stead!
> Repent thee not of thy fair precedent,
> Could make such men, and such a place repent:
> Nor may any fear to lose of their degree,
> Who in such ambition, can but follow thee.

Before long, however, Jonson and Overbury quarrelled violently, and
Jonson subsequently recalled that Overbury thereupon 'turned his mortal
enemy'. The incident was typical of Overbury, who had a reputation
for being 'a hot and violent spirit', 'full of bitterness and wildness of
speech and project'. In 1612 one acquaintance described him as having
'irritated and provoked almost all men of place and power by his extreme
neglect of them and needless contention with them upon every occasion'.
Robert Carr confirmed, after Overbury's death, that he was an impossible
character, declaring, 'I think he had never a friend in his life that he
would not sometimes fall out with and give offence unto.'[48]

Despite Overbury's difficult nature, it appeared unthinkable that there
could ever be a rift between him and Robert Carr for, as one commentator
put it, 'To the show of the world this band was indissoluble.' The pair
were extraordinarily close: in 1612, when writing to the Lord Treasurer
to thank him for some good office he had done Overbury, Carr declared,
'I must divide him, Overbury, from other men, and my thanks [are]
proportional to the value I put on him.' They were so inseparable that
people referred to Sir Thomas as Carr's 'dear Overbury'. There may
conceivably have been a homosexual element in their relationship. When
Overbury was dead Sir Francis Bacon (who perhaps was better attuned

than most in observing such nuances) referred to there having been 'an excess, as I may say, of friendship' between Carr and Overbury. James I's Master of Requests, Sir Roger Wilbraham, described Overbury as Carr's 'bedfellow, minion and inward councillor' and, though at the time men frequently shared beds without impropriety, the coupling together of the terms 'bedfellow' and 'minion' is suggestive. Overbury himself once suggested to Carr that one reason why the King disliked him intensely was because of Carr's 'loving me better than him'. Far from urging Carr to disabuse James of this idea, Overbury seemingly acknowledged that this was in fact the case. With typical insensitivity, Overbury suggested Carr should remind James that he was much older than him. Carr should then point out that it was only natural that he should be on such close terms with someone who was approximately his own age, for 'you are no old man yet, nor can delight in old company continually'.[49]

Carr was not only devoted to his friend, but he recognised that Overbury was far cleverer than he. He placed great reliance on his judgement, so much so, indeed, that Overbury came to be 'a kind of oracle of direction unto him'. Undoubtedly, however, Overbury also benefited from the friendship, for Carr loyally exerted himself to procure his friend's advancement. In September 1607 Overbury secured a welcome increase in income when he was leased by the Crown a salt production works at Droitwich, Worcestershire, part of the property of a man recently attainted for treason. On 19 June 1608 the King knighted Overbury, presumably at Carr's instigation. The same year, Overbury's father was made one of the circuit judges for Wales, and Carr may well also have been responsible for this promotion. In December 1609 Carr secured his friend some other favour, for it is recorded in the state papers that a bill concerning Overbury had been signed by the King as a result of Carr's importunity.[50]

At some point Overbury secured the post of sewer (or server) to the King. It is not clear exactly when this happened. It is conceivable that he had the office as early as 1606. When the King of Denmark visited England that year he gave Overbury some silver, which may have been because Overbury had waited on him at table.[51] It is more likely, however, that the appointment coincided with Overbury's knighthood in 1608.

At any rate, the award of this position was a great opportunity for Overbury to become on familiar terms with the King. There was every chance that James would develop a real fondness for him, for at mealtimes he was always very loquacious with his attendants. In 1601 a visitor to Scotland had reported, 'He speaks to those who stand around while he is at table ... and they to him. The dinner over, his custom is to remain for a time before retiring, listening to jests and pleasantries, in which he takes great pleasure.' In England James had kept up these habits, but unfortunately Overbury lacked the knack of ingratiating himself with his employer. He was an attentive listener, even jotting down remarks made by the King when eating. These were subsequently collected together under the title *Crumbs Fallen from King James's Table*. But, though initially James was well disposed towards Overbury – at the time of his appointment, the King had proudly pointed Overbury out to Queen Anne with the words, 'Look you, this is my new sewer' – on closer acquaintance, he did not warm to him. Overbury was evidently disappointed that his position as sewer did not prove a stepping-stone to further preferment. In 1609, 'to shift off discontents', he obtained leave of absence from court in order to travel in France and the Netherlands. When he returned in August, however, his relationship with the King did not improve.[52]

In contrast, the King's infatuation with Carr showed no signs of waning. Very gradually James even started to involve Carr in the conduct of state affairs. The practice came about because the King's councillors and secretaries generally stayed behind when James went on hunting expeditions. As a result the King needed assistance with his correspondence, which Carr was able to provide. Almost imperceptibly Carr began acting as an intermediary between James and his ministers. As early as April 1608 Carr had written to Salisbury, 'Those letters which you directed to me, I did present to his Majesty.' Once James had read and digested these, Carr passed his comments back to the Lord Treasurer.[53]

Realising the depth of James's attachment to Carr, Salisbury did his best to remain on good terms with the favourite. Carr initially seemed flattered. In 1608 he wrote to Salisbury, 'Your courtesy shall make me study by all means to give proof how sensible I am of your love, and how much I esteem the favours that come from you.' It was Salisbury who had suggested to James that Sherborne would make a suitable endowment for Carr. At the time James had been delighted: 'The more I think of your remembrance of Robert Carr for yon manor of Sherborne, the more cause have I to conclude that your mind ever watcheth to seek out all advantages for my honour and contentment,' he had enthused. He had also promised Salisbury that Carr himself would never forget his kindness, for 'He is more thankful in his heart to you than he can express.'[54]

Sadly, during the next two years, tensions developed between Carr and Salisbury. This may have been because Salisbury sought to persuade the King that he could no longer reward Carr on the same munificent scale as heretofore. Certainly, prior to the assembly of Parliament in February 1610, Salisbury told James that one reason why he had experienced difficulties during previous sessions was that the Commons had been annoyed by the 'harsh effects and ill order of your Majesty's gifts'. The French ambassador also claimed that the Council, under Salisbury's leadership, had been pressuring James to cut down, and that the Scots, realising that this would affect them adversely, decided to retaliate by undermining the Lord Treasurer.[55]

When Parliament met, fears that its members would prove refractory were vindicated. Salisbury had hoped to achieve a long-term solution of the King's financial difficulties by reaching an agreement with Parliament whereby James would undertake to surrender his rights to collect various feudal dues, in return for being awarded a guaranteed income. However, after prolonged wrangling, negotiations broke down, and Salisbury had to ask Parliament to suggest other ways of paying off the Crown's debts. During debates on the subject several MPs exhibited real anger at the way James had frittered away vast sums on undeserving persons. While not daring to censure the King directly, Thomas Wentworth vividly conveyed his disapproval by observing, 'We would be glad to hear of Spain that the King spent all upon his favourites and wanton courtiers.' John Hoskins made another hostile speech in which he deplored the King's financial position and hinted broadly that it was the greed of the Scots that was to blame. The King was furious at such insubordination: he wanted to send Wentworth to prison and, though with difficulty the Council dissuaded him from this, he determined to dissolve Parliament as soon as possible.[56]

One reason for this decision was that Robert Carr had told him that the Commons were planning to heap more abuse on the Scots, and that there was a scheme afoot to present a petition to the King begging him to send his countrymen home to Scotland. It is in fact improbable in the extreme that such a move was ever seriously contemplated, but Carr not only managed to persuade the King that it was imminent, but also convinced him that Salisbury had been aware of the situation, and had deliberately refrained from warning his master. For a time this cast a shadow over Salisbury's relations with the King and, though ultimately he managed to acquit himself of the charge that he had purposely misled James, some people felt that, after this Parliament, Salisbury no longer had the King's full trust.[57]

Carr was now in higher favour than ever. In early 1611 the King showed his utter disregard for public opinion by promising to give his favourite an additional £5,000, as well as simultaneously conferring large sums on the Scots Lords Fenton, Haddington and Hay. Responsible Englishmen were aghast at the King's behaviour, and some believed that he would soon come to his senses and rescind the grants. 'I do not hear they have yet received anything,' one courtier confided to a friend in February. 'Others conceive they shall not; all the world wisheth they may not.' These hopes proved illusory, however, and the money was soon handed over.[58]

On 25 March 1611 Carr's extraordinary ascent continued when the King raised him to the peerage as Viscount Rochester. He 'got the start of all his countrymen' by being the first Scot permitted to take a seat in the English House of Lords. A month later he was made a Knight of the Garter, and was described by the Venetian ambassador as being 'further in the King's graces than any other subject'. The ambassador commented maliciously, 'All this is displeasure to the English; all the same everybody is endeavouring to secure his favour and goodwill.' Rochester's prestige, and Salisbury's relative decline, was underlined by the fact that the former now 'had more suitors following him than my Lord Treasurer'.[59]

The implications for Salisbury were the more alarming because, with Overbury's encouragement, Rochester was seeking to interest James in an alternative political strategy to that hitherto advocated by the Lord Treasurer. The favourite began urging that when Parliament next assembled, James should entrust its management not to Salisbury, but to a corpulent country gentleman named Sir Henry Neville. Neville was a former ambassador to France who had been implicated in the second Earl of Essex's rebellion, and who had consequently spent the last two years of Queen Elizabeth's reign in the Tower. On James's accession he had been freed, but Salisbury had blocked his further political advancement. The King mistrusted Neville because, during the Parliament of 1610, Sir Henry 'had ranged himself with those patriots that were accounted of a contrary faction' to his ministers. Nevertheless, Rochester now maintained that, precisely because of these links with the opposition, Neville would control the Commons much more effectively than Salisbury had done. As one onlooker put it, 'The plot ... was, Sir H. Neville should undertake to deal with the Lower House, and then (so [long] as my Lord Treasurer would not intermeddle), there was no doubt but that better effects would come of the next session ... than did come of the former.'

It is clear that Overbury was the person who had incited Rochester to argue for Neville's promotion. A contemporary later noted that it 'was generally observed that Overbury carried [Rochester] on in courses separate and opposite to the Privy Council'.[60] For the moment the King was resistant to their schemes, but the pair were optimistic that, if Rochester persevered, James would ultimately accede to their wishes.

In March 1611 there were persistent rumours that Overbury was to be sent to Brussels as an ambassador[61] but nothing came of this. It is possible that Salisbury had deliberately set out to deprive Rochester of Overbury's political guidance by sending Overbury to serve abroad, and that Rochester succeeded in blocking the appointment by appealing to the King. If so, the episode may have misled Overbury into thinking that he would be able to evade unwelcome responsibilities with equal ease in the future.

Shortly after receiving his peerage Rochester was again able to help his friend by procuring a promise from the King that when the post of Treasurer of the Chamber became vacant, Overbury would be appointed. The current incumbent was Lord Stanhope, and Rochester was willing to pay him to resign the place so that Overbury could take possession at once. In the event Stanhope declined the offer, but Overbury could still console himself that he would succeed to the position in due course.[62]

However, in May 1611 Overbury's career suffered a severe reverse. Queen Anne had come to hate both Rochester and Overbury. However irksome she had found her husband's attentions to earlier favourites, she had never before seen him possessed by an all-consuming passion, but this time there could be no doubt she had been completely displaced in his affections. Apart from a very natural jealousy, she was also annoyed that James's constant deferring to Carr's wishes in patronage matters lessened her own influence in this area. The Venetian ambassador reported that Anne was incensed when Rochester persuaded the King to give a house in Scotland to a nominee of his, whereas she had wanted it to be presented to the Scots Chancellor. What she really found unendurable, however, was that Rochester afforded her scant respect. A French diplomat stationed in England subsequently reminisced that Rochester treated the Queen with 'insupportable contempt', deluding himself that she was of no account whatsoever. Even more foolishly, Overbury thought likewise and 'always carried himself insolently ... towards the Queen'.[63]

This turned out to have been a grave miscalculation. Towards the end of May 1611 Rochester and Overbury were walking together in the garden of Greenwich Palace. Queen Anne was watching them out of a window, when something happened to incense her. It is not clear what this was: one account states that she became furious when Overbury caught sight of her and failed to remove his hat; another version has it that she heard the two young men laughing, and assumed that they were making fun of her. At any rate, in a rage she went to see the King and 'with tears in her eyes' begged him to punish those guilty of insulting her. When the King appeared reluctant to take action of any sort, 'She cast herself on her knees and besought him not to suffer her to be so scorned and despised of his grooms, though she were content to suffer it from him.' In a state of near-hysteria, she threatened her husband that she would return to Denmark unless she had some redress. This unforeseen domestic crisis placed James in a dreadful quandary. Greatly agitated, he walked up and down, repeating in distress, 'Ah, woe is me, my Queen will go from me; my Carr, my Carr.' After the King had tried unsuccessfully to convince her that it was all a misunderstanding, Anne persuaded her eldest son to have an interview with his father, insisting that the incident could not be overlooked. Finding himself cornered, King James reluctantly agreed that Overbury and Carr should be summoned before a special meeting of the Council, who would investigate the matter.[64]

By this time the Queen had calmed down sufficiently to realise that it was most unlikely that James would give her satisfaction by disgracing Rochester. Overbury, however, was more vulnerable, for the King did not feel the same affection for him. 'The conclusion was, she finding herself not able to supplant Carr, which she desireth of all things in the world, turned all her force against Overbury.'

Anne wrote to Salisbury, who was to chair the Council enquiry into what had happened, making it plain that she expected '*that fellow*' (as she balefully referred to Sir Thomas) to suffer for his insolence. 'I recommend to your care how public the matter is now, both in court and city, and how far I have reason in that respect,' she told the Lord Treasurer, who doubtless derived a grim pleasure from reading this. When summoned before the Council both Rochester and Overbury strenuously denied having done anything to upset the Queen. Having heard what they had to say, the Council ruled that no action should be taken against Rochester, but that Overbury should be banished from court for an indeterminate period.[65]

This was a devastating blow to Overbury at a time when his prospects had never looked brighter. Fortunately for him, Rochester stood loyally by his friend. He protested at the way Sir Thomas had been made a

scapegoat, roundly telling James that 'if he would so far give credit to
the rage of a jealous woman [as] to banish a faithful and discreet servant
for his friendship, which was the only fault the Queen could impute
unto him, for his part he was resolute to share with him his fortune,
banishment or whatever it were'. In the event Rochester did not carry
out his threat to absent himself from court, but he continued to work
for Overbury's reinstatement, showing solidarity with Sir Thomas by
ostentatiously visiting him in his lodgings. By September Rochester's
remonstrances had secured for Overbury at least a partial restoration to
court. John More informed William Trumbull, 'During this progress,
there hath been some contestation between their majesties about Sir
Thomas Overbury's offence and, though her Majesty's displeasure be
not yet much mitigated, Sir Thomas begins to approach the court again,
his great friend Rochester much labouring in his behalf.'[66]

It was plain, however, that Overbury could not be officially readmitted
without the Queen's sanction. Realising that Rochester's entreaties to
the King were in themselves insufficient to secure this, Overbury had
to humble himself by sending a letter to Salisbury, asking him to
intercede between him and Anne. He wrote assuring him of his
'submission' to the Queen, and expressing a fear that 'her Majesty is
not fully satisfied of the integrity of my intent that way'. It is not clear
how Salisbury responded to this letter. Possibly he deemed it expedient
to help Overbury, even though he had little affection for him. At any
rate, in November 1611 it was reported that Overbury had been
permitted to return to court 'but neither into the Queen's sight, nor of
her side'.[67]

Although Anne had been prevailed upon to make this concession, her
hatred of Overbury remained implacable, and his restoration to court
was 'never but a palliated cure'. The incident had at least shown
Rochester that Anne should not be underestimated, and in the next few
months he sought to improve relations with her by asking the King to
grant her various favours. Some people believed that the Queen was
grateful for this, and that, by the spring of 1612, she and Rochester
were 'perfectly reconciled'. Others were not so easily deceived: in June
a knowledgeable Scottish observer reported that Rochester could not
'find the right way to please either the Queen or the Prince, but they
are both in the conceit of this court not well satisfied with him'.[68]

Queen Anne was by no means the only important person at court who
hated Rochester and Overbury. The Lord Chamberlain, the Earl of
Suffolk, detested the pair. This was partly for political reasons: as a

close ally of Salisbury, Suffolk would naturally have been displeased by the two young men's attempts to unsettle the Lord Treasurer. His antipathy to Rochester nevertheless went further, for he was filled with patrician contempt for this meanly bred, ill-educated Scot. He despised Rochester for the way he preened and simpered before the King, and was sickened by his flirtatiousness. Furthermore, while Rochester did not go out of his way to be rude, it infuriated Suffolk that this upstart saw no need to be unduly deferential towards more established figures at court. In 1611 the Lord Chamberlain wrote a remarkably frank letter[69] about Rochester. It was addressed to his old friend Sir John Harington, and Suffolk entrusted it to his son for delivery to ensure that it did not fall into the wrong hands. 'We are almost worn out in our endeavours to keep pace with this fellow in duty and labour to gain favour, but all in vain,' he sourly informed Sir John. Sardonically he described the shameless way James fondled his favourite in public, and how the young man encouraged him. Suffolk reported that the King was trying to make up for the deficiencies in Carr's education by teaching him Latin, growling, 'I think someone should teach him English too; for as he is a Scottish lad he hath much need of better language.' In the same tones of biting disdain, Suffolk went on to say that James was not alone in finding Rochester attractive, for the court ladies were 'not behindhand in their admiration'. The Earl then noted that, although there were men at court who would be outraged 'were Carr to leer on their wives', some husbands felt that it would be advantageous to their careers if they permitted him to ogle their ladies, and they even liked 'it well that they should be so noticed'.[70]

It was perhaps odd that Suffolk, who was reputed to be so understanding about his wife's liaison with Salisbury, should be so censorious about the way other men encouraged Rochester to flirt with their wives. This, however, was not the supreme irony of the letter. As Suffolk registered his aristocratic contempt for the libidinous young Scot, he was oblivious to the fact that the court lady who was most flattered by Rochester's attentions was his own daughter, Frances, Countess of Essex.

We do not know when Rochester first became interested in Frances. The only information we have on the methods he used to win her comes from a letter that Overbury wrote to him shortly before his death. In this Overbury reminisced about the time when Rochester 'fell in love' with Frances, although unfortunately he did not go into such detail as to permit a full reconstruction of these events. The letter makes clear that Overbury initially abetted Rochester in his pursuit of Frances, presumably because he assumed that once his friend had attained her, he would swiftly discard her. It was only when it emerged that Rochester's attachment to her was more serious than that, that Overbury took fright.

Overbury's alarm at this development was understandable, for he detested the whole Howard clan. Political differences accounted in part for his hostility, but it was sharpened by what one source describes as 'private malice'. He had never made any secret of his feelings, and had 'always professed hatred and opposition' to all Howards. He 'did much abuse the family' whenever an opportunity arose, saying 'that he hoped to live to see them all as low as now high'. He was habitually so insulting about them that some people were shocked that no male member of the family ever challenged him to a duel.[71] It is possible that Overbury initially encouraged Rochester to seduce Frances in the hope of ruining her reputation and bringing dishonour on her family. Certainly any suffering experienced by Frances as a result would have been to Overbury a matter of no account. As his poem *The Wife* makes plain, he believed that the onus fell exclusively on women to protect their virtue from male onslaughts, and that those who proved susceptible to temptation were objects ripe for exploitation.

It is not clear whether Overbury was a successful predator on women himself. Ben Jonson claimed that Overbury was 'in love with' the Countess of Rutland, and implied that one reason why he and Overbury quarrelled was that Overbury wanted Jonson to persuade the Countess to commit adultery with him. However, Jonson's reminiscences are far from reliable, and he is the only person known to have linked Overbury with a woman. After Overbury died his enemies spread a rumour that Overbury had had a terminal venereal disease but, when the case came to trial, the Attorney-General stressed that this was an unjust slur. 'As to dissoluteness, I never heard the gentleman noted with it,' he declared. 'His faults were of insolency, turbulency, and the like of that kind; the other part of the soul, not the voluptuous.'[72] While regarding himself as an authority on the qualities desirable in a wife, Overbury made little attempt to find himself such a paragon, preferring to condemn those who fell short of these standards than to settle down with someone who conformed to his ideals. He found it better to deal with women at one remove, deriving a vicarious pleasure from Rochester's love affairs, and monitoring their progress carefully by offering encouragement and advice.

At the outset of the courtship Rochester was in particular need of Overbury's assistance for, initially, Frances put up some resistance.

Overbury's literary experience proved invaluable in overcoming these 'difficulties'. He composed winning love letters on his friend's behalf, infinitely better phrased than the laboured prose that came from Rochester's pen. After receiving a few of these missives, Frances began to melt. Perhaps it was now, as it became apparent that their quarry was attainable, that Rochester and Overbury enjoyed exchanging jokes at Frances's expense. Years later, when Overbury and Rochester had fallen out because of Overbury's insults about Frances, Overbury reminded Rochester of the time when he 'would speak ill of her yourself'.[73]

Gradually Rochester had less need to use Overbury as his mouthpiece, and started to communicate directly with Frances. Overbury, however, had no doubt that his part had been crucial. He later told Rochester bluntly, 'You . . . won her by my letters,' refusing to admit that Rochester could have appealed to her on his own account. In fact, it was hardly surprising that Frances proved so responsive. Shackled to a husband for whom she had the utmost distaste, she now found herself pursued by one of the most eligible men at court. Since she was unaware that he looked on her as little more than a plaything, she grabbed at this chance for romantic fulfilment. There were, however, obvious problems. Adultery was an offence which came under the jurisdiction of the ecclesiastical Court of the Arches, which could impose degrading penances on those who committed this sin. A more immediate worry was the reaction of her husband and family if they found out. Her parents were aware that her marriage to the Earl of Essex was not happy but, far from being sympathetic, had indicated that they expected her to make the best of things. Admittedly, if Frances could have arranged things discreetly, they might not have disapproved in principle of an extramarital affair, but they were scarcely likely to condone a relationship with Rochester, since Frances's father utterly abhorred him. Unable to confide in her family at this juncture, Frances turned instead to her great friend and confidante, Mrs Anne Turner.

Anne Turner was a petite widow with 'a fair visage' and 'locks like golden thread'. She was in her mid-thirties, having been born in January 1576. Born Anne Norton, she came of an old Suffolk family with some claims to gentility: its members were entitled to bear arms with eleven quarterings, and the family crest was a greyhound's head with a gold collar. She was nominally a Catholic, although she later claimed that, after the exposure of the Gunpowder Plot, she had ceased attending mass. She had married Dr George Turner, a Catholic physician of repute, who may even have numbered Queen Elizabeth among his patients. Certainly in 1602, when the College of Physicians was demurring about electing him because of his religious sympathies, Sir Robert Cecil wrote to the college saying that his election would be pleasing to the Queen because, despite his non-conformity, 'he is no way tainted for malice or practice against the state'. Turner was duly elected, and at the time of his death in 1610 was acting as Treasurer for the college.[74]

It is not clear how Frances and Mrs Turner met. Mrs Turner would declare at her trial, 'She was ever brought up with the Countess,' but this sheds little light on the matter. Perhaps before her marriage she had some position in the Earl of Suffolk's household, and this was how she made his daughter's acquaintance. Subsequently, however, she was at pains to point out that Frances looked on her as a friend rather than an employee. After Frances's second marriage, Mrs Turner took up an invitation to come and live with her and her new husband, but she stressed that she did this 'not as her servant'. There is no doubt that the two women were remarkably close. Mrs Turner would later declare that Frances was 'as dear unto me as my own soul' and, when Frances wrote her a letter, she addressed her as 'Sweet Turner', and signed herself, 'Your sister, Frances Essex.'[75]

Frances had been very good to Mrs Turner when she had been widowed in 1610. Admittedly, Mrs Turner is unlikely to have been inconsolable at her loss. For some years prior to her husband's death she had been having an affair with Sir Arthur Mainwaring, a carver to Prince Henry, who had fathered three of her children. Dr Turner, it seems, had been aware of the situation, and had accepted it. At any rate, in his will he was amiable enough to leave Mainwaring a bequest of £10, implying that this should be spent on a wedding ring for Mrs Turner to be engraved with the motto, *Fato junguntur Amantes* (May the fates unite the lovers). Sadly for Mrs Turner, Mainwaring did not take the hint. He would have been quite a catch, for in 1609 he had been left a large estate worth £1,500 a year by his cousin, as well as additional cash and furniture, but he showed little inclination to share these assets with her.[76] He and Mrs Turner continued to see each other, and she sometimes claimed to be engaged to him, but Mainwaring could not be prevailed upon to make a formal commitment.

Marriage to Mainwaring represented Mrs Turner's only hope of security, for at Dr Turner's death she had been left 'in a desperate state' financially. She was also lonely on account of having suffered a fall in social status, 'other physicians neglecting to come to her as they would in her husband's time'. Her only independent means of providing for herself lay in selling the formula for a coloured starch that dyed ruffs and cuffs bright yellow. It was a fashion that had originated in France, but Mrs Turner had been so enterprising as to introduce it to England. Among the modish, yellow ruffs and cuffs had swiftly become mandatory, and were soon such a common sight that Ben Jonson claimed in *The Devil is an Ass* that even chimneysweeps and car-men 'are got into the yellow starch'. For some reason it was a fad that enraged traditionalists. One said that yellow ruffs might suit the French, as the 'colour did set off their lean sallow countenances', but it gave the English 'jaundice complexions'. The Dean of Westminster disapproved so violently that he actually sought to ban from his church ladies wearing yellow ruffs, and only abandoned the idea in the face of vigorous protests. But, though yellow starch was so popular with the fashionable elite, sales of the substance did not bring in enough to provide Mrs Turner and her brood with a comfortable living. In order to survive she had to rely on subsidies from Frances, who was by nature generous, or even careless, with money. Mrs Turner would later declare that she 'had no other means to maintain her and her children but what came of the Countess'.[77]

Such was Mrs Turner's desperation for Sir Arthur to propose that she was ready to coerce him by resorting to unorthodox means. In hopes of making Mainwaring less recalcitrant, she consulted the celebrated astrologer, necromancer and physician, Dr Simon Forman, who possibly had been an acquaintance of her late husband. Simon Forman was a small, red-headed man with a yellow beard and speckled complexion. Born in Wiltshire in December 1552, he was largely self-taught, for his father had died when Simon was only twelve and, thereafter, his formal education had been abandoned. Having been apprenticed to a general dealer, he picked up what knowledge he could by asking a schoolboy who lodged there to teach him by night what he had learned by day. He subsequently became a servant to two young gentlemen who were students at Oxford, and while at the university town he was able to study some more on his own account. After that he became a schoolmaster for a time, but in 1579 he embarked upon an exciting new career. In his diary he noted, 'This year I did prophesy the truth of many things which afterwards came to pass. The very spirits were subject unto me; what I spake was done.'[78] It was then that Forman decided to capitalise on these powers by establishing himself as a professional 'cunning man'.

'Cunning men', or wizards, were numerous in early seventeenth-century England. At the end of the sixteenth century it was estimated that they were comparable in numbers to the parish clergy. In Elizabethan

Essex no one is supposed to have lived more than ten miles from a known cunning man. In 1616, after it had emerged that the Countess of Somerset had been a client of several cunning men, Lord Chief Justice Coke mounted a purge of these practitioners of magic. Indignantly he informed the King that in London alone he had discovered 'thirteen imposters or wizards pretending to tell fortunes, to procure love to alter affections, to bring again stolen goods and such like deceits'. All were briefly imprisoned, and were released only after having provided sureties that they would not resume their activities.[79]

Sober-minded people lamented the prevalence of these charlatans, and the influence they exerted over their clients. In 1621 a future Bishop of Lincoln complained that it was 'scarce credible how generally and miserably our common ignorants are besotted' by belief in the power of wizards, charmers and fortune-tellers. Faith in their abilities was by no means confined to ill-educated sectors of society. Their enemies alleged that Catholic sympathisers were particularly credulous: not only had their religion already grounded them in superstition, but in some ways the rituals adopted for the conjuring of spirits were reminiscent of the Latin mass. However, pious Protestants were far from impervious to such beliefs. One Anglican minister admitted that 'seeking to witches and sorcerers was a common sin, even of hearers of the word', and certainly Forman numbered among his clientele senior clergymen such as the Dean of Rochester.[80]

Wizards were consulted for all manner of reasons, including requests to cure impotence, to locate lost property, to make children sleep or to bring luck at gambling. Sometimes the cunning man undertook to raise spirits who would assist him in carrying out these tasks. He was also frequently called upon to supply his clients with love philtres. Belief in the efficacy of these was widespread, even in educated circles: their effectiveness formed the subject of debates held at Oxford University in 1620, 1637 and 1653.[81]

Like many of his type, Simon Forman combined the practice of medicine with that of magic. For both these disciplines, a knowledge of astrology was essential. Qualified physicians did not dispute that the stars had a crucial bearing on health and well being, and doctors were accordingly required to be well versed in planetary lore. Different signs of the zodiac were believed to rule over different parts of the body, and it was agreed that celestial influences governed an individual's temperature, as well as the degree of moisture or dryness in his body. By casting a patient's horoscope, a medical practitioner discovered which planets dominated him or her, knowledge which was considered vital both when making a diagnosis and in selecting the most favourable time for treatment.

For Forman, however, astrology had wider applications. As well as treating patients who consulted him about their health, Forman was ready to foretell his clients' futures. His faith in his prophetic powers was such that he also conducted his own life according to his readings of the stars. In 1592, for example, he decided not to take as his wife a girl whose horoscope revealed she would 'play the whore privily'. He subsequently abandoned a plan to marry another woman when an astrological reading indicated an addiction to sodomy, of which Forman disapproved.[82]

Forman's chosen career was not without risk. The practice of medicine was officially confined to those licensed by the College of Physicians in London. This body jealously guarded its monopoly. While not disputing that astrology was a vital tool in medicine, they looked askance on unauthorised practitioners of the art. They claimed that such people lacked the necessary learning to make accurate interpretations of the stars, and had powers to imprison or fine individuals acting without the College's sanction.

Other areas of Forman's work were in theory still more hazardous. By a statute of 1604 the conjuring of spirits was declared a felony, punishable by hanging, and there were also numerous statutes against fortune-tellers. However, although black witches were often put on trial, people who practised magic without malevolent intent were not actively persecuted, and generally were tried only if caught defrauding clients of large sums of money. Nevertheless, men such as Forman were subject to irregular harassment by the authorities, and for this reason found it best to conduct their activities in secret.

Forman ran into trouble soon after he started practising his skills in Wiltshire, and in June 1579 he was imprisoned by a local magistrate for more than a year. After being freed he travelled for a time, but then returned to Wiltshire and resumed his activities. In Lent 1581 he was forced to desist after being bound over by Wiltshire Justices of the Peace and there ensued an interval in which he had to 'thresh and dig and hedge' in order to survive. Before long, however, he had started up again. He was again imprisoned in 1585, and suffered another term of confinement two years after that. Undaunted, he went to London in 1589, intent on setting up surgery there. For a time he had difficulty in making a living, and in 1590 he actually came near to starvation. Fortunately he survived this fallow period, and two years later he gained immense kudos during an epidemic of the plague. Fearing infection, many members of the College of Physicians had fled the disease-ridden capital, leaving the populace to fend for itself. Forman, however, had stayed behind. He created a sensation when he cured himself and members of his household of an illness diagnosed as the plague by lancing the sores that were a feature of the disease and administering liquors distilled by himself. At once others came to him, clamouring for treatment, and Forman repeated the formula with equal success.[83]

From that time on his reputation was assured. Forman's casebook became packed, and he was kept extraordinarily busy. Between 1597 and 1601 Forman cast over a thousand horoscopes; another indication of his industry is provided by his appointment book for 1598, which shows that on 20 February he saw six clients; on 22 February, five clients and on 24 February, seven clients. It was customary for Forman to cast a horoscope for each client, which always entailed elaborate computations.

During these years Forman was building up a distinguished clientele. It included the daughters of Queen Elizabeth's Lord Chamberlain, Lord Hunsdon; the Queen's lady-in-waiting, Lady Scrope; Lady Hoby and Lady Hawkins. He was also consulted by Lord Willoughby's daughter, Catherine Bertie, and by another Frances Howard, a distant cousin of the protagonist of this story, whose father bore the title Lord Howard of Bindon. Among his grander male clients were the naval commander Sir William Monson, Sir William and Sir Thomas Cornwallis and Sir Thomas Shirley. Intriguingly it appears that, during the reign of Queen Elizabeth, he once cast a horoscope for Frances's mother, Lady Suffolk, although it is not clear if this was at her instigation or at the request of another of his clients.[84]

Once Forman had acquired this formidable array of patrons, he became less vulnerable to attacks by officialdom. In his early years in London this had caused him some problems. In 1594 he was summoned before the College of Physicians, accused of unlawfully practising medicine. He was questioned about his knowledge of astrology, and his answers were condemned as deficient, his ignorance causing 'great mirth and sport among the auditors'. He was fined and forbidden to practise but, as usual, he ignored the injunction. Two years later the physicians again called him before them, and this time sent him to jail for his disobedience. No sooner was he freed than he resumed his practice, with the result that nine months later he found himself back in prison. This time, however, he was saved by one of his clients: Dr Blague, Dean of Rochester, interceded with the Archbishop of Canterbury, and Forman was let out of prison. He then moved to Lambeth in hopes of removing himself from the physicians' jurisdiction, but in 1603 he was again being harassed by the College. By this time, however, Forman had acquired powerful protectors. Frances, the daughter of Lord Howard of Bindon, was now married to the Earl of Hertford, and Lord and Lady Hertford promptly wrote to the Lord Chief Justice, protesting at Forman's treatment. The Chief Justice replied humbly that he had previously been prevailed upon by the physicians to grant a general warrant against Forman, but 'henceforth he would be better advised'. In June 1603 Forman gained an added legitimacy when the University of Cambridge conferred on him a doctorate and a licence to practise medicine and, thereafter, the physicians could not touch him. Permitted to practise unmolested, Forman grew prosperous. When he died he bequeathed his widow £1,200.

Forman's range of skills was astonishingly diverse. First and foremost, people came to him when they were ill. His fellow astrologer William Lilly testified that Forman was 'very judicious and fortunate' in treating sickness, 'which indeed was his masterpiece'. To modern eyes the treatment he advocated often appears dubious: when, for example, a clergyman named Dr Dove complained of suffering from 'a hoarseness and stuffing in his lungs that he cannot speak when he preacheth', Forman instructed him to purge himself. On the other hand there are areas in which Forman's unconventional ideas seem positively enlightened. He distrusted the teachings of Galen (the Greek physician and anatomist who lived in the second century AD), whereas the College of Physicians regarded these as sacrosanct. He also poured scorn on the idea that a patient's condition could be determined by an inspection of his urine, or 'judged by paltry piss', as Forman scathingly put it. When making diagnoses his reliance on astrology was not absolute, for he was also highly observant and intuitive, and he kept meticulous records.[85]

Starting in 1588 Forman had sought to enhance his prophetic powers through necromancy, or the conjuring up of deceased spirits. By 1590 he felt he knew enough to write a book on the subject, containing forms of prayer for summoning spirits good and evil. However, he never perfected the art to his own satisfaction. In 1596 he was still wondering 'whether I shall have that power in necromancy that I desire or bring it to effect?' The following year he noted that he had established contact with a spirit who had murdered its father. He reported that the apparition 'kept a wonderful ado, but we could not bring him to human form; he was seen like a great black dog, and troubled the folk of the house, and feared them'. With endearing honesty Forman added, 'But I saw him not. I saw the fire and then saw him in a kind of shape, but not perfectly.'[86]

Much of Forman's time was spent advising his clients on love matters. This was why Frances Howard's distant cousin and namesake consulted him. Before her marriage to Lord Hertford, she enquired of Forman whether the Earl of Southampton was in love with her, only to receive the discouraging reply that he bore her 'little good will'. The Dean of Rochester's promiscuous wife Alice Blague, who was 'given to lust and diversity of loves and men', likewise sought Forman's assistance over the conduct of her love life. Forman responded by fashioning for her a sigil in the form of a coral ring, which supposedly magically enhanced the attractions of its wearer. For another client 'the man with the cock was engraved', presumably a phallic figurine intended to inspire love in a designated person. Forman could charge a high price for such services. When Alice Blague asked Forman to secure her the love of a clergyman named Dean Wood, she gave him a down payment of 26s. 8d., promising Forman an additional £5 when Wood became 'full friend to her'.[87]

Some seers and alchemists held that it was only by leading a pure life that they could preserve their magical powers, but Forman did not subscribe to this view. He did not have sexual intercourse (or 'halek' as he mysteriously referred to it in his diaries) with a woman until he was thirty years old, but thereafter he compensated for his dilatoriness, having a series of mistresses as well as casual affairs. In 1599 he married Jane Baker, but he did not remain faithful to her. Nor did he observe a strict code of ethics at work, for he had affairs with several of his clients. Among these was Alice Blague, even though her husband, the Dean of Rochester, was a regular visitor to Forman's surgery. Another of the Doctor's conquests was Mrs Ellen Flower, who had originally consulted him to find out when her husband would return from sea, and had then found solace in Forman's arms for Mr Flower's absence.

Since Forman was as precise as ever in maintaining records of these encounters, we know the names of other female clients who slept with him, including Mrs Hipwell, Mrs Condwell (whose husband had been a witness at Forman's wedding) and Emilia Lanier, the former mistress of Lord Hunsdon. In his levels of sexual activity Forman could display prodigious energy: on 9 July 1607, for example, he had sex with one woman at 8 a.m., then with another at three that afternoon, and finally made love to his wife at nine in the evening.[88]

Forman seduced only a small minority of his clients. It is clear, however, that even when he had no sexual contact with women who consulted him, he did not treat them with purely professional detachment. Their belief in his occult powers predisposed his female clients to look on him with awe, making it easy for him to dominate them by sheer force of personality. Over the nobly born young ladies who came to see him, he sometimes assumed a quasi-paternal authority. The other Frances Howard (the future Countess of Hertford) called Forman 'father'. When Frances, Countess of Essex, came to him she soon began to do likewise, signing herself 'your affectionate loving daughter' when she wrote to him. Furthermore, even while imploring Forman in this letter to do all he could to make Viscount Rochester enamoured of her, she would declare, 'I must still crave your love, although I hope I have it, and shall deserve it better hereafter.' Her tremulous words demonstrate the mastery which Forman exercised over his clients, and the way he managed to keep them in a state of highly charged emotional subjection. It was an achievement perhaps not surprising from one whose position has been described as that of 'doctor, priest and psychoanalyst rolled into one', and who also claimed to have control over supernatural forces.[89]

It turned out to be beyond Forman's powers to bring Sir Arthur Mainwaring to marry Mrs Turner, although we are told that he did once induce in Mainwaring an extraordinary frenzy of lust. According to Arthur Wilson, Mrs Turner plied Sir Arthur with 'philtrous powders' supplied by Forman which 'wrought so violently with him that through a storm of rain and thunder he rode fifteen miles one dark night to her house, scarce knowing where he was till he was there'. Perhaps it was this feat which encouraged Frances to turn to Forman for guidance, although exactly what she wanted from him remains obscure. We know that she asked him to see that Viscount Rochester did not lose interest in her, begging, 'Keep the Lord still to me, for that I desire.' However, she may well also have asked Forman to work magic ensuring that her husband would remain incapable of consummating their marriage. Certainly the marital bed was an area which Forman deemed susceptible to his influence. In one of the manuals he wrote on the occult he recorded the procedure 'to tie a man not to meddle with a woman *et contra*'. His instructions were: 'In the time of matrimony take a point [a lace] and tie three knots thereon. When the priest says, "Whom God hath joined together, let no man separate," then they knit the knots, naming the party, saying, "Whom God hath joined together let the Devil separate. *Sara*, until these knots be undone." And he shall never meddle with the said woman. *Probatum*.'[90]

Since Forman had not been present at the marriage between Frances and Essex, he would have had to devise alternative measures, but doubtless he had something appropriate in his repertoire. Frances once mentioned that Forman had supplied her with 'jellies', and presumably these substances were intended either to stimulate desire in Rochester, or to disable her husband sexually. When Mrs Turner was arrested in 1615, a lead statuette of a copulating couple was found in her possession. It was assumed that this was one of Forman's products, used as part of some ritual enchantment. Although by that time Forman himself was dead, a search of his study yielded up other magical paraphernalia and 'cunning tricks', including pieces of parchment which allegedly were inscribed with the names of devils who would torment Rochester and Arthur Mainwaring 'if their loves should not continue'.[91]

Presumably Forman claimed credit for the fact that Rochester's admiration for Frances showed no signs of slackening. Unfortunately the doctor was less successful in freeing her from the attentions of her husband for, in the summer of 1611, Essex carried his wife off to his country estate, Chartley in Staffordshire. Frances was appalled at being marooned with her husband in what she termed 'this vile place'. She was by now passionately in love with Rochester, and she was terrified that his desire for her would wither while she was absent from court. Another anxiety was that Essex would at last succeed in making love to her, a prospect which not only filled her with revulsion, but which she feared would make Rochester angry with her. Her position was the more beleaguered because Essex had complained to her parents that she was failing to fulfil her matrimonial duties, and the Suffolks had made it clear to her that they considered her to be at fault. Evidently Essex had contrived to lay all the blame on her for their sexual failure, without mentioning any physical shortcomings of his own. Her family had warned her that she could not continue in this way, and Frances's brother had warned her that, since Essex was planning to stay in the country all winter, there was no question of a speedy return to court.

Ignoring pressure from her family to be more affectionate to her husband, Frances left Essex in no doubt at her resentment of the rustic existence he had imposed on her. Arthur Wilson recounted indignantly that, despite the fine summer weather, 'She shut herself up in her chamber, not suffering a beam of light to peep upon her dark thoughts. If she stirred out of her chamber, it was in the dead of night, when sleep had taken possession of all others.'[92]

Trapped and isolated as she was, Frances refused passively to accept her fate. She managed to maintain a lifeline between Staffordshire and London, smuggling out letters to Anne Turner and Dr Forman, in which she lamented her unfortunate condition and begged them not to

abandon her. Because of Frances's indiscriminate use of pronouns in
these documents, and her confusing references to 'My Lord' (Essex),
'the Lord' (Rochester), and 'the party' (Forman), it is sometimes hard
to be sure of her meaning. What is vividly conveyed, however, is her
utter misery at being yoked to Essex, her horror at the thought of
having to sleep with him, and the all-consuming nature of her passion
for 'the Lord'.

Having instructed Mrs Turner to 'burn this letter' (an admonition
which was ignored), Frances wrote:

Sweet Turner,
    I am out of all hope of any good in this world, for my father, my
mother, and my brother said, I should lie with him; and my brother
Howard was here, and said, he would not come from this place all
winter; so that all comfort is gone; and which is worst of all my Lord
hath complained, that he hath not lain with me, and I would not suffer
him to use me. My father and mother are angry, but I had rather die a
thousand times over; for besides the sufferings, I shall lose his [Roches-
ter's] love if I lie with him [Essex]. I will never desire to see his face, if
my Lord do that unto me. My Lord is very well as ever he was, so as
you may see in what a miserable case I am. You may send the party
word of all; he sent me word all should be well, but I shall not be so
happy as the Lord to love me. As you have taken pains all this while
for me, so now do all you can, for never so unhappy as now; for I am
not able to endure the miseries that are coming on me, but I cannot be
happy so long as this man liveth; therefore, pray for me, for I have
need, but I should be better if I had your company to ease my mind.
Let him [Forman?] know this ill news; if I can get this done, you shall
have as much money as you can demand, this is fair play – Your sister,
Frances Essex.[93]

To Forman she expressed herself in equally despairing terms:

Sweet Father,
    I must needs still crave your love, though I hope I shall have it, and
shall deserve it better hereafter. Remember the jellies, for I fear, though
I have no cause but to be confident in you, yet I desire to have that
remain as it is, yet will so continue it still if possible, and if you can,
you must send me good fortune. Alas, I have need of it, for now I am
a miserable woman. Keep the Lord still to me, for that I desire above
all things in this life, and be careful you name me not to anybody, for
we have so many spies, that all your wit you must use, and little enough,

for the world is against me, and I do fear the heavens favour me not; only happy in your love, and I hope you will do me good. And if I be ungrateful, let all mischief come to me. My Lord is lusty and merry, and drinketh with his men, and useth me as doggedly as ever before, and all the contentment he gives me is to abuse me. I think I shall never be happy in this world, because he hinders all my good, and will ever, I think. Remember, I beg for God's sake, and get me from this vile place. – Your assured, affectionate loving daughter, Frances Essex.[94]

Sadly for Frances, Forman would not be on hand much longer to provide comfort. He had always prided himself on his ability to foretell when people would die, and in early September 1611 he had a premonition that his own demise was imminent. According to the astrologer William Lilly, one Sunday evening at supper Forman's wife jokingly asked him whether she would outlive him. Although he appeared in perfect health, Forman sombrely replied, 'Oh Trunco [his nickname for his wife, meaning 'Body'], thou wilt bury me, but thou wilt much repent it.' When his wife enquired how long she would have to wait, he told her he would be dead ''ere Thursday night'. As the week went by Forman showed no signs of illness, and by Wednesday evening his wife was teasing him about his faulty prediction. Nevertheless, on the afternoon of Thursday, 8 September 1611, Forman was rowing himself across the Thames when he suddenly collapsed and died.[95]

Not long after Forman's death Mrs Turner appeared at his house. According to Forman's widow, Mrs Turner demanded that she surrender to her any papers in her late husband's study which related to the Countess of Essex and Viscount Rochester. Mrs Turner promised that the Countess would reward Mrs Forman for this whereas, if she refused to cooperate, the Council would doubtless order a search of Forman's house. They 'might find such things as might hurt' not only Rochester and Lady Essex, but also Mrs Forman, for the Council would probably then order that all Forman's property should be seized. In alarm, Mrs Forman handed over 'divers letters and papers', which Mrs Turner at once burned. However, as a precaution Mrs Forman kept back two of Frances's letters to her late husband, which subsequently were handed to the authorities.[96]

It is possible that Frances was already back in the capital by this time; certainly, despite her fears that she would be kept in Staffordshire all winter, she returned to London at some stage in the autumn. She and Mrs Turner wasted no time finding a replacement for Dr Forman. They approached two other conjurers, who operated in partnership, a

Mr Gresham and Dr Savory. Gresham was 'a very skilful man in the
mathematics' while Savory was subsequently described as one who 'had
no honest profession to maintain himself and maketh shew of profession
of physic'. When Mrs Turner was tried as an accessory to murder, it
was claimed that she had confessed that Savory had 'practised many
sorceries upon the Earl of Essex's person', but no such confession
survives. When Savory himself was interrogated on the matter, he gave
a much more guarded account of his activities. He maintained that Mrs
Turner had approached him and asked him 'to be earnest with Gresham
that Sir Arthur [Mainwaring] might marry her'. She had promised that
for these services, Gresham 'should have good satisfactions' and Savory
should be 'well contented', but in the event had paid them nothing. This
was understandable, since Sir Arthur showed little sign of renouncing
bachelordom, but Savory then tried to blackmail his client. He wrote to
her saying, 'If she would not satisfy me according as she did promise,
I would make it known unto Sir Arthur what she had been about
concerning him,' and also threatening to denounce her to the ecclesiastical Court of the Arches for having produced illegitimate children by
Mainwaring.[97]

It may be that Frances's involvement with these unpleasant characters
was only peripheral, for her love affair with Rochester was progressing
very satisfactorily without supernatural assistance. The indications are
that by the spring of 1612, if not before, he and Frances had become
lovers in the physical sense.[98] Although Rochester may well have
intended to abandon Frances once he had attained her, he did not do
so. In fact, far from breaking off the affair, he found himself pursuing
it with greater vigour.

Mrs Turner proved invaluable in helping Frances to arrange assignations with her lover. To facilitate their communications she suggested
that they avail themselves of the services of a former employee of hers
named Richard Weston. Weston was a man of about sixty whose 'sober
and fair outside' gave a misleading impression of his true character. He
had started out in life as a tailor, but had long since abandoned that
calling. At some time in the past he had narrowly escaped hanging on
charges of coining, having been discovered with a pocketful of counterfeit
sixpences. Luckily for him no witnesses had come forward to testify
against him, so charges had not been pressed. Since then he had been
employed for a time as a bailiff for Dr Turner. After the doctor had
died, he had remained in Mrs Turner's service, working at her house
in Paternoster Row.[99]

Mrs Turner now suggested that Weston could act as a messenger for

Frances and Rochester. Weston proved happy to perform this task, delivering Frances's letters to the favourite when the latter was staying with the King at Royston and Newmarket. On these occasions he 'brought answer back again by letter', handing the reply to Mrs Turner to pass on to Frances. Another time he delivered one of Frances's letters to Rochester at Hampton Court, and brought her back the verbal answer 'that my Lord would come'. When Frances learned this, she went with Mrs Turner and Weston to a 'house between Hammersmith and Brentford, over against a common and over against a smith's forge, into which house, being a farmer's house, the lady went'. Rochester joined Frances shortly afterwards, and 'they tarried together about an hour and a half at the least', after which Frances returned to London, and Rochester went back to Hampton Court. This encounter took place at two in the afternoon, but Weston was also present when Frances and Rochester had a nocturnal meeting at Mrs Turner's house in Paternoster Row, 'the Countess being there about half an hour before the Lord'.[100]

In the summer of 1612, Frances's trysts with Rochester were interrupted when her husband once again obliged her to retire with him to the country. There is conflicting evidence as to how long the separation lasted. In 1613, when Frances was seeking to have her marriage annulled, it was claimed that at this juncture she was absent from London for over four months, from midsummer to the end of October. According to this account, she and Essex first visited his grandmother in Warwickshire before progressing to Chartley. It seems, however, that after accompanying Essex on the first stage of the journey, Frances managed to slip away, promising to rejoin her husband at the first opportunity. On 11 August John Chamberlain reported from London, 'The Countess of Essex was going down to her Lord into Staffordshire, and some of her carriage was sent away, but she hath since changed her purpose and is come to this town, being in hand (as I hear) to buy or take Sir Roger Aston's house beyond Hounslow, that stands commodiously for many purposes.'[101] The last, seemingly innocuous, phrase was perhaps invested with a hidden significance. Chamberlain was exceptionally well informed, and may already have had some intimation that Frances needed a suitable location for clandestine encounters.

For Rochester, 1612 was a remarkable year. His relationship with Frances, which he had originally assumed would be merely diverting, deepened into something more serious. On the political front, great things were also happening. On 22 April 1612 Rochester was made a Privy Councillor. The announcement created a sensation, provoking spiteful comment in some quarters. John Barlee wrote sarcastically to a friend, 'The wise Carr is a counsellor of state to his Majesty, being thought fit at five-and-twenty. I pray you, keep your heart cool and your stomach unbuttoned, that it set you not afire with noble emulation.'[102]

Before long, however, Rochester had become still more influential. On 24 May 1612 the Earl of Salisbury died, and at once there was feverish speculation as to who would succeed him in the key positions of Secretary of State and Lord Treasurer. One observer reported, 'Here is extreme elbowing by great lords to bring in their friends to be secretaries,' and this meant that the atmosphere at court became still more febrile and competitive. To avoid causing resentment the King decided not to appoint a Secretary for the time being. He announced that he would do the job himself, boasting that 'he is prettily skilled in the craft ... and till he be thoroughly weary will execute it in person'. The King now assumed personal responsibility not only for the formation of foreign policy, but also for communicating his decisions to diplomats serving overseas. Naturally, however, James could not do all this without assistance of any sort. Since Rochester had aided him with his correspondence in the past, James decided it was time to entrust him with more weighty responsibilities. Despatches from ambassadors stationed abroad were now delivered to Rochester, who read them and then handed them on to the King. Later James would return the letter to Rochester, so he could 'answer by direction of his Majesty'.[103]

Despite Rochester's youth and inexperience, he now occupied a pivotal role. In July 1612, when Lord Sheffield wrote him a letter full of state business, he explained that he did so 'knowing your Lordship with the King doth manage for foreign affairs of this kingdom'. Rochester was also now awarded custody of the Signet, the seal traditionally held by the Secretary of State. This not only authenticated the King's letters, but had to be affixed to patents authorising royal grants. Previously the Signet had been entrusted to Sir Thomas Lake, one of the men who had hoped to be named Secretary, and he naturally resented having to part with it. Nevertheless, he thought it best to hide his anger with Rochester. Through gritted teeth Lake told Sir Thomas Edmondes, the English ambassador in France, 'The said courtier groweth potent in affairs here and therefore you shall do wisely to respect him hereafter.' Undoubtedly such forbearance was sensible. Rochester was now the 'man that does all', and the knowledgeable Scots courtier, Viscount Fenton, even insisted, 'His power is greater than any that ever I have seen in his place, and no man to gainsay him.'[104]

Some people assumed that once Rochester had served out a term of apprenticeship, the King would formally appoint him Secretary of State, but astute observers knew that the favourite's real ambitions lay elsewhere. Although he enjoyed wielding influence, the drudgery which was an inescapable part of a Secretary's existence was less to his taste. One of his more sycophantic correspondents correctly assessed the situation when he observed, 'I can hardly believe that ever so delicate a person would endure so great a pain.'[105]

If Rochester now found that he was kept busier than he could have wished, he was at least well paid, for the King continued to treat his favourite with reckless generosity. In February 1612 James awarded Rochester an annuity of £1,000, supplementing this with £15,500 conferred as 'free gift and reward'. Rochester used some of this money to buy land, and his holdings were further enlarged when James secretly transferred to him ownership of various Crown properties. Rochester's income was boosted higher by the grant of profitable offices. Following Lord Salisbury's death, he succeeded him as Bailiwick of Westminster, a post that brought with it £500 a year. Far more significant than this, however, was the promise he secured from the King in January 1612 that when the office of Chief Clerk of the Court of Common Pleas fell vacant, he and Sir John Harington would jointly succeed to it. Worth an estimated £3,500 a year, this was one of the most lucrative positions in the entire administration. Rochester had had his eye on it since 1608, intending that when he gained possession of it, he would pay a small amount to a deputy to carry out its duties, leaving him and Harington with ample proceeds to divide between them.[106]

By no means all of Rochester's wealth came directly from the Crown. Suitors who obtained favours at court through his intercession had always been aware that his assistance could not be had for nothing. Now that he was – as one courtier put it – 'the *Primum mobile* of our court, by whose motion all the other spheres must move, or else stand still', his services commanded an even higher premium. This led to claims by his enemies that he grossly abused his position, and that he built up a vast fortune through corruption. One hostile source alleged that 'using extraordinary covetousness and parsimony, he thereby heaped up to himself great store of money, and would not undertake any enterprise without he was well rewarded for his pains ... Offices in court that lay in his gift not bestowed without money; no pardon obtained without money; so that he was as great a bribe-taker as his mother [-in-law] the Countess of Suffolk.'[107]

In fact, compared to the excesses that characterised the latter half of James's reign, Rochester's handling of such matters appears almost restrained, at least at this stage of his career. Certainly Rochester prided himself on his moderation, and stressed that he did not exploit his influence as much as he could have done. In a letter written in October 1612 he pointed out that Sir John Roper, the present Chief Clerk of the Court of Common Pleas, had offered to vacate the office immediately if Rochester would persuade the King to make him a peer. Tempting though the prospect was of assuming the office at once, Rochester had declined the bargain, 'because I would not set titles to sale for my private ends'. Proudly the Viscount declared, 'Towards the nobility and towards all men may I justify myself that I am the courtier whose hand never took bribe, and that partly my estate can witness, which I have sought rather to preserve by moderate expense than to increase by unjust getting.'[108]

It is true that many of Rochester's contemporaries would have found his claim that he kept his spending in tight check a little hard to stomach. His statement that he never took bribes also requires clarification. There is no doubt that Rochester made money out of promoting the interests of individuals who wanted something from the King. Nevertheless, it was widely accepted that influential persons who exerted themselves in this way deserved some form of recompense and, providing due discrimination was exercised, and profiteering was kept within acceptable limits (which, admittedly, were never quantified), such practices were not viewed as inherently dishonest. Rochester felt that he satisfied these criteria. He claimed that, when recommending men to the King, he was not motivated solely by the prospect of personal gain, but also took other factors into account, such as whether they were competent or deserving. For this reason he felt justified in boasting that he had consistently sought 'to preserve love betwixt the King and his people, and ever to join his and the public good, and use my favour as much as [in] me lay towards the advancement of worthy men'. The Spanish ambassador, Don Diego de Sarmiento de Acuna, also claimed that Rochester never accepted payment from grateful suitors without clearing this with the King beforehand.[109]

Of their very nature, most of the transactions involving Rochester remain shadowy, so it is hard to gauge whether he was genuinely entitled to congratulate himself on his probity. We know that, in January 1613, Sir John Swinnerton told Rochester that if he secured him the contract to collect the customs duties on French and Rhenish wines, 'I will most thankfully give unto your Lordship yearly during the same lease the sum of £1,000 a year.' In the event Swinnerton did not secure what he wanted, and instead the existing leaseholders' tenure was extended. This could perhaps be adduced as evidence of Rochester's incorruptibility, were it not highly likely that he was on the payroll of the winning syndicate. Certainly when the customs farmers applied for a renewal of their lease, they informed the King that they had 'chosen the Lord Rochester, whose integrity we all know' to convey their terms to him.[110]

While there is no proof that Rochester received any remuneration on that occasion, in September 1613, when the lease of the sweet wine farm came up for renewal, he extorted a high price for his services. At that time a merchant named Lionel Cranfield offered Rochester 1,000 marks (just over £672) if he could obtain him the contract. Rochester let him know that another businessman was prepared to offer twice as much, and that Cranfield had no chance of success unless he matched this.[111]

So long as the customs were not collected by men who either deliberately defrauded the King, or imposed illegal exactions, Rochester could argue that the system enriched him without being detrimental to the public. Inevitably, however, the ruthless way he capitalised on his position with the King intensified the envy and resentment which others felt for him. In particular, men begrudged having to pay him substantial sums even when they had secured favours from the King without Rochester's assistance. Sir David Wood, a Scots servant of Queen Anne, was a case in point. Wood had obtained a suit from the Crown that he calculated would bring him £2,200. Just when he was congratulating himself on having secured so notable a prize, Rochester materialised and informed him that unless Wood paid him £1,200, he would see to it that the grant was never finalised. Naturally Wood was furious at this unexpected demand. Francis Bacon was another man who was annoyed by Rochester's depredations. In the autumn of 1613 Bacon applied for the position of Attorney-General. The King had already indicated that the post was his when Rochester suddenly 'thrust himself into the business for a fee'. Though Bacon paid up with as good a grace as he could muster, the incident left him seething.[112]

It was particularly unfortunate that Rochester frequently delegated Overbury to act as his agent when such delicate matters were in question. Overbury lacked the finesse to persuade an aggrieved party that Rochester's demands were reasonable, generally adopting an abrasive approach when he should have been emollient. Sir David Wood's fury at being asked to forego a sizeable slice of his profits was greatly exacerbated by the insensitive way Overbury handled the negotiations. Wood recalled later that, while they were haggling, he 'received some disgraceful words at the hand of Sir Thomas Overbury for which he meant to have given him the bastinado'.[113]

Overbury did not confine himself to acting as Rochester's business manager. Rochester had an indifferent intellect, and he found his new political responsibilities overwhelming. Unaccustomed to statecraft, he was left struggling with the massive amounts of paperwork and reading which the King now expected of him. Overbury, on the other hand, had an incisive mind, and found it easy to assimilate detailed information, or to reduce a complex document to its essentials. Unable to cope on his own, Rochester turned to Overbury for assistance. When despatches arrived from abroad, Rochester would pass them to his friend so that he could condense them for him. Years later a servant of Overbury's described the process, recalling an occasion when the English ambassador in Spain had sent a letter to the King. The sealed packet was first delivered to Rochester, who forwarded it unopened to Overbury. Overbury read the letter, 'took brief notes for my Lord ... and, sealing it again, sent both the notes and packets to him'.[114] Thus, by the time that Rochester took the letter to the King, he was familiar with its contents and capable of discussing it intelligently.

The arrangement meant that Overbury exerted a real, if unacknowledged, influence on state affairs. When summarising a document he could lay particular stress on one part, and this might well colour the King's interpretation of it. Despite the fact that he had no official position, he now enjoyed regular access to top-secret papers, many of which were never seen even by Privy Councillors. Before long he and Rochester were routinely exchanging such sensitive information that they developed a rudimentary cipher to be used in written communications, whereby all the leading figures at court were given their own sobriquets. While this was obviously a sensible security measure, there was also a more light-hearted side to it, for several of the nicknames they devised had humorous overtones. For example, since Sir Henry Neville bore a marked resemblance to the late King Henry VIII, Rochester and Overbury christened him 'Similis'. Other eminent persons were given slightly irreverent codewords. Thus the Queen was 'Agrippina', the Archbishop of Canterbury 'Unctius', the Earl of Pembroke 'Niger' and the Earl of Suffolk 'Wolsey'.[115]

In many ways it was inappropriate that a humble sewer should have so significant a role at the heart of government. Nevertheless, Rochester later claimed that the King knew what was going on and had no objection. And indeed, if Overbury had been more unassuming, the arrangement might have worked to everyone's satisfaction, but unfortunately it heightened Sir Thomas's already exaggerated self-esteem. Instead of contenting himself with acting as a loyal subordinate, he constantly reminded Rochester how dependent he was on him, maintaining that it was only on account of the work he put in that Rochester could satisfy the King as to his competence. He bragged that Rochester owed more to him than 'to any soul living both for ... fortune, understanding and reputation' and 'did not stick to upbraid this gentleman to his face, that he had neither wit nor discretion but what he put into him'. Worse still, Overbury left no one else in any doubt of the extent to which he dominated Rochester. Partly on account of this it began to be whispered that 'Rochester ruled [the King] and Overbury ruled Rochester', and when this reached James's ears, he was naturally furious. While excusing Rochester, he blamed Overbury for allowing such a perception to develop, and became 'much distasted with the said gentleman, even in his own nature, for too stiff a carriage of his fortune'.[116]

Once people became aware that Overbury was transacting so much confidential business, it led to speculation that he would shortly be appointed Secretary, the assumption being that he would 'fit himself ... to furnish the place ... by the practice and experience he is now in'. In view of the King's fixed dislike of Sir Thomas this was never a realistic prospect, and Overbury had the sense to understand as much. Instead he urged Rochester to persuade the King to give the job to their long-established political ally, Sir Henry Neville. Neville's appointment had the support of other influential men at court, including the Earl of Pembroke (like Rochester, a Privy Councillor) and the Earl of Southampton. Both believed that it would ease political tensions in the country by contenting those 'Parliament mutineers' who had criticised the King during the last session. The two Earls started attending meetings in Rochester's Whitehall chambers, at which all those who favoured Sir Henry's candidacy debated how best to achieve their ends.[117]

The Earl of Suffolk was displeased by Rochester's campaign on Neville's behalf. He had a rival candidate for the post of Secretary, leading one courtier to report that the matter had become 'a subject of notorious opposition between our great Viscount and the house of Suffolk'. Much more alarmingly, however, it brought Rochester into conflict with the King. James had never forgiven Neville for having opposed him in the Commons, and now he declared angrily that he would 'not have a Secretary imposed upon him by Parliament'.[118]

Overbury saw to it that Rochester did not accept this as final. Despite

complaints from the Council that the absence of a Secretary meant that
'matters find not that despatch that were to be wished', the position
remained vacant, and Overbury refused to drop Neville's candidacy
until another man had been chosen. For months the King kept everyone
in suspense. There were times when it did seem that he was contemplating appointing Neville, but he always drew back before committing himself. Contrary to Overbury's calculations, he did not grow
more amenable as time went by, and instead became irritated by
Rochester's dogged support of Sir Henry. It displeased James that his
favourite, who in the past had always been so tractable and obliging,
should now be so tiresomely persistent, and the King blamed Overbury
for the transformation. His anger was fuelled by Sir Thomas's many
enemies, who seized every opportunity to speak evil of him. Since
Overbury's obstreperous behaviour had also alienated many of the men
who had earlier worked with him to secure Neville's advancement, he
had very few defenders. Towards the end of 1612 Sir Henry Neville
wrote sombrely to a friend, 'There hath been much poison cast out of
late unto the King both against him [Overbury] and me, but more
especially against him and with more advantage, because I doubt [i.e.
fear] he hath given some advantage to take hold of, being, as you know,
violent and open.' Neville added that the King was now so exasperated
that he was even showing signs of disenchantment with Rochester.[119]

Rochester was able to retrieve the situation by nursing James devotedly
when the latter was struck down by a sudden illness. On 9 December
1612 Isaac Wake brought Sir Dudley Carleton up to date with what had
happened. 'Viscount Rochester's credit is on a sudden much increased
with the King after a time of pause or standing still,' he reported, 'and
now, some clouds being overblown that shadowed him a little, the sun
shines upon him fairer than ever. The occasion that favoured him was
a sickness of the King in this last journey where his old infirmity of
looseness [diarrhoea] took him somewhat troublesomely, if not dangerously. During ye indisposition of his Majesty, Rochester showed so
much care and diligence in continual waiting and attending as that the
King ... professed publicly that he saw well how truly Rochester loved
him, and that, if he lived, he should requite it in such a manner that
all the world should take notice of it.' But, though Rochester had
managed to redeem himself by rendering James personal service, the
same course was not open to Overbury, and the King's attitude to him
remained one of 'rooted hatred'.[120]

The Earl of Suffolk's detestation of Rochester was no secret, but his daughter Frances was not the only member of his family who harboured feelings of a very different nature for the favourite. The Earl of Northampton was also greatly taken with Rochester, and worked hard to establish a warm relationship with him. It is tempting to suggest an element of physical attraction in this. Northampton was a confirmed bachelor, 'more wedded to his book than his bed', but his fondness for nobly born young men attracted some comment. One observer noted that he was 'always attended (and he loved it) with gentlemen of quality, to whom he was very bountiful'. While there is no evidence whatever that he ever made physical advances, Northampton's letters to Rochester do give the impression that he was a little in love with the young man. He invariably addressed him as 'Sweet Lord' or 'Sweet Rochester', and the correspondence abounds with sickly assurances, such as 'No man lies nearer than yourself to my heart.'[121] Yet Northampton had too desiccated a soul to allow himself to be wholly guided by emotion, and he had other reasons for cultivating Rochester. He knew it would please the King if he befriended the favourite, but he also calculated that, if they merged forces, they would constitute a formidable political partnership. Furthermore, whereas in the past Northampton had been overshadowed by Salisbury, he was confident that he would have little difficulty controlling Rochester. Not only did the young man strike him as pleasingly malleable, but his vanity meant that he was susceptible to flattery, and no one knew better than Northampton how to exploit this.

Northampton first made known his liking for Rochester during the Earl of Salisbury's lifetime. In June 1611 he wrote to the King of his own 'inestimable love' for Rochester, and urged that he be given a seat on the Privy Council. Displaying his customary disloyalty to his colleagues, Northampton sighed that he only wished the current members of the Council were 'possessed of those dainty parts by nature, judgement and capacity which have enabled him and made him fit for use, whensoever it shall please you out of your own grace to call for him'.[122]

At the time nothing came of this, but when Rochester became a Councillor the following spring, Northampton was ready. He proved eager to initiate Rochester into the ways of government and, because Rochester was conscious of his own youth and inadequacy, he was grateful for such guidance. When Rochester was away on royal hunting expeditions, Northampton kept him informed of everything that happened in the Council chamber, and he also acted as Rochester's mentor in patronage matters. In August 1612, for example, Rochester consulted him as to whether he should grant Lord Dingwall's request to be made

Receiver of the Alienation Fines. On Northampton's advising against it, Dingwall's suit was rejected.[123]

The Earl of Salisbury's death had made inevitable a general reshuffle of court offices, and Northampton was able to draw Rochester closer because they shared an interest in the outcome. Northampton hoped to succeed Salisbury as Lord Treasurer and he promised Rochester that if he supported him in this, he in turn would help Rochester secure the prestigious office of Master of the Horse. Although these plans never came to fruition, Rochester was very interested by the proposal. In July 1612 an astute observer noted that Rochester was accounted 'a very great friend' to Northampton in his bid to gain the Treasury, 'and the greater friend because he sees his own preferment in the matter'.[124]

Northampton's success in binding Rochester to him was the more remarkable because the Earl was on appalling terms with all the other men at court with whom Rochester was closely affiliated. He was a bitter enemy of the Earls of Pembroke and Southampton, as well as Sir Henry Neville. Above all these, however, he loathed Sir Thomas Overbury, feelings which the latter reciprocated in full. With a mastery that came of long practice, Northampton now set about detaching his new protégé from his established allies.

In the late summer of 1612 events seemingly played into Northampton's hands when Rochester and Pembroke quarrelled. Northampton was delighted, and did all he could to make the rift permanent. When he heard that Pembroke was seeking a reconciliation, Northampton begged Rochester not to listen, telling him that it was impossible for one of his 'noble heart and spirit' to trust in the goodwill of a 'Welsh juggler'. To his chagrin, however, the two men overcame their differences that autumn, after Sir Henry Neville volunteered to act as an intermediary.[125]

Northampton next tried to turn Rochester against Neville. Neville was the steward of one of the King's properties and, on hearing that James was planning to sell it, he had written to the Chancellor of the Exchequer stressing that it was a very valuable piece of land and that a high price should be demanded. Annoyed both by the fact that Neville had heard of the deal and that he had felt entitled to interfere in the matter, Northampton wrote crossly to Rochester, 'He takes a glory to be thought of great understanding in those affairs, and thinks that tenderness in the point of the King's profit will be a great step to his advancement in another element [the Secretaryship].' Doubtless, Northampton was largely responsible for the fact that, by early 1613, Rochester was pushing less hard for Neville's appointment as Secretary.

He still maintained that Sir Henry had his full support, but observers concluded that his main priority was now to obtain the Mastership of the Horse on his own behalf, and that he would do nothing to jeopardise this.[126]

Much as Northampton wanted to foment hostility between Neville and Pembroke on the one hand and Rochester on the other, his overriding aim was to disrupt Overbury and Rochester's friendship. He knew that Overbury did not like the fact that he and Rochester were on good terms, and that Overbury would do everything in his power to alter the situation. Overbury's potential for causing damage was illustrated by an incident that probably occurred before Rochester became a Privy Councillor. A courtier named Sir Richard Morrison was hoping to secure the reversion of a court office currently held by a peer. He asked Northampton whether he could count on his support, and Northampton seemingly gave him a favourable reply. Nevertheless, when Northampton discussed the matter with Rochester, he expressed doubts as to whether it was appropriate for Morrison to be the next occupant of this post. Overbury learned of this conversation and passed on to Morrison an exaggerated version of it, pretending that Northampton was deliberately sabotaging his chances of gaining employment at court.

Before long Northampton noticed that Morrison was acting coldly towards him. When he asked him why, Morrison told him what Overbury had said. Northampton erupted in fury at this 'naughty and false imputation'. He said that he would not have minded if Morrison had been given an accurate account of his conversation with Rochester, but instead his words 'had ... been powdered by some malicious ingredients'. In his anger Northampton made some disparaging remarks about Overbury, the exact terms of which subsequently became a matter for dispute. Northampton maintained, 'I said less than many of my calling would have done upon a slander raised by an Overbury,' but Overbury heard differently. He alleged that Northampton had grossly insulted him, referring to him as a 'liar', 'base' and 'a rascal'. Overbury complained to Rochester, who was filled with indignation. He sent a fierce letter to Northampton, in which his affection towards Overbury was 'expressed with so strong a stream and so full a pen' that Northampton was alarmed. He became still more so when the King entered the argument, for Rochester had also protested to James about the way his friend had been dishonoured. The King promptly wrote to Northampton, rebuking him for having been so intemperate.

Northampton had to work hard to extricate himself from this imbroglio. He protested his innocence to the King, swearing in a

memorable phrase that he would never use offensive language, 'howsoever the wrongs of uncircumcised lips torture him'. He was adamant
that he had always treated Overbury with respect, 'not for himself ...
but as I find him visited in the favour of the person whom I love and
value above all men, next to your princely self'. The King accepted
these assurances, and before long Rochester also calmed down and
forgave Northampton. Nevertheless, the incident had given the Earl a
severe fright. As he said, it had proved that Overbury would do
'whatsoever he can ... to bring me within compass of false dealing
with this noble, choice and matchless friend my Lord of Rochester'.
Northampton believed that the only way of guarding against similar
attacks in the future was to find some means of prising Overbury and
Rochester apart.[127]

It is not clear exactly when Northampton became aware of one
potential area of friction between the two men, namely that Rochester
and Frances were in love and that Overbury disapproved. Very possibly
it was Frances herself who confided this secret to her great-uncle, in
the hope that he, alone of all her family, would favour this connection.
From the start, it seems, Northampton provided encouragement. In
May 1612 he concluded a letter to Rochester with some gentle teasing.
He explained that he was about to leave for his beloved house at
Greenwich, which he tenderly referred to as 'my mistress'. Playfully he
added that if Rochester 'had ever a mistress that you did love, or that
doth love Sweet Rochester (which I do not believe, because the ugliness
and deformity of your countenance, together with your ill grace and
weak brains, put you out of the love or liking of any woman that hath
dainty eyes)', then he wished 'that you were as near together, invisibly
but not insensibly'.[128] Could it be that there was a deeper subtext to
these apparent inconsequential remarks, and that Northampton was
subtly intimating that he knew about, and approved of, Rochester's
affection for his great-niece?

It may well be that it was not until much later in the year that
Northampton learned that Frances and Rochester had become close. At
any rate, whenever it was that he made the discovery, he viewed it as a
welcome development. Northampton's reasoning on the matter is not
hard to follow. So long as Rochester remained attached to Frances there
was an excellent chance that he would gravitate away from Overbury,
who was now urging his friend to terminate his relationship with a
woman he abhorred. Once Overbury had ceased to be in a position to
interfere, Rochester could be drawn ineluctably into the Howards' orbit.
Northampton was confident that, once he realised the advantages that

an alliance with Rochester would bring, the Earl of Suffolk's current hostility towards the favourite would fade. Northampton later confessed that he had long thirsted for 'an inviolable union' between the two men but said that, though he was 'ever of the mind that men which in their natures are not honest' – a barbed reference to Overbury – 'could not ever make a separation between those that are extremely honest', he had been unable to devise a way of effecting a rapprochement. Now, however, a solution offered itself. Frances would be the link between the two men, acting, in Northampton's words, as 'that dainty pot of glue that will make the bond more sure'.[129]

CHAPTER THREE

Shortly before Christmas 1612, the Earl and Countess of Essex shared a bedroom for the last time. The encounter took place at Salisbury House in the Strand, which belonged to Frances's brother-in-law. The Earl of Suffolk hoped that it would mark a fresh beginning for Frances and her husband for, although the marriage had so far been a disaster, Suffolk still would not accept that the situation was beyond salvage. For some reason, however, the events of that night went far to disabuse him of this idea.

Exactly what happened is unclear. Suffolk was under the impression that Essex was sleeping with Frances 'with a purpose to know her', but no one disputed that the sexual act did not take place. People sympathetic to Frances subsequently spread a story that, in bed that night, Essex 'labour[ed] a quarter of an hour to know her' and then said ' "Frankie, it will not be" and so kissed her and bid her goodnight.'

This may well have been a fabrication. Essex told his friend the Earl of Southampton and his uncle Lord Knollys that he had not even tried to consummate his marriage that night, 'for it was not in his heart to attempt that work, nor to deal otherwise than he had formerly'. In a conversation with the Archbishop of Canterbury he went further, blaming Frances for his bashfulness. He said that when they went to bed he had already 'forgiven all things' which had divided them in the past, 'but when they were alone, she reviled him ... terming him cow, coward and beast ... which things so cooled his courage, that he was far from knowing, or endeavouring to know her'.[1]

At any rate, there is no doubt that the evening was a failure. The Earl of Suffolk's concern deepened when he and the Earl of Northampton had a frank discussion with Essex. Also present were the Earl of Worcester and Essex's uncle, Lord Knollys, and the answers they elicited on this occasion left none of them in any doubt that the marriage of Frances and Essex was in the gravest trouble. As so often, we do not have exact records of what was said. Essex acknowledged that he had never managed to penetrate his wife and that 'although he did his best endeavour, yet he never could'. The conversation led the Earl of Suffolk to believe 'that the Earl [of Essex] had no ink in his pen, that himself had confessed that he could not know a woman'. Northampton also claimed that Essex 'confessed to impotency', and in his private correspondence he now dubbed Essex 'my good Lord the gelding'. Convinced at last that his daughter had been experiencing appalling privation, Suffolk resolved to take action. From having been determined that Frances must be coerced into making a success of her marriage, he now became intent on securing its dissolution, becoming 'so passionate' about this that 'till it had an end ... he lay as on a grid iron, broiling till the matter was accomplished'.[2]

By the end of the year Frances and Essex had ceased to cohabit. The following spring the Earl of Suffolk requested the King to appoint a commission empowered to nullify his daughter's marriage. He explained that, 'in her womanish modesty', Frances had hitherto concealed the fact that Essex had been incapable of consummating their union. Recently, however, 'false rumours of disobedience towards the said Earl' had forced her to reveal the true position. Suffolk declared that he was left with no alternative but to approach the King, 'forasmuch as any longer to dissemble or conceal this calamity of his house and to continue this so hard condition of his said daughter without pursuing such remedy as laws and the practice of all Christian policies in like case afforded neither sorted with good discretion nor the duty of a provident and loving father'.[3]

No mention was made of the Earl of Northampton's role in all this, but undoubtedly it was crucial. With his extensive knowledge of both canon and civil law Northampton was well qualified to advise his nephew on the feasibility of securing an annulment and, from the beginning, he worked tirelessly to ensure a successful outcome to the case. However, he did more than this. It was not enough that Suffolk now accepted that Frances had no future with Essex. Somehow the Lord Chamberlain had to be convinced that his daughter should take as her second husband Viscount Rochester, a man for whom Suffolk had always professed the most violent animosity. We do not know how this was achieved. It is possible that Frances herself pleaded with her father to let her marry Rochester, insisting that she could never be happy with anyone else. Northampton, however, was better placed to point out the political benefits that an alliance with the favourite would bring, and to persuade Suffolk that this was an opportunity too good to miss. Clearly, it was far from easy to overcome Suffolk's objections, and the process took some time. Nullity proceedings were already under way before Suffolk could bring himself to have any dealings with his future son-in-law, or to show him any goodwill. However, once contact had been established, the two men got on surprisingly well. After one meeting between them, Northampton wrote warmly to Rochester of his 'great satisfaction' in hearing of 'that fastness which I find already to be grown in your affections one to another'. While acknowledging that it was the love between Frances and Rochester that had made this development possible, Northampton felt he deserved credit for having expedited matters. He remarked complacently, 'It was the will of God that I should lead the way to my nearest friends by making them to apprehend that sweetness and goodness which now they find and taste.'[4]

It is possible that one reason why Suffolk proved so accommodating was that it had recently been brought home to him that Frances would go to desperate lengths to free herself from Essex. At the end of February 1613 it had emerged that Frances had become involved with a disreputable individual named Mary Woods. Her purpose in doing so was never conclusively established, but Frances's family were understandably embarrassed when the matter came to light. The discovery may well have convinced Suffolk that, unless Frances's marriage was ended by legal means, she would take extreme action, and the consequences of that would be incalculable. Certainly the Archbishop of Canterbury believed that it was the Mary Woods affair which galvanised Frances's family into pursuing the nullity, and that it was 'to shut that up, and so to free the Earl [of Essex] [that] this course was consented upon'.[5]

Mary Woods, otherwise known as 'Cunning Mary', came from a village near Norwich. She claimed to be skilled at palmistry, telling fortunes, and finding lost property with the aid of familiars. Sometimes she drummed up business by telling people that they were bewitched and then offering to free them from the ill effects of sorcery. She also volunteered to find husbands for spinsters, while at the same time nurturing ambitions of her own to marry Thomas Davy, an eligible neighbour 'who had a good land to maintain her withal'. Mary regarded it as no impediment that she already had a husband, a plodding individual named John Woods. She liked to boast that 'She would be divorced from her husband and she would have her door bored full of holes to the end her husband should see himself made a cuckold. But he should not come at her to hinder her at her sport.'[6]

Childless women often consulted Mary in the hope that she could provide them with charms to promote fertility. One such was Isabel Peel, to whom Mary gave a powder in a little taffeta bag which she claimed would make its wearer pregnant if hung about the neck. However, when Mrs Peel grew suspicious and 'ripped the taffety to see what powder it was', she found the contents to be 'but a little dust swept out of the floor'.[7]

It was inadvisable for Mary's dissatisfied clients to complain to the authorities that she had defrauded them because, when 'challenged of her lewd practices', she would retort 'that if they accuse her she will accuse them that they have practised with her to poison their husbands'. She was said to have carried out this threat 'very frequently'. Certainly in June 1612 she claimed to a Justice of the Peace that the wife of one Dr Suckling had approached her with a view to murdering her husband. The JP evidently took the view that Mary's accusations were untrue and it may have been to punish her for this that Mary was given a public whipping in Norwich.[8]

About a month before Christmas 1612 Mary Woods accompanied her husband when he went to London on legal business. In the capital she swiftly built up a flourishing practice, with 'many gentlewomen' visiting her lodgings in Clerkenwell. In early 1613 Frances heard about Mary's activities and invited her to come to see her at Salisbury House, where she was staying. Mary told her that, before doing anything for her, she must receive some guarantee of payment for, when it came to settling bills, grand ladies were apt to 'promise much and perform little'. As security, Frances gave her a diamond ring worth £60 which the Earl of Essex had purchased for her while on his travels. A few days later Mary went home to Norwich without returning the ring to its owner.[9]

In a panic, Frances sent a man named Richard Grimstone to Norfolk with instructions to retrieve her property. He managed to find Mary Woods but, since the latter had already sold the jewellery in London for a pittance, she could not hand it over. She warned Grimstone that, if the authorities were informed, she would say that Frances had given her the ring as a down payment for poison to murder Essex. Undaunted, Grimstone called in the local JP, and Mary was placed under arrest. However, Grimstone too was interrogated, for it struck the justice as suspicious that Frances should have entrusted an item of such value to Mary in the first place. Grimstone's explanation was that Frances had asked Mary to keep the ring safe for her while she attended a performance of a court masque. Pickpockets were always notoriously active on such occasions, and Grimstone said that Frances had feared lest 'the ring might be slipped off her finger' as she danced. Yet Grimstone's story did not command credence, not least because his claim that Mary Woods had been employed as a laundress at Salisbury House was soon revealed as false.[10]

Meanwhile, when Mary Woods herself was questioned, she insisted that Frances had given her the jewellery after requesting Mary to furnish her with a poison which 'would lie in a man's body three or four days' before taking effect, 'and that this poison was ... to be given to the Earl of Essex'. Mary said that she had originally promised to do as Frances wished, but she had then thought better of it and returned to Norwich.[11]

The authorities took this seriously enough to remove Mary to London for further questioning. Enquiries were being pursued even while the hearings for Frances's nullity were in progress at Lambeth. However, when Mary was next interrogated, in June, she changed her story. She now said that Frances had come to her because she was anxious to have a child, and that the ring had been handed over in payment for 'some privy powder' supposed to aid conception. When her interrogators demanded whether she was now telling them the truth, Mary answered cryptically, 'What was true she best knew in her own conscience.'[12]

There is no record of what happened to Mary Woods after this. It was fortunate for Frances that the woman already had a history of making unsubstantiated murder allegations, and hence her claims on this occasion were easily discounted. Yet the episode still discredited Frances, for her connection with this unsavoury character soon became common knowledge, and gave rise to shocked conjecture. John Chamberlain even believed that the resultant scandal would force the Howards to drop the nullity suit, but in the end the family brazened it out successfully.

It now seems idle to speculate whether there was any truth in Mary's claim that Frances was trying to poison her husband. Mary's subsequent explanation that Frances consulted her because she wanted to produce a baby is quite incredible, for by that time she and her husband had already separated, and it would have ruined her if she had become pregnant. On the evidence available it would, however, be uncharitable to assume that her real objective was murder.

Converting her father into an enthusiast for the match with Rochester may have been far from easy, but this was not the only – or even the greatest – challenge to Frances's powers of persuasion. Rochester himself had also been wary of committing himself to marry Frances, and had to be prodded into a betrothal. Showing great determination, Frances overcame his reservations, refusing to admit that there was any need for caution. A curious letter that Sir John Holles wrote years later to Rochester (or the Earl of Somerset, as he was by then) gives us an insight into how she did this.

Long after their marriage, Holles appears to have been present when a painful scene took place between the Earl and Countess of Somerset. For some reason Somerset then asked Holles to supply him with a written description of what he had witnessed. Holles complied, reminding Somerset that the subject under discussion had been 'your Lordship and your Ladyship's first coming together'. In Holles's hearing Somerset had told his wife that, 'notwithstanding several solicitations from her, it was not your [Somerset's] doing'. Presumably Somerset did not mean by this that he had started sleeping with Frances at her instigation; rather, he was claiming that he had married her under duress.

Holles then went into further details, recalling how Somerset had described a conference between himself and Frances which demonstrated the sort of emotional blackmail to which he had been subjected. This encounter had taken place shortly 'after my Lord of Essex had delivered her up to my Lord of Suffolk her father'. Frances had written to Rochester, asking him to meet her at Chesterford Park. When he had arrived he had found her sitting with the Duke of Lennox. Seconded by Lennox, Frances had then urged him to marry her, saying that there was nothing to stop them, now that 'she was a free woman'. Rochester had evidently been taken aback by this ultimatum, and had made numerous excuses. According to Holles, 'Your Lordship replied that you had yet made no fortune, that you were at the King's bestowing: and that he was hard to deal withal in any such matter; nevertheless, she pressing you still, and my Lord of Lennox in her behalf, your Lordship said you would try the King, how you could frame him thereunto.'[13]

Despite his reservations Rochester raised the matter with the King and, contrary to the favourite's expectations, the King proved delighted by the prospect of his marrying Frances. This might seem strange, considering James's own infatuated state. Oddly, however, James always appeared remarkably free from jealousy when his favourites acquired wives. He did not look on women as a threat, for he knew that he would continue to have first call on his favourites' time (almost immediately after Philip Herbert's marriage to Susan Vere, James had removed the bridegroom on a hunting expedition) and he probably thought he would retain priority in their affections as well. So long as it entailed no inconvenience to himself, James was a kindly man, who 'took delight to complete the happiness of them he loved', and he was therefore glad to bestow his blessings on the match. There were, however, additional reasons. As one observer noted, the Howard faction at court was 'the one to whom his Majesty inclines most'.[14] The prospect that Rochester might be tempted to forsake his former political allies in order to affiliate himself with the Howards could not have failed to please James. Above all it was obvious that if Rochester married a Howard, his dependence on Sir Thomas Overbury would be reduced, a development which the King would warmly applaud.

It is likely that James brought his influence to bear on the Earl of Suffolk, and that this partly accounted for Suffolk's willingness that Rochester should become his son-in-law. There is at least no doubt that the King assured Suffolk that Frances's marriage to Essex could be dissolved without difficulty. When her nullity suit later encountered problems, Suffolk and his followers gave out 'that what was done was performed by the King's direction, otherwise it had not been begun'. James himself virtually acknowledged as much, for he told the Archbishop of Canterbury that 'he set the course now in motion, and therefore if there were any error in it, he had done the Lord Chamberlain wrong'.[15]

By this time Sir Thomas Overbury had become seriously alarmed about the implications of Rochester's relationship with Frances. He now regretted having encouraged him to pursue her in the first place, and kept telling his friend that he must abandon her without delay. For a time, Rochester had managed to dissemble how serious his feelings for Frances were. Overbury later complained that Rochester had 'denied, concealed and juggled' with him in hopes of keeping him ignorant of how deeply he was involved. Overbury was too intelligent to be deceived for very long and, once he realised the true state of affairs, he became so offensive about Frances that Rochester had to ask him not to raise the subject again. Since Overbury simply ignored this prohibition, Rochester's friendship for him was subjected to an intolerable strain, and Sir Thomas's incessant abuse caused 'many breaches' between the two men.[16]

If we can believe evidence put forward at Rochester's trial, the bitterest row of all occurred sometime in March 1613. It was alleged that, having been on some nocturnal errand – very possibly an assignation with Frances – Rochester was returning to his rooms in Whitehall between one and two in the morning. He found Overbury waiting for him, pacing about in the Privy Gallery down which Rochester had to pass. Startled by this unwelcome apparition, Rochester asked, 'Are you there yet?' to which Overbury retorted, 'Am *I* here? Where have you been?' Then, when Rochester failed to answer, he demanded furiously, 'Will you never leave the company of that base woman?' Rochester denied that he had been with Frances, but Overbury brushed this aside, commenting bitingly, 'It is too manifest.'

The exchange (which one of Overbury's servants claimed to have overheard) grew still more heated as Overbury mercilessly harangued his friend. 'The King hath bestowed great honours and gifts upon [you] and you overthrow yourself and all your fortunes by haunting the company of that base woman,' he raged. He added that in view of the fact that Rochester intended 'to ruinate himself and his fortunes', he thought it best that he was no longer associated with him. He asked that Rochester promptly pay him £1,500, which he believed to be his share of the profits arising from a business deal he had recently conducted on Rochester's behalf, declaring that, once this matter was settled, their obligations to each other were at an end. Loftily he concluded, 'You shall stand as you can, and I shall shift for myself,' the implication being that Rochester would never survive at court without him. By now Rochester was so angry that the prospect of being free of his old friend seemed highly inviting, and he shouted he would have no trouble looking after himself.[17]

In the event, however, Rochester did not sever all connections with Overbury. Overbury would later recall that, following their quarrel, Rochester gave him an assurance 'that I should live in court, [that he] was my friend', and Overbury accepted this. Although for the time being the warmth had gone out of their relationship, Rochester's apparently conciliatory behaviour seemed to vindicate Overbury's assumption that the Viscount was too dependent on him to dispense with his services. When acquaintances questioned whether Rochester could really be so forgiving, Overbury had no hesitation in telling them they were wrong. Sir Dudley Digges later recorded that about this time he had suggested to Sir Henry Neville 'that my Lord of Rochester was desirous to be rid of Overbury'. Neville contradicted this, explaining 'that Sir Thomas Overbury was confident, and said often that my Lord of Rochester would not dare to leave him'.[18]

In reality, Overbury's confidence was misplaced, for Rochester was now infuriated with him. However, for reasons that are not altogether clear, Rochester feared the damage that Overbury would do if he cut him adrift. In particular, he was concerned that Overbury would manage to block his marriage to Frances, though how he would have achieved this was never specified. It seems probable that Rochester feared that Overbury would tell the Archbishop of Canterbury that Frances was guilty of adultery, and in these circumstances there would have been no question of her marriage being dissolved. And indeed, while he remained at liberty, Sir Thomas seems to have taken a tentative step in this direction, making some disclosure to Archbishop Abbot about Rochester and Frances. Rochester may also have been concerned that Overbury would incite the Earl of Essex to contest the nullity suit whereas, initially at least, it was hoped that he would not object to it. For these reasons Rochester decided that, for the present, he could not afford to alienate Sir Thomas. Instead he must be lulled into a false sense of security until a satisfactory way of neutralising him could be devised.

Frances was the person who had most to lose if Overbury was not curbed, and her hatred of him was correspondingly intense. Although there is no proof of this, it is possible that Rochester told her of his encounter with Sir Thomas in the early hours of the morning. If so, this alone would account for her loathing of the man, particularly since Overbury had cast the most grievous aspersion on her by referring to her as 'base'. Implying as it did that she was both immoral and low-born, the epithet was calculated to inspire the deepest rancour; one should bear in mind that when Northampton had allegedly applied the term to Overbury, the latter had immediately appealed to the King for redress. But Frances knew that Overbury was capable of more than verbal insults. She dreaded the possibility that he would act to stop her nullity going through, thus destroying her one chance of happiness. Furthermore, Frances may have feared that Overbury might yet persuade Rochester to break off relations with her. For the moment Rochester might maintain that the rift between him and Sir Thomas was irreparable, but he had deferred to Overbury for so long, and shown him such slavish devotion in the past, that it was not impossible that Overbury would reassert himself. Unless Overbury was kept away, he would lose no chance to denigrate her, and would constantly repeat his belief that she was a loose woman who was not fit to be Rochester's consort. Then, too, there was the worry that Overbury would convince Rochester that it would undermine his standing with the King if he married Frances. At present it was true that James appeared to have no objection, but Overbury clearly believed that before long his attitude would change. Frances knew that Rochester's initial reluctance to marry her had stemmed from his worries that by doing so he would displease the King, and so it was far from fanciful to think that Overbury would be able to exploit these fears.

Rochester evidently discussed with Northampton how best to deal with Overbury, and Frances may well have been present while they debated what to do. At one point it was proposed that someone should be prevailed upon to quarrel with Overbury, in the hope that, 'being of a hot and churlish disposition', Sir Thomas would seek a fight with his antagonist. In doing so he would contravene the King's ordinance against duelling, and this could be used as an excuse to imprison him. In the end the idea was rejected: at his trial Rochester said, 'It was once resolved somebody in court should fall out with Overbury and offer him some affront, but that was not followed.'[19] Frances, however, was not so easily deterred, deciding to press ahead with unilateral action. Showing the same remarkable spirit and determination that had manifested itself when she had pushed Rochester into agreeing to marry her, she approached Sir David Wood. The latter was the unattractive red-bearded Scot who bore a grudge against Overbury because of the insolent way he had sought to extort a fee of £1,200 after Sir David had secured a valuable suit from the Crown. On 13 April 1613[20] Frances summoned Wood to a private interview at Greenwich Palace. Coming briskly to the point, she told him, 'Sir David, I hear you have received great wrong of Overbury, and that you are a gentleman that can revenge ye wrongs as well as any.' She then explained that 'that man hath wronged not only yourself but myself and others exceedingly, and I would be glad that we were rid of him'. Sir David replied that he did not see what he could do, for he had already challenged Overbury to a duel and the latter had declined to meet him. Frances thereupon suggested that Wood waylay Overbury and murder him, offering to pay him £1,000 in blood money. Wood was disconcerted by her proposal, and said that 'for all the gold in the world he would not ... be a hangman to any man'. He did undertake to give Overbury a beating, promising that if Frances could provide him with a written guarantee from Rochester that he would not be prosecuted, he 'would give him [Overbury] the sounder knocks for her sake'. Since Rochester was unaware of this initiative, Frances could not provide Sir David with even this limited form of indemnity. All that she could promise was that, if he killed Overbury, she could arrange for Wood to be 'conveyed away' before he could be charged with murder. It was scarcely a very enticing proposal and Wood told her drily that 'he might be accounted a great fool if he upon a woman's word should go to Tyburn'. Despite this discouraging response, Frances persisted. She pleaded that Overbury was 'ever late at Sir Charles Wilmot's house, and as he came back late in the night you may take him out of the coach and kill him'.[21]

Since Wood remained obdurate, Frances's scheme came to nothing. However, there now existed an alternative strategy for dealing with Overbury. The King decided that Overbury should be sent abroad as his ambassador to France, the Spanish Netherlands, or Russia. It is not clear whether the idea occurred to James independently, or whether he adopted the plan after discussions with Rochester and Northampton. Certainly the proposal had much to commend it. Since a foreign posting ostensibly represented a promotion for Overbury, no one could say that he had been poorly treated but, at the same time, it would prevent Sir Thomas causing trouble at court or interfering in the nullity proceedings. The only problem was, when James sent the Archbishop of Canterbury to tell Overbury what he had in mind for him, Sir Thomas indicated he was not interested.

In some ways Overbury's lack of enthusiasm was understandable. Ambassadors were paid a yearly salary of £1,200, plus £400 for incidental expenses such as fees for couriers and informers. This allowance was barely adequate to cover the cost of maintaining a household in a foreign capital and, since payment was often severely in arrears, an ambassador could emerge from a stint abroad plunged in penury. Nor was there any guarantee that a lengthy term of duty overseas could pay dividends in terms of future advancement, for at court it was proverbial that 'absence is an enemy to preferment'. Unless he had friends in England who were ready to look after his interests and, when appropriate, to press for his recall, a diplomat might well face years of drudgery far from home with scant recognition for his services. Becoming ambassador to Russia would have seemed a particularly unpalatable prospect, for the country was looked on as both barbarous and remote. Unfortunately, once James had chosen someone to represent him abroad, the individual concerned had little option but to bow to his wishes. The more resourceful and well connected might find a friend who would plead that they were unsuited to the task but, if such intercessions failed, an outright refusal was likely to be construed as undutiful. In the circumstances, those named as ambassadors had to derive what comfort they could from the reflection that it was at least 'a place of honour and action' and to hope that, once they had endured the privations of overseas service, the King would offer them more congenial employment.[22]

Overbury, however, took a more defiant approach. He believed that, if he agreed to go abroad, he would fade into obscurity whereas, provided he stayed at home, his prospects were excellent. In view of the fact that he had recently quarrelled with Rochester and that the King had always disliked him, his optimism in this respect is mystifying. It is hard to assess whether it was his own arrogance and insensitivity that blinded him as to his true position, or whether it was duplicity on Rochester's part that misled him. Whatever the reason, a mere two hours before he was incarcerated in the Tower of London, he confided to Sir Henry Wotton that he conceived 'never better than at present of his own fortunes and ends'.[23]

James soon made it clear that Overbury could not evade his responsibilities so easily. Having had his initial overture rejected, he sent the Earl of Pembroke and the Lord Chancellor, Lord Ellesmere, to notify Overbury formally of the offer of the ambassadorship. The two peers told Sir Thomas that James 'had an intent to make use of his good parts and to train him for his further service', but even the implicit promise that this post would be a stepping-stone to a more rewarding position failed to tempt Overbury. According to one source, as an added inducement the King also sent a message that, on Overbury's behalf, he would purchase the post of Treasurer of the Chamber from Sir John Stanhope, enabling Overbury to enjoy the profits of this office even while on overseas service. Still Overbury remained intransigent. To Ellesmere and Pembroke he pleaded that he could speak only English, and therefore was unfitted to take up a diplomatic post. They told him that he was young enough to learn a new language and that, even if he failed to master it in time, he could employ secretaries who would act as his interpreters. Overbury then excused himself on grounds of ill-health, claiming that he was 'so exceedingly troubled with the spleen that if he had a long letter to write, he was fain to give over'. This too would not suffice, for Pembroke and Ellesmere suggested that 'change of air might be a special remedy for such infirmities'.[24]

At this stage Overbury should have recognised that he had no alternative but to obey the King but, with typical stubbornness, he persisted in his refusal. Furthermore, while it is unclear exactly how he expressed himself, it seems that he did so in an intemperate fashion, employing terms described as 'pregnant with contempt'. Another report refers to him having uttered 'undecent and unmannerly speeches'. Overbury himself subsequently came close to acknowledging that he had said things which might be considered disrespectful, though he pleaded in mitigation that he had been misunderstood. Writing to Rochester from the Tower, he pleaded, 'For my words, they were spoken as being surprised on the sudden, and spoken in regard of my sickness, and not of his [the King's] command.'[25]

When Pembroke and Ellesmere returned to the King and told him what had happened, James declared himself extremely angry. He argued that, by his summary refusal, Overbury had treated him with contempt. Having assembled the Council, he fumed that it was intolerable if 'he could not obtain so much of a gentleman ... as to accept an honourable employment', giving orders that Overbury should be summoned before the Council and then sent to the Tower. The King's instructions were swiftly carried out. Just after 6 p.m. on 21 April 1613 Sir Thomas Overbury was escorted from the Council Chamber by a clerk of the Council and two armed guards, who conveyed him to the Tower of London.[26]

Overbury's arrest caused a sensation. In particular there was intense speculation as to what this shocking event heralded for Viscount Rochester. Very few people were aware that he and Overbury were no longer on such close terms as before, and therefore it was assumed that Rochester would be devastated by what had happened. At the time of Overbury's arrest Rochester was thought to be recovering from a bout of fever, leading to the supposition that the King had seized the opportunity to move against Overbury while his best friend was bedridden. In the popular estimation Rochester was accounted ignorant of the fact that Overbury was to be offered an ambassadorship, let alone that he was in any danger of being imprisoned. Even well-informed observers, such as Lord Fenton, were sure that Rochester had been taken unawares, and that he 'was nothing acquainted with his Majesty's purpose in that'. Rochester's personal secretary, John Packer, likewise believed this, for he told Ralph Winwood that Rochester 'knew nothing till all was done and he [Overbury] gone, which your Lordship may imagine did much perplex him'.[27]

Many people concluded that, if James was prepared to humiliate Rochester in this way, this meant that the Viscount's own career was in jeopardy. However, the King soon made it clear that this was far from the case. John Chamberlain reported, 'Some take this as a diminution of my Lord Rochester's credit and favour, but the King told the Council he would not have it so construed, for that he had, and still did take, more delight in his company and conversation than in any man's living.'[28]

Gradually observers became aware that Rochester was not unduly upset by the treatment meted out to Overbury. Whereas when Overbury had last been in disgrace, Rochester had laboured unceasingly for Sir Thomas's restoration to court, he now seemed disinclined to exert himself. After a few weeks Lord Fenton had reached the conclusion that Rochester was 'able to forget Overbury before he offend the King'. By June 1613 Samuel Calvert could declare that Overbury had faded into oblivion for, 'Not a man enquires after him, nor doth the Lord C[arr] miss him.'[29]

Later, people revised their view of the part played by Rochester in Overbury's arrest. Whereas it had formerly been assumed that he had merely passively acquiesced in Sir Thomas's imprisonment, it was subsequently alleged that it was Rochester who was responsible for it in the first place. At his trial Rochester was accused of having incited Overbury to refuse to go abroad, knowing that this would result in him being sent to the Tower.[30] The Prosecution claimed that by this time Rochester's hatred of Overbury was so intense that it could not be assuaged merely by Sir Thomas leaving the country. Instead, Rochester wanted him to be confined in a secure place, so that he could poison him at his leisure.

In support of these claims it was pointed out that, while in the Tower, Overbury had written to Rochester reproaching him for having 'stayed me here when I would have been gone'. This was a seemingly damning piece of evidence, but it should be borne in mind that Overbury did not blame Rochester for his predicament until he had been in the Tower for several months, by which time his grip on reality was becoming decidedly precarious. At Rochester's trial Sir Dudley Digges testified that Sir Robert Mansel claimed to have seen a letter that Rochester had sent Overbury, encouraging him to reject the ambassadorial appointment. However, this letter was never produced in court, and Mansell was not even called upon to corroborate Digges's story. Digges also stated that he himself had seen Overbury shortly after the latter had heard that the King wanted to make him an ambassador. At the time Overbury had given Digges the impression that he could refuse to go abroad with impunity, as Rochester had promised to deflect the King's anger. Digges recalled, 'He found him [Overbury] to rely upon [Rochester] to be excused, saying "My Precious Chief knoweth the King's mind better than any, and I the mind of my precious chief".' In his defence, however, Rochester claimed that Overbury had merely pretended that he was being urged to remain in England, because he felt that this was the best way of justifying his own disobedience. Rochester insisted, 'Whereas it was urged [by the Prosecution] that I caused him to refuse the employment that was imposed upon him, it is not so, for I was very willing he should have undertaken it, but he not ... I should have been glad to have removed him, both in respect of my marriage and his insolence.'[31]

In apparent contradiction of this, the Prosecution could cite a letter that Rochester had written to the King while awaiting trial, in which he admitted that he had 'consented to and endeavoured' Overbury's imprisonment. He had stressed, however, that he had 'desired it for his [Overbury's] reformation, not his ruin', meaning that he had thought a jail term would make Overbury more tractable.[32] While the letter does add weight to the theory that Rochester was guilty of entrapment, it does not prove that it had always been his intention that Overbury would go to prison. In all probability he would have preferred it if Overbury had accepted an overseas posting, and it was only when it became clear that he would decline that Rochester came to favour a more brutal alternative.

At Rochester's trial it was implied that Overbury was not the only victim of trickery, for the King had effectively been duped into sending Sir Thomas to the Tower. Clearly, however, James cannot be absolved of all responsibility. It must be stressed that, at the time of Overbury's arrest, all onlookers concurred that James had acted with great deliberation. When passing the news on to a friend, Lord Fenton was positive that 'This matter is merely from his Majesty himself.' Holding out no prospect of Overbury's early release, he commented grimly, 'I think his Majesty will let the world see that yet for a time Rochester can make his despatches without the help of an Overbury.' Sir Thomas Lake likewise thought that the King's action had been carefully premeditated. He explained, 'His Majesty hath manifested that he hath long been of mind to have [Overbury] out of court, and so hath taken occasion to be rid of him.'[33]

Nobody queried whether James was really entitled to punish Overbury in this arbitrary fashion, a surprising lack of protest, considering that the King had arguably exceeded his sovereign powers. In the second volume of his great legal textbook, *The Institutes of the Law of England*, the jurist Sir Edward Coke declared, 'By the law of the land, no man can be exiled or banished out of his native country but either by authority of Parliament or, in case of objuration for felony ... by the Common Law. Therefore the King cannot send any subject of England against his will to serve him out of this realm, for that should be an exile.' Although this volume was not printed until 1642, the principle was applicable in 1613. Overbury had therefore been correct when he told Pembroke and Ellesmere that 'the King could not in law nor justice force him to forsake his country'.[34] It follows that his detention had no legal foundation. Since he had broken no law, there was no question of his being brought to trial, for the so-called 'contempt' which he had committed was not an indictable offence.

Throughout the reign, it is true, other men who had offended the King had been imprisoned at his pleasure, but their confinement had rarely lasted more than a week. Overbury's bewilderment at being treated with such severity was therefore entirely understandable. At one point he protested, "'Twas without example such an imprisonment upon a contempt.' After being confined in the Tower for a month he wrote to Rochester, 'Never man for such an offence as mine was restrained ... nay, such an offence as [the King] himself sought, for he knew afore they came I would not go such a journey.'[35] And indeed, despite the King's somewhat cavalier attitude to his subjects' constitutional privileges, he must have known that in Overbury's case an injustice had been done. On the day of Rochester's trial as an accessory to murder, the King was observed to be in a particularly agitated state. It is tempting to speculate that he feared that in his testimony Rochester would go into details about the events leading up to Overbury's arrest, proving that the King had been involved at every stage. It would have caused grave embarrassment to James if it had emerged that Overbury was imprisoned, not because of a spontaneous outburst of anger on his part, but as a result of a preconceived plan, whereby it had been determined in advance that Sir Thomas would be deprived of his liberty if he declined a posting overseas.

Unfortunately for Overbury, he was so unpopular that, when he was taken into custody, no one thought of objecting that this was a violation of his rights. The most common emotion excited by his arrest was jubilation that someone so arrogant should be humbled in this way. Samuel Calvert, for example, wrote to William Trumbull (who doubtless shared his satisfaction), 'You may observe how soon such aspiring minds fall down, scorched with the sun and their own weight.' Even when Overbury was kept in prison for much longer than expected, his predicament aroused no sympathy at court. Lord Fenton wrote callously to the Earl of Mar, 'We let him stick there, and it matters not how long.' Far from anyone voicing concern for Overbury, most people simply forgot all about him. By 3 June Sir Henry Wotton could report, 'Sir Thomas Overbury not only out of liberty (as he was) but almost now out of discourse.'[36]

One reason why people so quickly lost interest in Overbury was that everyone at court had become absorbed in the outcome of the nullity proceedings between Frances and the Earl of Essex. Before these began, Frances's family had been hopeful that her marriage could be dissolved

without undue difficulty. Prior to the case coming to court a meeting
had been arranged between the Earls of Suffolk and Northampton,
acting for Frances, and two representatives nominated by Essex, namely,
the Earl of Southampton and Essex's uncle Lord Knollys. From these
preliminary discussions it appeared that Essex did not object to his
marriage being annulled, providing this could be done without humiliating him. In particular it was stipulated that, while Essex was prepared
to acknowledge that he had not consummated his marriage to Frances,
he would not declare himself wholly impotent, for that would have
precluded him from taking a wife at a future date. Frances's representatives were confident that this would not cause a problem, and
that a formula could be devised which would ensure both 'that a
separation should be made and my Lord's honour every way preserved'.[37]

When the meeting was over Northampton went straight to Frances's
lodgings at court. Having brought her up to date with all that had
passed, he sat down to write the same news to Rochester. 'We are all
agreed to part fair,' he informed him gleefully. 'The case fell out to be
so clear in law as contradiction could not have profited, which makes
my Lord of Southampton a more indifferent arbitrator.' Northampton
related that Essex's representatives had been shown a series of articles
which the Howards intended should form the basis of Frances's nullity
suit. After inspecting these Knollys and Southampton had requested
only minor modifications, such as demanding the deletion of a clause
stating that, while they were living together, Frances did 'often times
crave copulation' with Essex. Silkily Northampton confided to Rochester
that, in view of the fact that the statement was 'a lie beyond measure',
he had been happy to comply. With a triumphant flourish Northampton
concluded that, now that these amendments had been incorporated,
there was 'no strife ... between either party in any points'. Because the
quill he was using was badly made, Northampton's handwriting in this
letter was less clear than usual, and this afforded him an opportunity to
make a sly pun at Essex's expense. He told Rochester, 'God will bless
the neat bargain, and here in this lady's chamber, from whence I write
now, I shall hope to find better pen and ink than I have at this present.'
In beautiful copperplate writing Frances appended a postscript of her
own: 'I am a witness to this bargain and set to my hand.' She signed
it, 'Frances Howard', emphasising that she should no longer be regarded
as the Earl of Essex's wife.[38]

Before long, however, it became apparent that the Howards had been
over-optimistic to think that matters could be amicably settled. It was
in fact surprising that they had been so confident of winning their case

for, at that time, the laws governing marriage were exceptionally rigid. In contrast to what had happened in almost all other Protestant countries, matrimonial law in England had never been subject to revision. Since the Reformation many German states, Scandinavian countries, Scotland and Calvin's Geneva had legalised divorce on grounds of adultery or desertion, albeit with the proviso that only the innocent party was permitted to remarry. In England similar changes had been contemplated during the reign of Edward VI. In 1551 a commission had been entrusted with the task of updating the existing body of canon law. They produced a new set of canons – known as *Reformatio Legum* – which sanctioned divorce in cases of adultery, desertion, or deadly hostility (cases where one partner had sought to murder the other). It was also stated there that, if one partner was unable to perform the conjugal act because of some bodily defect or the ill-effects of witchcraft, this constituted an impediment to marriage. But *Reformatio Legum* never became the law of the land. Not only were the proposals dealing with marriage controversial in themselves, but other sections of the code were so radical that they alienated influential figures. In 1571 an attempt to enshrine *Reformatio Legum* in statute was quashed. When English canon law was next revised, in 1604, the rulings on marriage were much more circumspect. Couples whose marriage had irretrievably broken down were permitted to apply to the ecclesiastical authorities for a judicial separation but, even if this was granted, neither party was permitted to remarry.[39]

The penalties for doing so were illustrated by the case of Penelope Rich who, coincidentally, was an aunt of the Earl of Essex. In her youth she had been forced to marry Robert, Lord Rich, a man whom she detested. After years of unhappiness she became the mistress of Charles Blount, Lord Mountjoy, producing five children by him. Towards the end of Queen Elizabeth's reign Lord Rich obtained a formal separation from his wife on the grounds of her adultery. Penelope continued her affair with Mountjoy, and initially it seemed that her unconventional way of life would not debar her from society. Following James I's succession, Penelope was taken up by Queen Anne, and Mountjoy was raised higher in the peerage, being created Earl of Devonshire by the King. It was only when she and Devonshire sought to put their liaison on an official footing that they found themselves in trouble. In December 1605 they married, but the validity of this union was never recognised. At one time there was even a possibility they might be tried for bigamy, but in the end the Attorney-General ruled that the marriage was unlawful and void in common law, but not felonious. Although they had escaped prosecution, Penelope and her husband were ostracised and disgraced. When Devonshire died in April 1606, Penelope was not permitted to inherit his property because she was not his lawful wife, 'but an harlot, adulteress, concubine and whore'. Penelope did not long survive her husband, following him to the grave within a year.[40]

Although divorce was not an option for English couples, it was theoretically possible to procure an annulment by recourse to the decretals relating to matrimony promulgated by Pope Gregory IX in the thirteenth century. It was stated there that, if a husband testified under oath that he was impotent, and his wife confirmed this, then their marriage could be considered void. The drawback was that, if the husband subsequently had sexual relations with another woman, this proved that he was guilty of perjury, and he would then be obliged to take back his former wife. This meant that there was little incentive for the male to be honest about any lack of physical prowess. If he was not prepared to make such an admission, the wife had no means of redress, for an unsupported statement by her that her husband was incapable was deemed insufficient to render their union null.[41]

However, in his commentary on canon law, Thomas Aquinas did provide an additional way out, for he declared that witchcraft could make a man impotent with one woman and virile with others. If husband and wife had lived together for more than three years without consummating their marriage, this could be taken as proof that the husband had been permanently disabled in this way, at least as far as that woman was concerned. In such cases the marriage could be dissolved by judgement of the Church, and both husband and wife permitted to form fresh unions. It was this which was seized upon by Frances's lawyers, as providing a means of honourable release for both parties. Although witchcraft was not mentioned in the articles which formed the basis for Frances's nullity suit (and still less was there any attempt to identify the person who had bewitched Essex), Essex was said there to be suffering from the same symptoms described by Aquinas. Witchcraft was the only legal explanation for this (although, in view of Frances's known involvement with Mary Woods, her family would have doubtless preferred it if another reason could have been put forward) and, when pressed, Frances's counsel agreed 'that it was that which they did mean'.[42]

It was Frances's misfortune that the Archbishop of Canterbury, who was chosen to preside over the nullity commission, was a 'stiffly principled' churchman who, from the outset, had the gravest qualms about the task entrusted to him. George Abbot was a man of humble origins who had been educated through the generosity of a private benefactor. Following his ordination, Abbot had become chaplain to Lord Buckhurst and then Master of University College, Oxford, but it was his appointment as chaplain to King James's influential Scots adviser, the Earl of Dunbar, that accounted for his later eminence. After leaving Dunbar's service, Abbot became Bishop of Coventry and Lichfield in 1609, and Bishop of London the year after that, but most people assumed that he would not rise higher than this. However, when the current Archbishop of Canterbury, Richard Bancroft, died in November 1610, Dunbar implored the King to name Abbot his successor. The prospect of Abbot's appointment caused ill-feeling among the rest of the episcopate. The man who had been widely predicted to become the next Archbishop was the eminent theologian, Lancelot Andrewes, Bishop of Ely, and he declared that he would not mind if the Archbishop of York or the Bishop of Winchester was given the place in his stead but, if Abbot 'had it, then he had wrong'. Most of the Council likewise thought Abbot an unsuitable choice, although, according to the Venetian ambassador, Robert Carr supported the appointment. If this was so, he would subsequently have cause to regret having meddled in the matter. However, it was Dunbar's intervention that weighed most heavily with the King. The Earl himself died in January 1611, but James decided to honour his memory by carrying out his wishes and, in March, Abbot was named Archbishop of Canterbury.

If few people were pleased by Abbot's elevation, the English Catholics had most cause to regret it, for his hatred of them was particularly virulent. On his appointment, the Venetian ambassador said Abbot was 'held their bitterest persecutor', and certainly, as Archbishop, Abbot strove hard to persuade the King to treat them with greater severity. In August 1612, he wrote an alarmist letter to James, saying that he feared some great popish conspiracy was afoot. His only evidence for this was that he had heard that a general fast had been ordered throughout Italy, and a similar event had preceded the Gunpowder Plot. He also wanted James to expel the Spanish ambassador, Don Pedro de Zuniga, alleging that he was fomenting disloyalty within the realm, and hinting that he had played a part in the powder treason. Most irritating of all, from the King's point of view, was Abbot's passionate insistence that Prince Henry must marry a Protestant. Despite the Archbishop's entreaties, by the autumn of 1612 it was widely believed that Prince Henry's betrothal to the Catholic daughter of the Duke of Savoy was imminent, and it was only the prospective bridegroom's unexpected death that forced these plans to be aborted. Nevertheless, although James had felt free to ignore the Archbishop, he was annoyed by his presumption. His anger proved short-lived, but Abbot would later ruefully recall that, at the time, he 'received some sharp words from the King for my labour'.[43]

Abbot's fanatically anti-Catholic stance and his detestation of Spain automatically meant that he was disapproving of the Howards, whose attitude towards these issues was so different. In November 1612 it was rumoured that there had been vehement clashes in the Council Chamber on some unspecified matter between Abbot and the Earl of Northampton. One potential cause of friction was that Northampton favoured more lenient treatment for recusants. In the summer of 1612 he took up the cause of the Catholic Lord Vaux and his mother, who were facing heavy penalties for non-conformity. He asked Rochester to speak to the King on their behalf, and that August he wrote thanking him for his 'charitable and compassionate intercession'. He said that it was now up to James to decide what action should be taken against them, but cautioned that mother and son remained fearful that 'the Metropolitan' would still make every effort to see they did not escape lightly.[44]

Abbot himself was emphatic that he did not allow personal or political considerations to influence him when presiding over the nullity suit. He solemnly protested, 'I bring with me ... a mind devoid of passion or any perturbation, which inclineth to no part for fear or for favour, for spleen or for hatred, from which, I thank God, in pronouncing of sentence I have ever been free.'[45]

Others, however, took a different view of the matter, alleging that Abbot's hostility towards the Howards coloured his outlook. The Tuscan ambassador Ottavio Lotti stated baldly that Abbot was 'an enemy of the house of Howard'. Furthermore, when the nullity suit encountered difficulties one observer attributed this to the fact that Abbot was 'exceeding partial against the Chamberlain [Suffolk] and, as it is said, for fear of some new allaye between [Lady] Essex and Rochester, whereof there is a great likelihood'. The King himself directly accused Abbot of being biased, claiming that 'the prejudice you have of the persons is the greatest motive of breeding these doubts into you'.[46] Undoubtedly this was too simplistic, for Abbot's scruples of conscience cannot be explained away simply as the product of malice. Nevertheless, in a case where there was so little hard evidence, and the legal position was so ambiguous, Abbot had to rely a great deal on his instincts in order to reach judgement, and in these circumstances his distrust of the Howards could not but be significant.

On 15 May 1613 the nullity commission convened at Lambeth Palace. There were ten commissioners in all. Apart from Abbot, these were:

John King, Bishop of London; Lancelot Andrewes, Bishop of Ely; Richard Neile, Bishop of Coventry and Lichfield; Sir Julius Caesar, the Chancellor of the Exchequer; Sir Thomas Parry, Chancellor of the Duchy of Lancaster; Sir Daniel Dunne, Dean of the ecclesiastical Court of the Arches; Sir John Bennet, Judge of the Prerogative Court of Canterbury; Dr Thomas Edwards, Chancellor of the Bishop of London, and Dr Francis James.

From the start Abbot was deeply uneasy. He had already had a private interview with the Earl of Essex, at which the young man had struck him as a very upright character. Essex had made it clear that he would not make a straightforward admission of impotence, declaring 'that he was resolved not to lay any blemish upon himself that way'. In the absence of this, Abbot could not conceive how the Howards intended to proceed, and it was only when lawyers acting for Frances submitted to the commission the articles which formed the basis for her application for an annulment, that the family's strategy became evident.

In accordance with the agreement reached beforehand between the parties, it was stated in the articles that Essex was in 'perfect estate of body'. Despite his inability to consummate his marriage, he was credited with 'power and ability to have carnal copulation with other women', for he sometimes 'had the motions of the flesh for carnal copulation, as he sayeth, and happily may believe and that truly'. The fact that, against her will, Frances was still a virgin, was attributed to 'a perpetual and natural impediment', which had prevented Essex from having sexual intercourse with her. When Abbot realised that he was being asked to believe that Essex suffered from a highly selective form of impotence, he was horrified. Darkly he observed to his fellow commissioners that the Howards 'had laid a very narrow bridge for themselves to go over'.[47]

Despite Abbot's misgivings, the case proceeded. To prove that Frances and Essex had slept with each other for the regulation three-year period, the Howards next called a succession of witnesses, who testified that they had seen the couple in bed together. This took some time, and it was 5 June before Essex was examined on his oath before the commission. At once it became apparent that the Howards' hopes that he would not contest the nullity suit were unfounded. It is not hard to think of reasons for his change of heart. Once it became public knowledge that he had never consummated his marriage, Essex had doubtless found himself a figure of fun in the masculine circles in which he moved, and now he was trying to retrieve his position. It also seems clear that his friends were inciting him to make difficulties. Lord Fenton, watching from the sidelines, confided to a colleague that 'Since the matter has been intended, it is thought that Southampton and Pembroke has made him go back again.'[48] However, the Earl of Southampton had earlier seemed amenable to the annulment, so he too had undergone a marked alteration. Perhaps he had become alarmed by the damage that was being done to his friend's reputation, and was simply trying to protect him from further dishonour. In all probability, however, the explanation was not so simple, but had its roots in the political situation.

By this time people were starting to suspect that Frances and Rochester were in love, and there was speculation that they would marry as soon as she was free to do so. Obviously this would entail additional humiliation for Essex, for if his wife at once found happiness with another man, it would merely underline his own shortcomings as a husband. From Southampton's point of view, however, there were other reasons why the union would be undesirable. For the last few months he and Rochester had worked together to try to obtain Sir Henry Neville's appointment as Secretary. By mid-1613, however, it was becoming apparent to informed observers that Sir Henry's chances of securing the job were dwindling. Southampton's own political career was also at a standstill: at the end of June it was reported that he was becoming increasingly resentful about the fact that he had never been made a Privy Councillor. Almost certainly Southampton attributed these failures to the fact that Rochester had started to align himself with the Howards, and he feared that if they forged a closer alliance, it would only worsen his own political isolation. At the beginning of August Southampton explained to a friend his present feelings about the annulment. He insisted, 'For the business itself, I protest I shall be glad, if it may lawfully, that it may go forward,' but he qualified this by admitting, 'Of late I have been fearful of the consequence, and have had my fears increased by the last letters that came to me.' While he did not elaborate on what these worries were, they were surely connected with the frustration of his political aspirations. Certainly the Earl of Northampton was sure that it was this which accounted for Southampton's conversion into an opponent of the annulment, for he told Rochester, 'He runs counter out of faction.'[49]

It may be that another important person at court had influenced Essex to become less cooperative about the annulment, for the Queen was 'supposed not to wish well to the business'. There were various reasons for this. For one thing, she hated Rochester, and was never happier than when causing him trouble. Besides this, she disliked the Howards intensely, and made no secret of her feelings. On one occasion – probably while the nullity was in progress – she pointedly excluded the

Earl of Suffolk from her coach when he attempted to accompany her as she drove away from Hampton Court. Claiming to have been offended because 'my Lord Chamberlain looked sourly on her', she instead invited the Earls of Southampton and Worcester to sit on either side of her. It was the Earl of Northampton, however, for whom she felt the greatest hatred. She and Northampton had clashed on several occasions in the past, and Anne had never forgiven him. When Sir John Swinnerton was attempting to obtain a lease of a lucrative customs farm the Queen had indicated that, if Swinnerton paid her debts, she would help him secure what he wanted. Northampton at once intervened to stop this, telling Rochester after he had done so, 'It were strange that at every piece of green cheese her mouth must water, and that her expenses should destroy the necessary means of the King's maintenance.' Some years before, Northampton and Anne had had a still more acrimonious encounter: during a heated exchange at Woodstock Northampton had told her, 'She was only the best subject, yet no less a subject than I.'[50] The prospect that the Howards might consolidate their power at court by forging a coalition with Rochester, another of her enemies, filled her with fury, and she did what she could to prevent it.

While there is no record that Anne had any contact with Essex at this time, she was certainly seeing a great deal of the Earl of Southampton, and so had ample opportunity to cause trouble. Northampton wrote irritably, 'Never man was so great with her as Southampton, for beside his private supping with her at Oatlands often times, she likewise caused a lodging to be made for him of purpose, and one of her beds to be set up for him.'[51] Knowing Anne's meddlesome disposition, it would be surprising if she refrained from making it known during these meetings that she strongly disapproved of the nullity proceedings.

When Essex appeared before the commissioners he did not dispute that his marriage had never been consummated. He admitted that he had unsuccessfully tried to do so 'divers times' during the first year he and Frances were together, and said that thereafter he had been disinclined to make any more attempts. However, far from confirming that during that first year Frances had repeatedly submitted herself to him in the hope of being penetrated, he maintained that sometimes she had rejected his advances. Furthermore, Essex answered one question in a way that gave the Archbishop of Canterbury the impression that he believed Frances had been unfaithful to him. Abbot recorded that when Essex was asked whether he thought Frances was *virgo incorrupta*, 'He smiled and said, "She saith so, and is so for me."' To Abbot this implied a degree of scepticism on Essex's part, but it is not surprising that he was the only member of the commission who understood it thus, for Essex's next answer was inconsistent with such an interpretation. When asked whether he believed that Frances was 'a woman able and fit for carnal copulation', he denied it, 'because he hath not found it'.[52]

Essex's embittered response threw the commissioners into confusion. When Bishop Neile of Coventry and Lichfield sought to clarify the position by questioning Essex in more detail about his physical abilities, he made little headway. Amongst other things Neile sought to establish whether Essex had ever had an erection, and whether he had ever experienced an emission of semen, but Essex remained obstinately silent in the face of these enquiries. His fellow commissioners were too embarrassed to give Neile the support he needed, for there was a feeling that it was unseemly for churchmen to probe too deeply into such matters. And indeed, when word of the Bishop's questions seeped out, there was 'much sport ... at the court in London'. It was only later, when the commissioners found that they had to reach judgement on the basis of imprecise information, that they came to regret their diffidence, and to wish 'that punctually his Lordship might have been held to give his answer'.[53]

Essex's evidence at least removed a fear in the mind of some of the commissioners that he and Frances were dishonestly colluding with each other, and that they were pretending that they had never consummated their marriage in order to gain their freedom. In other respects, however, his testimony was very damaging. Although he had offered no proof to substantiate his allegations, Frances's lawyers believed that decisive action was necessary to counter them. In order to refute Essex's claim that Frances was physically incapable of the sexual act, while simultaneously establishing that she was a virgin, they proposed that Frances submit herself to a gynaecological examination by a panel of midwives and married ladies.

In most subsequent accounts of the nullity proceedings it is alleged that Frances and her family were aghast when the commissioners imposed a requirement that she submit to a physical inspection. Numerous sources assert that the Howards knew that Frances was having an affair with Rochester, and that she had no chance of being pronounced a virgin. The story goes that the only reason that Frances came through this ordeal undetected was that her family requested that, to spare her embarrassment, she could be heavily veiled during the inspection. This meant that they were able to substitute another young girl in her place (named variously as the daughter of Sir Thomas Monson, or Frances's cousin, Mistress Fines), and it was she who underwent an examination. Anthony Weldon adds the salacious detail that, though the imposter was 'at that time too young to be other than *virgo intacta* ... within two years after, had the old ladies made their inspection, the orifice would not have appeared so small to have delivered such a verdict as they did'.[54]

In fact it is clear that the initiative about the inspection came from the Howard side. In an account of the nullity written by one of the commissioners, Sir Daniel Dunne, it was stated categorically that 'It was desired by the counsel of the said lady that matrons should make an inspection of her body.' Another report of the case claims that, in view of the fact that the Earl of Essex agreed that he had not consummated his marriage, an inspection to establish whether or not Frances was a virgin was 'held ... to be needless, yet she was searched'.[55]

The panel of inspectors comprised six in all. Two were professional midwives, 'expert in matter of marriage' and 'practised about the delivery of noblewomen'. The others were Lady Mary Tyrwhitt, Lady Alice Carew, Lady Dallison and Lady Anne Waller. Described as 'women fearing God and mothers of children', these gentlewomen allegedly 'came unwillingly' to the task. Nevertheless, their verdict vindicated Frances. In their report to the commissioners they 'testified they found her as straight as a child of nine or ten years of age', swearing that, as far as they could judge, she was both 'fit for carnal copulation and still a virgin'. Anthony Weldon declared that most people regarded the verdict as 'very strange', opining that the only way that the 'purblind ladies' could have reached their decision was by wearing 'spectacles ground to lessen' rather than improve their vision. However, if the ladies did make a mistake, they merely erred on the side of caution. Even in the twentieth century it is recognised that it is extremely difficult to establish through physical inspection whether or not a woman is a virgin.[56]

Having emerged from the inspection with her reputation intact, Frances next appeared before the commission in person. Her lawyers produced a written statement reaffirming that, despite her own efforts, her marriage had never been consummated. Interestingly, however, she made no claim that she was still a virgin. Initially some of the commissioners protested that this statement was not full enough but, after Frances's lawyers amended it slightly, it was deemed acceptable. Frances was not cross-examined, but merely took an oath on the Bible and then signed her statement.[57]

Essex was not prepared to let this pass. In early July his counsel made a submission to the commissioners on his behalf which was described as 'round and piquant'. Since this was later ruled inadmissible, and all record of it destroyed, it is impossible to be sure of its contents. However, it appears that, among other things, Essex argued that the matrons' verdict should be quashed. While not suggesting that they had been duped into inspecting an imposter, Essex's representatives contended that the midwives' examination of Frances had been insufficiently rigorous to enable them to reach an accurate conclusion. Furthermore, since the gentlewomen on the panel lacked professional expertise, they had been incapable of inspecting Frances independently, but had been obliged to accept the midwives' findings. It is clear that some of the commissioners shared these fears. At one point the Bishop of London complained to his colleagues 'that, he being with them, found that the ladies knew not well what to make of it; that they had no skill, nor knew what was the truth; but what they said was upon the credit of the midwives, which were but two, and I knew not how tampered with.'[58]

Despite such reservations, Frances's counsel was able to establish that the inspectresses' verdict should stand. Her lawyers argued that, though the midwives' conclusions were 'uttered but upon belief', their testimony afforded as 'substantial a proof as the law requireth'. To the charge that the midwives had not probed Frances sufficiently deeply it was countered that the report they tendered to the commission 'importeth a more precise search than by eye or sight', and it was therefore 'not to be doubted that the same likewise is sufficient'. As for the claim that, 'after the midwives had made search in their presence and reported that so they find it', the gentlewomen on the panel had merely endorsed their pronouncements, this was vehemently disputed. It was claimed that the gentlewomen had conducted their own examination, 'though the midwife proceeded further than the rest, as it was convenient for their science and knowledge, and for the danger that might have ensued if the matrons as the midwife had used their hands'.[59] Presumably it was on the basis of these representations that the Archbishop of Canterbury dismissed Essex's attempts to overturn the midwives' evidence.

Nevertheless, the Archbishop remained deeply unhappy. In particular he was concerned that there had never before been a case in English law in which a man had been recognised as impotent towards his wife but virile with other women. Sir Daniel Dunne, who from early in the proceedings showed himself 'a stickler for the nullity', contended that King Henry VIII's divorce from Anne of Cleves furnished the commissioners with the precedent they needed. Abbot was reluctant to accept this, pointing out that Henry was 'a strange prince in that kind', and that therefore it was inappropriate for English matrimonial law to be based on rulings in his favour. Eventually he agreed to consult the appropriate records but, when he did so, he became more set in his opposition, as he 'found not one word tending to the present case'. And indeed, it was true that Henry VIII's nullity suit was not strictly applicable to the one Abbot was hearing. At the time, Henry himself had submitted a written deposition to Convocation in which he implied that he had tried and failed to consummate his marriage. The King's physician, Dr Butts, also gave evidence that Henry 'thought himself able to do the act with other but not with her'. He explained that, when spending the night with Anne, Henry had often had wet dreams, proving to his own satisfaction that he was not impotent. However, when Convocation proceeded to annul Henry's marriage they did so, not on the basis of this testimony, but rather because Anne had earlier been precontracted to a son of the Duke of Lorraine, and this supposedly invalidated her union with Henry. In its ruling Convocation took note of the fact that Henry had not consummated the marriage, while stating that, had he succeeded in doing so, such congress would not have been legal.[60]

Bury's case, which was cited as another precedent by Dunne, also failed to satisfy Abbot. Bury's marriage had been annulled after he had acknowledged that an injury acquired out riding had left him impotent. When physically examined, it was found that he only had one testicle, 'and that no bigger than a bean', and this was thought to corroborate his story. However, after his marriage had been annulled, Bury took another wife, and produced a child by her. This automatically invalidated the grounds on which the nullity had been granted. Though Bury himself died shortly after, in a subsequent court case it was established that, at the time of his death, he and his first wife were still legally bound together. Far from convincing the Archbishop that this formed a reliable precedent, to his mind it merely confirmed that the Howards' case was untenable.[61]

Abbot was also fearful that, if he granted a nullity that enabled both parties to remarry, he would subsequently be besieged by other unhappily married couples, clamouring for the same treatment. With some asperity he told Sir Daniel Dunne, 'As soon as this cause is sentenced, every man who is discontented with his wife and every woman discontented with her husband, will repair to me for such nullities. If I yield unto them, here will be strange violations of marriages; if I do not, I must tell them that it was fit for my Lord of Essex, but is not so for you.'[62]

Abbot's most fundamental objection, however, was that he could not accept that Essex was physically incapable of consummating his marriage. He did not deny that, if Essex *was* impotent, the marriage should be dissolved. He acknowledged that 'Since marriage in young couples is for carnal copulation and procreation thereupon ... if this young nobleman be not able to perform those marital rights unto this lady, he doth her a very great injustice to retain her as his wife, and we shall perform a great part of injury and cruelty towards her if we do not free her of this burthen and yoke.' Nevertheless, since Essex maintained that he would be able to make love to another woman, the position was different. Since Abbot could not accept that witchcraft was responsible for Essex's condition, he concluded that Essex's failure to consummate the marriage was an act of will, arising simply from the fact that he did not love Frances. In Abbot's view it was this 'want of love which restrains all motions of carnal concupiscence, and not any impotence'.[63]

Abbot had various reasons for thinking, as he put it to the Bishop of Coventry and Lichfield, that the Earl of Essex was 'as able a man for a woman as any in England'. Essex's own assurances weighed very heavily with him, for the Archbishop believed him to be a God-fearing young man, and he did not think that 'so religious a nobleman' would lie on such matters. He also regarded it as significant that Essex's father had been renowned for his sexual prowess, and somewhat naively found it implausible that the current Earl's appetite could be so very different. More importantly, however, Abbot was told several stories which confirmed his belief that Essex was not afflicted by genuine impotence. The Earl of Northampton had no doubt of the identity of the persons who supplied Abbot with this anecdotal information. He wrote angrily to Rochester that he understood that Abbot and the Bishop of London were saying 'privately that they cannot believe an impotency in the Earl, hearing as much as they have done from great persons, which no doubt is the Queen and Pembroke'.[64]

While we do not know all the details of what Abbot learned from his informants, he did record one story which was passed on to him by 'a good friend', and which he considered noteworthy. One Sunday in September 'five or six captains and gentlemen of worth' visited Essex in his bedchamber. One of them started teasing the Earl about his inability, whereupon Essex 'rose out of his bed and, taking up his shirt, did show to them all so able and extraordinarily sufficient matter that they all cried out shame of his lady and said that, if the ladies of the court knew as much as they knew, they would tread her to death'.[65]

This incident may have been less telling than Abbot imagined. As an unmarried man who was himself utterly inexperienced in sexual matters, he did not realise that the ability to obtain an early morning erection prior to urinating is not necessarily indicative of sexual potency.

To Abbot these scraps of gossip seemed more conclusive than anything which contradicted his theory. He was unimpressed when the King confided that, on one occasion, 'some of the Earl's friends had put a woman to him and he would not touch her'. He was also dismissive of Essex's own admission that during the first year he had cohabited with Frances, he had 'divers times' unsuccessfully tried to make love to her. Abbot thought that these 'divers times may be twice or thrice and no more', and was more inclined to attach importance to Essex's statement that, during this period, Frances had sometimes repudiated him.[66]

The Earl of Northampton thought that if Lord Knollys and the Earl of Worcester revealed to the commission what Essex had said to them regarding his sexual inadequacy, it would clear up all doubts on the matter. Their evidence could not be lightly discounted, for both men would be very reluctant to say anything that might reflect badly on Essex. Knollys was Essex's uncle, while Worcester had no wish to displease the Queen by assisting the Howards.[67] At one point the King himself urged Abbot that Knollys and Worcester should be summoned before the commission but, unaccountably, neither of them was ever required to give evidence.

Abbot regarded it as a vital distinction whether it was a want of love or a physical deficiency that impeded Essex from fulfilling his marital duties, whereas others considered this irrelevant. Sir Daniel Dunne argued that it was needless to identify what had caused Essex's problem, as 'the sentence was to be given in general terms, not naming any particular impotency'. The King took much the same view, maintaining that a lack of copulation automatically nullified any marriage, and that it was immaterial 'whether the fault thereof hath been born with him or done to him by violence, or disease, or disproportion, or inaptitude betwixt the parties, or unnatural practices'.[68] In Abbot's view, however, such an interpretation was not consistent with the dictates of canon law.

Furthermore, although Essex had specifically told the commission that there was now no question of him ever loving Frances, Abbot maintained that the situation was not irretrievable. Since he took the view that Essex's inability to make love to Frances stemmed from his discontent with her, it followed that, if that discontent was alleviated, the other problem would right itself automatically. More realistic people could not subscribe to this analysis, for only the most blithe optimist could doubt the permanent nature of the young couple's ill-feeling for each other. Indeed, when Abbot suggested promoting a reconciliation between the estranged pair, the Bishop of Ely answered bluntly that if they were forced to live together, 'It might be the cause of poisoning and destroying one another.'[69]

From the start, when there had been a conflict of evidence, Abbot had been more inclined to believe Essex rather than Frances and, as the summer of 1613 progressed, Abbot's opinion of the young woman's character worsened steadily. Although his personal acquaintance with her was limited, during these months he 'heard many strange stories of the lady's carriage', which severely discredited her in his eyes. For one thing he learned of her involvement with Mary Woods, and he was also alerted to the fact that Frances and Rochester were already close and planned to marry. In July Sir Henry Neville warned Abbot that Frances had 'a new husband ... readily provided for her', and the Archbishop also remained mindful of 'a speech of Overbury's once to me in that kind'. Although the Archbishop did not say so directly, the inference is clear that he suspected Frances of adultery, and he certainly acknowledged that the unsavoury reports about her were too numerous to be disregarded. As he put it, 'These things, though out of charity I entertained not as absolutely true, yet the concurrence of them from so many made me that I could not condemn them.'[70]

Abbot's strong feelings against Frances manifested themselves when King James summoned him to Windsor in mid-July to discuss the progress of the nullity suit. When Abbot indicated that he believed everything that Essex had said, James reminded him that his testimony could not always be reconciled with what Frances had told the court. At this Abbot lost his temper and launched into an attack upon Frances, going so far as to condemn her for 'iniquity'.[71] The King was profoundly shocked by this outburst, and it was this that led to his subsequent accusation that Abbot was biased.

It would be wrong not to have considerable sympathy for Abbot. It was only after carefully scrutinising the relevant sections of canon law and numerous other authorities that he concluded that granting a nullity would be indefensible. As it became clear that he was opposed to a divorce, he was subjected to intense pressure from both the King and the Howards, and the fact that he would not change his mind despite fears that he would thereby incur lasting disgrace can be said to mark him as a man of formidable integrity. What was less commendable, however, was his total absence of compassion for Frances. Other members of the commission were moved by the plight of this young woman who had been condemned to a loveless existence before she was of an age where she could take responsibility for her own actions, but in Abbot such sympathy was totally lacking. When the King pointed out to him that, if the marriage was pronounced valid, Frances and her husband would 'be forcibly kept together, but never their persons or affections, and they still be forced to live in perpetual scandal or misery', this failed to worry Abbot. Rather, he took the view that, even if the couple were never reconciled and the marriage remained uncon- summated, 'It is no more but one lady doth want that solace which marital conjunction would afford unto her.' He urged that, in those circumstances, 'let her expect God's leisure in fasting and prayer and other humiliation'.[72] It is hard not to suspect that the prospect of Frances condemned to a lifetime of penitence and self-denial afforded him a certain grim satisfaction.

Another unattractive feature of Abbot's character was that, when other members of the commission expressed opinions contrary to his own, he invariably assumed they had unworthy motives. He formed a 'hard opinion' of Sir Daniel Dunne when he realised that he was in favour of granting a nullity, noting darkly that he had long regarded him as 'a man most corrupt'. He was furious when Sir Daniel made a speech to the commission explaining his position. 'I thought it was an audacious part that such a one as Sir Daniel Dunne was to teach us out of such poor grounds both what to do and how to do,' fumed Abbot, ignoring the fact that other members of the commission had indicated that they were interested in hearing what Dunne had to say on the subject. Even while condemning Dunne for speaking out of turn, the Archbishop was annoyed that the distinguished theologian Lancelot Andrewes failed to articulate his reasons for supporting the annulment. Abbot took this reticence to mean that Andrewes knew that his stance could not be justified. Abbot had initially been confident that Andrewes, Sir Julius Caesar and Sir Thomas Parry shared his abhorrence of the nullity, and when it emerged that they had shifted position, he concluded that they had done so in hopes of earning the King's approval. As for Bishop Neile of Coventry and Lichfield, Abbot not only thought he preferred to please the King than to obey his conscience, but also suspected him of acting from a crude determination to uphold the interests of the court faction he supported, being 'zealous of the house of Suffolk'.[73]

Although it was perfectly legitimate for Abbot to maintain that Essex did not suffer from impotence, he should have recognised that other members of the commission were entitled to hold different opinions.

Abbot was shocked when he heard that Lancelot Andrewes had told a friend that initially he had thought there were inadequate grounds to grant a nullity, and that he had changed his mind after being 'better instructed by the King' about 'the insufficiency of my Lord of Essex'. Abbot thought this proved that Andrewes had sold his soul for royal favour. It apparently did not occur to him that the reports which had led him to form a contrary conclusion were not necessarily more reliable than the information which had influenced Andrewes.

At one point Abbot had an angry exchange with Bishop Neile of Coventry and Lichfield after the latter attributed Essex's sexual paralysis to 'a natural impotency which was before the marriage'. When Abbot demanded why he thought this, Neile answered that he had 'heard divers particulars which are enough to persuade me, if they be true'. To this Abbot retorted, 'And I have heard as many to the contrary,' as if that settled the matter.[74] In reality, of course, the absence of scientific proof and the imperfect state of medical knowledge meant that none of the commissioners had anything very substantial on which to base their verdict. In the circumstances Abbot's certainty that he had reached the right conclusions was ill-founded, and he was certainly too hasty in claiming that his opponents were morally bankrupt.

Abbot was at least correct in thinking that those commissioners who believed that Essex suffered from impotence were guilty of inconsistency. If the Earl was afflicted in this way, in theory he should have been denied permission to remarry after his union with Frances had been nullified. Abbot intended to raise this point with his opponents by saying that if they thought Essex incapable of coition, 'Why then do you give him leave to marry again, that he who hath deluded and frustrated one may also delude another?'[75] The answer was, of course, that unless Essex had thought that it was in his interests to do so, he would never have made even a partial acknowledgement of physical inadequacy. Without such an admission on his part, Frances would have been tied to him for her entire lifespan, and those commissioners who pitied her situation believed that this would constitute a grave injustice. In the circumstances they thought it better not to question Essex's claim that he would be capable of consummating a union with a more suitable woman. In point of law their reasoning may not have been impeccable, but they were bending the rules in Essex's favour, rather than Frances's.

On 14 July, after it had become apparent that the nullity suit was in deadlock, the King summoned the commissioners to Windsor, and they spent more than three hours discussing the case with him. Sir Daniel Dunne sought to assure the King that the prospects for the nullity remained favourable, but Abbot would have none of this. When Dunne said that the Anne of Cleves divorce and Bury's case afforded reputable precedents, the Archbishop sharply contradicted him, and Dunne's remark that it would be a dreadful disgrace for the Lord Chamberlain and his daughter if their suit was rejected drew from Abbot the withering comment that 'They should have looked to that before they did begin it.'

Greatly worried by Abbot's intransigence, James took him aside for a private conversation. For the first time he made it plain that it was he who had encouraged Suffolk to bring the case in the first place but, though disturbed by this revelation, Abbot could not see that it altered anything. He begged the King to discharge him from the commission, but he left no doubt that, if James expected him to continue, he must do as his conscience dictated. Much perplexed, James told Abbot that the commission should reconvene the following day at Lambeth. If all the commissioners declared themselves in favour of the nullity, they should pronounce sentence to that effect. If, on the other hand, there were any dissenting voices, the case should be adjourned until further notice.[76]

When the commissioners met the following day it soon became obvious that there was no question of their unanimously consenting to the nullity. For the time being, therefore, matters were left in abeyance. Rochester, who had been anxiously waiting in London for the verdict, galloped down to Windsor to deliver the disappointing news to his master.[77]

That evening Abbot sat down to try to give the King a written summary of his objections to the nullity. He enclosed a memorandum drawn up by Sir John Bennet, in which the latter listed what he regarded as the legal weaknesses in the case put together by the Howards. The most controversial item set down here was the contention that Frances and Essex would not be entitled to a nullity until they had lived together for a further three-year period, for, according to Bennet's interpretation of the law, the triennial probationary period was meant to take place after legal proceedings had started. To Bennet's technical objection the Archbishop appended a treatise of his own, dwelling principally on why he found it impossible to accept that witchcraft could be responsible for Essex's poor relations with Frances.

Abbot began with the observation, 'Inasmuch as we firmly believe that scripture doth, directly or by consequence, contain in it sufficient matter to decide all controversies,' he found it curious that there was nothing in the Bible that could justify annulling a marriage because the husband had been physically disabled by witchcraft. Furthermore, while not denying that witchcraft might have adversely affected individuals in the past, he found it hard to believe that in these enlightened times, when popish superstition had been driven from the realm, it should still be so damaging. He thought it more likely 'that those who have embraced the gospel should be free from this *maleficium* [witchcraft], especially since amongst a million of men in our age, there is but one found in all our country who is clearly and evidently known to be troubled with the same'. However, even if one granted that Essex might be a victim of witchcraft, he found it odd that more effort had not been made to overcome its manifestations. Abbot did not go so far as to advocate that Essex should try a French folk remedy for impotence, namely, urinating three times through the keyhole of the church where he married.[78] Nevertheless, the Archbishop was adamant that, rather than merely passively accepting the consequences, Frances and her husband should have engaged in fasting and prayer to combat the forces of evil, or at least consulted doctors to see if Essex's infirmity would respond to medical treatment.

Abbot's missive infuriated the King. Until now, James had generally defended Abbot when Suffolk or Northampton claimed he was being obstructive, but the King's sympathy for him now diminished. For one thing, James was annoyed by Abbot's contention that scripture could settle all disputes, for this seemed to him 'preposterous, and one of the Puritans' arguments'. More importantly, however, it was fatal for Abbot to have written so dismissively of witchcraft, for this was a subject on which the King considered himself a leading authority. He was sure that in the past he himself had only narrowly escaped becoming a victim of witchcraft. Some years before James inherited the English crown, the Earl of Bothwell's private warlock was said to have conjured up the devil in North Berwick church. Witnesses described this apparition as having a beak-like nose and burning eyes and that, when ordered to 'kiss his arse', they found it 'cold like ice'.[79] When asked why he had never managed to harm the King, the devil answered regretfully in French, 'He is a man of God.' While in some respects this was reassuring, it had proved to James that satanic forces were conspiring against him. Anxious to find out more about his supernatural opponents, when a coven of witches was arrested in Edinburgh, the King 'took great delight to be present at their examinations'. James was startled when a witch named Jane Duncan obtained permission to whisper in his ear and then repeated to him *verbatim* a conversation he had had with the Queen on his wedding night. Fascinated and appalled by this evidence of witches' malign powers, James conducted further research into the subject, and in 1597 he published a book on it entitled *Daemonologie*. Abbot's scepticism about witchcraft suggested to James that he had not read this tract with the attention it deserved.

For the next few weeks James busied himself writing a response to Abbot. Angrily he rebutted Abbot's claim that witches could not harm members of the true church. 'To exempt this of our [religious] persuasion from the power of witchcraft is a paradox never yet maintained by any learned or wise man,' he chided, demanding why, if Abbot was correct, so many witches were arrested and sentenced to death in England every year? To the King it did not seem in the least implausible that Satan could 'so estrange the husband's affection' that he became incapable of making love, and it also struck him as logical that the powers of darkness could render useless 'a member ... wherein the devil hath his principal operation'. To Abbot's suggestion that Frances and Essex should seek to overcome their difficulties by fasting and prayer, James retorted that, for all Abbot knew, they might have tried this in the past, but now it was too late as 'no such cure is ... likely to succeed well except the parties' own hearts and desires be set thereupon'. He dismissed Abbot's fears that granting a nullity would cause a flood of similar applications from unhappily married couples. There were very few marriages which were not consummated, so few people would be affected by the ruling, but he considered it perfectly equitable to 'open a way of lawful relief to any person who shall chance to be distressed in that sort'. Lastly he treated with scorn Sir John Bennet's recommendation that Frances and Essex must live together for three more years before the commissioners considered the merits of their case. 'As for the triennial probation, I hope no man can be so blind as to make doubt whether that be taken before or after the suit be begun,' he wrote irritably.[80]

Although Abbot was warned by friends that the King planned to send him 'a sharp letter', he was kept in suspense as to its contents until after James returned to London from his summer progress. In the meantime he was informed that two more members were being added to the commission, namely, Thomas Bilson, Bishop of Winchester, and John Buckridge, Bishop of Rochester. Abbot was disgusted that these men had been selected. He had heard that Buckridge had already assured the King 'that he liked well of the nullity', and sourly commented that the Bishop doubtless conceived that 'This was a way to make him well esteemed, and to rise high in preferment.' As for Bilson, the Archbishop was sure he had been chosen because he had ties of obligation to the Howards and also bore 'an old grudge' against Abbot for having frustrated his own ambition to become Primate of all England. Abbot added bitterly, 'I heard of good credit and secretly that he was put in hope to be made a Privy Councillor; and the fame was general that for the father's labour [his] son should be made a knight.'[81]

The King now decreed that the commission should reassemble on 18 September. For Frances and her family the ensuing weeks were very tense. By this time it was widely rumoured that the Countess of Essex and Viscount Rochester were on exceptionally close terms with each other. In June John Chamberlain had reported, 'The world speaks liberally that my Lord of Rochester and she be in love one with another, which breeds a double question, whether that consideration be like to hinder [the nullity] or set it forward.' Later that summer Thomas Lorkin told a correspondent that Rochester 'showeth himself ... passionate in this business only in favour [of the Countess], with whom a new match would be presently concluded if the old one were now abolished'. Yet, though suspicions as to the true state of affairs were so widespread, the Howards were careful to do nothing that might confirm them. Writing confidentially on 23 August to a trusted business associate named Sir Arthur Ingram, the Earl of Suffolk declared, 'I have not made dainty to let you know of some more interest that I have, and may have, in my Lord of Rochester,' but he stressed that this was not something that 'I would avow publicly.'

One reason for such circumspection was that, if proof emerged that Frances and Rochester were romantically involved, it might prejudice the outcome of the nullity case. However, the Howards had other worries. Chief amongst these was a fear that their enemies might yet manage to deter Rochester from marrying into the family. It was this which led Suffolk to turn down a request from Sir Arthur Ingram that he should act as broker when part of the Sherborne estate was put on the market. Suffolk knew that Rochester stood to make money out of this transaction, and he did not want to annoy him by interfering. He told Ingram that he knew that an individual named Daccombe 'as knows I love him not' was 'a great enemy to any conjunction between my Lord and me, and hath already played his part so far in that' that Suffolk did not want to give him an opportunity to make further trouble. He was worried that 'if now I should persuade my Lord from his profit which he loves well, this knave and the rest of my good friends about him would so paraphrase upon this text as haply they might make him conceive that particulars of mine own would easily make me to think lightly of his good'. Rejecting Sir Arthur's application, he appealed to him, 'whether in this so tickle a world, it behoves me not to be wary?

A little time will give me security what to trust unto.'[82]

Clearly nervous that Rochester might yet abandon Frances, the Howards did all they could to keep alive his passion. Although prudence dictated that the young couple should not see much of each other till the nullity was settled, this increased the risk that Rochester would grow bored and seek the company of more available females. In the circumstances Frances's family did not think it wise to keep them apart for too long. On 14 August Northampton wrote anxiously to Rochester after the latter had said it would not be convenient for him to meet Frances at Cawsam, Lord Knollys's house in Oxfordshire. Rochester had proposed that instead an encounter should take place in London, but Northampton thought this too conspicuous, particularly since it would not be easy for Lady Suffolk to chaperone her daughter. He pleaded, 'London cannot be so fit in my Lady's absence, whom my Lord's affairs draw down for a while ... Audley End they take to be the better and fitter place, and freer from occasions of discourse in the meanwhile till the knot be tied.' However, Northampton was so anxious not to displease Rochester that he added that, if this arrangement did not suit him, 'My Lady [Suffolk] will come back presently [to London] and break off all her business.'[83]

Despite the best efforts of her family it was unavoidable that Frances and Rochester were separated for much of the summer of 1613, but at least her great-uncle could facilitate written communications between them. Their letters to each other were delivered by Northampton's couriers, and Northampton did not fail to stress to Rochester how much this meant to 'the pretty lady, who lives by the life of your letters as a chameleon doth by air'. When Rochester was dilatory about replying to Frances, Northampton nagged him to be more considerate. At one point he wrote reproachfully, 'From the lady I have not heard since the sending of my last, nor expect to hear till *un petit mot* from your fair hand awake her industry.' Besides this, Northampton took it upon himself to keep Rochester in a state of heightened erotic anticipation by alluding to the time when he and Frances would be able to sleep together without fear of the consequences. When Rochester apologised for having sent him a badly written letter, Northampton unctuously reassured him that reading it had caused him no pain, 'or rather, it were but that which a man takes in cracking a sweet nut to taste the kernel, or but like the pain my Lady Frances shall feel when the sweet stream follows'.[84]

Pending the resumption of the nullity proceedings the strain on all concerned was considerable, and matters were scarcely improved when

Essex became involved in a bitter dispute with one of Frances's brothers, Harry Howard. Howard had made some derogatory remarks about his brother-in-law – presumably relating to the latter's sexual performance – but unfortunately the person he had confided in 'treacherously revealed' to Essex what had been 'secretly imparted ... in trust' to him. On 20 August Essex challenged Howard to a duel, and Howard accepted the challenge. Someone sympathetic to Essex reported, 'The quarrel is deadly, being grounded upon the business of the Earl's lady ... If God save not this poor Earl, his life must pay for it, and so be the annullation of his marriage.' Certainly the Earl of Northampton seems to have hoped that Essex would be fatally injured in the confrontation, thus sparing Frances further problems. As a Privy Counsellor who had helped draft a royal proclamation against duelling, Northampton should have done all he could to prevent such an encounter, but to Rochester he expressed the hope that 'God the just judge will assist the right quarrel.' Northampton added maliciously, 'If my Lord [Essex] would draw his sword in defence of a good prick it were worth his pains, but never to make such a poor pudding's apology. I do scant persuade myself that a man can be saved that dies in defence of an ill prick.'[85]

In the end the two men never fought. Because duelling was illegal in England, the combatants had agreed to meet on the continent. When the King realised that Essex and Howard had left the country, he alerted his ambassadors in France and the Netherlands and, after their descriptions had been circulated, the pair were apprehended and brought safely back to England. However, although bloodshed had been averted, the acrimony engendered by the affair was not dispersed so easily.

On 17 September, the day before the nullity commission was due to reassemble, Bishop Neile of Coventry and Lichfield delivered to Abbot the King's answer to his treatise, plus a letter from James rebuking the Archbishop for being swayed by his personal hostility to the Howards. Neile later told the Earl of Northampton that he had discerned 'a great appalment' in Abbot's countenance as he read these documents. Nevertheless, much as it upset Abbot to have incurred the King's displeasure, he would not modify his stance on that account. He told Neile that unless various matters were clarified by Essex, he did not see how he could grant a nullity. At this stage Neile appeared in full agreement on this point. He suggested to Abbot that Essex should be recalled as a witness and the Archbishop willingly concurred.

The following day, when the commissioners reconvened, they agreed that Essex should be summoned before them for a second time. Unfortunately, before they could send for him, a message arrived from the King, forbidding them to proceed. James claimed that it would not be fair to recall Essex at this late stage because 'the said Earl, either being provoked by the late challenge between him and Mr Henry Howard, or otherwise instigated by the Earl of Southampton' would 'speak all things to hinder the nullity'. Exactly what he feared Essex would say was never established. We know, however, that Essex himself very much wanted to appear. At his request the Earl of Southampton went to see one of the newly appointed commissioners, Bishop Bilson of Winchester, to beg him that his friend should be recalled. When the Bishop asked him outright whether he thought Essex was capable of carnal conjunction, Southampton answered, 'No, *quo ad illam*' [i.e. as far as Frances was concerned] but then said that it was debatable 'whether strangeness in her as much as weakness in him was not the cause of want of execution'. Disingenuously Bilson did not reveal that the King had prohibited Essex's re-examination, claiming instead that such a procedure would be 'very unjust and impertinent, because after oath once taken, which is the highest form of proof, all further examinations were both by conscience and law prohibited'.[86]

It is possible that the Bishop was technically correct when he advanced this argument, but it had not occurred to him to raise this objection until after the King had intervened. In fairness to Frances it is undeniable that it would have been preferable if Essex had been pressed harder at his first appearance before the commission, for by now he was so embittered that there was little chance of him giving a fair account of what had transpired in the privacy of their bedroom. Obviously, however, the Howards' nervousness about what he might say does suggest that they knew he had genuine grievances, and the fact that the King was prepared to collude with them in order to suppress such evidence reflects extremely badly on him. Understandably, Abbot was deeply suspicious at the way he had been prevented from ascertaining what he wanted to know. He recalled saying to himself, 'Good Lord! What a case is this? Shall any truth be kept from us? Are they afraid to have all out? Do they only look to attain their own ends, and care not how our consciences be entangled and ensnared?' From that point, he resolved that he would never consent to the nullity.[87]

Determined that matters should not be further protracted, the King instructed Abbot that the commission must reach its verdict no later than 25 September. As the deadline loomed the Howards stepped up their efforts to secure a favourable outcome. Having alerted Rochester to the fact that Lancelot Andrewes had absented himself from the commission to attend to business in his diocese, Northampton asked

the Viscount to make sure that the King summoned Andrewes back in
time to cast his vote. He said that he was sure Andrewes did not mean
to let them down, but if this 'grave, judicious and learned judge' was
not present for the decision, 'the malicious crew' would claim that he
'had a mind to draw his head out of the collar'.[88]

The day before he was to pronounce sentence Abbot was summoned
to Whitehall to receive a final exhortation from the King. As Suffolk
and Northampton glowered at the Archbishop from the far end of a
gallery, James took Abbot aside and expressed a fervent wish that he
no longer had any doubts as to the merits of Frances's case. The Archbishop could hold out no such hope. He told the King, 'It was nothing
to me whether she remained wife to the Earl of Essex or married to
another man; but that I might not give sentence where I saw no
proof; that I had lived fifty-one years almost, and had my conscience
uncorrupted in judgment; that I knew not how soon I was to be called
before God, and I was loth against that time to give a wound to my
own soul.'[89]

The following morning Abbot rose before dawn to write a detailed
repudiation of the nullity suit. He knew that he could count on the
support of Sir John Bennet, Dr Thomas Edwards, Dr Francis James,
and John King, Bishop of London, and though by now it appeared
probable that they would be outnumbered by those commissioners who
would vote in favour of it, he was confident that he was in an unassailable
position intellectually. When Bishop King told the Archbishop that he
believed that if he supported the nullity, 'the devil would that night
fetch away his soul,' Abbot reassured him, 'I doubt not, in Almighty
God, but to batter their nullity to dust.' Having now 'resolved to speak
large, and home to the cause', he 'did long to be at the business'.[90]

As things turned out, however, Abbot was denied an opportunity to
express himself freely. Soon after the commissioners assembled on the
morning of 25 September they received a message from the King,
stating that each commissioner was to confine himself to declaring
whether he was for or against the nullity, without elaborating on his
reasons for this. Abbot was crestfallen at the restriction, but had no
option but to comply. When the verdicts were taken a majority of
seven to five commissioners declared themselves satisfied that Frances's
marriage should be annulled. Accordingly sentence was pronounced, to
the effect that, in view of the fact that 'some secret, incurable and
binding impediment' had prevented Essex from having carnal knowledge
of his wife, the marriage was 'utterly void and none effect'. Both parties
were declared free to remarry, albeit with the proviso that, 'as touching

other marriages' it was left 'to their consciences in the Lord' whether they were entitled to make such a commitment.[91]

The Earl of Essex was deeply resentful that the case had gone against him. Financial reasons partly accounted for this, for he was now required to hand back the dowry of £6,000 that Frances had brought him on her wedding day. In the hope of keeping his possessions intact, his grandmother lent him some of the money, but it turned out not to be enough. To raise the outstanding sum he was forced to sell a substantial area of woodland and to dispose of Binnington Manor, Hertfordshire.[92] On the other hand Essex was now freed from the obligation to make any provision for Frances in the event of him predeceasing her. This may well have relieved his estate of a heavy burden in the future but, faced with the immediate necessity of raising so much cash, Essex was in no mood to take this into account.

Essex's quarrel with Harry Howard also continued to fester, despite efforts by the King to make peace between them. On 26 September, the day after the nullity had been granted, the King convened a special court of honour. Both protagonists' seconds were required to give this body an account of the events which had resulted in a challenge being issued. Signed copies of their testimony were then shown to the King but, when Essex was asked to confirm it, he refused, saying that his second's version of events had been altered. Northampton told Rochester that Southampton had incited Essex to make difficulties, not because he had a genuine grievance but because he was annoyed that Sir Henry Neville had not been made Secretary. Northampton thought that Essex still hoped 'to shuffle swords' with Howard, as this would enhance his standing with the public. At Northampton's suggestion Rochester asked the King to intervene. As a result, on 11 October Essex was summoned before the Privy Council. Since he remained recalcitrant, he was confined to his London residence, and his brother (who was acting as his second) was sent to the Fleet prison. 'This sound reproof will put some water in their wine,' commented Northampton with satisfaction.[93]

There is no accurate way of gauging what the public thought about the nullity. According to Archbishop Abbot, 'Everyone spake acording to their fancies, but for the most part there was a detestation of the thing.' Certainly John Chamberlain was among those who considered that there had been a shameful miscarriage of justice. While the commission was sitting he wrote that if a nullity were granted, it 'in some sort were pity, as well for the example and consequence as for that I have heard from some that may know that all this business rises from wilfulness'. Sir John Throckmorton, the Governor of Flushing, was likewise scandalised that the case had ever been permitted to come to court. On 14 September he fulminated, 'This business of little grace doth much trouble both our politic and ecclesiastic government, and administreth but too much matter against us for our adversaries to sport themselves with.' While there is no certainty that such views were representative of public opinion, there are indications that the verdict caused widespread indignation lower down the social scale. Essex's father had been much loved by the populace and – in Northampton's words – as 'the son of a man whose name is yet among the vulgar rather than the better sort in some kind popular and plausible', the present Earl was also regarded with a good deal of affection. His humiliation at the hands of the Howards naturally displeased his admirers.[94]

Popular indignation found expression in a series of scurrilous rhymes that were widely circulated. The following is a typical example:

> There was at court a lady of late
> That none could enter, she was so strait
> But now with use she is grown so wide
> There is a passage for Carr to ride.

Another ditty ran as follows:

> This dame was inspected, but fraud interjected
> A maid of more perfection
> Whom the midwives did handle, whilst the knight held the candle
> O there was a clear inspection.
>
> Now all foreign writers, cry out on those mitres
> That allow this for virginity
> And talk of ejection and want of erection,
> O there is sound divinity!

As this rhyme suggests, the Bishops who had voted for the nullity became the butt of much ribald humour while, according to Abbot, there was 'a strange applauding and commending' of the dissenting minority. When the Bishop of Winchester's son was knighted shortly after the commission pronounced sentence, it was assumed that this was a reward for Bilson's endorsement of the nullity. Some 'merry fellow' promptly christened the unfortunate young man 'Sir Nullity Bilson'.[95]

From the Howards' point of view it was obviously regrettable that Frances had become an object of ridicule but, having secured the verdict they wanted, they could afford to ignore the taunts and witticisms. More worrying, however, was the possibility that the commission's decision might subsequently be reversed, meaning that there was a risk that, if Frances contracted a second marriage, it would be pronounced bigamous. There is no doubt that Archbishop Abbot cherished a hope that the nullity would later be overturned, and the threat was taken seriously by Frances's family and by Rochester. In a bid to ensure that the commission's findings were not questioned, there was talk of engaging someone to write an authoritative defence of the nullity. At one point the poet John Donne, who was in Rochester's service, contemplated producing such a treatise. However, when the Earl of Suffolk consulted Dr Stuart and Dr Bird, who had earlier acted as Frances's legal representatives, they vigorously advised against this course of action. They were adamant 'that it should by no means be meddled withal, but that things should die of themselves. But no questioning by writing, for so it might go on to the world's end, for one book might breed another.'[96]

Bishop Neile of Coventry and Lichfield then made the alternative suggestion that the sentence of nullity would acquire an added legitimacy if it was certified in Chancery and confirmed by King James personally. Once again the idea had to be abandoned after the King's Advocate declared bluntly, 'If the sentence were not good already, no confirmation could make it good.' Recourse to such an unusual procedure would merely 'proclaim that the sentence was defective' and 'make a great buzz in the world', whereas the priority should be 'to lay it asleep fairly'.[97]

Though the Howards had triumphed over formidable difficulties in procuring the annulment, there remained a danger that their victory would prove worthless. From one quarter, however, there was no longer any need to fear trouble. Those individuals who had agitated against the nullity ('the malicious crew', in Northampton's terminology) had by this time – again according to Northampton – 'lost their instrument',[98] Sir Thomas Overbury, for, on 15 September 1613, the latter had died in the Tower of London.

CHAPTER FOUR

W
hile awaiting trial Rochester would claim that he had hoped that a term of imprisonment would bring about Overbury's 'reformation, not his ruin'.[1] His explanation was regarded as risible, but possibly it did not deserve to be dismissed in so summary a fashion. It can be argued that Overbury's imprisonment did have a two-fold purpose. Obviously it kept him out of the way until Frances's annulment was settled, but it may also have been intended to achieve something more constructive. There were grounds for believing that a period in confinement would actually serve to reconcile Overbury to a match between Lord Rochester and the Countess of Essex. Once in prison, Overbury might be convinced that he could no longer afford to be an enemy of the Howards, for he could be told that his only chance of securing his freedom was to persuade the Earl of Suffolk to take up his cause with the King. Clearly, however, Suffolk would not be prepared to help him unless Overbury acted in a more conciliatory fashion. Overbury would have to drop his opposition to Rochester forming closer links with the Howards, and he would also have to apologise for the offensive comments he had made about the Lord Chamberlain's daughter. In return, Suffolk would ask the King to free Sir Thomas. Once Overbury had been released, he would remain under an obligation to the Lord Chamberlain, and hence would cease to be a nuisance.

When called upon to defend his actions, Rochester was adamant that this was all he had wanted to achieve by having Overbury incarcerated in the Tower. His accusers nevertheless insisted that from the first his intentions had been more malevolent. While agreeing that Rochester had been set on extorting an admission from Sir Thomas that he had maligned the Countess of Essex, this was represented as merely a preliminary objective on his part. It was alleged that, once Rochester had wrung an apology from Sir Thomas, it had always been his plan to proceed with Overbury's murder. One person summarised the position thus: 'the main plot [was], first to have [Overbury] confess and put under his hand the reparation of her honour, and that then he should die, before he could recant it'.[2]

The Earl of Northampton was another person who was determined that Overbury must retract the rude comments he had made about the Countess of Essex, and for much of the time that Overbury was in the Tower the Earl devoted a great deal of effort to achieve this result. It is not easy to assess the part played by Frances herself during these months. The Lieutenant of the Tower later admitted that he had a great deal of correspondence with both Frances and the Earl of Northampton regarding Overbury's treatment,[3] but unfortunately only one letter written by Frances survives on the subject. However, it does seem that, although Frances must have been aware that pressure was being brought to bear on Overbury to vindicate her honour, she had a separate agenda. Not only did she have little faith that Overbury's excesses could be curbed in future, but she was also not prepared to forgive Overbury for having insulted her in the past. Rather than waiting for Overbury to express contrition, she made at least one attempt to poison him in the Tower.

Rochester later claimed credit for having seen to it that Overbury was placed in reasonably comfortable quarters in the Tower, 'where he might have the best air, and windows both to the water and within the Tower'. In other respects, however, Overbury fared badly. Most prisoners in the Tower were not only permitted to be attended by their own servants, but could receive visitors whenever they wished. Overbury, in contrast, was declared 'close prisoner', which meant that he was not only placed in solitary confinement but could not even send out or receive letters. At Rochester's trial it was said that the 'strange manner of [Overbury's] confinement' was by his 'device and means', but Rochester denied this. He insisted that he had assumed that Sir Thomas would 'have liberty to speak with whom he would' while in the Tower, adding that it was 'against my intention to have him close prisoner'. Few people believed him, but it may have been true that he had not envisaged that Overbury would be so rigorously treated.[4]

While there is no evidence that Rochester made any attempt to improve Overbury's conditions, it does seem that the primary responsibility for the harsh restrictions placed on Sir Thomas lay, not with Rochester, but with the King. Later, this was successfully glossed over. At one of the Overbury murder trials the Lord Chief Justice sorrowfully observed, 'What a scandal they put on his Majesty ... that a gentleman and freeman, being only committed for a contempt, should be more straitly or closely kept than a traitor or bond slave, so that neither his father, brother nor friend might possibly see him.' At the time, however, the King had not only been aware that Overbury was being kept in isolation, but he rejected an application that he should be confined less stringently. On 13 May, three weeks after Overbury had been arrested, James was presented with a petition by Overbury's father, asking that since Sir Thomas was 'much damaged in his health by close imprisonment' he might see a physician and have a servant to wait on him. James agreed that one of his personal physicians, John Craig, could visit Overbury, but he would not let a servant move into the Tower with Sir Thomas. The courtier Sir Henry Wotton was taken aback by James's intransigence, commenting, 'When graces are managed so narrowly by a King, otherwise of so gracious nature, it doth in my opinion very clearly demonstrate the asperity of the offence.'[5]

At the time of his arrest Overbury was committed to the care of the Lieutenant of the Tower, Sir William Wade, who had overall responsibility for every prisoner there. As far as the Earl of Northampton was concerned, Wade was not an appropriate person to take charge of Overbury. Sir William was an upright but austere man who prided himself on his inflexibility, and it was unthinkable that he would connive at any underhand scheme which Northampton put to him. Thus much, at least, is clear. What is less easy to establish is exactly what Northampton had in mind at this point. Very possibly he simply wished to ensure that Overbury could be pressured into adopting a less obstructive attitude towards Rochester's marriage, and this could not be done without the active support of the Lieutenant of the Tower. It may be, however, that Northampton's plans extended as far as Overbury's permanent elimination, and this was the reason why he wished to remove Sir Thomas from Wade's custody.

Conveniently for Northampton, Wade was extremely unpopular, with few influential contacts at court, and there had also been 'continual complaints' about the manner in which he had executed his duties at the Tower. It is also possible that there had been some irregularity relating to his custody of King James's cousin Arbella Stuart, who at that time was a prisoner in the Tower. The upshot was that on 6 May 1613 Wade was called before the Council and dismissed from his post. To his fury Wade was told that under his jurisdiction there was 'more loose government and liberty given to the prisoners' than was considered fit. Wade later recalled that the Earl of Northampton particularly criticised him for 'using too much favour to Overbury and suffering him to lie in my lodging'. Wade thought this appallingly unjust. He prided himself that 'the Tower was never kept in better order in any time than it was while I served his Majesty there'. As for his treatment of Overbury, Wade was adamant that it was quite in order for the Lieutenant of the Tower to accord such privileges to a prisoner in his charge, particularly considering that the Lieutenant's wife and children had been absent at the time.[6]

That very day Wade was replaced by a Lincolnshire gentleman named Sir Gervase Elwes. The appointment caused general surprise, for Elwes was not obviously qualified to take on such an onerous post. Years before, he had briefly attended the Middle Temple when Nicholas Overbury, Thomas Overbury's father, had been studying there. Sir Nicholas later recalled Elwes as 'a dextrous and witty man' who had performed hilariously when cast as Lord of Misrule during the Christmas festivities at the Inns of Court. Apart from this, however, Elwes had never distinguished himself. He himself later acknowledged that his 'youth had been riotous and wasteful'. Later he had married and produced eight or even twelve children (accounts vary on this point), but fatherhood did not make him more responsible. Instead, Elwes became a compulsive gambler, whose custom it was to turn 'nights into days and days into nights'. 'Always, ill luck followed him' at the tables, but though on several occasions Elwes had made solemn vows to give up gambling, he always resumed before long. Within the last year Elwes had decided that his only hope of recouping his fortunes lay in coming to London to pursue a career at court. He had attached himself to the Howard faction, and had soon been made an Esquire of the Body and Gentleman Pensioner to the King. Nevertheless, he remained 'somewhat an unknown man' and his promotion to Lieutenant of the Tower took many people aback. John Chamberlain, who had encountered Elwes some years before while travelling in France, commented that he was 'of too mild and gentle disposition for such an office'.[7]

Before long it appeared that Chamberlain's strictures were justified. An indignant Sir William Wade heard that 'so soon as this Lieutenant was placed there, that liberty was given to the condemned men as they walked and talked together, played at cards and other pastimes, which liberty never before was seen there'.[8] Overbury, however, benefited from none of this, for he was kept strictly isolated, and the Earl of Northampton remained confident that Elwes would look after that particular prisoner in accordance with his wishes.

It is easy to understand why the Earl considered Sir Gervase so suitable for this task. Elwes was a man in a hurry, conscious that he had to make up for lost time and, as such, he was much less likely to be awkward than the cantankerous Sir William Wade. As a shrewd judge of character, Northampton was doubtless aware that Elwes was none too scrupulous by nature, correctly divining that, having acquired a precarious foothold on the ladder of office, Sir Gervase was not the sort of man who would jeopardise it by quibbling with those who had placed him there.

Elwes first heard that he had a chance of becoming Lieutenant of the Tower ten days before Wade's dismissal, when the Earl of Northampton sent a courtier named Sir Thomas Monson to discuss the matter with him. An enigmatic figure whose role in Overbury's detention and death has never been fully clarified, Monson was a crypto-Catholic and a close adherent of the Howards. He was later described by Anne Turner as 'a proud and odious man not loved in court', but he was high in the favour of James I because of his skill in handling the hawks and other birds of prey which afforded the hunting-mad King so much pleasure. Apart from being Master Falconer to the King, in 1611 Monson had been appointed Master of the Armoury at the Tower, and in consequence he exerted much control over the way jobs were allocated there. Besides this, he was a 'very good and ancient friend' of Sir Gervase Elwes, although Monson later stressed that he personally had wanted another man to replace Wade as Lieutenant, and that he had approached Elwes only in deference to Northampton's wishes. Monson told Elwes that the lieutenancy of the Tower would shortly be falling vacant and that, if Elwes was interested in succeeding to the post, 'my Lord of Northampton should work it'. Naturally such kindness did not come cheaply: if properly exploited, the lieutenancy was a lucrative position and Monson made it clear that, if Elwes wanted it, 'he must bleed' by paying £2,000 to those who obtained him the office. Elwes regarded this as a sound investment and set about borrowing the necessary funds from his uncle.[9]

Having cleverly arranged things so that he would make money out of an appointment he expected to be advantageous to him in other ways, Northampton went to the King and requested that Elwes should be made Lieutenant of the Tower. On its own, however, this was not enough. It was unthinkable that this important office could be disposed of without the approval of Viscount Rochester, and it was generally understood that he had promised another courtier that he should become Lieutenant on Wade's departure. Northampton advised Elwes to overcome this difficulty by requesting the Earls of Pembroke and

Shrewsbury to intercede on his behalf with Lord Rochester. Elwes duly did this and, on being pressed by Pembroke and Shrewsbury, Rochester agreed to support Sir Gervase. Later, however, it was alleged that this had been a charade, for there had never been any real prospect that Rochester would raise difficulties about Elwes's appointment. On the contrary, he had been as anxious as Northampton that Sir Gervase should be installed at the Tower.

On 6 May Elwes was named Lieutenant of the Tower. Ten days later he paid the first instalment of what he owed to those who had secured his preferment. Of the £1,700 handed over on this occasion, Northampton took £1,400, and the remaining £300 went to Monson. Elwes promised that he would pay the balance as soon as he could raise the money. At Rochester's trial it was alleged that he too had received £500 from Elwes in return for promoting him, but he vehemently denied this and no evidence was produced to show that he was lying.[10]

No sooner than Elwes had taken up his new position than Sir Thomas Monson asked him to put a different man in charge of Overbury. Monson wanted Overbury's current jailer replaced by Richard Weston, the disreputable individual who during the past year had helped the Countess of Essex and Viscount Rochester to meet secretly by delivering letters and messages for them. Two years later Monson was asked why he had put forward Weston's name to Elwes, and he answered that he had been requested to do so by both the Earl of Northampton and the Countess of Essex. At his trial it was alleged that Rochester also had been actively involved in Weston's appointment, although in his statement Monson made no mention of any dealings with the favourite on the matter. According to Monson, the Countess had told him that she wished Weston to become Overbury's keeper because this would please Mrs Anne Turner, who was Weston's former employer. When seconding his great-niece's application, the Earl of Northampton had assured Monson that Weston's appointment 'was fit for the King's service, and the King was contented therewith'. Accordingly Monson had raised the matter with Elwes, who duly agreed to take on Weston. Monson subsequently explained that he had understood that Northampton and Lady Essex were anxious that Overbury should have a reliable keeper who would prevent him from sending or receiving letters while in the Tower. However, it was later alleged that the real reason for Weston's appointment had been very different. In the lurid words of Lawrence Hyde, prosecuting counsel for the Crown, Weston was recruited because it was realised that he would prove 'a fit instrument to compass black murder that was so well acquainted with foul lust'.[11]

Weston later admitted that he had known from the start that his duties at the Tower would not be entirely straightforward. Prior to his appointment, Mrs Turner informed her former employee that if he gave Sir Thomas Overbury 'that which should be sent unto him', the Countess of Essex 'should reward him well'. Weston started work on 7 May and very shortly afterwards Mrs Turner summoned him to Whitehall for an interview with the Countess. As Mrs Turner looked on, Frances explained to Weston that, in return for a substantial reward, she wished him to administer to Overbury 'a water' which she would arrange to have delivered to the Tower. She said that it would do Sir Thomas no harm, but stressed that Weston must not sample the liquid himself. Weston later admitted that he 'at least suspected it should be poison'. Weston then returned to the Tower. A little later his son William, who worked at a haberdasher that supplied Lady Essex with fans and feathers, delivered to him 'in secret manner' a small glass phial, 'full of water of a yellowish and greenish colour'.[12]

Assuming that Sir Gervase Elwes had been informed of what was contemplated, Weston consulted him before proceeding further. That evening he encountered Elwes just before he took up Overbury's supper and he took the opportunity to ask, 'Sir, shall I give it him now?' Elwes naturally asked Weston what he meant, whereupon Weston showed him the liquid and explained that the Countess of Essex had instructed him to give it to Overbury. Elwes was utterly appalled. According to Sir Gervase's own account, he did everything in his power to convey to Weston the abhorrent nature of the deed he proposed to commit. 'I strake him down with my fist upon his knees,' Elwes later recalled. 'I did begin to terrify him with God's eternal judgments.' These stern words appeared to have an excellent effect. Still kneeling, Weston raised his hands heavenward and 'blessed the time that ever he did know' Sir Gervase. Satisfied that Weston had taken his lecture to heart, Elwes thought it unnecessary to say anything further. It was only the following day that he remembered that he had left Weston in possession of the poison and then he 'could not rest' until he had watched Weston pour it into a gutter in the Tower and break its glass container. Elwes now felt so confident that Overbury was safe that his only worry was that a dog would lick up the poison, with fatal results.[13]

Having taken these precautions, Elwes saw no need to report Weston to the authorities, or even to dismiss him. Instead he told Weston that he should pretend to the Countess and Mrs Turner that he had done as they wished, for Elwes did not want them to realise that their plan had gone awry. Having made Weston promise to warn him if further attempts were planned on Overbury, Sir Gervase assured him that 'If we would be secret, we two would laugh at them all.'[14]

With hindsight Sir Gervase acknowledged that his behaviour was at best foolish, at worst criminally irresponsible, but he insisted that he had not dared act otherwise. 'As ye times were, I had cause to respect my safety,' he would later say in his own justification. It is easy to understand why, as he put it, 'Ye cognition was grievous to me.' The Countess of Essex was a leading noblewoman with the most formidable connections and, to Elwes, it seemed unthinkable that anyone would believe that she was guilty of attempted murder. Even if he went directly to King James, her father, great-uncle and her admirer Viscount Rochester 'lived ... so near about the King, and [were] bound as much as ever subject was to prince' that they would surely persuade James not to listen to his story. Almost certainly it would be dismissed as a malicious fabrication, and Elwes would not only lose his job but would probably be severely punished.[15]

Nevertheless, while it would be harsh to condemn Elwes for keeping Weston's disclosures to himself, it is less easy to condone his decision that Weston should remain in charge of Sir Thomas Overbury. He would later justify this on the grounds that he could not dismiss him without giving an explanation to the people who had recommended him as Overbury's keeper, but he surely could have invented some plausible excuse for being rid of the fellow. Sir Gervase even argued that it had been in Overbury's own interest that Weston was retained. Elwes said he had been sure that his dissertation on the heinousness of murder had made a lasting impression on Weston and he also reasoned that Weston would realise that if Overbury now died unexpectedly, suspicion would automatically fall on him. In fact, of course, Weston was just as likely to conclude that since Elwes had shielded him until that point, he could continue to rely on his protection in the future. Lastly Elwes maintained that replacing Weston with another jailer would scarcely have made Overbury safer, for 'another, whom I did not know, might in time have come to be corrupted as well as he'.[16]

This was an astonishing admission of feebleness on Elwes's part but it may be that he was guilty of more than this. Despite his staunch insistence when his case came to trial that he did everything possible to deter Weston from harming Overbury, he might not have been so forceful as he pretended. According to Lord Chief Justice Coke (admittedly a man who sometimes could not resist distorting the truth, or exaggerating), Elwes admitted after his conviction that he had indicated to Weston that he would tacitly acquiesce in Overbury's murder. Far from being chastened by Elwes's remonstrances, Weston had told his superior that, sooner or later, 'they will have me give it him.' To this Elwes had merely responded, 'Let it be done so I know not of it.'[17]

As Elwes had advised, Weston told Mrs Turner that he had given Overbury the greenish fluid, assuring her 'that it had made him very sick and to vomit and cast extremely'. Cannily he then asked for his reward but Mrs Turner answered with asperity that he should not look for payment while Overbury was still living.[18] After that he did not hear from her for some time but, towards the end of May, she sent a sinister figure named James Franklin to have a talk with him.

'Doctor' Franklin was a most unprepossessing individual. He was 'a Yorkshireman, ... crook-shouldered, of a swarthy complexion', with a reddish beard and a 'wanton lock' of hair straggling down his misshaped back. His complexion was ravaged by venereal disease, which had left 'the marrow of his bones corrupted', and intermittently 'put him to great torment'. Franklin styled himself 'physician', but there is no evidence he had any formal medical training, and others labelled him a mere 'apothecary and druggist'. Mrs Turner had been introduced to Franklin by her maid Joanne, soon after the death of Dr Turner. Later she expressed a repugnance for him, 'He is so foul,' but as a lonely widow she had been less fastidious, and had become 'well acquainted' with him. Franklin, who boasted an ability to raise devils, may have offered to use his powers to help Mrs Turner snare Sir Arthur Mainwaring. Possibly she then introduced him to Frances, on the understanding that he would provide her with similar assistance with her love affair. Certainly Franklin subsequently claimed that Frances was grateful to him for having 'wrought the love between Rochester and her'. Franklin also hinted that it was he who had rendered the Earl of Essex impotent. While Frances's nullity suit was in progress, Franklin met a relation of his named Mercer, who was a former retainer of the Earl of Essex's late father. Mercer remarked, 'I am sorry that my old lord and master's son is found not able to content a lady.' To this Franklin replied, 'I have a hand in that business. I have a great friend of my Lady of Essex.' Shocked, Mercer demanded, 'But cousin, how can God bless you in this business?' only to be told, 'Let them talk of God that have to do with them.'[19]

Franklin was reputed to have poisoned his first wife, who died in agony after Franklin had given her a powder, supposedly for medicinal purposes. Franklin always denied this, not on the grounds that he had loved his wife, but because he had suffered financially through her death, and was hardly likely to have deliberately brought about this 'weakening to my estate'.[20] Perhaps, however, Mrs Turner had heard the rumours that Franklin had killed his wife and it was this which convinced her that Franklin would be prepared to supply her and Frances with poison.

Franklin later gave a graphic account of his dealings with Mrs Turner and Frances. He related that it was 'in a house near the Doctors' Commons' that Mrs Turner first mentioned Overbury's murder. She asked Franklin to obtain for her a poison that would not kill a man outright, but would 'lie in his body for a certain time, whereby he might languish away by little and little', and she gave him some money for its purchase. The first poison Franklin brought to her was a water called *aqua fortis*, also known as roseacre. Perhaps this was another name for sulphuret of arsenic, or what is now called realgar; it is more likely, however, that it was nitric acid. Mrs Turner reportedly tried this out on a cat. The creature soon began 'wailing and mewing as it would have grieved any to have heard her', finally dying two days later. Following this experiment, Mrs Turner ordered Franklin to confer about poisons with the Countess of Essex. At this meeting the Countess told Franklin that *aqua fortis* had such violent effects that it was bound to arouse suspicion if administered to Overbury, 'but what think you of white arsenic?' Franklin replied that that too was a very strong poison, whereupon the Countess demanded, 'What say you then to powder of diamonds?' Presumably she was referring to ground glass, but Franklin was unable to enlighten her as to its lethal properties, having to admit that 'he knew not the virtue thereof'. Angrily Frances told him 'he was a fool' and then, producing some gold, ordered him to 'buy her some of that powder'. Franklin duly produced this for her, but she subsequently ordered him to obtain other sorts of poison. In all, Franklin claimed to have supplied her with seven varieties: *aqua fortis*, mercury water, white arsenic, powder of diamonds, *lapis cosmatis*, 'great spiders' (an unidentified substance) and cantharides, or Spanish fly.[21]

Franklin's account is intriguing, but should be treated with the utmost caution. He had not the slightest regard for the truth and after his arrest he sought to save his own life by providing his interrogators with information which would enable them to prosecute other suspects. For this reason his evidence should be regarded as unreliable unless corroborated by other sources.

It was on Mrs Turner's orders that Franklin now liaised with Weston. Their meeting took place at the White Lion Tavern on Tower Hill. Franklin wanted to know whether Overbury was in good health, and Weston answered that he assumed Sir Thomas was far from well, as he

was regularly given enemas (or 'glisters') and also took a great deal of
medicine. At once it occurred to Franklin how this could be exploited.
He told Weston that an apothecary would be paid £20 to give Overbury
a poisoned glister. Weston asked whether it was the apothecary who
regularly visited Overbury in the Tower who would administer the
deadly enema, to which Franklin answered, 'No, another shall give it
him.' Weston claimed that when this meeting was over, he warned Sir
Gervase Elwes of this new danger to Overbury, and Elwes cautioned
him that if Overbury wanted colonic irrigation in the future, 'none
should come hither but the former 'pothecary or his man.'[22]

Before Sir Gervase Elwes took command of the Tower Sir Thomas
Monson had stressed to him that the Earl of Northampton and the
Countess of Essex were particularly anxious that Overbury should be
kept completely incommunicado. Monson insisted that 'neither letters
nor messages might be sent to him by any, nor from him to any other
whatsoever' and Elwes promised to be vigilant on this point. Despite
this we know that Rochester and Overbury regularly exchanged letters.
These may have been smuggled in without Sir Gervase's knowledge or,
alternatively, his original instructions could have been modified to the
effect that Overbury should be permitted to communicate with no one
other than Rochester. Overbury clearly thought that Elwes was unaware
of what was going on, but this may have been a deliberate deception on
the part of the Lieutenant. Although Rochester's letters have not
survived, Overbury's answers show that the Viscount was attempting to
convince Sir Thomas that it was in his interests to seek an accommodation with the Howards. There is therefore at least a possibility
that this correspondence took place with the blessing of the Earl of
Northampton. Indeed, it could be that one reason why Northampton
had found it necessary to eject Sir William Wade from his lieutenancy
was that, mindful of the King's order that Overbury should be kept
close prisoner, Wade had refused to let letters from Rochester reach
Overbury.[23] This had made it difficult to exert any form of leverage on
Sir Thomas, which was highly inconvenient, and it was therefore
desirable that someone less conscientious took custody of him.

Overbury's letters demonstrate that he had no conception how deeply
he had offended Rochester by his attacks on Frances. He blithely
assumed that Rochester was as devoted to him as ever, betraying not
the slightest doubt that while he was in prison, his friend's overriding
priority would be to secure his freedom. Furthermore, it appears not to
have occurred to him that, once he was free, their relationship might

rest on a changed footing. Instead he took it for granted that he would be reinstated as Rochester's political consultant and business adviser, and that Rochester would be as subservient to him as in the past.

Possibly Overbury was guilty of monumental self-delusion, but it seems more likely that in his letters Rochester was careful not to show any displeasure towards Sir Thomas. If Overbury thought he had forfeited Rochester's friendship, his bitterness would be such that there would be no question of his making amends to Frances and the Howards. Since this was the object of his imprisonment, it was essential that he be lulled into believing that he and Rochester remained on the same terms as before.

When writing to Rochester, Overbury was full of ideas intended to bring forward the date of his release. In one of his earlier letters, clearly written before 13 May, when the King agreed that Overbury should have access to a physician whenever he wished, Overbury explained why he was so keen to be inspected by a doctor. He believed that a doctor would be appalled by the state of his legs and that, when the King heard of this, he would be ready to free him on compassionate grounds. Unfortunately Overbury does not specify why his legs were in such a shocking state. Possibly he was suffering from varicose veins, which had caused leg ulcers, although Overbury's servants subsequently claimed that there were no sores on his body when he was sent to the Tower. At any rate, whatever the problem was, he was afflicted by it prior to his arrest. Overbury confided to Rochester that he would pretend to the doctor that the condition had developed since he had been in confinement, when in reality his legs 'were so afore'.[24]

Overbury then asked that, once the King had been warned of the decline in his health, Rochester should send him an emetic, or 'vomit', which would make him very sick. James could then be informed that Overbury had been struck down by another illness, providing Rochester with 'a new occasion ... to be importunate' about Overbury's release.[25]

Rochester did send Overbury an emetic in early May, which he obtained from Robert Killigrew, a mutual friend of theirs. It was taken to the Tower by a cousin of Overbury's named Giles Rawlins, whom Rochester had employed as a manservant on Overbury's recommendation. Rawlins accompanied the package with a note explaining that Rochester wanted Overbury to make himself sick so 'that he might have a ground to work upon for the speedier obtaining of his liberty'. However, when Overbury took the powder, it 'wrought but gently' with him, giving him no more than a mild case of diarrhoea. The morning after, Overbury wrote to Rochester that 'it worked only with me downward'. He still hoped that Rochester could persuade the King that his health was suffering as a result of his confinement; and was disappointed when Rochester informed him that James was unwilling to believe that Overbury was seriously ill.[26]

Overbury's next suggestion was that Rochester himself should take an emetic, enabling him to pretend that his distress at Overbury's predicament was making him unwell. We know that Rochester did take a vomit around this time, but his consequent indisposition did not have the results for which Overbury hoped. Rochester claimed that the King declared that he would not consider releasing Overbury until his favourite was restored to health, urging him 'to cure your sickness, if you would but do this you should obtain your ends sooner'. However, to his chagrin, Overbury was informed that when Rochester made a full recovery, the King began 'to slide back and talk to you of showing his favour otherwise'.[27]

Rochester evidently hoped that, in view of these setbacks, Overbury would be more willing to consider seeking a truce with the Howard faction, on the understanding that the Earl of Suffolk would then agitate for his release. Clearly Rochester made Overbury a proposition along these lines and, when Overbury replied, after he had been in prison nearly a month, he initially seemed quite enthusiastic about the plan. Stipulating only that the Countess of Suffolk must be kept in ignorance of these developments, Overbury outlined ways in which the Earl of Suffolk could help him. He suggested that Suffolk should go to the King and say that, having heard from the Lieutenant of the Tower that Overbury was 'every night so sick as he is ready to die', Suffolk had placed a man in the Tower to see if this was the case. Suffolk should pretend that this observer had confirmed that Overbury was desperately ill. Suffolk could then warn the King that, if Overbury did not survive, there was not only a danger that Rochester would die of grief, but it would also reflect very badly on Suffolk himself, 'for the world thinking me [Overbury's] enemy would lay his blood to my charge, which I would not have imputed to me for all the world'.[28]

However, having mused for a while in this fashion, Overbury abruptly let the matter drop. Although the idea had at first seemed appealing – 'Here is a plot exquisitely laid!' he exclaimed at one point – it soon dawned on him that Suffolk would agree to act as his broker only in return for significant concessions. Plainly Overbury would have to undertake that he would never again defy the Howards, as well as expressing regret for the manner in which he had traduced the Lord Chamberlain's daughter. This still struck him as too high a price to pay.

Fearing that it would make both himself and his friend objects of mockery he warned Rochester, 'Here is the caution of it, for your enemies insulting before, they never hoped for such a day of public glory.'[29] With that, he changed the subject.

Overbury still had faith that his release could be arranged without grovelling to his enemies. All that was necessary, in his view, was that Rochester must make it clear to the King that there was no chance that he would ever abandon his friend. Overbury argued that, once James accepted this, he would bow to the inevitable and let him out of jail. He believed that the King had imprisoned him in the first place because the Queen had told her husband that 'he durst do nothing to displease' his favourite, and by keeping him in the Tower he showed that he could still exert discipline on Rochester. However, providing that Rochester never wavered in his loyalty to Overbury, James would surely soon relent. Overbury wrote, 'Sure the reason he keeps me close thus long is to try all ways upon you alone, whether he can work your consent to a separation, for after the doors are open he thinks we will mingle thoughts again.' Rochester must therefore impress upon the King that there was not the least ambivalence in his feelings towards Overbury. Urgently Sir Thomas exhorted him to 'lose no hours to declare your resolution that God forsake you if ever you forsake me for any hope or fear'. Once James was convinced of this he would realise that it was pointless to keep the friends apart, particularly if Overbury promised that in future 'I will be reformed according to his instructions never to transgress, which he cannot but accept'.[30]

If James still appeared reluctant to restore Overbury's liberty, Rochester must take steps to coerce him. Rochester should threaten to 'quit all business' unless James conceded his demands. If that ultimatum failed, he should announce an intention 'to shut yourself up in a park and die'. Alternatively Rochester must take another powerful emetic, 'and be so dangerously sick that you must desire to speak with me before you die, tell him that is your last request to him, and so must continue till you have got me out'.[31]

Overbury concluded his letter with a despairing appeal. 'This do, rather than let me live here in this fashion, and my mind overthrow my body forever, do somewhat like an honest man and friend, though you never do more ... Alas, you bid me have a good heart, you must know that the best hearts can ever worst bear shame ... and for my part I wonder that you [go] abroad and are seen in the world, I lying here, for God refuse me if I be not so ashamed of staying here so long that now I never dare open the windows to look out.'[32]

Reading this agonised plea one can only feel pity for Overbury, who would subsequently have to endure four more months of imprisonment, and would then suffer a miserable death. Far from striving to free him, his so-called friend Rochester was quite content about the situation, and may well never have discussed Overbury's plight with the King. And yet Overbury's letters also make it clear that, in many respects, he only had himself to blame for his troubles. Even at this low ebb he retained the instincts of a bully, and the imperious way he addressed the man he expected to act as his deliverer strikes a far from sympathetic note.

It was not just that Overbury disdained to grasp the lifeline that rapprochement with the Howards might have afforded him. Astonishingly, he also assumed that he remained in charge of all Rochester's business at court, dismissing the possibility that Rochester was now rather better placed than he to exercise judgement in such matters. From his quarters in the Tower he issued a series of peremptory instructions about patronage matters, the details of which are now impenetrable, but which vividly convey his overbearing personality. 'I should be glad to hear William Udall's of Hyde's went on, for his sake no less than mine own,' he told Rochester in one letter; 'for the reversion after Fulke Greville for Jack Lidcote's boy, you may keep any other from having it, till a fit time to pass it for him; for Badger's stewardship, I would he had it; for Shirley's do somewhat, 'tis a fine suit'. It is clear that Overbury expected to be well rewarded for his managerial role. At one point he upbraided Rochester for being dilatory about exploiting an opportunity that he had pointed out to him. Overbury grumbled that he wished he had brought it to the attention of someone who would have acted faster, such as the Earl of Montgomery. Had that been the case (typically Overbury blithely overlooked the fact that Montgomery detested him), the deal would have already gone through, and Overbury would have claimed £5,000 in agent's fees, or more than forty per cent of the total proceeds.[33] Such missives gave little grounds for hoping that Overbury would come to recognise that he could not always monopolise Rochester as he had done in the past.

If Overbury had been more intuitive he could perhaps have helped himself by volunteering to spend time abroad once he had regained his liberty. Significantly, both the Earl of Southampton and Sir Henry Wotton believed that King James would not release Overbury unless Sir Thomas undertook to leave England, binding himself not to return without royal permission. Unaccountably, however, Overbury evinced a terrible dread of going out of the country, which incidentally makes it more likely that it was he who was responsible for his earlier refusal to serve as an ambassador, rather than being inveigled into it by Rochester. Now he begged Rochester to save him from even a short term of exile. 'By no means hear of my going at all beyond sea, though for an hour,' he wrote at one point, saying that if the King mentioned that he wished him to travel, he should be told that foreign air invariably exacerbated Overbury's health problems.[34]

Overbury's worst mistake of all, however, was to give no indication that he had modified his attitude to Lady Essex. In his letters to Rochester, he occasionally mentioned her in passing, referring to her as 'catopard'. The exact meaning of the term is debatable ('prostitute' is one suggestion) but clearly it was not a respectful appellation. Overbury's use of this nickname perhaps dated from the time that he and Rochester had delighted in making private jokes about Frances, but it was unwise of Overbury to think that he could still refer to her in this way without causing annoyance. In one letter Overbury once again referred to the possibility that the Earl of Suffolk might be ready to work for his release if he thought that this would earn him Rochester's lasting goodwill. Casually Overbury suggested, 'You might do well to write to the catopard to will her make her father sure, which except he think it will be a beginning of a perpetual friendship with you, 'twill not be.'[35] While perhaps not overtly offensive, the passage shows that Overbury was very far from seeking to placate the Countess, which undoubtedly would have been his wisest course of action.

In these circumstances it was not hard for the Earl of Northampton to keep alive Rochester's fears that Overbury remained implacably hostile towards Frances. At one point Northampton cautioned Rochester, 'To let you see that this negro will no more change his complexion than a leopard do his spots, I must let your lordship know what I receive secretly from the Lieutenant, that [Overbury] asketh many questions of my Lady Frances Howard, where she continues this summer, in what comfort she seems to be, what her friends conceive, how they are pleased and who comes to her. Thus much the poor lady is beholden to the gentleman more than she believes, for I dare undertake he thinks more of her than the Q[ueen] of Great Britain.'[36]

The apparent ease with which Rochester and Overbury kept in touch is mystifying, in view of the fact that close prisoners were theoretically forbidden to send or receive written communications. However, even close prisoners were permitted to have food and wine sent in from outside, either for personal consumption or to pass on to their jailers in the hope that this would result in better treatment. We know that

Rochester took steps to supplement Overbury's rations. Richard Weston later recalled that 'about a fortnight or three weeks after' his arrival at the Tower 'at divers times my Lord of [Rochester's] servants ... came to know how Mr Overbury did, and to know of Mr Overbury what he would have, either tart or jelly or wine'. 'According as he directed' these foodstuffs would then be delivered to the Tower, sometimes by servants of Rochester and sometimes by Overbury's own servants.[37] Perhaps, however, it was this seemingly legitimate traffic that enabled Overbury and Rochester to exchange letters. We know from Jacobean drama that it was a fairly standard ploy to send messages concealed in food to prisoners, who then were able to reply when the empty dishes were carried back to whoever had sent them. It may be that such an arrangement came into being while Overbury was in prison.

Admittedly there is a certain amount of evidence which militates against this theory. Weston would always maintain that these items were sent to Overbury merely to provide sustenance. He later stated that 'Sir Thomas Overbury did eat divers times some part of tarts and jellies and some he sent to Lady Elwes and her children.' Overbury himself informed Rochester that he intended to make gifts of food to the Lieutenant and his family. He instructed Rochester, 'You must give order presently and send for wine, jelly and a tart to be brought to me tomorrow ... and then for the jelly and the wine will I never have it up to my chamber at all, but have it conveyed ... to the Lieutenant's wife, which is the best way. So too for a cold pasty of venison, I will send it to the Lieutenant.' All this would tend to suggest that Overbury's requests for food to be sent to him were perfectly straightforward. Furthermore, if Lady Elwes and her children ate these gifts without coming to any harm, it would seem that there was nothing wrong with them. It may be, of course, that Elwes ensured that Overbury's offerings never reached his family, but Richard Weston also later stated that he partook of the tarts sent to Overbury at this time, and never felt ill in consequence.[38]

Another reason why it appears unlikely that tarts were used to smuggle letters to Overbury is that he and Rochester seem to have had little difficulty maintaining contact without resorting to such cumbersome procedures. At one point Overbury wrote to Rochester, 'He that brings me this letter brings no tart, which is ill lost' and this suggests that delivering letters presented no problem. Furthermore, when Rochester's servant Giles Rawlins sent Overbury the emetic made up by Robert Killigrew, he encountered no obstructions. He later stated that he wrote Overbury a note explaining what the powder would do to him and then 'sent in the vomit enclosed in the letter, by Weston'. Weston himself admitted that on several occasions a servant of Overbury's named Lawrence Davies asked him to pass on letters from Rochester to Overbury. The jailer testified that he did so, after showing them to Elwes and obtaining his authorisation.[39]

Whether or not Weston was telling the truth when he said that he did nothing without Elwes's permission is debatable. Presumably he was paid whenever he passed on letters to Overbury, and this illicit source of income would have acted as a powerful incentive to deceive the Lieutenant. Even so, there were times when Weston would not deliver letters to Overbury, either because he considered the risk unacceptable or because he was on bad terms with his prisoner. In late August 1613 Overbury's brother-in-law Sir John Lidcote told Rochester that Weston was currently refusing to let Overbury send out letters, 'by reason of some late falling out between them'. Because of Weston's recalcitrance, a recent letter from Rochester to Overbury had been delivered only 'with great difficulty', but Lidcote said he was sure that, within a few days, 'this vow of the keeper will be passed over, as many before have been.'[40] Nevertheless, the fact that Weston could be so uncooperative means that it would have made sense for Rochester and Overbury to devise a system of communicating that did not depend on the jailer, and it is possible that tarts and jellies were used.

Notwithstanding the evidence to the contrary, some passages in Overbury's letters appear to confirm that the food and wine sent to him served as a cover for clandestine correspondence. One of his letters to Rochester contains the request, 'I pray you, let me know tomorrow afore dinner whether that in the scurvy greasy bottle were legible' which suggests that he had been obliged to resort to subterfuge in order to reach Rochester. Furthermore, at one point Rochester evidently wrote to Overbury warning him that the King had become suspicious that they were communicating. Rochester suggested that Elwes must have told James that Overbury was receiving tarts and jellies and that this was how they managed to exchange letters. When replying, Overbury was adamant that Elwes had no idea that there was anything untoward about his food deliveries. As proof Overbury described a conversation he had had with Elwes a day earlier. 'He and I talking of news, I told [him] how ignorant I was of all things since I came in,' Overbury related. To Overbury's consternation, Elwes had queried this, saying, 'Nay, you have received wine and tarts.' Overbury had not let this pass. He picked up a Bible from a nearby table and 'swore upon it that none of all those things ever conveyed anything to me but themselves'. Elwes apparently accepted this, for 'he took the book straight again and swore he never suspected that they did'.[41]

Overbury may have prided himself on his perjury, which appeared to have worked so well but, in fact, in this game of bluff and counter-bluff it is exceptionally difficult to tell who was duping whom. It may be that Elwes was perfectly well aware that Rochester and Overbury were writing to each other, but he deliberately let Overbury think otherwise. Provided that Overbury believed that by exchanging letters he and Rochester were flouting the restrictions placed on him, his trust in his friend would be unshaken and he would be more ready to listen to Rochester's advice. However, if Sir Thomas suspected that Rochester was acting, not in defiance of his enemies, but in concert with them, he would never be prevailed upon to seek an accommodation with the Howards, which was the outcome that Rochester wanted.

It is true that parts of Elwes's own testimony appear to counter the theory that he connived at letters being smuggled in to Overbury. Sir Gervase would claim that, when offering him the job at the Tower, Sir Thomas Monson had warned him that Overbury would be sent tarts and jellies containing letters, and that the Earl of Northampton and the Countess of Essex had given instructions that on no account must these missives reach Overbury. Elwes insisted that he took these orders seriously: he said that, 'when any of these adulterated tarts or jellies came, though he thought it unlikely that letters should be in them, being liquid, he searched them'. He said that he only found a letter on one occasion, nestling inside 'one little dry coffin tart', and he claimed to have handed this over to the Earl of Northampton. Sir Thomas Monson supported Elwes's account, for he confirmed that he had passed on Northampton's and Frances's wishes that Overbury's jellies and tarts 'should be searched, lest there might be letter or writing in them'.[42]

Before long other tarts and jellies for Overbury began arriving at the Tower. These came from the Countess of Essex, although Overbury was supposed to think that Rochester had sent them as before. Several consignments of these tarts were carried to the Tower by a former employee of Sir Thomas Monson's named Simon Merston. He later stated that he received the tarts from Lady Essex's 'own hand ... at the Countess's chamber in Whitehall' and that he always surrendered them to the Lieutenant of the Tower in person, for 'so he was commanded to do and to no other'. The Countess also sent instructions to Weston regarding these tarts, telling him, as he afterwards recollected, 'to give Sir Thomas the tarts and jelly, but taste not thou of them'.[43]

Sir Gervase Elwes would later imply that he had never been told that these tarts came from Frances. In his somewhat disingenuous account of these events he confined himself to saying, 'There was an advantage taken of my Lord of Somerset's tenderness towards Sir Thomas Overbury who sent him tarts and pots of jelly. These were counterfeited, and others put to be presented in their stead.' Elwes then explained that, since he was on his guard after the first attempt to poison Overbury, he realised that something was amiss. Accordingly he kept back the tarts from Overbury, sometimes pretending that his wife and children had consumed them or, alternatively, replacing them with similar ones prepared by his own cook. Meanwhile, the tarts sent by Frances were stored in the Tower kitchen and Elwes said that his initial suspicions that they were poisoned were confirmed when they turned 'black and foul', while 'the jellies, with a little standing, would be furred'. Elwes maintained that he sought to stop more tarts arriving by ordering Weston to tell the boy who brought them that Overbury did not desire any more food from outside. At length, in mid-July, the supply of tarts ceased. By that time Rochester had left London, accompanying the King on his summer progress, and accordingly it no longer was feasible for Frances to send tarts to the Tower in his name.[44]

It is not easy to reconcile Sir Gervase Elwes's account with the fact that, when sending one batch of tarts to the Tower, the Countess of Essex enclosed a covering letter with directions for the Lieutenant. Like Frances's letters to Dr Forman and Mrs Turner, it is a somewhat incoherent document, in which the words 'he' and 'his' are used with such imprecision that it is difficult to grasp her meaning. Nevertheless, regardless of its many ambiguities, the letter became a key piece of evidence in the trials that followed. The letter ran:

Sir,

I pray you deliver not this thing till supper. I would have you change this tart in the place of his that is now come, and at four o'clock I will send you jelly, one pot, for I had but one sent to me. I was bid to tell you say that one pot was broken after the man had delivered. If he should know there came two pots, he must be answered so ... which I think he will not, for he cannot tell what is come now. This much now I was bid to tell you, that if he should send this tart and jelly and wine to your wife, then you must take the tart from her and the jelly, but the wine she may drink it if she will, for in that there is no letters, I know, but in the tart and jelly I know there is, as you shall know and from whom when we get the answer as that we shall to [sic] I know,

soon after he has gotten these. Sir Thomas Monson shall come this day
and then we shall have some other news. Do this at night, and all will
be well, I hope. If he send them to your wife then keep them for me, I
pray you.[45]

Two and a half years later, when Overbury's death was being
investigated, this letter fell into the hands of Lord Chief Justice Coke,
who was conducting the enquiry. Despite the fact that it was so vaguely
worded, he felt confident that he had correctly deciphered it. Annotating
the letter, 'This is expounded thus', he concluded that when Frances
referred to the tart and jellies containing 'letters', this was a codeword
for poison. The Countess's warnings to Elwes that his wife and children
must not eat the tarts and jelly betrayed her anxiety that they would be
accidentally poisoned. As for the person who had instructed the Countess
to send this message to Elwes, 'that must needs be Rochester, for none
could command her but he'.[46]

When Coke examined Frances on this matter, she seemingly verified
his interpretation. Underneath the copy of this letter in the Public
Record Office is appended a statement, purporting to be a confession
by Frances. According to this she agreed that when she ordered Elwes
to 'do this at night and all shall be well' she 'meant that the tarts and
jellies then sent wherein were poison should be given to Overbury that
night and then all should be well'. She also ostensibly acknowledged
that Rochester was the individual who had told her to issue these
instructions to Elwes, and likewise stated that when she had written, 'if
he should send this tart and jelly to your wife ...' the 'he' in question
was Rochester.

However, when the King had an opportunity to scrutinise the evidence
against Frances, he expressed misgivings about the reliability of this
confession. He pointed out that the phrase 'if he should send' must
logically apply to Overbury, and the fact that Frances had indicated
otherwise in her 'confession' cast doubt upon its accuracy. Accordingly
Frances was again questioned about her letter, and this time gave very
different answers. She confirmed that when she had written 'if he should
send' she had meant Overbury, and she also denied that it was Rochester
who had directed her to write to Elwes, saying instead that she was
acting on the orders either of Weston (which seems implausible) or the
Earl of Northampton.[47] Unfortunately she did not comment on the
claim that 'letters' meant poison, so it is unclear whether she was
prepared to let that section of her confession stand. However, it can be
contended that the later revisions prove that the whole confession was

seriously flawed, although it is a matter for conjecture whether Coke deliberately misrepresented what Frances had said or whether, having already decided to plead guilty, she simply found it easier to endorse everything he put to her.

If one discounts this confession the only real evidence that the tarts and jelly were poisoned rests on Weston's statement that the Countess warned him not to taste them himself. It is also noteworthy that, at some point, Frances appears to have put forward a completely different explanation as to why she had sent tarts to Overbury. The text of this confession is not extant but it was read out at Elwes's trial and a spectator there noted down its contents. In this report of the trial Frances is quoted as having 'confessed that she often sent [Overbury] tarts and jelly of purpose to intercept letters which were sent in Rochester's name. That the tarts and jellies were made in her father's kitchen, that she requested the Lieutenant to interchange the tarts that came from the Lord Rochester purposely to intercept letters'.[48]

When Overbury's death first came under investigation, it was Sir Gervase Elwes who volunteered the information that he thought tarts sent to Overbury had been poisoned. He had hoped to gain credit for having recognised the danger and for having protected Overbury by preventing him from eating the suspect offerings. However, this did not save him from being arrested and accused of having conspired with Frances to kill Overbury. At his trial Sir Gervase was less forthcoming on the subject of poisoned tarts. He sought desperately to defend himself from the charge that when Frances had written to him that the tarts contained 'letters' he had known that she meant poison. Elwes vehemently denied this, 'protesting ... that he knew nothing more by ye Lady of [Essex's] letters than that tarts should intercept letters, though he since thought and now perceives 'tis otherwise'. His words were brushed aside by Lawrence Hyde, prosecuting counsel for the Crown, who retorted, 'Why should the Lady of Essex intercept Rochester's letters when she laid with him every night almost?'[49]

In fact it seems quite plausible that Frances had become fearful that even from within the Tower, Sir Thomas Overbury would manage to undermine Rochester's affection for her and she therefore wished to disrupt communications between the two men. On its own, however, this explanation is insufficient for, in her letter to Elwes, she makes it clear that she *wants* the tarts containing letters to reach Overbury. Furthermore, Sir Gervase Elwes's insistence that he 'never knew any other meaning to the Countess's words in her letters but the bare literal meaning',[50] accorded ill with his claim that he nevertheless suspected that the tarts contained poison. Another incongruity is that Frances's letter suggests that she was confident that Elwes would obey her instructions. In view of the fact that he had reason to believe that she had already attempted to kill Overbury, it was curious that he had allowed her to think that he would be ready to do her bidding. The very fact that she was corresponding with him could be said to have compromised him.

The confusion is deepened by the defence put forward by Richard Weston at his trial for murder. Once again there is no official record of this, but Sir John Holles, who was present, maintained that Weston echoed Elwes's claim that Overbury was never allowed to taste the tarts sent by Frances. Holles quoted Weston as saying that the tarts 'which came from the Countess were thrown away by him and the Lieutenant, supposing them naught in regard of the colour, and that the Countess forbade him [Weston] to touch them; that these which came from [Rochester] were good, and of every one he [Weston] did eat his part ... and how [Overbury] died God knew, he knew not'.[51]

It is principally because of the shifts and contradictions in Elwes's evidence that it remains so difficult to assess the tarts' significance. The possibility cannot be discounted that Sir Gervase was guilty of a deliberate falsehood when he claimed that the tarts were poisoned, and that he knew that their real function was nothing other than to conceal letters. Elwes could have lied about this in the hope of being commended for his vigilance in preventing the tarts from reaching Overbury, and to emphasise his concern for the prisoner's welfare.[52] On the other hand, if Weston's defence is taken seriously, it would seem that Elwes was genuinely concerned that the tarts posed a danger to Overbury and was careful to keep them away from him. If so, however, the tarts cannot have contributed to Overbury's ill-health and subsequent demise.

When Rochester was tried his indictment stated that the tarts sent to Overbury contained mercury sublimate, but this seems incredible. Not only does mercury sublimate have such a strong metallic taste that the tarts would have been virtually inedible, but death would have ensued shortly after the poison had been taken. Francis Bacon was more plausible when he suggested that the tarts were poisoned with mercury water, a dilute solution whose effects would have been more lingering. Bacon noted mercury water was 'a poison fit for tarts, which is a kind of hotch pot, wherein no one colour is proper'.[53] However, while this was a valid observation, it may have been mere conjecture on Bacon's part that mercury water had been added to the tarts.

*

When Richard Weston was tried in 1615 for Overbury's murder it was claimed that, until assailed by illness in the Tower, Overbury had been a 'very healthful' man, and that he was quite fit at the time of his arrest. This was untrue, for it is clear that when Overbury went into the Tower, he was already suffering from various ailments. As he told Rochester in his letters, there was an unspecified problem with his legs which he hoped could be used to arouse King James's sympathy. In his letters he also mentions being afflicted by 'consumption' and *flatus hypocondriacus'*. He does not say what the symptoms were, although consumption should be taken to mean some form of wasting disease, rather than tuberculosis. These, however, were secondary complaints for, at the time of his arrest, the most persistent and debilitating condition to affect him was 'the spleen'. Overbury's servants subsequently testified that he had been receiving treatment 'for the spleen' prior to his imprisonment, and on Sir Thomas's arrival at the Tower Sir William Wade was so shocked by the 'indisposition of health' attributable to the spleen that he requested the King to permit Overbury to have one of his own servants to minister to him. It was 'not thought meet' by James to agree to this.[54]

In order to form some idea of what was meant by being 'troubled by the spleen' it is necessary to have an acquaintance with the medical theory current at the time. The human organism was held to be composed of four fundamental elements, or 'humours', each of which had its own distinctive properties. Blood, which came from the heart, represented heat. Phlegm came from the brain and represented cold. Yellow bile originated in the liver and represented dryness, while the spleen was the source of black bile, which represented wetness. Good health was thought to depend on keeping the four humours in equilibrium and when illness occurred it was generally ascribed to one or other of the quartet gaining a dangerous preponderance. Overbury in theory was burdened with an over-active spleen, and consequently suffered from an excess of black bile and wetness.

After Overbury had been in the Tower about nine weeks his condition became much graver. He wrote Rochester a series of letters describing what was wrong with him. Unfortunately all are undated, so the progress of his illness cannot be charted with any certainty. Nevertheless, internal evidence in some of the letters does provide clues as to when they were written.

It would seem that, either at the end of June or the beginning of July, Overbury experienced some bouts of fever. Before long, his temperature subsided but he was then assailed by numerous other symptoms. These differed from those which afflicted him as a result of his spleen disorder and bewildered him, since he considered them 'contrary to my constitution'. At some time in early or mid July he was stricken by acute nausea and diarrhoea. According to Richard Weston, it was just after the King went on progress, on 16 July, that Overbury 'vomited and purged so extremely' and Weston said that Sir Thomas complained that during this attack he passed 'threescore stools and vomits'. Besides this Overbury was tormented by a 'great heat ... in all my body', dreadful thirst, weight loss and 'loathing of meat'. His urine acquired a pungent aroma, becoming 'strangely high', as Overbury put it. His skin became unbearably sensitive: at one point he told Rochester, 'I never liked myself worse, for I can endure no clothes on and do nothing but drink.' After a visit from the doctor, he 'fainted and vomited'. He was in such pain that writing became an ordeal and he was left so weakened that he warned Rochester that, if he experienced a resurgence of his fever, it would undoubtedly kill him. By the third week of July he was 'sick unto death ... and the physicians that were there about him ... subscribed their hands that they hold him a man past all recovery'. Shortly afterwards he began to show a partial improvement.[55]

Prior to his arrest Overbury was receiving medical treatment for the problems his faulty spleen caused him. 'For the avoiding of rheum and ill humours', Overbury had in his left arm an incision, or 'issue', which facilitated bloodletting and was prevented from healing by the insertion of a small pellet of gold. Plasters impregnated with substances which could be absorbed through the skin were also applied to different parts of his body. While in the Tower he took a variety of other medicaments. Among these was the emetic which he requested Rochester to send him. Although Overbury reported immediately after taking it that it had had a limited effect, it might have been more deleterious than he realised. Certainly when Robert Killigrew supplied Rochester with a vomit made to the same formula he cautioned, 'I would not council your Lordship to take it unless the physicians do allow of it at this time, for though this be as good as any can be, yet there is no such medicine good for all persons at all times.'[56]

Early in his confinement Overbury told Rochester that if physicians were sent to tend him in the Tower, he would decline all treatment. He planned to tell them that his current ill-health was caused by despair at his imprisonment and 'till my mind is eased, no physic will cure my body.' Overbury hoped that the doctors would inform King James of this and this would arouse the King's compassion. However, since

Weston told James Franklin in late May that Overbury was taking a lot of physic and had frequent enemas, it is clear that Sir Thomas did not abide by this resolution. As his health deteriorated during the summer he submitted to a variety of different treatments. He was bled on at least one occasion and on 3 July he took the first of several cooling baths, designed to ease his skin inflammation. He was also taking a great deal of medicine. When in the autumn of 1615 Lord Chief Justice Coke was investigating Overbury's death, he interviewed Paul de Loubell, the French apothecary who made up drugs for Overbury's doctor. On Coke's orders de Loubell handed over the prescriptions that had been issued to Overbury while he was in the Tower. In all, these amounted to twenty-eight sheaves of paper.[57]

Overbury's reliance on his doctors had grave implications at a time when medical science was primitive to the point of barbarism. In early seventeenth-century England medicine was still dominated by the ideas of Hippocrates and Galen. The concept of disease as an entity was only imperfectly understood, for in general illness was presumed to arise from an imbalance in the humours. To correct this physicians sought to purge the offending humours through forcible evacuation, relying largely on bloodletting, emetics and laxatives. These drastic remedies, combined with an ignorance of the causes of infection and an utter disregard for hygiene, often constituted more of a threat to the patient than his original malady.

Stories abound which illustrate the damage done by physicians. In March 1613 John Chamberlain wrote to a friend, 'I have been purged four or five times within this fortnight, and whereas when I entered into physic I complained only of want of appetite and a kind of heaviness all over ... I am now come to that pass that my stomach is quite gone ... my head extremely distempered and my sleep utterly lost ... so that I am now come to mine old opinion that physic ... doth ordinarily more harm than good. And yet, I have the advice of a man well reputed of, and one that studied five years at Padua.'[58]

At least Chamberlain lived to regret having called in a doctor, but others were not so fortunate. In February 1615 Chamberlain reported that when Lady Cheke complained of an itch in her arm, her doctor recommended that she be let some blood. 'By mishap the Queen's surgeon pricked her too deep and cut an artery which ... in a few days grew to a gangrene' and killed her. Similarly when Sir Robert Owen died in June 1617 Chamberlain noted, 'It is thought the physicians did so weaken him with letting blood and purges that they made an end of him.' Such occurrences were by no means uncommon. When Lord

Hay's wife died of measles in June 1614 Sir John Holles attributed this to Dr William Butler's 'presumptuous physic', and commented 'not improperly a physician may be in the list with the gout, dropsy and palsy and other such murthering diseases, for they kill more I think than all the alphabet doth besides'.[59]

The physicians were also 'much blamed' after the death of Prince Henry from what is now known to have been typhoid fever. In desperately seeking to cure him, the doctors succeeded only in increasing his sufferings. Throughout his illness the poor Prince was not only repeatedly bled but, 'for easing of the extreme pain of his head, the hair was shaven away and cupping glasses applied to lessen and draw away the humour and superfluous blood to the head, which he endured with wonderful patience'. On the eleventh day of his illness, 'a cock was cloven by the back and applied to the soles of his feet'. Neither this, nor the newly killed pigeons which were likewise spread over him, could bring about any improvement.[60]

Several doctors appear to have visited Overbury in the Tower, including Dr Micham, Dr John Craig, Dr Nessmith, and Dr Allen. However, the physician who ministered to him most frequently during these months was Theodore Turquet de Mayerne, the most fashionable doctor in the country. Mayerne (as he was always called) was regarded very highly in court circles, notwithstanding John Chamberlain's caustic observation that he had 'failed as often in judgment' as any of his colleagues. Born in 1573 near Geneva, Mayerne had studied medicine at the universities of Heidelberg and Paris. Having qualified as a doctor at the age of twenty-four he took up residence in Paris, where he became a successful lecturer. He commended to his students the use of chemical remedies, which brought him into conflict with other members of the Parisian medical establishment, who claimed that such remedies were injurious to patients. Mayerne was provoked into publishing a treatise defending his methods. He stressed that, contrary to the accusations levelled against him, chemical remedies in no way contravened the teachings of Galen, 'the master of physicians', and he charged the Paris doctors with jealousy towards him because he was an outsider.[61]

Mayerne first came to England in 1606. On being presented to the King by a peer whom he had treated in Paris, he was appointed the Queen's physician. Before long he returned to Paris but in 1611 James recalled him, and named him his personal physician. Mayerne quickly acquired a distinguished and wealthy clientele. Rochester was numbered among his patients, consulting Mayerne over an attack of dyspepsia in 1611. Mayerne's reputation remained intact even after the death of

Prince Henry, despite the fact that his rival Dr William Butler castigated his handling of the case, censuring him for giving the Prince a purge the day after he sickened, which Butler claimed 'dispersed the disease ... into all parts'.[62]

The treatments ordered by Mayerne could be fearsome. It was his belief that 'most often it is the bitterest medicines which work the best' and, in accordance with this maxim, he customarily prescribed extraordinarily foul concoctions. When a patient applied to him with breathing difficulties, Mayerne advised that 'a syrup made with the flesh of tortoises, snails, the lungs of animals, frogs and crawfish, all boiled in scabrous and coltsfoot water, adding at the last sugar candy, will prove very useful'. Mayerne was also a believer in the restorative properties of 'mercurial medicines, taken inwardly', which is noteworthy in view of the fact that Overbury's death was ultimately attributed to mercury poisoning. To encourage the healing of a fistula scar, Mayerne urged a patient to use a mercury water 'made of mercury sublimate, freed of its corrosive spirits by tin, according to art'.[63]

Intriguingly, Mayerne also left records of the treatment he thought should be followed by a patient who was afflicted by 'hypochondriacal distempers', which perhaps was the same thing as the '*flatus hypo-condriacus*' of which Overbury complained. In making his diagnosis, Mayerne had no doubt that the patient's spleen was at the root of the problem. He identified the cause of the distemper as 'a melancholy humour ... generated in the liver ... wrought upon in the spleen ... but also mixed in the veins' which 'extended as far as the brain'. Mayerne pronounced that 'that troublesome heat of the palm of your left hand and the sole of your foot doth plainly show the power of your spleen, affecting the upper as well as the nether parts, also the intense dryness of your mouth'. As for the 'stupor and numbness' in the patient's arms and legs and his intermittent 'fluttering of tongue', Mayerne was confident that that 'may be constituted to proceed from the reciprocal flowing of that juice from the spleen to the brain, and contrary ways back again, which oftentimes introduces grievous symptoms'. Moving on to the treatment he considered appropriate, Mayerne commanded, 'Let vomits lead on the first and main battle, as well for their efficacious removing of filth of the first regions of the body, as also to remove by their specific efficiency ... future impediments'. The most suitable emetic for the purpose was one composed of an 'infusion of *crocus metallorum* made in canary wine', and this solution should be taken at least three or four times.[64]

To ensure a speedy recovery, Mayerne also recommended opening a vein, and then keeping it open by artificial means, thus facilitating the expulsion of undesirable humours. We know that Overbury had just such an 'issue' in his arm, and Mayerne acknowledged that these often proved efficacious. However, he was emphatic that issues in the arms 'are in no way comparable to those which are made in the shoulders'. He explained that, after nicking the patient between the shoulder-blades, the physician should insert in the wound 'and closely press down, five or seven peas, applying a sticking plaster upon them ... which doth powerfully strengthen and confirm the parts'. In cases of hypochondriacal distemper it was also desirable to remove the dressing daily and anoint the backbone with balsam of earthworms or bats.[65]

In his book, *Medicinal Counsels*, Mayerne set down the recipe for balsam of bats. The primary ingredients were 'three of the greater sort of serpents or snakes cut into pieces, their skins being first stripped off; twelve bats; two very fat sucking puppies; one pound of earthworms washed in white wine; common oil; malago sack; sage, marjoram and bay leaves'. After all these had been boiled together, two pounds of hogs' lard was to be stirred in. Once the wine had evaporated, and the animals had started to disintegrate and putrefry, the fat was to be pressed out, and then, 'the marrow of a stag, an ox's legs, liquid amber, butter [and] nutmegs' was mixed in to make a balsam. After this had been applied regularly to the backbone, the final stage of the treatment was 'an emollient and detergent glister' containing 'lenitive electuary and honey of dog nettles', which was to be injected 'in a morning about three hours before dinner'.[66]

Mayerne and the apothecary he employed, Paul de Loubell, were absolved of all responsibility for Overbury's death. Possibly, however, it was wrong to have exonerated them. There are indications that, while in the Tower, Overbury occasionally felt concern about the adverse effects of the medical treatment he was undergoing. Under examination Sir Gervase Elwes mentioned that, at one point during his captivity, 'Sir T. Overbury was very angry with his apothecary at certain vomits which he had.' Furthermore, the King himself apparently heard that Overbury was dissatisfied with Mayerne. This emerges from a letter written to Rochester by Overbury's brother-in-law, Sir John Lidcote. Towards the end of July 1613 Lidcote was permitted to visit Overbury in the Tower, and he subsequently wrote to inform Rochester how the prisoner was faring. Lidcote reported that though the medication prescribed by Mayerne had so far made Overbury feel dreadful, Sir Thomas had no doubt that ultimately it would prove beneficial. Lidcote insisted, 'My brother utterly misclaims that he ever had any mistrust in Mayerne's physic [and] therefore humbly prayeth your Lordship to remove that apprehension of the King that which he speak to Sir Robert Killigrew. My self was rather to shew the distemper that the violent working of the physic had brought him to it, than any mistrust he had of it.'[67]

Obviously, in the absence of forensic evidence, it is not possible to state with any certainty that Mayerne inflicted serious harm on Overbury. Nevertheless, at the very least, his methods must have sapped Overbury's resistance to ill-health at a time when he was already debilitated by depression at his incarceration. It is perfectly plausible, moreover, that the consequences were much graver than this, and that Overbury should be included among the innumerable casualties of seventeenth-century medicine.

Perhaps, however, it is unfair to single out Mayerne for blame, for Overbury was also consulting other practitioners. The apothecary de Loubell said that when he visited Overbury in the Tower, 'he saw sometimes waters and other things' which Sir Thomas had not obtained from him.[68] In particular we know that Overbury was imbibing a patent medicine called *aurum potabile*, or 'drinkable gold'. This was the invention of a chemical empiric with no medical qualifications named Francis Anthony.

Aurum potabile was fabricated by an immensely complicated process. First, tin was heated until reduced to ashes, and then these were mixed with red wine vinegar and distilled. This produced a fluid which Anthony named 'the menstruum', which was then blended with salt and finely ground gold, and heated until all the liquid had evaporated. After this the residue was pulverised and, once reduced to powder, boiling water was poured on top of it. After being stirred the solution would separate: a thick sediment would settle on the bottom of the container, while a 'fine white calx' floated to the surface. This scum was skimmed off and combined with more of the menstruum. The mixture was left to rest for two or three days, after which a clear liquid was poured off. This too was distilled, producing a honey-like syrup known as 'the tincture'. This in turn was heated until it turned into a black earth-like substance. Once this had been ground finely and mixed with canary wine, it was ready for consumption.[69]

Anthony wrote that, by following this procedure, gold was altered 'from the compacture and solidity of his primitive body ... into a subtle, penetrant and volatile nature', and he prided himself on having thereby perfected 'an universal medicine'. He contended that 'Whereas the original of most diseases springeth from ... a distemperature, being especially in the first qualities, hot, cold, moist or dry, there is not reason to the contrary but that one medicine ... may be sufficient for the rectifying of all and every such distemper'. It was Anthony's boast that *aurum potabile* 'refresheth, vigorateth and strengtheneth the heart; restoreth and increaseth the vital spirits; advanceth the force and generation of good blood; multiplieth genitive seed and hability of prolification in both sexes, banishing sterility, preventing abortions, and providing quick, easy and safe deliveries in childbed'. According to Anthony, the potion not only cured plague, dropsy, jaundice, extreme cough, insomnia, consumption, convulsions, colic in babies and palsy, but it also worked well as a prophylactic.[70]

As proof of *aurum potabile's* miraculous properties Anthony cited several remarkable case histories, such as that of a patient who had been in grave danger from a malignant fever. After being given *aurum potabile* he fell into a deep slumber. While sleeping he 'voided through his mouth four live worms, long and round', awaking refreshed and free of fever. Another of Anthony's successes was Thomas Wheeler of Waltham, a sixty-seven-year-old man who had been so seriously ill for a month that the church bells had tolled for him. After taking three spoonfuls of *aurum potabile* he 'had a vomit of a great quantity of slimy humours' and then, 'by sensible degrees, he recovered health'.[71]

Anthony's claims were controversial. Because he had no licence to practise medicine, he had several skirmishes with the College of Physicians. In 1600 he was examined before them and forbidden to practise and, when he disregarded their injunction, he was imprisoned. The following year he was imprisoned again after one of his patients died but, once freed, he resumed his activities. In 1610 the College commissioned one of its members called Matthew Gwinne to write a tract refuting Anthony's claims about *aurum potabile*. Maintaining that there was no such thing as a panacea, Gwinne declared that metallic medicines were not superior to animal or vegetable compounds and that, anyway, Anthony's methods did not dissolve gold or make it digestible. Despite this, Anthony's business continued to flourish. In 1612 the college abandoned plans to prosecute him but, two years later, his methods again came under scrutiny after a dying theologian named Dr Sanderson attributed his demise to *aurum potabile*. However, no action was taken and though in 1616 there was more talk of instituting proceedings against Anthony, the matter was not pursued further.[72]

The most sustained attack on Anthony was made in 1623 by Dr John Cotta. In a treatise entitled *Cotta contra Antonium* he asserted that most of the so-called cures effected by Anthony were fictional, and that, even in cases where recovery had followed a dose of *aurum potabile*, this was wholly fortuitous. Worse still, Cotta alleged that, far from being a magical elixir, in some circumstances *aurum potabile* was positively harmful. He adduced the case of Dr Hickman, Chancellor of the diocese of Peterborough, who had suffered from consumption. On the recommendation of Anthony he had taken some *aurum potabile*, whereupon his pains worsened, his belly and legs swelled up, and he had died shortly after. Another casualty was Lady Markham, who had been ill but not in serious pain when she consulted Anthony. After being dosed with *aurum potabile* she underwent 'a miserable durance of intolerable torture, not only grievous unto all beholders and friends, but unto the master of *aurum potabile* himself, who professed his own sorrow and repentance for the dispensation thereof'.[73]

When Overbury's death came under scrutiny, the authorities discovered that he had had access to *aurum potabile*. Accordingly Anthony was interviewed. He denied having supplied Rochester with *aurum potabile* to be despatched to Overbury, but admitted having dealings with a servant of Sir Thomas. Anthony said that this man came to him when his master was sick, wanting to know whether '*aurum potabile* was good against poison?' Anthony replied that it was (though it is not clear whether he thought it conferred immunity or acted as an antidote once poison had been taken), and the servant had bought two ounces of the potion and paid £10 for it. The servant later returned and told Anthony's wife 'that it had done his master good', and purchased another two ounces.[74] This, incidentally, is the only instance where Overbury is depicted as having shown anxiety about being poisoned.

It is not clear if Anthony's account was truthful. Despite his denial of doing business with Rochester, the latter definitely supplied Overbury with some of Anthony's medicine. On 26 July 1613 Sir John Lidcote wrote to Rochester that Overbury 'hath taken all your Lordship's *aurum potabile* and is entered into another glass, and surely findeth much good of it'.[75] In the final analysis, however, it does not really matter if Overbury obtained his *aurum potabile* through Rochester, or whether he sent a servant to deal directly with Anthony. The crucial thing is that, while in the Tower, Overbury was taking a dubious nostrum which had never been subject to scientific appraisal, and which may have been highly dangerous.

At no point during the Overbury murder trials was it suggested that Sir Thomas had been unwittingly harmed by medical treatment. Instead, his death was confidently ascribed to poison. The poisoned tarts and jellies which were supposedly sent to him throughout his imprisonment were by no means the only deadly substances alleged to have been administered to him during this period. In particular it was claimed that Rochester had taken advantage of Sir Thomas's readiness to take emetics to trick him into taking a powder which was supposed to have only mildly disagreeable effects but which was, in reality, white arsenic.

As has been seen, Rochester did send Overbury at least one emetic, which had been made up for him by Sir Robert Killigrew and delivered to the Tower by Giles Rawlins. However, no one disputed that this had been an essentially harmless formulation, which had not even worked as powerfully as Overbury had wanted. In contrast the deadly vomit, containing arsenic, was said to have been supplied by James Franklin and conveyed to the Tower in all innocence by a servant of Overbury's named Lawrence Davies.

It was Lawrence Davies who first aroused the authorities' interest in the powder. Quite early in the investigation into Overbury's murder Lord Chief Justice Coke interviewed Davies, who told him that there had been several occasions when he had delivered letters from Rochester to Overbury at the Tower. Once, when handing such a letter to Weston (who was to pass it on to Sir Thomas), Davies noticed that a small packet of white powder had fallen out and he had picked this up and reinserted it in the folded letter. Weston – who could not read – wanted to know what was written in the letter, so Davies had a quick look at it. According to Davies, Rochester there told Overbury 'that the powder would make him sick but that should be a cause for him to move the King the rather for his liberty'.[76]

Davies said that, the day after delivering this letter, he again saw Weston. Weston told him that during the night Overbury had been terribly sick and he showed Davies 'the loathsome stuff' that Overbury had vomited. Davies was so alarmed by this that he wished to take it away and show it to Rochester, but Weston would not permit this, saying, 'It was an unfit sight to show him.' Davies furthermore alleged that, after Overbury was dead, he had another encounter with Weston and that on that occasion, 'he saw in Weston's hand part of the white powder' which had been in Rochester's letter. Weston said that he intended to give this back to Rochester.[77]

Davies's statements formed a major part of the Crown case against Rochester, but he cannot be taken for an altogether trustworthy witness. Davies had been in Overbury's service for eight or nine years and Overbury's father said that of Sir Thomas's two servants, Davies 'was the ancienter and the higher then in esteem'. Nevertheless, it appears that not all of Overbury's family had such a high opinion of Davies. It is perhaps relevant that, towards the end of Overbury's life, his brother-in-law, Sir John Lidcote, expressed doubts as to the reliability of 'Lawrence' (presumably Lawrence Davies), and suggested that Overbury find an excuse to send the man away from London. Lidcote feared that in some way Lawrence was betraying Overbury and, though there is nothing to indicate why he thought this (or, still less, whether he was justified in doing so), it does not inspire confidence in Davies's integrity.[78]

There are other, rather stronger, reasons for questioning Davies's honesty. It would be wrong, no doubt, to make too much of the fact that he apparently saw nothing wrong in illicitly reading letters which had been entrusted to him, for Jacobean drama suggests that this was a universal failing of servants at this period. It is, however, significant that – for reasons which will be explained later – Davies had cause to bear a grudge against Rochester. This may have made him willing to fabricate evidence against him. An illustration of the way in which Davies was ready to stretch the facts is provided by his testimony regarding Overbury's refusal to serve as an ambassador. When first interviewed he said merely 'that he hath heard (but of whom he remembereth not) that Sir Thomas Overbury would have ... gone over according to his Majesty's pleasure but that he was dissuaded by the Lord of Rochester'. At Rochester's trial, however, Davies made the much more damaging assertion that he had seen a letter which Rochester had sent Overbury, urging him not to take the post.[79]

The time at which this powder was allegedly delivered to Overbury does not fit with the way his illness developed. When Davies first mentioned this powder to the authorities he was vague about exactly when he had sent it to Overbury, saying 'the time he certainly knows not'. In a subsequent examination, however, Davies became more specific, telling his interviewers that this took place 'three weeks after Sir Gervase Elwes came to be Lieutenant of the Tower'.[80] This meant that the powder would have been delivered about 1 June. According to Davies, Overbury was immediately assailed by chronic sickness. However, Overbury's letters show that, although he wanted it to be thought that he was gravely ill, at this date he was not suffering from anything other than the complaints which had bothered him when he entered the Tower.

It is true that this observation is undermined by the fact that, at various points during the trials for Overbury's murder, it was suggested that the powder was administered somewhat later. However, the evidence relating to this is contradictory. Different accounts of the trial state that the powder was taken on 1 June, 3 June or 5 June. In the section of his book *The Institutes of the Law of England* which deals with Overbury's murder, the Lord Chief Justice Sir Edward Coke states that the arsenic was given on 1 June, which is perhaps significant in view of the fact that Coke was familiar with every detail of the case and was intimately involved in the preparation of indictments. Elsewhere, however, the date is variously given as 'the last of June', 1 July or 2 July. This would certainly tally better with the onset of Overbury's symptoms. Unfortunately it is impossible to establish conclusively which was the date advanced by the Prosecution. One must bear in mind that our knowledge of the trials derives from the reports of spectators, which would have been scribbled in haste and which may well contain errors. Furthermore, it is not even certain that the Prosecution showed much consistency when suggesting dates on which poison was administered. At one of the trials a prosecutor actually declared that this was a point of little significance, airily asserting, 'Neither mattered it much to show the direct time of poison or to name the thing that did the act; let it suffice that it was done, whether by this or that poison it skills not'.[81]

Overbury's other servant, Henry Peyton (whose evidence will be dealt with later), and Giles Rawlins (the cousin of Overbury who was employed by Rochester) did what they could to support Lawrence Davies's story. Rawlins would later recall a conversation which had taken place between him and Davies on the subject of Sir Thomas Overbury. According to Rawlins, Davies remarked 'that he hoped [Overbury] was not so ill as he made shew of', and then he told Rawlins that he had recently delivered an emetic to Overbury from Rochester. Rawlins said he was surprised by this as 'his Lordship did not acquaint me with this as he did with the former, nor do I know from whom he had it'. After Overbury was dead Rawlins and Davies met again and this time – so Rawlins claimed – Davies reported that Weston would shortly be coming to see Rochester in order to give him 'a paper of powder'.[82]

Rawlins may have been telling the truth about all this. Nevertheless, it must be borne in mind that he was anxious to defend himself from the imputation that he had been too supine about the death of his close relation and benefactor, Sir Thomas Overbury. We have it on Rawlins's own admission that, when the enquiry began into Overbury's murder, he was 'taxed by divers that, being so near of blood, and having been preferred by him to his lord's service, that he did not strive in it'.[83] Plainly, he was anxious to make up for what he saw as his past remissness and, in these circumstances, he may not have adhered to the strictest standards of accuracy when giving evidence.

There is no disputing the fact that, shortly after the death of Sir Thomas Overbury, a meeting took place between Richard Weston and Viscount Rochester.[84] What is less readily apparent is what transpired on this occasion. Davies would have it that Weston wanted to return to Rochester what remained of the powder sent to Overbury, but this rests only on his authority. For what it is worth, Weston himself vigorously denied that anything of the sort took place at their encounter. After his arrest he agreed that, while he had been working at the Tower, Davies had brought letters there from Rochester to Overbury, but he was adamant that none of these letters contained 'any paper with any white powder ... or that he after Overbury's death redelivered to my Lord of Rochester the residue of the powder that remained'.[85]

While it would obviously be unwise to rely too much on Weston's testimony, it is by no means implausible that he went to see Rochester simply because he hoped to receive some remuneration for having looked after Overbury in the Tower. This was what Giles Rawlins assumed when he found Weston waiting outside Rochester's court apartments (which was rather odd, if Davies had really mentioned that Weston intended to return a powder). Rawlins later explained, 'I did let his Lordship know that [Weston] was without and that I believed he expected some reward, but I desired his Lordship to give him nothing because of his negligence in his service to Sir Thomas Overbury'. Rochester agreed that Weston could be shown into his bedchamber and the two men had a brief discussion. The content of this remains a mystery. After revealing that Weston 'made no long stay' with Rochester, Rawlins had to admit, 'What words passed betwixt them ... I do not know, for I stood not near and their discourse was too low to be heard far off.'[86]

Davies's allegations received partial confirmation from another source, albeit a highly dubious one. While awaiting trial in 1615 James Franklin provided the authorities with a colourful and detailed account of the methods used by Overbury's enemies to kill him. He agreed that arsenic had been sent to Overbury in a letter but he maintained that this was merely one of a myriad of toxins that Overbury was ingesting at this period. Franklin declared, 'There were continual poisons given him in all his meats ... and that Overbury being once desirous to eat of a pig, they provided him a pig, and in the sauce they put white arsenic ... Sir Thomas Overbury did eat neither broth nor sauce for the most part but that there was poison put into it, so prepared to lie in his body before it wrought ... The white powder which was sent to Sir Thomas Overbury was white arsenic and was sent to him in a letter. The poison being heavy worked upwards and downwards and laid to lie long in the body before it killed him ... Sir Thomas Overbury never eat salt but it was poisoned with white arsenic, and that the salt was provided by Mrs Turner and prepared by her in her chamber. And once, Sir Thomas Overbury being desirous to eat of a partridge, and the sauce being water and onions, cantharides, being black, was strewed therein instead of pepper.[87]

Reading this list, the chief mystery is that Overbury did not succumb sooner to these murderous onslaughts. The Attorney General Francis Bacon's explanation for this was that Overbury accumulated so much poison within his system that he acquired a partial immunity to it.[88] However, there may have been a different answer, for it is very possible that Franklin's allegations were malicious fabrications, volunteered in the hope of earning himself mercy.

When Rochester was brought to trial for his part in Overbury's murder, the Prosecution contended that his malign intent towards the deceased was proved by the fact that, during Sir Thomas's captivity, various individuals had sought to convince Rochester that Overbury was danger-ously ill, and that Rochester had reacted with chilling indifference. The most graphic evidence to this effect came from Overbury's servant Henry Peyton. Peyton deposed that, when Sir Thomas was 'very sick after the receipt of the powder' delivered by Davies, Overbury had asked Peyton to carry to Whitehall a letter from him to Rochester. At the door of Rochester's lodgings Peyton was relieved of this by Giles Rawlins, who took it in to his master. Having read the letter, Rochester came out to have a word with Peyton. According to Peyton, when Rochester asked how Overbury was, he answered bluntly that Sir Thomas was sick. 'How sick?' Rochester asked, to which Peyton replied, 'Very sick'. 'Very sick indeed?' queried Rochester, whereupon Peyton insisted, 'Yea my Lord in great danger of death, for he hath had threescore purges and vomits in one day.' Peyton's alarming bulletin left Rochester unruffled. As the indignant manservant related, 'My Lord of Rochester cried "Pish!" and so smiling turned about and left this examinant.'[89]

The apothecary Paul de Loubell also claimed that, after he had visited Overbury in the Tower, he had been summoned to Whitehall by Rochester, who wished to know more about Overbury's condition. De Loubell maintained that on three separate occasions he warned Rochester that Overbury was gravely ill, but had been puzzled by the lack of concern with which Rochester greeted this. At his trial Rochester vehemently disputed de Loubell's allegations. He said that he had only laid eyes on de Loubell on one occasion, pointing out that there were no other witnesses who could establish that they met more frequently.[90] His protests were unavailing, but perhaps it was unfair that de Loubell's assertions were so widely accepted. When interrogated about Overbury's death the apothecary had presumably been terrified that he would be held responsible. In the circumstances it would have been understandable if he had pretended that he had done everything possible to draw attention to Overbury's failing health, only to be rebuffed by Rochester.

In contrast to his angry rejection of de Loubell's claims, Rochester neither confirmed nor denied that the exchange described by Peyton had happened. This may have been merely an oversight on his part, but it could also be taken as a tacit admission that such a conversation, or something approximating it, had taken place between them. Even so, this does not necessarily constitute proof that Rochester was utterly callous about Overbury's sufferings. After all, Rochester knew that Overbury had been taking emetics, and it must also be remembered that Overbury had confided to Rochester that he intended to exaggerate his physical debility in the hope that this would engage the King's sympathy. It was therefore excusable that Rochester remained sceptical when told that Sir Thomas was alarmingly ill.

There are also indications that Rochester was receiving information from another source which gave a very different picture. Throughout Overbury's captivity the Earl of Northampton sought to convince Rochester that he should not be worried about Overbury's physical condition. At some stage in the summer of 1613 Northampton wrote to Rochester, 'Sir Thomas Overbury continues hearty and eats heartily, expressing great contentation in some messages of comfort he hath lately received.' If this was written before late June, there was nothing very exceptionable about it, but by the end of August it does seem that Northampton was wilfully misrepresenting the extent of Overbury's frailty. By that time Overbury had finally been persuaded to write to the Earl of Suffolk. In his letter to the Lord Chamberlain he apologised for not writing at greater length, explaining that his illness had left him so debilitated that doing so would have taxed him too greatly. Perhaps fearing that Rochester would be so disturbed by this that he would no longer acquiesce in Overbury's imprisonment, Northampton glossed over this passage. He assured Rochester, 'I will note unto your Lordship [Overbury's] infinite hypocrisy in pretending weakness, for in his life the Lieutenant never knew him better or in more hope of recovery.'[91]

If it is possible to make allowances for Rochester's lack of concern about Overbury's health, his behaviour towards Overbury's parents is harder to defend. As has been seen, it was in response to a petition from Nicholas Overbury that the King agreed that physicians should visit Overbury whenever necessary. Following this, however, Rochester had told Mr Overbury that he should not approach the King again on his son's behalf, as he himself was better placed to agitate for Sir Thomas's release. Nevertheless, as time went by and Overbury remained in the Tower, Mr Overbury presented another petition, begging James to free his son. The King indicated that he would consider the matter (it is not clear whether he later formally rejected the application) but Rochester told Mr Overbury that it had been misguided of him to submit this plea. He reiterated that matters must be left in his own hands, and warned that further intervention from Mr Overbury would only 'stir [Sir Thomas's] enemies up against him'. He would not even permit Overbury's mother, who had come up to London in hopes of seeing her son, to seek permission to visit him in the Tower, claiming that 'that might protract his delivery'. Rochester wrote urging her to return to the country, promising that, before she reached home, her son would be a free man. When details of all this emerged at Rochester's trial it aroused the utmost repugnance, for people were appalled by the callous way that he had abused the Overburys' trust in him. Bishop Godfrey Goodman even maintained that Mr Overbury's testimony was 'that which made most against' Rochester.[92]

When Overbury was extremely ill in July 1613 his brother-in-law, Sir John Lidcote, begged Rochester to ask the King to allow Lidcote and Robert Killigrew to visit the sick man. Rochester obliged and the King gave his assent although, by the terms of their warrant (which was signed by Northampton and several other councillors), they were not permitted to talk to Overbury alone but had to do so in the presence of the Lieutenant of the Tower. When Elwes ushered Lidcote and Killigrew into Overbury's room they were alarmed by his appearance, for they found him 'very sick in his bed, his hand dry, his speech hollow'. Overbury told them that he wished to draw up a will, and Lidcote promised to make the necessary arrangements and to return with the document ready for Overbury's signature the following day. When the allotted time for the visit had elapsed Killigrew was shown to the door by Elwes, but Lidcote was able to stay behind and exchange a surreptitious word with his brother-in-law. Urgently Overbury asked Lidcote whether he thought Rochester 'juggled with him, or not', taking

Sir John by surprise, for at that time it had not occurred to him that Rochester was playing Overbury false. He just had time to whisper that he still had faith in Rochester when Elwes suddenly realised that the two men were conducting an unauthorised conversation. Furious, he swore at Sir John for abusing the privilege accorded him, ordering him to leave at once. When Lidcote and Killigrew next presented themselves at the Tower in the hope of seeing Sir Thomas a second time they found that their entry warrant had been rescinded, although Lidcote was allowed to send Overbury's will in for him to sign.[93]

On 26 July Lidcote wrote to Rochester reporting how he had found Sir Thomas, while of course omitting to mention that Overbury had expressed any doubts about him. Lidcote felt able to assure Rochester that there were grounds for cautious optimism for, though there was no doubt that Overbury had been gravely ill, he was now 'more comfortable in himself than he was'. 'He ... eateth broth every day and therefore we hope well of him,' declared Lidcote, adding that the *aurum potabile* provided by Rochester was undoubtedly doing Overbury much good. In conclusion he effusively assured Rochester that 'the greatest comfort I can give him [Overbury] is the assurance of your Lordship's favour, of which he hath had so long and noble a trial as we cannot doubt the continuance thereof, for which, how much both himself and all his friends stand charged in duties to your Lordship I cannot express.'[94]

By this time Overbury had been in prison for more than three months but he showed few signs of mellowing towards the Howards. Since Rochester was now accompanying the King on progress, the Earl of Northampton decided it was up to him to make Overbury more tractable. He wrote to Rochester telling him that he need not bother himself further about Overbury for he, Northampton, would soon reduce Sir Thomas to conformity. Promising that, as with 'all things you commit to my love and care,' he would give the matter his full attention, Northampton assured the younger man that he would keep him apprised of any developments. He wrote soothingly, 'I find not that your Lordship need to use many instruments while I am here and speak with the Lieutenant when I list for, so far as my wit and industry can work, your directions shall come to a speedy and sound execution.' He explained that he had briefed Elwes very thoroughly as to what was required of him and the Lieutenant was now 'very perfect in his part'.[95]

Elwes's allotted role was to convince Overbury that it was in his own interests to reach an accommodation with the Howards, a task to which the Lieutenant applied himself with vigour. Elwes began by telling Overbury that he would remain in prison for a very long time unless he humbled himself before the Earl of Suffolk. At first Overbury was sceptical, pointing out that he had committed no crime and that therefore the King was bound to release him before too long, but Elwes worked hard to disabuse him of this idea. He told the prisoner that the Earl of Northampton had been present when the judges had discussed his case and, on that occasion, the Lord Chief Justice had pronounced that Overbury's offence constituted 'as high a contempt as a subject could commit'.[96]

Elwes also had to overcome Overbury's conviction that it would be pointless to approach Suffolk, as the latter hated him so much that he would be hardly likely to respond favourably. Elwes countered that Suffolk wanted nothing more than to settle his differences with Rochester and, if Overbury offered to bring this about, he would earn the Lord Chamberlain's lasting goodwill. Elwes added winningly that Suffolk was well aware 'both of the greatness of [Overbury's] wit and the strength of his interest in my Lord's [Rochester's] affection', and therefore it was unthinkable that he would spurn Overbury's advance.[97]

Overbury still argued that such self-abasement was unnecessary, clinging to the hope that Rochester would prevail on the King to release him without Suffolk being involved in any way. Elwes would have none of this, telling his charge that Rochester was so despairing of achieving anything on his own that he had already steeled himself to ask Suffolk for his help. According to Elwes, Rochester had begged the Lord Chamberlain to tell the King that Overbury had suffered enough. Elwes said that Suffolk's response showed that he was by no means as implacable as Overbury assumed for, while the King was staying at Salisbury on his summer progress, he had raised the matter with James. So far nothing had come of this, but Elwes now prodded Overbury into writing to the Lord Chamberlain, thanking him for his initiative on his behalf.

Overbury reluctantly agreed that it was incumbent on him to make some sort of acknowledgment to Suffolk but the letter he penned in consequence was hardly a fulsome expression of indebtedness. With frigid courtesy Overbury thanked Suffolk for being 'an earnest mediator to his Majesty for my liberty', conceding that, 'considering things past', he had more reason to be grateful for this kindness than if he had received it 'from one from whom I could have hoped for it'. Explaining that he was still so weak that he was 'not able to write much', Overbury concluded with the tepid undertaking that, if Suffolk persisted in his attempts to restore his liberty, 'I will ever after be as faithful to you as your Lordship's own heart.'[98]

The letter was despatched as Overbury wished but Elwes ridiculed the idea that these empty assurances would be of any interest to Suffolk. He stressed that, if Overbury hoped to receive meaningful aid from the Lord Chamberlain, he would have to be a good deal more forthcoming. Overbury refused to see the logic of this, protesting that Suffolk's exertions on his behalf had so far yielded very little result. Elwes retorted that Overbury 'might thank his own cold answer to my Lord' for that, for Suffolk 'being drawn so far as he was already come, merely at the instance of my Lord of Rochester, did expect that Sir Thomas Overbury would have met him with stronger demonstrations of gratitude'.[99]

Still Overbury wriggled on the hook but he was gradually coming round to the view that he had no alternative but surrender. After a particularly lengthy discussion with Elwes on this subject he suddenly 'desired the Lieutenant to leave him to the night's thoughts', prompting hopes that he was close to yielding. Sure enough, after reflecting overnight, he called Elwes to him and said that he would make a renewed attempt to propitiate Suffolk. Accordingly Overbury drafted a letter to the Lord Chamberlain which he thought was sufficiently placatory without being demeaning but, when he showed it to Elwes, the latter still dismissed it as too equivocal. Berating Overbury for writing in such 'a dainty manner', which was 'of no greater effect to satisfy my Lord ... than the first', Elwes 'endeavoured to put him from his ifs and ands'. At last Overbury agreed that he could not afford to be so circumspect and 'resolved to write with a fuller pen'.[100]

Unbeknown to Overbury, Elwes gave a full account of all this to the Earl of Northampton and he, in turn, apprised Rochester of what had taken place. Passing on the news that Overbury had finally written to Suffolk a letter in appropriately ingratiating terms, Northampton commented sarcastically, 'Thus at last the mouse is born, of which the mountain was in so long and sharp travail, and in better shape than was likely in the beginning of the labour.'[101]

In his letter Overbury once again thanked the Lord Chamberlain for having interceded on his behalf with the King at Salisbury. He observed that he knew that Suffolk had acted at the behest of Rochester, and that he hoped that this signified that they were now on better terms. He concluded with a solemn assurance that 'I profess upon my faith and salvation that it shall be my endeavour, to the uttermost of my friendship, to continue that friendship between your two Lordships firm and inviolable'.[102]

The letter was rushed to Suffolk at Audley End and elicited a swift answer. Suffolk had been carefully tutored as to how he should respond to Overbury's advances – the Earl of Northampton assured Rochester, 'The Chamberlain ... hath his lesson by heart in the very words of your Lordship's direction to me' – and he carried out these instructions faithfully. On 23 August he wrote a cordial letter to Overbury. He promised that he would use his influence to persuade King James to release Sir Thomas, although he added the caveat that he knew that the King was still highly offended with Overbury and that, therefore, 'I conceive your freedom must be a work of some time.' As for Overbury's offer 'to mediate a fast friendship between Rochester and myself', Suffolk expressed keen enthusiasm at the prospect, heartily assuring Sir Thomas that he would hold him to this undertaking when he was out of the Tower.[103]

It is not clear by what contrivance this letter reached Overbury in the Tower. Obviously the most plausible assumption is that a servant of Suffolk or Northampton simply handed it to Elwes so he could pass it on to Overbury. However, it is not inconceivable that more circuitous methods were employed. Could the letter have been delivered to Overbury in a tart and, if so, could this provide the key to Frances's enigmatic letter? In that letter Frances makes it plain that an unnamed third party – who could easily have been Northampton – had instructed her to see that Overbury received the letters contained in the tarts and jellies she was sending. She also appears eager to see Overbury's answer, 'as that we shall ... I know, soon after he has gotten these'. The explanation still leaves some passages of the letter obscure (and is also undermined by the consideration that Elwes said that no tarts arrived at the Tower for Overbury after the King's departure on progress), but is hardly more fanciful than that advanced by Lord Chief Justice Coke. While it remains an unlikely hypothesis, it should not be altogether excluded.

Overbury was thrilled by the Lord Chamberlain's missive. He had held out so long against compromise with the Howards that his sudden capitulation, which promised to yield such positive results, had an exhilarating effect on him. Chuckling at the absurdity of the situation, the Earl of Northampton informed Rochester that Overbury was now in a state of virtual euphoria. 'This medicine of my Lord Chamberlain's hath purged choler, as the doctors say, to the very dregs,' he crowed. 'The melancholy doubts upon delay are vanished, my Lord ... The Lieutenant is the man whom Sir Thomas Overbury vows to magnify above all worthy friends of the world for the sound advice he gave.'

Northampton was sure that Rochester would derive further amusement from the fact that Overbury's only fear was that Rochester would resist his attempts to effect an alliance with the Earl of Suffolk. Overbury had gravely told Elwes that it would require persistent effort on his part to make Rochester amenable to such a scheme for, 'impressions ... that hath been long in festering crave time to be cured'.[104]

Such was Overbury's delight that he could not restrain himself from writing another letter to the Earl of Suffolk, expressing his joy that their misunderstandings were at an end. He declared that his sole regret was that 'unhappily, I have been a stranger thus long unto your Lordship' and, once again, he implored his new patron to do all he could to expedite his release. Noting that Suffolk had cautioned that obtaining his freedom would 'be a work of some time', he begged 'that your Lordship will be pleased, as much as in you lies, to shorten that time, which I crave of your Lordship not only for my liberty itself, but principally for my health's sake'. Overbury explained that, though he was by no means so ill as he had been earlier in his imprisonment, the 'air and solitariness of this place will not suffer my strength to grow but slowly, which change of air will quickly recover'.[105]

Overbury also wrote to his servant Lawrence Davies enclosing a copy of Suffolk's letter to him. He asked Davies to duplicate this and send one copy to Viscount Rochester (for Overbury had no conception that Rochester knew all that had been going on) and another to his father, 'to let him see that my business is now come to a certainty and will have a short end'. In great excitement Overbury commanded Davies to 'desire him to make haste back out of his circuit, for I hope to be at Bourton afore him, and let my uncle William write to my uncle that I hope to meet him without fail at Bourton at Michaelmas, or sooner if he will come'. He also asked Davies to tell his mother 'that I never longed more to see her and I hope I shall do shortly. For my health, I thank God I grow better again'. Overbury added as an afterthought that his parents should not take seriously Suffolk's warning that there would be some delay before the King would assent to his release. He proclaimed confidently, 'For that word in the letter ("sometime") is no long time, a week or ten days'.[106]

It is almost unbearably poignant to think that, within three weeks of writing this joyous note, Overbury was dead. His confidence that his tribulations were at an end proved misplaced for, though it did not occur to him that the Howards could be anything other than satisfied by the way he had prostrated himself, several members of that family still viewed him with the most profound mistrust. The Earl of

Northampton, for one, was acutely disturbed by the possibility that Overbury might soon be released. Writing to Rochester to tell him of Overbury's submission to Suffolk, Northampton would not accept that Overbury was acting in good faith, fretting that he still discerned 'great restriction and reservation' in Sir Thomas's avowals. While not daring to state outright that he would be happier if Overbury was dead, Northampton sought subtly to attune Rochester's mind to this idea. He told Rochester that his esteem for Elwes had deepened after the latter had sent him a letter containing the comforting reassurance that they had nothing to worry about, even if Overbury regained his strength, for, if he did not abide by his promise to 'do good offices between your Lordship and my Lord Chamberlain ... your Lordship that in your nature are most noble and honest will account him an arrant knave'. Northampton continued that Elwes had nonetheless taken the view that, ideally, the problem would not arise, for there was still a chance that Overbury 'shall not recover at all, which he thinks were the most happy and sure charge of all, for he finds in him many times, as he says, certain flashes that express a very strong affection to some persons that wish not well to this amity'.[107]

From this one can deduce that Northampton was worried that, now that Overbury had modified his stance towards Suffolk, Rochester would argue that there was no longer any excuse to keep him locked up in the Tower. In one of his letters to Northampton Sir Gervase Elwes alluded to these concerns when he observed, 'Rochester's part I shall much fear, until I see the event to be clearly conveyed.' At his trial Elwes was asked to account for this remark and he explained that, having 'heard and known of that great league that was between' Overbury and Rochester, 'I might well think, suspect and fear whether [Rochester] would always countenance these projects for [Overbury's] restraint.'[108] It was presumably unease on this point that had led Northampton to assure Rochester that Overbury had been lying when he had told Suffolk that he was far from well, fearing that Rochester would press harder for his friend's release if he believed him to be in poor health. However, Rochester should perhaps have managed to gauge the true state of affairs because, almost immediately, Northampton contradicted himself about this. It was later in the same letter that Northampton mentioned the possibility that Overbury would 'not recover at all', not hiding the fact that such an outcome would afford him considerable relief.

What concerned Northampton more than anything was that, although Overbury had been driven to be more deferential towards Suffolk, he had expressed no regret for his past behaviour towards Frances. On 23

August Northampton asked Elwes to tell Overbury that he expected him to make amends for this. The following day Overbury wrote to Northampton, saying that he understood that Lady Essex had 'been informed of some speeches of mine wherein I should wrong her honour'. He acknowledged that he had sometimes been less than polite about Frances but implied that this had been a response to provocation from her, and furthermore insisted that he had always stopped short of being intolerably offensive. He explained that Rochester and others had often informed him 'with what bitterness her Ladyship would speak of me and, out of the sense of that, 'tis possible I may have spoken with less respect of her than was fit; but that I ever touched her in ... her honour, far be from me'. He wrote that, if he was required to apologise in person, he was ready to 'tender as much' to both Frances and her mother, concluding with a condescending assurance that, 'For my Lady of Essex, if I might only be freed of her ill-will for time to come, there shall be no man readier to respect and honour her than myself.'[109]

This conditional undertaking, which came close to suggesting that Overbury was more of an aggrieved party than Frances herself, was not at all what Northampton had been seeking. Before long Elwes came back to Overbury and indicated that he must do better. Overbury, whose self-esteem was still so rampant that he could not comprehend how his recantation could have been found wanting, was genuinely taken aback. Elwes recounted, 'After some silence, he took the Bible and protested his innocence', pointing out in some indignation that 'he had justified her honour already'. 'Alas', said Overbury plaintively. 'What will they do with me?' Elwes – who clearly relished his role in the humbling of this proud man – responded, 'So refine you that there shall be no question of your pureness hereafter.'[110]

Overbury was momentarily subdued by that but, as Elwes was taking his leave, he suddenly burst out that 'He would say in general that [Lady Essex] was so worthy, she was a wife [fit] for any man, but to say she was a wife worthy in particular of my Lord Rochester, he would never say it, lest my Lord should condemn me for valuing his worth.' Elwes withdrew without comment, hoping that after pondering the matter, Overbury would be more sensible. However, when Elwes returned he found Sir Thomas 'not in fear, but in fury', having worked himself into a rage at the way he was being harried. He raged not only against Northampton but also against the Countess of Suffolk, blustering that 'he feared as little to die as they to be cruel'.[111]

As yet Overbury was not ready to criticise Rochester as being responsible for his predicament. Nevertheless, if Lawrence Davies can be believed, Overbury wrote to Rochester shortly afterwards, making it plain that he still thought it would be a grave mistake to marry Frances. Davies was asked to deliver this letter to Rochester and, as usual, he could not resist having a surreptitious look at what was written there. When later asked to summarise its contents Davies stated that Overbury declared that he remained ready 'to be a means of friendship between Rochester and others ... but concerning the marriage he would never advise him'.[112]

It may have been the receipt of this letter that finally convinced Rochester that Overbury was utterly incorrigible. So exasperated was he that, when Overbury's brother-in-law Sir John Lidcote came to see him, he did not hide that he had lost all patience with Sir Thomas. He expressed annoyance about the 'unreverent style' in which Overbury had addressed him and said that the two of them 'should never be as we had been'. Rather foolishly he asked Lidcote to keep these remarks to himself but Lidcote was not prepared to oblige. Although in late July he still had had complete faith in Rochester, he had subsequently become convinced that the Viscount was guilty of the most monstrous duplicity. The turning point had come when he had paid an earlier visit to Rochester to discuss Overbury's case. Pretending to be upset that the outlook for Overbury remained gloomy, Rochester had heaved what Lidcote described as 'a counterfeit sigh'. Lidcote said he suddenly realised that Rochester was being insincere when, 'at that instant, he smiled in my face'.[113]

On 27 August Lidcote had written to Overbury warning him that he was the victim of a wicked deception. 'Never any man was so cosened as you are', he declared, dismissing the idea that Overbury had anything to gain through cooperation with the Howards. 'My Lord Chamberlain is not so foolish to think that you will deny to yield to anything for your liberty but, when all is done, it will be pretended the King's wrath will keep you there,' he told his brother-in-law. Nevertheless, although he had no doubt that Rochester was one of those plotting to prolong Overbury's imprisonment and that 'There is no honest quarter to be held with him,' he advised Overbury against upbraiding his former friend for having betrayed him so grossly. Instead he urged Sir Thomas to pretend that he still trusted Rochester implicitly, for a confrontation at this stage would be singularly unwise.[114] Unfortunately, when Lidcote followed up this letter by passing on to Overbury Rochester's latest comments about him, Overbury could no longer contain his bitterness. He wrote Rochester a long and anguished letter, accusing him of treachery and ingratitude and threatening revenge.

'I understand that you told my brother [Lidcote] that my unreverent style should make an alienation betwixt you and me hereafter,' Sir Thomas opened menacingly. He demanded to know how Rochester could have the gall to say 'that you would be less to me, to whom you owe more than to any soul living, both for your fortune, understanding and reputation'. He professed outrage that after the tribulations he had endured, including his earlier exile from court and 'now, five months miserable imprisonment', Rochester could dare 'to make so poor a pretence to say you will alter toward me for the style in my letters'. Overbury warned that this feeble excuse could not justify Rochester's treatment of him, 'your sacrificing me to your woman, your holding a firm friendship with those that brought me hither and keep me here' and his failure 'to make it your first act of any good terms with them to set me free and restore me to your self again'. Overbury continued that until now he had always suppressed all doubts about Rochester's loyalty, even though it had mystified him that 'notwithstanding my misery, you visited your woman, frizzled your head never more curiously, took care for hangings and daily were solicitous about your clothes ... held day traffic of letters with my enemies without turning it to my good, sent me nineteen projects and promises for my liberty, then at the beginning of the next week sent me some frivolous account of the miscarriage of them and so slip out of town; and all this ill nature showed me by the man whose conscience tells him that trusting to him brought me hither'. Now, however, there could be no denying that Rochester had abused his trust in the most abhorrent fashion.

Overbury then announced that he had devised a means of striking back at Rochester. He claimed to have written a full account of all their dealings in the past, providing details of the way he had promoted Rochester's career, and of the 'secrets of all kinds' that had passed between them. He had also set down how he had assisted Rochester to court and seduce Frances, and how they had subsequently quarrelled when Rochester had refused to renounce her. Overbury maintained that he had made several copies of this document and that he had sent one 'to all my friends noble', urging each of the recipients to circulate it widely. Since Overbury had by this time alienated his former friends at court, this threat was perhaps not so intimidating as he imagined. Nevertheless, Overbury expressed confidence that the effect would be devastating, and that Rochester would be covered in ignominy for his base conduct. He exulted, 'Thus, if you deal thus wickedly with me, I have provided, whether

I die or live, your nature shall never die, nor leave to be the most odious man alive'.[115]

The odds are that Overbury was bluffing when he asserted that he had already written and sent out this fearsome indictment of Rochester. Certainly no trace of such a document survives. In these circumstances, it was nothing short of madness on Overbury's part to write this declaration of hostile intent. Since it merely confirmed how dangerous he would be if given his liberty, the Earl of Northampton could hardly have hoped for a better justification for keeping Overbury in confinement. As for Viscount Rochester, it would be alleged at his trial that this letter furnished him with the ultimate motive for murder.

Shortly after this all communications ceased from Overbury. Giles Rawlins later recalled that, whereas earlier in Overbury's imprisonment, he had frequently caught a glimpse of Sir Thomas gazing out of his room in the Tower, from about the beginning of September, 'he could never see him at the window, albeit he often attempted it and desired it.' This may have been a consequence of new security measures introduced by Sir Gervase Elwes. On 27 August Sir John Lidcote wrote to Rochester that it had lately become almost impossible to maintain contact with Overbury, which he thought might have something to do with the fact that the Lieutenant had recently closely questioned Overbury about whether any letters had been delivered to him. Lidcote suggested that, during an earlier conversation with the Lieutenant, Overbury must have let fall some remark 'which perhaps savoureth of some intelligence', and this had alerted Elwes to the fact that letters were getting through to him.[116] One cannot discount the possibility that Lidcote was being disingenuous when he wrote this and that, because he now mistrusted Rochester, he wished to discourage him from communicating with Overbury. On the other hand, because of Overbury's recalcitrance, it may have been true that Elwes had placed further restrictions on him.

The most likely explanation, however, is that at the end of August Overbury became so ill that he was no longer capable of writing letters. When he wrote to Rochester on 27 August Sir John Lidcote believed that Overbury was maintaining his recovery from his earlier illness. However, it must have been about that date that Sir Thomas suffered a serious relapse. Rochester was informed of the deterioration in his condition and he thereupon wrote to Dr Theodore Turquet de Mayerne (who was in Bath) to request his advice. On 31 August Mayerne replied by letter that he was sorry to hear that the prisoner was suffering a recurrence of his illness, and that he had begun to vomit, but that there was nothing he could do at present. He suggested that Overbury wrote to him himself for, if he was given a fuller account of Sir Thomas's symptoms, he might, even from this distance, be able to divine what was wrong.[117]

We do not know whether or not Mayerne returned from Bath in time to pay Overbury a final visit in the Tower. What is clear, however, is that Overbury's last bout of illness differed from the earlier attacks in one significant respect. After his death one person who saw his body stated that Overbury had a large ulcer, or sore, on his back. There is evidence that, in the days leading up to his death, this caused him considerable pain. He kept the ulcer covered by a plaster, which was periodically changed. A few hours before he died he asked Weston to put a new one on for him, but Weston was not permitted to look at the afflicted part. Instead Overbury kept himself covered by his bedclothes, and Weston had to grope about under them, while Sir Thomas shouted directions as to where the dressing should be applied. It was an awkward procedure, and Weston could not avoid hurting Overbury in the process. The jailer told Northampton that Overbury was in such agony that he swore loudly when Weston 'did but touch the place whereon he laid the plaster'. When passing this on to Rochester, Northampton showed no compassion for Overbury's sufferings. Instead he declared it reprehensible that Overbury should have dared to utter such profanities on what turned out to be his deathbed.[118]

The fact that Overbury was a patient of Dr Mayerne, who regarded issues in the back as a sovereign remedy, raises the possibility that, while in the Tower, Sir Thomas had agreed to supplement the existing issue in his arm with another one between his shoulder-blades. If so, it is surely a permissible hypothesis that such a wound (which Mayerne directed should be kept open by the insertion of five or seven peas)[119] could have become gangrenous, and that Overbury died not from poisoning, but from septicaemia.

What, then, of the deadly enema which was said to have been administered to Overbury, and which supposedly killed him? In theory, the ailing Overbury decided that it would do him good to have an enema and, when his enemies heard of this, they bribed an apothecary's boy to fill the syringe with mercury sublimate in place of the therapeutic solution prepared by the apothecary. Sir Gervase Elwes was the first person to claim that this was how Overbury was murdered. When called upon to reveal what he knew of Sir Thomas's death he stated that 'That which wrought it ... was a glister.' He alleged that, after Overbury was dead, Weston 'confessed to me, here was his overthrow', adding that

Overbury's apothecary 'had a servant who was corrupted; twenty pounds, Weston told me, was given'.[120] Ostensibly this seems straightforward enough, but Elwes's testimony requires thorough probing. When examined, Richard Weston himself would claim that he had first heard that Overbury was to be poisoned in this way months before Sir Thomas's death, when he had had a drink with Franklin at the White Lion Tavern. Weston said that he had promptly warned Sir Gervase of this threat, who had given orders that only Overbury's recognised apothecary should be permitted access to him. Even if Weston was lying, and he did not tell the Lieutenant what Franklin had said until after Overbury's death, it does not follow that Franklin's proposal had been put into practice.

From the point of view of Sir Gervase Elwes, there were definite advantages to claiming that it was an enema which finally killed Overbury. Elwes believed that, if this was established as the cause of death, he could not be accounted negligent for failing to protect his prisoner. At his trial he argued that he had been powerless in the face of such villainy, pleading, 'If [Overbury] were poisoned with a glister, it could not have been prevented, though he had lain in his Majesty's chamber. For how honest ye physician be, yet an apothecary or his servant may be corrupted, which all the guards in the world could not prevent.'[121] In the hope of absolving himself from all responsibility for Overbury's death, Elwes may have seized upon what Weston had told him, and pretended that Franklin's nefarious scheme had become reality.

Doubts as to whether Overbury really met his end in this gruesome fashion are reinforced by the fact that the identity of the apothecary's boy remains a complete mystery. During Weston's trial he was airily described as 'another man unknown, being apothecary'. For a more precise identification of this elusive figure one is forced to turn to Anthony Weldon's book, *The Court and Character of King James I*. Weldon records there that the apothecary's boy was named Reeve and states that, after the murder, he fled to Brussels. Arthur Wilson and William Sanderson relate similar stories in their books on the Jacobean Court, with the variation that, in these works, the fugitive apothecary's boy is said to have escaped to the town of Flushing, in the Netherlands. However, none of these sources can be considered truly authoritative. At no point in Weldon's book (which was written years after Overbury's murder and not published till 1650) does he disclose how he discovered the name of the apothecary's boy. It is also noteworthy that Weldon never says that Reeve administered a poisoned enema to Overbury. Instead he states that Reeve, 'having, under his master, made some of those desperate medicines', took fright and ran away when Overbury sickened, 'or else his master sent him out of the way'. According to Weldon it was Richard Weston and James Franklin who gave Overbury the *coup de grâce* by suffocating him with his bedclothes. Weldon adds the further detail that some time after Overbury's death, Reeve returned to London and himself set up as an apothecary, dying only shortly before Weldon finished his memoir.[122]

The only contemporaneous evidence that would seem to confirm the existence of the apothecary's boy comes from a deposition given in November 1615 by a man named Edward Rider. Rider was the landlord of Dr de Loubell, father of Paul de Loubell, the apothecary who made up prescriptions for Dr Mayerne. In the early autumn of 1615, just after the official investigation into Overbury's death had started, Rider went to de Loubell senior's house to collect the rent. Of his own accord de Loubell raised the subject of Overbury, protesting, 'They went about to prove him poisoned but ... he was not poisoned, but died of a consumption proceeding of melancholy by reason of his imprisonment.' De Loubell then went on to speak 'very hardly against those that went about to prove Sir Thomas to be poisoned, saying that the glister which they pretend was the cause of his death (for which his son was called into question) was prescribed unto him by Dr Mayerne and that his son had made it according to his directions, not once speaking of his [son's] man to have any hand in it'.

A week later Rider had another chance encounter with Dr de Loubell and his wife when they were out walking. This time, Rider started talking about Overbury, remarking, 'It is now too manifest that he was poisoned.' Rider then went on to say 'that it was done by an apothecary's boy [who lived] in Lime Street, near to Mr Garret's'. Rider later recounted that he had said this casually, 'as if I knew not that it was his son's boy, although I knew it was his son's boy that did the deed'. When Mrs de Loubell heard this she exclaimed in visible consternation, 'Oh, *mon mari*! ... That was William whom you sent into France.' Watching de Loubell carefully, Rider noticed that his teeth began to chatter at his wife's observation. In some agitation he then admitted to Rider that his son had once employed a young English lad who had left the apothecary's service after complaining that de Loubell was a hard master. De Loubell senior had subsequently supplied the boy with a letter of recommendation to be shown to a friend of his in Paris who might be prepared to take the boy on as an employee.[123]

This, one would have thought, would have given the authorities a most promising lead, both as to the identity and whereabouts of the missing apothecary's boy. Inexplicably, however, there appears to have been no attempt whatsoever to follow up the information volunteered by Rider. Paul de Loubell was examined on several occasions but there is no record that he was ever asked if he had employed a boy named William, or if the latter had at any time given Overbury a glister. Nor is there any indication that Dr de Loubell's friend in Paris was ever contacted to see if he knew what had become of the boy. Edward Rider's statement has been carefully preserved among the state papers, but no use was made of it at the time and he was not asked to testify at the murder trials. Far from throwing light on Overbury's death, his deposition merely serves as an additional source of puzzlement.

The apothecary's boy appears a still more insubstantial figure if one bears in mind that at no point did Richard Weston – who allegedly was 'standing by and assisting him whilst he put [the glister] up into [Overbury's] guts' – admit to any knowledge of him. It will be recalled that Weston said he had passed on to Sir Gervase Elwes all that Franklin had said about bribing an apothecary's boy to poison Overbury. Elwes had thereupon decreed that Weston must never permit anyone other than 'the former 'pothecary or his man' to give Overbury treatment. Weston insisted that these orders were meticulously followed, and that 'No other came at any time, or gave any glister to Sir Thomas Overbury.' Intriguingly, during a separate examination, Weston agreed that Overbury had been given an enema two or three days before he died, but he was emphatic that this was 'given him by Paul de Loubell'. If Sir John Holles is to be believed, Weston stuck to his story at his trial, 'absolutely denying that any apothecary meddled with Overbury, saving the 'pothecary appointed by Mr Mayerne, or that he had the glister given him, which Franklin propounded'.[124]

Obviously Weston might have been lying in the hope of escaping the gallows. On the other hand, if an apothecary's boy had really been admitted to the Tower to give Overbury an enema, Weston's logical course would have been to deny all knowledge that the glister was poisoned, rather than maintaining that the incident never occurred. It would arguably have been in his own interests to give his interrogators a detailed description of the youth, so that he could be located and accused of the murder. In fact, whenever the apothecary's boy was mentioned, Elwes showed utter bewilderment, and could never be brought to accept that such a person ever existed. It all tends to the conclusion that the apothecary's boy was a convenient phantom, designed to distract attention from the many weaknesses in the Crown's case.

*

According to Weston's indictment, the deadly enema was given to
Overbury on 14 September 1613. That evening Overbury was in fearful
pain. In his own account of Overbury's last hours Weston testified 'that
he came to him in the night ... for he heard him groan exceedingly'.
He said that, in hopes of making him more comfortable, he transferred
Sir Thomas to another bed, but this afforded no relief to the dying
man. At dawn the next day Overbury sent him out of the Tower to buy
some beer to slake his thirst. Weston was gone for only a quarter of an
hour but, when he returned, at seven o'clock in the morning of 15
September, he found that Overbury had died in his absence.[125]

When Sir Gervase Elwes was told what had happened he immediately
informed the Earl of Northampton. Rochester was also given the news,
though we do not know by whom. For reasons that are not altogether
clear Northampton sent someone on whom he could rely to view
Overbury's body in the Tower. Having had this man's report, he relayed
it to Rochester, dwelling on the distasteful details with unmistakable
relish. Mirthfully he told Rochester that, having made his inspection,
his emissary had commented that 'for his own soul's health, he would
not have forborn that spectacle of corruption'. Despite the fact that so
little time had elapsed, the body already smelt appallingly obnoxious,
and was decomposing abnormally quickly. Northampton then related
that twelve pustules had been visible on Overbury's stomach, 'every one
as broad as a threepence and raised above the belly the height of a small
button, of colour yellow, but not likely to have broken suddenly'. On
Overbury's back there was 'a long plaster, newly changed', but what
had struck the observer as particularly singular was the fact that the
back 'from the shoulders down, was all of the colour of dark tawny,
most strange and ugly to behold'. During the inspection it was proposed
that the plaster should be removed to show what was underneath, 'but
the stink was so intolerable' that no one present could bring themselves
to perform the task.[126]

A coroner's inquest was also held on Overbury's body, and a verdict
of death by natural causes returned. Although the Tower came under
the jurisdiction of the coroner of the City of London, the inquest was
conducted by the coroner of Middlesex. Later it was implied that Elwes
had called in this man on the understanding that he would be willing
to overlook evidence of foul play. It is perfectly plausible, however, that
this was a genuine procedural error on Elwes's part. The coroner
subsequently had his verdict certificated in the Exchequer, rather than
in the Court of King's Bench, as he should have done, but again there
is no reason to think that this was done in order to prevent the facts

coming to light. The original papers were lost but, when subsequently questioned, the coroner had no difficulty remembering what he had seen at the Tower. Though his report differs in some details from that given by Northampton's informant, in essentials it is remarkably similar.

The coroner recalled empanelling a jury comprising six warders from the Tower, and six other men. These persons viewed the body, which they found 'as bare as, in effect, it was consumed away, having nothing but skin and bone'. The coroner was perhaps less squeamish than those who had viewed the body before him, for he evidently removed the plaster affixed to the dead man's back. Beneath it, 'he found a black ulcer of the breadth of two fingers, and all black round about it, betwixt the two shoulderblades.' The only other things he thought worthy of comment were that 'in the brawn of the left arm he had an issue, kept open with a little pellet of gold ... and, on the belly of him, two or three blisters of the bigness of peas, and yellow as amber'.[127]

These formalities completed, the next step was to bury Overbury. Overbury's brother-in-law Sir John Lidcote asked that the body could be released so that the dead man's family could give him a decent funeral. Hearing of this, the Earl of Northampton sent the Lieutenant a carefully phrased letter. He reported that Viscount Rochester, 'desiring to do the last honour to his deceased friend', had urged that Lidcote's request be granted. 'Herein my Lord declares the constancy of his affection to the dead,' Northampton observed mellifluously, before delicately intimating that he thought it preferable that Overbury should be interred without any ceremony. Without directly forbidding it, Northampton queried whether there were any precedent for a man who had been kept close prisoner at the time of his death being buried outside the Tower. The Earl then raised a more practical consideration, for the reports regarding 'the unsweetness of the body' enabled him to affect concern that 'the keeping of him above ground must needs give more offence than it can do honour.'[128]

In case Sir Gervase failed to take the hint, Northampton followed this up with a more explicit letter. At noon on the day that Overbury died he instructed Elwes that, once Sir John Lidcote (together with three or four other friends of Overbury, if they made themselves available) had been shown the body, no time should wasted burying it in St Peter ad Vincula, the chapel attached to the Tower. 'If they have viewed, then bury it by and by; for it is time, considering the humours of that damned crew, that only desire means to move pity and raise scandals', Northampton commanded urgently. 'Let no man's instance move you to make stay in any case and bring me these letters when next I see you'. However, Elwes neglected to carry out this last injunction and Northampton evidently forgot to remind him.[129]

Apart from this Elwes punctiliously fulfilled all Northampton's instructions. When Lidcote came to the Tower Elwes told him that he was not authorised to release Overbury's body to his family. In protest, Lidcote refused to have anything to do with Overbury's burial. He refused even to provide a coffin for his late brother-in-law, forcing Elwes to find one himself. Overbury was placed in it loosely wrapped in a sheet for, even after this brief passage of time, the body smelt so appalling that no one was prepared to wind him in a shroud. The interment took place between three or four on the afternoon of the day Overbury died. Elwes later acknowledged that this might seem suspiciously quick, but pleaded that, such was the stench from the body, 'I kept it overlong, as we all felt'.[130]

After Overbury's death the rumour was spread that he had died of venereal disease, and that his body had putrefied at such a pace because it was 'leprosed with vice'. Despite this, from the start 'there ... went a murmur' that Overbury had been murdered, but this was mainly 'the speech of ... vulgar people', and appeared to have no chance of being taken seriously in more elevated quarters. With hindsight, however, the fact that Overbury's corpse deteriorated so rapidly was taken as a sure sign of poisoning, which traditionally was supposed to have this effect on its victims. The body was described as having 'looked like poison itself', but this may have been misleading. Some authorities believe that arsenic poisoning actually delays decomposition, though others, admittedly, dispute this. Fast decomposition is often associated with diseases which have caused changes in fluids and tissues prior to death, whereas these processes often have not taken place in victims of poisoning. It is true that, in Overbury's case, this might not have applied, for he in theory had been poisoned over a long period with numerous small doses, which could have caused a premature degeneration in his fluids and tissues.[131]

Even if there had been a full autopsy on Overbury it could not have produced conclusive proof that he had been poisoned, for it was not until the late eighteenth and early nineteenth centuries that chemical tests were invented capable of detecting the presence of the more common mineral poisons. In some ways this absence of forensic evidence enhanced the position of the Prosecution. During the Overbury murder trials it was contended that, since poisoning was a 'work of darkness', no one could expect definitive proofs to be produced regarding the types of poison used, or the methods of administering them. Unfortunately, at a distance of nearly four hundred years, the available data does not permit one to draw more precise conclusions.

In summarising the evidence as to whether or not Overbury was poisoned, one must acknowledge that much of it is unsatisfactory. Even if Overbury *was* sent poisoned tarts and jellies, one cannot be sure that he tasted them. The allegations that Rochester sent Overbury arsenic in a letter do not stand up well to scrutiny. Although Overbury *was* given an enema two or three days prior to his death, it is unlikely that this was poisoned, as it was administered by Paul de Loubell, whose honesty was not in question. The apothecary's boy who supposedly gave Overbury the glister of mercury sublimate appears to have been chimerical. As for the evidence of James Franklin, this should in fairness be discounted.

And yet it is undeniable that, at various times during his imprisonment, Overbury suffered symptoms which are consistent with poisoning. The symptoms of arsenic poisoning include vomiting, faintness, loss of weight, loss of appetite, diarrhoea and intense thirst. Skin eruptions are also common in victims but, though these can take the form of blisters, they typically consist of a thickening of the skin on areas such as the palms of the hands and soles of the feet. The yellow pustules observed on Overbury's stomach are unlikely to have been produced by this process. Pigmentation of the skin is another frequent feature, which may assume the form of dark brown or blackish patches. However, the description of the discolouration affecting Overbury's back suggests that this covered a much larger area than is normal in cases of poisoning. Probably it was caused simply by normal post mortem hypostasis, or the accumulation of blood in one area that develops once circulation has ceased. Overbury's symptoms could also have been caused by mercury poisoning. Among its indications are dehydration, vomiting, diarrhoea, emaciation and, sometimes, skin eruptions, all of which were experienced by Overbury. Lastly, cantharides poisoning gives rise to acute thirst, diarrhoea, nausea, hot skin and smelly urine, reminiscent of the 'strangely high ... water' of which Overbury complained during his illness.[132]

If Overbury's body was exhumed, it might be possible to establish whether he had in fact been administered certain poisons. Although at the trial of Richard Weston it was stated, quite falsely, that Overbury was 'very unreverently buried in a pit, digged in a very mean place', Sir Thomas's remains still lie in St Peter ad Vincula, the chapel attached to the Tower. Inorganic poisons, such as arsenic and mercury, do not break down with time and, moreover, when administered in large quantities, are stored in the bones. In theory, therefore, it might now be possible to detect traces of these substances in Overbury's skeleton. If so (and provided that one could exclude the possibility that the bones had been contaminated by arsenic in the soil), it would be a highly significant finding. However, it would obviously be controversial to disturb Overbury's remains, and it is highly unlikely that an exhumation will ever be authorised. Without forensic proof, we must still rely on deduction to determine whether or not Overbury was poisoned.

It can hardly be disputed that poison intended for Overbury was sent to the Tower on at least one occasion, when Richard Weston's son handed to his father the glass phial of liquid. It could be argued that, since Overbury subsequently died in a manner strongly suggestive of poisoning, it is too much to expect anyone to believe that his demise was occasioned by anything other than this. Nevertheless, the absence of firm evidence does mean that this should not be regarded as a foregone conclusion. There are other possibilities which merit consideration. One has already been mentioned, namely that Overbury died from septicaemia secondary to a gangrenous ulcer. Alternatively his death could have been iatrogenic – i.e., caused by medical treatment. Overbury's symptoms are also consistent with late onset diabetes which, in its uncontrolled form, is fatal. If he was suffering from this it would have resulted in weight loss, intense thirst and, very possibly, infections of the skin and urinary tract. The infected urine would not only smell very strongly, but might in itself result in septicaemia, with attendant fever and vomiting.

Another possibility is that Overbury was murdered but that the immediate cause of death was suffocation rather than poisoning. It will be recalled that in his book, Anthony Weldon alleged that Weston stifled Overbury with his bedclothes. There is some contemporary evidence which supports this theory, which will be examined later.

There is no record of the Countess of Essex's reaction when she learned of the death of the man she so detested, but it cannot be doubted that it afforded her the liveliest satisfaction. As for the Earl of Northampton, he did not hide the fact that he saw the news as a cause for celebration. Writing to Rochester shortly afterwards he declared joyously, 'God is gracious in cutting off ill instruments before the time wherein their mischiefs are to be wrought, and certainly, by somewhat I hear muttered, this factious crew had a purpose, in case he could by any means have been gotten out, to have made some strange use of him.'[133]

It is rather more difficult to evaluate Rochester's feelings. A servant of Frances's, called Mrs Horne, subsequently declared that Rochester was 'never more gladder of anything in this world when he heard that Overbury was dead', but we do not know what she saw to convince her of this. At the time it was other people's perception that Rochester was deeply upset by the loss of Sir Thomas. One courtier reported, 'Rochester takes it so heavily that he kept his chamber on the news thereof.' This was the impression that Rochester himself sought to convey when writing letters of condolence to Overbury's family. To Overbury's father he declared himself shattered at being deprived of a friend 'such ... as I will never have hereafter, nor expect to find amongst men'. Apologising for not having written sooner, he explained that he felt 'justly guilty' about Overbury's death, 'for I cannot deny that your son's love to me and to honest causes, got him malice from so many. And those enemies so purchased cast knots upon his fortunes and wrought him that disgrace with his master as hath brought forth this unfortunate effect'. In a separate letter to Overbury's brother Giles, Rochester reiterated his distress at the tragedy, and said that the only consolation he could offer was that he intended to take great trouble advancing the careers of Overbury's family, thus demonstrating to those that 'belonged to him, how high a value I set on himself'.[134]

At Rochester's trial the Attorney-General read out his letters to Overbury's parents and then commented, 'By this, you see my Lord's dissimulation'. The odium incurred by Rochester on this account is understandable for, in view of the manner in which he had connived at Overbury's imprisonment, his expressions of sorrow when Sir Thomas died do seem nothing less than rank hypocrisy. And yet it is possible that his regret at Overbury's passing was not entirely simulated. There are unmistakable indications that, towards the end of Overbury's life, Rochester was increasingly troubled by the prospect of detaining Overbury in the Tower for much longer. Not only did Elwes express concern on this score but, when Northampton wrote to the Lieutenant after Overbury had died, he stated that it had been Rochester's intention to see King James on his next visit to Theobalds, 'to have given his strongest strain for [Overbury's] delivery'.[135] Northampton may have been habitually disingenuous but one should not automatically assume he was lying on this occasion. Besides this, Rochester's calling in of Dr Mayerne at the end of August, and his wish that Overbury should be accorded a proper burial, do suggest that he retained some residual attachment to Overbury. Their relationship had been too intense to be severed without emotion, so it is conceivable that Rochester's expressions of regret to Nicholas Overbury were more candid than is usually imagined.

Apart from his family, few people mourned Sir Thomas Overbury. When informing an acquaintance of Overbury's death, the letter-writer John Chamberlain commented brusquely, 'He was a very unfortunate man, for nobody, almost, pities him and his very friends speak indifferently of him.'[136] At that point Overbury seemed fated to be swiftly forgotten; no one could have predicted that, within three years, he would visit on his enemies posthumous retribution.

CHAPTER FIVE

The verdict of the nullity commission meant that Lady Frances Howard – as she was now styled – was free to remarry, and few people doubted that Viscount Rochester would be her next husband. At court that autumn the prospective union formed 'the chief subject of discourse', the assumption being that the wedding would take place quietly at Audley End, 'without shew or publication till they think good'. But, though originally Frances's family had thought it advisable that the nuptials should be fairly discreet, in early November there was a change of plan. The King had been expected to go to the wedding without his wife, who had been so disapproving of the nullity proceedings. Suddenly, however, Queen Anne indicated that she too was willing to attend. To avoid inconveniencing her it was agreed that the wedding would take place at Whitehall during the Christmas holidays. This meant that the celebrations would be more elaborate and prolonged than had earlier been envisaged. Despite the fact that the Crown was so short of money that even the salaries of the King's guard and royal messengers were badly in arrears, James announced that he would bear the costs of the wedding himself.[1]

Considering it inappropriate that Frances, who formerly had been an earl's wife, should suffer any diminution in rank on remarrying, King James took steps to remedy the situation. On 4 November 1613 a solemn ceremony was held at which Viscount Rochester was invested with the title Earl of Somerset. Many people assumed that this would be the prelude to his being raised still higher in the peerage. John Chamberlain heard that the favourite would shortly be created Marquis of Orkney, 'that his mistress may be a better woman (if it may be) than she was before', as he sarcastically put it.[2] In fact these prophecies proved inaccurate.

'All the talk now is of masking and feasting,' John Chamberlain told a friend as the wedding date neared but, despite the Howards' seemingly buoyant demeanour, they were plagued by an underlying disquiet. They were nervous that, even at this late stage, there would be attempts to stop the marriage going ahead, and they took what precautions they could to prevent such a challenge being mounted. Eight days before the wedding Archbishop Abbot was surprised to receive a visit from Bishop Neile of Coventry and Lichfield. The latter requested the Archbishop to grant a special licence for Frances to marry the Earl of Somerset, thus obviating the need for the banns being read beforehand. When Abbot icily enquired why it was desirable to depart from the normal procedures, Neile reminded him of an incident that had occurred soon after the death of Prince Henry, when a lunatic had created a disturbance by stripping naked in the King's chapel. Neile voiced fears that, if the banns were read out, something equally unfortunate might happen, causing Abbot to reflect wryly that, given the circumstances, 'it was no mad body that they should need to stand in fear of', but people in full possession of their senses. The Archbishop was able to decline Neile's request on the grounds that the matter came within the jurisdiction of the Bishop of Bath and Wells, who was Dean of the King's chapel, and it was therefore incumbent on him to make a decision. In the event the Howards decided not to press the issue. The Sunday before the wedding, the banns were read out as usual and all worries proved groundless as 'there was nothing but fair weather'.[3]

However, a crisis of a different sort was only narrowly averted. As Keeper of the Game in Greenwich Park, Northampton enjoyed lifetime tenure of a lodge there, but the Queen coveted the property for herself. In the autumn of 1613 Northampton heard that Queen Anne had made known her intention 'to drive me out of Greenwich'. Initially he was clear that he would not budge for her, as he loved his house there and had spent a great deal of money improving both that and the park around it. Queen Anne, however, was not easily deterred, and was ready to use every weapon at her disposal. Having agreed to be present at Frances's wedding, she suddenly indicated that, after all, she would boycott the festivities unless her wishes with regard to Greenwich were gratified.[4]

Realising that it would be highly damaging if Anne so conspicuously absented herself, Northampton felt he had no alternative but to capitulate. In martyred tones he wrote to Somerset, leaving him in no doubt of the immensity of the sacrifice he was making. 'Since the Queen, inflamed with passion and rage, should, out of her hatred of me, disorder the main state of the proceedings as they stand now and distemper you, rather than this tempest should be raised to your prejudice, that are as dear to me as my own life, spare not, sweet Lord, to cast me overboard,' he begged. 'Believe me, sweet Lord, that in case she were but crossed in this injurious and exorbitant demand she would eschew the marriage. She would fall again to railing publicly as at this instant she doth still privately. She would with rage and fury put all forms out of frame.'[5]

In the end, however, Northampton did not have to renounce the house he loved so much. On 20 December 1613 he was confirmed in his office of Keeper. Although the Queen was cheated of her desire to possess his house at Greenwich, some way was found of placating her so that she did not carry out her threat to stay away from the wedding.

On 26 December 1613 Frances's wedding to the Earl of Somerset was celebrated in the Chapel Royal, Whitehall. Not only was this the same place that Frances had been married to the Earl of Essex, but the service was conducted by the Bishop of Bath and Wells who, as Dean of the Chapel, had also officiated on that earlier occasion. To John Chamberlain the congruities between this and the ceremony that had preceded it appeared singularly tasteless. 'All the difference was, that the King gave her last time, and now her father,' was his acerbic comment. The protagonists, however, gave no hint of embarrassment. Frances defiantly reaffirmed her maiden status by wearing her hair unbound in the manner of a virgin bride, 'pendant almost to her feet', as one commentator sourly put it. The Dean of Westminster preached the sermon, in which he not only paid tribute to the young couple, but heaped praise on the bride's family, particularly the Countess of Suffolk or 'the mother-vine (as he termed her)'.[6]

The wedding presents acquired by the couple were magnificent and costly, 'more in number and value than ever I think were given to any subject in this land' in the estimate of John Chamberlain. The King outdid everyone by bestowing jewels worth £12,000 on the new Countess, but other guests did not lag far behind in generosity. As befitted the architect of the match, the Earl of Northampton was the most munificent. He gave plate worth £1,500, plus a sword for the bridegroom in a 'most curiously wrought and enamelled' scabbard. The gold hilt of the sword alone was said to have cost £500. Other notable presents included a set of silver dishes from the Queen; 'a whole furniture or implements of a kitchen of silver' from Sir Arthur Ingram; 'six goodly candlesticks' from Sir Thomas Lake, valued at £700; and, from the Earl of Nottingham, a basin and ewer of gold which the King of Spain had earlier presented to him. When later assayed by London goldsmiths this

turned out to be made of impure metal but, even so, the total worth of
the wedding presents (excluding the King's contribution) came to
£12,000. This far exceeded the tally notched up at Frances's first
marriage, which at the time had seemed so sensational.[7]

The marriage was followed by lavish celebrations. In his verse
epithalamium, written in honour of the occasion, John Donne lyrically
described the merrymaking that took place in the Whitehall banqueting
house that night:

> The tables groan, as though this feast
> Would, as the flood, destroy all fowl and beast,
> And, were the doctrine new
> That the earth moved, this day would make it true;
> For every part to dance and revel goes.
> They tread the air, and fall not where they rose.[8]

At eleven o'clock, the audience took their seats for a masque that
Thomas Campion had written specially for the wedding. According to
John Chamberlain, the performance did not fulfil the high expectations
entertained of it. Afterwards he 'heard little or no commendation of the
masque . . . either for devise or dancing, only that it was rich and costly'.
Certainly the Agent of Savoy, who was present, found the show tedious
and unimpressive, even though 'the scenes and the expenses were
lavish'. Inigo Jones was abroad at the time and, in his absence, the
masque was designed by Constantine de Servi, a Florentine who lacked
Jones's genius. At one point six male masquers were lowered to the
stage standing on a cloud but, though beforehand it had been anticipated
that this would be 'a marvellous thing', the outcome was disappointing.
Gleeful that a national of a rival Italian state should have acquitted
himself so badly, the Agent of Savoy reported, 'When it came down,
one could see the ropes that supported it, and hear the pulleys, or rather
wheels, making the same noise as when they raise or lower the mast of
a ship.'[9]

Although the masque was clearly a failure in terms of spectacle and
entertainment, it was more successful as propaganda. It opened with
four squires dolefully explaining that twelve knights had wanted to
come from every corner of the globe to celebrate this wedding but, *en
route*, they had been abducted by four wicked fiends, named Error,
Rumour, Curiosity and Credulity. After an interlude of frenzied dancing
by these malign creatures, the three Destinies appeared, carrying a tree
of gold. Setting it before Queen Anne, they invited her to break off one
of its branches explaining that, in doing so, she would break the spell

by which the knights were held captive. When the Queen did as she was asked, the twelve knights materialised, as if by magic, and then performed a lengthy sequence of dances, expressive of their joy at that day's wedding. By involving Queen Anne in the drama, Campion sought to transform her – at least in the courtly perception – from a passive spectator into a benevolent patroness of the young couple. Whatever Anne's misgivings at being prevailed upon to make this endorsement, it was a gesture loaded with symbolic significance.[10]

When the masque came to an end the Queen was led out to dance by the Earl of Pembroke, who had been cast as one of the twelve knights in Campion's entertainment. It was a pairing that seemingly reiterated the message that even those who had been most vehemently opposed to the dissolution of the Essex marriage were now happy that Frances Howard and Robert Carr had been joined in matrimony. The other knights also took partners from among the audience, and the bride herself was one of those chosen to dance a galliard.[11]

By the time the dancing had finished it was past two o'clock in the morning. In his verse tribute hailing the new Earl and Countess of Somerset, John Donne speculated on the exhaustion felt by the bride when finally she found herself alone with her husband. For her the night's activities were by no means over for, as Donne observed, instead of snatching a few hours' sleep,

> Thy self must to him a new banquet grow
> And you must entertain
> And do all this day's dances o'er again.

Donne assumed that not only would Frances have been wearied by the events of a day replete with emotion and excitement but that she would also be overcome by bashfulness at the prospect of her sexual initiation. Nevertheless, he hoped she would succumb to her husband's advances with becoming wifely compliance:

> ... As friends look strange,
> By a new fashion, or apparel's change,
> Their souls though long acquainted they had been,
> These clothes, their bodies, never yet had seen;
> Therefore at first she modestly might start,
> But must forthwith surrender every part
> As freely, as each to each before, gave either eye or heart.[12]

Charming as Donne's lines are, it was perhaps not wholly apposite to depict the consummation of this marriage as an ordeal for an inexperienced woman. After all, Frances was not quite the *ingénue* that Donne imagined.

The King, at least, did not have to rely on poetic fancy to form an idea of how the wedding night had gone. Unable to contain his curiosity, the next morning he visited the newly-weds in bed. Extravagant as ever, he compensated for this intrusion by supplementing his already generous wedding gift with another jewel worth £3,000.[13]

Even now the marriage celebrations were far from over for, at court, the entire Christmas season was devoted to fêting the happy couple. The day after the wedding the King, Prince Charles, the bridegroom and others ran at the ring, a contest preceded by a dialogue between two Cupids, who each claimed credit for having fostered the love between bride and bridegroom. On 29 December Ben Jonson's *Irish Masque* was presented, featuring the adventures of a group of Irish rustics who had crossed to England to pay their respects to the newly-weds. John Chamberlain considered the actors' shambling gait and 'mimical imitation' of an Irish brogue to be insulting, deploring the fact that, at a time of heightened political instability in Ireland, Jonson had seen fit 'to exasperate that nation by making it ridiculous'. The King, in contrast, was so delighted by the entertainment that he requested it be repeated a few days later.[14]

On New Year's Day there was a tournament at which the rival teams were respectively decked out in the colours of the bride or bridegroom. Three days later the Lord Mayor of London was coerced into feasting the couple. When it had first been suggested to him that he should entertain them, the poor man had protested that his house was not big enough, only to be told that he could commandeer for the occasion the biggest hall in London. Merchant Taylors Hall was duly requisitioned and the City agreed to bear the expenses of this enforced hospitality. On the evening of 4 January there was a magnificent procession through the streets of London as the court made its way by torchlight towards the City. The male guests rode on horseback, 'well mounted and richly arrayed, making a goodly shew; the women all in coaches'. Frances was in the most luxurious vehicle of all, having just taken delivery of 'a goodly new rich coach'. Unfortunately her husband did not possess a set of horses fine enough to merit being harnessed to this new acquisition. An approach was made to Sir Ralph Winwood, a diplomat who nurtured ambitions of becoming Secretary, in the hope that he would consider lending the bride his magnificent team of thoroughbreds. Gallantly Sir Ralph responded 'that it was not for such a lady to use anything borrowed', begging the Earl of Somerset to accept the animals as an additional wedding gift. For a time Somerset demurred, protesting that, in view of the fact that Winwood had already presented him with a gold basin and ewer, this new offer was excessively generous. However, since Sir Ralph would not hear of a refusal, the Earl deferred to his wishes and took the horses 'in very good part'. Frances was accordingly transported in style to her destination, where a splendid banquet was followed by the presentation of Thomas Middleton's *Masque of Cupids*.[15]

On 5 January yet another masque – the *Masque of Flowers* – was put on at Gray's Inn in honour of the Somersets. The cost of £2,000 was borne by Sir Francis Bacon, as a token of his gratitude for having recently been appointed Attorney-General. Another prominent legal figure, Solicitor-General Sir Henry Yelverton, offered to defray Bacon's expenses with a contribution of £500, but Sir Francis would not hear of his largesse being diluted. He insisted that 'his obligations are such, as well to his Majesty, as to the Great Lord and to the whole house of Howard, as he can admit no partners'.[16]

As if four masques written for her benefit were not enough, other poets bestirred themselves to garland Frances and her husband with verse tributes. The majority of these were conventional panegyrics, eulogising the bride's beauty and virtue, and extolling her husband's fine qualities. A few, though, touched on more controversial matters. William Terracae wrote a forty-page verse analysis of the issues arising from the nullity case, entitled *A Plenarie Satisfaction*. While on the whole strongly sympathetic to Frances, he did acknowledge that her behaviour to Essex had deviated from the ideals of humility and subservience enjoined on wives at the time. However, having censured Frances for

> ... disobedience and unhearty shows
> Of duteous spousal love unto her Lord

he qualified this tentative criticism by stressing that these 'frailties' were 'adventitial, not of thy true essence', and could in no way eclipse her 'natural virtues'.[17]

In his poem, *Andromeda Liberata*, George Chapman took a less defensive stance. He rounded on Frances's detractors and berated them for questioning her purity, railing against the 'ungodly vulgars' who, in defiance of 'Kings and their peers', had spread scandal and salacious gossip. He urged that it was time for

> All vicious rumours, and seditious jars
> Bane splitting murmurs and detracting spells

to be consigned 'with curses, to the blackest hells'.[18]

Chapman chose to expound his theme in allegorical form, using the mythological story of Perseus and Andromeda to illustrate the trials endured by Frances. According to legend, Andromeda was a princess who seemed destined to fall prey to a ravening monster which was terrorising her father's kingdom. Her father had tied her up and left her to be devoured by the creature, having been told that only by making this expiatory offering could he spare his people further suffering. Just in time, Perseus appeared to free the princess and slay the monster. Unhappily, Chapman's treatment of the story was open to misinterpretation. When he bewailed the plight of Andromeda, 'bound to a barren rock', this was thought to be a snide reference to the Earl of Essex. The monster itself was taken to represent those bishops who had voted against the nullity. It was also unfortunate that, in the course of defending Frances, Chapman highlighted various matters which would have been best left to fade into oblivion. His indignant comment that:

> The monstrous world would take the monster's part
> So much the more and say some sorcerer's art
> Not his [Perseus's] pure valour, nor her innocence
> Prevailed in her deliverance

was perhaps particularly inopportune, in view of Frances's known connections with Mary Woods.

The Earl of Suffolk evidently took the view that the poem was a serviceable piece of propaganda, for he was one of four councillors who licensed the poem for printing. Following its publication, however, there was such a furore that Chapman felt impelled to issue a *Justification*, insisting that his poem was not meant to be offensive. Chapman was adamant that he had never entertained 'so far-fetched a thought in malice' that his allegory could be taken 'to the dishonour of any person now living', and lamented that his work had stirred up 'seas too extreme ... to be calmed so soon'. Interestingly, it would seem that the Earl of Somerset was annoyed with Chapman for having caused him embarrassment. Part of Chapman's *Justification* took the form of a verse dialogue between the poet himself and an imaginary interlocutor, who cautions him,

> Your Perseus is displeased and slighteth now
> Your work as idle and as servile you.

In his defence, the poet acknowledges that his work had lost him many friends, but expresses a hope that the Earl of Somerset was endowed with sufficient insight to understand the poem's true meaning and to reject the misconceptions surrounding it.[19]

At last the hectic whirl of celebrations ceased and the Earl and Countess of Somerset settled down to married life together. Having overcome the difficulties that had conspired to keep them apart, there now seemed no bar to their future happiness. Somerset was on the best of terms with his father-in-law, the friction between them having been long since replaced by an easy familiarity. In early 1614 Suffolk concluded a letter on political affairs to his son-in-law with an affectionate admonition to 'kiss Frank once more for my sake, with the hazarding of getting a curly-pated boy'.[20]

Contrary to Overbury's predictions, the King's attachment to his favourite had in no way been weakened by his marriage. Somerset's political power continued unabated: in February 1614 John Chamberlain reported, 'Nothing of any moment is done here but by his mediation.' Far from being jealous of Frances, James was so well disposed towards her that Arthur Wilson could later claim that she was 'the King's favourite, as well her husband'. In February 1614 the King honoured the young couple by spending the night at Chesterford Park, which Somerset had rented. Three months later James was strikingly solicitous when Frances suffered a brief illness: John Chamberlain reported that there was 'much care and respect had of her, both by her Lord and the King'.[21]

At this stage the only flaw in the young couple's early married rapture was that they were too often separated. When the King went on hunting expeditions, Frances had to remain behind with the majority of the court, while Somerset accompanied his master. During her husband's absences, Frances pined for him. The Earl of Northampton did his best to make things easier: when writing to Somerset on council business he was able to pass on fond messages from 'a bedfellow that more longs for you than is expressible'. 'Time seems long, but necessity is predominant,' Northampton consoled Somerset in one such letter, assuring him that while he was away, the 'pretty creature' he had married kept him 'ever in her eye and her part imaginative'. On another occasion he confided to 'witty Mercury' – one of his pet names for Somerset – that, while he derived 'no small comfort' from the knowledge that when he wrote to King James on policy matters, 'I have so worthy and so wise a friend to recommend the business ... yet I must confess I am not sorry when I hear your Lordship is removed from thence.'

This was because 'I know that Mercury is then removed to that pretty nymph' who had such infinite 'happiness in holding him'.[22]

Whenever possible Somerset slipped away from his master to be with Frances, but these breaks were often fleeting. Once, Frances persuaded Somerset to send the King a plea that she be permitted to enjoy his company for a while longer. Apparently confident that the King would take such a request from her in good spirit, Somerset wrote whimsically, 'Sir ... There is a stranger here of this enchanted place that offers me her intercession to get your Majesty's leave. I know not what may beget this confidence, unless she measure her strength the same in everyone as she finds it with me. And yet I may remember that there has passed divers tokens and letters betwixt you which are signs of some secret goodwill. This way, may I hope to get this favour, for which she puts her hand to this paper with no difference nor alteration but as if we were in one degree equally bound to call and account ourselves your Majesty's most obliged creatures and servants, R. Somerset, Fr. Somerset.'[23]

The continuing absence of a Secretary of State meant that much business relating to the conduct of foreign affairs was left in the hands of the Earl of Somerset. Unfortunately, because he had so much to deal with, some aspects of government were neglected, and the situation could not improve until a Secretary was appointed. The King still refused to consider employing Sir Henry Neville and the Earl of Suffolk took the view that the best alternative would be Sir Thomas Lake, who had extensive administrative experience. Suffolk may have assumed that, now that Somerset was his son-in-law, he would not oppose Lake's candidacy, but the favourite proved to have different ideas on the subject. He was determined that the post should go to his protégé Sir Ralph Winwood, who currently was serving as English agent to the States-General in Holland. It was not a popular choice: Winwood was a 'harsh and austere' man, who lacked affability, and who had antagonised 'the tender ears of this age' by being 'too plain a speaker'. Somerset, however, felt sure that he could depend upon his loyalty, for Sir Ralph had been a client of his since 1612, or even earlier. Despite Winwood's reputation for abrasiveness, he had made slavish professions of devotion to his patron. In an early letter to him he had promised, 'If it shall please your Lordship to call me nearer to [the King's service] ... the respectful care which I have of your honour, which I profess will stand deeply engaged ... will give me courage and constancy to continue in the course which truth, honour and honesty will tread before me.'[24]

Somerset believed it essential to instal a dependant of his own in this key position, thus confirming that political advancement could only be achieved through him. Furthermore, though he welcomed the prospect of being disencumbered of tedious routine work, he was anxious that a new Secretary should not encroach overmuch on his current power. It would be impossible to prevent Sir Thomas Lake assuming his full responsibility for the conduct of foreign affairs, but Somerset believed that it would be easier to control Winwood. It was little short of perverse of Somerset to think this for, far from being easily dominated, Winwood struck other men as dangerously opinionated. While fighting for his appointment, Somerset himself told Winwood, 'Your enemies have objected enough against you and, lastly, that you are too violent, which signifies in court language not malleable to their use.'[25] Having obtained what he wanted, Somerset would discover to his cost that Sir Ralph's reputation for stubbornness was by no means ill-founded and he paid a terrible penalty for having so foolishly underestimated him.

It was all the more odd that Somerset failed to foresee the friction that would develop between them, for their views on policy matters were scarcely convergent. Winwood was a militant Protestant who took great pride in having negotiated the terms of treaties binding England to Holland. He believed passionately that England's interests would best be served by a further commitment to the Dutch alliance, and was vehemently opposed to any form of rapprochement with Spain, the power which posed the greatest threat to Dutch independence. However, drawing closer to Spain was precisely the policy that Somerset would come to favour, thus placing a severe strain on his relationship with Winwood.

Somerset's insistence that Winwood be made Secretary so irritated his father-in-law that, for a time, it was 'like to have made a breach' between the two men. At length, however, the matter was settled in a manner acceptable to both parties. On 29 March 1614 Winwood took his oath as Secretary, while Sir Thomas Lake was accorded the con-solation prize of being made a Privy Councillor. One observer com-mented of the outcome, 'My Lord of Somerset hath so great a power of prevailing with the King as never any man had the like, otherwise you would have judged it almost impossible that Sir Ralph could have been brought into that place, considering that he was violently opposed by most of the Lords [of the Council].'[26]

It is possible that, in fighting so hard for Winwood's appointment, Somerset was motivated by something other than his desire to dem-onstrate his muscle in patronage matters. Later there were persistent

Double portrait engraving of the Earl and Countess of Somerset, by Renold Elstrack, probably produced at the time of their trials in May 1616.

Anne of Denmark. The Queen resented her husband's favourite and opposed the marriage between Robert Carr and Frances Howard.

Frances, Countess of Somerset. Portrait attributed to William Larkin.

King James I. James disliked Sir Thomas Overbury
and ordered his arrest in April 1613.

The lively portraict of the Lady Francis Countesse of Somerset

Frances, Countess of Somerset. This engraving by Simon van der Passe shows why she had the reputation of being one of the most beautiful ladies at court.

Sr THOMAS OVERBURY.

Sir Thomas Overbury, by Silvester Harding. Extremely unpopular in his lifetime, Overbury was mourned after his death as 'a man of absolute integrity'.

Frances's first husband, Robert Devereux, third Earl of Essex. His failure to consummate the marriage led the Earl of Northampton to dub him 'my good lord the gelding'.

Miniature of Robert Carr, Earl of Somerset, after the manner of Hilliard.

Effigy of the Earl of Northampton
on his tomb in the chapel of
Trinity Hospital, Greenwich. Had
Northampton not died in 1614,
he would almost certainly have
been tried for his part in the
death of Sir Thomas Overbury.

The Earl of Suffolk, the father
of Frances Howard, who 'lay
as on a grid iron, broiling' to
procure an annulment of his
daughter's marriage to Essex.

Dr Simon Forman, the astrologer and quack consulted by Frances and Mrs Turner.

Dr Theodore Turquet de Mayerne, the fashionable physician who attended Overbury in the Tower.

Bulfinch del.   Godfrey Sc.

DR. SIMON FORMAN,

ASTROLOGER.

Engraved from the Original Drawing
in the Collection of the Right Honble
LORD MOUNTSTUART.

Theo: de Mayerne Eques Auratus
Baro Albonæ in Aula Magnæ Regis Britanniæ
Archiatrorum Comes.   Anno Ætatis 82.
W. Elder sculp.

Vera Effigies Viri clariss EDOARDI COKE
Equitis aurati nuper Capitalis Justiciarij
ad Placita coram Rege tenenda assignati

The Chief Justice of the Court of King's Bench, Sir Edward Coke. Coke conducted the investigation into Overbury's death and also presided as judge at several of the resulting trials.

The picture of the vnfortunate gentleman, Sir Geruis Eluies Knight, late leiftenant of his Maiesties Tower of London.

The Lieutenant of the Tower, Sir Gervase Elwes, going to his execution flanked by two divines. The sympathetic heading reflects the widespread compassion for Elwes's fate.

MRS ANNE TURNER,
Executed Nov? 15th 1615, for the Murder of Sir Tho? Overbury.
From a very rare Print.

Woodcut of the penitent Mrs Anne Turner on her way to the gallows at Tyburn.

Portrait by William Larkin of George Villiers, the beautiful young man who replaced Somerset as the favourite of King James I.

Letter sent by Frances to Sir Gervase Elwes while Overbury was in the Tower. She gives Elwes instructions relating to a tart and jelly containing 'letters'. This may have been a codeword for poison. In the margin are scribbled comments by Sir Edward Coke. At the foot of the page is the confession supposedly made by Frances when examined by Coke on 8 January 1616. She subsequently retracted part of this statement.

rumours that financial considerations were involved. Winwood, of course, had presented Somerset with his fine team of horses, and this gesture clearly did not fail to commend him to the favourite. However, Bishop Godfrey Goodman heard that further sums of money changed hands in connection with Winwood's appointment. He claimed that 'Somerset was well paid for Winwood's office by the Hollanders', who wished for someone sympathetic to their interests to be placed in power. In his memoirs Simonds d'Ewes retailed a different story. According to him, when Winwood later turned against the Earl of Somerset, the latter accused him of ingratitude. To this Sir Ralph retorted 'that for his Secretary's place he might thank seven thousand pounds ... which he gave him'.[27] There is no way of knowing whether or not these stories are apocryphal. One thing, however, is certain: Winwood later became a key agent in Somerset's downfall so, if there were any truth in the assertions that the Earl arranged his promotion in return for monetary gain, he could not have made a worse bargain.

The coldness that had arisen between Suffolk and Somerset over the choice of Secretary did not last long and the pair were soon as cordial as ever. The two men's liking for each other was reinforced by the fact that they worked together well, enjoying a shared political outlook. What was ironic, however, was that the Earl of Northampton, who had orchestrated their alliance, now found himself being elbowed aside by them. Although as a political novice Somerset had been happy to submit to Northampton's tutelage, he now found it easier to bypass the elder statesman and deal directly with his father-in-law. Suffolk was by nature expansive and relaxed, whereas his uncle Northampton's approach was more cautious and fussy, a tendency that of late had irritated Somerset. Furthermore, by the spring of 1614, Northampton was far from well, and this made it easier for his nephew and Somerset to exclude him from their confidence. In late February the Council convened at Northampton's house, but thereafter he ceased to attend its meetings. It was given out that this was on account of his frail health, but at least one court onlooker formed the impression that the decline in his political influence had left Northampton 'more sick in mind than body'.[28]

Certainly Northampton was painfully conscious that his relations with Somerset were no longer what they had been. In the past Northampton had thought it a trifling matter if, at his request, Somerset had persuaded the King to confer a knighthood on some man. Now he was pathetically grateful when Somerset did this for him, writing humbly that, although 'the matter itself be not great, yet I confess that I should have received a great wound upon the quailing'. Cringingly he added, 'I am not ignorant what strange conceits and fantasies have crept of late into vulgar conceits concerning us and would have been sorry that such a demonstration raised new ground for rumour.'[29]

The fact that Northampton's opinions no longer counted for much was cruelly illustrated by the way that Parliament was summoned in the spring of 1614. Northampton took the view that the session would be disastrous for the King unless the Council carefully prepared for it beforehand, but Somerset and Suffolk were much more sanguine about how things would turn out. They believed that, provided the Crown sought to address minor grievances by putting forward a legislative programme which would be both 'moderate to the King and yet attractive to' the House of Commons, this would provide sufficient 'inducements to get the good we look for'.[30]

Parliament assembled on 6 April 1614. At once Northampton's forebodings were proved correct, for the House of Commons was furious at being asked to grant the Crown substantial funds. Instead of proceeding with the subsidy bill, they began to debate 'impositions' – the term for duties imposed on merchandise without parliamentary sanction. Such disrespectful things were uttered in the course of this debate that on 3 June the King warned the House that he was contemplating dismissing them. Undeterred, various members went on to make 'seditious speeches', which 'neither spared King nor Queen'. The worst offender was John Hoskins, who stated that the only way of avoiding a massacre comparable to the Sicilian Vespers was for James to send his Scots subjects back to Scotland. At this the King lost patience. He dissolved Parliament on 7 June, having apparently been warned that, unless he acted quickly, the Commons would commit still greater excesses and 'would rip up his life and the life of his greatest favourites'.[31]

Later, suspicions developed that Hoskins had been incited to make his inflammatory speech in order to provoke the King into dismissing Parliament. Sir Charles Cornwallis was arrested in connection with the matter, but it was widely believed that the Earl of Northampton was the man who was really responsible. When questioned, Cornwallis denied this, and it remains disputable as to whether he was telling the truth or not. It has also been hinted that Somerset had encouraged Hoskins's conduct, but the evidence linking him to the intrigue is still more tenuous. If Northampton *did* deliberately sabotage the Parliament in 1614, his reasoning may have been that, if money was not forthcoming from that quarter, King James would have no alternative but to betroth his son to a Spanish infanta, who would bring with her an enormous dowry. We do at least know that, in early June, King James consulted Northampton, complaining that the House of Commons was out of control. Northampton appears to have urged him to dissolve Parliament immediately. Soon afterwards Northampton informed the Spanish ambassador of this discussion, satisfying the ambassador that, as ever, the advice he had given had been 'in keeping with the good of Christianity and the advantage and service of Spain'. A week after Parliament's dismissal the Earl rode into London from Greenwich 'as it were in triumph', 'gallantly attended with no less than sixty gentlemen on horseback'.[32]

Northampton's triumph proved short-lived. For some time he had suffered from 'a wennish tumour' on his leg, which of late had become dangerously swollen. His doctors advised him to have it surgically removed, 'whereupon it grew so angry that it gangrened and made an end to him'. The surgeon who lanced the growth was somehow infected by the vile matter that poured from it, and himself became grievously ill. For two days after the operation Northampton lay in a bedchamber pervaded by the stink of corruption. Realising that death was inevitable, he was given extreme unction. Four months earlier he had been secretly received back into the Roman Catholic Church by a priest sent by the Spanish ambassador, who had heard his confession and administered the sacrament. Now that he had nothing to lose, Northampton did not trouble to conceal where his loyalties lay in religion. His will began with a statement that he died a true Catholic.[33]

One of Northampton's last acts was to write to the Earl of Somerset for, though he had been hurt by the way that Somerset had treated him in recent months, Northampton bore him no malice. In a very shaky hand he wrote, 'Dear Lord, My spirit spends and my strength decays. All that remains with my dying hand [is] to witness what my heart did vow when it gave itself to your Lordship as to the choice friend whom I did love for his virtue, not court for his fortune.'[34]

We do not know what Somerset's feelings were on reading this letter. Undoubtedly Frances had been close to her great-uncle so when he died, on 15 June 1614, his death cannot have failed to sadden her. There is every reason to think that Somerset, too, had been fond of the old man but, from a business point of view, he may well have found it something of a relief that his former mentor would no longer be there to nag him. Somerset now looked on himself as an experienced man of affairs and he had begun to find it a trifle oppressive to have Northampton constantly hovering over him. He was wrong, however, to think that he could manage without Northampton's expert guidance. In the coming months Northampton's wiliness and intuition, his skill at identifying and disarming enemies, and his experience at overcoming crises, would all have proved invaluable. The fact that Northampton was no longer on hand to help Somerset was one reason why the latter was soon floundering.

Even prior to Northampton's death there had been speculation that the King intended to appoint the Earl of Suffolk Lord Treasurer. This was despite the fact that Northampton was known to covet that position above all others, and to be deeply wounded at the prospect of being passed over. Now that Northampton was beyond minding about such matters, the King saw no reason to delay further. On 10 July 1614 he announced that Suffolk would be the new Lord Treasurer and that the Earl of Somerset would replace him as Lord Chamberlain. When he presented the two noblemen with the white staves which were the emblems of office, the King made a short speech, speaking of both of them with the warmest approbation. Contrasting Suffolk favourably with his late predecessor Lord Salisbury, who had been so witty and plausible and yet could never solve the Crown's financial problems, the King declared that, this time, 'He had made choice of a plain honest gentleman who, if he committed a fault, had not rhetoric enough to excuse it.' Moving on to the chamberlainship he said fondly 'that, forasmuch as it was a place of great nearness to his person, he had therefore made choice of him thereto who of all men living he most cherished, my Lord of Somerset'. When Somerset knelt down to take his staff, the King addressed him as 'friend Somerset', 'with the most amiable condescension that might be' imagined.[35]

Having forged a successful alliance with the Howards while preserving intact the King's favour, Somerset appeared invincible. As Sir Roger Wilbraham, a former Master of Requests to Queen Elizabeth, put it, this was the time 'when the house of Suffolk was at the highest pitch: himself Lord Treasurer, his son-in-law the Earl of Somerset Lord High Chamberlain and the most potent favourite in my time: Lord Knollys, another son-in-law, Treasurer of the Household ... The Lord Walden, his eldest son, married to the heir to the Earl of Dunbar', as well as being Captain of the Gentlemen Pensioners. In other circumstances it might have been undesirable for Suffolk to give up the post of Lord Chamberlain. As Lord Treasurer he would see less of the King, and his switch of office entailed a 'remove from the King's privacy to a place of much distraction and cumber'. However, by 'leaving a friend in his room', it was thought he had effectively protected himself, for Somerset should have been able to ensure that Suffolk did not 'take cold at his back, which is a dangerous thing in a court'. The King himself later pointed out to Somerset that, by virtue of their occupancy of these two key positions, which in many respects perfectly complemented each other, he and Suffolk enjoyed extraordinary power. 'Do not all court graces and place come through your office as Chamberlain and rewards through your father-in-law that is Treasurer?' he asked Somerset. 'Do not ye two, as it were, hedge in all the court with a manner of necessity to depend upon you?'[36]

And yet Somerset was more vulnerable than appearances suggested. For one thing, he was a man with many enemies. Some people had assumed that Somerset's integration into the Howard family presaged an end to the bitter divisions which had split the court until then. 'Here is a general reconcilement between my Lord of Howard and my Lords of Pembroke, Southampton etc. in this conjuncture,' one optimistic soul had written at the time of Somerset's wedding to Frances.[37] In reality, however, the factions had merely regrouped under different leaders.

The Earl of Pembroke was chief among those who resented Somerset's and the Howards' pre-eminence. His anger stemmed from the fact that he had expected to replace Suffolk as Lord Chamberlain and, though he was told that he could count on being promoted when the next great office of state fell vacant, this had failed to pacify him. Apart from the Earl of Montgomery, who also considered his brother had been badly treated, Pembroke enjoyed the support of Archbishop Abbot, who still felt aggrieved about having been out-manoeuvred during the divorce case. Besides this, he regarded Somerset as unsound about religion. Whereas Abbot's hatred of popery was as virulent as ever, the Spanish ambassador was delighted to hear that Somerset was 'not ... ill inclined towards the Catholic religion, nor does he wish to persecute the Catholics'. The tensions generated by this issue were illustrated by a clash between the two men which occurred in May 1615. In Council the Archbishop begged the King to execute some priests, 'saying his safety required it', but, after discussion, it was agreed that the priests should merely be confined in Wisbech Castle. Somerset later assured the Spanish ambassador that he had given orders that they should be well treated. In the eyes of Archbishop Abbot, Somerset now represented 'the height of evil', and he was ready to countenance anything that might dislodge him from power.[38]

Other influential figures at court nurtured grievances against the Earl of Suffolk and, in view of Somerset's close ties with his father-in-law, their enmity automatically extended to him. Lord Fenton had hoped to obtain a valuable concession relating to wool exports and, when this failed to go through, he blamed the Lord Treasurer. Sir Thomas Lake had swallowed his disappointment at not being made Secretary because he had understood that he would shortly be created Chancellor of the Exchequer. He therefore regarded himself as monstrously ill-used when, in the autumn of 1614, the post went to another man. Suffolk's nephew, the Earl of Arundel, was annoyed that he had not been the sole beneficiary of the Earl of Northampton's will, for the late Earl had bequeathed a substantial part of his estate to Suffolk and his male heirs. This compounded Arundel's festering resentment of the way that, earlier in the reign, Suffolk had cheated him out of much of his patrimony.[39]

Somerset had also managed to turn Secretary Winwood into an enemy, no mean achievement considering the way he had furthered Sir Ralph's career. The trouble arose because Somerset refused to delegate to Winwood, preventing him from playing any part in the conduct of foreign policy. Whereas it was customary for the Secretary to receive letters from diplomats stationed abroad, and then to pass them on to the King, Somerset insisted that all correspondence must pass through his hands, bypassing Winwood altogether. In July 1614 it was reported that Somerset was continuing 'to receive all the packets, to order the despatches and, in a manner, disburthens the Secretary of the whole care of foreign affairs'. When Winwood suggested to Somerset that he should enter into a correspondence with William Trumbull, the English agent in Brussels, he was told condescendingly, 'He should not need to trouble himself with the care thereof, for [Somerset] would do whatsoever was requisite.'[40]

Having imagined that he had gained a great prize in the Secretaryship, Winwood now found that he was little better than a political eunuch. His situation was indeed peculiarly humiliating: Sir Thomas Edmondes reported, 'The world thinketh that he hath no cause to take any comfort in his new preferment, in respect that the authority thereof is so much abridged.' The office to which he had aspired for so long had turned out to be 'rather an indignity than a dignity' and Winwood's first reaction on learning the conditions attached to his employment was to suggest he would be better off if he resumed his post in the Low Countries. Later he thought better of this and pretended to subordinates that he did not really mind being denied responsibility. When he wrote to Trumbull, confirming that letters should be addressed to Somerset, he maintained that he had no objections. 'I stand not upon ceremony,' he declared, unconvincingly, 'I aim at nothing but the good of H.M.'s service and the prosperity of his crowns ... You must be content, as we all are, to accommodate yourself to the condition of the times.' Inwardly, however, he was seething, and determined not to let the matter rest. Bit by bit he managed to claw back some of the power that Somerset had appropriated for himself. By late 1614 several ambassadors had started addressing their despatches to him. The following June John Chamberlain warned his friend Dudley Carleton (who was English ambassador to Venice) that he risked antagonising Winwood if he persisted in writing to Somerset rather than the Secretary, as other diplomats had long since discontinued the practice.[41] However, though by patience and resolve Winwood had succeeded in carving out a niche for himself, he was angered that he had had to work so hard to attain even a fraction of the influence that was his rightfully. The upshot was that he considered that, because of Somerset's scandalous treatment of him, all his obligations to the favourite were negated.

Somerset had also neglected lesser men at court who had attached themselves to him in the hope of advancement. The trouble was, supervision of a patronage network was time-consuming and required attention to detail and Somerset was too lazy to devote sufficient effort to the task. In the past, of course, Overbury had often handled such matters for him but now his expertise was no longer available. Northampton, too, had watched Somerset to ensure that he did not neglect his obligations. In early 1614, for example, he had gently chided Somerset for having forgotten about an undertaking to secure a client of his a favour from the King, which now looked set to be awarded to another individual. Northampton wrote carefully, 'For my part I know neither of the competitors but, finding that the world expected grace to one of them from you, which is a kind of engagement, and that the matter in your absence is laid in sleep, I presume to tell your Lordship that it stands you somewhat upon to stir in it again.'[42] With Northampton gone, there was no one on hand to issue Somerset with such timely reminders.

In a letter of advice written to a subsequent favourite of King James, Francis Bacon set out guidelines about how to handle patronage matters, stressing that this was of fundamental importance. Bacon counselled the favourite to devote an hour or two every day to sorting petitions and also to set aside a daily time to receive suitors. Sir Francis was emphatic that, if there was little chance of a petition being granted, it was best to make this clear without delay. 'Believe it Sir,' he told his pupil. 'Next to the obtaining of the suit, a speedy and gentle denial (when the case will not bear it) is the most acceptable to suitors. They will gain by their despatch, whereas else they shall spend their time and money in attending; and you will gain in the ease you will find in being rid of their importunity.'[43] Somerset lamentably failed to observe these precepts. Not only could he be unforgivably dilatory with his clients, but often he also held out hopes to them which failed to materialise.

A case in point was that of William Trumbull, who was serving as English agent in Brussels. Somerset promised to obtain for him a post as Clerk of the Council but in August 1613 another man was sworn in to the position. Somerset's secretary protested to his master that, in view of the assurances he had received, the news would 'somewhat astonish' Trumbull. To this Somerset blustered that the announcement was not really such a setback for Trumbull. He claimed that the new incumbent would not occupy the post for long and that, in due course, Trumbull would become Clerk of the Council. Trumbull must therefore have been shaken to the core when, a month later, he received a letter from Somerset rebuking him for being so demanding. 'It is fit you consider the many that have their hopes and pretences, very justly, for H.M.'s favour and ... how many there be whose hopes go unprovided,' Somerset pontificated. 'Men of your cast especially can but hope – unless your merits be extraordinary – to have the ordinary course kept with you, which is to be remembered in those places which are of a size and capacity with the person ... This is to show you how your desires must not come so stuffed.'[44]

John Donne was another man who fared poorly after putting his trust in Somerset. In the spring of 1613 Donne had reluctantly decided that his only hope of having a successful career lay in entering the Church. At that point, however, he was presented to the favourite, who asked him to do clerical work for him and promised to obtain Donne an administrative position. Unfortunately nothing of the sort happened. In the summer of 1614 Donne wrote to Somerset, begging him to redress the situation. He pointed out that more than a year had gone by since Somerset had dissuaded him from being ordained, but he remained without secular employment. Somerset continued to insist that he would not have to wait long but, in January 1615, Donne finally lost patience. He took holy orders and at once was appointed Chaplain-in-Ordinary to the King.[45]

As a result of such episodes Somerset began to acquire the reputation of a man who consistently failed to perform as much as was expected of him. In April 1615 John Chamberlain told Dudley Carleton, 'Truly, I doubt that you have leaned too long upon a broken staff that cannot or will not or (I am sure) hitherto hath not given support to any that relied upon it and, in respect thereof, neglected those that in all occasions would have stood more firmly to you.'[46] So long as the King's attachment to Somerset remained unshakeable, this did not really matter but, when a rival appeared on the scene, Somerset was deeply vulnerable.

It is possible that Frances also bore a share of the blame for the fact that her husband came to be perceived as someone who promised much and delivered little. There are indications that suitors sometimes made applications to Frances in the hope that she would encourage Somerset to help them. On these occasions, it seems, Frances was far too free with assurances of what she would achieve for them, and it naturally caused acute disappointment when nothing came of her promises. For instance, Sir Thomas Edmondes had been one of the contenders for the post of Secretary of State, and Frances deluded him into thinking that she could secure the job for him. After Winwood's appointment Edmondes's brother wrote bitterly to a friend, 'Some ten days before the determination of the business, [Sir Thomas Edmondes] was made hopeful to the last hour by the young Countess of the preferment, which was only to draw him to the utmost.'[47]

The implications are that expectant suitors were beguiled into giving Frances money in the belief that they were making a sound investment. Even when their hopes proved groundless, they were not offered a refund. Sir Thomas Lake's anger at his failure to become Chancellor of the Exchequer may have been sharpened by having paid Frances a substantial sum on the understanding that this would guarantee that the post went to him. In March 1616 Sir John Holles sombrely reminded the Countess that it was scarcely surprising that Lake had turned against her and her husband, bearing in mind the '£2,000 you had of Sir Thomas Lake for a courtesy which was never performed'.[48]

Somerset compounded the sin of exerting himself too little for his supporters by being ever more acquisitive on his own behalf. Furthermore, in his eagerness to enrich himself, he became less discriminating than in the past as to how he made money. Since his marriage his outgoings had rocketed (in October 1614 John Chamberlain estimated that, during the previous twelve months, Somerset had spent 'above £90,000'), and possibly his father-in-law may have encouraged him to be more ruthless about maximising his assets. Whereas in the past Somerset had boasted that he would never be a party to the sale of titles, by late 1613 he saw nothing wrong in accepting £24,000 on the understanding that, on the death of Lord Darcy – who had no direct male heirs – his barony would be conferred on his son-in-law.[49]

Towards the end of his life the Earl of Northampton had become worried that Somerset was no longer exercising the same degree of judgement about such matters as he had earlier in his career. In early 1614 he wrote deploring the fact that Somerset had been granted permission to pursue people for monies owing on Crown lands which had been granted to their families generations earlier, and for which payment was still outstanding. Trenchantly Northampton told Somerset that the proposal would be 'a canker to the commonwealth and thought likely to gall three thousand people, heirs, executors and administrators of men dead long since'. He made it plain that he thought it wrong for individuals to be exploited in this way unless the Crown accrued the benefit, lamenting, 'These ways of sucking satisfaction by private persons out of subjects' fortunes hath been so dangerously scandalous in this state as I shall pray you from my heart that no man persuade your Lordship to dip your hand, that is spotless, into that pitch.'[50]

It is not clear if Northampton's firm words deterred Somerset from pursuing the matter further. The following year, however, the favourite became involved in a corrupt transaction with a syndicate of customs farmers. A group of London merchants was hoping to file a lawsuit against the farmers, who bribed Somerset to prevent the case from coming to court. A subsequent Lord Treasurer declared that this was 'the last and most hated act that ever [Somerset] did, his marriage and Overbury's death excepted'.[51]

The leading members of the coalition ranged against Somerset were, for the most part, a selfish and venal bunch, motivated primarily by greed and thwarted ambition. Nevertheless, the fact that Somerset no longer observed the same standards of conduct that he had imposed on himself earlier in the reign meant that they could imply that their opposition to him was highly principled, and stemmed largely from a desire to curb court corruption. As Somerset's loyal supporter Sir John Holles noted in disgust, the favourite's enemies 'accordingly to the manner of new brooms, promise a cleanly house'.[52]

On 3 August 1614, while staying at Apethorpe in Northamptonshire on his summer progress, King James encountered an exquisite young man from Leicestershire named George Villiers. Aged nearly twenty-two, Villiers had a face framed by chestnut curls and was endowed with singular charm and grace. His mother had given him an education designed to enhance his natural assets: unworried by his failure to master Latin, she had chosen 'rather to endue him with conversative qualities and ornaments of youth, as dancing, fencing and the like'. At the age of sixteen he had travelled to France, where he had acquired more courtly accomplishments, including a high level of equestrian skills. What initially commended him to the King, however, was his appearance, which was of godlike perfection. One observer declared him 'the handsomest bodied man in England', while another person 'saw everything in him full of delicacy and handsome features', singling out his hands and face as being 'especially effeminate and curious'. In addition he had an innate poise and distinctive bearing which were extraordinarily alluring. As one contemporary reminisced, 'From the nails of his fingers, nay, from the sole of his foot to the crown of his head, there was no blemish in him. And yet his carriage, and every stoop of his deportment, more than his excellent form, were the beauty of his beauty.'[53]

James was instantly attracted to this vision of beauty and resolved to see more of Villiers. On 2 September, less than a month after the King had made Villiers's acquaintance, the knowledgeable Lord Fenton reported that this new arrival at court 'begins to be in favour with his Majesty'.[54]

Somerset's enemies were quick to grasp the opportunity that had presented itself. A conclave was held by the Earl of Pembroke at Baynard's Castle, attended by the Earls of Montgomery, Hertford, Bedford and some others. Together these men determined to use Villiers to undermine Somerset. To ensure success they provided the impecunious young man with the wherewithal to make the most of his attractions. One of the anti-Somerset faction, Sir John Graham, borrowed £100 from Sir Arthur Ingram to clothe Villiers as becomingly as possible. 'Thus backed, our favourite needed not to borrow.' Whereas before, Villiers had possessed only one threadbare suit, he was now magnificently attired in the height of fashion. With youth on his side he cut a dazzling figure and, in aesthetic terms at least, he easily outshone the Earl of Somerset.[55]

James was so delighted with Villiers that in November he planned to make him a Groom of the Bedchamber. Somerset acted promptly to block the appointment. He protested to the King, insisting that the position should instead be given to William Carr, an illegitimate son of his brother's. Villiers had to make do with the lesser office of cupbearer, but this was far from being the setback that Somerset expected. For those familiar with the classics, Villiers's new job was not without symbolic significance: Jove's catamite Ganymede had been cupbearer to the Gods. On a more prosaic level, Villiers's duties brought him into much more frequent contact with the King, who found him a most beguiling companion. Because Villiers was required to serve the King his drink, 'he was naturally much in his presence, and so admitted to that conversation and discourse with which that prince always abounded at his meals'. Villiers knew instinctively how to keep his master amused and the King listened enraptured as the young man talked entertainingly about life at the French court, and other enthralling topics. That December John Chamberlain learned that the highlight of the Christmas festivities would be a masque costing £1,500. The King had promised that he would bear the costs of the production, 'the principal motive whereof is thought to be the gracing of young Villiers and to bring him on the stage'.[56]

If Somerset had been sensible he would have made way gracefully for Villiers, as Montgomery had done for him seven years earlier. Not only would the King have been grateful if the emergence of a new favourite could have been managed without any unpleasantness, but in some ways Somerset should have welcomed the freedom that such a change would bring him. Of late he had grown reluctant to share the King's bedchamber and James would not have minded so much about this if Somerset had been less critical of his interest in Villiers. Had James been left to order his life as he wished, Somerset would also have been able to spend more time with his wife and family, a prospect which Frances, at least, would have found delightful. Furthermore, it was highly unlikely that Somerset's influence would be seriously eroded by the rise of Villiers. As a Privy Councillor and Lord Chamberlain he was in a position of immense strength and, even if James's feelings for him became less ardent than in the past, there was every likelihood that the King would show him at least as much affection as he had to other discarded favourites. While it was possible that Somerset's power would not be so monolithic as before, it would never have been whittled away completely. Lord Fenton, for one, had no doubt that Villiers represented little threat to Somerset. He prophesied that the only outcome of James's liking for this young man would be rather 'to kindle a new fire than extinguish an old one'.[57]

Foolishly, however, Somerset reacted with fury to the rise of the interloper. He berated the King for disloyalty, claiming that his own position at court was becoming untenable. He alleged that the King was tacitly encouraging men who were plotting his downfall, accusing James of failing to object when Somerset's enemies told him that 'one man should not rule all'. Having identified Sir John Graham as one of Villiers's foremost backers, Somerset insisted that the King treat him with marked coldness. For the sake of peace James complied but, even then, Somerset did not cease to load him with bitter recriminations. To

James's distress his favourite repeatedly made painful scenes late at night, subjecting his master to 'furious assaults' which so upset the King that he would then be tormented by insomnia. What James found most unforgivable, however, was that he could detect hardly a trace of affection behind Somerset's angry diatribes. Instead of appealing to the King that he naturally found it painful to be supplanted by a younger man, he acted as though James had no right to exercise a preference in the matter. He implied that he would not permit the King to behave in this fashion, and that James would regret it if he sought to defy him.

Sometime in early 1615 James wrote a letter to Somerset, described by the nineteenth-century historian S. R. Gardiner as 'perhaps the strangest which was ever addressed to a subject by a sovereign'.[58] The King opened by rebutting Somerset's accusations that he was nourishing faction, stating firmly that he could not envisage trusting any man as much as he had trusted Somerset. He acknowledged that Somerset deserved to have such confidence reposed in him considering his unfailing discretion (or 'secrecy above all flesh', as James put it) and his concern to uphold the King's honour and profit. Recently, however, Somerset had become possessed by a 'strange frenzy' of 'passion, fury and insolent pride', which quite obscured his better qualities. James admitted that, in view of their past intimacy, Somerset was entitled to use 'an infinitely great liberty and freedom of speech unto me ... yet to invent a new art of railing upon me, nay, to borrow the tongue of the devil ... that cannot come within the compass of any liberty of friendship'.

James lamented that Somerset's 'fiery boutades', 'uttered at unseasonable hours', were interspersed 'with a continual dogged sullen behaviour towards me', which made him a less than pleasant companion. What the King found most objectionable, however, was that Somerset gave him the impression 'that ye mean not so much to hold me by love hereafter as by awe, and that ye have me so far in your reverence as that I dare not offend you or resist your appetites'. James warned that, though until now he had tolerated these 'mad fits' on the part of Somerset, the latter should not delude himself that he could continue to act this way with impunity.

The King stressed how much Somerset's behaviour pained him, affirming, 'Never grief since my birth seized so heavily upon me.' He added that, unless things improved, his health would be endangered, and this would have grave implications for the kingdom's stability. He explained that he felt obliged to confront Somerset because their angry exchanges late at night had been overheard by numerous royal attendants.

If it appeared that the King was prepared to endure such disrespectful treatment, his authority would inevitably be damaged. Somerset must therefore indicate by 'exterior signs' that he felt remorse for his behaviour. Above all, however, Somerset must dispel all suspicion that he believed it in his power to bully the King into conforming to his wishes. 'Never think to hold grip of me but out of my mere love, and not one hair by fear,' he cautioned Somerset. Grimly he warned the Earl that if he disregarded this injunction, 'all the violence of my love will in that instant be changed in[to] as violent a hatred'.

'God is my judge, my love hath been infinite towards you,' James avowed solemnly, saying that it was this alone that had enabled him to bear Somerset's provocations. 'Let me be met then with your entire heart, but softened with humility,' he urged reasonably. 'Let me never apprehend that ye disdain my person or undervalue my qualities (nor let it not appear that any part of your former affection is cooled towards me).' The King was adamant that, provided Somerset acted in a more seemly fashion, his pre-eminence at court was assured during James's lifetime. 'Hold me thus by the heart, ye may build upon my favour as upon a rock that shall never fail you, that shall never fail to give new demonstrations of my affections towards you,' the King promised.

Addressing Somerset's fears that he was about to be displaced by his youthful rival, James insisted these were groundless. He gave an undertaking that he would 'never suffer any to rise in any degree of my favour except they may acknowledge and thank you as a furtherer of it, and that I may be persuaded that they love and honour you for my sake'. James added that, in any case, he did not intend to permit any man to come within 'the twentieth degree of your favour'. This, however, was not just out of consideration for Somerset's feelings, for James acknowledged that he had been at fault in having exposed himself to the risk of being so abused by a subject. Sombrely he declared, 'Although your good and heartily humble behaviour may wash quite out of my heart your by past errors, yet shall I never pardon myself, but shall carry that cross to the grave with me, for raising a man so high as might make one to presume to pierce my ears with such speeches.'

James concluded this dignified but in many ways extraordinarily generous letter with a reminder that Somerset had a clear choice, and that it was up to him to shape his own destiny. 'It lies in your hand to make of me what you please,' he reiterated, 'either the best master and truest friend or, if you force me once to call you ingrate, which the God of Heaven forbid, no so great earthly plague can light upon you.'[59]

That Somerset failed to heed this explicit and yet far from harsh admonition is a testament to his stupidity. Instead of amending his conduct he continued to act as if he was the wronged party, pestering the King to give him further gestures of support, and bombarding him with 'desperate letters'. With insufferable arrogance he even told James he could no longer hold him in 'inward affection', while maintaining that he would remain the King's dutiful servant. In exasperation James wrote that he failed to understand how the two things could be reconciled, making it plain that his patience was almost exhausted.[60]

Meanwhile the cabal promoting Villiers had been far from idle. With incredible effrontery, they even persuaded the Queen to give them her backing although, understandably, she initially had been reluctant to do so. Much as she detested Somerset, she had been 'bitten with favourites both in England and Scotland' and at first could not muster any enthusiasm at the prospect of another young man engaging James's affections. When first approached by Villiers's aristocratic sponsors, she told them that she thought it unlikely that he would turn out to be a marked improvement on his predecessors. This prompted the intervention of the Archbishop of Canterbury for, odd though it may seem that the most senior churchman in England should wish to use his influence to procure the King a new male favourite, Abbot's hatred of Somerset made him ready to do so. 'Knowing that Queen Anne was graciously pleased to give me more credit than ordinary,' he urged the Queen to commend Villiers to her husband.

To begin with it seemed that Abbot would be unable to overcome Queen Anne's reservations. 'My Lord,' she told him scornfully, 'You and the rest of your friends know not what you do. I know your master better than you all ... If this young man be once brought in, the first persons that he will plague must be you that labour for him, yea, I shall have my part also. The King will teach him to despise and hardly entreat us all.' Undaunted, Abbot persisted, arguing that 'George was of a good nature, which the other was not' and that, even if Villiers's character degenerated once he was sure of the King's favour, it would be a long time before he became as odious as Somerset. In the face of these entreaties, and the representations of those other noblemen who were thrusting Villiers forward, Queen Anne relented, promising to do all she could to further Villiers's advancement.

Since James and Anne were said to be 'never in better terms and liking than at this time', her recruitment by the pro-Villiers faction was significant. Her chance to strike came on 23 April 1615, St George's Day, when the King came with his son to her bedchamber for a family gathering. The Queen had prearranged that Villiers should be waiting nearby and, when she judged the time correct, she summoned him to join the royal family. Taking a sword from Prince Charles, she knelt before the King and implored him to use the weapon to knight 'this noble gentleman, whose name was George, for the honour of St George, whose feast he now kept'. The King was taken by surprise (Bishop Godfrey Goodman claimed that, such was James's neurotic terror of assassination, he initially flinched on seeing the Queen wielding a naked blade), but he did not take long to recover. Delighted to be presented with a request that accorded so well with his own desires, the King not only knighted Villiers but announced that he would appoint him a Gentleman of the Bedchamber.[61]

Word of this reached Somerset, who had positioned himself outside the door of the Queen's bedchamber. Desperately he sent in a message begging the King to raise Villiers no higher than Groom of the Bedchamber. Others saw to it that his plea was unsuccessful: Abbot and Villiers's other supporters were also stationed close enough to encourage the Queen to 'perfect her work', and Villiers was duly sworn in as a Gentleman of the Bedchamber. Shortly afterwards he received further signs of royal favour when the King gave him the right to sell a barony to the highest bidder and conferred on him a pension of £1,000 a year.[62]

Utterly frantic at Villiers's rise, Somerset decided that the only way he could counter it was by achieving a diplomatic triumph. For some time the King had been considering betrothing his son Prince Charles to a Spanish infanta. From James's point of view, such a union was an attractive prospect primarily because the bride would bring with her an enormous dowry that would ease the Crown's financial difficulties. Unfortunately religious differences posed a problem, for the King of Spain would undoubtedly be wary of marrying his daughter to a Protestant. He would not even contemplate such a step unless James made various concessions, such as relaxing the persecution of his Catholic subjects. In the eyes of those Englishmen who viewed the Roman Church with fierce loathing, such a bargain would amount to a pact with antichrist, for they feared for the survival of their own religion unless the English Catholics continued to be severely subjugated. Nor were such worries entirely groundless: the Spanish ambassador to England, Don Diego de Sarmiento de Acuna (referred to henceforth as Sarmiento), prophesied that, within a few years of Prince Charles marrying a Spanish princess, the Catholics in England would outnumber Protestants.[63] Nevertheless, although King James recognised that an influential section of the governing class was violently opposed to a

Spanish marriage, the idea still appealed to him. Since early 1615 the English ambassador to Spain, Sir John Digby, had been instructed to make informal enquiries in Madrid to see on what terms the Infanta's hand might be offered. In the belief that the King would be eternally grateful to any man who brought the matter to a successful conclusion, Somerset sought to set himself up as the architect of the Spanish marriage by wresting control of these negotiations from Digby.

In mid-April 1615 Sarmiento received a visit from an antiquary named Sir Robert Cotton. Cotton's extensive collection of rare manuscripts and legal records gave him a scholarly insight into many aspects of government and Somerset frequently sought his advice on diverse subjects. Cotton also secretly harboured Catholic sympathies, and Somerset therefore selected him as an appropriate intermediary for his dealings with the Spaniards. Cotton told Sarmiento that Somerset and King James had sent him to say that James was very keen to proceed with the Spanish marriage, but that he feared that Sir John Digby had little enthusiasm for the project. When recording this discussion, Sarmiento quoted Cotton as saying, 'The King considered Digby was not a good negotiator because he was a great friend of the Archbishop of Canterbury and the Earl of Pembroke, who were of the Puritan faction.' Cotton said that this made it hard for the King to be as accommodating as he wished about alleviating the condition of the English Catholics, 'because it might be that the ambassador would discover it to these other people and would thereby cause commotions and rebellions in this kingdom'. Cotton claimed that, instead of communicating through Digby, the King would rely on Somerset to secure a satisfactory outcome. All that James needed was an assurance that the King of Spain would not make unreasonable demands of him, and then he would at once give Somerset a commission to finalise the details with Sarmiento.

Sarmiento was sceptical about much of this, for he found it hard to believe that James was truly so distrustful of Sir John Digby. He suspected that the person who was really anxious to exclude Digby from the negotiating process was Somerset. Sarmiento wrote home, 'Because Somerset is not a friend of Sir John Digby, he is trying to take the negotiation out of his hands, thinking that, merely by treating concerning it, Digby will gain influence, and much more if it is concluded by his means; and that he himself will obtain authority if it passes through his own hands, and that he will thereby preserve the favour of the King, of which he has suspicions.'[64]

Shortly after his first visit to Sarmiento, Sir Robert Cotton was arrested. Sarmiento heard that the King complained that Cotton had exceeded his instructions by expressing such a wholehearted commitment to the Spanish marriage. Somerset's enemies hoped that he would be blamed for Cotton's indiscretion, but the trouble soon passed over. When examined, Cotton maintained 'that the King himself gave him his instructions to speak as he did, as he believes ... but that it may be he misunderstood him'. His explanation was accepted and he was restored to liberty.[65]

Meanwhile, in Spain Digby was still engaged in negotiations. In May 1615 he sent home a list of the conditions which the Spanish would impose before agreeing to the marriage. When James first read these demands, they struck him as excessive. Among other things the Spaniards stated that all children resulting from the union must be baptised and educated as Catholics, that English Catholics should be free to attend mass in the Infanta's chapel, and that the penal laws against recusants should be suspended. In shock, James scribbled a series of negative comments on Digby's despatch but, shortly after this, Sir Robert Cotton again visited Sarmiento on Somerset's orders, giving him the impression that James had little objection to the terms set by the Spaniards. 'They tell me that the King has read them at different times in their presence without finding difficulty with them, with the exception of the education of the children specifically in the Catholic religion,' Sarmiento reported.[66]

It is hard to tell how truthful Cotton and Somerset were being about this. It may be that James really did fear that, if he left things in the hands of Sir John Digby, his son would lose the Infanta, and he therefore encouraged Somerset to take matters further. On the other hand, Somerset may have deliberately misrepresented James to the ambassador, hoping that, once the negotiations had acquired sufficient momentum, it would be easy to overcome James's doubts about the marriage. At any rate, even if Somerset had the King's authorisation for what he was doing, he was pursuing a high-risk strategy. It soon became known at court that he was an enthusiastic advocate of the Spanish marriage (even though the full extent of his involvement in the negotiations could only be guessed at) and this made men such as Pembroke, Abbot and Winwood hate him more obsessively than ever. Their campaign against Somerset began to assume the dimensions of a crusade, and they convinced themselves that both national security and religious considerations made it imperative that they crush him. Others felt likewise, with the result that, instead of being recognised for what they were – an ambitious clique intent on securing their own interests – Villiers's supporters began to be hailed as an 'aggregation of good patriots'.[67]

Villiers's installation as a Gentleman of the Bedchamber in the face of Somerset's protests advertised to all at court that the latter no longer monopolised the King's favour. In early May a follower of Somerset's named Sir John Holles noted, 'There is a new favourite springing who makes much noise and great expectation, that all the fortune followers in that place seem to be distracted.' After weighing up the position many courtiers concluded that Somerset was already a spent force, and that they would do better to ingratiate themselves with Villiers. Less than three weeks after Villiers's promotion Sir John Holles estimated that, in terms of supporters, 'the new man exceeds in number', although it still seemed to him that Somerset 'weighs more'. Holles was a man of principle who considered it unacceptable to detach himself from a court patron to whom he had earlier offered fealty. Nevertheless, at this stage he considered that he was not merely behaving correctly from an ethical point of view but also as regarded his own interests. He reasoned, 'It may be the King's affection [to Villiers] and others' malice to the other will bring forth something in his behalf, yet not in that proportion as he shall be able to raise a Chamberlain and a Treasurer ... out of the book of life.'[68]

By late spring the atmosphere at court had become so confrontational that even a traditional display of pageantry served as an occasion for the two factions to defy each other. The King had recently created Lords Knollys and Fenton Knights of the Garter. Because he was married to another of the Earl of Suffolk's daughters, Knollys was automatically ranged among Somerset's supporters, whereas Fenton was one of his foremost opponents. Prior to their initiation ceremony the two Knights were scheduled to process together on horseback from London to Windsor. Each was to be accompanied by mounted followers, assuring onlookers of an impressive spectacle. On this occasion, however, a spirit of undisguised rivalry dominated the proceedings, with great significance being attached to how much support each peer could muster. Joining the train of either Knollys or Fenton was looked on as a public declaration of support for their respective faction, and the cavalcade enabled onlookers to judge with some precision how loyalties were allocated. Accordingly both sides took immense pains to recruit an impressive retinue.

On the day of the procession Knollys and Fenton each managed to assemble over three hundred followers, with Knollys's men wearing black and white feathers in their caps, while Fenton's troupe sported plumes of grey and yellow. In the end it was not easy to decide which put on the better show, for there was numerical parity and both peers succeeded in marshalling behind them an equal proportion of noblemen and prominent court figures. The verdict of one observer was that 'Fenton's people were generally better apparelled, with many more chains of gold and better horses,' while Knollys's contingent were 'the better marshalled and ordered'. The King did not permit Sir George Villiers to ride in the procession but, as he stood at James's side watching the twin phalanxes of horsemen set out for Windsor, no one had any doubt as to which group Villiers supported. Relating all this to a friend, John Chamberlain commented apologetically, 'These particularities were not worth the repeating, but that the matter is come to that pass that every little thing is observed now they were grown as it were to siding and open opposition.'[69]

Although the Howards acquitted themselves well on this occasion, there could be no disguising that Somerset's standing at court was not what it had been. By the end of May even the optimistic Sir John Holles had to admit with regard to the two favourites, 'The new seems to grow daily and, from the old, a general defection'. Men who had been regarded as loyal dependants of Somerset were now switching allegiance. When accused of ingratitude they put the blame squarely on the Lord Chamberlain, robustly alleging that 'their well deservings have received neglects and injuries'.[70]

Somerset was already acutely aware that he was being undermined at court but, that summer, he began to be troubled by something far worse. In the words of Sir Gervase Elwes, by July 1615, 'It should seem there was lately some whispering that Sir Thomas Overbury's death would be called in question, which came to the ears of some whose conscience might accuse them.' How this came about is a mystery: later, the authorities sought to imply that a scandal, which had lain dormant for nearly two years, somehow spontaneously regenerated itself, but it may be that the process was more contrived. At any rate Somerset heard something which made him nervous. At this stage it may not necessarily have occurred to him that he could ever be suspected of murder. His fears may rather have centred around the possibility that his discreditable role in plotting Overbury's imprisonment would be brought to light and he wished to guard against this. In a bid to protect himself he re-established contact with Overbury's former servant, Lawrence Davies. Somerset's eagerness to seek out this man was in itself suspicious for, during the past two years, he had studiously ignored him. After

Overbury's death Davies had asked the Earl of Somerset for a job but – as Davies later complained – 'the Earl never listened to him, nor did he ever receive any kindness for his dead master's sake'. It was only in July 1615, 'not long before the progress' in Davies's recollection, that Somerset sent to him his servant Giles Rawlins and, 'pretending some special, private cause', asked Davies to hand over 'all such letters, copies of letters and other writings as had heretofore passed betwixt the Earl and Overbury' that were in his possession. For some reason Davies had hoarded a large collection of Overbury's correspondence. He surrendered the majority of these letters, 'to the number of thirty or thereabouts', but reserved two or three as a precaution.[71]

By this time Somerset was not the only person who felt disquieted by recent developments. Overbury's former jailer, Richard Weston, Mrs Anne Turner and – one may surmise – Frances had all become agitated by what was being said about the death of Overbury. In their anxiety they did various things which seemed only to confirm their guilt.

Immediately upon Overbury's death Richard Weston had quit his job at the Tower. As has been stated, a little later he had a brief interview with Somerset, but thereafter he did not see the Earl again. He did, however, have further dealings with both Mrs Turner and Frances. Whether or not Weston had actually administered poison to Overbury, he had led Frances and Mrs Turner to believe that he had done so and, in keeping with this, he sought payment for his services. Not long after the death of Sir Thomas Overbury, Weston 'demanded of Mrs Turner a reward according to promise, for that he had told [Mrs Turner and Frances] that he had given [Overbury] the poison'. To his dismay and astonishment Mrs Turner fobbed him off, declaring, 'My Lady hath no money.'

Not unnaturally Weston was not satisfied. When he was first engaged as Overbury's jailer, Frances had not only promised him money but had told him that, if he gave satisfaction, she would arrange for him to be made a pursuivant, a court office with an estimated income of £200 a year. Determined that she should at least be held to this, he accosted the Countess at her Whitehall lodgings. Boldly he 'desired to have the pursuivant's place according to the Countess's promise', but Frances remained infuriatingly evasive. She 'answered that she could not help him to it, but that Mrs Turner would give him somewhat'. In fact, according to Weston, it was a long time before he received any money, though it is impossible to say whether this was because Frances was genuinely short of cash, or because she had hoped to avoid paying him anything. At length, 'about a year after Sir Thomas Overbury's death', he was paid £100 'in gold, in twenty shilling pieces'. In the early summer of 1615 he was given an additional 'four score pounds in gold'. Weston subsequently deposed that 'All this he received by the hand of Mrs Turner ... delivered in secret, no person being present.'[72]

In the spring of 1615 Frances became pregnant. That summer she spent a lot of time at a house named Grays, near Henley, which Somerset had either borrowed or rented from his brother-in-law Lord Knollys. Mrs Turner was a permanent fixture, having moved in with the Somersets following their marriage. As the summer progressed, the two women became increasingly uneasy about gossip suggesting that Overbury had been murdered. In July Mrs Turner contacted Richard Weston, insisting that they meet as soon as possible. After one encounter at an inn at Hogsdon, on 24 July they had another conference in London, Mrs Turner having travelled up from Grays for the occasion. Together they discussed what Weston should say if he was questioned as to why he had been appointed Overbury's jailer. They also decided that Weston should try to find out whether suspicion had yet fallen on them and they agreed that the best way of doing this was to confer with Sir Gervase Elwes, who was still Lieutenant of the Tower.

The following day Weston saw Elwes at the Tower. We do not know what sort of reception he was given. Perhaps, as on other occasions, Elwes offered him an expensive wine called sack, generous treatment which was later cited as proof that Elwes approved of all that Weston had done while working for him. Unfortunately the only account we have of this meeting is Elwes's, and that lacks detail. He later declared that Weston came 'to sound me whether he could perceive that I had got any inkling of this ... foul fact or not and, if I had, whether he could perceive any desire to have it reaved into [sic] or not'. Sadly, Elwes gave no clue as to the reply he gave, or whether Weston was reassured or disturbed by it. When the interview had ended Weston saw Mrs Turner to tell her what he had learned, and she then returned to the country.[73]

Elwes himself was far from easy in his mind at this juncture. In court he would later reveal that, about this time, 'considering with myself, and doubting [i.e. fearing] that something had been done to Overbury', he decided to bring up the matter with his old friend Sir Thomas Monson. He told Monson that he thought that 'Sir Thomas Overbury had some ill measure in his death' and asked Monson if he could throw any light on the matter. Monson 'protested that he knew nothing of it', adding that he hoped his son 'might never prosper if I am any way guilty or acquainted with ye death of Overbury'. Since in the past Elwes had frequently chided Monson for being too indulgent to his child, the fact that Monson was ready to make such a solemn oath convinced him that he was not lying.[74]

It could be argued that, since Frances, Mrs Turner, Weston and Elwes were all in such a state about the growing suspicions that Overbury had been murdered, this in itself proves their involvement for, otherwise, they would have had no cause to worry. In the case of Frances and Mrs Turner, however, one must bear in mind that Weston may have deceived them by telling them that he had given poison to Overbury, leading them to believe, quite falsely, that it was this which killed Sir Thomas. As for Weston, even if he had not, in reality, murdered Overbury, the fact that at one time he had been willing to do so meant that he would find it difficult to exonerate himself if accused of murder. His anxiety to discover what was being said about Overbury's death, and to find out whether Elwes was planning to cause trouble, was therefore understandable.

Elwes's evidence prompts further reflections. He claimed that, when he discussed the matter with Sir Thomas Monson, he merely *feared* that Overbury had been murdered. Similarly, Elwes said that when Weston came to see him on 25 July it was because he wanted to find out whether Elwes 'had got any inkling of this foresaid foul act'. Both these statements suggest that, until that point, Weston had not told Elwes that Overbury had been given a deadly enema by a corrupt apothecary's boy for, obviously, if Elwes had been aware of this, he could hardly have doubted that Overbury had been murdered. And indeed, Elwes himself made precisely this point in the course of his trial. He urged, 'Weston came from Grays to sound me ... if I had any inkling of the business. If I knew it, if I had a hand in it, what need to be sounded?'[75]

Of course Weston could have revealed to Elwes during their July meeting how Overbury had died but, in that case, very little time elapsed between Elwes gaining a clear idea of what had happened to Overbury and his revealing it to the authorities. If that was so, at his trial he would surely have pointed out in his own defence that he had exposed the murder as soon as he was in a position to do so. In fact he never said this. The omission reinforces the suspicion that at no time did Weston tell Elwes that Overbury had been murdered in this way and that Sir Gervase was merely improvising when he put forward the theory that it was a poisonous enema which ultimately did for Overbury.

Somerset, meanwhile, was engaged in a struggle at court which in

retrospect convinced many people that he knew himself guilty of
Overbury's murder, and wished to evade the consequences. In the
summer of 1615 he asked the King to grant him a royal pardon that
would indemnify him for various crimes which, in the past, he may
unwittingly have committed. To modern eyes such behaviour is certainly
indicative of a guilty conscience, but it would be rash to assume
automatically that Somerset sought this pardon because he feared being
prosecuted for murder. Feeling that his enemies were closing in on him,
he may rather have believed himself vulnerable to accusations of financial
malpractice, and it was this against which he wished to protect himself.
Certainly the Venetian ambassador believed this to have been the case,
for he reported home that Somerset was 'said to have appropriated a
considerable quantity of the Crown jewels' and that it was 'to assure
himself against this and every other charge' that he asked for a pardon.
At his trial Somerset himself said something very similar, protesting,
'There were divers reckonings for money and jewels and the first pardon
was desired in no other respect.'[76]

Furthermore, it was by no means unheard of for prominent statesmen
to take precautions of this nature. In 1619 a manual printed for aspiring
courtiers went so far as to urge readers to adopt such measures.
Reflecting that 'the estate and condition of courtiers is very slippery and
uncertain' on account of being vulnerable to 'fraudulent accusations and
malicious detractions of wicked men', the anonymous author advocated
that the successful courtier should 'well and wisely shift for himself and
... covenant or compact with his prince that he will vouchsafe unto
him a general pardon'. During Somerset's trial, when his attempts to
secure a pardon were adduced as proof of his guilt, some of the peers
on the jury openly disputed this. 'My Lord Wentworth and others said
that such pardons were usual.'[77]

Somerset's first attempt to obtain a pardon ended in ignominious
failure. This was in no way the fault of the King for, when Somerset
begged him for a pardon, James at once had one drawn up and signed
it. However, when the document was submitted to the Lord Chancellor,
Lord Ellesmere, he refused to pass it under the Great Seal. Ellesmere
was a stern Protestant who disliked Somerset intensely, and he claimed
that it would be unconstitutional for him to authenticate the document.

The King remained supportive of Somerset. On 20 August he came
to a meeting of the Council where both Somerset and Ellesmere were
present. When the Council had finished dealing with all business on the
agenda Somerset rose and, as prearranged with the King, addressed
James. He declared 'that the malice of his enemies had forced him to

ask for a pardon', and he asked the King to command the Lord
Chancellor to explain why he did not think him entitled to one. In reply
James 'spoke at length in praise of Somerset . . . saying that he had done
very well in asking for a pardon, and that he had granted it to him with
great pleasure'. He insisted that Somerset had nothing to fear during
his lifetime for, as King, he would protect him from his enemies, but a
pardon would prevent Somerset being ruined once Prince Charles was
on the throne.

Addressing the Lord Chancellor, James declared that neither Ellesmere nor any other councillor could turn him against Somerset,
although – in an aside that Somerset would have done well to have
heeded – he qualified this by adding, 'Somerset alone could do it, if he
became truly unworthy' of the affection James had for him. The King
then commanded the Lord Chancellor to seal the pardon immediately,
but Ellesmere remained defiant. Throwing himself on his knees, he
begged James to reconsider, saying that the pardon was 'without a single
precedent' and that its clauses were so loosely worded that it would give
Somerset the freedom to embezzle all the King's property, should he
desire to do so. Ellesmere said that if he sealed this pardon he would
need a similar one for himself, freeing him from the consequences of
his action, and that, otherwise, he could not comply with the King's
order. 'With this, the King grew very angry, saying that he ordered him
to pass it, and that he was to pass it.' He then stalked out of the Council
Chamber and returned to his private apartments. However, when the
Queen was informed what had happened, she at once sought out her
husband. 'She and the enemies of Somerset were so busy with him and
perplexed him so' that James abandoned his demand that Ellesmere seal
the pardon.[78]

This was a major setback for Somerset but he refused to accept
defeat, doggedly resolving to pursue the matter further. He enlisted the
help of Sir Robert Cotton, who could draw on the resources of his
extensive library, and who often furnished Somerset with precedents
when 'things were to be done in the state which he doubted whether
they were lawful and expedient'. Since Ellesmere had alleged that
Somerset's pardon was the first of its kind, Cotton urged Somerset to
overcome that objection by copying the wording of pardons issued to
earlier statesmen, such as William Wykham, Bishop of Winchester and
Cardinal Wolsey. The new pardon that Cotton drafted went further
than the last one, featuring murder and accessory to murder among the
crimes against which Somerset was indemnified. Somerset then renewed
his efforts to make James sign it, considering this vital not merely

because of the immunity from prosecution it would confer on him, but also because it would enable him to recover the prestige he had lost when Ellesmere and the Queen thwarted him.

The text of this pardon does not survive. At Somerset's trial the Lord Chief Justice claimed that Somerset had sought to disguise its extensive nature by listing first the petty crimes which he could commit with impunity, and burying the more controversial items in the midst of dense legal verbiage. Perhaps this was unusual but, considering Sir Robert Cotton's scholarly and meticulous nature, it seems more likely that he accurately reproduced the text of earlier pardons. As things turned out, however, the matter remained academic, for Somerset had not managed to secure the King's signature for his pardon at the time he was arrested. His efforts to protect himself had only served to undermine him further. While Somerset was awaiting trial William Trumbull commented, 'The pardon sought to be obtained by the Earl of Somerset ... will (as I suppose) be a very strong evidence to prove him faulty.'[79]

At the end of July the King left London on his annual progress. Yet even while James was taking what was, in effect, his summer vacation, the tensions and rivalry that had been so evident in recent weeks showed no signs of subsiding. Sir John Holles warned Somerset that his enemies were as malevolent as ever, cautioning, 'This progress promiseth them a rich harvest, be it by crossing you or by furthering themselves.' As James moved across Hampshire and Wiltshire, people watched carefully to see whether he stayed more frequently with members of one or the other faction, for his acceptance of hospitality was taken as a crucial indicator of his feelings. The Howards were delighted when James consented to be entertained by Lord Salisbury at Cranborne, by Suffolk's eldest son Lord Walden at Lulworth and Bindon, and at Charlton Park by Sir Thomas Howard. For Somerset, however, the greatest triumph came when the King made Thomas Bilson, Bishop of Winchester, a member of the Privy Council. Bilson had been looked on as a Howard follower ever since the nullity hearings and, for some months, Somerset had been unsuccessfully begging the King to appoint him Lord Privy Seal. While Bilson's seat on the Council was less than what Somerset had originally sought for him, the appointment was hailed as a significant victory. Sir John Holles had no doubt that it would greatly enhance Somerset's standing. 'It is an unanswerable argument of your flourishing and well-managed greatness,' he exulted. 'At my coming into the country, everyone gave your cause for lost, and had found out a rising sun, in whose light they rejoiced ... so much had the omnipotent Chancellor possessed them in stopping the pardon ... with which his friends were full fraught ... Now that the wind is turned, their discourse is also turned.'[80]

In fact Bilson's appointment was scarcely the cause for rejoicing that Somerset imagined for another – and far more momentous – event had occurred simultaneously. Bilson's elevation to the Council took place at Farnham Castle, the episcopal palace of the See of Winchester. As George Villiers would remind King James, years later, it was at Farnham that, for the first time, 'the bed's head could not be found' between Villiers and his sovereign.[81]

It was towards the end of the progress, according to Anthony Weldon, that Somerset rejected a final attempt to bring about an accommodation between him and Villiers. Since we have the story only on Weldon's authority, it may well be invented, but it is not inherently implausible. Weldon claimed that James asked Sir Humphrey May, who was on good terms with both Somerset and Villiers, to prevail on Somerset to be less hostile towards his rival. May duly sought out Somerset and told him that Villiers was intending to make a respectful submission to him whereby, if Somerset was amenable, the younger man would declare himself his 'creature'. May urged Somerset to accept the overture, explaining that, if he did so, 'Your Lordship shall still stand a great man, though not the sole favourite.' When Somerset still appeared unwilling, May told him that the King had asked him to act as a mediator, but even this failed to make an impression. Half an hour later Villiers called on Somerset. He said courteously that, if Somerset would extend him his protection, he would regard himself as being permanently obligated to him. 'Your Lordship shall find me as faithful a servant unto you as ever did serve you,' Villiers promised, but Somerset reacted with venom to this polite undertaking. Harshly he retorted, 'I will none of your service and you shall none of my favour. I will, if I can, break your neck and of that be confident.'[82] It was mad, self-destructive behaviour on the part of Somerset. If he had been more reasonable, his position would have been virtually unassailable, but by acting in such a petulant and wilful fashion he inevitably alienated his sovereign.

It was while the King was on progress that Sir Ralph Winwood decided to probe Sir Gervase Elwes about the death of Sir Thomas Overbury. Exactly why he judged that this would be a rewarding exercise remains hazy. In his memoir of the period, William Sanderson claims that the missing apothecary's boy fled to Flushing after Overbury's murder and that, while in the Netherlands, he 'told the tale to Trumbull' who, in turn, passed this on to Winwood. Arthur Wilson echoes this story, adding the detail that the boy became ill while abroad and that he poured out a confession on his sickbed, which was then relayed to Winwood. Anthony Weldon differs slightly from the others, claiming that Winwood received the first intimation of Overbury's fate from the Countess of Shrewsbury, who was herself a prisoner in the Tower. According to this version, Elwes had become friendly with the Countess because he hoped that she would commend him to her sons-in-law, the Earls of Arundel and Pembroke. Sir Gervase was unwise enough to tell her that Overbury had been murdered, whereupon she informed Winwood. However, the apothecary's boy (whom, it will be recalled, Weldon identified as 'one Reeve') also plays a part in Weldon's story. He states that, while in exile, Reeve 'fell in company with Trumbull's servants at Brussels, to whom he revealed it [and] they to their master, who examining the boy, discovered the truth'. Weldon claimed that Trumbull then crossed to England to tell Winwood and the King of his discovery.[83]

None of these stories can be corroborated. The correspondence that Trumbull sent from the Netherlands contains no hint that he had uncovered the truth about Overbury's murder, but it may be that letters he sent on the subject were destroyed by the recipients. However, it is clear that, contrary to Weldon's assertions, Trumbull was out of the country when the murder investigation was initiated. On 21 August 1615 Winwood informed him that the King had granted him permission to return to England to attend to his private affairs, but Trumbull did not even set out from Brussels till late September, by which time the enquiry was in full progress.[84] Though Trumbull was delighted by Somerset's downfall, there is no proof that he instigated it. What it was that inspired Winwood to make his move remains a mystery. Perhaps he simply acted on instinct, and was amply rewarded for doing so.

Winwood did not confront Elwes directly about Overbury, but instead tackled him in a more oblique manner. He enlisted the Earl of Shrewsbury – another prominent opponent of Somerset – to inveigle Sir Gervase into volunteering incriminating information. Cunningly they exploited Elwes's vanity and ambition to render him more pliable. This emerges clearly from an account written by Sir Gervase that autumn (known as his 'apology') seeking to justify his actions prior to Overbury's murder, as well as his part in its exposure. Here Elwes related that in the late summer of 1615 the Earl of Shrewsbury (who was a long-standing acquaintance) told him that, 'out of a noble respect towards me continued from youth', he wished to recommend him as an able man to Secretary Winwood. Flattered at being sought out in this way, Elwes had no doubt that this represented an excellent opportunity. However, his complacency was shattered when Shrewsbury informed him that Winwood had declined to have anything to do with him, on the grounds that it was impossible 'to contract friendship with one upon whom did lie a sore suspicion of Overbury's death'. Elwes was naturally appalled to find that his reputation lay under such a shadow. In horror he began to wonder whether other members of the Council regarded him with suspicion, realising that, if this was the case, his career was effectively over. Worse still, it occurred to him that, before long, an official enquiry might be held into Overbury's death. If evidence of foul play emerged during this, he, as Lieutenant of the Tower, would be held accountable. He reasoned that the only way he could absolve himself was to give an account of what happened, presenting his own conduct in as favourable a light as possible.

Accordingly Elwes told Shrewsbury that 'I was unworthy [of] his Lordship's love, or any man's, such a blemish lying upon me, and that I would be ready, even in Mr Secretary's presence, to free [myself from] so foul a suspicion.' Shrewsbury said that Winwood would be very interested in hearing all that Elwes had to say on the matter, and that he would arrange a meeting. Soon afterwards Elwes presented himself at Shrewsbury's Whitehall chamber, where Winwood was waiting. As he later recorded it was there, in the presence of 'we three only, I made ye relation'. According to Simonds d'Ewes, Elwes revealed much more than Winwood had ever hoped, going 'even beyond his expectation'.[85]

Elwes noted that this took place the day after King James was entertained by Shrewsbury so, if it could be established when that happened, it would provide a date for the meeting. Afterwards Winwood and Shrewsbury waited for the right moment to inform King James of what Elwes had said to them. According to Lord Carew, the King was told while he was still on his summer progress, staying with the Earl of Southampton at Beaulieu. We know that James was at Beaulieu on 21 August, so it must have been around that time that the news was broken. James gave instructions that Elwes should 'freely set down in writing' all that he knew about the death of Sir Thomas Overbury. Elwes thereupon wrote a summary of what he had confided to Winwood and Shrewsbury. Two copies of this document exist, one dated 2 September 1615, and the other eight days later. The later date has generally been presumed to be the correct one but, in all probability, wrongly.[86]

Elwes opened by stating that he personally had nothing to fear from writing this declaration. Indeed it would seem that at this stage his main concern was that he would incur criticism for making disclosures damaging to the people who had advanced him, rather than for withholding information. With this in mind, he begged the King to ensure that his reputation as a man of honour did not suffer as a result of his revelations.

Having explained that he had employed Richard Weston at the request of Sir Thomas Monson, Elwes related how, shortly after he had started work at the Tower, he had deterred Weston from poisoning Overbury's supper. He said that, having done this, he had encouraged Weston to deceive 'them who had set him on work' by pretending that Overbury had suffered fits of 'extreme castings [i.e. vomitings] and other tokens'. Elwes then described how tarts and jellies purportedly sent from the Earl of Somerset to Overbury had been swapped with others, which Elwes deemed suspicious. Accordingly he had ensured that these items never reached Overbury and, as a result of these precautions, he had felt confident that his prisoner was in no further danger. Only when it was too late had he realised that Overbury's need for medical treatment had made him vulnerable to the machinations of his enemies. Elwes stressed that neither Dr Mayerne nor his apothecary, Paul de Loubell, had been involved in any wrongdoing. He explained that, after Overbury's murder, Weston had confessed to him that a servant of the apothecary had been bribed £20 to poison Overbury with a glister. 'Who gave it, who corrupted the servant, or what is become of him, I can give your Majesty no intelligence,' Elwes insisted, declaring that the only person whom Weston had named as 'a principal actor in this business' was Mrs Anne Turner.

'I have herein obeyed your Majesty's command, setting down the truth,' concluded Elwes, before nervously acknowledging that it was 'peradventure not the whole truth'. He nevertheless maintained that he had included 'whatsoever is fundamental', and said that he would be willing to give full answers to any further questions.[87] Elwes would soon find out that he had taken on more than he had bargained for, for Winwood and his colleagues had by no means finished with him. For the moment, however, his statement was perfectly adequate for their purposes, since the King now had no alternative but to order exhaustive enquiries into the death of Sir Thomas Overbury.

CHAPTER SIX

In his statement to the King Elwes had not mentioned either the Earl or Countess of Somerset. Nevertheless, from the start the King was aware that 'great persons' were believed to be implicated in Overbury's murder. Presumably Winwood had informed him that the Somersets were both suspects. To his credit James never doubted that the matter had to be further investigated. Critics of the King later claimed that he sanctioned this, not from a desire to see justice done, but because Somerset had been so obstructive about James's relationship with Villiers that the King welcomed an excuse to be rid of him. Simonds d'Ewes asserted that, having 'fixed his eyes upon the delicate personage and features of Mr George Villiers', the King 'was the more easily induced to suffer the Earl of Somerset to be removed from his court and presence to the Tower of London'. Anthony Weldon was positive that 'had Somerset complied with Villiers, Overbury's death had still lain raked up in his own ashes'. This, however, was mere conjecture. In fairness to the King it should be noted that he appeared genuinely appalled by the possibility that Overbury had been murdered, making it hard to believe that he would ever have been prepared to overlook a crime of such magnitude. At one point during the enquiry he wrote, 'We cannot satisfy our own conscience if any course should be left unattempted whereby the foulness of so heinous a fact may be laid open to the world.'[1] Such words convey a strong sense of his horror at what was unfolding. It is idle to speculate whether he would have acted differently if he had remained as devoted to Somerset as formerly. Perhaps the issue would simply not have arisen: one wonders if Winwood would have dared delve into Sir Thomas Overbury's death if Somerset's star had not already been waning.

James at once issued instructions about what should be done, urging that Richard Weston, Anne Turner and the apothecary and doctor who had tended Overbury should be questioned. The indications are that at this stage he still hoped that these enquiries would exonerate the Somersets. The Attorney-General Sir Francis Bacon later stated that James initially suspected that 'wicked persons of mean condition' might be deliberately telling lies in order to 'alienate his mind' from Somerset. Seeming confirmation of this is provided by the memorandum the King wrote after reading Elwes's story. There James noted that if, upon investigation, Elwes's allegations could not be substantiated, 'then there must be a foul conspiracy ... for the finding out no pains is to be spared. The punishment ... will be the best example that ever came in my court.' Nevertheless, James was adamant that the only means of clearing the Somersets' name lay in mounting a thorough investigation, 'for when innocency is not clearly tried, the scar of calumny can never be clearly cured'.[2]

James had good reason for hoping that it was untrue that Overbury had been murdered. In theory the King had been responsible for Overbury's welfare for, as a prisoner in the Tower, Sir Thomas had been 'out of his own defence and in the King's protection'. The fact that Overbury had been imprisoned on spurious grounds in the first place, and that he had been kept in close confinement on James's orders, must also have weighed heavily on the King's conscience. However, James never publicly acknowledged this and, during the ensuing trials, there was no suggestion that the King had cause to reproach himself. Instead it was given out that he was greatly grieved at the way that Overbury's enemies had tricked him into imprisoning Sir Thomas. During one court case Lord Chief Justice Coke declared, 'The heinousness of it hath made the King's eyes shed tears and his bowels to yearn.' Coke also claimed that at one point James had demanded, 'Shall I be made the instrument to effect their cruelty? Spare neither sex, nor honour, nor degree, place nor persons till you come to the root.' Whether James truly expressed himself in such melodramatic terms may be doubted.[3]

In mid-September Richard Weston was arrested and locked up in the residence of Sir Thomas Parry, a Privy Councillor and the Chancellor of the Duchy of Lancaster. To cow him into submissiveness Weston was left in solitary confinement for several days but, on 27 September, he was finally questioned by four Privy Councillors. Besides Parry, the interrogation was carried out by the Chancellor of the Exchequer, Fulke Greville, Lord Zouch and Secretary Winwood. When asked to account for the death of Sir Thomas Overbury, Weston initially insisted that it was due to natural causes. He maintained that while taking a stroll in the Tower garden Overbury had caught a chill which had been aggravated when he came inside and 'sat so long in a window that he was never well after'. The nearest he came to conceding that Overbury's illness had been artificially induced was his admission that on one occasion Overbury had taken 'a potion', following which 'he had threescore stools and vomits'. When his deposition was read out to him, Weston qualified this by saying he was 'not certainly assured of that number'.[4] Nevertheless the same phrase would recur in other written statements taken in the course of the murder enquiry.

At this stage Weston's interrogators made no comment but, the following day, they returned and put it to him that he had once had a conversation with Sir Gervase Elwes about poisoning Overbury. Taken aback, Weston 'first ... utterly denied it', but could not get anyone to believe him. He then agreed that he had once shown Elwes a phial of liquid 'which he, this examinant, did not like'. He said that Elwes had berated him for having anything 'to do with such a thing', causing him to dispose of the glass and its contents. When asked who had supplied him with the phial, Weston said 'one Franklin', and indicated where the latter could be located.[5]

When next interviewed, on 29 September, Weston made further admissions. He now revealed that it was Mrs Turner who had asked him to give Overbury the liquid, explaining that she had told him that, if he did so, 'The Lady Somerset should reward him well.' Sir Gervase Elwes was then led in to see the prisoner and the statement he had submitted to the King was read to Weston. Hearing this, Weston acknowledged 'that all and every the said particulars are true'.[6]

Meanwhile the Countess of Somerset and Mrs Turner were in a fearful panic, having learned that Weston was in confinement. James Franklin later related that, shortly after Weston had been taken into custody, he received a summons at ten o'clock at night to present himself at Frances's Whitehall apartment. When he arrived there he found Frances with her husband and Mrs Turner, but the Earl of Somerset then withdrew into another room nearby. In great agitation Frances informed Franklin that Weston had been arrested and that he had 'confessed all' already. It was inevitable, she said, that Franklin would himself shortly be arrested and she told him that, in that event, his only hope of survival lay in denying everything. 'If you confess anything you will be hanged,' she cautioned him, swearing that 'By God, if you confess, you shall be hanged for me, for I will not be hanged.' 'No Madam,' interjected Mrs Turner mournfully, 'I will be hanged for you both.'[7]

In his account of this meeting Franklin said that, at this point,

Frances left the room 'to speak with one whom he verily believes to be my Lord of Somerset'. Having supposedly consulted her husband, she returned to issue fresh warnings about revealing nothing under questioning. She told Franklin 'that the Lords [who would] examine him would promise him a pardon to confess, but believe them not, they will hang thee when all is done'.[8] Franklin then took his leave. As Frances had prophesied, shortly afterwards both he and Mrs Turner were arrested.

Now that Weston had mentioned the Countess of Somerset by name, the King decided that the enquiry must be entrusted to a legal expert who could probe more deeply into the matter. The man chosen for the task was the Chief Justice of the Court of King's Bench (referred to in common parlance as the Lord Chief Justice), Sir Edward Coke. Now aged sixty-three, Coke (who was known, by virtue of his office, as Lord Coke) was a formidable figure. Tall and forbidding, with a long oval face, he was the country's leading authority on jurisprudence. Having earned vast sums in the course of his legal career, he was now acknowledged to stand 'for wealth and law wit above all of memory'. One contemporary described him as 'an oracle of the law', and he would later be hailed by a colleague as '*monarchia juris*' – 'King of the law'. King James was said to have observed, somewhat irritably, that Coke was 'one [who] seemed to eat, drink and evacuate nothing but law'. Certainly Coke's exhausting daily schedule left him little time for domestic life, or any other form of recreation. Since his student days he had invariably risen at 3 a.m. in order to extend his working day. He retired at nine in the evening, after hours of toiling at his desk or in the law courts, punctuated only by brief respites at mealtimes. Coke was famed for being 'of wonderful painstaking'. He had won his very first case – a libel suit – by catching out the lawyer on the opposing side who had quoted from a faulty English translation of the relevant statute, rather than consulting the original text in Latin. Though at times 'so fulsomely pedantic that a schoolboy would nauseate it', Coke had gone on to win great renown as a lecturer at one of the Inns of Court, characteristically enjoining his students always 'to read to the statutes at large and not to trust to the abridgements'. Now he would bring all his energy to bear on the investigation into the murder of Sir Thomas Overbury, later boasting of having taken 'at least three hundred examinations in this business'.[9]

Coke's reputation was magnified by the legal Reports he issued annually between 1600 and 1616. He had started compiling these while still a student at the Temple, recording details not just of cases he had witnessed, but of others about which he had tirelessly gathered information. These manuals were invaluable at a time when the law had not been properly codified, relying largely on maxim and legal rule when no statute could be found in the Parliamentary Rolls on which to base judgement. It is true that some of Coke's comments and conclusions were deemed controversial in some quarters, but even Sir Francis Bacon, who hated Coke, had to acknowledge in 1616 that if they had not been published, English law had been 'by this time almost like a ship without ballast'.[10] In 1628 Coke would also publish the first part of his magisterial survey of English law and legal history, *The Institutes of the Law of England*. After his death in 1634, three other volumes were published, posthumously confirming Coke's eminence as a jurist. Nevertheless, although Coke's legal knowledge and powers of recall were unrivalled, he could not always resist the temptation to abuse his position, making dubious rulings in the knowledge that few would dare challenge a man of his authority. This trait would be particularly noticeable in the coming months when, in his eagerness to secure convictions for Overbury's murder, he sometimes evinced scant regard for justice.

Earlier in his career Coke had established himself as a fearsome prosecutor. He had been appointed Attorney-General in 1594 and, as such, had been responsible for presenting the Crown's case in several celebrated treason trials. He had prosecuted the second Earl of Essex and the gunpowder plotters but perhaps his most ferocious performance came soon after King James's accession, when Coke was called upon to prosecute Sir Walter Ralegh for treason. The Crown's case was in fact decidedly weak, but Coke sought to compensate for the lack of evidence by heaping the most vitriolic abuse upon Ralegh. He labelled him 'a spider of hell' and 'a monster', spluttering at one point 'Thou art the most vile and execrable traitor that ever lived ... I will make it appear to the world that there never lived a viler viper on the face of the earth than thou.' At the end of the trial Ralegh was found guilty, but in some ways Coke's attacks proved counterproductive. The spectators at the trial were so shocked by Coke's aggressive manner that at one point they even hissed him and, although until then Ralegh had been highly unpopular with the public, Coke's harsh treatment converted him into an object of sympathy. Now Coke would prove as relentless against those thought to have had a part in Overbury's murder as he had in the past against suspected traitors. An enemy of the Lord Chief Justice remarked sourly that his new role as 'chief inquisitor' was one ideally

suited to 'the malignity of his nature ... his delight having always been
to trample on the unfortunate'.[11]

In 1606 Coke had been promoted, becoming Chief Justice of the
Court of Common Pleas. His career now took a new turn for, whereas
as Attorney-General he had acted as a slavish servant of the Crown, as
a judge his first loyalty was to the Common Law of England. Conceiving
it as his duty to protect its privileges against royal encroachment, during
the next seven years he clashed with the King on several occasions.
Amongst other things he disputed the right of the Prerogative Court of
High Commission to arrest offenders or try certain cases, and established
that the Crown could not make new laws by issuing proclamations. He
so annoyed the King that in 1613 it was decided to transfer Coke to
become Chief Justice of the Court of King's Bench, which dealt with
felonies and criminal cases. In theory this was a more prestigious post
than that which Coke had previously occupied, but it was also less
lucrative. An enemy of Coke's remarked complacently to King James
that Coke's removal 'to a place of less profit ... will ... be thought ...
a kind of discipline for opposing himself in the King's causes'. A few
days later Coke was offered the consolation of being made a Privy
Councillor, but the preferment was conferred on him largely because
the King hoped that Coke would 'thereupon turn obsequious' and cease
to cause difficulties for him in legal matters.[12] So far it seemed he had
been right in this for, in the past two years, Coke had shown signs of
becoming more tractable to royal wishes.

Nevertheless, in view of Coke's turbulent and unpredictable record,
the King should perhaps have anticipated that his conduct of the
Overbury murder investigation would prove troublesome. In fact, according to the Spanish ambassador, Sarmiento, James had no such worries.
The ambassador claimed that James appointed Coke because, while he
was a man of unquestioned authority, he was also regarded as a 'creature
and intimate friend of Somerset', who could be relied on to accord the
Earl fair treatment. This turned out to have been a miscalculation. As
Sarmiento described it, 'in no more than three days', Coke became
'excited and bloodthirsty in the investigation', showing a ruthless
determination to achieve the results he wanted.[13]

Various reasons can be advanced as to why Coke proved so fierce in
his pursuit of those accused of Overbury's murder. One should not, of
course, exclude a wish to see justice done, and indignation for the
sufferings of the victim. However, a desire to win public esteem may
also have motivated him, for Coke was 'desirous of credit with the
people' and he knew that a successful conclusion to this case would

bring him acclaim throughout the country. Such opportunities did not often present themselves for, in the acerbic words of Francis Bacon, Coke had 'in his nature not one part of those things which make men popular, being neither liberal, nor affable, nor magnificent'. It was therefore 'by design only' that he could commend himself to the populace. Having been entrusted with a cause ideally suited to his purposes, Coke exploited this skilfully. As the enquiry progressed he revelled in the admiration and attention which focused on him, being described at one point as 'wonderfully fattened with the success and glory of his appointment'.[14]

Coke had other grounds for being vindictive towards those who now came under his scrutiny. The Chief Justice had a virulent hatred of Spain so, when evidence came to light of Somerset's dealings with the Spanish ambassador, he reacted in an almost rabid fashion. Then again, Coke had a deep detestation of Catholics, and the fact that several of the suspects in this case (notably Sir Thomas Monson and Mrs Turner) were Catholic sympathisers served to inflame him further. During the trials held as a result of his investigation, he several times declared that there was an explicit link between Catholicism and crimes of this nature. 'Poison and popery go together,' he once stated darkly. At other times he described poisoning as 'a popish trick' and branded Frances's alleged use of the codeword 'letters' to mean 'poison' as 'a trick of popish equivocation'.[15]

Coke ensured that it was impossible for the King to restrain him, for he claimed that it would constitute improper interference if he was required to supply James with detailed information regarding the progress of his enquiry. 'In matter of blood I never acquainted Queen Elizabeth with particular proof or circumstance, but she ever left it to the ordinary and indifferent course of justice and law,' Coke declared at the beginning of the investigation. James meekly accepted Coke's conditions, although Coke seems to have had no legal foundation for enunciating this doctrine. The result was that, until a suspect was brought to trial, James remained in ignorance of the Crown's case against that person. On 2 November 1615 the Tuscan ambassador's secretary, Pompilio Gaetani, reported, 'The Lord Chief Justice does not trust anybody and therefore not even the King knows exactly what is going on.' Nearly a month later Coke wrote to his master, 'I humbly beseech your Majesty to pardon me in that I express not particulars against any that shall be hereafter arraigned, for evidences lose a great part of their force if they be evident or known before the trial.'[16]

It could be argued that Coke was wise to take these precautions, and that his independence would have been seriously compromised if he had been obliged to report back to James more frequently. Nevertheless, because Coke was able to withhold information on the case from all but a tiny circle of men, he was in a position of immense power, and there were times when he wielded this unscrupulously. At various intervals he made wild public pronouncements hinting that, if the perpetrators of this crime had remained at liberty, Overbury would merely have been the first of many victims. There was no evidence whatever to support these statements but, since Coke so jealously guarded what he knew on the subject, no one was in a position to contradict him. His alarmist utterances were expressly designed to whip up hysteria and to heap odium on the suspects and, as such, bordered on a perversion of the course of justice.

In fairness to Coke it should be noted that, when questioning suspects, his manner was probably milder than in the courtroom. He himself was adamant that 'My fashion is in examinations always to deal gently with everybody.' At his trial Richard Weston confirmed this, acknowledging that his written depositions had been 'taken with mildness and gentle means, without any threatening and hard words'.[17] Doubtless Coke found that prisoners were more apt to incriminate themselves if handled with restraint, particularly in view of the fact that, at trials, it was usual practice to quote short extracts from written examinations. This often made it appear that the prisoner had made more damaging statements than would have appeared if the words had been set in context.

From what can be discovered of Coke's interrogation methods, it would appear that he relied greatly on leading questions, which gave the person being interviewed a strong idea of the answers he was seeking. For example, the list of questions which Coke put to James Franklin on 26 November included the demands, 'Was not something given to a cat to see whether it would kill her?' and, 'The Earl of Somerset, whether he speak not with you?'[18] Since by this time Franklin was eagerly cooperating with the authorities in the hope of averting his execution it is scarcely surprising that he at once confirmed that Coke was right to think this.

Furthermore, the depositions of other witnesses give the impression that Coke was instrumental in shaping their statements. As has been said, in his examination of 27 September Richard Weston declared that when Overbury became ill, he complained of having passed 'threescore stools and vomits'. This phrase, or something very like it, then featured repeatedly in the evidence submitted by other witnesses. The apothecary Paul de Loubell denied when questioned 'that ever Sir Thomas Overbury found fault with him for having threescore stools and vomits'. Overbury's manservant Henry Peyton claimed that he had warned Rochester that Overbury was extremely ill, having 'had threescore purges and vomits in one day'. Perhaps Peyton had independently learned of this extraordinarily precise estimate of Overbury's bowel movements. However, it is hard to resist the conclusion that Coke put words into the mouth of the individual being interviewed on this and other occasions.

On 1 October Richard Weston was once again interrogated, and made his fullest statement to date. He now revealed that, almost immediately after he had been made Overbury's jailer, Mrs Turner had brought him to Whitehall to see the Countess of Essex. The Countess had instructed him to give a water to his prisoner and, shortly afterwards, he had received a phial of liquid. This had been delivered to him by his son, and not by James Franklin, as Weston had earlier pretended. Weston said that it had weighed heavily on his conscience ever since he had lied about this, while stressing that his son 'was in no way privy or suspecting that it was poison'. Then he went over the incident when Elwes had found him with the phial, and described how the Lieutenant had deterred him from administering Overbury the contents. He explained that he had nevertheless told Mrs Turner that he had followed her orders, and that Overbury was very ill after eating the poison. Weston then turned to the tarts which Lord Rochester had sent to Overbury, noting that not only Sir Thomas but also Elwes's wife and children had suffered no ill-effects after eating these. He also reported his conversation with Franklin at the White Lion Tavern, insisting that, because Franklin had stated that Overbury would be poisoned by an unknown apothecary, great care was taken to see that only Overbury's regular apothecary was granted access to him. Finally he confessed that after Overbury's death, the Countess had arranged for him to be paid a total of £180.[19]

Five days later Weston supplemented this confession with an account of how he had aided Rochester and Lady Essex to arrange their adulterous encounters. These revelations provided no insights into Overbury's murder, but Coke realised they could be utilised to blacken Frances's character. Furthermore, when presiding at later hearings, he would more than once assert that there was an automatic connection between marital infidelity and acts of homicide. At a hearing held on 10 November he stated categorically that 'poison and adultery go together'. During the trial of Sir Gervase Elwes he would likewise declare that 'a man shall seldom see an adultery of an high degree ... but accompanied with murder'.[20]

Following her arrest Anne Turner had been placed in the custody of a London alderman and, at his house, she too was repeatedly examined by the Lord Chief Justice. She proved much less forthcoming than Weston. She said that she had no knowledge of Weston's receiving instructions to give Overbury a potion and insisted that it was untrue that she had handed him sizeable sums of money. She also denied having discussed Sir Thomas Overbury with James Franklin, even though Franklin had apparently admitted as much to the authorities. She stood by her story even when Franklin was brought before her to avow 'his former confessions to her face'. She conceded only that she had once sent Franklin 'to enquire of Weston how he did, but not to know how Sir Thomas Overbury did, for that she had no acquaintance with him'. Next, Weston was produced by her interrogators to declare in her presence that she had paid him £180, 'showing the place and other circumstances'. Still Mrs Turner could not be shaken. Stubbornly she swore 'that she will never confess it, as long as she lives'.[21]

Mrs Turner's resistance to interrogation doubtless owed something to the sustaining messages she had received from Frances while in detention. The day after she was taken into custody, Frances had sent a servant to pass on her best wishes and to assure Mrs Turner that she should 'be of good cheer and that she should want nothing'. A few days later she sent her friend a diamond ring and cross, promising that 'My Lord would go to court within three or four days to procure her delivery.'[22]

After being in confinement for nearly a fortnight Mrs Turner herself petitioned Coke to grant her bail. In her application she lamented the great distress and inconvenience which she had suffered ever since 'the malicious and scandalous accusations' of her 'suborned adversaries' had caused her to be deprived of her liberty. She requested that, since she had no doubt that Coke must now be satisfied of her innocence, he would free her so that she could attend to her 'poor fatherless children'. It would seem that, as Frances had promised, the Earl of Somerset asked the King to order Coke to release Mrs Turner, but James offered only cautious assistance. He wrote to Coke saying that he understood that Mrs Turner wished to be bailed and that, if it was customary to offer bail in murder cases, her request should be granted. 'If there be no ground of their guiltiness apparent, we would be loth to refuse unto her that which in like cases is usually granted to others,' he commented, but added that he left the decision to Coke's judgement. As a result Mrs Turner stayed where she was, for Coke had no intention of freeing his prime suspect. Somerset's failure to help her merely added to the perception that he was in serious trouble. From Royston, where the

King was in residence, the Earl of Arundel wrote on 11 October, 'What becomes of the matter in question, about Overbury's death, is not yet made known, but it is doubted it will not prove well, because the Lord Chief Justice hath refused to bail Mrs Turner, notwithstanding so great instance hath been made.'[23]

Meanwhile Coke was interviewing other individuals suspected of being connected with the death of Overbury. Sir Thomas Monson was asked why he had urged Sir Gervase Elwes to employ Richard Weston as Overbury's jailer. He replied that he had done so at the request of the Earl of Northampton and Lady Essex, adding that it was these two who had caused him to warn Elwes to watch for letters secreted in tarts for Overbury. Having given these answers, Monson for the time being was not detained further, but he remained under suspicion. As yet Sir Gervase Elwes also remained at liberty, but he was repeatedly interrogated. He confirmed what Monson had said about searching tarts for correspondence, and he also gave more details about the suspicious tarts and jellies that arrived from the Countess, and which became furred if left standing.[24] Unfortunately, though the testimony he gave here was quoted during Weston's trial, the original examination is missing from the state papers.

Besides this Coke questioned the apothecary Paul de Loubell, although, frustratingly, he does not appear to have asked him whether any employee of his was ever permitted to administer a glister to Overbury. Nor does any examination of Dr de Mayerne survive, but it would be curious if he was not questioned, particularly in view of the fact that the King had expressly stated at the outset of the investigation that Overbury's physicians should 'be spoken unto', and that 'Mayerne must be asked the state of the prisoner's body when last he saw him.'[25]

Coke also interviewed Giles Rawlins, Overbury's cousin who was in Somerset's service. He related how he had sent Overbury the vomit concocted by Robert Killigrew, adding that he had been troubled by the rumours that Overbury had come to a violent end, and that numerous friends had reproached him for his failure to do anything about this. Overbury's own servant, Lawrence Davies, was the next to be questioned. At his first examination, on 3 October, he revealed that Overbury had been very excited after receiving the letter from the Earl of Suffolk, which he thought presaged his release. Four days later Coke spoke to Davies again, and it was then that the latter made the much more serious allegation that a packet of white powder had been enclosed in a letter which he delivered from Rochester to Overbury.[26]

This was the first firm evidence that linked Somerset with Overbury's murder. Having uncovered this, Coke decided that the matter was too grave for him to deal with on his own. He resolved to ask the King to name additional commissioners to share the burden with him, and set off for Royston, where James was in residence. When Coke appeared there, at eight o'clock on the morning of 11 October, his arrival created a sensation. The legal term had just started and it was unheard of for the Lord Chief Justice to leave London while the courts were in session. After being closeted with Coke the King agreed that three more prominent individuals should join the commission of enquiry chaired by the Lord Chief Justice. They were the Lord Chancellor, Lord Ellesmere, Lord Zouch and the Duke of Lennox, and James believed that this constituted a well-balanced grouping. Although Ellesmere was a known enemy of Somerset, Lennox had always been looked on as 'a friend well-affected to him', while Zouch was 'a man void of all partiality'.[27]

Hot on Coke's heels came the Earl of Somerset, who materialised at Royston three hours after the Lord Chief Justice. His presence excited almost as much comment as Coke's had, for it was known that he had reached London only late the night before, having previously been staying at his house in the country. Such was his haste to see the King that he came on horseback, instead of travelling more comfortably by coach, as was his custom. He hoped to dissuade James from appointing Ellesmere to the commission, claiming that the fact that a confirmed enemy of his had been appointed would be taken to mean that he had irrevocably forfeited the King's favour. In desperation he reminded the King that Ellesmere had been on the commission which had sentenced to death James's mother Mary Stuart, suggesting, quite preposterously, that this showed he was unfit to wield judicial responsibility. Somerset also claimed that it was unprecedented for Privy Councillors to undertake an investigation of this nature and hinted that James risked alienating the entire Howard family unless he treated Somerset more sympathetically.

The King reacted coldly. Shortly after this he wrote Somerset a letter, explaining in detail why he was rejecting his plea. He declared that in a case of suspected murder, it was his duty to see that it was looked into by someone who could be counted on to make the most rigorous enquiries. Having made his choice, it was unthinkable that he alter it at the instance of the party under scrutiny. He treated with contempt Somerset's attempt to turn him against Ellesmere by alluding to his part in Mary Stuart's execution, and the King was equally unmoved by the insinuation that the Howards would be angered if he did not comply with Somerset's wishes. James told Somerset that it was actually in his own interests that the enquiry should be conducted by someone known for his severity, for only a person who commanded universal respect had any chance of vindicating those currently under suspicion. However, he made it clear that he now feared that it was unlikely that Somerset would be completely exonerated, for his behaviour was hardly that of a man who knew himself to be innocent. Bluntly James told Somerset that ever since 'the beginning of this business both your father-in-law and ye have ever and at all times behaved yourselves quite contrary to the form that men that wish the trial of the verity ever did in such a case'.[28]

Presumably Somerset had already left Royston by the time James delivered this rebuke. In his book, Anthony Weldon gives an account of how the King and Somerset parted, on what proved to be the last occasion that either laid eyes on the other. Weldon maintained that, when Somerset left Royston, he was given little clue that he was on the brink of a cataclysm, for James lulled him into a false sense of security by feigning slavish affection. When Somerset kissed the King's hand, prior to departure, 'The King hung about his neck, slabbering his cheeks, saying, "For God's sake, when shall I see thee again? On my soul I shall neither eat nor sleep until you come again." ' The Earl said he would return within three days, whereupon James said eagerly, ' "Shall I, shall I", and then lolled about his neck.' Accompanying Somerset downstairs, he continued to kiss him, asking him to send his love to Frances. As soon as Somerset had left the house the King's manner changed abruptly: 'I shall never see his face again,' he declared with grim finality.[29]

Weldon claimed to have witnessed this leave-taking personally, and to have been apprised of James's last remark by two Gentlemen of the Bedchamber. Nevertheless, his account is hard to credit. The murder enquiry had already placed relations between the King and Somerset on an extremely tense footing, even if James had not yet rejected Somerset's plea to alter the commission's composition. In the circumstances it seems implausible that James would have seen fit to act in such an effusive manner.

Meanwhile, in London, the commissioners were continuing their enquiries. On 13 October Overbury's other servant, Henry Peyton, described the late night exchange he had overheard at Whitehall between Overbury and Rochester. Archbishop Abbot was also doing his best to assist the commissioners. 'On suspicion of importing Popish books', Abbot had recently arrested Dr Savory, whom Frances and Mrs Turner had consulted after the death of Simon Forman. Having talked with him, the Archbishop found that Savory had 'some entanglement' with the matter under investigation. He therefore handed his prisoner over to the Lord Chief Justice for further questioning.[30]

Coke was currently engaged on a new quest, for he wished to gain possession of the wax effigies 'and other things of as bad consequence' which had been used by Frances and Mrs Turner in magical rituals. Somehow Coke established that Weston had disposed of several such items to an acquaintance of his named Simcocks. When summoned before Coke, Simcocks surrendered this material to him.[31] However, Simcocks was able to provide Coke with more than this, for he proved willing to testify that Weston had told him various things which showed that the Earl of Somerset had been responsible for the death of Sir Thomas Overbury. As a result Simcocks would become a key prosecution witness at Somerset's trial.

Once back in London Somerset began making frantic efforts to extricate himself from danger. As has been said, a few weeks earlier he had asked Lawrence Davies to hand over to him any letters of Overbury's that he had retained. Now he once again contacted the manservant to check whether there was any further correspondence in his possession. By this time Somerset was uncomfortably aware that he had given Davies little cause to be helpful to him, so he clumsily sought to make amends. He sent Davies £30, saying that this was at the request of Giles Rawlins, and hinted that he would soon provide him with permanent employment. He acknowledged lamely, 'True it is, I have heretofore been moved to retain thee but, out of sight, out of mind, and so I forgot thee; but now I will remember thee. Hast thou any more writings?' Davies said that he had two or three in the country and promised to produce them, but Somerset was offering him too little and too late to buy his loyalty.[32]

When the Earl of Northampton had died, Sir Robert Cotton had been charged with sorting out his affairs. After clearing out the late Earl's study, Cotton had returned to Somerset all the letters he found from him to Northampton. For some reason Somerset now decided that it was undesirable to keep these and, on 16 October, he 'burnt the whole bundle'. However, he preserved the letters which Northampton had written to him. He also kept the letters which Overbury had sent him from the Tower, and decided to place both these and Northampton's letters in the keeping of Sir Robert Cotton. However, he and Cotton agreed that, in some places, Overbury's letters needed excising. We do not know what it was about them that Somerset considered objectionable. At his trial Somerset said merely that 'some parts were cut off as impertinent', and he never offered a fuller explanation. Cotton also undertook to insert dates on Overbury's letters, assuring Somerset that if this was done, the letters could later be used to clear him from the imputation of murder.[33]

On 16 October Somerset did another suspicious thing. Using his authority as a councillor, he signed a warrant empowering a pursuivant to break into a house where Richard Weston's son lodged. Once inside, the pursuivant was to locate a trunk containing letters, and bring it to Somerset. The pursuivant duly entered the house with a constable, telling him that they were looking for documents relating to the marriage settlement of one Mrs Mary Hind, a sister of Mrs Turner. When the box was opened, the constable noticed that Mrs Turner's name was on several of the documents. The pursuivant then carried off the trunk and delivered it to Somerset. It is not known what became of it or its contents.[34]

At his trial Somerset explained that he had signed the warrant at his wife's request. In one account he is quoted as saying that Frances had implored him to do this 'for Mrs Turner's sake' but, according to other reports, he asked his listeners to accept that, as a result of what Frances told him, he had really thought that the documents belonged to Mrs Hind.[35] Not surprisingly such claims were treated with scepticism, for it is difficult to believe he would have taken such urgent measures unless he thought that the material in the trunk compromised either himself or Frances.

Within hours the commissioners were informed of Somerset's action, probably by the constable who had accompanied the pursuivant. Fearing that Somerset was trying to tamper with the evidence, and angered also by the discovery that Frances was still seeking to send heartening messages to Mrs Turner, the commissioners decided that the Earl and Countess could no longer remain at liberty. On 17 October they ordered Somerset to be confined to his Whitehall apartments. Restrictions were also placed on Frances (by now over seven months' pregnant), requiring her to stay in a room provided for her in the house of Lord Knollys. Having secured the Earl and Countess, the commissioners felt the time had come to act on their findings. On 18 October they informed the King that all was in readiness for the trial of Richard Weston, on a charge of murder.[36]

The very next day, 19 October, Weston's trial opened at the Guildhall in London. Instead of a single judge presiding, seven commissioners sat in judgement. The most prominent of these was Coke, the Lord Chief Justice.

There are numerous accounts of the case but, unfortunately, there can be no certainty as to their accuracy. Unlike today, criminal trials at this date were not recorded verbatim in an official transcript. Instead we have to rely on the reports taken down by spectators, which may well be misleading. One man who compiled an account of Weston's trial for a friend's benefit concluded with the comment, 'These are ye notes as I could take ... I adventured to let you see them as they are.' When controversial passages occur in accounts such as this it is difficult to assess whether the proceedings have been reproduced correctly, or whether the person making the record had become muddled. For example, in the account of Weston's trial that was later printed in *State Trials*, there is mention of the white powder sent to Overbury in a letter, with the comment that this 'white powder, upon Weston's confession, was poison'.[37] In fact at no time had Weston made such an admission. However, it is not clear if it was the reporter who was at fault here, or if the Prosecution had really asserted this. Such ambiguities ensure that our knowledge of what transpired at these trials is inevitably flawed. It is probable that some details of what went on are missing, while other passages may well be travesties of the original.

In seventeenth-century England the accused in a criminal trial started at a terrible disadvantage. The burden of proof rested with the accused, for there was no presumption of innocence. In prominent cases acquittals were virtually unknown, for juries were conscious that verdicts of innocent were looked on as implicit criticisms of the sovereign in whose name the case had been fought. At Somerset's trial the fact that he had been indicted at all was cited by the King's counsel as 'the first argument ... to prove him guilty'.[38] In his *Institutes*, Edward Coke expressed great pride that the English system of justice offered the accused a chance to speak in his own defence, which differed from procedure on the continent. Nevertheless, the prisoner might well find it hard to exploit this privilege. He was permitted no legal counsel, but had to expose the weaknesses in the Crown's case without expert assistance of any kind. Prior to the trial the accused was kept in ignorance of the evidence that would be presented against him, and so was unable to prepare his defence beforehand. Pen and ink were customarily denied him during the hearing, forcing him to speak from memory when addressing the allegations made against him. Nor was it admissible for the accused to deal individually with points as they were raised against him. Instead he had to wait until the Prosecution had marshalled all the evidence and then somehow produce a coherent defence that encompassed every accusation.

In most cases the majority of the Crown's evidence consisted of reading out the written depositions of individuals examined earlier. It was rare for the Crown's witnesses to testify in person and, when they did, the accused was not entitled to cross-examine them. It was also very difficult for an accused person to call witnesses in his own defence. Theoretically it should have been possible to do so for, in 1606, Parliament had passed a law granting that in certain circumstances an accused person should enjoy 'the benefit of such witnesses as can be produced for his better clearing and justification'. In his *Institutes*, Coke argued that this was a fundamental right and there was 'not so much as *scintilla juris* against it' but, in practice, the defendant was often obstructed from summoning witnesses. In the course of the Overbury murder trials Sir Thomas Monson requested that the Earl of Suffolk should give evidence on his behalf, and the Earl of Somerset wanted Sir Robert Cotton to appear for him. Neither request was successful: Coke ruled that, rather than testifying in person, it sufficed for the Earl of Suffolk to write a letter in general terms to the effect that he could think of nothing to clear Monson. As for Cotton, he could not be summoned to testify on oath because charges might have been pending against him, and he was therefore not an acceptable witness. Only in 1868 was an accused given statutory authority to call witnesses on his behalf. Almost twenty years before, in 1849, defendants had gained the legal right to know in advance the case against them.[39]

It also accords oddly with modern notions of justice that the investigating magistrate – in this case, Coke – should be permitted to preside as a judge at the trials of those charged as a result of his enquiries. Furthermore, it was perfectly acceptable for the judge, no less than the prosecuting counsel, to abuse the prisoner and to interrupt him when speaking in his own defence. During the trials for Overbury's murder, Coke did not disguise his hostility towards those brought before him, and made no pretence of keeping an open mind as to the rightful outcome. On 10 November, when several cases connected with the matter were still pending, Coke announced in the Court of Star Chamber that he could 'boldly affirm that there were none brought into question of this great business of poison but such as in his soul and conscience were apparently guilty'.[40]

There was, however, one respect in which those accused of poisoning Overbury could count themselves fortunate. Poisoning was regarded as a crime alien to the English character and hence peculiarly abhorrent.

In the *Institutes*, Coke claimed that there was no record of any convictions for poisoning between the reigns of Edward III and Henry VIII, a span of roughly two hundred years. However, in 1531 there was a celebrated case of poisoning which Henry VIII considered 'so odious' that he decreed that poisoning should be regarded as a species of high treason, rather than a mere felony. Accordingly he 'inflicted a more grievous and lingering death than the common law prescribed, viz that the offender should be boiled to death in hot water'. In order to prolong the agony, it was specified that the murderer was 'first to be put in at the tiptoes' and then immersed 'by little and little'. Several individuals suffered this penalty in the reign of King Henry, including a young serving girl named Margaret Davie. There is no doubt that their deaths were peculiarly horrible. During the reign of Queen Elizabeth one MP recalled being taken as a child to see a poisoner being publicly executed, and he said that the memory still haunted him. However, as Coke noted, this law 'was too severe to live long', inspiring such revulsion that it was repealed in the reign of Henry's son, Edward.[41] As a result poisoning was reclassified as a felony, and the penalty for it was hanging.

After Weston was led into court the clerk of the court read aloud the indictment, outlining the charges against him. First, it was alleged that on 9 May 1613 Weston had poisoned Sir Thomas Overbury's broth with liquid rosealgar. Next, he was said to have administered Overbury white arsenic in powdered form, as well as feeding him tarts and jellies poisoned with mercury sublimate. Lastly, he was accused of being 'present and aiding' when an unknown apothecary gave Sir Thomas a glister of mercury sublimate. When the clerk of the court had finished, Weston was asked how he pleaded, and he replied, 'Not Guilty'. Then, in accordance with established procedure, he was asked 'how he would be tried', to which the required response was, 'By God and my country.' Weston declined to utter the correct formula. To the consternation of all present he 'said he had referred himself to God and would say no more'.[42]

Weston's unexpected obstructiveness threw the court into confusion. In theory this meant that the case could not be proceeded with for, though Weston could be punished for his refusal to enter a plea, he could not be convicted of the crime for which he stood indicted unless he had signified his willingness to face the charges. It was precisely because the course adopted by Weston posed so serious a threat to the functioning of the legal system that the penalties reserved for it were terrible. Those who refused to plead in court were subjected to *peine forte et dure*, or death through weight, cold and hunger. The prisoner was spreadeagled with a sharp stone 'placed under the ridgebone of his back', and then weights were laid on top of him. At first these would not be heavy enough to endanger his life but, every day, they would be progressively increased until the breath was crushed out of him. After each daily test of endurance the prisoner suffered the further torment of being exposed to the elements naked. His diet would be below subsistence level, for he would be fed nothing other than the coarsest bread available, and the only water offered him would come from the nearest 'sink or puddle to the place of execution'. Even so, on days when he had bread, he would be permitted no water, and bread would be denied him on the days he had fluid. People had been known to survive eight or nine days under this regime of torture but, when death came, it was looked on as a mercy.[43]

Surprisingly there were people who, knowing the penalties, deliberately opted to defy the courts by not pleading. In 1609, for example, Ralph Bathurst was pressed to death after standing mute on a charge of murder.[44] The motive in such cases was generally the desire to hand on property to a wife or children, for the goods of those who stood mute could not be sequestered by the Crown, unlike those of persons condemned of felony. As far as Weston was concerned, however, this could not have been the incentive, for he had few possessions. The logical assumption was that he had been suborned – possibly by offers to look after his family – by others suspected of complicity in Overbury's murder. Their aims were obvious: the law decreed that, unless the person charged as principal in a case of murder had been convicted, it was not permitted to instigate proceedings in a common law court against others suspected of being accessories.

At first Coke sought to reason Weston out of his defiance. 'For the space of an hour' he and his colleagues on the bench sought to persuade the prisoner to plead, telling him 'that it was a favour of law to have his trial'. Coke told the prisoner of instances when individuals who had initially stood mute had agreed to plead and had then been acquitted. In contrast, 'there was no hope of life' if he continued his present policy. Having explained in detail what lay in store for Weston should he remain obstinate, Coke begged him not to expose himself to 'the extreme torment of pressing'. All to no avail, for Weston remained silent. Incensed at being frustrated in this unlooked-for manner, Coke gave vent to his fury in a vicious outburst. He raged at Weston that he had always 'used him fairly and kindly in all his examinations ... yet now he must needs tell him plainly that he was one of the vilest varlets that ever lived, that he had been ... a messenger to sorcerers and witches, a poisoner and a murderer, and now would be a murderer of his ... soul and body by being mute'.[45]

Having delivered himself of these strictures, Coke began analysing Weston's reasons for remaining silent. Ominously he pronounced, 'This is but a Machiavellian trick to save certain accessories, by whom it seemeth you have been dealt with thus to do, knowing that there is no hope for you to live, and the law being that they cannot be arraigned until you the principal be tried. You do it not for your sake, you have no goods or lands to save, but for their sake.' The Chief Justice then vowed that, for all that, these miscreants would not escape justice. 'There be many and great accessories, but it shall not serve their turn; it will be the worse for them,' he fulminated. 'Your great lord and your lady are now in safe custody as you are ... You, Weston, have been their pandar and bawd.'[46]

When Coke had finished haranguing the prisoner, it was assumed that he would adjourn the proceedings. Not at all, however, for Coke had no intention of relinquishing this opportunity of publicising his discoveries. Despite Weston's failure to enter a plea, Coke boldly invited the Prosecution to present the evidence, in order 'that God might be gloried, his Majesty honoured, and the truth revealed'. The decision was of questionable legality but, 'the rest of the judges, being asked their opinion, consented'. Coke later took pains to justify his action. At the end of the trial, 'he cited and showed that by the laws of the land, they ought and were bound' to continue the hearing. Coke also assured the King that his ruling had been 'to the great satisfaction of the auditory, which we might well discern by their gestures'. However, it is clear that the unorthodox procedure did not meet with universal approval. In his closing speeches at the trial Coke referred balefully to 'certain critics' who 'found much fault for that the examinations were read, the prisoner standing mute'.[47] Coke still vigorously defended his decision but, to the supporters of Somerset, it provided confirmation that his enemies were too intent on his destruction to have any regard for legal niceties.

The King's chief counsel, Lawrence Hyde, opened for the Prosecution. He began by stating baldly that the Earl and Countess of Somerset had been the 'principal movers' behind the murder of Sir Thomas Overbury. He said that Overbury had incurred 'the malice of the Countess' because he had strived to prevent her marriage. Hyde went on to describe Rochester's encounter with Overbury outside his Whitehall apartment, relating how Overbury had referred to Frances at that time as 'a base woman'. Hyde then amazed those present by adding, 'and so rightly termeth her for, although she is sprung of an honourable house, yet she is proved to be a corrupt branch and, if she be cut off, that house will prosper the better'. The spectators in the courtroom considered Hyde's 'boldness very observable' in saying this. Accustomed to members of the nobility being accorded an automatic deference, they were astounded that, even when so grave a crime was under consideration, Hyde should dare to make such pejorative remarks about a high-born lady.[48]

Hyde proceeded to outline how Overbury had been offered an ambassador's post, stating that, had Rochester not intervened, Overbury would have accepted it. However, since he refused it, he was imprisoned, and the Countess thereupon arranged for Richard Weston, who had previously acted as her 'procurer and bawd', to become Overbury's keeper. At this Coke, who knew the details better than anyone, affected theatrical amazement. 'What! Are you sure of that?' he roared, and Hyde gravely confirmed that there could be no doubting it. Hyde then resumed that Mrs Turner had instructed Weston to administer to Overbury a substance that should be sent to him. Shortly afterwards Sir Gervase Elwes had met Weston carrying a phial of suspicious liquid. On that occasion Elwes had prevented him from giving it to Overbury but, a day or so later, Weston put it in Overbury's broth. Overbury at once began to vomit and purge, and he became iller still after receiving a powder from Rochester which turned out to be arsenic. Weston also received tarts from the Countess of Essex, who ordered him not to taste them. Accusingly Hyde told Weston, 'These tarts were taken from you by Mr Lieutenant and, ye same being kept but a while, were strangely furred and appeared to be corrupted with poison. Others were given by you Weston unto Overbury in the name of my Lord of Rochester for, if he had known they had come from her, he would never have eaten of them.' Hyde continued that, as Overbury's sufferings intensified, he grew more bitter against Rochester. He wrote to him, threatening that one day he would be even with him but, 'Then came ye glister which gave him sixty stools; thereof he died.' Hyde noted that although Overbury's servants had testified that, prior to his imprisonment, he had 'a clean and sound body', his corpse was covered in 'blains and blisters' and 'looked like poison itself'.[49]

When Hyde had concluded, the evidence on which he had based his assertions was set out in more detail. Selections from Weston's own confessions were read out, as were extracts from the examinations of Overbury's servants, Anne Turner, Elwes and Sir Thomas Monson. Sir Dudley Digges appeared in person to testify that he knew that it was at Rochester's instigation that Overbury had refused to become an ambassador. What created perhaps the greatest sensation, however, were the revelations contained in Weston's confession of 6 October, when he had given details of Frances's and Rochester's illicit meetings for adulterous purposes. The court official who had to read this out was so embarrassed at being called upon to publicise material which dishonoured the Countess of Somerset that he deliberately lowered his voice, so that only people sitting near him could catch what he was saying. Coke would have none of this: repeating that Frances was 'a rotten and corrupt branch of her family', he ordered the official to read the document at full volume, to enable all present to hear everything.[50]

Weston's refusal to enter a plea meant that the jury could not return a verdict. Accordingly, once the evidence had been rehearsed, Coke announced that there would be a three-day adjournment. Nevertheless, going ahead with the trial had been by no means a futile exercise. One onlooker commented that, although Weston had 'remained mute, he was condemned as guilty in the judgment of all the hearers, and the accessories also'. Coke did not fail to point out to the King that, if no further action was taken against those named as Weston's accomplices, it could not fail to cause a scandal, 'the cause being so public, the auditory consisting of many thousands and, by this time, spread far and wide'. Admittedly, if Weston remained silent, it would not be possible to try the other offenders in a common law court, but Coke hoped that acts of attainder could be passed against them by Parliament.[51]

Obviously, however, it would be preferable if Weston could be prevailed upon to plead. In the interval before the next hearing no effort was spared to achieve this. Weston was removed to the Sheriff of London's house, where his hands and feet were manacled. Having thus ensured that he would be in great physical discomfort, senior churchmen were called in to apply spiritual pressure.

The King was profoundly disturbed by the news that Weston's trial had proved inconclusive. He agreed that he must have been suborned and Sir Ralph Winwood told Coke that 'His Majesty will hold it in you, my Lord Chief Justice, a masterpiece of service if your industry and diligence can discover by whom Weston was practised to stand mute.' James proposed that Coke should examine the Somersets on the matter, urging him to 'remonstrate unto them how unworthy a thing it is in the state they now stand to heap sin upon sin, and to charge their consciences with the apparent danger of the damning of the soul of that miserable wretch'. He also suggested that Weston should be brought face to face with both the Somersets and Mrs Turner, to see if this caused anything further to emerge. Coke cited legal reasons for rejecting this idea. On 22 October the commissioners informed James that 'as the case hath been proceeded in and now standeth ... there cannot be any such examination or confrontation without great inconvenience and scandal of all the former examinations and proceedings'.[52]

At this stage it still appeared that Weston was not going to change his mind. No less a person than the Bishop of London was called upon to convince Weston that he must abandon this sinful course of action but, after much 'painful but fruitless labour', he had to admit failure. The Bishop of Ely, Lancelot Andrewes, was the next to attempt the task but, after a lengthy session with him, Weston remained as obdurate as ever. Baffled, Andrewes suggested that Weston might prove more responsive if a Catholic priest was fetched out of prison to speak to him, but the prisoner answered indignantly that 'if the Bishop of London and the Bishop of Ely could not do it, neither Jesuit nor priest could do it'. All seemed lost until the morning of 23 October, the very day scheduled for the trial's resumption. At last, 'by the instance of the Holy Ghost', and after a conversation with the Sheriff of London's servant, Weston's resolution crumpled. Commenting that he hoped that those in power 'would not make a net to catch little birds and let the great ones go', he indicated that he was willing to face trial.[53]

That afternoon, in the Guildhall, Weston entered a formal plea of 'Not Guilty', this time following correct usage. Lawrence Hyde then recapitulated what he had said at the earlier hearing. Once again he described what had led to Weston's appointment at the Tower, and how Elwes had met him carrying the poison. Hyde said Elwes had discouraged him from using the poison at that time, but he had not confiscated it 'and, albeit [Weston] now denieth he ever gave the poison yet ... he delivered it; he confessed to Mrs Turner he had done it, saying it made [Overbury] very sick and to vomit often'.[54] After Hyde had again alleged that Weston had aided the apothecary to give the fatal enema, the examinations were read out as at the first arraignment. The only new development was that, while the court had been in recess, Sir David Wood had been interviewed by Coke, and he had revealed how Frances had attempted to persuade him to waylay and murder Overbury. This examination was now read with the others.

After this Weston was asked what he had to say in his own defence. Not surprisingly, in view of the fact that he was an elderly illiterate with no experience of public speaking, his courtroom address was far from articulate. Much was later made of the fact that he did not suggest that what he had said under examination had been misrepresented, but, since he had never admitted to killing Overbury, this signified little. Unfortunately we do not know exactly how he sought to prove his innocence. The most detailed account says merely, 'He seemed to excuse himself in a kind of ignorance or unawares ... and finally could say nothing that had any colour of material or substantial point to excuse or argue innocency in him.' At one point he started to explain what had happened after he had received the phial of suspicious liquid. At once Coke, or one of the prosecuting lawyers, broke in to ask why Weston had initially claimed that he had received it from James Franklin, when in reality it was Weston's son who had delivered it. The wretched Weston faltered that he had done this 'to save his child', but the interruption served both to unsettle him and brand him a liar.[55]

Tantalisingly, one source does suggest that Weston defended himself more vigorously than most reports lead one to believe. Somerset's loyal supporter Sir John Holles was in the courtroom and he, at least, felt that Weston's defence deserved to be taken seriously. Holles recorded that Weston began by denying that Overbury had ever had any dealings with any apothecary other than de Loubell. He also said that Overbury never ate any of the tarts that were sent to him by the Countess of Essex. Weston agreed that Overbury had eaten the tarts that came from Rochester, but these could not have been harmful, because Weston himself had partaken of them. Weston concluded helplessly, 'How he died, God knew; he knew not.' Hearing this, Holles (whose affiliation to Somerset admittedly predisposed him to hope for an acquittal) believed that Weston had succeeded in casting serious doubt on the allegations levelled at him. Sir John was overheard remarking that 'If he were of the jury, he would doubt what to do,' an observation that later landed him in trouble.[56]

The jury did not share Holles's reservations. They withdrew 'and within a short space returned' to announce that they had found Weston guilty. With relish Coke then pronounced the mandatory sentence for murder, namely, that Weston should be taken from prison to a place of execution and hanged by the neck till he was dead.

On 25 October, a mere two days later, Weston was hanged at Tyburn. A large crowd came to watch, for public executions were popular spectacles, valued not only as a deterrent to crime but also as potentially uplifting experiences for the law-abiding. The condemned man was permitted to address the crowd from the scaffold, although it was understood that he must not use this opportunity to justify himself, or to claim he had been wrongly convicted. Instead convention dictated that the speech acknowledged his own sinfulness and expressed deep repentance, becoming themes from one standing on the threshold of eternity. As it happened, Weston decided not to say any last words to the spectators. This did not necessarily signify resentment at the fate ordained for him. Sir Edward Coke later stated that, after his conviction, Weston had been stricken by remorse. He had begged that Sir Thomas Overbury's father might be permitted to see him (though elsewhere Coke recorded that it was Nicholas Overbury who 'sent for' Weston) and, when Mr Overbury had entered his cell, Weston had fallen on his knees and begged forgiveness.[57] If so, however, Weston now felt no need to say anything further.

As Weston stood waiting for the hangman to perform his office, there was a last-minute interruption. Sir John Holles and another follower of Somerset's, Sir John Wentworth, rode up on horses and tried to make Weston break his silence. Hoping that the condemned man could be prevailed upon to say something that proved Somerset's innocence, Wentworth demanded 'in a ruffling and facing manner' whether it was true that Weston had poisoned Overbury. Holles seconded his plea, urging Weston 'to discharge his conscience and so satisfy the world'. Poor Weston, anxious only that his ordeal should be over as soon as possible, refused to answer. Reproachfully he said to the officiating sheriff, 'You promised me I should not be troubled at this time.' Wentworth nevertheless repeated his question, whereupon Weston said stolidly, 'I die not unworthily, my Lord Chief Justice hath my mind under mine hand and he is an honourable and just judge.' Desperate to escape further harassment, Weston pleaded, 'Hang me!' to the executioner, 'presenting also his body forward'. The hangman duly pushed him off the ladder, at which Sir John Holles 'in an indignation turned about his horse and said he was sorry for such a conclusion'.[58]

When the authorities learned of this, they took immediate action. Wentworth and Holles were arrested and on 10 November they were brought before the Court of Star Chamber. Alongside them was a Scots Gentleman of the Privy Chamber named Lumsden, whose offence was slightly different. Described by Lord Chief Justice Coke – for reasons that remain obscure – as 'a pandar to the Earl of Somerset', Lumsden had arranged for the King to be presented with a paper he had written following Weston's first arraignment. In this Lumsden (who had not personally attended that hearing) was not only bitterly critical of the Lord Chief Justice but also claimed that Weston had rejected the statements attributed to him in his written depositions. Like Wentworth and Holles, Lumsden was now accused of acting in a manner calculated to bring justice into disrepute. For their temerity, the trio were all fined large sums and sentenced to a year's imprisonment. None of them served their full sentence, being released after less than two months. Nevertheless, their punishment served to deter others from voicing criticisms of the way the Overbury murder trials were conducted. This was precisely what the authorities had intended: Coke had presided at the Star Chamber hearing (which in itself was unfair, considering that the three men before him had cast aspersions on him) and, when pronouncing sentence, he menacingly declared that he hoped that henceforth gentlemen would 'take heed how they fell into discourses of these businesses when they be at their chambers; for, in the proceedings of these great businesses and affairs, if a man speak irreverently of the justice thereof, the bird that hath wings will reveal it'.[59]

Following Weston's execution, more people were detained in connection with Overbury's murder. Sir Thomas Monson, who had been allowed to go free when first questioned, was now placed in custody to await trial. He had sought to save himself from arrest by telling the King that the welfare of the royal falcons would suffer if he was not on hand to tend them but, though it was an ingenious ruse, it was insufficient to keep him out of prison. Sir Gervase Elwes now found that his part in exposing Overbury's murder had not protected him from being prosecuted for it. On 25 October he was deprived of his post of Lieutenant of the Tower and confined in the house of a London alderman. Shocked by this development, and fearful that his family would starve if he was convicted of a capital offence and his goods confiscated, he became, for a time, ill with worry. Besides this, Sir Robert Cotton was interrogated, though not about Overbury's murder. The King had somehow heard that Cotton had communicated 'divers secrets of state' to the Spanish ambassador and, on 26 October, he instructed that Cotton was to be questioned. Cotton succeeded in convincing his interrogators that these suspicions were groundless and he was released shortly afterwards.[60]

At the end of October the commissioners informed the King that, in view of the fact that they had found 'matter ... pregnant against the Earl of Somerset for being accessory to the poisoning of Sir Thomas Overbury before the fact done', it was fitting that he should be removed to the Tower of London. Having agreed to this, the King ordered that Somerset should also be stripped of his seals of office and other 'ensigns and ornaments of the King's favour'. On 2 November Lord Wotton came to collect these from Somerset at his Whitehall lodging. Somerset handed over the seals in his possession, and then pointed out his Lord Chamberlain's staff, propped up in a corner. Bitingly, 'Lord Wotton rejoined that the order he had received from the King did not purport that he was to take the staff, but that the Earl was to give it.' After this humiliation Somerset was conveyed to the Tower of London, setting out by barge but transferring to a coach shrouded in black velvet when it proved too dangerous to negotiate London Bridge's rapids.[61]

Because the Countess of Somerset was heavily pregnant, for the time being she was spared imprisonment in the Tower. Instead she was temporarily reinstalled in the Whitehall apartment which her husband had vacated. Then, because of fears that this was not secure enough, she was shifted to Lord d'Aubigny's house at Blackfriars. She was placed in the charge of a London alderman named Sir William Smithe and, at once, Frances set out to make herself agreeable to him and his family. She offered to feed Smithe and his wife and a daughter at her own expense, thus freeing him from the necessity of hiring a cook. One might have thought that Smithe would have been alarmed by the prospect of having all meals provided by a woman alleged to be an arch-poisoner, but this was far from the case. Humbly he professed himself most grateful for 'my Lady's noble offer to find me meat'. Unfortunately, it soon emerged that Frances had undertaken more than she could perform. Despite the huge sums of money that had accrued to him in the course of his career, Somerset had also incurred heavy debts. Now that he was in disgrace, his creditors were seeking to foreclose, and Frances had been left with no cash whatever at her own disposal. Merely in order to equip the house at Blackfriars, Smithe had had to send one of Somerset's servants to cadge £10 from the Earl of Suffolk and Lord Knollys, to be spent on wood, coal and beer. Even this was a hazardous operation, for the servant had stood surety for his master's debts, and there was a real prospect that he might be seized by Somerset's creditors in the street.[62]

Frances was now effectively isolated. Soon after taking charge of her, Smithe permitted her to send a gentleman to Somerset in the Tower, 'to see or know how her Lord did', but he promised the commissioners this would not be repeated. When Frances made another attempt to communicate with Mrs Turner, begging her to 'be not grieved though the lady [Somerset] was in prison', the message was intercepted.[63] Even if it had reached Mrs Turner it would have been of little use to her, for her position was now so desperate that cheering words from Frances had become irrelevant.

On 7 November 1615 the arraignment of Anne Turner took place in the Court of King's Bench. In her indictment she was charged with 'comforting, aiding and assisting' Weston in the poisoning of Sir Thomas

Overbury. At the outset of the trial Mrs Turner conducted herself as
though sure of being acquitted. Her composure doubtless arose from
the reflection that she had given nothing away under questioning and,
of course, she had no means of anticipating the devastating material
that had been amassed against her by the Prosecution. Indeed, it had
even been kept from her that Weston had been convicted and hanged
for the murder. For the hearing she had taken great care with her
appearance, and was immaculately turned out in a black baize dress. At
her throat a yellow starched collar provided a defiant touch of colour
and the finishing touch was added by a smart hat, perched on an
elaborate hairstyle. At once Coke, who was again presiding, saw to it
that her confidence was shattered. He declared – on what authority is
obscure – that, although it was fitting that women should cover their
heads in church, 'ye laws of ye land' did not permit them to wear hats
in court. Mrs Turner was compelled to remove the offending headgear,
ruining her hairstyle in the process. Now flustered and dishevelled, she
attempted to restore some semblance of dignity by covering her head
with her handkerchief.[64]

Once again it was Lawrence Hyde who was the principal prosecutor.
After some preliminary remarks about 'the wickedness and heinousness
of poisoning', he introduced the subject of Mrs Turner's dealings with
Dr Forman. He accused her of employing Forman to bewitch both
Viscount Rochester and Sir Arthur Mainwaring, revealing incidentally
that Sir Arthur had fathered three of her children. Hyde marshalled a
good deal of evidence to support his assertions. Forman's widow testified
in person 'that Mrs Turner and her husband would be sometimes three
or four hours locked up in his study together'. Mrs Forman had also
supplied the commissioners with various papers and supplementary
material which were now exhibited. Most damaging of all were the
letters which Frances had sent from Chartley to Mrs Turner and Dr
Forman in the summer of 1611. These of course had no bearing
whatever on the death of Sir Thomas Overbury, but were considered
eloquent testimonies to the depravity of Frances's character. One person
considered the letters 'impossible for the wit of man to answer with a
clear conscience', while another commented that they demonstrated
'how abusively her lust wronged those great judgements' that supported
the annulment of Frances's marriage to Essex.[65]

In addition, assorted artefacts and magical paraphernalia were
produced by the Prosecution. Among these was a doll in wax, 'very
sumptuously apparelled in silks and satins'. This supposedly had featured
as a prop in Forman's incantations, although one person present said it

was simply a miniature mannequin used by dressmakers 'to teach us the fashion for ladies' tiring and apparel'. Other items did lend themselves to a more sinister interpretation. 'There was shown in court two pictures of black lead, a man and woman naked, belly to belly, in bestial fashion.' Besides this, a parchment with the names of the Trinity written on it profanely was shown to the court, as well as another parchment which had a piece of human skin attached to it. On this was written the 'particular names' of the devils 'who were conjured to torment the Lord Somerset and Sir Arthur Mainwaring' if they proved faithless. The audience were fascinated when the Prosecution produced another document, purporting to be a list kept by Forman of 'what ladies loved what lords in court' but, to their disappointment, Lord Chief Justice Coke would not permit this to be read out. Gossip had it that his prohibition was due to the fact that, when this list was passed to him for inspection, his own wife's name was the first he saw mentioned.[66]

The exhibits were viewed avidly by the spectators, who were greatly stimulated at being made privy to such dark secrets. As the items were being displayed, there was a loud crack from one of the scaffolds. The atmosphere by now was so febrile that this 'caused great fear, tumult and confusion ... everyone fearing hurt as if the devil had been present, and grown angry to have his own workmanship showed by such as were not his own scholars'. The commotion lasted nearly a quarter of an hour, and it was only after order had been with difficulty restored that the rest of the weird miscellany was held up for inspection.[67]

Since Forman had died two years before Overbury, none of this had any relevance to the case under consideration. The sole purpose of dredging up these unsavoury details was to blacken Mrs Turner's character and to predispose the public to believe that she was capable of murder. The ploy was wholly successful. Simonds d'Ewes even claimed that though Richard Weston, James Franklin and Sir Gervase Elwes were pitied by the public for having been drawn into the murder plot at the behest of the Countess of Somerset, Anne Turner was 'less regarded' because she was 'worthy to be abhorred as a diabolical woman who had used sorceries to draw Sir Arthur Mainwaring to her bed'. Nevertheless, in order to obtain a conviction, the Prosecution could not dwell exclusively on this salacious material. Having dealt with the subject to his satisfaction, Hyde declared portentously, 'Thus much for witchcraft; now for poisoning.'[68]

Unfortunately there is no very full account of this part of the proceedings. Various examinations which had been read out at Weston's trial were repeated at this hearing. Other depositions were read out from acquaintances of Franklin, describing how Franklin had displayed an unhealthy curiosity about the properties of various poisons. The letter which Frances wrote to Sir Gervase Elwes about tarts and jellies containing letters was also quoted, and Coke declared 'that those words *letters* were private tokens between the Countess and the Lieutenant ... to give notice what things were poisoned and what not'.[69]

Mrs Turner was a broken woman by the time the Prosecution finished, and was in no state to defend herself coherently. Once she had grasped that Weston had already been executed, the discovery 'so much dejected her that in a manner she spake nothing for herself'. When Coke asked her what she had to say in her own defence, promising 'all patience and hearing', she merely 'denied all absolutely and entreated favour'. Ruthlessly Coke swept her protestations aside. 'Denial is no good excuse for then every delinquent would escape,' he told her. He then made some comments of his own on the case to the jury, before directing another stream of abuse at Mrs Turner. In apocalyptic tones he thundered that she personified seven deadly sins: she was 'a whore, a bawd, a sorcerer, a witch, a papist, a felon and a murderer, the daughter of the devil Forman'. He concluded by exhorting her 'to repent, and to become a servant of Jesus Christ, and to pray to him to cast out those seven devils'.[70]

The jury then withdrew to consider their verdict, surprising no one when they found Mrs Turner guilty. When Coke asked the poor woman if she had anything further to say, she 'could not speak anything for weeping'. Coke's colleague Judge Crook accordingly pronounced sentence of death, telling Mrs Turner that she ought to be grateful, as 'she had had a very honourable trial by such men as he had not seen for one of her rank and quality'.[71]

The outcome of the trial was as the authorities desired, but it was still hoped that more information could be drawn out of Mrs Turner. The King commanded that 'for the better manifestation of the truth and the salvation of her soul', her execution should be delayed until divines had spoken with Mrs Turner. If she proved unwilling to unburden herself to Protestant clergymen, Catholic priests could be taken from prison to counsel her.[72]

On 10 November a Protestant minister named Dr Whiting visited Mrs Turner at her place of confinement. He found her in a despairing state, and scarcely capable of rational discourse. Sobbing bitterly, she acknowledged herself 'to be a most vile, abominable and monstrous sinner' but, when urged to give details, she expressed reluctance to reveal more to a Protestant churchman. 'Why should I confess to them

that will not give me absolution?' she demanded sharply. Whiting told
her that his powers were greater than she realised and that, providing
she repented, he could shrive her 'as much as any priest, yea, as much
as the Pope himself'. At length 'after many exhortations and pressing
of her', she began to be more forthcoming. She confessed 'that she
knew of the poisoning of Sir Thomas Overbury before it was done, and
kept it secret, and denied it upon her examination in respect she would
not hurt that lady of Somerset who was (said she) as dear unto me as
my own soul. And therewithal wept and lamented exceedingly, and
mentioned the Earl of Northampton.' In fearful distress she wailed that
she had gained no relief from these admissions. 'Now that I have
confessed it, where is the comfort?' she asked piteously but, somehow,
Whiting managed to give her 'such ghostly consolation' that she agreed
to renounce the Catholic faith and receive communion according to the
rites of the Church of England.

The following morning Whiting returned to administer the sacrament
to Mrs Turner and he was much gratified when she told him that her
conscience had been greatly eased by having talked with him. Following
up his advantage, Whiting begged her to be more frank. Mrs Turner
then made some rambling observations, in the course of which she let
fall the name of Sir Thomas Monson. At once Whiting asked her
'whether his hand was in the business?' By now Mrs Turner was too
crushed in spirit to deny this. 'If you will have me say so, I will,' she
answered listlessly, but Whiting judged it best not to pursue the matter
further. He regarded it as more promising when she once again alluded
to the Earl of Northampton, declaring, 'If any were in it that I know,
it was the Lord Privy Seal.' Eagerly Whiting put it to her that she must
know a great deal about his part in the murder but Mrs Turner
disappointed him by responding apathetically, 'Conclude what you will.'

Though Whiting begged Mrs Turner to tell him something of real
substance, the rest of her confession was little more revealing. When
asked to provide details of the role played by the Earl and Countess of
Somerset, she asked in surprise, 'But have you not [enough] against
these already?' She did make a few intriguing comments, but these do
not appreciably enlarge our knowledge of what happened to Overbury.
Whiting noted that she told him that 'She saw the jellies in my Lady's
chamber to go to Sir Thomas Overbury, but neither knew who made
them nor who carried them ... She confessed she delivered money to
Weston but no such matter as was spoken against her ... She confessed
that Weston told her he was set on work to poison Sir Thomas Overbury
and that all the house [i.e. Rochester's household] said when [Overbury]

was first cast in prison, he would never come out again ... She said that Weston, being asked a little before Overbury's death whether he were dead, "No" said he, "Not yet, but now I will go and send the knave away packing. I will pull away his pillow and then be gone." [73]

Even if Mrs Turner had made the most detailed revelations about the manner in which Overbury met his death, these could not have formed part of subsequent criminal proceedings, for it was a legal maxim that confessions made after conviction could not be used against those facing trial on related charges. Nevertheless, as far as the authorities were concerned, sending Dr Whiting to her had been an eminently worthwhile exercise. Although her statement was not admissible as evidence there was no objection to alluding to it in general terms and, when doing so, it was possible to intimate that her admission of guilt had been very far reaching. Thus at the trial of Sir Gervase Elwes, Lord Coke declared that to Whiting Mrs Turner had 'confessed the act of poisoning persons and all circumstances freely'. As a result, although the details of what she had said were kept secret, the public developed the perception that it had been of great significance. For example, the annalist William Camden noted that, when with Whiting, Mrs Turner 'confessed every particular (and more) which she had denied before the bench'.[74]

Yet, quite apart from the consideration that it would be wrong to attach too much importance to a statement made when Mrs Turner was in so abject a frame of mind that she declared herself willing to parrot any suggestion that was put to her, the most noteworthy aspect of her 'confession' is that it was so limited. Despite her professed readiness to volunteer information, her remarks cast little enlightenment on the death of Sir Thomas Overbury. Although she admitted that she was aware of an intention to kill Overbury, she was singularly uninformative about exactly who was responsible, or the methods used to poison him. Perhaps the most interesting part of her statement lies in her claim that Weston, when chided for incompetence, implied that he would suffocate Overbury with his pillow. Years later Overbury's father Nicholas Overbury stated that this was indeed how his son had met his end, for he asserted 'that Weston, to his poisoning, added smothering of Sir Thomas Overbury with a pillow lest his pain should make him roar too loud'. It is possible that, when Nicholas Overbury talked with Weston after the latter's conviction, Weston disclosed this to him. Both Anthony Weldon and Simonds d'Ewes heard that it was asphyxiation rather than poisoning which ultimately accounted for Overbury and it may well be that their information was correct.[75]

Once it appeared that there was nothing more to be gleaned from Mrs Turner, her execution was set for 14 November. Interest in Overbury's murder was such that 'an infinite number' of people flocked to Tyburn for the hanging. These included 'many men and women of fashion', who 'came in coaches to see her die'. They were not disappointed by the performance put on for them. The execution of an attractive woman was of course of interest in itself, even if, at the age of thirty-nine, Mrs Turner had become too 'lean and long-visaged' to be called beautiful.[76] What gave the greatest satisfaction, however, was her speech from the scaffold, which was a model of its kind. It inspired not only compassion but also the satisfying recognition that, by atoning for her sins in this way, Mrs Turner would attain eternal redemption.

Mrs Turner began by acknowledging that 'she had deserved death' and that she 'came thither to die for the fact for which she was condemned'. Having announced that she died a Protestant, she said she had derived great comfort from having partaken of the sacrament for the first time in many years. When closeted with Dr Whiting, Mrs Turner had shown some bitterness towards the Earl and Countess of Somerset ('O my Lady Somerset, woe worth the time that ever I knew her!' she had lamented. 'My love to them and to their greatness have brought me to a dog's death'), but now she manifested no resentment. On the contrary, she asked whether she might pray 'for that poor lady'. Dr Whiting, who was on hand to offer spiritual solace, answered that this would be 'a charitable deed', for the Countess 'had need of her prayers'. Having offered up devotions on Frances's behalf, Mrs Turner entreated the 'forgiveness of all the world and that she might be an example of all men living'. Movingly she deplored the vanity and corruption of the fashionable world, 'crying out heartily ... of ... swearing, wanton living ... and the pride of the court', and singling out powdered hair and yellow starch as worthy of especial reprehension. One prim young man expressed a hope that, now that the woman who had introduced yellow starch – 'which so much disfigured our nation and rendered them so ridiculous and fantastic' – had denounced it in such terrible circumstances, it would cease to be popular. In fact the fashion proved extraordinarily resilient, and people were still inveighing against it years later.[77]

Finally Mrs Turner begged God to bless her children and then she knelt while the Lord's Prayer was recited. After the noose had been tightened around her neck, her hands were bound with silk ribbon, and the black veil covering the back of her head was pulled over her face by the executioner. As silence fell, 'the cart was driven away and she left hanging, in whom there was no motion at all perceived'. That evening her brother, who was a servant to Prince Charles, came and took down her body so that it could be accorded a decent burial at the church of St Martin-in-the-Fields.[78] One can only hope that he, or Sir Arthur Mainwaring, recognised an obligation to support her children.

It was about this time that important new evidence fell into the hands of the commissioners. As has been stated earlier, in late October Sir Robert Cotton had been called in for questioning on suspicion of having supplied the Spanish government with documents and information. Fearing that his house would be searched while he was in detention, he had entrusted the cabinet containing Somerset's correspondence to a lady named Mrs Farnworth. She, in turn, had deposited the box with her former landlord, a Mr Holland, who lived in Cheapside. When Cotton was set free he asked Mrs Farnworth to return his property, and she duly requested Holland to surrender the cabinet. Holland, however, was aware that Cotton had given her the cabinet and, 'considering the rumours of the time multiplied', decided not to give it up. Instead he decided to see whether its contents were of interest to the commissioners in Overbury's case. Having been unable to locate Lord Coke, who was attending a service at St Paul's, Holland delivered the cabinet to Lord Zouch. Zouch treated it as a matter of such urgency that he sent word to Coke that he must leave before the sermon and, as soon as the Lord Chief Justice arrived, the box was broken open.[79]

Inside they found letters which the King, the Earl of Northampton and Overbury had written to Somerset. We do not know the contents of the King's letters, for Coke returned these to James, and they did not form part of the evidence at Somerset's trial. It is clear, however, that James was perturbed to learn that Somerset had secreted them away, perhaps suspecting that the Earl intended to use them to blackmail him in some way. Before his trial Somerset sought to allay the King's fears, explaining that he had given the letters to Sir Robert Cotton so that he could redeliver them to the King. James was dubious about this, commenting that, if Somerset had really wanted to return his letters, he could have done so prior to his removal to the Tower, rather than committing them to Cotton's custody.[80]

A brief inspection of the remaining letters in the casket sufficed to convince the two commissioners that those written by Overbury had been tampered with. Not only were parts of them missing, but dates had been added in another hand. At once Sir Robert Cotton was re-arrested and questioned. He soon acknowledged that he had amended the letters, explaining that, the day after Weston's arraignment, he had 'cut and dated them by my Lord's direction'. As far as one can gather, his object had been to try to show that Overbury remained in good health long after the dates on which, according to Weston's indictment, poison had been administered to him. Without doubt this had been an extraordinarily misguided action on Cotton's part. The letters seem to have been altered in such an amateurish fashion that it was unlikely anyone could have been taken in for long and, once the deception was exposed, it merely served to discredit Somerset. Predictably, at his trial, his attempt to distort the evidence was adduced as a powerful argument of his guilt.

On 16 November 1615 there was held Sir Gervase Elwes's trial. Like Mrs Turner he was accused of being an accessory to murder, charged with the 'malicious aiding, comforting and abetting' of Richard Weston. Once again Coke sat in judgement and, at the start of the trial, he made an introductory speech, intimating that dramatic revelations would emerge in the course of this hearing. 'You, my masters, shall hear strange and stupendous things, such as the ears of men never heard ...' he promised. 'Whether it hath brim or bottom I yet know not, I yet cannot find it.' Lawrence Hyde followed, and he too heightened the excitement by claiming, quite without foundation, that the murder plot was now known to have been much more serious than previously imagined. Wildly Hyde stated, 'This wickedness of poisoning, had it not been prevented in time, although it began in Overbury, it would not have ceased with his destruction, but that his Majesty's person, ye Queen and ye whole state should have felt thereof.'[81]

The Crown's case against Elwes can be summarised as follows: firstly, it was alleged that, although the Lieutenant had ineffectually reproved Weston when he found him carrying a phial of poison, he had not prevented the keeper from giving it to Overbury that evening. Furthermore, after discovering that Weston intended to murder Overbury, Elwes had not dismissed him, but had continued to treat him as a favoured employee. In addition, Elwes had knowingly let Overbury eat tarts containing poison. In support of this, the letter sent by the Countess of Essex to Elwes (it is not clear, incidentally, how the commissioners had gained possession of this) was cited. It was claimed that there had been an understanding between them that, when she wrote to him, she would substitute the word 'letters' for 'poison'. Lastly, Elwes was accused of having colluded in the death of Overbury for personal gain. A few days before Overbury died, Sir Gervase had ordered Overbury's servant to deliver to the Tower a fine set of hangings belonging to Sir Thomas. The Prosecution alleged that Elwes had done this because he had been forewarned that Overbury was about to receive a poisoned glister and, if a prisoner died in the Tower, all the possessions he had with him were automatically forfeited to the Lieutenant.[82]

The Prosecution made good use of the cache of letters from the Earl of Northampton which had been found in the cabinet entrusted to Sir Robert Cotton. At earlier trials there had been no suggestion that Northampton had been in any way involved in Overbury's murder. Now, however, Lawrence Hyde stated baldly that Northampton ('Yea, that late Northampton, of whom such a base practice would not have been believed') had plotted Overbury's death with the Somersets. Hyde lamented that, 'the more's the pity', it was impossible to proceed against Northampton, but he consoled his listeners that the dead Earl was currently 'at a higher bar'. Fortunately, however, Northampton had left 'registers ... under his own hand that he was foully and shamefully guilty in devising, contriving and executing this foul fact'. These could now be laid before the court.[83]

From the surviving accounts of Elwes's trial it would seem that, to create the maximum impact, bowdlerised versions of Northampton's letters were read out, omitting parts that militated against the theory that he had conspired to kill Overbury. After being edited in this way, the extracts paraded in court created an appalling impression. The court learned that Northampton had boasted of coaching the Lieutenant 'that he might the better act his part for the adventure in which he dealeth'. Northampton's comment that he would 'love [Elwes] better for ... his conclusion' that it would be preferable if Overbury did not recover from his illness was also construed as seriously incriminating. Northampton's gloating description of Overbury's corpse, and his offering up of thanks to God for 'cutting off ill instruments', increased the general revulsion.[84]

Almost as damaging was a letter which was produced from Sir Gervase Elwes to Northampton. In this Elwes related how Overbury had asked in perplexity what the Howards wanted of him, to which the Lieutenant had replied that they wished to refine him. Turning on Elwes, Lawrence Hyde thundered, 'Your refining of him, Sir, was flat poisoning.'[85]

Although it was scarcely relevant to Elwes's case, another letter from Northampton to Rochester was quoted, in which Northampton assured his 'sweet lord' that, far from being a torment to him, deciphering Rochester's handwriting was 'no more than ... my niece's pain in the silver dropping stream of your pen'. As Coke declaimed the 'beastly and bawdy' phrases, the disapproval was palpable, and the Lord Chief Justice artfully pretended that the letter contained other material which was still more distasteful. Having finished the most indelicate passage, he declared that he would refrain from reading further 'for the bawdiness of it'.[86]

There was profound shock in the courtroom that Northampton, who had been respected for his celibate way of life, should have evinced such a ribald sense of humour. One of the spectators declared that he would not have believed that such disgusting language 'should come from the mouth of a Christian man'. Another commented in outrage that 'it would turn chaste blood into water to hear the unchaste and unclean phrases that were contained' in Northampton's letters.[87]

It was now up to Elwes to try to save himself by speaking in his own defence. Acutely aware of how much was at stake, for a time Elwes remained quiet, in order to collect his thoughts. A tense silence fell as the spectators waited eagerly to see how he would seek to clear himself, 'all standers-by having great expectation of what he should speak, because my Lord Chief Justice promised they should hear strange matters that day as ever ears did hear'. At length, 'with a temperate voice and fair carriage', Elwes began his address.[88]

He started by observing that he had once heard Lord Coke declare in the Council Chamber that the plight of the accused in a criminal trial never failed to excite his compassion. As Coke had pointed out on that occasion, the unfortunate individual had 'to answer on the sudden to multitudes of particulars laid to his charge, having no knowledge before he come there what will be said against him, nor may have any counsel against ye King's to defend him, nor is admitted to write anything for his memory, nor may answer to ye points as they are objected until all are enforced and burdened upon him'. Bitterly Elwes told Coke that, contrary to his claim that he 'always pitied the cause of such a one ... you have not observed your own rule in my cause'. Far from showing himself mindful of the prisoner's welfare, 'You have paraphrased upon every examination, you have aggravated every evidence and applied it to me, so that I stand clearly condemned before I be found guilty.' Elwes agreed that 'If I be so vile a man as your Lordship conceives me,' he deserved to die. Nevertheless, he hoped to convince the jury that it was otherwise, even though he would 'not tell a lie to save my life'.[89]

After these introductory remarks Elwes began systematically to counter the evidence against him. He was adamant that, at their encounter of 9 May 1613, he had prevented Weston from poisoning

Overbury, describing how he had impressed upon him the iniquity of murder. 'If you call this comforting and abetting, to terrify a man for his sins ... and to abhor and detest the act, then I am an abettor and comforter of Weston,' Elwes reasoned. He explained that he had kept Weston on as his employee out of 'charity', claiming that he had treated him kindly in order to ensure that Weston kept his promise not to harm Overbury. He now acknowledged that this had been an error on his part, but urged in mitigation that 'it was indiscretion, yet not worthy of death'.[90]

Turning his attention to the poisoned tarts, Elwes insisted that he had prevented the prisoner from eating these. He said that he had stored the tarts in his kitchen. When he noticed that they had become black and furred with mould, he had ordered his cook to make new tarts for Overbury and to throw away the originals. As for the letter he had received from Frances, Elwes claimed that at the time it had not occurred to him that it had any hidden meaning, although he now thought differently.[91]

Elwes did not deny that Northampton's letters afforded proof of some kind of conspiracy against Overbury. Nevertheless, he argued that this did not necessarily mean that it had been intended to murder Sir Thomas. The plan was merely to keep Overbury locked up until he 'might agree to their purposes concerning the marriage to be had between Rochester and the Countess'. Elwes pointed out that, when his own letters had been read in court, 'You never find that I write anything of tarts and jellies but only of my task with Overbury and, God knows my heart, it was with no ill intent to him, but that I thought to carry ye matter so even as that it should have been his peace and mine too.'[92]

Elwes then said that he could produce letters from the Earl of Suffolk and Sir Thomas Monson, showing that they too had been involved in the scheme to make Overbury amenable to the marriage. At one point Suffolk had called Sir Gervase to his lodging at Whitehall and emphasised that the sole aim of the plotters was to repair his daughter's honour. 'If in this I was foul, my Lord Treasurer was as foul as I,' Elwes defiantly asserted.[93]

Lastly, Elwes argued that it was he who had revealed that Overbury had been poisoned in the first place, and he was hardly likely to have done this if he had known himself to be responsible for the crime. Furthermore, nearly two years after Overbury had died, Mrs Turner had sent Weston to him to find out how much he suspected about the death of Sir Thomas Overbury, and they would hardly have needed to do this if Elwes had been fully apprised of all that had happened.[94]

Elwes's defence, which had lasted two hours, contained some inconsistencies and did not address every point raised by the Prosecution. Nevertheless, for a man who had claimed that his memory was 'not good when it is at the best', he had performed exceptionally well under pressure, and many of the spectators were sufficiently impressed to hope for an acquittal. One person present was sure that 'all men that brought thither indifferent ears both wished him innocent and expected the conclusion should leave him as they wished'. Another concurred that 'no man thought he should have been found guilty'. Lord Coke took a different view of the matter. Protesting furiously that 'he never knew any man with more impudence make a weaker defence than he did', he proceeded to demolish Elwes's arguments.[95]

Firstly, he dismissed Elwes's contention that he deserved the credit for alerting the authorities to the poisoning, declaring that it was Sir Ralph Winwood who had caused the matter to come to light. Then the Lord Chief Justice raged at Elwes for having cast baseless aspersions on the Earl of Suffolk. Expressing no interest in the letters which Elwes had said would clarify the part played by Suffolk, Coke twisted Elwes's words to suggest that the Lieutenant had sought to implicate the Lord Treasurer in Overbury's murder when, in fact, Elwes had merely claimed that Suffolk was no more guilty than he was. Coke professed the highest indignation that a nobleman could be so slandered. 'You are indicted and so is not he; you have had evidence given against you, and so hath not he; I have not throughout all this business found anything to touch the honour of that noble gentleman,' he chided Elwes.[96]

Coke then unsheathed a still more devastating weapon. James Franklin had now been in custody for nearly two months. He had clearly been examined during that time but appears to have revealed little of significance. However, having brooded on his position, he had decided that his best chance of saving his own life lay in making graphic revelations. Accordingly, that very morning at five o'clock, he had sent Coke a message saying that, moved by 'conscience and perplexity of mind', he wished to volunteer a full confession. Coke had at once gone to see him and had taken down a written statement. With a flourish Coke now 'drew out of his bosom' this document, warning, 'It is such a one as the eye of England never saw, nor the ear of Christendom never heard.'[97]

Franklin's confession contained much that was sensational. It was here that he claimed that the Countess and Mrs Turner had ordered him to obtain no less than seven varieties of poison, and that these had been incorporated in Overbury's food in many ingenious ways. He claimed that the Countess of Somerset's maid, Mrs Horne, her Groom of the Chamber, Stephen Clapham and a servant of Mrs Turner's referred to as 'the toothless and trusted Margaret', were all involved in the murder plot. Sir Thomas Monson 'was a messenger about this poison' and, as for Elwes, Franklin was positive that he too was 'acquainted therewith, for he hath seen letters from Sir Gervase Elwes to the Countess, testifying so much'. Franklin said that Frances had often asked him to read these letters to her, because she had difficulty deciphering Elwes's handwriting. In general Franklin was vague about what had been said in these letters, but he did remember a particular phrase once used by Sir Gervase, 'viz, this scab he is like the fox, the more he is cursed, the better he fairs'.[98]

Exactly what Elwes had meant when he wrote this cannot be stated with any certainty. Another imponderable is whether Franklin was telling the truth when he said that Frances regularly showed him Elwes's letters, or whether he merely caught a glimpse of one when visiting the Countess and was able to quote, to great effect, a stray sentence. At any rate, Elwes's reaction when he heard his own words was one of complete dumbfoundment. He stood 'stricken as if with a thunderbolt'. Smiting his breast, he was overheard murmuring, 'Then Lord have mercy upon me.' Utterly nonplussed, 'He knew not what to answer, or to make of his own letters.' It was enough to seal his fate. The jury went out and 'shortly after returned' to announce that they had found him guilty. Once again it fell to Coke to pronounce sentence of death, and Elwes was taken away to await execution.[99]

When informed of the verdict, the King expressed satisfaction, while voicing doubts as to whether or not Elwes was still harbouring secrets. He directed the commissioners to use 'all means possible to move him to clear his conscience of all that he knoweth in this foul business'. Accordingly the services of Dr Whiting were once again enlisted. When he visited Elwes to offer 'ghostly comfort', he found the condemned man full of contrition. Under Whiting's gentle probing Elwes acknowledged that he had once written the Countess a letter which had contained the words cited by Franklin, 'and that it was agreed between the Earl of Northampton, the Countess of Essex, Thomas Monson and him that this word (scab) should be the by-word in all their letters and callings to express Sir Thomas Overbury'. Unaccountably Whiting was content with this explanation, and he did not press Sir Gervase to enlarge on his dealings with these three persons. However, the clergyman did succeed in prompting Elwes to make some general admissions. The Lieutenant now acknowledged that he was culpable in three respects.

The first was that 'he knew and concealed the wretched purpose to poison Sir Thomas Overbury', keeping it secret out of a desire for worldly advancement. Secondly, he had been guilty of 'uncharitableness' towards Overbury, for he had conspired to draw 'tickets and writings from him according to those letters and promptings given unto him by the Earl of Northampton and the Countess of Essex'. Lastly, he agreed that 'many things had slipped from his pen suspiciously and unadvisedly, whereof he can make no good account and in some of them was matter sufficient to condemn him'.[100]

As in the case of Mrs Turner, Elwes's conversations with Dr Whiting were in some respects disappointing. Everything he said tended merely to confirm what had already come to light, rather than providing new insights. However, on 18 November Elwes did write to inform Lord Coke that 'God hath called to my remembrance' some more details concerning the Earl of Northampton. He described the letters which Northampton had sent him immediately after the death of Sir Thomas Overbury and suggested that Northampton's anxiety that the deceased man should be buried in haste showed that he had indeed been 'acquainted with the practise'.[101]

On the afternoon of 19 November Elwes was informed by Dr Whiting that he was to hang the following morning. Struggling to come to terms with the grim news, he 'desired to be private' and then 'cast himself grovelling on his bed' for a period of introspection. Two hours later Whiting returned with a colleague, Dr Felton, still hoping that Elwes could provide them with further information. When the two clergymen enquired about Elwes's state of mind, he answered despairingly, 'I have ... ripped myself up from my cradle, and have found myself to be a most horrible, vile and beastly sinner, and one that had abused all the gifts and graces that ever God of his mercy had bestowed on me, turning them to wantonness and the serving of my own concupiscence.' Seizing on his desolation, the divines told him that he could still hope for eternal salvation, providing that he was keeping nothing from them. Even at this late stage Elwes did manage to reveal some 'other things' to them. However, when the divines passed on details to Coke, the only disclosure he thought worthy of record was Elwes's admission that Weston had warned him that, sooner or later, he would have to poison Overbury, to which Elwes had answered, 'Let it be done so I know not of it.'[102]

The following morning Elwes was led out to execution. The King had instructed that he should not suffer at Tyburn, but that he could hang outside the Tower of London, where a 'lusty tall gibbet' had been erected. James had also agreed to waive his right to seize all Elwes's property following his conviction for a felony, thus saving the Lieutenant's wife and children from destitution. This comforting knowledge enabled Elwes to face death with dignity. Flanked by the two divines who had earlier ministered to him, he marched purposefully to the gallows. He mounted the hangman's ladder and, having sat himself on a rung, addressed the crowd.

Elwes began by apologising for having pleaded innocent at his trial. He said that, until recently, he had genuinely thought that he had done nothing wrong when he had concealed the attempt to murder Overbury. Only after his conviction had his confessors revealed to him 'the ugly face of his sin, which was great and bloody'. He thanked God that he had been vouchsafed this timely awareness. If he had perished in an accident on the Thames, or some such mishap, he would have faced ceaseless torment for his failure to recognise the evil in him. As it was, he had been granted an opportunity for repentance. He now hoped that angels were on hand 'to carry his soul within ten minutes to those eternal mansions where he should see his saviour'.[103]

Elwes blamed Sir Thomas Monson and the Earl of Northampton for having lured him into this wickedness. He begged his audience to learn from his mistake, and never to let anyone, no matter what their rank, persuade them to commit ungodly actions. Cautioning his listeners against arrogance and conceit, he said that it was apt that his own 'obsequious quill' had been the cause of his downfall, for he had taken inordinate pride in his writing ability, which undoubtedly had displeased the Almighty. Without noticeable self-pity he observed that he believed that if Franklin had not mentioned his letter to the Countess, he would have escaped conviction. However, he did not try to explain why he had written the passage referred to by Franklin. Instead he confined himself to saying that, prior to the trial, he 'utterly had forgotten' penning those compromising words, 'protesting that he could not yet bring to mind why he wrote any such letter to the Countess'.[104]

Rather than dwelling on the crime for which he had been convicted, Elwes felt more comfortable uttering pious platitudes. Those present were content to indulge him. At one point he urged, 'Profane not the Holy Sabbath of the Lord, nor his good creatures ... In serving God, you must not only read the scriptures but join practice therewith.' He lamented that he had wasted so much money at the gaming tables, saying that he believed that God had brought him to this extremity because he had once prayed that he might be hanged if he ever again played for money, only to resume gambling shortly afterwards. Numerous friends of the Lieutenant's had come to see him die and when he caught sight of Sir Maximilian Dallison, with whom he had spent hours at the tables, Elwes singled him out for especial attention. Reproachfully he intoned, 'You know Sir Maximilian, what gaming we have had, and how we have turned days into nights and nights into days. I pray you in time to leave it off and dishonour God no more by breaking his sabbaths, for he hath always enough to punish, as you now see me, who little thought to die thus.' Shaken, Sir Maximilian promised that he would never forget what Elwes had said to him.[105]

Having finished his address, Elwes covered his face with his hands for a few minutes of private prayer. This done, he said a final farewell, imploring those present to pray for him. Then, having held out his hands to be tied, with great deliberation he uttered the words, 'Lord Jesus receive my soul.' It was the signal the executioner had been waiting for: it had been prearranged that Elwes would say this when he was ready for the hanging to proceed, and at once the hangman tipped him off the ladder. To ensure a speedy death a servant of Sir Gervase tugged on one of his feet, and an assistant to the hangman seized hold of the other. Their intervention had the desired effect for, 'after hanging a small distance of time, his body not once stirred or moved, only his hands, being tied with black silk riband, a little stirred and moved'.[106]

Meanwhile, Coke had not been idle. Following Franklin's allegations that various servants of both Mrs Turner and Frances had been caught up in the plot, the Lord Chief Justice had diligently pursued this new line of enquiry. There is no evidence that the Countess of Somerset's maid, Mrs Horne, was questioned. She was an eminently respectable lady who for some time had been seeking to leave Frances's service, and Coke appears to have accepted that Franklin's accusations against her were baseless. However, Mrs Turner's maid Margery (or Margaret) Ewen and Lady Somerset's Groom of the Bedchamber Stephen Clapham were both interviewed. In the end neither was charged as accessory but, in different ways, both 'fortified [Franklin's] testimony'.[107] Whether or not these frightened menials were telling the truth, or whether they were inventing stories to placate the authorities remains, of course, a matter for conjecture.

Margaret Ewen declared that, on his visits, Franklin brought Mrs Turner 'salt, sugar and arsenic as she thinketh'. It was also she who first told the authorities that she had seen her mistress 'put a water into a white cat that kept a-mewing and was pitifully tormented by it'. Coke then referred this point back to Franklin. The latter readily confirmed that 'after he had brought some [poison], he understood that part was given to a cat, and they found it too violent and sent it back'.[108]

Stephen Clapham knew nothing about his mistress having been supplied with poison. However, he testified that Franklin had been a frequent visitor to her Whitehall apartments and that 'he did often let Franklin into the Countess's bedchamber before she was up'. While this had little direct bearing on the murder case, Coke professed disgust that 'such a wicked fellow' and a carrier of venereal disease could be granted admittance to a noblewoman's bedroom. He saw it as further proof of Frances's depraved character and was confident that others would share his outrage.[109]

Franklin himself was re-examined on 17, 20, 22 and 26 November. Among other things, he agreed that he had been in the habit of paying Frances early morning visits. He confided that the only times he had been denied access was when Rochester had spent the night with her. On those occasions, he said, Mrs Turner was sent to talk to him, a sure sign that 'My Lord Rochester lay there.' Interesting though this was, it was made plain to Franklin that what Coke really wanted was concrete information incriminating the Earl of Somerset in Overbury's murder. Franklin did what he could to oblige. It was at this point that he described to Coke how he had been summoned to Whitehall by Frances following Weston's arrest. For the first time he made the damaging claim that Frances had retired for a consultation with her husband before advising him how to conduct himself if taken into custody. Franklin also said that, shortly before Overbury died, he had had another discussion with Frances at Whitehall, when she had been most indignant that Overbury was still alive. Stressing the urgency of the situation, she had shown him a letter that she had recently received from Rochester. It contained the testy comment, 'I marvel at these delays and that the business is not yet despatched.' Franklin was ready to swear that 'the business' in question was the poisoning of Overbury.

In addition Franklin alleged that, shortly after this, Frances had shown him another letter from her lover. In it Rochester had warned that Overbury would be released from the Tower within two days and that 'then they should all be undone'. According to Franklin, Frances responded by sending for Weston and berating him for his failure to kill Overbury. Resentfully Weston had protested that this was scarcely his fault, for he had 'given him that that would have killed twenty men'.[110]

Franklin had clearly hoped that, in return for these revelations, the commissioners would drop the case against him. This was a delusion. Since evidence given after conviction was not admissible, Coke had refrained from prosecuting Franklin until he had gained all that he wanted from him. However, once 'he had discovered sufficient matter against the Earl of Somerset', the Lord Chief Justice saw no reason to delay further.[111]

Franklin was brought to trial on 27 November. He had the effrontery to plead innocent to the charge of being accessory to murder but his own confessions, which were read out in court, were more than sufficient to convict him. When invited to put forward a defence, he 'spoke little and to less purpose'. While admitting that he had supplied the Countess with poisons, he claimed he had been ignorant of what she had meant to do with these substances. Not surprisingly he failed to convince the jury. They were equally unimpressed by Franklin's claim that he could not be held responsible for his actions as he 'was so haunted by the Countess of Somerset that he could not rest'. He contended that 'those two women, what with their gifts, what with their fair speeches were able to seduce any man', and that, though it was unfortunate 'that he had not had grace to withstand their charming tongues', he should not be blamed for having been led astray by them. His arguments were dismissed. After a mere quarter of an hour's conferring, the jury found Franklin guilty. Having made 'a brief exhortation to the prisoner', Coke passed sentence of death on him.[112]

As far as Franklin was concerned, however, all was not yet lost. As he was taken away he was heard to say mysteriously, 'There were greater persons in this matter than yet were known.' As he had calculated, the commissioners decided to look into this and the trusty Dr Whiting was sent to sound Franklin on the subject. To Whiting, Franklin spewed out a preposterous farrago of lies and insinuations. Things were made easier for Franklin because rumours were already flying around the capital that the late Prince of Wales, the Earl of Salisbury and even the Queen had all been poisoned. In this climate the most outrageous fantasies were deemed worthy of attention. As his questions to Franklin indicated, Whiting had clearly heard these stories and was willing to accept there was some truth in them. As a result, Franklin was able artfully to exploit his credulity.

Franklin's aim in this was plain. 'I can make one discovery that should deserve my life', he told Whiting at one point, refusing to disclose his dark secrets until his death sentence had been rescinded. He warned Whiting that a great deal still remained hidden, saying that 'although the Lord Chief Justice hath found and sifteth out as much as any man could, yet that he is much awry and has not come to the ground of the business; for more were to be poisoned and murdered than are yet known and he marvelleth that they have not been poisoned and murdered all this while'. He pointed out that the identity of the man who gave Overbury the glister still remained a mystery, and hinted that he could solve it. 'I think next the powder treason there was never such a plot as this is,' he declared solemnly. 'I could discover knights, great men and others. I am almost ashamed to speak what I know.'

Although Franklin did his best to be as enigmatic as possible, he did claim that the Countess of Essex had been abetted in her crimes by her parents, and that the Lord Treasurer 'was as far in as himself'. When Whiting put it to him that Frances was very young to have masterminded such a plot on her own, Franklin gravely concurred with this. 'No, no,' he said emphatically. 'Who can think otherwise? For the lady had no money, but the money was had from the old lady, one day £200 and another day £800, for we wanted no money.'

Gaining confidence, Franklin started hinting that Somerset had murdered Prince Henry. He said that, at Whitehall, Mrs Turner had once pointed out to him a physician with a red beard who had supplied poison for this purpose. Franklin implied that Somerset's next victim was to be the King's daughter Elizabeth, who was married to the Elector Palatine and lived in Germany. 'The Earl never loved the Prince nor the Lady Elizabeth,' said Franklin sorrowfully. Tremulously Whiting asked whether it was true that Franklin was to be paid £100 to go on a mission to the Palatinate. At this Franklin sucked on his teeth and responded, 'An hundred! Nay, five hundred! I will not say how much.' By now thoroughly agitated, Whiting remarked that the Queen had lately been ill, and the two children she had borne in England had died in infancy. 'Soft, I am not come to it yet,' was Franklin's intriguing answer. He was categoric that he could substantiate all his allegations. 'If I cannot prove these things I should be ten thousand times more the son of the devil than now I am; but God hath sent me now more grace than so to do,' he assured Whiting.[113]

By this means Franklin did succeed in postponing his execution because, for a time, the commissioners were convinced that they could learn much from him. Nevertheless, Franklin would have been downcast if he had seen the letter which Coke sent the King on 29 November. This made it plain that this state of affairs was only temporary. 'For Franklin, he is only reserved for a time, to give some light of this work of darkness,' the Lord Chief Justice explained. 'But the hour of your justice and the wickedness of the man is such as long continuance of his life cannot consist together and, therefore, after a convenient time, when as much as can be is extracted from him, execution shall be done and your Majesty never troubled therewith.'[114]

However, although Coke was clear that Franklin did not merit a reprieve, this did not mean he was sceptical about his allegations. On the contrary, when the King wanted to know whether Franklin had said anything to suggest that he himself was at risk of poisoning, Coke gave him only partial reassurance. While conceding that 'this villainy ... concerns not your Majesty's own royal person', he warned 'some overture is made of some wicked attempt ... aginst some that be near and dear unto you'.[115] Even when Franklin failed to produce a shred of evidence to support his claims, Coke clung to an obsessive belief that what he was investigating was not a straightforward case of murder, but an evil of monstrous proportions.

By his inventiveness Franklin had gained a few extra days, but time was running out for him. On the afternoon of 8 December he was told that his execution was set for the following morning. Initially 'he seemed to be in a great chafe' about this but, after a time, he cheered up 'and danced carantoes up and down his chamber'. With grisly humour he started swinging by his arms from an overhead beam, saying, 'tomorrow they should see how gallantly he would hang'. Sadly it soon emerged that his swaggering demeanour owed more to an incorrigible belief that he could yet cheat the noose than to an acceptance of the fate in store for him. Earlier he had confided to Dr Whiting that, on the numerous occasions he had cast his own horoscope, he had seen nothing to indicate that he would end his life on the gallows. Though he had added mournfully that 'therein the devil hath deceived me', he plainly still clung to the hope that he would escape hanging.[116]

The next morning Whiting came to the prison to comfort the condemned man. For his benefit, Franklin put on a show of remorse, coupled with further cryptic hints that he was the repository of deep secrets. When asked by Whiting how he felt, Franklin answered reverently, 'The better for him and his prayers,' declaring that 'Wheresoever I dine today, I doubt not but to dine with the Lord Jesus.' Earlier Franklin had had angry exchanges with one Dudson, a witch hunter. Now he made it up with him, telling him 'where to find witches', which Dudson had wanted to learn from him.

Having prepared the ground in this way, Franklin again began alluding to hidden mysteries. He warned that 'there were three other great lords in this foul fact not yet named' but, when pressed to identify them, he would 'by no means discover it'. Whiting said that the Lord Chief Justice would find them out anyway, but Franklin could not be drawn to divulge details. '*I think so too*,' was his only comment. Then he once again spoke with foreboding of the perils that faced the royal family. 'God bless the King, for he has many enemies; God bless the Queen for she was bewitched three years ago,' he muttered fervently.

At this point the public executioner was brought in to see Franklin. 'Art thou the man that shall hang me? Thou lookest like a man to do better service,' cried Franklin jovially. He said that, in weeks to come, he hoped the hangman would be kept busy despatching 'some great or noble ones that shall follow after'. Seizing the fellow by the hand, Franklin gave him money, as was customary, and implored earnestly, 'When the time shall come do me a kindness: hang me finely and handsomely.'[117]

On being led out of his prison Franklin leaped into the cart 'with a great show of resolution', but his equanimity soon deserted him. At the gallows he behaved so oddly 'that all men thought him either mad or drunk'. When the executioner placed the rope about his neck, Franklin seized it and tried to put it on the hangman, laughing manically as he did so. At the second attempt the executioner was able to slip the noose over Franklin's head, whereupon Franklin cuffed him on the ear. Once this undignified tussle had concluded, Dr Whiting called for silence, so that Franklin could say a few words. An expectant hush fell, but Franklin remained obstinately mute. When Dr Whiting sought to prompt him by calling out his name Franklin merely turned and, with exaggerated courtesy, doffed his hat to him. To break the awkward silence Whiting suggested that Franklin doubtless wished to confess his fault, but Franklin answered curtly that this was not the 'place nor time to make exclamation'. Even now, however, he still cherished hopes of saving himself by pretending to know more about the plot's inner workings. Franklin's coffin stood waiting for him, and, patting this significantly, he ventured, 'There are yet some left behind and great ones too, but let that pass, I'll never name them while I breathe.' This time no one was taken in by these transparent 'shifts to spin out his life a while longer'. Franklin was still muttering unintelligible remarks when the cart was driven away, leaving him hanging. 'Thus he died, never heard to pray one word.'[118]

Sir Thomas Monson's trial as an accessory to murder had been scheduled for 30 November but, as the date neared, there could be no denying that the Crown's case against him was extraordinarily threadbare. A document in Coke's hand, headed *Against Sir Thomas Monson*, shows just how few incriminating facts he had succeeded in amassing. A rumour even gained currency that the King had observed that, though there was a certain amount of circumstantial evidence, there was 'not one unanswerable argument to prove him guilty'.[119] This was certainly a correct assessment but the King is unlikely to have made the comment in view of the fact that he had no idea of what the proofs against Monson were, inadequate or otherwise.

On 29 November Coke told the King he intended to defer Monson's trial, while insisting that this was 'not in respect of any innocence I find in him'. He maintained that he merely wished to ensure that statements by Monson could be used at the trials of the Earl and Countess of Somerset whereas, if he were convicted prematurely, anything he said after his arraignment could not form part of the evidence. 'I really am persuaded he can discover secrets worthy and necessary to be known, and he may be a good witness in some points which he affirmeth against the Countess,' Coke reasoned. Furthermore, once Frances heard that Monson was denouncing her, this might in turn be 'a mean to whet her tongue against him'. Coke assured the King that there was no prospect of Monson escaping justice: 'He cannot be in a better case than he is but in worse he may be.'[120] On 30 November Coke went through the charade of having Monson brought to the Guildhall, supposedly to be tried, and then adjourning the hearing on the grounds that the courtroom was overcrowded. Four days later Monson was brought back before the court, but the proceedings did not progress very far before being abruptly halted.

It is possible that one reason why Coke paused at this point was that he was nervous that, given the chance, Monson would put forward a vigorous and well-argued defence. He had already indicated that he wished the Earl of Suffolk to be on hand near the Guildhall, so that he could give evidence on his behalf. In particular there were two questions which Monson desired Suffolk to answer, namely, whether he could confirm that it was Northampton who had picked Sir Gervase Elwes to be Lieutenant of the Tower, and whether Elwes had been chosen as 'an instrument to make Overbury submissive to my Lord Treasurer and his house for the former wrongs done them'.[121]

Coke did not go so far as to deny that Monson had the right to ask these questions, but he plainly did not want the Lord Treasurer to testify in open court. However, when the King heard that Monson believed that Suffolk could clear him, he insisted that the Earl should be asked if there was any truth in this. While Coke dared not disobey, it is obvious that he did not question Suffolk at all rigorously. On 29 November Coke assured the King, 'Concerning the vouching of the

Lord Treasurer, I have not been slack in that which your Majesty doth require, for I have it under his hand.'[122] In fact Suffolk had done no more than to provide Coke with a written statement to the effect that he was not aware of anything which had any bearing on Monson's case. If Monson's trial had not been adjourned, it is debatable whether it would have been feasible to fob him off with this bland disclaimer.

Instead, at the Guildhall on 4 December, Monson had no sooner entered his plea of 'Not Guilty' than Coke announced that he was postponing the hearing. Not wishing it to be thought that the murder investigation was losing momentum, Coke implied that the reason was that Monson was now suspected of treason. Accordingly Monson was to be removed to the Tower, so that this 'business of a higher nature' could be unravelled. Coke was adamant that ultimately Monson's plea of innocence would be overturned, reminding those present that Richard Weston, Mrs Turner and Sir Gervase Elwes had all denied guilt, only to die repenting their evil deeds. Addressing Monson harshly, Coke told him that his attempts to drag the Earl of Suffolk into this sorry affair were utterly reprehensible. The Lord Treasurer, said Coke indignantly, 'hath ever been honourable'. Then he read to the court Suffolk's letter, which stated baldly: 'After my hearty commendations, I have heard that Sir Thomas Monson thinks I can clear him, but I know nothing of him to accuse or excuse him, but I hope he is not guilty of so foul a crime.'[123]

Monson refused to be intimidated. Stoutly he replied, 'I do not accuse the Lord Treasurer, nor calumniate him, for I know he is very honourable, but I desire to have an answer to my two questions.' 'You shall hear more of that when the time serveth,' retorted Coke irritably, telling Monson that his best course would be to confess all, for 'there is more against you than you know of'. 'If I be guilty, I renounce the King's mercy and God's; I am innocent,' returned Monson defiantly, a response that brought down on him the wrath of all the judges sitting on the bench that day, as well as the Counsel for the Prosecution. Coke roared, 'You are Popish!' as if that explained everything. Another judge of the Court of King's Bench, Justice Doderidge, contributed somewhat contradictorily, 'It is an atheist's word to renounce God's mercy.' Lawrence Hyde then chimed in that Monson was 'as guilty as the guiltiest' and that, 'if he did not prove him to be [as] guilty of the death of Sir Thomas Overbury as Weston was ... he would never be seen to speak at any bar any more'.[124] In the circumstances this was a rash undertaking, and one that Hyde conveniently forgot when it proved beyond him.

Coke saw to it that no one thought he was abandoning the trial because the evidence against Monson was so meagre. While declining to be specific, he alluded darkly to the terrible dangers that would have overwhelmed the country if this conspiracy had not been thwarted. Every Englishman, he declared, was 'much bound to God and to his deputy on earth, the King, for their great deliverance'. He said that, though it would be premature for him to 'discover secrets', he had seen letters which 'make our deliverance as great as any that happened to the children of Israel'. Naturally these sweeping remarks aroused feverish speculation. All were convinced that terrible things were yet to be revealed, even if there was puzzlement as to their nature. 'We believe the judgment seat, only doubt what the deliverance may be, equal to that of the children of Israel,' was one bemused comment. People could talk about nothing else and in late November Francesco Quaratesi (who had replaced Lotti as Tuscan ambassador) reported that the Privy Council had ceased to transact business, because their attention was riveted on this affair. It was assumed, however, that the suspense would not last much longer. Surely all would be made clear when the Earl and Countess of Somerset were brought to justice, as was anticipated would happen before Christmas. As Sir John Throckmorton put it, 'Then we shall undoubtedly be able to see into the bottom of this and their other wicked practices.'[125]

CHAPTER SEVEN

T he extravagant remarks uttered by Lord Chief Justice Coke during the recent arraignments had fostered a perception amongst the public that Overbury's death had not been an isolated case of murder, but had formed part of a gigantic conspiracy. The most absurd rumours proliferated, as even sober-minded individuals spread alarmist tales of the mayhem that would have been unleashed if the Somersets had had their way. Treason, black magic and regicide were merely some of the crimes alleged to have been contemplated or committed, and people all over the country shudderingly congratulated themselves on having narrowly escaped a terrible fate.

It was a universal assumption that Frances had resorted to witchcraft to render the Earl of Essex impotent but Somerset, too, was believed to have dabbled in the occult. The Tuscan ambassador's secretary, Pompilio Gaetani, reported that the Earl had poisoned Overbury after consulting a wizard who had warned him that one man posed a serious threat to him. The wizard had been unable to name the person in question but he had shown Somerset an enchanted mirror, in which Overbury's face had been displayed.[1]

Prince Henry's death was now widely attributed to poison. An unfortunate matron named Mrs Saul actually grew frantic with terror that she would be accused of having killed the Prince. In May 1612 Somerset had employed her to prepare a banquet which the Prince had attended. Now Mrs Saul became apprehensive that her cooking would be held responsible for the young man's demise, which had occurred six months afterwards.[2]

The good lady's fears proved groundless, but suspicions against Somerset were not so easily dispelled. Indeed there were people who were prepared to believe not only that Somerset had poisoned the Prince, but that he had planned to do away with the entire royal family. It was put about that Frances was merely feigning pregnancy with a cushion, and that she had intended to pass off as her own a child borne by Mrs Turner's sister. This would have provided a pretext for the King and his family to have been summoned to a lavish christening feast. There, every one of them was to have been poisoned. An earnest young man assured a correspondent that 'So soon as ye poison should have taken effect,' the English Catholics 'should all of them have been in arms with their whole power against ye Protestants ... Presently upon these hurly-burlies ye Tower should have been betrayed and five hundred Spaniards let into her ... Nay, further, the City should have been set on fire with wildfire in nineteen places ... and there should have followed a sudden and unexpected massacre of all Christian professors throughout the realm.' Another story had it that, once poison had been administered to King James, his wife and Prince Charles, 'Mrs Turner should have gone over to have been dry nurse to the Palsgrave's child, and Franklin should have accompanied her to do like villainy there.' In this manner, the Stuart dynasty would have been utterly extirpated.[3]

Although Frances was now portrayed as the incarnation of villainy, her family stood loyally by her. While she was under confinement at Whitehall her brother, Harry Howard, made several attempts to see her, hoping to pass on affectionate messages from Lord and Lady Suffolk. Unfortunately some of her family's attempts to defend her merely landed them in trouble. The Earl of Suffolk's second son, Thomas Howard, protested loudly when his sister and brother-in-law were arrested, saying that if justice was always so rigorously administered, the prisons would be overflowing. He offered to fight anyone who impugned his sister's honour but, in doing so, he merely drew on himself condemnation for daring 'to speak of drawing swords, especially in the court, in favour of these foul things'. Declaring that Howard's behaviour savoured of 'sedition and mutiny', the King sent him to the Fleet prison, although he was free again by the end of November. Frances's mother Lady Suffolk also somehow incurred the King's disapproval, and was ordered to retire to Audley End and stay there. The Earl of Suffolk was sufficiently concerned to seek an audience with the King to beg that the rest of his family would not have to suffer for the mistakes of one of his children. James reassured him that he had no intention of victimising them unfairly.[4]

It was perhaps fortunate that the Earl and Countess of Somerset themselves had little means of knowing what was being said about them. Pending the arrival of her child, Frances remained under house arrest at Blackfriars, while her husband was kept in close custody in the Tower. Virtually their only contact with the outside world was formed when they were interrogated by Coke and the commissioners. Sadly, while we know the questions which were put to them on at least some of these occasions, their answers are not so well recorded. Whereas the written examinations of many other suspects questioned in connection with Overbury's murder are preserved in the public records, few statements by the Somersets survive in their original form. For the most part we can only reconstruct what was said by reading the extracts quoted at their trials, and it is by no means certain that these were accurately reported.

The Earl of Somerset was questioned in the Tower on 25, 28 and 30 October. At his first examination he agreed that he had sent Overbury a powder at the Tower, but he insisted that this had been 'wholesome and good physic'. On 28 October he stated that he had never laid eyes on Richard Weston until after Overbury was dead, a claim to which he adhered tenaciously at all times thereafter. On 30 October he was questioned about the role he had played in securing Sir Gervase Elwes's appointment as Lieutenant of the Tower. He acknowledged that, at the instigation of the Earl of Northampton, he had requested the King to appoint him.[5]

After this it would seem that the commissioners refrained from questioning Somerset for a period. He was left isolated and ignorant of developments taking place outside the Tower, and was thus not even aware that others implicated in Overbury's murder were being tried and executed. During these weeks he made several attempts to communicate with the King. He begged that either Lord Knollys or Lord Hay could be sent to him, so he could relay to James 'some matter ... fit for his Majesty to know'. He refused to tell the commissioners what this was (which they considered 'no small affront' to their authority), saying only that it did not relate to 'the criminal part of the cause for which he is restrained', nor was it 'any suit to divert the course of justice for himself or any other'. Although the King's curiosity was aroused, for the time being he resisted sending an emissary to the Tower.[6]

Frances was also questioned during this period, but our knowledge of how she answered is still more fragmentary than is the case with Somerset. On 28 October she told the commissioners that the only people who sent tarts and jellies to Overbury in the Tower were her husband and herself. She may have gone further than this. When defending himself at his trial, Somerset alluded to this confession, claiming that his wife had said of those tarts that some were 'wholesome and some not, and that she sent him unwholesome ones'.[7] However, while it is possible that it was now that she made this admission, most indications are that at this stage she declined to acknowledge that she had played any part in poisoning Overbury.

Certainly when Coke made a further attempt to interview her in late November, she refused to cooperate. At Blackfriars she was kept in less strict seclusion than Somerset in the Tower and, from her servants, she heard details of the arraignments and hangings as they occurred. Understandably the news greatly upset her but, even in this demoralised state, she had been incensed to learn that, at Weston's trial, Coke had arranged for details of her premarital affair with Rochester to be made public. So affronted was she by the disrespect shown her that the next time Coke came to see her, she refused to talk to one who had so grievously dishonoured her. The Lord Chief Justice retorted that she had dishonoured herself when she had repudiated her first husband but Frances imperiously silenced him. 'Don't try to trick me like you tricked those poor people you had executed,' she told him contemptuously. 'Go away, because my life belongs to the King.' With that, she swept back to her room, leaving Coke fuming.[8]

One reason why Coke could not exert further pressure on Frances was that she was now in the final stages of her pregnancy, and hence could not be handled insensitively. As it was, for much of the time she was observed to be 'very pensive and silent and much grieved'. This was understandable enough, in view of what Sir John Holles described as the 'comfortable birth and childbed' which awaited her: 'the child born to misery, and the mother to the gallows, if she outlive the pains of her travail'. There were even fears that she might deliberately try to harm herself and so escape justice. It was Mrs Turner who had first alerted the authorities to the possibility, for she told Dr Whiting 'that the Countess of Somerset would not be hanged, for she would die in childbed by a wet cloth upon her belly after her delivery'. These suicidal tendencies seemed confirmed when Frances's custodian Alderman Smithe reported that, 'laying her hand upon her belly', the Countess had declared, 'It is my death that is looked for and my death they shall have.' The King gave urgent orders that she was to be attended only by highly competent midwives, who would 'be answerable that at her delivery she do not miscarry, either by her own wilfulness or the malice of any other'. These precautions sufficed to prevent anything untoward happening. On 9 December Frances gave birth to a baby girl, apparently without any complications. A few days later the child was christened 'without ceremony' at the nearest church, being named Anne in the hope that the Queen would take this as a compliment.[9]

The Earl of Somerset was still not permitted to see either Frances or his new daughter. In desperation he may have tried to write to his wife, but the attempt merely resulted in his confinement becoming more rigorous. Until this point Somerset had been permitted two of his personal servants, named Coppinger and Andrew Fargus, to look after him in the Tower. These two bribed a jailer to provide them with pen and paper, and then offered him more money to smuggle a letter out of the Tower. The jailer refused to perform this further service, so Somerset's servants burned the letter. When this came to light, Coppinger and Fargus were arrested and, when questioned, were evasive about the contents of the letter. They were imprisoned and, though Somerset was permitted to replace them with servants of his own, from now on two servants of the Lieutenant's were also on duty, 'to observe their behaviour'. Somerset himself was also called before the commissioners for further questioning. Probably he was now informed for the first time of the trials and executions that had already taken place, as well as learning that the casket containing letters from Overbury and Northampton was now in the hands of the commissioners. Whereas until now he had generally remained in good spirits, 'upon his return from the Lords he was much troubled and dejected'.[10]

Originally it had been assumed that Somerset's trial would follow soon after those of the other offenders, with 5 December being mentioned as a likely date for the hearing. By mid-December, however, it was clear that it would not take place 'until the season's distractions be over'. At court Somerset's enemies gave themselves over to merriment, and with good reason for, undoubtedly, they had much to celebrate. On 22 December the Earl of Pembroke replaced Somerset as Lord Chamberlain, in which capacity he presided over the Christmas festivities. On 3 January Sir George Villiers was named Master of the Horse, a post which Somerset had long coveted, but which had always eluded him. Sir John Holles prophesied that there would be numerous other beneficiaries from Somerset's misfortune. 'What other chips be gathered from the fall of this great oak I know not,' he wrote bitterly. 'Every bird of them will carry some straw or other to his nest.' Sure enough, on New Year's Day 1616, a friend could congratulate William Trumbull on having at last been appointed Clerk of the Council. Sir John Throckmorton was hopeful that the outlook was as rosy for other men who until recently had been overshadowed by Somerset. In early November 1615 he wrote to Lord Lisle, 'I trust that this great man's fall will raise your Lordship and some of your noble friends to your just and worthy demerits.' Two days later he put in his own claim for preferment, observing to Lisle that, since there were now 'many good things in his Majesty's gift again, I beseech your Lordship take this occasion ... to move for something for me unto his Majesty'.[11]

The jubilation at Somerset's fall was given artistic expression when the Earl of Pembroke commissioned Ben Jonson to write a masque to commemorate his appointment as Lord Chamberlain. The result was *The Golden Age Restored*, an allegorical piece whose theme was the expulsion from Britain of a group of iron-age conspirators. These corrupt and unworthy beings are driven out by the Goddess Astraea, the embodiment of Justice and Mercy, who inaugurates a new Golden Age and era of prosperity. The parallels with the recent upheavals at court were obvious and, if the Tuscan ambassador, Francesco Quaratesi, is to be believed, an added piquancy was provided by the fact that the Earl of Essex was among the masquers. Although the King had been ill with gout he made a special effort to be present. The masque was deemed such a success that a second performance was given, at the end of which the Queen, who had also been unwell, 'was pleased to dance'. This was not only 'a good sign of her convalescence' but also an indication of her happiness at the new dispensation.[12]

For the Somersets, Christmas 1615 was a less joyful affair. On 18 December the King had finally given in to Somerset's importunities and despatched Lords Knollys and Hay to see him in the Tower. James had been intrigued by Somerset's claim that he wished to communicate some 'matter of great importance' that was not connected with Overbury's death, but this turned out to have been a ruse on Somerset's part. When Knollys and Hay arrived, Somerset at once attacked the King for having 'dealt rigorously with him' by imprisoning him in the Tower. He complained that, since he was not accused of treason, he should have been confined in some nobleman's house, apparently without seeing any irony in the fact that he had acquiesced in Overbury's incarceration in the Tower for a much lesser offence. He demanded that he be informed of the evidence against him and asked that, rather than being brought to trial, his wife should instead 'be kept in some private corner all the days of her life, since she is the mother of a child'.[13]

For ten days the King made no response. Then, on 29 December, he sent a message to Somerset via the Lieutenant of the Tower, Sir

George More. He denied that he had been at fault in confining
Somerset to the Tower, for the decision had been in the hands of the
commissioners. They had certainly not been premature about removing
him there, for the fact that Somerset had remained at large for as long
as he did had caused 'a great murmur among the people that justice
was stayed'. Furthermore it was ridiculous to claim that he should
merely have been placed under house arrest, for while this would have
been appropriate if he was suspected of committing some minor crime,
'the offence for which he is in question is a murther of the foulest
kind, near approaching unto treason (he that was murthered being my
prisoner) and the proofs against him alleged by the commissioners
very pregnant'.

James likewise rejected Somerset's request to be apprised of the
evidence against him, saying that there was no reason why he should
not stand trial. If he was innocent, 'upon trial he will be cleared',
whereas if he was guilty Somerset's sole hope of salvation lay in
confessing his fault and pleading for mercy. The King also poured
scorn on Somerset's suggestion that Frances should be kept permanently secluded without having undergone a trial. There was as yet
no certainty that she was guilty, and a formal hearing was necessary
to determine this. The King warned that 'if it shall plainly appear that
she is very foul as is generally conceived and reported', he saw no
reason why sentence of death should not be carried out. However, he
failed to see why Somerset should object to this, having 'just cause to
be glad that he is freed from so wicked a woman'. Only if Frances
acknowledged her guilt and showed proper penitence would James
consider showing mercy.

It is not clear how Somerset received this message. One may
surmise, however, that Sir George More informed Frances of at least
part of what James had said and, having absorbed the implications,
she took a decisive step. A few days after Christmas she addressed a
humble message to the King, begging that he send her 'two persons
from amongst those whom he trusted most, to whom she might speak'.
On 2 January the King ordered Viscount Fenton and the Earl of
Montgomery to visit her. She then made a full confession to them,
acknowledging that she was responsible for Overbury's murder but
stressing that her husband was entirely innocent. The Spanish ambassador, Sarmiento, reported, 'She spoke to them plainly, confessing the
part which she had taken in desiring and aiding the death of Overbury,
as being a girl aggrieved and offended by the most unworthy things
which he had said about her person, but that the Earl of Somerset –

who at that time was not yet her husband – neither knew anything about it, nor took any part in it. She had rather guarded and kept the secret from him because she held him to be a very true friend of Overbury ... For all this, she threw herself at the feet of the King, begging for his grace and pity.'[14]

On 8 January Lord Chief Justice Coke returned to interview Frances. This time she did not refuse to speak to him. From a list compiled by Coke we know at least some of the queries he put to her on this occasion. First and foremost, he interrogated her as to the meaning of the letter she sent to Elwes, asking, ' "If he send" – who is meant?'; 'Who did bid you say that he sent but one?' Besides this, she was questioned about whether she had intended to send Franklin to the Palatinate, and to identify the person who had written a list of poisons in a Roman hand, which Franklin had claimed she had shown him at one point. We know very little about the answers she gave. At Somerset's trial (or at least, according to one account of it) part of her confession of 8 January was read out, and there Frances was said to have admitted 'that she received all the poisons from Mrs Turner etc., that she kept them in her chamber at Whitehall, whither the Earl had oftentimes resort'. She also, as we know, went some way to clarify her letter to Elwes. On 8 January Coke attached to his copy of the letter some statements by Frances relating to it. It was now that he recorded that when she had written 'if he should send', she had been referring to the Earl of Somerset, 'for he used to send many jellies and tarts to him'. The document goes on, 'She confesses that by these words in her letter, "Do this at night and all shall be well," she meant that the tart and jellies then sent wherein were poison should be given to Overbury that night and then all should be well.'[15] However, as has already been mentioned, these statements must be regarded with extreme caution. The fact that Frances subsequently retracted part of this confession might be thought to invalidate it altogether. It must also be borne in mind that when she made this confession, she had had a baby less than a month earlier. Almost inevitably she would have been suffering from post-natal depression and exhaustion. Perhaps, in these circumstances, she simply found it easiest to agree to whatever interpretation Coke chose to put on her letter.

Sir Thomas Monson's trial had been scheduled to resume on 9 January. The expectation was that the Somersets would be tried shortly after him but, suddenly, all further hearings were postponed to enable Coke to pursue a new line of enquiry. This related to Somerset's clandestine dealings with Spain, to which Coke had been alerted largely as the result of a misunderstanding. Coincidentally, by early January the King had been apprised by Sir John Digby, his ambassador in Spain, that Somerset and Sir Robert Cotton had been negotiating with Sarmiento. Through an informant, Digby had learned that Somerset had told Sarmiento that he would see to it that Digby was discredited if he sought to obstruct a Spanish marriage treaty. The informant also revealed that Somerset had assured Sarmiento that the King 'might be drawn to condescend unto' the Spaniards' terms for the marriage.[16] In December 1615 Digby had sent a letter disclosing all this to the King and, when it arrived in England early in the New Year, James at once summoned Digby home so that he could discuss the matter further. However, it does not appear that James informed Coke of these developments. The document that convinced Coke that Somerset was a Spanish agent was a much earlier letter from Digby to the King, which Coke found among Somerset's correspondence.

Ironically, this letter did not in fact incriminate Somerset at all. Digby had written it in 1613, just after discovering that several important people at the English court were receiving Spanish pensions. At the time of writing he was still unaware of their identities. It was only at the end of the year that he had returned to England to reveal to James that the recipients included the late Earl of Salisbury, the Earl of Northampton, the Countess of Suffolk, and the Admiral of the Narrow Seas, Sir William Monson, who was Sir Thomas Monson's brother. James had decided to take no action against those involved.[17] He did, however, show the letter to Somerset, who had filed it away among his own papers. When Coke had found the despatch in Somerset's casket of letters, he had leaped to the wrong conclusion. He decided that Somerset had intercepted the letter on its arrival from abroad, and that Somerset had prevented it from reaching the King because he himself was in the pay of Spain, and did not want James to know this.

Coke's deduction was incorrect, but it is at least possible to follow his reasoning. Unfortunately he did not stop there. Coke's hatred of Spain verged on the pathological: in 1621 he would declare in Parliament that nothing good ever came out of Spain, 'No, nought but traitors ... There came the great armada out of Spain to make King Philip monarch of all christendom, came while we were treating of peace with Spain. The first plague among our sheep was brought by Spanish sheep to England. So also *morbus Gallicus* [syphilis] by Spaniards from Naples.' Having established to his own satisfaction that Somerset was an inform-ant of Sarmiento's, Coke took this as proof that Somerset's ultimate

purpose was the utter subversion of all King James's dominions. Coke
set down his views on the subject in a memorandum written in early
1616. Having noted that Digby had 'certified in most secret manner
under seal to our sovereign Lord the King divers secrets of state for
the preservation and safety of the King and this kingdom', Coke
extrapolated from this various unwarranted conclusions. He stated
boldly, 'Somerset did falsely and traiterously compass and imagine the
death of the King and Queen. And for the better and speedier performance thereof . . . [did] falsely and traiterously discover to Don Diego
Sarmiento de Acuna . . . the said secrets of state, to the end that the
safety of the kingdom might be traiterously prevented and that the King
and kingdom might, by this treacherous revealing of secrets, fall to utter
ruin and destruction.'[18]

Coke was determined to find further evidence to corroborate his
theories. Early in the New Year Sir Robert Cotton was once again taken
into custody and questioned about his dealings with the Spanish
ambassador. Sir William Monson, the brother of Sir Thomas Monson
whom Digby had named as a Spanish pensioner, was also removed to
prison. He had long been reviled in strongly Protestant circles. As
Admiral of the Narrow Seas, it was his responsibility to prevent Dutch
attacks on Spanish shipping and the rigorous way in which he carried
out his duties had led to muttering that he was 'Spanish in his affections'.
His arrest was a source of great satisfaction to his enemies, with Sir
John Throckmorton commenting, 'I never had a good opinion of that
man.'[19]

It became clear that the Somersets would not be tried until after Sir
John Digby had returned from Spain and been interviewed by the Lord
Chief Justice. However, to indicate that the King was as resolute as ever
that justice would be done, on 19 January the Somersets were formally
indicted as 'accessories to murder before the fact done'. Coke presided
over this brief hearing, at which a summary of the evidence was
presented before a jury of 'seventeen knights and esquires of Middlesex'.
They returned a verdict that the case against the Somersets needed
answering.

Once the legal process had reached this stage it was no longer possible
for Coke to keep the King in ignorance of the evidence amassed by
him. The Crown's case was now placed in the hands of the Attorney-
General, Sir Francis Bacon. To enable Bacon to prepare for the trials,
Coke had to release to him all the relevant documentation. At once
there was a change of emphasis. Whereas Coke had had an agenda of
his own, and had brought a demonic energy to bear on the case in the

hope of creating a momentum that the King would be powerless to check, Bacon had a more measured approach. While no less ambitious than Coke, and in some ways more brilliant, Bacon believed that the path to advancement lay in unreservedly placing his prodigious intellect at the disposal of the Crown. In keeping with this, it was his guiding principle during the months to come that the trials of the Earl and Countess of Somerset must be conducted in a manner agreeable to his sovereign.

This did not mean that he would show more partiality towards Somerset than had Coke. In the past, it is true, Bacon had been looked on as an adherent of the Earl's, but he had fawned on him only in order to further his career, and he felt no awkwardness about turning on him. Nor was this surprising, for Bacon's past behaviour showed that he was capable of much greater betrayals. At the end of Queen Elizabeth's reign, Bacon had played a prominent part in the prosecution for treason of his friend and benefactor, the second Earl of Essex. It was an episode that had proved that, though Bacon was wise in many ways, his moral sense was curiously defective. It was Bacon's tragedy that an ability to distinguish between right and wrong, which came to simpler men instinctively, was the most poorly developed of his faculties.

Having perused the evidence, Bacon concluded that the Crown had a good chance of securing Somerset's conviction, but only by concentrating on essentials. He was exasperated by the way that Coke had become distracted by absurd conspiracy theories for, in doing so, he felt that the Lord Chief Justice had placed the Crown's entire case in jeopardy. A jury of peers was likely to be less docile than those who had tried the other defendants and, unless the evidence was very compelling, they would merely be irritated if asked to believe hysterical and outlandish allegations that Somerset had poisoned the Prince of Wales and had similar plans for the remainder of the royal family.

When outlining all this to the King, Bacon avoided overt criticism of the Lord Chief Justice. Nevertheless, he managed to convey that he considered such arrogance and lack of moderation on the part of Coke to be utterly typical. Bacon must have relished passing these barbed comments, for he and Coke had detested each other for years. In the reign of Queen Elizabeth Bacon had persistently been worsted by Coke when competing for office. In 1593, when Bacon had been aged thirty-two (Coke was nine years older), he had hoped to be made Attorney-General. Coke had not only secured the appointment for himself but had then – so Bacon believed – prevented him from being awarded the lesser post of Solicitor-General. Matters became worse when both men had sought the hand in marriage of the same rich widow, a contest from which Coke once again emerged victorious. One day, in the Court of Exchequer, the bitterness between them had flared up when Coke made some self-congratulatory comment. Bacon snapped that it was unfitting that he should dwell in this way on his own greatness, prompting the crushing rejoinder, 'I think scorn to stand upon terms of greatness towards you, who are less than little, less than the least.' Stung, Bacon retorted, 'Mr Attorney, do not depress me so far, for I have been your better and may be so again.'[20]

As yet Bacon had not achieved his ambition of superseding his rival. However, in recent years, he had steadily gained the King's confidence, whereas Coke had experienced an unmistakable loss of favour. In 1613 Bacon had at last been appointed Attorney-General. It was he who had then advised the King to transfer Coke from the court of Common Pleas to King's Bench, a move which ostensibly represented an advancement, but which Bacon knew would not be to Coke's liking. Realising who was responsible, Coke had shortly after confronted Bacon on the matter. 'Mr Attorney, this is all your doing,' he said accusingly. Bacon did not trouble to deny it. Jovially he told Coke, 'Ah, my Lord, your Lordship has all this while grown in breadth. You must needs now grow in height, or else you would be a monster.'[21]

The feud between the two men had had its roots in personal antipathy. Nevertheless, it was sustained by a fundamental difference of principle, for their views on law were incompatible. Coke believed passionately in the supremacy of English common law. In contrast, for Bacon, one of the law's primary functions was to bolster the authority of the Crown, a stance with which the King concurred enthusiastically. In theory it was an issue which had little relevance to Somerset's case. However, in the next few months, Bacon's willingness to defer to the King, which differed so markedly from Coke's determination to exclude him from the enquiry, was indicative of the contrast in their philosophies. In preparing for the trial Bacon elected to work with the King in close consultation. It was also partly to please James that Bacon decided to concentrate on those aspects of the case which were least contentious.

On 19 January 1616 Bacon had an audience with the King at which they discussed Somerset's case. The King first sought a reassurance from his Attorney-General that, if Somerset was brought to trial, he would be found guilty, for an acquittal would have been looked on as a deep humiliation for the Crown. James also appears to have expressed concern that the trial might cause difficulties for him by touching on matters which he did not wish to be made public. One can only speculate as to what he had in mind. Possibly James may already have been anxious that, unless caution was exercised, Somerset would be provoked into attacking him when testifying. Alternatively he may simply have felt strongly that any attempt to link Somerset with matters such as the death of the Prince of Wales would be a travesty of justice, and he refused to let the Crown be associated with it.

On 22 January Bacon wrote to the King, addressing these concerns. He began by stating, 'The evidence upon which my Lord of Somerset standeth indicted is of a good strong thread, considering impoisoning is the darkest of offences.' Nevertheless, 'the thread must be well spun and woven together, for Your Majesty knoweth it is one thing to deal with a jury of Middlesex and another to deal with the peers'. He told James that, at present, he foresaw two problems. The first was that he did not think it sufficient simply to rehearse again the evidence that had featured in earlier trials for, 'the same things, often opened, lose their freshness, except there be an aspersion of somewhat that is new'. Unfortunately, by alluding to the country's miraculous deliverance, the Lord Chief Justice had created expectations that Somerset's trial would be marked by lurid revelations. Inevitably, when these failed to materialise, the effect would be anti-climatic and things would 'seem less than they are, because they are less than opinion'. Confident that he had said enough to damage Coke in James's eyes, Bacon did not labour the point. Instead he merely commented that, while he much commended the Lord Chief Justice's 'great travails', it was regrettable that through 'over-confidence', Coke had subjected matters to 'a great deal of chance'.

Next, Bacon dealt with the King's wish that some way must be found of 'confining' the evidence against Somerset. He urged James to exercise particular care when choosing a Lord High Steward to preside over the commission of peers who would try Somerset. It was essential, Bacon stressed, to appoint someone who was not only authoritative but who could be counted on to 'moderate the evidence and cut off digressions'.[22]

Meanwhile Coke and his colleagues on the commission of enquiry were doing everything possible to secure a confession from Somerset. On 22 January he was again examined at the Tower, and he provided his interrogators with a key to the codenames which he and Overbury had given prominent court figures when writing to each other. On 4 February the commissioners returned with a long list of further questions. Among other things, Somerset was asked to provide details of the circumstances leading to Overbury's arrest, and to reveal whether the had been aware of Frances's hatred for Overbury. The commissioners also wanted to know why he had sent Overbury a powder in the Tower, and from whom he had obtained it.[23] There is no record of Somerset's answers to these queries. Clearly, however, what he said fell far short of the admission of guilt that the commissioners wanted. Hoping to startle Somerset into being more forthcoming, Coke told him that his trial was expected to be held very shortly. This came as a shock to Somerset: he had clung to the belief that the King would never subject him to such an ordeal, particularly since he had so stubbornly maintained his innocence. He also knew enough about the workings of the legal system to realise that, if charges were pressed, he would have scant chance of being acquitted. Greatly disturbed, he asked Coke for leave to write to the King. This time, his request was granted.

It was scarcely a generous concession, for Coke had an instinct that Somerset might inadvertently incriminate himself when writing to James. His letter could then be used as evidence against him. Initially, however, the results were disappointing. Somerset phrased his letter with extreme care, avoiding writing anything which could be construed as an admission of wrongdoing. Greatly irritated, Coke reported to the King that, while Somerset was dictating the letter, if 'any word casually fell from him in the least degree tending to any submission to your Majesty, he would cause it to be put out'. In high ill-humour Coke remarked that he thought this 'strange' conduct on Somerset's part, and that the King would find Somerset's comments 'not worthy of the time your Majesty shall bestow in reading them'.[24] As the sequel proved, however, Somerset had been wise to express himself so guardedly.

Annoyed that his efforts had so far proved unavailing, Coke told Somerset that if he wished to help himself he must show more humility. Unluckily for him, Somerset allowed himself to be persuaded. On 7 February he wrote the King another supplication, this time couched in more submissive language. The original letter is lost but we can ascertain its gist from reports of Somerset's trial (where it was read out) and also because Coke summarised its contents soon after seeing it. In essence, the letter was an appeal from Somerset to James not to bring him to trial. He wrote that, considering he had been, 'if not the first, yet inferior to very few' in the King's favour, he had hoped to be spared this, particularly in view of the fact that he had committed no offence against the King or state. Regarding Overbury's murder, he insisted that he was 'clear from that foul fact'. He nevertheless acknowledged that 'the presumptions may be strong against me, in respect I consented to and endeavoured the imprisonment of Sir Thomas Overbury (though I desired it for his reformation, not his ruin)'. Ruefully he agreed that, 'the same being enforced by wit and art against him, the extent of law

might take hold upon him'. He therefore begged the King to show him
'mercy' by not subjecting him to a trial. Having sought permission to
bestow his lands and goods on his wife and child, he asked the King to
pardon Frances, 'having confessed the fact'. In conclusion he requested
James to send his cousin, Sir Robert Carr, and Lord Hay to see him.[25]

According to Coke, the letter contained another passage, but no other
source makes mention of this. Coke claimed that Somerset said of his
offence that 'If it were done by him ... and if he should have fallen
into any error concerning the same, yet he might be thought to have
been transported thereunto either by force of his affection to his so
much desired wife, or through the jealousy of the practices of Overbury,
and not by the malice of a wicked heart.' Coke exulted, 'Of these and
some other passages in this discourse, good use (thanks be to God) may
be made of them.' Certainly if Somerset had expressed himself thus, he
came close to compromising himself. However, at Somerset's trial, there
was no reference to these words, which gives rise to a suspicion that
Coke invented, or at least exaggerated, them. In contrast, other sections
of this letter were put to good use. When preparing for the trial, Francis
Bacon noted that it could be interpreted as 'both a confession of the
practice and out of his own mouth a concession ... that the practice of
his getting Overbury into the Tower is an invincible argument of his
guiltiness'.[26]

Next day, Coke and the commissioners returned to the Tower to try
to make Somerset elaborate on his admission 'that he, with others,
assented to the imprisonment of Sir Thomas Overbury'. They failed,
and Coke was reduced to taunting the Earl about Pembroke having
replaced him as Lord Chamberlain. It was the first that Somerset had
heard of this but, if Coke had hoped it would unsettle him, he was
disappointed, for the Earl absorbed the news with composure. He
equally showed no emotion when Coke told him (without divulging
details) that Frances had made a full confession, urging him to do
likewise. All Somerset said, according to Coke, was that 'he was sorry
that his wife was guilty of so foul a fact'. Still hoping to avoid a trial,
Somerset now proposed that he should be given a chance of proving
his innocence in a more informal manner. He suggested that he could
be apprised of the evidence against him and, providing he could give a
convincing explanation for anything that appeared suspicious, a public
trial would be unnecessary. Coke rejected the idea peremptorily, telling
Somerset 'that neither did his request stand with the course of justice,
neither had the like been granted ... to any in the like case before'.[27]

However, though Coke would not hold out any hope to Somerset that his trial would be abandoned, by this time other people were anticipating such an outcome. Coke might bluster that, when questioned, Somerset had 'made direct answers which we take in some points very material',[28] but the fact remained that the Earl had yet to acknowledge his guilt. As a result there began to be a perception that the murder enquiry was stagnating. At court a hard core of Somerset's enemies – among whom should be numbered Coke himself, Secretary Winwood and the Archbishop of Canterbury – remained determined that Somerset should be tried, but it was not known if the King shared their commitment. In view of the fact that a date had yet to be set for the hearing, many courtiers began to doubt that matters would be taken further.

The outlook for Somerset was improved by the fact that there was a growing disunity among his enemies. Astonishingly, the Queen, who had always been so inveterate against him, was now experiencing a definite change of heart. This was typical of her contrary nature. Ironically, Overbury had recognised this aspect of her character, and had sought to exploit it while in the Tower. He had written to Rochester, 'Her nature is, if it be well followed, now others would oppress me, to be as much for me as afore she was against me.' He had hoped that she might be prevailed upon to speak up in his favour but, in his case, nothing came of this. Now, however, the Somersets benefited from her streak of perversity, for she became 'of another humour' towards them. On 22 February the Tuscan ambassador, Quaratesi, reported, 'The Queen is now said to favour the Earl and Countess, even though previously she was bitterly opposed to them.'[29]

More importantly the Lord Chief Justice was now locked in conflict with his most senior colleague on the commission of enquiry. In February the aged Lord Chancellor Ellesmere had fallen ill and, 'supposing him on his deathbed' (as an enemy of Coke's uncharitably put it), Coke had mounted an opportunistic attack on him. He claimed that, under Ellesmere's direction, the Court of Chancery had regularly exceeded its powers, ruling on cases which fell within the jurisdiction of other law courts. If these allegations had been proved, Ellesmere would have been liable for heavy penalties, including the confiscation of much of his property. However, when news of these developments was given to him on his sickbed, 'choler ... revived him' and he made it plain that he would vigorously defend himself. Now that there promised to be 'a shrewd battle' between these two eminent legal figures, it appeared increasingly unlikely that they could continue to work together to secure Somerset's downfall.[30]

Other opponents of Somerset had also fallen out with one another. The Earls of Arundel and Pembroke had recently quarrelled over an inheritance. Furthermore, of late Arundel had been assailed by qualms that the destruction of Somerset would entail the ruin of his Howard cousins and so, out of family feeling, he had become less eager to attack him. The Tuscan ambassador reported that Pembroke was so concerned by this change of attitude that he was intriguing to exclude Arundel from the commission of peers who would sit in judgement on Somerset, should his case come to trial. Besides this the ambassador noted that several influential figures who had earlier assisted George Villiers's rise to prominence were showing signs of disenchantment with him. On 15 February he reported, 'Some of Somerset's enemies are disgusted with the new favourite because he doesn't appreciate the fact that his power is due to them.'[31]

On 23 February Somerset's loyal supporter Sir John Holles confirmed Quaratesi's observations. He wrote cheerfully, 'This mountain of my Lord of Somerset's begins to fall again, like an empty bladder, which the Lord Chief Justice's breath only blew up to that monstrous magnitude ... The wind begins to tack about, and the new faction, though from private interests falling asunder into parts, yet all parts seem to wish well to the afflicted ... My Lady of Somerset's friends have access to her and the Lord in the Tower carries himself very well, with good temper and, for aught I can hear, is out of gunshot.' Holles sought to accentuate this trend by approaching the King through an intermediary, urging that, since the evidence against Somerset was purely circumstantial, it was inappropriate to proceed with his trial. During the next few weeks knowledgeable observers considered that things were continuing to improve for the Somersets. On 30 March Sir Dudley Carleton declared, 'Those that were at the bottom of fortune's wheel I hear are halfway up again.' There were also persistent rumours that Lady Suffolk would soon be welcomed back at court. King James, however, gave no indication as to what he intended to do next, forcing Holles to admit, 'No man knows the King's heart.'[32]

Men such as Coke, whose enmity towards Somerset had not abated in the slightest, eagerly awaited the return from Madrid of Sir John Digby, hoping that he would reveal matters which would make Somerset an object of universal execration. In the event, however, Digby imparted little of interest. He reached England on 20 March, and at once was closeted with the King for a two-hour interview. He then saw the Lord Chief Justice, who eagerly interrogated him, but Digby insisted that Coke had misinterpreted his letter about Spanish pensioners. Somewhat testily the ambassador later wrote to the King, 'I must confess unto your Majesty that I am of opinion that the coming of this letter unto my Lord Coke's hands hath been the cause of his aggravating matters very far; for he having there found mention made of the discovery of your Majesty's secrets, of great sums of money bestowed upon your Majesty's principal ministers, of Spanish pensions, of the selling of my despatches etc., either conjectured these things to have been absolutely held back from your Majesty, or else, lighting upon them in the prosecution of the business concerning my Lord of Somerset, made a wrong application of them to him.'[33]

Sir Francis Bacon (who was proceeding on the assumption that Somerset's trial would go ahead, even though the King had yet to make up his mind) was almost as disappointed as Coke that Digby had unveiled nothing of significance. Unlike Coke, he did not delude himself that Somerset's dealings with the Spanish ambassador could be taken as proof of his involvement in a nefarious scheme to betray King and country. Nevertheless, he was sure that if more could be found out about Somerset's links with Spain, it would provide a means of discrediting him. Bacon perceived – not without satisfaction – that Digby would be reluctant to discuss the matter further with Coke. The ambassador had been appalled by the outrageous manner in which Coke had sought to distort the facts to fit his own demented vision, and was now anxious to prevent the Lord Chief Justice from gaining access to any more state secrets. However, Bacon believed that Digby would understand that he was a man who would responsibly handle confidential information. He therefore requested King James to order Digby to cooperate with his own enquiries. He explained that, though Digby might protest that he knew of no evidence suggesting that Somerset was in the pay of Spain, he might be able to provide some clue to indicate that Somerset had been rewarded by Sarmiento. 'I am sure that no man was liker to be a pensioner than Somerset, considering his mercenary nature, his great undertaking for Spain in the match, and his favour with his Majesty,' argued Bacon.[34] The King gave the necessary authorisation but, contrary to Bacon's expectations, Digby proved incapable of telling him anything that could be used against Somerset.

Bacon then turned to other sources in the hope of obtaining what he wanted. Sir Robert Cotton had already been questioned about his meetings with Sarmiento and had given a somewhat guarded account of what had passed between them. Although he said nothing to suggest that Somerset had done anything detrimental to English interests, Bacon remained anxious to pursue the matter further. On 17 April Bacon went to the Tower with all the commissioners except Coke (who had now been excluded from this aspect of the enquiry, presumably because he had shown himself incapable of approaching the subject rationally). They demanded that Somerset tell them all that had gone on between him and Sarmiento, but Somerset was considerably less forthcoming than Cotton had been. He declined to say anything about his attempts to promote a marriage treaty and, while this did 'much aggravate suspicion against him', it left the commissioners with nothing on which to proceed.[35]

They next tried asking him outright whether he was a pensioner of Spain. In high indignation Somerset protested that 'he had such fortunes from his Majesty as he could not think of bettering his conditions from Spain'. Lacking independent evidence to the contrary, the commissioners had to accept his assurances. In fact Sarmiento's correspondence reveals that Somerset was not being strictly truthful on this matter. It was correct that, to date, he had never received any money from Spain. However, prior to his arrest, he had submitted a demand to Sarmiento that the Spaniards pay him £1,500 annually, matching the pension that had been allocated to the late Earl of Salisbury. Sarmiento had subsequently obtained clearance from his superiors to make such payments, but he had not handed over the first instalment at the time Somerset was taken into custody.[36] Fortunately for Somerset, the commissioners had no way of knowing that he and Sarmiento had come to this arrangement. In the absence of any proof as to its existence, Somerset's financial connection with Spain, which Coke had assumed would prove so damning, could not be raised at his trial. Accordingly the commissioners quietly abandoned this line of enquiry.

On 4 April 1616 Frances was moved the short distance from Blackfriars to the Tower of London. It was a development that took her and many others by surprise, in view of the fact that at court the animus against her seemed to have withered. John Chamberlain believed that the King had been angered because the Countess of Suffolk had recently reappeared at court, presuming she would be welcome, and it was this which had precipitated James's decision. Frances was 'given so short warning that she had scant leisure to shed a few tears over her little daughter at the parting'. Nevertheless, 'she carried herself every way constantly enough' and her composure was shattered only when, on her arrival at the Tower, she learned that she had been allocated the same room that Overbury had occupied. Then she became hysterical and 'did passionately deprecate and entreat the Lieutenant that she might not be

lodged in Sir Thomas Overbury's lodging'. Obligingly the new Lieutenant, Sir George More, moved out of his own quarters so that she could
occupy these until the rooms which Sir Walter Ralegh had recently
vacated could be made available.[37]

Frances's transfer to the Tower was scarcely a heartening omen, but
it did not mean that proceedings against her and her husband were
imminent. At one point, 15 April was mentioned as a likely date for her
trial, but this proved without foundation. The fact was the King had
yet to make up his mind about what action should be taken against the
Somersets. The only thing he was clear about was that, come what may,
neither of them should be executed. Apart from that he could not decide
whether to proceed with their trials or to impose sanctions of a more
informal nature. In this dilemma he turned to the Attorney-General.
On 28 April Bacon wrote a paper for the King, outlining his alternatives.

Bacon stated that, providing Somerset confessed that he was responsible for Overbury's murder, the King had three choices. He did not
have to bring the Somersets to trial at all, but could accept as sufficient
a humble submission, in which they prostrated themselves before the
King and implored his mercy. However, to prevent a public outcry at
such favourable treatment, the couple must be permanently disgraced,
and there must be an 'utter extinguishing of all hope of resuscitation of
their fortunes and favours'. Another possibility was to try the Somersets,
but to halt proceedings before judgement was passed. Alternatively the
sentence could be rescinded, thus ensuring not only that Somerset's life
was saved, but that his lands and goods were not subject to forfeiture.
Thirdly, the Somersets could be tried and sentenced, and their property
confiscated, but the King could spare them the death penalty.

When annotating this document, the King indicated that he favoured
the second alternative of halting the trials before sentence was given.
Unfortunately the situation was complicated by the fact that Somerset
was still maintaining his innocence. Bacon noted that, if Somerset failed
to confess, the King's options were considerably narrower. The trials
must proceed, and Bacon assumed that the King would not think it
appropriate to prevent judgement being passed on the offenders. In fact
it turned out that the King would still have preferred this to happen,
providing that such a course could 'stand with the law'. Bacon duly
promised to look into this, but was doubtful that he could find a legal
precedent. The Attorney-General was nevertheless confident that, if the
Somersets were tried and convicted, the King would be within his rights
if he remitted the death sentence. In view of the confessions already
made by Frances, it was logical to assume that she would plead guilty

and, in that case, 'her penitency and free confession' afforded 'ground of mercy'. If Somerset pleaded innocent, this could not apply to him, but Bacon argued that the King would be justified in sparing his life because 'the nature of the proof ... resteth chiefly upon presumptions'. In these circumstances, 'There may be an evidence so balanced, as it may have sufficient matter for the consciences of the peers to convict him, and yet leave sufficient matter in the conscience of a King to spare his life.' Bacon assured his master that in order not to circumscribe his freedom in this respect, he would take great care 'so to moderate the manner of charging [Somerset] as it make him not odious beyond the extent of mercy'.[38]

Bacon did not overlook the remote possibility that the peers would acquit Somerset. He told the King that this would be an eventuality 'which I would be very sorry should happen', but which need not be looked on as utterly disastrous. Even if absolved of murder, there were 'many high and heinous offences (though not capital)' which warranted Somerset being brought before the Council's own court, Star Chamber. Pending an appearance there, he could be confined in the Tower. The King endorsed this suggestion, approvingly annotating Bacon's text, 'This is so also.'[39] Unfortunately there is no way of identifying the transgressions to which Bacon alluded. Presumably they related either to Somerset's handling of the Spanish marriage negotiations, or some form of financial malpractice.

The fact that Frances had already acknowledged her part in the murder should have simplified Bacon's task considerably. In fact Bacon suspected that parts of her confession were misleading. It would seem that he pointed out the most serious discrepancies to the King, although Bacon was so consummate a courtier that he later praised James for having alerted him to the problem. Concern centred on Frances's confession of 8 January, when she had elucidated for Coke's benefit the letter she had sent to Sir Gervase Elwes. As will be recalled, Frances had claimed that she had been alluding to Somerset when she had written, 'If he should send ... ' but, to a dispassionate observer, it appeared inconceivable that this could be so. The King and Bacon agreed that Frances should be re-examined so she could clarify this point. When Coke heard this he objected vigorously that there should be 'no casting back to the business', but the King overruled him. On 29 April a chagrined Lord Chief Justice accompanied Bacon and the other commissioners to the Tower, where he heard Frances contradict her former confession on two crucial points. She denied that the phrase 'if he should send' had referred to Somerset and, furthermore, said that the person who had instructed her to write to Elwes had not been Somerset, but either Weston or Northampton. A satisfied Bacon reported all this to the King: 'His Majesty is found both a true prophet and most just King in that scruple he made,' he wrote unctuously, 'for now she expoundeth the word "he" that should send tarts to Elwes's wife to be of Overbury and not of Somerset ... For the person that should bid her, she sayeth it was Northampton or Weston, not pitching upon certainty, which giveth some advantage to the evidence.'[40]

Bacon promised that he would order the prosecuting counsel at Somerset's trial to take account of this by refraining from implying that Frances had written this letter on Somerset's orders. All this would seem to suggest that Bacon was scrupulously correct in his handling of the evidence, and that both he and the King were determined that Somerset should be treated fairly. And yet when one examines what actually occurred at Somerset's trial, it is less easy to feel that he was dealt with equitably. When Frances's letter was read out, no mention was made of the fact that she had said she was acting under the directions of either Weston or Northampton. While it was never explicitly stated that it was Somerset who had dictated what she wrote, those present in the courtroom inferred this. An example is provided by Edward Sherburn's account of Somerset's trial. When transcribing the part of Frances's letter where she had written, 'I was moreover bid to tell you that if he did send you any wine,' he noted in brackets, 'by which was meant the Earl of Somerset'. Similarly Lord Compton, one of the peers who was trying Somerset, confronted him on this issue, saying, 'My Lady in her letter writes, "I was bid to bid you do this." Who should bid her but you my Lord?' Though Bacon and his colleagues on the Prosecution knew that Frances had supplied an answer to this question, they kept this to themselves.[41] Indeed it is hard not to suspect that Bacon's eagerness to question Frances about her suspect confession derived primarily from a belief that it would reflect badly on Coke if she revised what she had said earlier, rather than because he wished to discard evidence that might be unsound.

In fact what Bacon considered most unsatisfactory about Frances's confessions was not that they featured admissions which were demonstrably false, but that they did not go as far as he considered desirable. He was disturbed by her attempts to exonerate her husband, and determined that she must not be given a chance to repeat such things in public. He resolved to discuss with the judges whether if, at her trial, Frances made 'any digression to clear his Lordship', she could be 'interrupted and silenced' by whoever was presiding over the hearing. Clearly, however, it would be preferable if Frances did not even try to make any inconvenient utterances. One way of avoiding this would be to attack Somerset only in her absence. Ostensibly out of concern for her welfare, Frances could be removed from the courtroom once the trial had started, freeing Bacon to cast as many aspersions on Somerset as he wanted.

Bacon explained all this to George Villiers in a letter written on 10 May. He cautioned him that he thought it probable that if Frances heard anything at her trial that implied that Somerset was guilty, 'she might break into passionate protestations for his clearing'. Although this could 'be justly made light of, yet it is better avoided'. Therefore, after conferring with the Lord Chancellor, he proposed that before he started discussing the case in court, the Countess should, 'in respect of her weakness, and not to add further afflication, be withdrawn'.[42] For some reason, however (perhaps the King demurred, when Villiers showed him this letter), this plan was not followed: Frances was present throughout all the proceedings against her. Instead, in his courtroom address, Bacon refrained from expatiating on Somerset's guilt, claiming that it would be more appropriate to reserve the evidence for Somerset's own trial. The tactic worked, insomuch as Frances's trial passed off without her making any embarrassing outbursts.

On 24 April 1616 summonses were sent to twenty-five peers who had been chosen to sit as jurors at the Somersets' trials. Among them were several of Somerset's known enemies, the most notable of whom were the Earls of Pembroke, Montgomery and Worcester, and Lord Lisle. It was also an ill omen for Somerset that Lord Chancellor Ellesmere was named as the Lord High Steward who would preside over the hearing. Equally significant was the fact that the Earl of Arundel, who was regarded as sympathetic to Somerset, did not feature on the panel of jurors. However, those chosen to serve were by no means universally hostile to Somerset. During a break in Somerset's trial one of the peers on the jury, the Earl of Rutland, sent him refreshments, which seems indicative of a friendly regard for the accused. Questions asked during the proceedings by Lords Wentworth, Darcy and Compton also show that, quite properly, they had not decided in advance whether Somerset was innocent or guilty. Clearly their verdict was determined by weighing up the evidence, rather than being a foregone conclusion.

At last the King nerved himself to make a decision about the Somersets. It was given out that the Countess's trial would be held on

15 May, and that her husband's would take place a day later. Nevertheless, James was still profoundly unhappy at the prospect of Somerset proclaiming his innocence in court. He remained most anxious that the Earl should enter a plea of guilty and, accordingly, pressure on Somerset was intensified. On 3 May he was once again interrogated, and he made one new admission which was considered significant. When asked whether he had sent Frances letters about Overbury during the summer of 1613, when he was accompanying the King on progress, Somerset initially denied this. Then he changed his mind, saying that perhaps he had mentioned Overbury in his letters, although he could not recall details. At his trial the Prosecution claimed that Somerset volunteered this much only because he feared the commissioners had gained possession of these letters, and he thought it better to make vague admissions than to be exposed as a flagrant liar. Nevertheless, although the commissioners might congratulate themselves on having forced Somerset to compromise himself further, this fell far short of the unqualified confession which the King was seeking. It became clear to James that the impasse would not be broken without some new initiative on his part.

On 9 May, and 'in such secrecy none living may know of it', King James sent a message to Somerset in the Tower. The bearer was probably Somerset's cousin and namesake, Sir Robert Carr. The latter had Somerset to thank for his position in Prince Charles's household, but he was now on somewhat distant terms with his kinsman and could be relied upon to do the King's bidding. As far as can be gathered the King told Somerset that, providing he confessed, not only would his life be spared, but his wife and child would be treated more favourably. Somerset evinced not the slightest interest in this offer: he indicated that he looked on it as a far from powerful inducement and that, anyway, he remained confident of clearing himself in court.[43]

Following this disappointing response, pressure of a different sort was applied to Frances. On Sunday 12 May the ever obliging Dr Whiting was engaged to hold a private service of worship in Frances's chamber in the Tower. In his sermon he enjoined her to 'clear confession', by which was meant a confession which incriminated her husband. Immediately after this the Lieutenant of the Tower informed Frances that her trial would take place the following Wednesday. He too told her that it was not only her 'Christian duty' to 'deal clearly' touching her husband, but that it would be 'good for them both' if she did so. The effect was far different from what had been hoped for. The shock caused Frances to be seized by 'a sudden vomiting ... together with a looseness', which incapacitated her for several days.[44]

On 13 May the King made another attempt to wear down Somerset's resistance. He asked the Lieutenant of the Tower to pass on a message that, if Somerset acknowledged his guilt, 'I will not only perform what I promised by my last messenger, both towards him and his wife, but I will enlarge it.' He added, 'I mean not that he shall confess if he be innocent, but ye know how evil likely [unlikely] that is.' He asked More to point out to Somerset that though he now maintained that he would never be found guilty, only the previous February he had told Coke 'his cause was so evil likely as he knew no jury could [ac]quit him'. The King concluded by requesting More to tell Somerset, 'as from yourself', that Frances was expected to 'plead weakly for his innocency', and that the commissioners were confident that, before going to trial, she would reveal everything about the part played by her husband in the murder.[45] As we know, this was completely untrue, and this dishonourable stratagem merely reveals the depths of the King's desperation. Humiliatingly, the ploy proved unsuccessful. In the face of all these blandishments, Somerset kept up an obstinate silence.

After the commissioners had paid Somerset another visit, and that too had failed to move him, the King decided he had no alternative but to postpone the first of the two trials until 23 May. Frances's illness was used as a reason, and it was also given out that more time was needed because the Earl of Somerset had recently sent a message to James 'to the effect that he wished to discover and declare great matters'. In reality, of course, the very converse was the case, and the Spanish ambassador, for one, had no illusions as to the true position. He wrote home that he did not doubt that the delay had been caused by the commissioners' desire 'to find fresh proofs, and that they might urge him again to confess his faults'.[46]

On 17 May the Duke of Lennox and Lord Hay were sent to Frances, 'persuading her afresh to declare what she knew against her husband. She said that, with respect to Overbury's death, she had declared and confessed her own fault, and had even enhanced it, in order to have more to work upon the pity and clemency of the King, but that she did not know that the Earl was guilty of this or anything else'.[47]

The two noblemen then went to see Somerset. Hay had formerly been on good terms with the prisoner – it will be recalled that the then Robert Carr may have been acting as squire to Hay when he broke his leg in the tiltyard – but the relationship was no longer cordial. The Earl of Northampton, who had hated Hay, seems to have caused the rift by revealing that, in conversation with a friend, Hay had 'after a frank manner, opened his mislike of the matching of this sweet lady [Frances] with my sweet lord'.[48] Despite the coldness that had ensued, the King hoped that the memory of Hay's earlier kindness, joined with the fact that they were compatriots, would encourage Somerset to listen to him.

Lennox and Hay began by speaking approvingly of the way that Frances had thrown herself on the King's mercy. They said that, because she had been so candid, there was every chance that she would not be executed, and they begged Somerset to follow her example. The Earl countered that he thought it strange that they should praise the King for his clemency, when it was still intended to bring his wife to trial, a humiliation he had assumed she would be spared. As for himself, he insisted he had been 'badly treated without cause' and, for the first time, he hinted that, unless proceedings against him were dropped, the King would have reason to regret it. In a tone of unmistakable menace he warned his interlocutors that he had expected better 'from the prudence of the King and of those who counselled him' for, if he was tried, 'he would say that which he knew in his own defence, without the King being able to complain of it, since he was the cause of it'.[49]

We can only guess at what Somerset had in mind. The most likely hypothesis is that he was contemplating revealing the part played by the King in Overbury's imprisonment, which would have been highly embarrassing for James. Lennox and Hay, who had no idea what Somerset meant, were nevertheless horrified by the veiled threats he was making. Hay said firmly that 'he should abstain from talking this way, and that he saw in his face that he was guilty and that he thought he could see the confession in his mouth and even in his lips'. While acknowledging that Somerset's recent ingratitude had so annoyed him that he had actually urged the King to imprison him, Hay implored the Earl 'to speak it out, and take the advice of a man who, at that moment, was speaking to him as a brother and faithful friend'. With icy politeness Somerset replied 'that he had always wished to serve him, and he regretted that he had not been as successful in this as he wished'. He conceded that, because of his past obligations to Hay, 'he was bound to take his advice, and to follow it as far as possible'. Nevertheless, 'a confession of what had never been could not be in his mouth nor anywhere else'. For three hours Lennox and Hay laboured to convince Somerset of the futility of further denials but, at length, they admitted defeat and departed.[50]

That night the Lieutenant of the Tower resumed the argument, trying 'with no more effect, to accomplish the same object'. All that happened was that Somerset repeated his warning that, unless the King was careful, he could make things unpleasant for him. Sir George More passed this on to King James, who answered by letter. Wearily he wrote, 'I am extremely sorry that your unfortunate prisoner turns all the great care I have of him not only against himself, but against me also, as far as he can. I cannot blame you that ye cannot conjecture what this may be, for God knows, it is only a trick of his idle brain, hoping thereby to shift his trial. But it is easy to be seen that he would threaten me with laying an aspersion upon me of being in some sort accessory to his crime.' James insisted he would not submit to this intimidation, arguing that, if he cancelled the trials at this stage, it would indeed suggest that there was something about Overbury's murder which he wished kept hidden.[51]

Though determined to withstand Somerset's blackmail, James was sufficiently disturbed to ask Francis Bacon for advice on how best to control his former favourite. According to Anthony Weldon, a melo-dramatic scheme was adopted. Weldon claimed that, throughout Somer-set's trial, two men with cloaks were standing behind him, ready to throw them over his head and muffle his words if he tried to say anything that reflected on the King adversely. Clearly this was untrue but, from Bacon's papers, we know that there were other contingency plans to prevent Somerset causing James embarrassment. Bacon pro-posed that, when Somerset arrived at Westminster Hall, the Lieutenant should deliver a stern lecture while they waited for the prisoner to be called into the courtroom. The Attorney-General noted, 'The Lieutenant should tell him roundly that if in his speeches he shall tax the King, that the justice of England is that he shall be taken away and the evidence shall go on without him, and all the people will cry away with him, and then it shall not be in the King's will to save his life, the people will be so set on fire.' If Somerset disregarded this warning and said anything which threatened to bring dishonour on the King, then the Lord Steward must intervene. If it proved impos-sible to silence the prisoner, he must 'be told that, if he take that course, he is to be withdrawn, and evidence to be given in his absence'.[52]

Because of Somerset's intransigence, the trials were put back one more day. On the evening of 23 May Lord Hay paid his former protégé another visit and once again urged him to confess everything. Then, 'seeing that there was no hope of that, [he] counselled him, with very lively arguments, to moderation and patience, so as not to break bounds or meddle with what did not concern him, since, by this, he would oblige the King; strongly assuring him ... of the King's affection and goodwill towards him, again assuring him that, if he did not do this, he would risk all'.[53]

Despite his failure to secure an undertaking that Somerset would behave circumspectly at his trial – much less a confession – the King resolved to wait no longer. Just before eight o'clock in the morning of Friday 24 May the Countess of Somerset was taken by barge from the Tower of London to be tried in Westminster Hall. Attorney-General Francis Bacon had long deliberated about the wisdom of trying her before her husband. If Somerset's trial had preceded hers, and he had been found guilty, it would not have mattered if the Countess had proclaimed his innocence at her own hearing for, once a conviction had been obtained, it could not be overturned on that basis. There was also a chance that, if Somerset's turn came first, he would 'be in the better temper, hoping of his own clearing, and of her respiting'. Conversely, if he came to court in the knowledge that his wife had already pleaded guilty without attempting to exonerate him, there was no predicting his behaviour.[54] On balance, however, Bacon had concluded that there was a better chance of securing Somerset's conviction once his wife had publicly admitted her guilt. The Countess was therefore the first to face her accusers.

According to one observer, Frances appeared unconscious of the gravity of the occasion. It was claimed that, as she rode by barge upriver, 'she looked very merrily and smiled'.[55] However, once at the bar of Westminster Hall, surrounded by tiered rows of spectators, and facing the scrutiny of judges and peers, all trace of levity vanished. As the indictment was read out, cataloguing Weston's crimes and alleging that she had procured them, she quivered and wept openly. When called upon to return a formal answer to the charge of being accessory to murder, it was in a notably subdued manner that she entered her plea of guilty.

Despite the fact that she stood accused of a terrible felony, Frances still enjoyed the protection of her rank. In contrast to those unfortunates whose cases had already been heard, she was treated throughout the proceedings in an almost deferential manner. When Attorney-General Bacon rose to address the courtroom, he began by praising the Countess for confessing her crime. This marked her out from the other low-born offenders, who had lacked the nobility to acknowledge their evil actions. 'Those meaner persons upon whom justice passed before, confessed not; she doth,' he argued, adding, 'I know your Lordships cannot behold her without compassion. Many things may move you: her youth, her person, her sex, her noble family, yea, her provocations ... but chiefly her penitency and confession.'[56]

Bacon then delicately intimated that it was most unlikely that the Countess would hang for her crime. He observed that, so far in the reign of King James, the only members of the nobility who had been sentenced to death had been Lords Cobham and Grey, who had been convicted of treason. Since the penalty had not been carried out, the natural inference was that Frances would escape execution, particularly in view of the fact that the two peers' offences had been directed against the King and state. In contrast, the Countess's criminality was much narrower in character, having merely brought about 'the death of a particular subject'. Furthermore, unlike Cobham and Grey, the Countess and her husband had been high in the King's favour. By bringing them to justice King James had demonstrated that he was 'the best King in the world' whose 'affections royal are above his affections private', but his former closeness to these malefactors seemed likely to temper his severity.[57]

Bacon declined at this hearing to go into details about the murder. He observed magnanimously, 'I will enforce nothing against a penitent, neither will I open anything against him that is absent.' In fact, of course, his reticence was prompted by the fear that if he was too outspoken against Somerset, Frances would vigorously rebut the allegations. Instead Bacon confined himself to summarising events which took place after the murder. He first deplored the way that Overbury's death had initially been ascribed to venereal disease. Then he described how Elwes had been persuaded to disclose what he knew, and how this had led to Weston's arrest, Coke's investigation and the subsequent trials and executions. In conclusion, having read out the directions issued by the King at the start of the murder enquiry, he claimed that the delay in bringing the Somersets to court was due to 'weighty grounds and causes', which concerned state security rather than the case under consideration. Having tantalised his audience with this enigmatic pronouncement, he brought his address to a close by praying the Lord Steward to deliver judgement.

Before Ellesmere complied, the clerk of the court asked the Countess if she could think of any reason why sentence of death should not be passed on her. 'In a most humble, yet not base manner', Frances gave her answer. Apologising that 'the conduits of her voice were hindered with tears and sorrow of heart', she said merely, 'I can much aggravate, but nothing extenuate, my fault. I desire mercy and that the Lords will intercede for me to the King.' She spoke so low that Ellesmere could not catch her words, but Bacon repeated them for him, 'with some amplification'.[58]

Having satisfied himself that she had nothing further to say, the Lord High Steward proceeded to pronounce the death sentence mandatory in cases of felony. He did so, however, 'with compassion', promising that, having witnessed 'the humility and grief' she had manifested, the Lords would mediate on her behalf with the King. Though Ellesmere had no choice but to decree that she 'be hanged by the neck till she were stark dead', the terrible words were 'so sweetened by the delivery' that few people present expected the sentence to be enacted. The prisoner herself 'heard it without much amazement'. Having once again curtsied deeply, she was led out, 'in a constant and comely guise'. It is possible, however, that she was so calm only because she had not fully taken in what had happened. The proceedings had been 'all done in an hour and a half' and one account states that, at her departure, she did not realise that her trial was over. This is verified by another observer who reported, 'It seemeth she did not rightly understand it for, when she came into the barge, she asked what the Lords had said and being told by the Lieutenant she was condemned, she took on extremely, and would have gone back again to deliver some paper she had in her pocket.' Perhaps she was upset at having missed her opportunity to exculpate her husband but, if so, the mistake could not be corrected. As the Countess registered the fact that she was now a convicted felon, 'she returned back to the Tower with a heavier countenance than she came'.[59]

On the whole Frances had created a favourable impression at her trial. It is true that Edward Sherburn criticised her demeanour as being 'more curious and confident than was fit for a lady in such distress'. However, when writing to another correspondent he revised this, conceding, 'She behaved herself so nobly and worthily as did express to the world she was well taught and had better learned her lesson.' Surprisingly Sir Ralph Winwood also commended her dignity and poise, noting, 'The Lady carried herself with such modesty and temperate assuredness as did work in the hearts of the assistants much commiseration of her unhappiness.' As for a courtier named Edward Palavacino, he was positively smitten by the spectacle of this beautiful young woman brought before this solemn tribunal. In adulatory tones he declared 'the prisoner's behaviour truly noble ... fashioned ... with so much sweetness, grace and good form, as if all the graces had heaped their whole powers to render her that day the most beloved, the most commiserated spectacle, and the best wished unto that ever presented itself before a scene of death'.[60]

*

The Countess's trial could not have gone more smoothly, and the King could justly feel relief at the result. That evening, however, an unforeseen crisis occurred. When told to prepare himself for his appearance in court the following day, the Earl of Somerset told the Lieutenant of the Tower, Sir George More, that he would not present himself for trial. He said that the only way of getting him to Westminster Hall would be to drag him there by force. Sir Anthony Weldon later claimed that Sir George More told him himself that, when he informed the King of this, in the early hours of the morning, James had burst into tears. In Weldon's version, the desperate King then instructed the Lieutenant to tell his prisoner that James was as affectionate as ever towards him and that, though as a formality Somerset must stand trial, there was no doubt of his acquittal. Weldon alleged that Somerset was deceived by this and agreed on these terms to submit himself for judgement. By the time he realised his mistake, it was too late to escape.[61] In fact, though More may have mentioned to Sir Anthony the last minute difficulties caused by Somerset, it is clear that the King and the Lieutenant coped with them in a manner far different from that alleged by Weldon. A holograph letter of the King survives, instructing More how to deal with the emergency. From this it is evident that, though James was naturally concerned by More's 'strange news', he was in no way panic stricken.

James wrote that he would send Sir Robert Carr and Lord Hay to reason with Somerset for one last time. If that had no effect, More 'must do your office', using coercion if that was the only way of taking Somerset to court. James stipulated that the only circumstances in which he would countenance any postponement of the proceedings would be if More believed Somerset to be 'either apparently sick or distracted of his wits'. In that case the hearing could be put back by two days, after which it would be easier to tell if the prisoner's symptoms were feigned. Such firmness paid off but, clearly, More had no easy task persuading Somerset to cooperate. Somerset did not arrive at Westminster Hall until nearly ten o'clock, almost two hours after the hearing was scheduled to begin. Sir Ralph Winwood claimed that, even to achieve this, More had had 'to threaten to carry him by force if willingly he would not go'.[62]

Once again the Hall was packed to capacity. Edward Sherburn reported that there were 'more ladies and great personages than ever, I think, were seen at any trial'. The Earl of Essex was prominent among these. During the previous day's hearing he had done his best to make himself as inconspicuous as possible, but today he flaunted his presence.

Making no attempt to hide his exultation at Somerset's discomfiture, he positioned himself so that he 'stood full in his face'.[63]

The anticipation of the spectators had been heightened by the widespread belief that the charges which Somerset faced would not merely relate to Overbury's murder, but would extend to treason, witchcraft and espionage. Even so sober and well-informed a person as Sir John Throckmorton thought that Somerset would be accused of selling secrets to Spain, poisoning the King's children and 'procuring by sorcery to inveigle the King's heart so as he should have no power to deny him anything'. Nevertheless, although Lord Chief Justice Coke believed he had uncovered a mass of evidence implicating Somerset in such matters, the Attorney-General Bacon had no intention of utilising it. In Bacon's opinion many of Coke's findings were little more than 'loose conjecture', and he believed that it would actually undermine the Prosecution's case to include such 'frivolous things'. To guard against being accused of having 'omitted divers material parts of the evidence', on 5 May he listed for the King those items he planned to discard. They included an allegation that Mrs Turner had given Dr Forman a waxen image of a young man which – so Coke believed – had been a representation of the late Prince of Wales. Also rejected was the claim that at Whitehall Mrs Turner had pointed out to Franklin a physician with a red beard, whom she claimed had poisoned Prince Henry. As Bacon observed, even if there was any foundation for these stories (which he clearly doubted), neither had any real bearing on Somerset's case and placed undue weight on testimony given by Franklin after conviction. Agreeably aware that his comments could not fail to damage Coke, Bacon explained that he feared that it would debase the solemnity of the proceedings to feature 'evidence which touches not the delinquent or is not of weight'. Of no less significance was the fact that, if he made use of such material, Somerset might be so infuriated that he would say something offensive, when the King's anxiety to avoid this had led him to give orders that the prisoner should not be unnecessarily goaded.[64]

Nevertheless, because of the speculation and excitement that the trial had generated, Bacon felt that it was not enough to attribute Overbury's murder to a mere dispute over a woman. Conscious that a belief had been inculcated in the public that there was more to it than that, he feared that the Crown's case would be deemed disappointingly meagre unless he could offer a more weighty explanation. Bacon told the King, 'It is most necessary to establish that the malice [of Somerset for Overbury] was a deep malice mixed with fear, and not only matter of revenge upon his lady's quarrel.' The problem was, how to achieve this without so inflaming public opinion that Somerset's execution became unavoidable. Bacon had ruled out accusing Somerset 'by way of aggravation, with matters tending to disloyalty or treason'. Not only was there little evidence to justify such charges, but Bacon feared that, if provoked in this way, Somerset would retaliate by making personal attacks on the King. In these circumstances Bacon decided that it would be best to present Somerset's actions as being inspired, not just by anger at the obstruction of his romance with the Countess of Essex, but by dread that Overbury would destroy him by betraying political secrets.

The beauty of this approach was that there was no need to specify what the secrets in question were. It was enough to demonstrate that, by virtue of his friendship with Somerset, Overbury had had access to confidential information. It could then be argued that, when the two men had fallen out, Somerset had felt vulnerable to Overbury's threats of exposure. The details could remain mysterious: Bacon was confident that it would suffice if, 'by some taste that I shall give to the peers in general, they may conceive of what nature those secrets may be', and that further elaboration would be unnecessary.[65]

Standing before the bar in Westminster Hall, the Earl of Somerset presented a very different spectacle from the smooth-cheeked youth who, nine years earlier, had so entranced the King. Though his hair was as tightly curled as ever (on 21 May the French ambassador reported that in the Tower Somerset was devoting his usual attention to crimping his locks artificially), the experiences of the last few months had left him gaunt and haggard, 'his visage pale, his beard long, his eyes sunk in his head'. Eschewing the peacock raiment of his heyday, he was dressed in a 'plain black satin suit'. Despite the warm weather, he wore over it a cloak of black velvet. His Garter insignia, or 'George', which hung about his neck as a defiant reminder that he had formerly been the King's most trusted intimate, provided the only ornamentation.[66]

The clerk of the court having issued the command, 'Robert Earl of Somerset, hold up thy hand,' the indictment was read aloud. This stated that Richard Weston had been proved to have administered poison to Sir Thomas Overbury in four different ways, namely, poison in broth, poisonous powder, poisoned tarts and a poisoned glister. The Earl of Somerset was charged with having 'stirred up, moved, commanded, abetted, aided, hired, counselled and assisted the said Weston in the execution hereof' and was therefore indicted as an accessory before the fact of Sir Thomas Overbury's murder.[67]

While the indictment was recited Somerset 'three or four times whispered' to the Lieutenant of the Tower, who was standing behind him. When the reading had finished, the prisoner was asked how he pleaded and, 'making an obeisance to the Lord High Steward', Somerset answered firmly, 'Not Guilty.' The clerk of the court next demanded, 'How wilt thou be tried?' to which the Earl replied 'By God and the country.' Then, realising his mistake, he corrected himself by saying, 'By God and my peers.'[68]

As Lord High Steward, Ellesmere then addressed Somerset. He promised that the court would listen to all he had to say in his own defence, but urged him not to lie in hopes of saving himself. 'Remember', warned Ellesmere, '... God is the God of truth ... To deny that which is true increases the offence; take heed lest your wilfulness cause the gates of mercy to be shut upon you.' There was general surprise when, contrary to normal procedure, Somerset was told that he would be permitted pen and ink so that he could take notes which would aid him to draw up his defence. It is unclear why he was granted this concession; possibly the King was responsible. Yet Somerset remained acutely aware that he was still at a terrible disadvantage. At some point he asked permission to deal with the evidence against him point by point, rather than having to wait till the Prosecution had finished presenting its case. The application was rejected on the grounds that 'the manner of our trial is to lay down the whole evidence together'.[69]

One of the three members of the Prosecution team, Henry Montague, now made some introductory remarks. He began by saying that the instigator of any crime was far more reprehensible than the person who carried out his instructions. 'My Lord,' he thundered to Somerset, 'I affirm boldly it was Weston that poisoned but you that persuaded.' Though Weston's hand had done the deed, 'the naughty and mischievous contriving of it was in this Lord's heart'. Somerset therefore stood indicted of 'procuring Weston four several times to deliver four several poisons to Sir Thomas Overbury, which he took and thereof he died'.[70]

This prompted an intervention from the Lord High Steward. Ellesmere explained to the peers that the question at issue was not the precise dates when poison was given, nor the sort of poison employed. What mattered was whether Overbury had been killed on Somerset's orders. Lord Chief Justice Coke who, like the other judges, was seated near Ellesmere, 'seconded the Lord High Steward'. He announced that it was unrealistic to expect the indictment to be absolutely accurate. Provided that the peers were satisfied that the substance of it was correct, that was sufficient.[71]

The Attorney-General, Francis Bacon, then rose to deliver a lengthy oration. He began by declaring that he knew that the peers would require 'sound and sufficient matter of proof' before condemning a member of their own privileged community. He promised to furnish them with this, and to do so without making unfair 'invectives' against Somerset. The King himself had enjoined such restraint on Bacon and his colleagues, and Bacon said that this did not worry him, 'this being such a cause as shall not need any aggravation'. Even though the crime under consideration was 'a work of darkness' and poisoning 'the most secret manner of murdering', Bacon was confident that, 'so far hath the finger of God shewed itself in the discovery of this close and obscure complot that I shall without any great difficulty direct your Lordships with the lantern of truth and carry it before you upright and safe from the blasting winds of any frivolous evasions or weak pretences of the prisoner'.[72]

Bacon next passed some general observations on the 'nature and greatness of the offence' being tried. Murder, he said, was the greatest of crimes apart from high treason, and 'the foulest of felonies'. What made this one worse, however, was that it was 'murder by impoisonment'. Besides this, the victim had been a prisoner in the Tower, 'a thing that aggravates the fault much'. Poisoning, asserted Bacon, was a cowardly and subversive crime alien to the national character, 'a foreign manslayer fetched from Rome ... an Italian revenger, a stranger to the records of England'. There were three aspects of poisoning which made it 'grievous beyond other murders'. The first was that its victims were seized unawares as they sought refreshment, supposedly 'in full peace'. Next, Bacon condemned the crime as 'easily committed, easily concealed and, on the other side, hardly prevented and hardly discovered'. Furthermore, it often extended beyond 'the destruction of the maliced man', claiming accidental victims who happened to be dining with the poisoner's real enemy.[73]

The very nature of the crime meant that evidence relating to it tended to be looser in character than that put forward when other offences were tried. 'If in all cases of impoisonment you should require testimony, you were as good proclaim impunity,' Bacon claimed. Because the law recognised this, it was valid to convict those accused of 'works of darkness' without being shown 'such apparent proofs as in other open and visible sins'. It was for this reason that the Lords need not concern themselves as to whether Somerset's indictment was correct in every particular. Indeed Bacon went further than Ellesmere by saying that the peers were not required to devote any consideration at all to the manner of Overbury's death. That question had already been settled, for 'all the world by law is concluded to say that Overbury was impoisoned by

Weston'. Instead they merely had to decide whether it was Somerset who had procured the deed and abetted the murderer. This could have been in any one of a number of ways: buying, preparing or supplying poison were all obvious acts of abetment, but Somerset was also guilty if it could be shown that he had done anything 'to give the opportunity of impoisonment ... or to stop and divert any impediments that might hinder it ... with an intention to accomplish and achieve the impoisonment'.[74]

Bacon then applied himself to setting the murder in context. He described the devoted friendship that had once existed between Somerset and Overbury, and how Overbury had dominated and over-awed the younger man. 'This friendship rested not only in conversation and business of court, but likewise in communication of secrets of state,' Bacon affirmed, explaining that, while Rochester had been acting as provisional Secretary of State, he had revealed all manner of the King's confidential business to Sir Thomas. At this point Somerset demanded angrily why Bacon was dwelling on 'these impertinent and by matters, done by the King's commandment?' Bacon answered that he did it to show 'that, as there were common secrets between you, so there were common dangers'.[75]

Bacon next detailed how the close bond between the two men was transformed into mortal hatred after Rochester's 'unlawful love' for the Countess of Essex made him set on marrying her. Sir Thomas 'touched her with unchaste life', Bacon noted, but he urged his listeners not to assume that this denoted a superiority of character on Overbury's part. On the contrary, 'so far was he from cases of conscience in this matter' that he actually boasted of having assisted Rochester's conquest by penning letters for him.[76]

These animadversions on Overbury represented a marked departure from the policy followed at the earlier murder trials. There, Overbury had always been referred to in admiring terms as a worthy gentleman who, unhappily, had offended the King, but whose talents and fine qualities were undisputed. At Weston's trial, for example, Lawrence Hyde described Sir Thomas as 'a gentleman of good descent ... a man of exceeding civil and virtuous conversation'. During Mrs Turner's trial, Lord Chief Justice Coke went so far as to speak 'of the love the King bare unto' Overbury, notwithstanding his imprisonment. Now, however, Bacon had to ensure that it remained possible for the King to reprieve Somerset after conviction, and for this it was necessary to depict Overbury in a much less favourable light. At this point, therefore, Bacon launched a devastating attack on the deceased man. He averred that

Overbury '(to speak plainly) had little that was solid for religion or moral virtue, but was a man possessed with ambition and vainglory'. His opposition to the marriage with Lady Essex derived not from high principle but because he 'was loth to have any partners in the favour of my Lord of Somerset'. Remorselessly Bacon continued, 'And certainly (my Lords), howsoever the tragical misery of that poor gentleman Overbury ought somewhat to obliterate his faults yet, because we are not now upon point of civility, but to discover the face of truth to the face of justice, and that it is material to the true understanding of the state of this cause, Overbury was naught and corrupt.'[77]

Having delivered himself of these strictures, Bacon resumed his narrative. He declared, 'When Overbury saw that he was like to be dispossessed of my Lord here ... by whose greatness he had promised himself to do wonders,' he 'dealt violently with him to make him desist [from marrying], with menaces of discovery of secrets and the like'. As a result of this threatening behaviour, 'two streams of hatred' were directed towards Overbury. One came from the Countess of Essex, 'in respect he crossed her love and abused her name, which are furies to women'. 'The other, of a more deeper and more mineral nature' welled up in Somerset, caused by fears that, if Overbury 'did break from him and fly out, he would mine into him and trouble his whole fortunes'. The third member of the unholy alliance dedicated to securing Overbury's downfall was the Earl of Northampton. The latter, desiring 'to be first in favour with my Lord of Somerset, and knowing Overbury's malice to himself and his house, thought that the man must be removed and cut off'.[78]

'So it was amongst them resolved and decreed that Overbury must die,' Bacon stated flatly. Having considered and then rejected a plan to have Overbury murderously assaulted, they hit on poison as the most satisfactory method of disposal. However, it was first necessary to place Overbury in confinement, 'for then they could not miss their mark'. Here Bacon was on dangerous ground, for there must be no hint that the King had acted improperly in sending Overbury to the Tower. Bacon skated over the difficulty with sinuous grace: he ably conveyed that, once Overbury had been incited to defiance, the King could not have responded other than he did. 'My Lords,' he observed gravely. 'No Man is imprisoned without a cause; the law of England would have all free; some ground therefore must be raised to abridge Overbury of his liberty.' By arranging for Overbury to be named as an ambassador, the conspirators hit upon the perfect contrivance, enabling them to 'animate him to commit a contempt in refusing that employment, for which he might be committed'.[79]

Pressing on, Bacon mentioned briefly the installation of Elwes and Weston at the Tower, which created the ideal conditions for the conspirators to effect their scheme. Once Overbury was sealed in an environment where he was uniquely vulnerable, 'then was the time to execute the last act of this tragedy. Then must Franklin be purveyor of the poisons and procure five, six, seven several potions to be sure to hit his complexion. Then must Mrs Turner be the [es]say mistress of the poisons to try upon poor beasts what's present [fast-acting] and what works at distance of time. Then must Weston be the tormentor and chase him with poison after poison: poison in salts, poison in meats, poison in sweetmeats, poison in medicines and vomits, until at last his body was almost come by use of poisons to the state that ... the force of poisons were blunted upon him, Weston confessing when he was chid for not despatching him that he had given him enough to poison twenty men.' Meantime, while seeing to it that Overbury remained in prison, Rochester distracted him with 'continual letters, partly of hopes and projects for his delivery, and partly of other fables and negotiations'.[80]

Having finished his résumé, Bacon stated that the evidence against Somerset fell into four sections. The first task of the Prosecution was to establish a motive by demonstrating that there existed between Somerset and Overbury 'a root of bitterness, a mortal malice or hatred mixed with deep and bottomless fears'. Secondly, it was incumbent on them to prove that Somerset was 'a principal actor' in Overbury's murder, and that he was involved 'in all those acts which did conduce to the impoisonment and which gave opportunity and means to effect it'. Next, Bacon said it could be proved that Somerset's 'hand was in the very impoisonment itself'. This was shown by the fact that Somerset not only delivered to the Tower some of the poisons which killed Overbury, but then showed acute interest in Overbury's state of health, 'calling for despatch' when Overbury lived longer than expected. Lastly, Somerset's behaviour subsequent to Overbury's death was indicative of his guilt. Not only he had concealed and destroyed vital evidence, but he had also sought a pardon from the King which would have indemnified him from prosecution.[81] Bacon announced that he would deal with the first two heads himself, leaving the others to his colleagues, Sir Henry Montague and Randall Crew.

Bacon first set out to demonstrate that Somerset had come to hate and fear Overbury. In support of this he produced Henry Peyton's written description of the row he had overheard between Rochester and

Overbury at Whitehall. Peyton was then called in person to confirm his
original account. He supplemented it by relating how he had warned
Rochester that Overbury was gravely ill in the Tower, and how this had
elicited nothing more from the defendant than a contemptuous 'Pish!'
Perhaps because Peyton was nervous, several of the peers on the jury
found his testimony less than convincing. 'The Lord Darcy of the
North, Wentworth and Compton said these were but presumptions and
no clear evidences.'[82]

An examination of Overbury's other servant, Lawrence Davies, was
then read. Unfortunately the original is not in the Public Record Office,
and the only text we have is that printed in *State Trials*. We cannot be
certain that it is accurate. According to this, when examined by Coke,
Davies recalled hearing his master say that he would have accepted the
post of ambassador had Rochester not dissuaded him. Davies also
maintained that he had seen a bitter letter which Overbury had sent
Rochester while in the Tower, saying that Rochester was now even with
him. At this point in the interview Davies appeared to have suffered a
loss of nerve, for he admitted that he thought Rochester 'never saw
those passages'. At the trial Somerset tried to exploit this, interjecting,
'I pray you, my Lords, note he says I never saw those passages.'
Somehow Bacon managed to gloss over the confusion. According to
State Trials he countered, 'It is true: for those letters were lost, but
after found by him who knew them to be his Master Sir T. Overbury's
hand.' Though this explanation seems less than convincing, it appears
to have gone unquestioned.[83]

After this two letters written by Overbury were exhibited. No copy
survives of the first so, once again, one has to rely on the version in
State Trials. In this Overbury writes threateningly to Rochester from
the Tower, upbraiding him for letting him 'lie in this misery' and
expressing incredulity that such treatment could be 'the fruits of common
secrets, common dangers'. 'Drive me not to extremities,' he pleads, 'lest
I should say something that you and I both repent. And I pray God
that you may not repent the omission of this my counsel in this place
where I now write this letter.'[84]

The second letter was the anguished screed which Overbury wrote
after Rochester had declared that Overbury's 'unreverend style' made it
impossible for them to remain friends. There could be no denying the
shocking nature of this searing tirade, in which Overbury bemoaned the
way that Rochester's love for the Countess of Essex had caused a rift
between them, ranted at him for ingratitude and threatened to reveal to
the world his baseness and disloyalty. On its own it went far to justify

the Prosecution's contention that Somerset had cause to regard Overbury with 'mortal malice, coupled with fear'.[85]

There was more to come however, as Bacon now made first use of the testimony of John Simcocks. Simcocks, it may be recalled, was an associate of Richard Weston's who had surrendered to Coke various wax effigies and other items believed to be invested with ritualistic significance. When examined, Simcocks had furnished Coke with details of various conversations he claimed to have had with Weston on the subject of Sir Thomas Overbury. Since hearsay evidence was admissible, the Prosecution was able to put his testimony to good use. Bacon accordingly read out a statement by Simcocks declaring that Weston had boasted of having 'private access to my Lord of Somerset, and that [Somerset] bade him look well to Overbury, for, if ever he came out, one of them must die'. Simcocks was present in court to attest to the accuracy of this. He struck one observer as 'a man of some fashion and good understanding' and, from the credence which was accorded to all he said, one may deduce he put on a polished and plausible performance. Only Lord Wentworth showed a hint of scepticism, demanding whether Simcocks had known Weston for a long time. 'He and I were of ancient and familiar acquaintance long since,' Simcocks answered smoothly. Thereafter his veracity went unquestioned.[86]

The next evidence put forward reflected Bacon's conviction that the Crown must establish that Overbury had posed a threat to Rochester because of what he knew. To support this a statement from Lawrence Davies was read out, describing how despatches on foreign affairs had regularly passed through Overbury's hands. Bacon observed, 'Thus you may see there were no mean secrets betwixt my Lord and Sir T. Overbury, that might rather cause him to fear him than the hindrance of his marriage.' He claimed that further proof was afforded by the crude cipher which Rochester and Overbury had used in their communications. No matter that the code was amateurish and bordered on the infantile; according to Bacon, it savoured of some sinister intrigue and showed that Rochester and Overbury 'made a play both of King, court and state, and that their imaginations wrought upon greatest men and matters'.[87]

Having dealt with motive, Bacon alleged that Somerset had first contemplated getting rid of Overbury by embroiling him in a duel. After that plan had been rejected, assassination was considered. As proof, Bacon produced the testimony of Sir David Wood, the Scots courtier whom Frances had invited to ambush and kill Overbury. Wood's written examination made it clear that he had had no dealings with

Rochester on this matter. Presumably, however, Bacon expected that the peers would take it that Frances had been acting on his orders when she approached Sir David.

Bacon then moved on to the circumstances of Overbury's arrest, claiming that Rochester had been 'principal practiser ... in a most perfidious manner ... to get him into the Tower'. Sir Dudley Digges, who had already testified to good effect at Weston's trial, once again took the stand to declare that Overbury had initially led him to believe that he would accept the diplomatic post. He had therefore been surprised when Sir Thomas subsequently 'sent ... word by Sir R[obert] Mansel that he had changed his mind'. Digges added that Mansel claimed to have seen 'a letter from the Lord of Somerset to Overbury that dissuaded him', but he himself had not been shown this. Digges seemed slightly embarrassed by the inadequate nature of his evidence. He expressed puzzlement that 'Mr Attorney hath called me so far out of the country for this small testimony', while apparently not seeing fit to summon Sir Robert Mansel. Nevertheless, no other witness could add anything to what Digges had said. Bacon's only other means of proving that it was Carr who had contrived Overbury's arrest was to read the petition that Somerset had sent the King from the Tower, acknowledging that he had 'consented to and endeavoured' Overbury's imprisonment.[88]

Bacon next declared that it was Somerset who had secured both Sir Gervase Elwes and Richard Weston their places at the Tower. It was of course true that Somerset had played some part in Elwes's appointment but, ostensibly at least, this had been largely at the prompting of the Earl of Shrewsbury. In one of his examinations Elwes himself had suggested that this circuitous procedure had been an elaborate sham, designed to suggest that Somerset had not taken a personal interest in his promotion. This was the explanation that Bacon now put forward. He argued that the real position had been very different and that, long before the intervention of Pembroke and Shrewsbury, Somerset had determined that Elwes would have the job.[89]

Linking Somerset to Weston's appointment was rather more of a challenge. When interviewed, Somerset himself had stated categorically that he had never laid eyes on Weston until the latter came to see him, shortly after Overbury's death. To overturn this claim Bacon drew attention to Weston's own statement that, on numerous occasions in the year preceding his employment at the Tower, he had acted as a messenger between the Countess of Essex and Lord Rochester. Bacon also quoted testimony given by Sir Thomas Monson, even though, on the face of it, this failed to show that Rochester had been responsible for Weston's appointment. Monson had said that it was at the request of Lady Essex and Lord Northampton that he had urged Elwes to take on Weston, making no mention of Rochester. However, Bacon implied that it would be idle to think that the latter had not also been involved, for a matter such as this was 'a business the lady's power could not reach unto'.[90]

At this point the testimony of John Simcocks once again proved crucial in convincing the court that Somerset had lied. To devastating effect Bacon quoted an examination of Simcocks, which suggested that Weston and Somerset had been on the most familiar terms. In this Simcocks insisted that while working at the Tower, Weston had had frequent meetings with Rochester. The jailer's visits had been kept secret from Giles Rawlins, Overbury's cousin, but Weston had told Simcocks all about them. Weston saw so much of Rochester that he had volunteered to use his influence with the favourite to procure Simcocks a lucrative suit. In addition – so Simcocks said – Weston had confided that Rochester regularly rewarded him with liberal quantities of gold. Simcocks recalled that on one occasion Weston had chortled that it baffled him that people had a high opinion of Overbury's intelligence for, though Overbury put great trust in Rochester, Weston knew that 'there was no man hindered his liberty but he'.[91]

Simcocks's evidence proved remarkably persuasive. When the time came to defend himself, Somerset reiterated that he 'did not so much as know' Weston until after Overbury was dead. He objected that Simcocks's 'depositions ... were but by hearsay and could not be sufficient testimony', but his protestations were deemed hollow. Although the reason is not altogether clear, it was Simcocks's account that carried more conviction.[92]

Bacon then accused Somerset of having rendered Overbury incapable of protecting himself by cutting him off from his family and friends. To prove the point, Overbury's father appeared in person and tellingly revealed how Rochester had forbidden him to petition the King for his son's release. His account inspired widespread revulsion, which only increased when Rochester's letter urging Overbury's mother to return to Gloucestershire was read out. The letters of condolence Rochester had written to Overbury's grieving parents conveyed an equally appalling impression, indelibly branding the prisoner as an arch-dissembler and hypocrite.

No less damning was the oral testimony of Overbury's brother-in-law, Sir John Lidcote. For the benefit of the court he described his last visit to Overbury in the summer of 1613, when Overbury had manifested doubts as to whether he was being deceived by Rochester. Bacon hammered home his advantage by alleging that it was Rochester who had initially issued the order that Overbury was to be kept in solitary confinement. He claimed that under examination Sir Thomas Monson had stated quite clearly, 'My Lord of Northampton and my Lord of Somerset gave orders to keep [Overbury] close prisoner.' This evidence would appear very strong, were it not for the fact that none of the examinations of Sir Thomas Monson preserved in the state papers contain any such words. On 5 October 1615 Monson had declared that it was the Earl of Northampton and the Countess of Essex who gave orders that no one should have access to Overbury, 'and that neither letters nor messages should come to him nor from him'. He said nothing to suggest that Rochester had been involved at any stage.[93]

Bacon then contended that while Overbury was being 'plied with poisons' in the Tower, Rochester had 'thirsted after news' of his condition, displaying extreme impatience when Sir Thomas did not succumb as speedily as expected. Bacon grounded this primarily upon testimony submitted by Dr Franklin. Franklin had deposed that Frances had once shown him a letter that Rochester had written her while absent from London. In this Rochester had 'wondered [that] these things were not yet despatched' and had warned that 'Overbury was like to come out within a few days if Weston did not ply himself.' At this, said Franklin, the Countess had summoned Weston and berated him, causing the latter to protest that he did not understand why Overbury was still alive when 'he had given him poison enough to have killed twenty men'.[94]

More proof was provided by a statement allegedly made by Sir Gervase Elwes, to the effect that the Countess of Essex often wrote to him wanting to know 'how Overbury did, that she might certify the court'.[95] Like several other of Elwes's examinations, this has been lost, and so cannot be checked. Bacon also made use of the written testimony of the apothecary Paul de Loubell. The latter claimed to have been summoned by Rochester on three separate occasions, and that each time Rochester had questioned him closely about Overbury's state of health. Lastly, Bacon cited Somerset's own statement of 3 May. It was then that Somerset had retracted his earlier claim that he had never raised the subject of Overbury in his letters to Frances and admitted that he might, after all, have mentioned him.

In conclusion Bacon offered to prove that throughout Overbury's imprisonment, Somerset 'bore him in hand with other pretences'. Bacon explained that, 'in respect Overbury had a working brain', it was necessary to keep him preoccupied with thoughts of 'his delivery and the terms of his coming out'. Accordingly, 'there was a continual negotiation with Overbury ... to make him by some recognition under his hand to free the lady's honour and to make him (after his liberty) an instrument of good offices towards the lady and her friends'. All this was nothing but an elaborate masquerade designed 'to set Overbury's head on work and to keep him from breaking out into clamours and discoveries of secrets'. Northampton's letters to Rochester provided the evidence for this. Various passages were quoted, including that where Northampton had boasted that as a result of his coaching, the Lieutenant of the Tower was 'very perfect in his part'. Also read out was the letter where Northampton mused that he would always love the Lieutenant 'for his conclusion ... that either Overbury would recover and do good offices betwixt my Lord of Suffolk and you [i.e. Rochester] ... or else that he shall not recover, which he thinks the most sure and happy change of all'. From this it could hardly be doubted that some form of double dealing was being practised at Overbury's expense. As Bacon put it, 'There was one thing pretended, and another thing intended.'[96]

Satisfied that he had covered everything, Bacon announced, 'Here my part ends.' Lord Ellesmere took this chance to beg Somerset to change his plea, observing that, having heard what had been said, and knowing that there was as much to come, he could hardly imagine that he would be found innocent. 'My Lord,' said Somerset with dignity, 'I came with a resolution to defend myself.' Realising that there was no prospect of bringing the proceedings to a speedy close, Ellesmere signalled that there would be a short intermission. Like the rest of the peers, the Lord High Steward 'went out of the court to ease himself', but it does not appear that Somerset was afforded much respite. One account reports that 'in the meantime the Earl drank wine and did eat a little suckets' but there is no mention of his being permitted either to sit down or to relieve his bladder.[97]

After this short break another respected lawyer, Sir Henry Montague, took over the Prosecution. It fell to him to prove that Somerset had been directly involved in Overbury's death, no easy task, since the evidence relating to this was perhaps the most unsatisfactory part of the Crown's case. In recognition of this Bacon had declared that Somerset's personal participation was 'more than needs be proved' for him to be found guilty as charged.[98]

Montague's opening words were little more than crude abuse. He proclaimed to the court, 'I have not known, heard, or read of any one felony more foul ... than this now in judgement; nor in so foul a matter did I ever see so fair, so favourable, so gracious a trial.' Indignantly he continued, 'Yet is this man, this prisoner, incapable and insensible of this great favour, of which stupidity I can yield no reason but that his hardness of heart is doubled upon him; and he that dares to enterprise so odious an evil, both to God and man, is not now ashamed to persist in a careless regard of what follow it.'[99]

Once he had finished castigating Somerset, Montague proceeded to his proofs. He alleged that there were two counts of poisoning that could be directly laid at Somerset's door, the first being that the Earl had tricked Overbury into taking arsenic. This claim was supported by James Franklin's deposition that 'the white powder which was sent to Sir Thomas Overbury was white arsenic ... sent to him in a letter', and by Lawrence Davies's statement that Overbury became very ill after he received a letter from Somerset containing powder. Montague then referred to a written examination of Somerset. Since the original text is lost, *State Trials* provides the only source. During this examination (the date of which is unknown) Somerset apparently acknowledged that he had sent Overbury a powder via Davies (possibly in a letter), while insisting that 'it was the same that he had had before of Sir R. Killigrew, and sent by Rawlins'.[100]

Montague then alleged that Somerset had sent Overbury poisoned tarts. As proof, Frances's letter to the Lieutenant was read out, and the peers were allowed to conclude that she had written this on Somerset's orders. Next, a confession supposedly made by Frances on 1 January was produced. It is not clear if this had been taken down by Fenton and Montgomery when they visited her early in the New Year, or whether it in fact formed part of her interview with Coke, a week later. Two versions of it exist in trial accounts, both maddeningly brief. According to the report printed in *State Trials*, Frances admitted that when she wrote to Elwes, 'by "letters" she meant poison'. In Edward Sherburn's account of the trial, the wording is less definite: 'being demanded what she meant by "letters", she answered, "perhaps poison"'.[101]

With this Montague sat down, leaving it to his colleague, Randall Crew, to conclude the Crown's case. Crew embarked on his task with gusto, bringing a touch of melodrama to the proceedings by invoking the vengeful shade of Sir Thomas Overbury. 'My Lord of Somerset,' he intoned. 'Methinks I hear the ghost of Overbury crying to you in this manner: "*Et tu quoque Brute!* did not you and I vow friendship of souls? Did not you sacrifice me to your woman? ... Have not I waked that you might sleep, cared that you might enjoy? Have not I been the cabinet of your secrets? ... Have I done all this to suffer thus by you? ... *Et tu quoque Brute*!'

Crew was required to demonstrate that Somerset had taken various steps to evade prosecution, actions which were hardly those of an innocent man. The majority of the evidence dated back to the autumn of 1615. Crew began by describing how, that September, Franklin had been summoned late at night to the Countess of Somerset's chamber, and had found her in a panic because of Weston's arrest. After a brief discussion the Countess had retired for what Franklin had assumed was a consultation with her husband. On her return she had warned Franklin that on no account must he reveal anything to the authorities. Crew based all this on Franklin's account, but he was able to produce a certain amount of corroboration for it. In her examination Mrs Turner's maid, Margaret Ewen, had deposed that it was she who had led Franklin to the Countess's apartment on that night. She had also testified that she was sure that the Earl of Somerset was there at the time. Still more damaging for Somerset was a confession attributed to Frances herself, in which she acknowledged 'all that Franklin said concerning her discourse with him, and that my Lord was with her that night'.[102]

Crew then examined Somerset's actions in the days before his arrest, which could hardly be interpreted as anything other than attempts to impede the commission of enquiry. Crew began by relating how Somerset had signed a warrant authorising a constable and a pursuivant to break into the house where Weston's son lived in order to seize papers relating to Anne Turner. These papers subsequently disappeared. Crew then described the steps taken by Somerset to obtain Overbury's correspondence from Lawrence Davies, and revealed that Somerset had paid the manservant £30 'to stop his mouth'.[103] Next, Crew drew attention to Somerset's own admission that on the eve of his arrest, he had burned all the letters he had written to Northampton. Fourthly, Crew was able to show that the letters sent from Overbury to Somerset had had false dates put on them by Sir Robert Cotton.

Crew further contended that Somerset had made such persistent efforts to secure a pardon because he knew that, otherwise, he was liable to be prosecuted for Overbury's death. Crew claimed that usually pardons prominently displayed the major offences voided, 'but in this pardon, they began with the least and mingled the great crimes, as if they would shuffle them in undiscerned'. According to Crew, the petition which Somerset had addressed to the King from the Tower served as additional proof that he was guilty. Indeed the very fact that he had begged to be spared a trial should be looked on as an 'implicative confession'.[104]

With that the case for the Prosecution was completed. By now it was after eight o'clock, and Somerset had been on his feet since ten that morning. Inevitably he would have been suffering from exhaustion and stress, which cannot have been eased by the knowledge that his life now depended on his making a lucid and well-argued defence.

Before Somerset could say anything, the Lord High Steward made one more attempt to persuade him to admit his guilt. He said that there was still 'great hope of the King's mercy' provided that Somerset 'mar not' his chances by putting forward a mendacious defence. He warned that although 'I think there never was, nor is a more gracious and merciful King than our master,' by doing so, Somerset risked putting himself beyond hope of redemption.

Somerset was not to be swerved from his purpose. Firmly he declared, 'I am confident in mine own cause and am come hither to defend it.' Regretfully, therefore, Ellesmere readied himself to listen to his arguments. He promised Somerset a fair hearing, quoting St Paul's words to Festus: 'Speak boldly, for we will hear you this day.' He assured Somerset, 'My Lord, be not troubled with yourself to imagine your answers will be abridged by time. It is indeed very late, but we will borrow some hours of the night; we will think no time too long so long as you shall be able to reply.' The Lord High Steward's only caveat was that Somerset should avoid 'frivolous circumlocutions', an injunction which was doubtless intended to serve as a reminder that Somerset should refrain from casting aspersions on the King.[105]

The Spanish ambassador heard that, during the Prosecution speeches, Somerset 'wrote much' with the pen and ink provided, but organising his material intelligently proved to be beyond him. As he began his speech he admitted that neither his memory nor his notes were good enough to permit him to deal methodically with the evidence put forward, and that, therefore, he would answer at random the points made against him. This erratic approach was not successful. He made his defence 'very confusedly, insisting most upon those particulars which were least material'.[106]

Somerset started by agreeing that he had consented to Overbury's imprisonment 'to the end that he should make no impediment in my marriage'. He nevertheless stressed that, 'for the contriving his death, he did not so much imagine the same'. He moreover insisted that he had taken great care that Overbury was allocated salubrious quarters within the Tower, where it should have been possible for Overbury 'to speak with whom he would'. 'So you see,' Somerset argued, 'it was against my intention to have him close prisoner.'[107] He failed, however, to excuse his advice to Overbury's parents, or to explain who it was who had ordered Overbury into close confinement. One reason for his silence may have been that it was impossible to do so without attacking the King.

Somerset did not deny that he and Overbury had had a bitter falling out. He commented that it was hardly surprising that their friendship had not lasted, for Overbury was a notoriously quarrelsome man. He gave examples of earlier occasions when Overbury had behaved particularly unreasonably, before going into details of 'how insolently Overbury opposed himself' to his proposed marriage, and 'what opprobrious and dishonourable terms' he had used about Frances. However, Somerset said that though this had naturally embittered their relationship, it was nonsense to suggest that he feared Overbury would ruin him by betraying secrets. While it was true that Overbury had helped him to process despatches from abroad, this had been done with the King's permission, and had not provided Overbury with a means of keeping him in subjection. 'For other secrets, there were never any between us,' Somerset affirmed.[108]

Somerset also denied that he had dissuaded Overbury from accepting the embassy posting, 'for I was very willing he should have undertaken it, but he not'. He said he had been relieved when the Archbishop of Canterbury had urged Overbury to go, and had hoped that this counsel would prevail. Regarding Digges's evidence, he said that Overbury had deliberately misled Sir Dudley into thinking he would go, when in fact he had never had any intention of doing so. Somerset claimed, 'Overbury came to me and said, "I will tell Sir Dudley Digges I will undertake this embassage, that he may so return answer to my Lord of Canterbury; but then you must write to me not to do so, and so take it upon you."' This was all that Somerset had to say on the subject, leaving it unresolved whether he had in fact written such a letter.[109]

The Earl agreed that he had sent Overbury tarts, but insisted that there had been nothing wrong with them. If poisoned tarts had reached Overbury, they must have come from his wife. At this point there was an interruption from one of the more hostile jurors, Lord Lisle, who attacked Somerset for having failed to prevent Frances from intercepting his tarts and substituting them with her own. 'If you had sent him good tarts, you should have seen them conveyed by a trusty messenger,' he cried.[110]

Not deigning to answer this, Somerset denied having been present when Franklin had visited Frances in their quarters at Whitehall. 'If Franklin knew me so well, and that I was privy to the plot, why should then my wife and I (as he pretends) when he was there, speak so closely, and always out of his hearing and sight?' he demanded.[111]

Dismissing de Loubell's claim to have talked with him about Overbury, he said that he had only ever seen the apothecary once. He also repeated that he had never met Weston until Giles Rawlins had brought the man to see him shortly after Overbury's death. This prompted Randall Crew to remind Somerset that Weston himself had confessed that, prior to taking up his position at the Tower, he had been 'a common deliverer of messages and letters between him and his lady. That he carried the message for their meeting between Hammersmith and Brentford, and for their meeting at Mrs Turner's house.' Somerset answered, 'That might be so, but he never saw his face to his knowledge.' He insisted that Weston had always handed the letters to his own servants to pass on, and said that these men would be prepared to vouch for this. His suggestion was ignored, for his servants were never called before the court. Somerset's explanation was regarded as utterly unconvincing, with one spectator noting, 'This was but a colour [pretence], for it was before proved that Weston was not only a carrier of letters betwixt Rochester and the Countess of Essex, but also a messenger and had private conference.'[112]

Somerset fared no better when he addressed the crucial subject of the powder, failing to persuade the court that this had been an innocuous emetic. He agreed that he had sent Overbury a powder via Davies, saying that 'he had the same of Sir Robert Killigrew, that it was good and wholesome ... [and] that the quantity was so small as gave [Overbury] but one stool'. Sir Randall Crew disputed this, and 'offered to prove that the powder which he had of Sir Robert Killigrew was not the powder which was sent to Overbury'. Sir Randall said that Killigrew had three times supplied Somerset with powders, but these had all been accounted for: 'the first was lost, the second [Somerset] took himself ... the third he sent by Rawlins to Overbury'. Where, then, had he obtained the fourth powder? All that Somerset could say 'was, it was of the same powder'.[113]

Somerset attempted to clarify the situation by producing a letter which Overbury had written to thank him for sending a powder 'which had wrought very gently and well, and that he would take no more'. Sir Randall Crew dismissed this, saying that this letter referred to the powder delivered by Rawlins, and did nothing to refute the contention that that sent by Davies was toxic. This threw Somerset into confusion:

'he was much perplexed, and still kept anchor-hold by the letter, having continual recourse unto it, not being able to tell from whom he had the powder which he sent from Davies'. Crew, however, was sure that it had been supplied by Franklin. He reminded the jury that Franklin himself had admitted that Overbury had been sent white arsenic in a letter. Helplessly, Somerset pleaded, 'I do not think you can take Franklin for a good witness.'[114]

Remorselessly Crew then pointed out that the date on the letter had been subsequently inserted by Sir Robert Cotton. Somerset insisted that this had not been done with any intent to deceive, but that he had merely 'caused ye true date, according to ye time he received it, to be set down'. He said that it had been Cotton's idea to date the letters, on the grounds that they 'might prove useful to me at this time'. He also claimed that he had been following Cotton's advice when he had sought a royal pardon in the early autumn of 1615. 'Having had many things of trust under the King, and custody of both the seals, I desired by this means to be exonerated,' he explained. After his first attempt to secure a pardon had failed, Cotton urged him to overcome this setback by pressing for one that was wider still, based on those granted by past monarchs. Somerset stressed that he bore no responsibility for the wording of the document, which had been drawn up by Cotton and other legal experts.[115]

To this it was objected that Cotton had told his examiners that he had merely been following Somerset's orders. Since he was unable to cross-examine Cotton on the matter, this confounded Somerset. Despairingly he remarked that he wished Cotton could have testified in person, 'to clear many things which now be obscure'. Crisply the Attorney-General interjected that this was out of the question in view of the fact that Cotton was currently 'held for a delinquent'.[116] In fact, as charges were never pressed against Cotton, there was not really any valid objection to his giving evidence.

Somerset then attempted to overturn Franklin's testimony. Interestingly, he conceded that during the 1613 summer progress he might have sent Frances a letter containing the comment that he 'marvelled the matter was not despatched'. Nevertheless, this had not related to Overbury's murder. 'He hoped their Lordships did conceive he had other business to be despatched in those days than such a foul business, and he thought that Franklin's examinations were not sufficient proofs to ... prove that was ye business.' He said that what he had actually been alluding to was the proposed 'reconciliation between Overbury and the Howards', but this explanation met with the open contempt of Lord

Chief Justice Coke. The trial had been peppered with his derisive interjections, and he now snorted angrily 'that the more the Earl stirred to defend himself, the more he mired himself.' Refusing to be deflected, Somerset argued that Frances might have let Franklin glimpse this letter because she thought that the doctor would aid her more readily if it appeared that the royal favourite 'had a hand' in the plot to kill Overbury.[117]

While agreeing that not all of Franklin's evidence was invented, Somerset vehemently repudiated the Doctor's allegation that he had written in more explicit terms about the urgency of killing Overbury. Somerset implored the peers to consider that, at that time, 'being the most affectionate to Frances, the means how they might lawfully enjoy the marriage bed being then consulted, he had much occasion to write unto the Countess secrets of moment, perhaps concerning Overbury, yet not coasted on the red sea of blood or death' as alleged by 'that perjured Franklin'. Above all Somerset denied that he had ever written to Frances expressing concern that 'if Weston did not play his part', Overbury would be released within days. 'If this letter be to be produced, if Frances ever confessed that I did ever send such a letter unto her, I am then guilty and convicted without excuse; but I call heaven now to witness, I never wrote any such letter, neither can any such be produced,' he asserted defiantly. 'Let not you, then, my noble peers, rely upon the memorative relation of such a villain as Franklin ... I humbly desire you to weigh my protestations, my oath upon my honour and conscience against the lewd information of such a miscreant for, my Lords, both in his life and death he proved atheistical.'[118]

Such moments of passion on Somerset's part were all too rare, for in general his defence fell far below this standard. When trying to explain why he had sent the pursuivant to requisition Mrs Turner's papers, he said that he had done so at the request of his wife, who 'told him that there were divers papers and bonds concerning Mrs Hind, and prayed him ... that he would send a warrant to search for those papers and so bring them away'. He protested that he did not think he was abusing his powers as a councillor by putting his name to the warrant for, before signing, he had consulted his secretary Packer, who had assured him that he was acting legally. His explanation was greeted by another devastating aside from the Lord Chief Justice: witheringly Coke sneered 'that he was a fit man to be a Counsellor of State who required counsel of his secretary'.[119]

Somerset made no more headway when he attempted to convince his peers that Northampton's letters had been misinterpreted. He assured the court that Northampton's boast about having prompted the Lieutenant in his part referred to the late Earl's 'endeavour to make Overbury be a good instrument betwixt my Lord of Suffolk and me; and to that end those whom [Overbury] thought to be his principal enemies should be the only causers of his freedom'. He pointed out, 'If I had thought those letters of my Lord of Northampton dangerous to me, it is likely I would never have kept them.' Unfortunately this merely prompted the reflection that he *had* destroyed his own letters to Northampton, perhaps because he realised their compromising nature. Somerset maintained that, on the contrary, 'he wished he had those letters, for they would make for him', but he was at a loss to explain why he had burned them, if they reflected so well on him. He attempted to shrug this off by saying that 'he did not so delight in his own lines that he would keep them for monuments', but this was little short of puerile.[120]

Somerset did not hide the fact that he considered it unfair that the petition he had addressed to the King while in the Tower had been used as evidence against him. 'When I writ it, I did not think thus to be sifted,' he commented bitterly. While not seeking to retract the statement that he had consented to and endeavoured Overbury's imprisonment, he said that he had assumed that his admissions would be for the King's eyes only. He was particularly indignant that his humble language, and his plea that James show him 'mercy' by sparing him a trial, had been taken as indicators of his guilt. In fact, 'he knew himself clear, as he there protested, but he doubted' how he would fare in a court of law. Furthermore, when appealing to the King on such a matter, he could hardly have expressed himself otherwise than respectfully. Even so, when drafting the petition, it had occurred to him that craving 'mercy' struck rather too abject a note and he had suggested to the Lieutenant of the Tower that he should alter that sentence. Sir George More had told him that the wording could not be bettered, 'upon whose approbation he let it pass'.[121]

Somerset had now spoken for rather than more than an hour and, though conscious that his audience had yet to be won over, he was obviously faltering. Trying to recall stray items that he had left uncovered, he sought to distance himself from Elwes's appointment. He was adamant that 'he never moved his Majesty herein, he only at the instance of the Earl of Shrewsbury gave way unto it'. He insisted that he had not made any money out of Sir Gervase's promotion and that 'If any man used his name [for] particular gain unto himself thereby, it was more than he knew.' Nor was there anything sinister about Sir William Wade being removed from the lieutenancy, for it was well known that he had been dismissed for incompetence. After this Somerset was left bereft of inspiration. 'More I cannot call to mind, but desire favour,' he finished lamely.[122]

Opinion was unanimous that Somerset had performed lamentably. There was even a school of thought that, by putting forward a defence that had been confused, meandering and inarticulate, Somerset had actually made matters worse for himself. The historian William Camden recorded, 'Some think if he had put himself upon the trial of his peers and he had not answered at all, but left them to the evidences, it might have gone better for him.' Sir John Holles echoed this view, reporting, 'The observing standers by rather found the weakness of his answers and defences to prejudice him than the fact with which he was charged.' The Spanish ambassador dismissed Somerset's address as 'lukewarm and dispirited', while Sir Ralph Winwood mockingly declared, 'Never man spake more poorly for himself than this man did.' Edward Sherburn was equally censorious, telling a friend, 'His answers were poor and idle, as many of the Lords his peers shook their heads and blushed to hear such slender excuses come from him of whom much better was expected.'[123]

Sir Francis Bacon felt so confident of victory that he thought it unnecessary to summarise the Crown's case, as was customary at the end of hearings. It only remained for Somerset to utter a final despairing appeal. Addressing the peers directly, he declared, 'As the King hath raised me to your degree, so he hath now disposed me to your censures. This may be any of your own cases and, therefore, I assure myself you will not take circumstances for evidence for, if you should, the condition of a man's life were nothing ... For my part, I protest before God I was neither guilty of, nor privy to, any wrong that Overbury suffered in this kind.' It was one of the few times that day that he communicated well with his audience. The Spanish ambassador commented that it was only in these last moments that Somerset 'spoke to the point', but this belated burst of eloquence was not enough to save him.[124]

As the peers withdrew to consider their verdict, Somerset was removed to a small room adjoining the hall. For a brief but tense period the lords deliberated, at one point asking Lord Chief Justice Coke and Sir Henry Hubbart, Chief Justice of the Court of Common Pleas, to confer with them. After half an hour the peers filed back to their places, and Somerset was led in to hear their decision. Already he had guessed the worst. While out of the hall he had taken off his George and Garter, saying that he had always worn them with honour, and he did not want to suffer the humiliation of being stripped of them.[125]

One by one Lord Ellesmere addressed the peers by name. He repeated the same formula twenty-two times: 'Robert Earl of Somerset hath been indicted for the murthering and poisoning of Sir Thomas Overbury, hath pleaded not guilty, put himself for his trial upon God and his peers; what say you, is he guilty of this felony and murther or no?' A majority verdict would have been sufficient to convict Somerset, but the peers' decision was unanimous. In turn each peer removed his hat and stood up to make his answer. It was always the same: 'Guilty my Lord.'[126]

Once again Somerset was ordered to hold up his hand. When he had done so, the Lord Steward asked whether he could give any reason why judgement should not be passed. Conscious that he had spoken poorly, Somerset sought to make up for his failure by adding to what he had said earlier. He declared, 'He doubted not but his peers had done according to their conscience, but he thought himself clear in his own conscience. [Un]happily (he said) through the weakness of his memory he had omitted to answer some things which made them to condemn an innocent man.' He appeared about to launch into a new defence, beginning, 'For that Simcocks said ...' but the Attorney-General at once protested that this was out of order. Once a verdict had been reached, the case could not be reopened, and Bacon begged the Lord Steward that 'some course might be taken' to prevent such an unorthodox procedure. Ellesmere complied, urging Somerset 'not to insist upon that, but rather to implore for mercy'.[127]

Somerset duly subsided, leaving Ellesmere free to pronounce sentence. 'Robert Earl of Somerset,' he began, 'Whereas thou hast been indicted, arraigned and found guilty as accessory before the fact of the wilful poisoning and murder of Sir T. Overbury, you are therefore to be carried from hence to the Tower, and from thence to the place of execution where you are to be hanged till you are dead. And the Lord have mercy upon you.'[128]

Even Somerset's enemies conceded that, though his defence had been weak in content and poorly delivered, he had shown a notable 'constancy and undaunted carriage in all the time of his arraignment'. Now that all seemed lost, his dignity did not desert him. The Spanish ambassador reported that when sentence had been passed on him, the Earl 'kissed his hand and made a reverence with a look such as he might have had if he had been much favoured'.[129]

CHAPTER EIGHT

ing James was in residence at Greenwich Palace on the day of Somerset's trial, near enough to London to be notified swiftly as to the outcome, but not so close that there could be any suggestion that he had sought to influence the proceedings. More than one courtier reported that, throughout the day, the King was noticeably agitated, until news was finally brought to him that Somerset had been convicted. On 31 May Edward Sherburn informed a friend, 'I will not omit ... that the day of the late Earl of Somerset's arraignment, his Majesty was sometimes sad and discontented, as he did retire himself from all company and did forbear both dinner and supper, nothing giving him contentment until he had heard what answer the late Earl had made. It seemed something was feared would in passion have broken from him. But, when his Majesty had notice that nothing had escaped him more than he was charged to answer to the business then in hand, his Majesty's countenance was soon changed and he hath ever sithence continued in a good disposition.'[1]

Anthony Weldon told a similar story. In his historical memoir of James's court he recorded that 'those who had seen the King's restless motion all that day, sending to every boat he saw landing at the bridge, cursing all that came without tidings, would have easily judged all was not right, and there had been some grounds for his fears of Somerset's boldness but, at last, one bringing him word he was condemned ... all was quiet'. Although Weldon is often unreliable, the fact that in this instance his account is corroborated by Sherburn's obviously adds to its credibility. However, it should be noted that on that day James was not in such a disturbed state that he was incapable of transacting business. On the afternoon of Somerset's trial the King had a long audience with the Spanish ambassador, Sarmiento, at which they discussed matters relating to Prince Charles's marriage.[2]

From the letter which Francis Bacon wrote to the King on 28 April 1616 it is clear that, by that time, the Attorney-General already knew that James had no intention of executing the Somersets. However, apart from Bacon, hardly anyone was aware of this. Accordingly there was fevered speculation as to whether the death sentences would be carried out. Shortly after the trials Sir John Holles told his son, 'All eyes are turned upon the King, whether punishment or mercy will close up his justice.' On 31 May Edward Sherburn wrote, 'Generally it is reported that his Majesty will show mercy to the lady but the late Earl shall be speedily executed.' It was thought that the only favour James would show Somerset would be to heed his plea made at the end of the trial that he be granted 'a death according to my degree', permitting him to be beheaded rather than hanged. It was also believed in some quarters that the execution would take place within the walls of the Tower, in front of a select group of witnesses. This was not to spare Somerset humiliation but because it was feared that 'if he dies in public, he may say something which will give pain to someone'.[3]

While most people assumed that Frances would be reprieved (the Tuscan ambassador thought that the King would not only take into account her youth and the provocation she had endured from Overbury but also the fact that she was 'one of the most beautiful women in court'), a minority of observers were convinced that she would suffer the same fate as her husband. They argued that the King was bound by a 'solemn protestation made at the first discovery of this business that the severity of the law should be visited upon offenders', as well as by the consideration that it was unfair that she should escape, 'seeing so many have already suffered'. Others took the view that, if the King was set on executing Somerset, he could hardly spare his wife. Sarmiento reasoned, 'If she does not die, being the principal, it will not be right that the Earl should die, being condemned only on presumption.' It was also rumoured that the Earl of Essex was urging the King not to show mercy to his former wife. He was said to be maintaining that his marriage had been wrongfully annulled and that, since he could not lawfully remarry during Frances's lifetime, his line was 'in danger of extinction' unless she was executed.[4]

While only a few people thought that the Countess's life was in real danger, in the week following the trials, her husband's execution was daily expected. Sir John Holles noted angrily, 'Some have been so confident of the ill that day by day they watch the Tower, lest the execution should be stolen from them.' On more than one occasion crowds congregated on Tower Hill in the belief that Somerset was going to be led out to meet the axeman. Each time, they proved mistaken.[5]

After a week had passed it started to dawn on Londoners that they were to be denied the spectacle that they had anticipated with such excitement. On 14 June John Gerard informed a friend that, although until recently 'there was a general expectation of [Somerset's] execution ... now, all such rumours are blown over and nothing but mercy spoken of'. John Chamberlain noted that when Sir Thomas Monson's trial – which had been set for 7 June – was once again postponed, this made 'the world think that we shall hear no more of this business'. Soon afterwards the Earl and Countess of Suffolk deemed it safe to return to London. They had retired to Audley End for their daughter's arraignment, 'not being able through grief to abide so near a place where their shame and dishonour should be laid open' but, by 14 June, Sir John Holles could declare, 'My Lord Treasurer holds up his head again.' In the Tower, Somerset was still kept isolated, but his wife was permitted visits from her sister Lady Knollys, who regularly brought her baby daughter to see her.[6]

On 13 July Frances was granted a royal pardon. The death sentence on her was formally lifted although, as yet, she remained subject to imprisonment at the King's pleasure. The grounds alleged were fourfold. First, it was stated that the King had been moved to mercy in recognition of the long service of her father and her 'noble progeny'. The fact that Frances had voluntarily confessed her crime, and that, upon her conviction, the peers had promised to intercede for her provided further mitigating circumstances. Finally, because Frances had not been guilty of murder but had been condemned as an accessory who, moreover, had been enticed to commit evil 'by the procurement and wicked instigation of certain base persons', it was fitting to exercise leniency.[7]

The Earl of Somerset did not, as yet, receive a pardon. Nevertheless, his conditions of imprisonment were gradually relaxed, making it plainer than ever that there was no question of his execution. By 19 July he had been granted 'the liberty of the Tower', meaning that he was free to move about within its precincts. To the astonishment of many people, he was not even expelled from the Order of the Garter. As he strutted about the Tower, he could be seen still wearing his George, causing John Chamberlain to wonder about the reaction of foreign princes who were honorary Knights of the Garter on finding that they shared membership of this supposedly elite fraternity with a convicted felon.

Prior to the Somersets' trials Sir Francis Bacon had assured the King that there would be little public indignation if their death sentences were waived. He was confident that, because 'the blood of Overbury is already revenged by divers executions', there could be no grounds for protest, an argument that blithely overlooked the manifest injustice of failing to punish the Somersets for a crime for which others had previously paid the ultimate penalty. Besides this, Bacon considered 'the great downfall of so great persons carrieth in itself a heavy punishment and a kind of civil death, although their lives be not taken', but this was too cerebral a concept to be embraced widely.[8]

In court circles, it is true, there was some sympathy for Somerset, even from individuals who had little affection for him. Edward Palavacino was surprised to discover that 'where a man converseth he finds ... [Somerset] is the most pitied and well wished ... that ever I yet heard of'. The general public, however, proved less forgiving. Following the trial of Richard Weston, 'the common people had expressed their joy for the justice done', assuming that others named in connection with Overbury's murder would be treated as severely. As the bells had rung out throughout London, the populace were heard declaring 'that the King should have subsidies and whatsoever he would require'. The Lord Mayor and aldermen had sent word to the King of the 'great comfort' the proceedings had afforded them, 'acknowledging their great happiness in living under the government of such a King'.[9] Now, however, it emerged that these celebrations had been premature. Although the strength of popular feeling had undoubtedly helped to convince James that the Somersets must face trial, the couple's survival after being convicted made it painfully apparent that the King's justice was not visited equally upon all. As Weston had prophesied, it was the 'little birds' who had been caught in the net, while the great ones fared better.

In his memoirs Sir Simonds d'Ewes recalled, 'It was much pitied that Sir Gervase Elwes, Weston and Franklin had suffered, who were merely instruments to execute that murder which the Countess of Somerset had originally plotted and principally acted, and yet that she and her husband should escape.' Some of the resulting bitterness found expression in abusive verses and ballads, which were widely circulated. The following, which satirises Somerset's humble birth and calls for his execution, provides a typical example:

> From Carr a carter surely took his name
> Or from a carter surely Carr first came
> Sith Carr and Carter then so well agree
> Let none them part till they at Tyburn be

Where Carr with Carter when you there do find
Take ter from Carter but leave Carr behind.[10]

Such was the indignation that on one occasion the Queen actually
found herself at the centre of a minor riot. On 20 July 1616 John
Chamberlain reported that when the Queen was out driving in her
coach with the Countess of Derby, Lady Ruthin and Lord Carew, a
mob had formed after it was rumoured that the Countess of Somerset
and her mother were inside the vehicle. 'People flocked together, railing
and reviling and abusing the footmen and putting them all in fear,'
Chamberlain informed his correspondent. The crowd was not pacified
when the Countess of Derby sought to persuade them they were
mistaken. Lord Carew then offered to step outside and calm them but
the Queen would not let him, fearing he would be violently handled.
The disturbance subsided only when the mob saw the coach return
through the gates of Whitehall.[11]

Those resentful at the privileged treatment accorded Somerset could at
least console themselves that, as a convicted felon, he had been stripped
of his titles (and was accordingly referred to as 'the late Earl of Somerset)
and that his property was forfeit to the Crown. Anger would have
doubtless been much greater if it had been appreciated that James had
sought to restore these to Somerset, and to grant him a pardon even
'before his lady had hers'. The only reason why this had not happened
was that, 'out of cursed heart', Somerset rejected the terms offered
him.[12]

Following Somerset's arrest in the autumn of 1615, James had given
orders that an inventory be taken of his possessions, in readiness
for their confiscation. The resulting document, dated 29 November,
catalogued the furniture, works of art, clothing and jewellery contained
in his Whitehall apartment. As well as providing an insight into
Somerset's taste in pictures (his art collection included works by Titian,
Veronese and Tintoretto, recently acquired in Venice), it vividly conveys
the splendour of his wardrobe. The list features nearly thirty cloaks and
more than forty doublets or jerkins with matching pairs of hose.
Garments individually described include: 'one cloth of silver doublet,
cut upon taffety; a doublet and bullion hose of crimson satin, laced,
with embroidered satin; a doublet of striped cloth of gold and silver,
cut with yellow taffety; a doublet and long hose of black taffety, cut
upon tinsel with two embroidered laces; a scarlet cloak, embroidered
with seagreen silk and lined with seagreen velvet; a black cloak of uncut

velvet laced with four embroidered laces and with black satin raised; a scarlet cloak, embroidered with crimson and lined with crimson velvet'. Also inventoried were Somerset's six horses (awarded by the King to various courtiers) and two coaches, one lined with crimson velvet and the other with cloth embroidered with black velvet. Somerset's gold and silver plate was valued at over £15,000, although much of this had already been pawned.[13]

Yet the aforementioned items were by no means Somerset's most valuable assets, for he had also accumulated extensive lands. After the death of Prince Henry, the King had once again bestowed the Sherborne estate on Somerset. The Earl had also acquired lands in Westmoreland and Northumberland which had been seized by the Crown in 1571 following the Earl of Westmoreland's treason. The King had not parted with these for nothing: John Chamberlain heard that the price was £40,000, to be paid in instalments. This later enabled Somerset to claim that 'he had never lands of gift from the King', which conveniently overlooked the fact that the foundations of his fortune had been laid when James had originally presented him with Sherborne. These, and other holdings, now reverted to the Crown.[14]

The King had hoped that, once Somerset had been found guilty, he would follow the example of others tried before him and acknowledge that he had been rightfully convicted. This proved unfounded. Though preachers were sent to the Tower to urge the Earl to confess, he continued 'firm in denial'. His stubbornness meant that the King could not pardon him for having expressed remorse for his crime. John Chamberlain reported that the King was much perplexed that whereas 'all the rest that have gone before ... so frankly confessed the matter, he only should continue so confident'.[15]

Immediately after his trial, the King refused to receive direct communications from Somerset. It would seem that James attempted to force Somerset to approach him through George Villiers, but the Earl flatly refused to do such a thing. 'My cause nor my confidence is not in that distress as for to use that mean of intercession,' he declared proudly.[16] Faced with this instransigence, the King relented.

A few weeks after his conviction Somerset sent the King a tortuously worded letter, lamenting that 'all this while I have received nothing to comfort me from your Majesty'. Throughout, his tone was one of injured innocence. Far from conceding that he had cause to censure himself, he came close to castigating James for having permitted his case to come to trial. 'That whereupon I was judged, even the crime itself might have been none, if your Majesty's hand had not once touched upon it, by which all access unto your favour was quite taken from me,' he pronounced reproachfully. While acknowledging that, technically, 'both life and estate are forfeited to you by law', he made it clear that he expected the King to exercise his prerogative of mercy. Almost casually, Somerset implied that, by suggesting that his life should be spared, he was not asking much of James. Airily he wrote that 'the resistance is not great' to such an act of clemency, all possible objections having been 'taken away by your Majesty's letting me loose to the utmost power of law'. Furthermore, numerous people had already been executed for the crime, 'which yieldeth to the world subjects of sorrow, rather than appetite to more blood'. This, however, was not all, for Somerset also wanted the King to restore intact his entire estate. In his view such a demand was in no way excessive. 'I have voluntarily departed from my hopes of pension, place, office,' he loftily explained to James. 'I only cleave to that which is so little as that it will suffer no paring or diminution.'[17]

Somerset's plea met with an encouraging response. In early July the King sent Lord Hay to see him in the Tower. Hay explained that James 'was sorry for what had passed', but that it had not been within his power to 'hinder the course of justice'. This would have been the case even if it had been his own son who was suspected of murder. However, now that Somerset's trial was concluded, James intended to 'do what he might by law or otherwise' to 'repair him again'. Hay promised Somerset that James was ready to 'restore unto him his liberty and his honour in as complete a degree as he had them before, and to give him his pardon'.[18]

Shortly after this, Somerset's father-in-law, the Earl of Suffolk, accompanied by various other noblemen and councillors, visited him in the Tower. In his capacity as Lord Treasurer, Suffolk outlined in greater detail the settlement that was on offer. Suffolk confirmed that Somerset 'should have a pardon as full and advantageous as lawyers could devise or the law could give, that all his debts should be paid, all his goods restored him, excepting ... two or three jewels which the queen had taken'. However, Somerset's lands would only be partially restored to him. The King intended to dispose of most of these to favoured courtiers, and Somerset's estate in the north of England had already been earmarked for Prince Charles. Nevertheless, Somerset would be compensated with lands elsewhere which produced an equivalent income. Somerset's property in Northumberland and Westmoreland had an estimated annual yield of £5,000. The King would match this by returning lands which Somerset had formerly owned in Northamptonshire, worth £1,000 a year, supplementing this with additional holdings with an aggregate income of £4,000. Realising that Somerset would probably think that his estate in the north had been undervalued, Suffolk reassured him that the settlement would be more lucrative than these figures might suggest. 'My Lord,' said the Lord Treasurer cheerfully, 'You know who is Lord Treasurer, assure yourself that land shall be none of the worst. I shall undertake to make it worth unto you £6,000 *per annum*.'[19]

This would have guaranteed Somerset an income of £7,000 a year but, incredibly, he spurned it. He was adamant that he would accept nothing less than the restitution of his northern estate, 'which was such as he had made special choice of as fittest for him ... out of many other things worth more offered him and he let pass'. 'Reposing confidence in his Majesty's favour and gracious promises' made to him by Hay, Somerset flattered himself that, before long, the King would concede to his demands. In fact the matter was allowed to lapse. Since King James was not prepared to issue a pardon until a financial settlement had been reached, Somerset stayed in the Tower, still technically under sentence of death and deprived of all his wealth.[20]

In early June 1616 the 'inferior rabble' who had been detained as a result of the murder enquiry were set free. These included Coppinger and Fargus, the two servants of Somerset arrested after they had tried to smuggle letters out of the Tower. It is probable that Dr Savory, 'Toothless Margaret' and the Countess of Somerset's Groom of the Chamber, Stephen Clapham, had also been kept in prison until this date. The following month Sir William Monson was released. Although there had never been any likelihood that he would be charged in connection with Overbury's death, there had been a general expectation that he would be tried for 'Spanish reckonings and some undue connivencies while he was Vice Admiral'. This turned out to be false. For the moment, his brother Sir Thomas Monson remained in the Tower, fiercely proclaiming his innocence to anyone who would listen.[21]

Sir Robert Cotton was also freed at the beginning of June, a development that took many people by surprise. John Gerard commented to a friend that he had not expected his release, 'since foul matters at the arraignment [of Somerset] were proved against him, as counselling and advising my Lord Somerset how to clear himself, for which purpose he antedated some of Sir Thomas Overbury's letters'. According to Simonds d'Ewes, only the fact that Cotton had 'great friends' at court had prevented him from being 'swallowed up' by this affair. Even so, it cost him £500 to secure his freedom.[22]

The position of Cotton and the others was undoubtedly improved by the fact that, by June 1616, Sir Edward Coke had fallen into disgrace. Having first undermined his position at court by his ill-advised attempt to challenge Lord Chancellor Ellesmere, he had then infuriated the King by refusing to abandon a case which had potentially adverse implications for the royal prerogative. When summoned to Whitehall on 6 June, Coke, alone of all the judges, refused to modify his stance. As a result, on 30 June he was suspended from the Privy Council. In addition he was barred from going on his summer circuit as an assize judge and was ordered to spend the coming months revising contentious pronouncements that he had inserted in his annual law reports. Coke declined to make any significant alterations to the published text, with the result that, on 14 November 1616, he was dismissed from the post of Lord Chief Justice.

The official reason given for Coke's dismissal was that he had offended the King by his 'perpetual turbulent carriage' when adjudicating on cases concerning the ecclesiastical courts and prerogative royal. However, it was whispered that there had been more to it than that. John Chamberlain reported, 'The world discourses diversely how he could run so far into the King's displeasure, and will not take the alleged causes for sound payment, but stick not to say he was too busy in the late business [the murder enquiry], and dived further into secrets than there was need.' John Gerard believed that Coke's 'harshness in the carriage of this poisoning business' had earned him many enemies in court, and certainly the Earl of Suffolk must have experienced great satisfaction when it fell to him to suspend from his place on the Privy Council the man who had so relentlessly pursued his daughter and son-in-law.[23]

Gossip, however, hinted that something more sinister than this had caused Coke's fall. In some quarters it was actually said that Coke had uncovered the truth about Prince Henry's death, and that it was the King's determination that this should not come out that had led him to dismiss Coke. Some fantasists went so far as to allege that in his 'rhetorical flourishes' during the murder hearings, Coke had insinuated that the King had ordered Overbury to be killed after discovering that it was Sir Thomas who had poisoned the Prince.[24] This was, of course, nonsense: even Coke would have baulked at uttering such an inflammatory statement which was not supported by a shred of evidence. The only way in which the Overbury murder case had any connection with Coke's dismissal was that his unbalanced and strident conduct throughout the enquiry had exasperated the King and undermined his faith in Coke's judgement. This made him the less inclined to tolerate other misdemeanours and lapses on Coke's part.

The Earl and Countess of Somerset led a fairly privileged existence within the Tower. Since April 1616, each had been permitted to retain the services of a cook and butler, and an additional small staff of personal servants ministered to their other needs. Before their trials, and for some weeks afterwards, they were kept separately, but within a short time this was relaxed. As early as 25 July Edward Sherburn heard, 'The Lord of Somerset and his lady do enjoy one another's company and conversation both at bed and board.' A month later the King agreed that the Lieutenant of the Tower should 'lodge them as near one to the other as may conveniently be' and that, if Sir George More thought it appropriate, they could share the same quarters. The upshot was that Somerset came to occupy the Bloody Tower, where Sir Walter had been housed early in his imprisonment, while Frances was confined in an adjoining set of rooms to which Ralegh had later been transferred. Lord Carew reported, 'All doors are open between them.' That November Carew revealed that, as a result of being so cosily accommodated, the couple had 'agreed so well as she is with child'. About this time others also heard that Frances was pregnant but either they were misinformed or Frances later miscarried, for she never had another child.[25]

By this time both Somersets were permitted to receive visitors. Lady Knollys continued to see her sister regularly and more distant relations also came to the Tower. Frances's cousin Lady Anne Clifford paid more than one visit as well as corresponding with her. In April 1619 Lady Anne accompanied Lady Windsor and another cousin of Frances's, Mr Sackville, to the Tower, later noting in her diary that when with Frances, 'we saw her little child'. The devoted Sir John Holles assiduously visited his former patron, Somerset, but it is not clear whether many others showed similar loyalty. Apart from this the Somersets enjoyed the companionship of other inmates of the Tower. John Chamberlain heard that the Earl of Northumberland was 'much in their company, framing himself altogether to be friendly and sociable'.[26]

Within a year of his trial, Somerset's financial position had been clarified, though not entirely to his own satisfaction. By late 1616 the King had disposed of much of Somerset's former lands, conferring his northern estate on Prince Charles and allocating Sherborne to Sir John Digby. This forced even Somerset to recognise that he was now unlikely

to regain these possessions. His family and friends implored him to
make alternative provision for his wife and any children (this was about
the time that Frances was rumoured to be pregnant) by asking the King
to fulfil the undertakings made on his behalf by Suffolk and Hay. With
typical crassness, Somerset refused to petition the King directly about
this, on the grounds that doing so 'might ... imply an assent on his
part to that which had been done with his estate'. Instead he grudgingly
consented that his wife could write to Lord Hay, requesting him to take
up the matter with James. This oblique approach produced disappointing
results. The King agreed to make financial provision for Somerset, but
the terms were less generous than those proposed earlier in the year.
Once again the King signified that Somerset could repossess his former
lands in Northamptonshire, but it was now estimated that these produced
an income of only £900 a year. Besides this, James agreed that Somerset
should have the rental income from Crown lands let for £3,000 a year.
This would have left Somerset with an annual income of under £4,000,
whereas the initial figure mentioned had been £7,000.[27]

Somerset only had himself to blame for this deterioration in his
prospects. All experienced courtiers knew that if they received a promise
from the Crown it was essential to ensure that the grant passed the
Great Seal without allowing the monarch time to reconsider. Nevertheless, Somerset could still have retrieved the situation if he had been
slightly less obtuse. The Earl of Suffolk told him that, if he did not
want to settle for this lesser amount, he must 'use means, and that by
his own suit, to have the King put in mind of his first directions'. To
the despair of his father-in-law, Somerset still claimed that this would
demean him, 'and would not be induced to make any such suit'. As a
result Somerset had to make do with this pared down settlement, which
passed the seal in March 1617. About this time his debts were also paid,
with a free gift from the Crown of £5,083. Despite the fact that he
should have counted himself fortunate not to have been deprived of all
worldly goods (not to mention his life), Somerset merely felt aggrieved
by the treatment he had received. Even more bizarrely, he still did not
relinquish all hope of having his former estates restored to him in full.[28]

Though Somerset considered that the King should feel guilt for the
way he had behaved, the truth was that James was too besotted with
George Villiers to devote much thought to his fallen favourite. In August
1616 the King had conferred on the young man the title of Viscount
Villiers. Two months later John More told William Trumbull, 'The
Lord Villiers is in greater grace than ever the Lord Somerset was

thought to be.' The following January Villiers was raised higher in the peerage, as Earl of Buckingham. A month later he became a Privy Councillor. By this time he was already a rich man. The King had originally intended to give him Somerset's forfeited Sherborne estate but, perhaps out of superstition, Villiers had declined it, 'praying the King that the building of his fortunes may not be founded upon the ruins of another'. Instead he was given lands of comparable value elsewhere. As ever, the King was not in the least inhibited about publicly displaying his affection for his latest object of desire. In September 1617 he complacently confessed 'to loving those dear to me more than other men'. He then announced to his Council, 'You may be sure I love the Earl of Buckingham more than anyone else ... I cannot be blamed: Christ had his John and I have my George.' In January 1618, the month Buckingham was created Marquis of Buckingham, the Venetian ambassador was surprised by the King's undisguised rapture when watching Buckingham dance. At the end of the performance, James patted his favourite's cheeks and kissed him, 'with marks of extraordinary affection'.[29]

Despite James's transparent devotion to Buckingham, what remained of the Howard faction at court harboured hopes that his passion would prove transient, and that, if things were managed skilfully, Buckingham could be supplanted by a new favourite under their control. It was chiefly the Earl and Countess of Suffolk – with, it would seem, the support of Somerset from within the Tower[30] – who schemed to bring this about. Sir William Monson had an epicene son whom it was thought the King would find enticing. Accordingly the Suffolks and their allies 'took great pains in tricking and pranking him up'. He was fitted out in fine clothing while Lady Suffolk cherished the young man's complexion by 'washing his face every day with posset curd'. Monson was then instructed to parade about before the King. In February 1618 Nathaniel Brent reported that Monson was taking 'all occasion to present [himself] to his Majesty's view', adding that the young man's ambition was 'so palpable as it causeth much laughter'. However, by making himself so conspicuous Monson managed to annoy the King, who began to find his presence intrusive. The Lord Chamberlain, the Earl of Pembroke, was sent to tell Monson 'that the King did not like of his forwardness and presenting himself continually about him; that his father and uncle were not long since called in question for matters of no small moment; that his own education had been in such places and with such persons as was not to be allowed of'. Monson was therefore ordered to stay away from the King.[31]

The faction promoting the young man concluded that the King had taken against him because he suspected that, like other members of his family, Monson had Catholic leanings. To disabuse James of this idea, Monson ostentatiously received communion at the hands of the Archbishop of Canterbury on Easter Day. Soon afterwards he applied to the King for permission to travel abroad, explaining that 'he could live with no contentment here, being debarred his presence'. By this time James's irritation with Monson had subsided. He refused him leave to go abroad, protesting that it was 'more than he knew' that Monson had been denied access to him. Naturally Monson's supporters were encouraged by this development but, as it turned out, Monson never posed a serious threat to Buckingham's pre-eminence. Buckingham remained sole favourite for the rest of the King's life although, when he left England to accompany Prince Charles to Spain in 1623, he did take the precaution of ensuring that Monson was out of the country at the same time.[32]

By attempting to oust the favourite, the Suffolks had merely succeeded in angering him. He proved a dangerous enemy. In the summer of 1618 Buckingham informed the King that persons owed money by the Crown could never obtain payment from the exchequer unless Lady Suffolk had been bribed. Enquiries were mounted and, in July 1618, the Earl of Suffolk was forced to resign the office of Lord Treasurer. In October 1619 the Suffolks were prosecuted for corruption in the Court of Star Chamber. They vigorously denied the charges but the evidence was overwhelming and they were found guilty on all counts. The Earl of Suffolk was fined £30,000 and sentenced to be imprisoned at the King's pleasure. After a mere ten days in the Tower he was released and his fine was subsequently reduced to £7,000. The King might have been prepared to remit even this sum had it not been for the fact that Suffolk had angered him by placing his lands in the hands of trustees and removing all furniture from his houses to prevent seizure by royal officials. Nevertheless, although Suffolk was not treated with undue severity, his fall destroyed his political influence for ever.

Suffolk's imprisonment, which coincided with the incarceration of Secretary of State Sir Thomas Lake on unrelated charges, led to jokes that, since the Tower now housed a Lord Treasurer, a Lord Chamberlain and a Secretary, it was possible to hold a Council meeting there. By this time the Earl of Somerset had settled comfortably in his quarters at the Tower, which he had altered and improved at his own expense. In other respects, however, his life was less happy, for there are indications that he and his wife were no longer on good terms. In June 1617 John Chamberlain reported 'a great jar' between the Countess of Somerset and her husband. Perhaps this related to the Countess's encouragement of a courtship between Lord Hay and the Earl of Northumberland's daughter, Lucy Percy. Disapproving of Hay as an upstart Scot, the Earl of Northumberland had refused to sanction a betrothal, and instead insisted that Lucy came to stay with him in the Tower. By this time Northumberland had taken rather a fancy to the Countess of Somerset and so, while his daughter was with him, he encouraged her to visit Frances, calculating that this would afford him 'the better access himself'. The Countess – who, after all, had herself risked a great deal to marry the Scotsman of her choice, and who also had good reason to be grateful to Lord Hay – covertly assisted Hay's pursuit of Lucy Percy. She enabled them to meet under the pretext of visiting her, with the result that Lucy decided to marry in defiance of her father's wishes. Northumberland was furious at the way he had been duped. He turned on the Countess, telling her she was nothing but 'a young bawd'.[33] It may be that Somerset supported Northumberland, and that it was this that led to the disagreement between him and his wife.

Possibly the rift was soon repaired, but in October 1618 Chamberlain learned that the Somersets had had an even more serious falling-out. The reason he gave was that Somerset 'had taken her tripping' meaning, presumably, that he had caught Frances being unfaithful. Whether there was any truth in this is impossible to say. Since Somerset could never have been far away, and bearing in mind that visits to the Tower generally took place either under the supervision of the Lieutenant or his wife and daughter, one would have thought that Frances would have had very few opportunities for adultery, but perhaps she seized whatever chance she could. Since Chamberlain did not elaborate, one can only speculate as to what his information was. However, Chamberlain did say that the Somersets had quarrelled so bitterly that separation had been discussed.[34] If so, nothing came of this. The Somersets continued to live together at the Tower, but it may be that they were never fully reconciled.

About three years after this Buckingham purchased a house from Frances's brother-in-law, by this time promoted from his earlier title of Baron Knollys to that of Viscount Wallingford. Wallingford agreed to sell at a reduced price provided that Buckingham prevailed on the King to release the Somersets. As a result, on 17 January 1622 they were freed from the Tower. The document authorising their release stipulated that, for the time being, they should remain 'confined to some convenient place'. On leaving the Tower they were ordered to take up residence at either Grays or Cawsam, one of Wallingford's two houses in Oxford and, once they had made their choice, to remain within three miles of the property. This, however, was only a temporary arrangement. By September 1623 Somerset had acquired a house at Chiswick, which was to be his home for many years. Since his furniture and much of his art collection had been restored to him (the exceptions being various Italian paintings which Somerset had not paid for at the time of his fall, and which had reverted to the agent who had purchased them on his behalf), he was able to decorate it in style. However, it seems that his movements were still subject to restriction. In August 1624 Sir John Holles wrote to Somerset describing a play he had recently seen in London, in a manner that suggests that Somerset was unable to go to the theatre himself.[35]

By this time Somerset was on the brink of obtaining a formal pardon. Earlier that summer he had swallowed his pride and petitioned Buckingham (now elevated to a Duke) to raise the matter with the King. On 7 October 1624 Somerset's pardon was finally sealed. Its terms were less extensive than Somerset had desired, for he had been hoping for nothing less than a complete reversal of the indictment. Nevertheless it meant that Somerset was no longer subject to any penalty for his crime (although he did have to give an undertaking that he would not resume his seat in the House of Lords) and the optimistic Sir John Holles consoled the Earl that 'time and occasion may enlarge it'.[36]

Somerset was now able to move about more freely. We hear of him paying a visit to Lord Dorset's house, and going with his wife to see Sir John Holles in London. Surprisingly poets and playwrights occasionally dedicated works to him, as they had at the height of his prosperity. The poet George Chapman, who had greeted the Somersets' nuptials with his poem on Perseus and Andromeda, dedicated to Somerset his edition of *The Crown of all Homer's Works*. William Davenant likewise dedicated the play *Albovine* to Somerset, a somewhat pointed gesture, perhaps, in view of the fact that the play took as its subject the downfall of a king's male favourite who was overthrown by scheming courtiers. Even more bizarrely, Abraham Darcie 'humbly consecrated' a book on the Howards entitled *Honour's True Arbour* to 'the immortal goodness and greatness' of the Countess of Somerset.[37]

The fact that struggling writers occasionally accorded Somerset such outward marks of respect should not be taken to mean that his pardon truly eradicated the stain of his conviction. There was no question of his returning to court and the circle that he moved in was decidedly limited. On those occasions when he ventured beyond Chiswick, he risked embarrassing encounters with hostile individuals. In June 1629 Sir John Holles was incensed when 'one Booth, a seller of aquavitae' abused Somerset outside Holles's London residence, calling him 'rascal, with other reviling speeches'. Having discovered that Booth was affiliated in some way to the royal household, Holles appealed to the Lord Chamberlain to chastise the offender. 'The misdemeanour to a noble man and a companion of the order is not to be passed without exemplary punishment', Holles fulminated, but it is not clear whether the Lord Chamberlain accepted that disciplinary action was warranted.[38]

Having secured his pardon, Somerset's next task was to impress upon the King that the financial endowment provided for him in 1617 was less than what had earlier been promised. Sir John Holles was relieved that Somerset was at last bestirring himself about this, gently chiding the Earl for having 'hitherto been somewhat too slow' in the matter. Initially it appeared as if Somerset would succeed in his mission. When his claims were brought to the King's attention, James declared (according to Somerset, at least) that 'what Somerset had to demand of him in that matter, he should have it, if he had so much land in England'.[39] It turned out, however, that Somerset had been too dilatory about bringing his suit. Shortly after this the King fell ill. On 27 March 1625 he died at Theobalds, without having done anything to satisfy Somerset's claims.

With the accession to the throne of King Charles I, Somerset's prospects looked much more bleak, for Charles had always disliked his father's former favourite. Somerset did, however, have one inestimable – if unlikely – friend at court. Towards the end of King James's life the Duke of Buckingham had succeeded in becoming Prince Charles's best friend and, in consequence, his supremacy at court spanned two reigns, an unprecedented feat for a favourite. Now that Somerset no longer posed any sort of threat, Buckingham was prepared to be magnanimous to a former member of his own 'profession' who found himself in difficulties.

Admittedly Somerset's first attempt to enlist the aid of Buckingham met with a courteous rebuff. Somerset later recalled that Buckingham acknowledged that he had cause for complaint and indicated that he would have liked to help, were it not for the fact that the King was currently so short of cash. Somerset nevertheless persisted, claiming that his desires could be satisfied in a manner 'nothing prejudicial to the King'. Buckingham then agreed to do what he could for his 'unfortunate predecessor' (as Somerset described himself when writing to him). Sir John Holles was sure that Somerset's affairs would prosper now that things were 'proceeding from a favourite to a favourite'. In August 1628 Buckingham visited Somerset at Chiswick and was affability itself. He assured Sir John Holles – who was present – that in future he would devote himself to 'dispersing all clouds of mistakings and of heretofore misbelief'.[40] Unfortunately for Somerset death once again intervened: on 23 August Buckingham was struck down by a lone assassin.

Deprived of his invaluable support, Somerset found the climate at court less sympathetic. Far from showing any sign of wishing to add to Somerset's property, King Charles appeared disposed to relieve him of some of what he currently possessed. In 1629 Somerset was called before the Court of Star Chamber and accused of distributing a pamphlet designed to bring the monarchy into disrepute by implying that the King intended to introduce various objectionable policies. Sir John Holles believed that the King wanted to impose a swingeing fine but, in the end, Somerset was able to prove that he was the victim of a misunderstanding and the case was dropped. However, in May 1633 the King mounted a fresh assault after it emerged that, at some time in the past, Somerset had, through 'I know not . . . what brokage', purchased for a fraction of its true value a jewel from the royal collection which dated back to Roman times. 'With sharp reprehension' he was summoned before the Council and ordered to surrender it to the King, a command he obeyed 'with great reluctation'.[41]

Such setbacks were without question minor compared to the penalties imposed on others implicated in Overbury's murder or, indeed, on men convicted of lesser crimes. Nevertheless Sir John Holles was furious that Somerset should be subjected to such harassment, fretting that this injurious treatment might undermine the Earl's health. When Somerset was unwell in September 1630, Sir John indignantly told his son, 'My Lord of Somerset's sickness questionless comes from a grounded deep discontent, in regard of the hard and unworthy usage he hath received.'[42]

Evidence is scant as to whether Somerset's domestic life afforded him any consolation for the reverses he received in other areas. As has been said, even before they were freed, he and his wife were reported to be getting on badly. Once they moved to Chiswick, the fact that Holles always included in his letters to Somerset a courteous salutation to the Countess perhaps provides some ground for thinking that the marriage had not totally broken down. On the other hand Holles's description of the altercation that took place at an unspecified time between Somerset and his wife at Clerkenwell House would seem to indicate that their life together was less than harmonious. It was on this occasion, in the presence not only of Holles but also the Countess of Suffolk, that Somerset taunted his wife that their 'first coming together' had been in response to 'several solicitations from her', rather than at his own instigation. He also reminded her of the pressure she had brought to bear on him when he had suggested that a marriage might be unwise.[43] Perhaps this was an isolated outburst on the part of Somerset, but the fact that he later requested Holles to produce a written account of what he had witnessed shows that he did not regard it as an incident best forgotten.

While there is no way of knowing how frequently Somerset gave vent to his feelings, it is scarcely surprising that the Earl could not always resist engaging in angry recriminations. The fact that, while awaiting trial in the Tower, Somerset had proposed that his wife 'might be kept in some private corner all the days of her life'[44] suggests that already he was filled with anger and disgust about what she had done, and these feelings can only have been accentuated once it emerged that his life as well as hers would be ruined as a result. Since Somerset was a man by nature disinclined to accept that he had contributed to his own misfortunes, he almost certainly blamed Frances entirely for what had befallen him, and his festering sense of grievance must inevitably have corroded his affection for her. Indeed the wonder is not so much that the marriage reportedly came under strain but that, when first reunited after their trials in the Tower, the couple resumed living together with every appearance of amiability, and it was only later that tensions surfaced.

The Countess of Somerset's feelings for the husband she pursued with such tenacity remain utterly unfathomable. As has been said, John Chamberlain insinuated that she was inconstant to Somerset while in the Tower, but without more information it is difficult to judge the truth of this. Arthur Wilson also alluded to the 'common rumour' that, once freed, she found some 'new object' for her affections but he admitted that, equally, it might have been Somerset's 'inclining to reluctancy' towards her that caused an estrangement between them. Even had the facts indicated otherwise, Wilson would no doubt have liked to believe that she was incapable of remaining faithful, which fitted in with his own depiction of her as an incorrigible voluptuary. While a little vague as to the cause, Wilson was at least positive that the marriage was a failure. With obvious satisfaction he pronounced, 'That love that made them break through all oppositions ... grew so weak that it pined away and they lived long after (though in one house) as strangers to one another.' The author of *The True Tragi-Comedie*, a drama inspired by these events, likewise believed that Frances 'lived after her enlargement long under the same roof with Somerset, yet unconcerned as a wife, he looking upon her as the author of his fall'.[45]

Simonds d'Ewes heard a slightly different story: it was 'very credibly related' to him that Frances developed some medical condition which prevented her from having sexual relations with her husband. He was told 'that, soon after the birth of her daughter she was disabled by the secret punishment of a higher providence and that, though she lived near upon twenty years after it, yet her husband the Earl of Somerset never knew her'.[46] The astrologer William Lilly reports something very similar. Possibly early symptoms of the cancer which ultimately killed Frances, or complications following childbirth did result in gynaecological problems which inhibited her from intercourse. It is equally plausible, however, to attribute the story to wishful thinking on the part of moralists who found it only proper that a woman who – according to common perception – was driven by lust should be denied the sexual pleasure that meant so much to her.

Men with this cast of mind also found a pleasing symmetry in the fact that, at the age of only forty-two, the Countess of Somerset was killed by 'a disease in those parts' 'below the girdle' which she had allegedly abused so wantonly. On 22 August 1632 Frances died 'in very great extremity' at Chiswick, attended by a local minister. Arthur Wilson set down a repellent account of the torments she suffered in the course of her last illness. Gloatingly he recorded how 'that part of her body which had been the receptacle of most of her sin grown rotten (though she never had but one child) the ligaments falling, it fell down and was cut away in flakes, with a most nauseous and putrid savour which, to augment, she would roll herself in her own ordure in her bed, took delight in it'.[47] Wilson's evident relish in her agonies, and his insistence that she derived depraved pleasure from her incontinence, merely shows the depths to which her detractors could sink in their determination to demonise her.

Wilson may have gleaned at least some of his information from his one-time employer, the Earl of Essex. Certainly the latter took a keen interest in the death of his former wife, preserving among his papers an autopsy on her carried out by, among others, Dr Mayerne. From this it appears that Frances had suffered from both breast and uterine cancer. There was a large tumour 'under the right pap' which 'had penetrated and wrapped itself about the ribs on the inside'. The womb was 'cancerous in the whole body of it'.[48]

There is nothing to indicate whether Somerset felt sadness or relief on losing his wife. His family life now centred on his daughter, Lady Anne Carr, who, at the appropriate time, assumed her place at court like other earls' daughters. By her late teens she had grown into 'a most fine young lady' and in 1635 it was reported that William, Lord Russell, son of the fourth Earl of Bedford, was in love with her. Unfortunately the Earl of Bedford (who had been one of the peers who had tried Frances, although illness had forced him to absent himself from Somerset's arraignment) set himself against the match, ordering his son 'to choose anywhere but there'. However, Lord Russell would not renounce the young lady and, rather surprisingly, in 1636 the King intervened, telling Bedford that since the young couple remained so devoted, he hoped that they would be permitted to marry. This forced Bedford to give his consent, but he still hoped to prevent a betrothal by stipulating that Somerset must provide his daughter with an enormous dowry of £12,000. Though shocked by the demand, Somerset refused to be defeated by it. Taking his daughter to see the King's Lord Chamberlain, the Earl of Pembroke (formerly the Earl of Montgomery, who had succeeded to his brother's title when the latter died in 1630), he declared that, however ruinous it proved, 'he chose rather to undo himself than to make her unhappy'. To raise some of the money he sold his Chiswick House and its contents to Pembroke, who had once been considered an enemy of Somerset, but who now proved ready to act as 'a great mediator in this business' of Anne's marriage.[49]

The sale raised only a small portion of the sum required but, by February 1637, Somerset believed himself to be in a position to negotiate with Bedford. He proposed that if Anne married Russell, he would hand over to Bedford an initial payment of £1,000 supplemented by a further £9,000 six months later. When Somerset died, a final instalment of £3,000 would be released. Bedford agreed to this, and on 11 July 1637 Lord Russell and Lady Anne Carr were married at St Benet's Church, London.

The outcome left the young couple 'wonderful happy, for they exceedingly well love one another' but the financial arrangements which had sealed their union proved less durable than their affection. As promised, Somerset had produced £1,000 prior to the marriage, but he subsequently reneged on his outstanding obligations. Partly this was because he had hoped to raise money by mortgaging lands in Scotland expected to pass to him at some time in the future, but then the current tenant's family contested Somerset's right to the property, making it impossible for him to use it as security. However, this was not the only reason why Somerset failed to honour his engagements, for he had committed himself to Bedford on the assumption that, before long, the King would make up the shortfall between the financial settlement first proposed for him, and that eventually awarded. Whether Somerset had any justification for believing this is less clear, but in view of the King's evident distaste for him it seems likely that his hopes were unrealistic. Indeed, in 1635 it had actually been proposed to prosecute Somerset in the Court of the Exchequer in connection with a loan of £60,000 which, it was alleged, had been repaid to England by Henry IV of France, and which Somerset had then embezzled.[50] The case had never come to court, but the fact that the King harboured such suspicions makes it seem highly implausible that he could ever have contemplated adding to Somerset's fortune.

Despite this, Somerset remained convinced that, in time, the King could not fail to admit that he deserved compensation. In a petition submitted to Charles some time after May 1641, Somerset declared that he had been assured by his acquaintances at court 'that, whatsoever he had to demand justly of your Majesty, or should make appear to have been meant of him by your father, you would do him right in it'. It turned out that his optimism was misplaced. Although Somerset expressed confidence that he 'hath more proofs to shew than any other that he hath deserved well of the King your father, or your Majesty, and of all these three kingdoms', Charles never recognised the justice of his claims.[51]

Somerset's failure to pay his daughter's dowry caused a coldness between them, as well as embroiling him in a lawsuit with the Bedford family. The friction arising on this account can hardly have been eased when in 1642 his son-in-law (who by this time had become fifth Earl of Bedford) had to pay £1 to 'a silk man in Cheapside' who 'demanded money as due to him from the Earl of Somerset'. Somerset came to feel so bitter towards his daughter that, during the Civil War, when Royalist troops ransacked his house and seized some tapestries, he alleged that Anne and her husband had organised the raid, having long coveted these hangings.[52] In July 1645 he died while the Civil War was still in progress. As the relic of another era, he was not mourned widely; in fact, his death occasioned as little sadness as had Overbury's, a generation earlier.

*

It is, quite simply, impossible to ascertain the full truth in the case of Sir Thomas Overbury. For one thing, important pieces of evidence are missing. These include the letters which Somerset wrote to Northampton and which Somerset burned on being ordered into confinement. The papers bearing Mrs Turner's name which were in the trunk seized by the pursuivant and delivered to Somerset were also, presumably, destroyed. It is equally noteworthy that, while Overbury was in the Tower, numerous letters passed between the Countess of Somerset, Sir Thomas Monson and the Lieutenant of the Tower (in one statement Elwes referred to 'all their letters') but only one of these subsequently came to light. Furthermore, although most of the letters which Overbury sent to Rochester from the Tower were preserved, it was never clearly established how much these had been altered by Sir Robert Cotton.

Despite these lacunae, the Crown still managed to prove its case to the satisfaction of most contemporaries. However, our difficulties in judging the strength of that case are compounded by the fact that by no means all the evidence which was gathered at the time remains available. Some of Elwes's examinations are no longer extant, and almost all the statements made by the Earl and Countess of Somerset (including, crucially, Frances's confessions) have disappeared. If these documents could be consulted, it might well have a significant bearing on our understanding of the affair.

Such testimony as we do have is, of course, not necessarily reliable. Many of the key prosecution witnesses were themselves suspects who had good reasons for lying. The most obvious example is James Franklin, who certainly was ready to fabricate the most outrageous stories in the hope of saving his life. It does not automatically follow, however, that everything he said was false.

Assessing the accuracy of Sir Gervase Elwes's testimony is in some ways particularly problematic. Among his contemporaries his fate excited widespread sympathy. Even after the expectations for his acquittal proved mistaken, Elwes continued to be perceived by many people as an unfortunate who had been sucked into the business through little fault of his own. The normally uncharitable Sir Anthony Weldon was sure that Elwes was 'truly no otherwise guilty but that he did not discover it at Weston's first disclosing it'. Weldon had no doubt that Elwes had genuinely been determined to protect Overbury, but had been deceived by Weston, who promised not to harm the prisoner and then 'gave those poisons after sent without acquainting the lieutenant'.[53]

However, this was not a universal belief. One spectator at Elwes's trial was unimpressed by his claims to have been an unwitting participant in the conspiracy, writing hostilely that Elwes relied on 'smooth terms and cunning carriage to persuade ye auditory of his innocence'.[54] And indeed, his defence failed to address various salient points. In particular he proved incapable of explaining why the Countess of Somerset had felt it necessary to tell him that tarts and jellies destined for Overbury contained 'letters'. His claim on the scaffold that he could not remember why he had written the sentence beginning 'the scab is like the fox' was also extraordinarily lame.

It is perhaps significant that the Earl of Somerset came to believe that, of all those tried, Sir Gervase Elwes was the individual most grievously at fault. In the letter he wrote to the King shortly after his conviction Somerset expressed resentment that Elwes's widow had been permitted to retain her late husband's property while his own estate was still liable for forfeiture. According to Somerset, Elwes was 'the worst deserver in this business, an unoffended instrument who might have prevented all after mischief; but for his own ends suffered it and by the like arts afterwards betrayed it'.[55] In short, although Elwes's evidence is central to any reconstruction of the Overbury murder case, it may be that it is as unreliable as Franklin's.

Sir Thomas Monson's role in the intrigue remains exceptionally difficult to disentangle. In some respects he appears to have been a pivotal figure. In her letter to Elwes the Countess of Somerset wrote, 'Sir Thomas Monson shall come this day and then we shall have some other news', a comment that suggests that he was a vital link in the chain of conspiracy. Elwes himself declared that, like Northampton and the Countess, Monson had been privy to the arrangement to refer to Overbury in letters by the codename 'scab'. Furthermore, on the scaffold Elwes recalled that 'he had notes and instructions from time to time from the Earl of Northampton and Sir Thomas Monson for the usage of his prisoner'. According to Sir John Throckmorton, in this final speech Elwes was very bitter towards Monson, 'openly accusing' him and Northampton of 'drawing him to this villainy which brought him to that shameful end'.[56]

It seems incontrovertible that Monson was in some way involved in the plan to force Overbury to be less objectionable towards the Howards; the real question is whether he was an accomplice to murder. James Franklin claimed that he was, insisting in one statement that 'Sir Thomas Monson was a messenger about ... poison, and acquainted therewith.' Franklin subsequently deposed that, not infrequently when he visited the Countess of Essex, he 'hath been shifted into another room, happening sundry times to be with the Countess when Sir

Thomas Monson came unto her, till the said Monson were gone, and that then the Countess would send for ... Franklin and impart unto him such matters as had passed between her and the said Monson'. As always with Franklin, however, there is no way of knowing whether this was anything other than fantasy. The fact that Monson's trial was not pursued suggests that Franklin's testimony against him was considered suspect.

Apart from Franklin's depositions, evidence linking Monson to Overbury's murder was decidedly limited. He had played a part in securing the appointment of both Weston and Elwes. He also admitted that he had once told Richard Weston that the Countess of Essex wished to see him, but he insisted that he had no idea why she desired this meeting. This scarcely amounted to a strong case against Monson. Nevertheless, it should be noted that Sir John Holles believed that if Monson's trial had proceeded, an acquittal would have been unlikely. He reasoned, 'If guilty seeming presumptions in these modern times be received for good evidence ... at the Lord's [Somerset's] arraignment, I conceived them strongest against [Monson].'[57]

Somerset himself appears to have felt resentful that Monson was spared trial, while he had to undergo the full legal process. In his letter to the King Somerset referred balefully to persons who, 'if they had come to the test ... should have drunk of the bitter cup as well as others'. Monson and, perhaps, Sir Robert Cotton fell into this category. Interestingly, many years after his son's death Sir Nicholas Overbury claimed to have been instrumental in the decision not to proceed with Monson's trial. He reminisced to his grandson 'that himself favoured Sir Thomas Monson, though accessory to his son's death, for old friendship sake'.[58]

After the last adjournment of his trial in early June 1616, Monson remained in the Tower for some months. However, in October he was freed on bail. Soon afterwards, desiring 'that his innocency might appear to the world and likewise that he might be discharged of the said indictment', he petitioned that the evidence against him might be reviewed. This was done, with the result that Solicitor-General Sir Henry Yelverton and Lord Chancellor Ellesmere informed the King that, because most of the evidence against Monson was conjectural, 'to rip up those matters now will be neither agreeable to ... justice nor to the mercy used by your Majesty towards others'. They advised James to issue Monson with a pardon to which he could formally plead.[59]

On 12 February 1617 a hearing was held for this purpose in the Court of King's Bench. On being asked whether he would accept the proffered pardon, Monson replied in the affirmative, even though he acknowledged that this might seem strange. The grant of a pardon implied that some crime had been committed, whereas he had always maintained that he had done nothing wrong. He had also repeatedly declared that he looked forward to his case being tried in court, where he would have an opportunity to prove his innocence. However, he pointed out that the wording of this particular pardon 'shows plainly that not any diffidence of me but insufficiency of the processes and evidences against me have been the sole occasion of this course of proceeding'. Lest any doubts remained, he proclaimed roundly, 'I am guiltless of the blood of that man ... guiltless of the fact, guiltless of the procurement thereof, guiltless of the privity or consent thereto.' Sir Henry Montague, who had succeeded Coke as Lord Chief Justice, concurred with this, observing, 'It is true as you say that every pardon is an implied confession of the fact, but yours is not so, but is a declaration of your innocency.'[60]

In theory, at least, Monson had been completely exonerated. In reality, the fact that in early 1618 the King reproved Monson's nephew William for his forwardness by reminding him that his uncle Sir Thomas had been 'not long since called in question for matters of no small moment' shows that Monson's association with the murder case had left a lasting blemish on his character. Having previously enjoyed regular access to the King, he was not readmitted to the royal presence till 1620. On his arrest in 1615 he had been dismissed from his court employments. Though in 1618 he was given the minor consolation of being made Steward of the Duchy of Lancaster, and awarded another small grant in 1625, he suffered financially as a result of losing his former offices. While Monson was fortunate in comparison with others caught up in the Overbury murder case, he did not emerge unscathed from the episode.

Northampton's death in 1614 saved him from being called to account for his part in Overbury's murder. Nevertheless, in his absence, he was confidently stated to have played a key part in it. At Somerset's trial Sir Francis Bacon averred, 'The extreme hatred that this malicious and unbounded fellow [Overbury] beared to the Lady and the house of Howard ... moved my Lord of Northampton to say, "Overbury must die."' Sir Nicholas Overbury was equally certain that Northampton had 'plotted the poisoning'. Long afterwards Sir Nicholas told his grandson that the Earl 'had doubtless suffered if he had not died between the murder and the discovery of it'. Sir John Holles, though convinced of

Somerset's innocence and doubtful whether the case against Weston had been proven, was profoundly shocked by those letters of Northampton's which were read out at Sir Gervase Elwes's trial. Holles thought they demonstrated that Northampton was 'the chief mover and encourager of this foul business', and Simonds d'Ewes likewise believed that the letters 'left a foul stain of suspicion' upon Northampton.[61]

However, when analysed, the evidence against Northampton is scarcely conclusive. His letters to Rochester prove beyond doubt that he had a motive to murder Overbury, and it is of course relevant that in one of them Northampton actually muses that he would welcome it if Overbury were to die. Nevertheless, while it is obvious that it was Northampton who coordinated and controlled the process whereby Overbury was to be coerced into aligning himself with the Howards, it would be rash to equate this with a determination to murder Sir Thomas. It should be recalled that Northampton had a lifetime's experience of confounding his enemies, which he had done on innumerable occasions without recourse to such unsubtle methods. There is nothing to suggest that Northampton ever had any dealings with James Franklin, or that he had procured poison from other sources. Such evidence as there is against him is purely circumstantial, and can be reduced to three counts. He was responsible for placing at the Tower not only Sir Gervase Elwes (which might have had an innocent explanation) but also of Richard Weston, a much more dubious action. In addition the letters Northampton wrote to Elwes immediately after Overbury's death leave no doubt that he was desperate that Overbury should be buried in haste, and his anxiety is hard to account for unless he was aware – or at least suspected – that foul play had taken place. Lastly, the Countess of Somerset's statement that it may have been Northampton who told her what to write in her letter to Elwes would serve as a powerful argument of his guilt, were it not for the fact that her admission was so vague.

It is regrettable that Northampton died before these matters came under investigation. If called upon to justify himself in court, he would surely have done so more ably than Somerset at his trial. As a seasoned orator, endowed with the powerful intellect and mastery of detail that Somerset so conspicuously lacked, Northampton could have been depended upon to put forward a cogent and well-argued defence. Since he also excelled at equivocation and had been schooled in deception since early adulthood his account would, very likely, have been mendacious and self-serving. Nevertheless, his version of events might well have clarified much that is currently obscure.

*

Assessing the culpability of the King with regard to this affair is by no means a straightforward task. In the last century Andrew Amos, a professor of law at Cambridge, actually contended that responsibility for Overbury's murder should be laid at the King's door. Amos was convinced that it was James who arranged for Dr Mayerne to poison Overbury, but he advanced little evidence to support his belief, and the theory is untenable. Amos's book *The Great Oyer of Poison* is useful because it reproduces many of the primary sources relating to the murder case (though these documents are haphazardly arranged and, in some cases, inaccurately printed) but his analysis of these events merely adds to the confusion surrounding them.

Nevertheless, while James was innocent of murder, this episode scarcely redounds to his credit. It is clear that James was responsible for the decision to imprison Overbury. Whether he merely responded impetuously when Overbury refused to serve abroad, or whether the King coldly pre-meditated his arrest, remains enigmatic. It is not inconceivable that James actually encouraged Rochester to tell Overbury that he should reject the posting, and then used Overbury's rebuff as an excuse to send him to the Tower. Once Overbury was in confinement the King's treatment of him was extraordinarily unrelenting. By mid-July 1613 James cannot have been unaware that Overbury was seriously ill but he did not see fit to set him free, or even to permit one of Overbury's servants to wait on him. This aspect of the matter was never discussed in public, but many people at court knew what had happened, and James was conscious that his actions laid him open to suspicion. This was one reason why the King did not do more to protect the Somersets. In December 1615, when Somerset was begging James not to bring him to trial, the King explained why it was impossible for him to grant this request. He noted, 'If . . . I should have stopped the course of justice against [Somerset] in this case of Overbury, who was committed to the Tower and there kept a close prisoner by my commandment, and could not have been so murthered if he had not been kept close, I might be thought to be the author of that murder and so made odious to all posterity.'[62]

The fact that James fulfilled his duty by bringing Somerset to justice is in itself a powerful argument that he was in no way connected with the attempts on Overbury's life. Nevertheless, James's agitation on the day of Somerset's trial does indicate that he feared that something would be revealed there which would reflect badly on him. It has sometimes been suggested that James was worried that Somerset would disclose the homosexual nature of their relationship, but Somerset would have had to be insane to do something so utterly destructive, which would undoubtedly have brought about his own ruination. The most plausible hypothesis is that James feared that Somerset would go into details about the events which led to Overbury's arrest, and that the part played by the King at that time would then become a matter of record.

The question of the Earl of Somerset's guilt is perhaps the greatest enigma arising from the Overbury murder case. Somerset himself remained adamant that he was the victim of an injustice. At the close of his trial he had remonstrated with the peers who had found him guilty, desiring 'them to consider that it was but the testimony of two men of bad condition [presumably he was referring to Franklin and Simcocks] that had condemned him'. When he wrote to the King a few weeks later he was more inclined to attribute his conviction to his own weak performance when speaking for himself. He told James, 'I fell rather for want of well defending than by the violence or force of any proofs, for I so far forsook myself and my cause as that it may be a question whether I was more condemned for that or for the matter itself.' Interestingly, the King himself may well have harboured doubts that justice had not been done. According to Sir John Holles, James 'oft alleged ... that he was not satisfied in the trial'.[63]

The fact that Somerset so stubbornly maintained his innocence, even after conviction, might appear significant, were it not for the fact that an inability to recognise when he was at fault was one of his most marked characteristics. At the very least he was guilty of betraying a friend, but he could never bring himself to express remorse even for that. Nor was he averse to lying when it suited him: he claimed that he had never sought payment from Spain for his services, when in reality he was awaiting the first instalment of a Spanish pension at the time of his arrest. Possibly other claims he made were equally untruthful, but the evidence is lacking which could establish this.

Although the case against Somerset was purely circumstantial, by the standards of the time he had had a fair trial, and in general con-temporaries were satisfied that his conviction was sound. John Chamber-lain, for one, was sure that the verdict was correct, registering his belief that 'by all circumstances and most pregnant (yea almost infallible) probabilities, he be more faulty and foul than any of the company'. Edward Palavacino was equally certain that Somerset bore the primary responsibility for Overbury's murder, declaring, 'According to my capacity, and by the proofs read I dare say it, the lady come into the business by him and his means.'[64]

Others thought that Somerset had not been directly involved in the murder conspiracy, but that he had learned what had happened after Overbury was dead and had then acted criminally in attempting to protect those responsible and falsify evidence. The anonymous author of *The True Tragi-Comedie* affirmed, 'Concerning the poisoning ... the general opinion of that time did acquit him of all knowing till after the fact.' Anthony Weldon also subscribed to this view, declaring, 'Many believed him guilty of Overbury's death, but the most thought him guilty only of the breach of friendship (and that in a high point) by suffering his imprisonment which was the highway to his murther; and this I take to be of the soundest opinion.'[65]

There is a real possibility that Somerset was wrongly convicted, but it is difficult to feel much sympathy for him. Overbury's death provided Somerset's enemies with the perfect means of destroying him, but if it had not been for Somerset's arrogance and ineptitude his downfall would not have been so eagerly sought. Once deprived of the guidance of intelligent mentors such as Overbury and Northampton, his fundamental lack of talent and discernment became painfully apparent, as he systematically squandered the advantages that had accrued to him as a result of his youthful good looks. His mismanagement and neglect of his patronage obligations, and his needless antagonism of potential allies undermined him at court. When he compounded this by alienating the King, he became acutely vulnerable. There is no sign that Somerset ever recognised his deficiencies in this respect. After his conviction the mulish way he handled the negotiations relating to his financial settlement shows that his faith in his own abilities never wavered, and that he had learned nothing from painful experience.

When reviewing Somerset's career some memoir writers of the period were surprisingly generous in their treatment of him. Arthur Wilson took the view that, rather than being inherently evil, Somerset was corrupted by his wife and her family, and that 'if he had not met with such a woman he might have been a good man'. Anthony Weldon reached a similar conclusion. He declared of Somerset, 'Surely he was the most unfortunate man in that marriage, being as generally beloved for himself and his disposition as hated afterwards for his linking himself in that family; for in all the time of this man's favour, before this marriage he did nothing obnoxious to the state, or any base thing for his private gain.' Weldon went so far as to assert that, had it not been for Somerset's ill-advised union with the Howards, 'otherwise had he been the bravest favourite of our time.'[66]

It would be wrong to attach too much significance to these remarks.

Nostalgia for the time when Somerset was in power was caused not so much by recollection of Somerset's virtues but because he benefited by comparison with the Duke of Buckingham. At one time Buckingham had been hailed as an agent of reform, and his early supporters such as the Earl of Pembroke and Archbishop Abbot had fondly imagined that Buckingham would discourage the King from pursuing an alliance with Spain. In the event, Buckingham turned out to be a Frankenstein's monster, whom his own creators were powerless to control. Anthony Weldon wrote bitterly, 'Since his first being a pretty, harmless, affable gentleman, he grew insolent, cruel and a monster not to be endured.' At court, abuses such as sale of titles and awarding of monopolies became more common than in Somerset's day. Far from seeking to deter the King from drawing closer to Spain, Buckingham enthusiastically endorsed the policy of procuring Prince Charles a Spanish bride. Before long, those who had been Buckingham's most ardent promoters came to regret their part in his advancement. As early as September 1616 the Earl of Fenton noticed that Buckingham had 'lost much affection of his particular friends and generally of all men'. In later years many of the grandees who had supported the young man at the outset of his career – such as Pembroke, Abbot and the Earl of Arundel – became Buckingham's antagonists in the House of Lords. In the Commons, Sir Edward Coke led the opposition against the Duke, on one occasion denouncing Buckingham as 'the grievance of grievances'.[67]

As condemnation of Buckingham grew more strident, attitudes softened towards Somerset, whose excesses seemed minor when set beside the Duke's. Comparing the two favourites in his memoirs, Simonds d'Ewes found much to praise in Somerset's record, while bitterly denouncing his successor. According to d'Ewes, had Buckingham 'followed my Lord of Somerset's example in some particulars, the Church and Commonwealth had fared better, and his memory had doubtless been more accepted with posterity; for I have heard Sir Robert Cotton affirm that some hundreds of monopolies and projects by which the Commonwealth was oppressed, were refused by my Lord of Somerset, and for the present dashed, which afterwards all passed by Buckingham's means; that Somerset suffered no honours to be conferred but rarely, and that upon persons of noble extraction and fair revenue; whereas my Lord of Buckingham, without regard of person or condition, prostituted all honours under the degree of a marquis to such as would buy: that whereas the former favourite advanced none of his name or kindred to undeserved preferments or unmeet honours, the latter invested so many of his name, kindred and alliance with high titles, as many of them were

enforced to be burthens to the Crown or Commonwealth'.[68] By a
supreme irony, the royal favourite who was a murder victim was more
reviled than the one convicted of murder.

If the judgement of contemporaries was somewhat ambivalent towards
the Earl of Somerset, this was not the case with the Countess. In almost
every memoir of the period she is portrayed as an evil and vicious
woman whose involvement in a spiral of sin led by a natural progression
to murder. Arguably, it is right that she should have been depicted thus.
In contrast to her husband, there seems little room for doubt that she
was responsible for Sir Thomas Overbury's murder. It is true that the
evidence relating to the poisoned tarts and jellies is confusing and
inconclusive, but the reason for this was probably that the Countess
herself took the precaution of destroying everything liable to incriminate
her. Even so, her surviving letter to Sir Gervase Elwes is undeniably
suspicious. It also would seem indisputable that immediately after
Weston took up office at the Tower she sent him a liquid, and it is
reasonable to assume that this was poison. The fact that she had earlier
attempted to persuade Sir David Wood to assassinate Overbury proves
that she wanted Overbury dead and that she was sufficiently ruthless to
pursue this objective. Furthermore, while the claims of Mary Woods
and Samuel Calvert that she had tried to murder the Earl of Essex are
unsubstantiated, it is certainly a striking coincidence that such allegations
had been levelled against her in the past.

The text is missing of the confession made by Frances on 1 January
1616 to Lords Fenton and Montgomery (it is not even certain that her
words were written down), but we have it on authoritative report that
she admitted to them that she had murdered Overbury. There is likewise
no full record of her confession to Lord Chief Justice Coke, a week
later, but on that occasion it appears she was equally willing to
acknowledge her culpability. Any last vestiges of doubt should surely
be dispelled by the fact that at her trial she pleaded guilty.

Nevertheless, there are two points which should be borne in mind.
Some weeks after Frances had confessed to Fenton and Montgomery,
she was asked to add to what she had told them by testifying that
Somerset had been involved in the conspiracy. She refused, saying that
not only was she ignorant of anything detrimental to her husband but
that, when 'she had declared and confessed her own fault', she 'had
even enhanced it, in order to have more to work upon the pity and
clemency of the King'.[69] It is – just – possible that similar considerations
made her plead guilty to a crime that she had not in fact committed.

From what had happened to previous defendants, she would have known that if she pleaded innocent, there was scant chance of an acquittal. It had also been made very clear to her that if, after denying the charges, she was convicted and sentenced to death, the King would not see fit to exercise his prerogative of mercy.

It is, admittedly, highly unlikely that Frances should have unprotestingly allowed herself to be condemned as a murderess if she believed that she had no part in Overbury's death. There is, however, another possibility. The Countess may well have assumed that Overbury was killed by poison that she had procured, but it does not follow that she was correct in thinking this. After Sir Gervase Elwes had deterred him from adding to Overbury's food the liquid supplied by Frances, Weston pretended to her that he had administered it as planned. Similarly, Frances was given no reason to think that the tarts and jellies she sent to the Tower were failing to reach Sir Thomas. Naturally, therefore, when Overbury fell ill, she would have assumed that poison was responsible but, since both Elwes and Weston insisted that the prisoner never tasted her food, she may have been mistaken.

It could be argued that the question is academic: if not a murderess in fact, Frances was a would-be murderess. In moral terms this amounts to much the same thing. That she became a notorious figure is scarcely to be wondered at but, even so, some of the excoriations heaped on her were undeserved. It is notable that many of these attacks laid undue emphasis on her supposedly lustful nature, an aspect of her character which, once fixed on her, served as confirmation that she was inherently wicked. During her own trial Frances was protected by the King's order that 'no odious or uncivil speeches should be given' against her, but the process whereby her sexual transgressions were magnified in order to whip up opprobium against her had started at Weston's arraignment. On that occasion her adulterous meetings with her lover were made public in a deliberately humiliating fashion, and the Prosecution followed this up by referring to her as a 'filthy woman' who was 'lewd and malicious'.[70] It is significant that although Somerset's private conduct was on a par with hers, it was never attacked in such offensive terms.

Later commentators took up the theme with glee, embellishing it by claiming that Frances had always been incurably licentious. In his *Detection of the Court and State of England* Roger Coke (a grandson, as it happened, of Sir Edward Coke) confidently stated that the Countess was a woman 'intolerably bent' on carnality, while another anonymous chronicler of the period described her as possessed of an 'insatiate appetite'. The same account stressed that her career of promiscuity began very early and that, even while the Earl of Essex was travelling on the continent, 'She continued most inconstant, of a loose life, suffering her body to be abused and others to make shipwreck of her modesty and to abrogate the rights of marriage.' When Essex returned her behaviour did not improve: 'She ran at random and brought herself into the contempt of the world ... Almost all men spake of the looseness of her carriage.' Anthony Weldon was equally emphatic that Frances was renowned for her immodesty. He recorded that when, in 1613, the midwives and matrons declared her a virgin, their findings were regarded as utterly astounding, since it was common parlance 'that her way was very near beaten so plain, as if *regia via* [the King's highway] and, in truth, was a common way before Somerset did ever travel that way'.[71]

By dwelling on Frances's sexual rapacity these authors were able to draw a wider moral from her story. Once shaped to their requirements, Frances ceased to be a complex individual responding to a highly unusual set of circumstances. Instead she assumed more of a symbolic status, emblematic of her sex's innate corruptibility and tendency to excess. She illustrated that, once women deviated from the standards of purity enjoined on them by a patriarchal society, the consequences were incalculable, and her disrespect for human life was viewed as simply a logical extension of her earlier career as sexual predator. Simonds d'Ewes was typical in thinking that her infidelity formed the natural prelude to her committing sins that were still more grievous, declaring gravely, 'By this example, as in many others, we may see plainly that the conscience being once emasculated and cauterised by lust and whoredom is then prepared and fitted for the commission of witchcraft, murder or any other villainy.'[72]

Frances may have lacked the passivity and subservience considered proper in a woman of her time, but nor did she conform to the stereotype imposed on her. For some reason contemporaries found it insufficient to stigmatise her as a murderess; instead Frances had to fit into the established mould of an evil woman. As a result, rampant promiscuity was automatically numbered among her vices. Nevertheless, however satisfying the image, it hardly accorded with reality, for the claim that Frances was possessed of an insatiable lust is not warranted by evidence. As has been seen, rumours of an affair between Frances and Prince Henry only became current long after both the supposed protagonists were dead. Nor is there anything to suggest that she conducted herself improperly while Essex was abroad. It seems likely that, when her marriage to Essex was causing Frances deep unhappiness, she began sleeping with Rochester but, even on this point, some doubt exists. The only detailed information regarding Frances's and Rochester's adulterous encounters is provided by Weston, who described how he delivered letters on their behalf which led to their meetings at Hammersmith and Paternoster Row. At least one authority considers Weston's statement suspect, pointing out that at no time did Mrs Turner acknowledge Weston's part in arranging such assignations. In her confession to Dr Whiting she recalled rather that it was Northampton who enabled the lovers to maintain contact, declaring that 'all letters that came from the Lord of Somerset to the Lady came in the packet of the Earl of Northampton, and from him she had them'. This is an interesting objection, but it is nevertheless undermined by Somerset's own testimony at his trial. There, he went far to verify Weston's evidence by referring to an occasion before their marriage when he and Frances 'met at Hammersmith'. Furthermore, although it would have been greatly to his advantage if he could have established that Weston never acted as a messenger between him and Frances, Somerset never contended this. When reminded that Weston had delivered letters to him from the Countess, Somerset responded, 'That might be so but he never saw his [Weston's] face to his knowledge.'[73]

Against this it must be conceded that Northampton's letters written in the spring or summer of 1613 suggest that at that stage he, at least, assumed that the relationship between Rochester and his great-niece remained unconsummated. Though lubricious in tone, his arch reference to the exquisite pain that Frances would feel 'when the sweet stream followeth' allows of no other interpretation than that he believed that she had yet to be deflowered. In itself, however, this does not constitute proof that Frances remained a virgin until her marriage to Somerset. Although she knew that her great-uncle viewed her liaison with Rochester with avuncular indulgence, prudence and good taste would surely have inhibited her from furnishing this elderly bachelor with graphic details of their couplings.

Even if Frances did sleep with Rochester while she was technically the Earl of Essex's wife, this scarcely justifies the claim that she was a notorious whore who had been serviced by innumerable men long before she surrendered to Rochester's advances. The likelihood is that Somerset was her sole sexual partner. Indeed if one accepts the claim that he ceased to sleep with her shortly after their trial, it would mean that during the whole of Frances's life she was sexually active for no more than three or four years. However, it could be said that this is immaterial, for today our perception of Frances is formed by other considerations. The fact is that Frances did in all probability plot Overbury's murder, and it is this which accounts for her reputation as a wicked and scheming woman, devoid of humanity. Nevertheless, there are several mitigating factors. Her marriage to Essex was a source of profound unhappiness and if it had not been dissolved she faced years of utter misery. Since the marriage was unconsummated she was denied not only physical fulfilment but also the consolations of motherhood, and it is understandable that the prospect of spending the rest of her life with a man she abhorred reduced her to despair. Had Frances been a model of Christian womanhood she should, no doubt, have resigned herself to her fate, but from a modern perspective it is less easy to condemn her lack of stoicism. Even Simonds d'Ewes conceded that this mockery of a marriage was 'a real and true affliction to the lady', and his criticism centred on the fact that she initially found solace in adultery, instead of seeking 'that divorce which was afterwards procured'. D'Ewes was positive that had she 'not satisfied her inordinate lust by that unlawful means, she had never been plunged into that deluge of sin with which she was afterwards overwhelmed',[74] but this was a simplistic view, which owed everything to hindsight. It should be recalled that when Frances first confided her marital difficulties to her family they were adamant that she would have to make the best of her situation, and the fact that her problems would later be resolved by obtaining an annulment would at that stage have seemed inconceivable. In the circumstances, it is amazing that, as far as can be ascertained, Frances refrained from sleeping with Rochester until some time in 1612.

It could be argued that though Frances's situation merits our compassion, resorting to murder was not only inexcusable but also unnecessary. Theoretically, once Overbury was in the Tower, he could not damage her in any way. Provided that he remained in prison until her annulment was secured, the matter would have been settled and he would have been powerless to interfere. If one accepts this, the inference is that Frances acted not out of a practical concern that Overbury was going to sabotage her future, but in a spirit of pure vindictiveness, to punish him for the insulting things he had said about her. Nevertheless, it would be mistaken to underestimate Overbury's capacity for harm. It is clear that Archbishop Abbot hoped that the verdict of the nullity commission would be challenged at a later date and if that was a possibility Overbury would have represented a threat whenever he was let out. Alternatively, if Overbury was set free after she had secured her annulment, but before Frances had become Somerset's wife, there was still a chance that Overbury would persuade Somerset to give her up.

In many ways Frances was a remarkable woman, differing radically from the conventional pattern of docile femininity which seventeenth-century females were expected to follow. Everything indicates that she had great strength of will and a fiercely independent spirit. This is shown not only by the determined way she pressured Rochester into marrying her but also by her approaching Sir David Wood to ask him to assassinate Overbury. If James Franklin's accounts of her dealings with him have any factual basis, they too demonstrate her purposefulness and tenacity. Unfortunately, given the limitations imposed on women at this time, the only legitimate outlet for her energies lay in marriage and the family, and when these aspects of her life proved unsatisfactory she applied herself obsessively to remedying the situation. While Frances was exceptional in the dedication and ruthlessness she brought to bear on the problem, it was recognised as natural that women minded more about such matters than their male counterparts. It is significant that Francis Bacon found it necessary to claim that Somerset's principal reason for killing Overbury was his fear that Sir Thomas would disclose compromising secrets whereas, in Frances's case, her concern that Overbury planned to disrupt her marriage was looked on as sufficient motivation. While it was regarded as inconceivable that love alone could drive a successful man to murder, women were held to be more susceptible to such passions.

However, in one way at least, Somerset, no less than his wife, was a victim of sexist prejudice. Despite the fact that Frances was clearly capable of acting on her own initiative, preconceived ideas about the incompetence of women led people to discount her abilities to an extent where they simply refused to accept that she could have formulated and executed a complex murder conspiracy without male guidance. The only acceptable explanation was that she had been acting on Somerset's orders, as the Tuscan ambassador, Francesco Quaratesi, noted. Following Somerset's conviction he recorded, 'As the Earl was so in love with the Countess and so close to her, the judges assumed the Countess would not have taken such an action without consulting him.'[75]

Obviously it is legitimate to feel indignation that, by virtue of her noble birth, the Countess of Somerset escaped execution for a crime for which humbler individuals had to pay the full penalty. The injustice becomes still more glaring when one considers the sort of offence for which other men suffered the death penalty. In 1619, for example, a poor labourer was hanged after being caught holding dogs for two men who were poaching the King's deer; he had been paid sixpence for his services. Nevertheless, while in some respects Frances can be considered to have occupied a grotesquely privileged position, nothing can detract

from the fact that hers was an essentially tragic story. By modern
standards her aspirations were hardly excessive, but in order to fulfil them
she was driven to extreme measures. Her desperate action purchased her
rather less than two years' happiness. Although the ultimate outcome
can be said to have justified Overbury's predictions that she would be
a disastrous wife for Somerset, there is every indication that until
scandal overwhelmed them in 1615 the couple's marriage was successful.
However, when the murder was exposed, she forfeited the love of the
man for whom she had gambled everything. Her husband's aversion to
her seems to have been inspired not by the fact that she was a murderess
but because she had wrecked his career, for he gave her no credit for
the fact that, despite the utmost pressure on her, she had loyally sought
to prevent blame being attached to him. Though her life was spared,
one can readily believe the claim of William Sanderson that, after her
trial, 'She was dead whilst living, being drowned in despair.'[76] Without
condoning murder, one can hardly say that such sufferings were undeserved. Nevertheless, it is the ultimate irony of the Overbury murder
case that the Countess of Somerset, who has been traditionally displayed
as villainy incarnate, an evil and unscrupulous woman devoid of conscience or compassion, should emerge as perhaps the most sympathetic
figure in the story.

The Overbury murder case was the greatest scandal of James I's reign
and, arguably, the greatest court scandal to have occurred at any time
in English history. While the trials were in progress, the entire country
was absorbed by what was happening, almost to the exclusion of other
business. On the morning of the Countess of Somerset's arraignment
one young man reported, 'Here is now such a hurrying to Westminster
Hall as it distracts everybody's mind from anything else'. But it was not
just in England and Scotland that the affair caused a sensation. Foreign
ambassadors supplied their masters with detailed accounts of the progress
of the murder enquiry and the subsequent hearings. In October 1615
Sir John Throckmorton, a government official stationed in Holland,
announced, 'It is most true that not only Flushing but all the world far
and wide are full of that business of Sir Thomas Overbury's death.' He
claimed that the affair had altered foreigners' fundamental perception
of England: 'They begin to brand and mark us with that hideous and
foul title of poisoning one another, and ask if we become Italians,
Spaniards or of what other vile, murderous nation,' he reported. Few
people shared the view of Sir John Holles that an insignificant incident
had been artfully exploited to destroy the Earl of Somerset and that 'no

age hath seen so small a cause afford so many uses'. Instead the case inspired the utmost horror and revulsion, and the crime was judged 'second to none but the powder plot'.[77]

Although in seventeenth-century England there was no daily press to regale its readership with lurid trial accounts and revelations about the defendants, the affair inspired an outpouring of popular literature. This ranged from moving elegies on Overbury to scurrilous rhymes about the Somersets. Overbury himself acquired posthumous literary fame as a result of the publicity generated by his murder. By 1616 his poem *The Wife*, first issued in late 1613, was already in its seventh imprint. One admirer expressed a hope that Overbury's poetic works would serve as a lasting memorial to him, immortalising his name so that his

> ... fame's extent
> Fill every part of this vast continent.

A typical elegy on Overbury was that which was printed in 1616 as an epilogue to a tract entitled *The Just Downfall of Ambition, Adultery and Murder*. The anonymous author hailed Sir Thomas as

> ... in all parts a man complete,
> Great in regard, in goodness far more great
> Who, like a star in Britain's court did shine,
> Learned in the laws, both human and divine,
> A scholar full of gentlemanlike parts
> Whose noble carriage won a world of hearts ...
> So courteous, valiant, sober and so wise
> And one that (fawning) could not temporise
> So well proportioned, of such comely feature
> So fully fraught with a true honest nature
> So hopeful and so loving and beloved
> Whose life and actions every tongue approv'd,
> That expectation marked him out to be
> A man of absolute integrity,
> Of zeal, capacity and eminence
> To serve his God, his country and his prince.

At Somerset's trial Sir Francis Bacon sought to counter the growing tendency to idolise Overbury. Anxious that, otherwise, hostility towards the Somersets would reach such a level that the King would have no choice but to execute them, Bacon urged his listeners to bear in mind that Overbury was 'naught and corrupt; the ballads must be amended for that point'. His words made little impression. Though Overbury

had been almost universally disliked while alive, in death he had attained
iconic status. For years he continued to be viewed as a paragon whose
annihilation in the prime of life was a tragedy for his country. Even as
an old man Sir Nicholas Overbury was venerated for having sired such
a noble being. In 1637 Sir Nicholas confided to his grandson that his
son was still so revered that in town he himself was 'often pointed at
by way of honour in the street: "There goes Sir Thomas Overbury's
father." '78

While Overbury's memory was honoured with laudatory verses the
Somersets, conversely, were vilified in rhymes and libels. Most of these
mocked the Earl as a dim-witted and vulgar upstart, while hurling more
coarse abuse at Frances. One such offering proposed a fitting epitaph
for Somerset:

> Here lies he that once was poor
> Then great, then rich, then loved a whore
> He wooed and wedded but in conclusion
> His love and whore was his confusion
> A page, a Knight, a Viscount and an Earl
> All four were married to one lustful girl
> A match well made, for she was likewise four
> A wife, a witch, a murtheress and a whore.

In another, Somerset's rise and fall was charted in scornful couplets:

> Thy lands are gone, alas they were not thine
> Thy house likewise, another says 'tis mine
> Then where's thy wit? alas 'tis two years dead
> Then where's thy wife? another did her wed.
> Art thou a man or but some simple parts?
> Nothing thy own but thine aspiring heart;
> Ralegh's thy house, Westmoreland's thy lands
> Overbury thy wit; Essex thy wife demands
> Like Aesop's jay each bird will pluck his feather
> And thee strip naked, exposed to wind and weather
> But yet thy friends to keep thee from the cold
> Have mured thee up in London's strongest hold.

A third anonymous versifier displayed similar ribald humour when
offering a variation on the same theme:

> The wealth he got to make his means great
> Not from his purchase came, but knightly feat

The land his late made lordship did profess
Was Westmoreland's and Ralegh's known distress ...
Ye spouse he had to grace his nuptial bed
Was Essex's wife without a maidenhead
She was ye lady killed his lecherous itch
Before inscribed whore, wife, widow, witch
Ye wit whereby he got all but his wife
Was his poor knight whom he bereft of life
This wife undid what all those did before
And left him lord of nothing but a whore.[79]

Their convictions for murder meant that the Earl and Countess of Somerset attained eternal notoriety but the Overbury murder case had much wider reverberations. The fact that such a wicked deed was committed by a man towards whom the King had not only displayed such marked affection, but had loaded with honours, riches and public office raised serious questions about James's judgement. Direct criticism of the King was of course unthinkable, but the system which had produced Somerset did not escape condemnation. The case further blighted the reputation of the court as a whole by enhancing the impression that it was fundamentally rotten. In the eyes of some people the murder of Sir Thomas Overbury was merely an extreme manifestation of the corruption and dishonesty that were recognised features of court life. It served as confirmation that the institution which stood at the nation's core, and which supposedly provided the kingdom with an inner strength and cohesiveness, was in fact a source of moral pollution.

There was not even comfort in the fact that Overbury's murder had been exposed by men who themselves were prominent in the court hierarchy. Far from being inspired by moral outrage or compassion for the dead man, most saw bringing Somerset to justice as a means of advancing their own careers. During Somerset's trial Bacon declared that Overbury had opposed his marriage not out of high principle but as a result of baser concerns. 'All was but miserable bargains of ambition,' Bacon commented scornfully,[80] but those who orchestrated Somerset's fall were motivated by equally squalid passions.

The disgust and disenchantment with the court which the case inspired was reflected in some of the elegies penned on Overbury. One man who bewailed the loss of Sir Thomas observed of the courtly regime that it would induce despair in all the King's loyal subjects

> ... t'observe how virtue draws faint
> Wise men kept low, others advanced to state
> Right checked by wrong, and ill men fortunate.

Another lament for Overbury upbraided Providence for acting in an unfathomable manner, complaining that at court Chance's blind hand

> ... thy benefits erroneously disburse
> Which so let fall ne'er fall but to the worse
> Whence so, great crimes commit the greater sort
> And boldest acts of shame blaze in the court;
>   ... honour disgraced
> And Virtue laid by fraud and poison waste
> The adulterer up like Haman and so sainted
> And females' modesty (as females) painted.[81]

Anthony Weldon echoed such sentiments, alleging that Overbury's murder was symptomatic of larger failings endemic in a society 'worthless and corrupt in men and manners'. To him this 'grand business' encapsulated its era, and he dubbed it 'the gross production of a then foul state and court, wherein pride, revenge and luxury abounded'.[82]

NOTES

ABBREVIATIONS USED IN THE NOTES

BL   British Library Manuscript Room

BL Add.   Additional Manuscripts in British Library

BL Harl.   Harleian Manuscripts in British Library

Bod.   Bodleian Library

Cal. Ven. Calendar of State Papers and Manuscripts relating to English affairs in the Archives and Collections of Venice

CSPD   Calendar of State Papers, Domestic Series

CUL   Cambridge University Library

DNB   Dictionary of National Biography

HMC   Historical Manuscript Commission

PRO   Public Record Office

SP   State Papers in the Public Record Office

ST   A Complete Collection of State Trials, ed. William Cobbett, Volume II

PROLOGUE

1 ST 915; ibid 927
2 McClure II, 1
3 ST 953–54
4 Wilson, 57; Bod., Smith 17, fo. 30; SP 14/83/38, fo. 62v
5 ST 953–54

CHAPTER ONE

1 Frances's date of birth is given as 31 May 1590 in two astrological schemes: BL Sloane Mss 1683 fo. 176, Bodleian Ashmolean 243 fo. 162. However, in another astrological scheme in the Bodleian (Ashmolean 174 fo. 149) Frances is said to have been born on 26 August 1591. During the nullity proceedings of 1613 her father stated that, at the time of her marriage, Frances was 'above thirteen years of age' and that she was 'now above twenty-two years old' (ST 794). I have taken this as accurate, ignoring the statement printed ST 785 that Frances was thirteen at the time of her marriage, and in 1613 was aged twenty-two or twenty-three, because the arithmetic does not fit. Bearing in mind Suffolk's statement, I have taken the date of Frances's birth as 31 May 1590.

2 Birch I, 42–43

3 Jonson, *Masques and Entertainments*, 67; Birch I, 43

4 See Jonson, *Masques*, 59–79; Birch I, 42–43

5 Jonson, *Masques*, 77

6 Jonson, *Masques*, 63; Fraser 12; Stone, *Crisis*, 659; Alexander Niccholes, *Discourse of Marriage and Wiving* (1620), 11

7 Stone, *Crisis*, 653

8 Stone, *Family and Fortune*, 284; McClure I, 281; ST 810

9 Stone, *Family and Fortune*, 268–69; Robinson, 89

10 Stone, *Family, Sex and Marriage*, 180

11 Lodge III, 100–101; McClure II, 187–88; Ashley, 26

12 McClure I, 273, 385

13 Wilson, 55; ST 814

14 D'Ewes in Halliwell I, 88; Lodge III, 149, 152; d'Ewes in Halliwell I, 74

15 Wilson, 43

16 HMC Salisbury XXI, 47

17 Cal. Ven. X, 26; Snow 21–22

18 Cecil, 365

19 DNB Howard; Robinson, 89; Stone, *Family and Fortune*, 269–70; Harington I, 336; Stone, *Family and Fortune*, 270–71

20 Peck, *Northampton*, 23

21 Stone, *Family and Fortune*, 272; Hervey, 22

22 Drury, 20, 3; Robinson, 92; Stone, *Family and Fortune*, 283; Akrigg, *Letters*, 250

23 Wilson, 43; Akrigg, *Letters*, 257; Peck, *Northampton*, 8; BL Add. 25348, fo. 6v

24 Rowse, *Homosexuals in History*, 45; *Complete Peerage*, Northampton; Peck, *Northampton*, 11, 6

25 Peck, *Northampton*, 6, 12, 15, 6; BL Add. 25348, fo. 6; Weldon in Scott I, 333

26 BL Cotton Titus C VI, fo. 480; *Sidney Papers* (ed. A. Collins, 1746), II, 215; Dalrymple, 233
27 Ashton, 4; Dalrymple, 116
28 Dalrymple, 28–29
29 *Truth Brought to Light*, 267
30 Winwood II, 92–93; Peck, *Northampton*, 178; ibid 35; ibid 146
31 Peck, *Northampton*, 133, 26, 29
32 SP 14/69/56, fo. 70; Peck, *Northampton*, 135
33 CUL Dd 3 63, fo. 35; BL Cotton Titus C VI, fo. 80
34 McIlwain, 32; Bruce, 31, Gardiner I, 193; Wilbraham, 60
35 Harington I, 393, 396
36 Akrigg, *Letters*, 288; Willson, 168
37 BL Add. 25348, fo. 6v; Cal. Ven. X, 42; Lodge III, 194
38 Carter, 125–27; Loomie, *Toleration and Diplomacy*, 50; Mattingly, 261
39 Loomie, *Jacobean Catholics* I, 157
40 Winwood II, 92–93; Lodge III, 104; Stone, *Family and Fortune*, 284
41 Mathew, *Jacobean Age*, 51; Tillières, 6; Mathew, *Jacobean Age*, 163–64, 329
42 Weldon in Scott I, 338; Clifford, 6; Loomie, *Jacobean Catholics* I, 157; Cecil, 365; Tillières, 6; Akrigg, *Letters*, 234
43 Amos, 221; Loomie, *Jacobean Catholics* I, 71
44 Loomie, *Toleration and Diplomacy*, 26; Loomie, *Jacobean Catholics* I, 81; Loomie, *Toleration and Diplomacy*, 36; Carter, 127; Loomie, *Toleration and Diplomacy*, 33–34
45 Winwood II, 175
46 Hurstfield, Joel, and Smith, A.G.R. (eds.), *Elizabethan People: State and Society* (1972), 163; HMC *Mss of the Duke of Rutland at Belvoir Castle* (1888) I, 107; Harington I, 170; Marotti, 215; Bald, 103; Zagorin, 44
47 Harington I, 143; Zagorin, 45; Halliwell II, 388; Wotton, *Life and Letters* I, 507; Bald, 161
48 McIlwain, 33
49 Hutchinson, 42; Halliwell II, 325–26
50 Clifford, 16; Harington I, 351–52; HMC Downshire II, 379
51 DNB Arthur Wilson; Wilson 186, 146; Osborne in Scott I, 280; Prestwich, 18; Aubrey, 297; McClure I, 487; Peyton in Scott II, 369; Lee, 68
52 McClure II, 217; ibid I, 626; ibid I, 334; ibid II, 203; DNB Knollys
53 Willson, 194; HMC Salisbury XIX, 22; Lee, 62; Nichols I, 444
54 Harington I, 349–51
55 Goodman I, 199; Stone, *Crisis*, 569; McClure I, 252–53; Winwood III, 181; McClure I, 424–25
56 Stone, *Family, Sex and Marriage*, 521; Schreiber, 10
57 Halliwell II, 348; Dent, 48–49; HMC Downshire III, 28; Strickland IV, 122; *Truth Brought to Light*, 279

58 Akrigg, *Letters*, 243; Dietz, *Receipts and Issues*, 158–60; Peck, *Court Patronage and Corruption*, 35; Akrigg, *Letters*, 292; HMC Downshire III, 28; Gardiner II, 108; McClure I, 538

59 Sanderson, 407

60 Amos, 217; ibid, 221

61 Wilson, 56; Lodge III, 192; Lindley, 64, citing HMC Salisbury XXI, 157

62 Wilson, 56; BL Add. 25348, fo. 4v; Jonson, 126, 128

63 McClure I, 302, 300; ST 807; Wilson, 56

64 D'Ewes in Halliwell I, 87; ST 805; Wilson, 162; Snow, 17

65 Sanderson, 385; ST 932; ST 822; HMC Downshire II, 182

66 HMC Downshire II, 353; See McClure I, 507, Snow 106

67 McClure I, 475

68 ST 787; BL Harleian 39, fo. 427v–428, see also Bodleian, Rawlinson C 64, fo. 3 (the version of Essex's statement given at ST 787 is clearly slightly inaccurate); ST 786–87; BL Harleian 39, fo. 427v

69 Sanderson, 385; Bodleian Rawlinson D 361 fo. 11v, 13v

70 *Desiderata Curiosa* ed. Francis Peck (1779), 466; Wilson, 162

71 ST 791

72 HMC Downshire II, 328

73 D'Ewes in Halliwell I, 90; BL Add. 25348, fo. 4v

74 Strong, 80; Devereux II, 222

75 D'Ewes in Halliwell I, 90–91; Wilson, 56

CHAPTER TWO

1 Ashton, 115; Willson, 33

2 Willson, 36; ibid 41–42

3 Bingham, *James VI of Scotland*, 55; McIlwain, 23

4 Ashton, 34; DNB Esme Stuart

5 Willson, 85, 99

6 Weldon in Scott II, 2

7 Goodman I, 39–40; Weldon in Scott II, 332–3; Schreiber, 140–41; McClure I, 238

8 Lodge III, 119; Winwood II, 43; McClure I, 238, 241; Stone, *Crisis*, 440

9 Osborne in Scott I, 218; Clarendon I, 74

10 Sanderson, 410

11 *Truth Brought to Light*, 268; Cuddy in Starkey, 191

12 BL Add. Mss. 25348, fo. 3v; Harington I, 395; Tillières, 2; Saslow, 194

13 Weldon in Scott I, 374–75; Wilson, 54; Harington I, 398

14 HMC Salisbury XIX, 456; Cal. Dom. 1603–10, 385; Cuddy in Starkey,

187; Ashton, 5; Spedding XIII, 27; Cuddy in Starkey, 187, 199

15   Cuddy, in Starkey, 193; Lodge III, 251; HMC Salisbury XIX, 305
16   HMC Salisbury XIX, 269 n; Gardiner II, 46
17   Weldon in Scott I, 371; Harington I, 392; Tillières, 4
18   McIlwain, 45; Harington I, 392; Osborne in Scott I, 275
19   Oglander, 196; R. Coke, 87; Goodman I, 18
20   Osborne in Scott I, 276; Harington I, 392; Osborne in Scott I, 275
21   Osborne in Scott I, 275; Bourcier, 92–93
22   Akrigg, *Letters*, 337; Lockyer, 22
23   Bourcier, 92–93
24   B. R. Smith, 43–44
25   E. Coke, *Third Part*, 58–59
26   B. R. Smith, 51; Burg, 6–7
27   McIlwain, 20; Akrigg, *Letters*, 315; d'Ewes, 92–93
28   Holles I, 141–42
29   Wilson, 158–59; McClure II, 243; Rowse, *Homosexuals*, 71
30   BL Harleian 646, fo. 59–59v (omitted from printed version of d'Ewes autobiography, edited by Halliwell)
31   Gardiner, *Parliamentary Debates in 1610*, 11
32   Akrigg, *Letters*, 240; Cuddy in Starkey, 190; HMC Portland IX, 113
33   Winwood II, 217
34   Wormald, 207
35   Goodman I, 215; Weldon in Scott I, 376
36   Holles I, 72–73; Amos, 220; BL Add. 25348, fo. 3v
37   Holles I, 72–73
38   Sanderson, 383; BL Add Mss 15476, fo. 92v; Winwood III, 479
39   BL Add. Mss. 15476, fo. 92v; SP 14/82/46 fo. 59; *Truth Brought to Light*, 293; Overbury, 223–51
40   See Overbury, 33–45
41   Patterson, 20; BL Add. Mss. 15476, fo. 93
42   Overbury, 53; ibid 58–59
43   Overbury 138; ibid 118
44   D'Ewes in Halliwell I, 76
45   Weldon in Scott I, 374; Goodman I, 215–16; ST 974; Aubrey, 417; BL Add. Mss. 25348, fo. 5v
46   HMC Downshire II, 103
47   HMC Downshire IV, 83
48   Overbury, xxxi–xxxii; Patterson, 16; Amos, 129; Huntington Library, Ellesmere Mss. 5979, fo. 6; HMC Buccleuch I, 131; ST 993
49   Halliwell II, 336; HMC Salisbury XXI, 340; HMC Downshire III, 83; ST 973; Wilbraham, 116; BL Harleian 7002, fo. 283v
50   ST 973; CSPD. 1603–10, 372; ibid. 567
51   BL Add. 34738 fo. 17
52   Ashton, 4–5; BL Add. Mss. 15476 fo. 92v; *Truth Brought to Light*, 293

53 HMC Salisbury XX, 150

54 HMC Salisbury XX, 150; Akrigg, *Letters*, 311

55 Peck, *Mental World*, 145; Notestein, 569n.

56 Gardiner, *Parliamentary Debates in 1610*, 144–45

57 HMC Salisbury XXI, 264–65; Goodman I, 41; Notestein, 433

58 Dietz, *Receipts and Issues*, 168; HMC Downshire III, 28

59 HMC Downshire III, 47; Cal. Ven. XII 142, 135; HMC Buccleuch I, 101–02

60 HMC Buccleuch I, 101–02; Huntington Lib. Ellesmere Mss. 5979, fo. 6

61 HMC Downshire II, 31, 44; Birch I, 108

62 BL Stowe 172, fo. 28

63 Wilson, 79; Cal. Ven. XII, 142; Tillières, 4; Huntington Lib. Ellesmere Mss. 5979, fo. 6

64 Wilson, 79; Goodman I, 216; HMC Downshire III, 83

65 Goodman II, 145; HMC Downshire III, 83

66 HMC Downshire II, 83; ibid, 138–39

67 Goodman II, 143–44; HMC de l'Isle and Dudley V, 65 (though dated incorrectly); HMC Downshire III, 180; McClure I, 314

68 Wotton II, 19; McClure I, 346; HMC Mar and Kellie, 40–41

69 It should be noted that the attribution of this letter to Suffolk is debatable. It has been suggested that the Thomas Howard who signed it was not Suffolk, but his son. Undoubtedly it is hard to believe that a man who occupied Suffolk's high office at court could have expressed himself in such intemperate terms. However, the fact that the author says that the letter will be delivered by his son rules out Thomas Howard the younger, as in 1611 he did not have a son old enough to perform this task. I have therefore accepted that the Earl of Suffolk wrote the letter.

70 Harington I, 395–97

71 Sanderson, 384; ST 974; Goodman I, 216; Bod. Ashmolean 824, fo. 28v

72 Patterson, 20; Spedding XII, 300

73 Winwood III, 479

74 Halliwell II, 336; Amos 49–50; ibid 221; Clay, 67; DNB Turner

75 ST 935; SP 14/82/1; SP 14/83/19; ST 931–32

76 ST 931; Amos, 221; HMC Downshire II, 185

77 Halliwell II, 336; Jonson, *The Divell is an Ass*, Act I Sc. I l. 112; Wilson, 59; McClure II, 294; ST 936

78 Rowse, *Forman*, 280

79 Thomas, 244–47; SP 14/86/49, printed Amos 397–40

80 Thomas, 244–47; 272

81 Thomas, 226

82 Rowse, *Forman*, 75–76

83 Rowse, *Forman*, 45–46
84 Thomas, 307; Rowse, *Forman*, 83, 22, 236, 226
85 Rowse, *Forman*, 140–41, 50
86 Rowse, *Forman*, 85
87 Rowse, *Forman*, 120, 127, 87–88, 129
88 Rowse, *Forman*, 120, 52; Stone, *Family, Sex and Marriage*, 548–50
89 ST 933; Stone, *Family, Sex and Marriage*, 550
90 ST 932; Rowse, *Forman*, 73
91 ST 933
92 Wilson, 57
93 ST 931–32
94 Bod. MS Willis 58, fo. 242–43 (differs slightly from version printed in ST 932)
95 Lilly, *History of his Life and Times*, 16
96 ST 933; Chester City Record Office, CR 63/2/19 fo. 10
97 ST 792; Halliwell II, 346; SP 14/82/51 fo. 66; SP 14/82/101 fo. 164
98 SP 14/82/34; ST 973
99 ST 912; Wilson, 70; SP 14/82/33, fo. 44; SP 14/82/1
100 SP 14/82/34, fo. 45
101 ST 989; McClure I, 377
102 Nichols II, 442
103 HMC Downshire III, 436; McClure I, 354–55; HMC Mar and Kellie, 40–41
104 Cuddy in Starkey, 209; BL Stowe 173 fo. 20; HMC Mar and Kellie, 46
105 SP 14/70/46, fo. 96
106 HMC Salisbury XXI, 327; Dietz, *Receipts and Issues*, 160; Akrigg, *Letters*, 327–28; McClure I, 351; Akrigg, *Letters*, 307; McClure I, 331, 367
107 Birch I, 191; Halliwell II, 401–02
108 Egerton Papers, 455–56
109 Egerton Papers, 455–56; Gardiner, *History of England* II, 212, quoting Sarmiento-Lerma, 26 Dec. 1615
110 SP 14/72/1, fo. 1, 3
111 CUL Dd 3 63, fo. 63
112 SP 14/82/84, fo. 110; Spedding XI, 393
113 SP 14/82/84, fo. 110
114 ST 981
115 BL Add. Mss. 15476, fo. 94v; BL Harleian 7002, fo. 281
116 Amos, 157; Winwood III, 479; Amos 128; McClure I, 443; Wotton II, 19
117 HMC Buccleuch I, 113; HMC Mar and Kellie, 51; McClure I, 359
118 Wotton II, 19; McClure I, 359
119 McClure I, 409; HMC Buccleuch I, 131

120 SP 99/11 fo. 178; Winwood III, 475
121 Sanderson, 393; Wilson, 73; BL Cotton Titus C V fo. 110
122 SP 14/64/23, fo. 28
123 Peck, *Northampton*, 33
124 HMC Mar and Kellie, 42
125 Birch I, 191; SP 14/70/46 fo. 96; HMC Buccleuch I, 131, 118
126 CUL Dd 3 63 fo. 9–9v; McClure I, 401, 404
127 BL Cotton Titus C VI fo. 82–83
128 SP 14/69/56, fo. 70
129 CUL Dd 3 63, fo. 44

CHAPTER THREE

1 CUL Dd 3 63, fo. 31; ST 819
2 ST 787; ibid 806; CUL Dd 3 63, fo. 53; ibid fo. 37; ST 810
3 ST 792; SP 14/72/134, fo. 240v; BL Harleian 39, fo. 416v
4 CUL Dd 3 63, fo. 44
5 ST 818
6 SP 14/72/133, fo. 228; SP 14/72/49, fo. 104; SP 14/71/60, fo. 118
7 SP 14/72/133, fo. 238
8 SP 14/72/49, fo. 104; SP 14/69/69, fo. 106
9 SP 14/72/53, fo. 109; SP 14/72/133, fo. 238
10 SP 14/72/49, fo. 104
11 SP 14/72/53, fo. 108
12 SP 14/74/3, fo. 6
13 Holles III, 510–11
14 Akrigg, *Letters*, 250; Wilson, 68; HMC Mar and Kellie, 52
15 ST 819, 814
16 Winwood III, 479
17 SP 14/82/47, fo. 60–60v
18 SP 14/83/9
19 CUL Ee IV 12, fo. 5; Bod. Ashmolean 824 fo. 30; ST 982
20 In SP 14/82/84, fo. 110 Wood said that he had a meeting with Frances on the day the King and Queen went with Princess Elizabeth to the town of Rochester; Nichols II, 611 gives this as 13 April.
21 SP 14/82/84, fo. 110–110v
22 Birch I, 189; ibid. 95
23 Wotton II, 20
24 McClure I, 443; Wotton II, 19–20; Winwood III, 447
25 Wotton II, 19–20; SP 14/72/146; BL Harleian 7002 fo. 286v
26 Winwood III, 447; Wotton II, 19–20
27 HMC Mar and Kellie, 51; Winwood III, 448
28 McClure I, 441

29 HMC Mar and Kellie, 52; HMC Downshire IV, 125
30 Amos, 129
31 Winwood III, 479; ST 982; SP 14/82/71, fo. 90; ST 993
32 ST 982–83
33 HMC Mar and Kellie, 51; SP 14/72/146, fo. 258v
34 Bowen, 398–99; McClure I, 448
35 BL Harleian 7002, fo. 285; ibid fo. 283
36 HMC Downshire IV, 125; HMC Mar and Kellie, 51; Wotton II, 29
37 ST 805
38 CUL Dd 3 63, fo. 31–31v
39 See Phillips; Stone, *Road to Divorce*, 302–3; Kelly 280
40 Stone, *Road to Divorce* 307; Lindley, 88
41 See Emil Richter and Emil Friedberg, *Corpus Juris Canonici*, (1881), II, 704–708
42 See Thomas Aquinas, *Opera Omnia* (Parma, 1858), VII, 984–86; ST 810
43 HMC Downshire III, 31; Welsby, 38; CSPD, 1611–18, 144; ibid. 138; ST 821
44 McClure I, 394; SP 14/70/46, fo. 96
45 ST 845–46
46 Crino, 259; HMC Mar and Kellie, 53; ST 861
47 ST 806; SP 14/72/134, fo. 240–40v; ST 786; ST 806
48 For date of Essex's evidence (given incorrectly in State Trials) See Bod. Rawlinson C 64, fo. 2v; HMC Mar and Kellie, 51
49 Birch I, 248; ibid 252–53; Winwood III, 475; CUL Dd 3 63, fo. 52v.
50 BL Cotton Titus C. VI, fo. 136–36v; CUL Dd 3 63, fo. 39v
51 CUL Dd 3 63, fo. 10
52 ST 807, 787
53 ST 816
54 Halliwell II, 357; Weldon in Scott I, 389
55 BL Harleian 39, fo. 420; Lambeth MSS 2877, fo. 159
56 ST 804; BL Harleian 39, fo. 420v; ST 807; BL Cotton Vitellius CXVI part i, fo. 98; BL Harleian 39, fo. 431v; Weldon in Scott I, 388–89; Glaister and Rentoul, 411–12
57 BL Harleian 39, fo. 422; ST 808
58 ST 810; ibid 807
59 BL Cotton Vitellius CXVI, fo. 98v, 124
60 ST 812; Kelly, 270–72
61 ST 849
62 ST 811–12
63 ST 846; ibid 854
64 ST 842; CUL Dd 3 63, fo. 53
65 ST 822
66 ST 814, 854

67 CUL Dd 3 63, fo. 53
68 ST 811; ibid 799
69 ST 816
70 ST 818
71 ST 802
72 ST 801, 857
73 ST 813; ibid 839
74 ST 818; ibid 823
75 ST 857
76 ST 813–14
77 Birch I, 269
78 Darmon, 33
79 Ashton, 40
80 ST 801–02
81 ST 817
82 McClure I, 461; Birch I, 269; West Yorkshire Archive Service, Leeds, Temple Newsam Correspondence 20/382
83 CUL Dd 3 63, fo. 23
84 CUL Dd 3 63, fos. 21, 45, 35
85 CUL Dd 3 63, fo. 37v
86 CUL Dd 3 63, fo. 52v
87 ST 822, 842
88 CUL Dd 3 63, fo. 52
89 ST 825
90 ST 821, 826–27
91 *Case of Insufficiency Discussed*, 31–32
92 Snow, 69
93 CUL Dd 3 63, fo. 50–51v
94 ST 829; McClure I, 475; HMC Downshire IV, 200; CUL Dd 3 63, fo. 50
95 James L. Sanderson, *Poems on an affair of state* in Review of English studies, New Series, Vol XVII (1966), pp 57–61; Lindley, 99, Chester City Record Office, CR/63/2/19, fo. 14; ST 829
96 ST 834, 829, 841; 832
97 ST 837–38
98 CUL Dd 3 63, fo. 52

CHAPTER FOUR

1 ST 983
2 Bod. Tanner 299, fo. 198
3 SP 14/83/49
4 ST 993, Spedding XII, 319; ST 993

5   ST 927; Wotton II, 24
6   McClure I, 452; SP 14/81/84, fo. 142–142v
7   BL Add. Mss. 15476, fo. 93v; Birch I, 379; ST 945; Bod. Tanner 299, fo. 199; ST 943; Amos, 217; HMC Downshire IV, 105; McClure I, 452
8   SP 14/81/84, fo. 142–142v
9   Bod. Ashmolean 824, fo. 30; SP 14/83/21, printed Amos, 219–21; Weldon in Scott I, 412; DNB Monson; Bod. Tanner 299, fo. 199v; SP 14/84/11, fo. 24; Bod. Ashmolean 824, fo. 30; ST 984
10 Bod. Tanner 199, fo. 198v; Bod. Smith 17, fo. 31
11 SP 14/82/30, fo. 40; SP 14/82/20, fo. 24; ST 916–17
12 SP 14/81/118, fo. 202; SP 14/82/3, fo. 3; SP 14/82/19, fo. 23
13 Bod. Willis 58, fo. 228v; HMC Buccleuch I, 160; Bod. Tanner 299, fo. 199; SP 14/82/3, fo. 3; Bod. Tanner 299, fo. 199
14 Bod. Tanner 299, fo. 199
15 Bod. Tanner 299, fo. 195; Bod. Willis 58, fo. 236v
16 Bod. Tanner 299, fo. 195
17 SP 14/83/49, printed Amos, 215–16
18 SP 14/82/3, fo. 3–3v
19 Halliwell II, 372; Amos, 50; HMC Salisbury XII, 25; SP 14/83/38, fo. 62; ST 933; SP 14/83/21 printed Amos, 219–21; SP 14/82/3, fo. 3v; SP 14/83/1, fo. 1; SP 14/83/38, fo. 62v; ST 933–34
20 CSPD 1611–18, 337; SP 14/84/19, fo. 33
21 SP 14/83/70, fo. 129; Christison, 266, Huntington Lib. Ellesmere 5979 fo. 1, ST 913 says Overbury given poison called rosealgar; SP 14/83/73 printed Amos, 388; SP 14/83/70, fo. 129; SP 14/83/38, fo. 62
22 SP 14/82/3, fo. 3v
23 SP 14/81/20, fo. 24; SP 14/81/84, fo. 142v
24 BL Harl. 7002, fo. 281
25 Ibid
26 SP 14/82/24, fo. 32; BL Harl. 7002, fo. 281v
27 BL Harl. 7002, fo. 283
28 BL Harl. 7002, fo. 282v
29 BL Harl. 7002, fo. 282v
30 BL Harl. 7002, fo. 285v; ibid fo. 283
31 BL Harl. 7002, fo. 283v, 284
32 BL Harl. 7002, fo. 284
33 BL Harl. 7002, fo. 285v
34 Winwood III, 475, Wotton II, 22; BL Harl 7002, fo. 281v, 286
35 BL Harl. 7002, fo. 286
36 CUL Dd 3 63, fo. 44
37 SP 14/82/3, fo. 3
38 BL Harl. 7002, fo. 284; Holles I, 96–97

39 BL Harl. 7002, fo. 284; SP 14/82/24, fo. 32; SP 14/82/34, fo. 45v

40 BL Harl. 7002, fo. 291

41 BL Harl. 7002, fo. 284v

42 SP 14/82/30, fo. 40; SP 14/82/20, fo. 24

43 SP 14/83/32, fo. 43; SP 14/82/19, fo. 23

44 HMC Buccleuch I, 160–61; ST 939, 922

45 SP 14/86/6, fo. 13

46 SP 14/86/6, fo. 13

47 Spedding XII, 266, 282

48 Bod. Willis 58, fo. 234

49 Bod. Tanner 299, fo. 199v

50 ST 939

51 Holles I, 96–97

52 The historian S.R. Gardiner subscribed to this view. See Gardiner, *History of England* II, 183, 183n

53 ST 961; Christison 369

54 ST 919; BL Harl. 7002, fo. 286v; SP 14/82/23, fo. 28; SP 14/81/84, fo. 142v

55 BL Harl. 7002, fo. 286v, 287; SP 14/82/5, fo. 6, SP 14/81/111, fo. 202; BL Harl. 7002, fo. 287, 288; Birch I, 269 (Birch dates this letter 29 August 1613 but this cannot be correct as it was clearly written during the week after 15 July 1613); confirmation that Overbury was ill at this time is supplied by HMC Buccleuch I, 139, where he is described in a letter of 20 July as 'shut up close and very sick'.

56 ST 918; SP 14/82/2, fo. 2; SP 14/82/46, fo. 59; BL Harl. 7002, fo. 281v

57 BL Harl. 7002, fo. 281; ibid fo. 288; ST 921–22; SP 14/82/22, fo. 27

58 McClure I, 439

59 McClure I, 578; McClure II, 79; Holles I, 57

60 Nichols II, 479

61 DNB Turquet de Mayerne; McClure I, 341; Mayerne, 13

62 DNB Turquet de Mayerne; McClure I, 388

63 Mayerne 7, 29

64 Mayerne 22, 23, 25

65 Mayerne 6, 27

66 Mayerne 36–38

67 ST 922; BL Harl. 7002, fo. 288v

68 SP 14/81/22, fo. 27

69 Anthony in *Collectanea Chymica*, 73–78

70 Anthony, *Apology or defence of ... aurum potabile*, 19, 1, 6, 112–13; 77, 79, 84, 93, 102

71 Ibid 26, 57

72 Clark, 202–203

73   Cotta, 94–95
74   SP 14/82/118, fo. 187
75   BL Harl. 7002, fo. 288v
76   SP 14/82/39, fo. 51
77   ST 988; SP 14/82/39, fo. 51
78   SP 14/82/46, fo. 59; BL Add. 15476, fo. 93; SP 14/72/145, fo. 257
79   SP 14/82/46, fo. 59; Amos, 132
80   SP 14/82/39, fo. 51; ST 988
81   For instances where an early date is given for the administration of powdered arsenic see: Amos, 144; ST 917; HMC Downshire V, 518; Coke, *Institutes* III, 49–50; for a later date see: ST 913; ST 924; BL Sloane 1002, fo. 9; BL Add. 35832, fo. 5v; Bod. Ashmolean 824, fo. 28
82   SP 14/82/24, fo. 32–32v
83   SP 14/82/26, fo. 35
84   Rochester admitted this, ST 994
85   SP 14/82/34, fo. 45v
86   SP 14/82/24, fo. 32v
87   SP 14/83/38, fo. 62–62v
88   ST 975
89   Amos, 131
90   ST 986 (though ST 996 says Rochester admitted meeting de Loubell twice)
91   CUL Dd 3 63, fo. 44; ibid fo. 49
92   ST 984; Goodman I, 220
93   ST 985; BL Harl. 7002, fo. 288v
94   BL Harl. 7002, fo. 288v
95   CUL Dd 3 63, fo. 21, 35
96   CUL Dd 3 63, fo. 48v
97   Ibid
98   BL Harl. 7002, fo. 289v
99   CUL Dd 3 63, fo. 48v
100 CUL Dd 3 63, fo. 48–49
101 CUL Dd 3 63, fo. 48
102 BL Harl. 7002, fo. 290
103 CUL Dd 3 63, fo. 49; BL Harl. 7002, fo. 290v
104 BL Harl. 7002, fo. 291v
105 BL Harl. 7002, fo. 291
106 SP 14/81/23, fo. 29
107 CUL Dd 3 63, fo. 49–49v
108 ST 938–39
109 BL Harl. 7002, fo. 290v
110 Bod. Willis 58, fo. 231v
111 Bod. Willis 58, fo. 231v–232; BL Cotton Titus B VII, fo. 486

112   SP 14/82/39, fo. 51
113   Winwood III, 478; ST 985
114   SP 14/72/145, fo. 257
115   Winwood III, 478–79
116   SP 14/82/26, fo. 35; BL Harl. 7002, fo. 291
117   SP 14/74/54, fo. 110v
118   CUL Dd 3 63, fo. 53v
119   Mayerne, 6
120   HMC Buccleuch I, 160
121   Bod. Tanner 299, fo. 195
122   SP 14/82/71, fo. 88v; Sanderson, 414; Wilson, 80; Weldon in Scott I, 404–405, 385–86
123   SP 14/83/12, printed Amos, 168–70
124   SP 14/82/3, fo. 3v; SP 14/82/34, fo. 45v; Holles I, 96
125   SP 14/82/3, fo. 4
126   CUL Dd 3 63, fo. 53v
127   SP 14/82/2, fo. 2
128   Winwood III, 481
129   Winwood III, 482
130   CUL Dd 3 63, fo. 53v; Winwood III, 482
131   Spedding XII, 300; BL Add. 35832, fo. 6; Blyth, 7
132   Glaister and Rentoul, 508; Simpson, 262–63; Glaister and Rentoul 651; Blyth, 500
133   CUL Dd 3 63, fo. 53v
134   SP 14/84/10, fo. 19; HMC Downshire IV, 205; Bod. Tanner 299, fo. 201; BL Add. 39288, fo. 14
135   ST 985; Winwood III, 481
136   McClure I, 478

CHAPTER FIVE

1   HMC Downshire IV, 260; McClure I, 481–82; ibid 484, 487
2   McClure I, 484
3   McClure I, 487; ST 839–42
4   BL Cotton Titus C VI, fo. 95v
5   CUL Dd 63, fo. 39–39v
6   Wilson, 72; McClure I, 495
7   Crino, 259; McClure I, 496–98
8   Donne, 113
9   McClure I, 496; Orell, 304
10   Lindley, 137–38; Thomas Campion, *Works*, ed W.R. Davis (1969), 268–277
11   Orell, 305

12 Donne, 114
13 Crino, 259
14 Nichols II, 717, 721; McClure I, 498
15 McClure I, 499
16 McClure I, 492–93
17 Lindley, 91, 124, 132–33
18 Chapman, 185–92
19 Lindley, 135; Chapman, 185–92
20 BL Cotton Titus F IV, fo. 341
21 McClure I, 510; Wilson, 71; McClure I, 516; ibid 534–35
22 BL Cotton Titus C VI, fo. 88; ibid fo. 101v; ibid fo. 95
23 BL Add. 19402, fo. 116
24 McClure I, 480; ibid 608, 492–93; HMC Buccleuch I, 103–04
25 HMC Buccleuch I, 119
26 HMC Downshire IV, 385
27 Goodman I, 257; d'Ewes in Halliwell I, 70
28 HMC Downshire IV, 362
29 BL Cotton Titus C VI, fo. 107
30 BL Cotton Titus F IV, fo. 341
31 SP 99/16, fo. 108
32 See Wotton II, 38–39, Peck, *Northampton*, 209, Moir, 140, Roberts and Duncan, 491, Peck, *Northampton*, 210n., Seddon, 65; Loomie, *Jacobean Catholics* II, 38; McClure I, 541, Birch I, 323
33 McClure I, 541; Loomie, *Jacobean Catholics* II, 38–39
34 CUL Dd 3 63, fo. 16
35 Wotton II, 38–39; Birch I, 335–36
36 Wilbraham, 115; Wotton II, 41; Akrigg, *Letters*, 339–40
37 HMC Downshire IV, 252
38 Birch I, 336, 339; Gardiner, *Certain Letters of Gondomar*, 152; Loomie, *Jacobean Catholics* II, 48; Rushworth I, 456–57
39 Holles I, 74–75
40 Birch I, 337
41 HMC Downshire IV, 385; Holles I, 77; HMC Downshire IV, 476; Wotton II, 46; Lee, 182
42 BL Cotton Titus C VI, fo. 88
43 Spedding XIII, 16, 28–29
44 HMC Downshire IV, 176, 193, 195
45 Bald, 272–73, 293–94
46 McClure I, 592
47 HMC Downshire IV, 356
48 Holles I, 120
49 McClure I, 480; ibid 489
50 BL Cotton Titus C VI, fo. 122
51 Prestwich, 197

52 Holles I, 72–73
53 Lockyer, 10; Goodman I, 225; d'Ewes in Halliwell I, 166–67; Prestwich, 171–72
54 HMC Mar and Kellie, 26
55 Sanderson, 456; d'Ewes in Halliwell I, 86
56 McClure I, 559; Clarendon I, 12; McClure I, 561
57 HMC Mar & Kellie, 58
58 Gardiner, *History of England* II, 320
59 Akrigg, *Letters*, 335–40
60 Akrigg, *Letters*, 341
61 HMC Mar and Kellie, 59; Goodman I, 224; Rushworth I, 256–57
62 Rushworth I, 256–57; for two other, rather less colourful accounts of Villiers's knighthood and promotion see HMC Downshire V, 202 and 206; McClure I, 602
63 Gardiner, *Narrative of Spanish Marriage Treaty*, 286–87
64 Gardiner, *Certain Letters of Gondomar*, 157–58
65 Ibid 164
66 Loomie, *Jacobean Catholics* II, 51
67 HMC Downshire V, 284
68 Holles I, 66
69 McClure I, 599
70 Holles I, 70
71 HMC Buccleuch I, 161; Amos, 148
72 BL Add. 35832, fo. 6; SP 14/82/3, fo. 3v, 4v
73 Bod. Willis 58, fo. 229; HMC Buccleuch I, 161
74 Bod. Tanner 299, fo. 200
75 Bod. Willis 58, fo. 236
76 Gardiner, *Certain Letters of Gondomar*, 175; Bod. Smith 17, fo. 32
77 A., 27–28; Bod. Smith 17, fo. 32
78 Gardiner, *Certain Letters of Gondomar*, 167–68
79 Goodman I, 215; Bod. Smith 17, fo. 32; HMC Downshire V, 387
80 Holles I, 78
81 Lockyer, 22
82 Weldon in Scott I, 407
83 Sanderson, 414; Wilson, 80; Weldon in Scott I, 403–405
84 See HMC Downshire V, 319, 349, 359
85 Bod. Tanner 299, fo. 194; d'Ewes in Halliwell I, 69
86 Carew, 16; HMC Downshire V, 319; HMC Buccleuch I, 160–61; SP 14/81/86
87 HMC Buccleuch I, 160–61

CHAPTER SIX

1 SP 14/81/88, fo. 149v; Weldon in Scott I, 408; d'Ewes in Halliwell I, 70; Akrigg, *Letters*, 346
2 Bod. Smith 17, fo. 30; SP 14/81/88, fo. 149–149v
3 Spedding XII, 310; Bod. Willis 58, fo. 225
4 SP 14/81/111, printed Amos, 177
5 SP 14/81/111, printed Amos, 178
6 SP 14/81/118, fo. 202
7 HMC Salisbury XXII, 29; SP 14/83/70, fo. 129v; Amos, 389
8 ST 991; SP 14/83/70, fo. 129v; Franklin's confession of 20 November 1615 is missing
9 Wilbraham, 117; Bowen, 266, 420; *True Tragi-Comedie* (BL Add. 25348) fo. 17; Aubrey, 26; Bowen, 7; Spedding XII, 302
10 Bowen, 52, 329
11 Bowen, 167, 182; Holles I, 88
12 Campbell I, 276
13 Gardiner, *Certain Letters of Gondomar*, 170
14 Gardiner, *Certain Letters of Gondomar*, 170; Bowen, 330; Holles I, 93–94
15 ST 1031; ST 930; Bod. Willis 58, fo. 240v
16 SP 14/81/90, fo. 151; Crino, 266; SP 14/83/74, printed Amos, 388–90
17 Bod. Tanner 299, fo. 200v; SP 14/82/96, printed Amos, 375
18 SP 14/83/66
19 SP 14/82/3, fos. 3–4v
20 SP 14/82/34, fo. 45–45v; ST 1031; Bod. Willis 58, fo. 224
21 SP 14/82/1, fo. 1; SP 14/82/21, fo. 26
22 SP 14/82/36, fo. 48
23 SP 14/82/45, printed Amos 189–90; HMC Buccleuch I, 162; Hervey, 96
24 SP 14/82/30, fo. 40; SP 14/82/20, fo. 24; ST 927
25 SP 14/81/88, fo. 148
26 SP 14/82/26, fo. 35; SP 14/82/23, fo. 28; SP 14/82/39, fo. 51
27 Hervey, 96; Molyneux, 75
28 Akrigg, *Letters*, 343–45
29 Weldon in Scott I, 411–12
30 SP 14/82/51, fo. 66
31 SP 14/82/55, fo. 70
32 Amos, 148
33 CUL Ee 4 12, fo. 7; ST 991; Amos, 155
34 ST 991; Amos, 149; CSPD, 1611–18, 317
35 ST 995; HMC Downshire V, 509; Amos, 155; CUL Ee 4 12 fo. 8v
36 SP 14/82/62; SP 14/82/58; SP 14/82/60; SP 14/82/62

37 BL Add. 35832, fo. 6v; ST 917
38 HMC Downshire V, 518
39 Bowen, 123; ibid 468n; Stephen I, 226, 228
40 ST 1031
41 Coke, *Institutes* III, 48; ST 1031; J.E. Neale, *The Elizabethan House of Commons* (1949), 410
42 ST 912–13; BL Add. 35832, fo. 4v
43 Chester City Record Office CR 63/2/19; ST 914
44 CSPD 1603–10, 535
45 ST 913; BL Add. 35832, fo. 4v; Amos, 372; Lambeth Palace 663, fo. 180
46 BL Add. 35832, fo. 4v
47 Lambeth Palace 663, fo. 180v; ST 929; SP 14/82/71, printed Amos, 372; ST 929
48 BL Add. 35832, fo. 5; ST 915
49 BL Add. 35832, fo. 5v; ST 915–18
50 Crino, 264–65
51 Lambeth Palace 663, fo. 181; SP 14/82/72, printed Amos, 372
52 SP 14/82/91, fo. 123; SP 14/82/74, printed Amos, 378; Akrigg, *Letters*, 346; SP 14/82/89, fo. 119
53 SP 14/82/78, fo. 101; SP 14/82/96, printed Amos, 375–76; ST 927
54 ST 924
55 ST 928
56 Holles I, 96; ST 1028
57 ST 1026; SP 14/83/40, fo. 64
58 Holles I, 103; ST 1028
59 ST 1032, 1034
60 Crino, 271; ibid 266; HMC Buccleuch I, 162
61 SP 14/82/58, printed Amos, 41; Camden, 644; Cal. Ven. XIV, 65; Crino, 268
62 SP 14/82/115, fos. 183–4
63 Ibid; SP 14/82/117, fo. 186
64 ST 930–31; Chester City Record Office CR 63/2/19, fo. 9v
65 ST 931–32; Egerton Papers 471; Birch I, 380
66 ST 933; Weldon in Scott I, 418
67 ST 933
68 D'Ewes in Halliwell I, 87; Chester City Record Office CR 63/2/19, fo. 10
69 ST 934
70 ST 933–34; HMC Salisbury XXII, 23
71 ST 936
72 SP 14/83/17, fo. 30
73 SP 14/83/21, printed (not entirely accurately) Amos, 219–21
74 Bod. Willis 58, fo. 225v; Camden, 645

75   BL Add. 15476, fo. 93; Weldon in Scott I, 385–86; d'Ewes in Halliwell I, 86

76   Amos, 223; ST 936; BL Add. 15476, fo. 93v

77   Amos, 220–21; SP 14/83/32, fo. 53; Akrigg, *Jacobean Pageant*, 197

78   Amos, 224; Birch I, 377

79   ST 979; Amos, 132–33

80   Molyneux, 76–77

81   Bod. Willis 59, fo. 224–25; Bod. Tanner 299, fo. 196

82   ST 935; Bod. Tanner 299, fo. 197; Bod Willis 58, fo. 229

83   Bod. Tanner 299, fo. 196; Bod. Willis 58, fo. 227v

84   ST 936, original letter in CUL Dd 3 63, fo. 35v; Bod. Willis 58, fo. 231, original letter CUL Dd 3 63, fo. 49–49v; ST 937, original letter CUL Dd 3 63, fo. 53v

85   Bod. Willis 58, fo. 231v; Bod Tanner 299, fo. 196v

86   ST 936, original in CUL Dd 3 63, fo. 35; Bod. Willis 58, fo. 230

87   Bod. Willis 58, fo. 230; Birch I, 381

88   Bod. Tanner 299, fo. 198v

89   ST 938

90   ST 938; Bod. Willis 58, fo. 235v

91   ST 939

92   ST 939; Bod. Tanner 299, fo. 199

93   ST 940; Bod. Tanner 299, fo. 199v

94   ST 940

95   Bod. Willis 58, fo. 227; Birch I, 377; BL Add. 28640, fo. 153v; Bod. Tanner 299, fo. 200v

96   Bod. Willis 58, fo. 237

97   ST 941

98   Bod. Willis 58, fo. 239; SP 14/83/38, fo. 62

99   Birch I, 377; SP 14/83/49, printed Amos, 213–24; ST 942

100   SP 14/83/73, printed Amos, 214

101   SP 14/83/48, fo. 73

102   Amos, 215–16

103   Birch I, 378–79

104   ST 945; Birch I, 380

105   ST 943–44

106   ST 947

107   SP 14/84/4, fo. 19; Amos, 388

108   BL Stowe 396, fo. 153v; HMC Salisbury XXII, 27–28

109   HMC Salisbury XXII, 27; SP 14/83/73, printed Amos, 389

110   SP 14/83/70, fo. 129–129v – text of original examinations missing

111   SP 14/83/73, printed Amos, 388

112   BL Stowe 396, fo. 155v; ST 948; SP 14/83/38, fo. 62v; HMC Salisbury XXII, 28; BL Stowe 396, fo. 154v; SP 14/83/70, fo. 129v

113   For Franklin confession to Whiting see Spedding XII, 338–39; also ibid 289

114 SP 14/83/73, printed Amos, 391–92
115 Amos, 391
116 Egerton Papers, 476; Spedding XII, 339
117 Amos, 225–27
118 Egerton Papers, 474–76
119 SP 14/84/9, fo. 16; SP 14/86/36, fo. 71
120 SP 14/83/85, printed Amos, 391
121 SP 14/84/11, fo. 24
122 SP 14/83/85, printed Amos, 391
123 Birch I, 384; ST 950
124 ST 950; HMC Downshire V, 383–84
125 ST 949; BL Sloane 1002, fo. 71v; HMC Downshire V, 382; Crino, 270; Birch I, 382

CHAPTER SEVEN

1 Crino, 269
2 SP 14/83/60, fo. 91
3 SP 14/83/53, fo. 81; Chester City Record Office CR 63/2/19, fo. 5; BL Add. 28640, fo. 153v
4 SP 14/82/115, fo. 183; Crino, 266; HMC de l'Isle and Dudley V, 341; HMC Downshire V, 371; Crino, 267
5 Amos, 144; ibid, 137; Huntington Library Ellesmere 5979, fo. 11
6 SP 14/83/55, fos. 83, 85; SP 14/83/65, fo. 97
7 Amos, 144–45; ST 994
8 Crino, 272
9 Birch I, 381–82; Holles I, 94; Amos, 220; SP 14/83/43, fo. 68; SP 14/83/63 fo. 95; HMC Downshire V, 383
10 HMC Downshire V, 382; ibid, 388
11 Holles I, 94; HMC Downshire V, 395; HMC de l'Isle and Dudley V, 340, 344
12 Lindley, 163; Crino, 275; HMC Downshire V, 404
13 Camden, 645; Molyneux, 107–110
14 Gardiner, *Certain Letters of Gondomar*, 177–79
15 SP 14/86/7, fo. 14; Amos, 143; SP 14/86/6, fo. 13
16 SP 94/21, fos. 203–05
17 Gardiner, *History of England* II, 216–17
18 Bowen, 387; SP 14/86/51, fo. 93
19 HMC Downshire V, 387, 411
20 Spedding XII, 232; Campbell I, 260
21 Bowen, 294
22 Spedding XII, 231–32
23 SP 14/86/38, fo. 73

24 Amos, 398–99
25 ST 982–83; Amos, 399–400; Huntington Lib. Ellesmere 5979, fo. 10
26 Huntington Lib. Ellesmere 5979, fo. 10
27 SP 14/86/49, printed Amos, 411–12
28 Ibid
29 BL Harleian 700 fo. 285v; Holles I, 116, Crino, 289
30 Holles I, 116–18
31 Crino, 279–80
32 Holles I, 116; ibid I, 120, 122–23; HMC Downshire V, 459; Holles I, 124
33 Spedding XII, 262–63
34 Spedding XII, 265
35 HMC Buccleuch I, 163; Spedding XII, 270
36 Spedding XII, 270; Carter, 127, 282n
37 McClure I, 619
38 Spedding XII, 276–79
39 Spedding XII, 279
40 Spedding XII, 285, 282; ibid XII, 270; ibid XII, 282
41 Amos, 144–45; ibid, 158
42 Spedding XII, 291
43 Akrigg, *Letters*, 350–51
44 Spedding XII, 291; SP 14/87/24, fo. 34
45 Akrigg, *Letters*, 351–52
46 Gardiner, *Certain Letters of Gondomar*, 182
47 Ibid
48 CUL Dd 3 63, fo. 23v–24
49 Gardiner, *Certain Letters of Gondomar*, 183
50 Gardiner, *Certain Letters of Gondomar*, 183–84
51 Akrigg, *Letters*, 352–3
52 Spedding XII, 295–96
53 Gardiner, *Certain Letters of Gondomar*, 184
54 Spedding XII, 296
55 HMC Downshire V, 517
56 Spedding XII, 297
57 Spedding XII, 298–99
58 SP 14/87/29, fo. 68; HMC Downshire V, 511; ST 957; HMC Downshire V, 511
59 Bod. Smith 17, fo. 30; HMC Downshire V, 514; SP 14/87/34, fo. 75; HMC Downshire V, 514; Bod. Ashmolean 824, fo. 27; HMC Downshire V, 511; ibid 517
60 SP 14/87/27, fo. 56; SP 14/87/29, fo. 68; HMC Downshire V, 514; SP 14/87/34, fo. 75
61 Weldon in Scott I, 422–23
62 Akrigg, *Letters*, 353–54; HMC Downshire V, 514

63 SP 14/87/27, fo. 56–56v
64 Spedding XII, 288–89
65 Spedding XII, 287
66 PRO 31/3/51, fo. 42; ST 967
67 ST 967; Bod. Ashmolean 824, fo. 27
68 ST 968
69 Ibid; Bod. Ashmolean 824, fo. 28
70 Amos, 123; CUL Ee 4 12, fo. 3v
71 CUL Ee 4 12, fo. 3v; ST 969
72 Spedding XII, 307; Amos, 124–25
73 Spedding XII, 308–10; Amos, 126
74 Spedding XII, 311
75 Spedding XII, 312; CUL Ee 4 12, fo. 4v
76 Huntington Library Ellesmere 5979, fo. 2; Spedding XII, 314
77 Bod. Willis 58, fo. 212; HMC Salisbury XXII, 22; Spedding XII, 313–14
78 Spedding XII, 314
79 Amos, 129; CUL Ee 4 12, fo. 5
80 Spedding XII, 316
81 Spedding XII, 317
82 ST 978–79; Bod. Smith 17, fo. 31
83 ST 979
84 ST 979
85 ST 976
86 HMC Downshire V, 519; Egerton Papers, 471; ST 981
87 ST 981; Huntington Library Ellesmere 5979, fo. 7
88 ST 982
89 Huntington Library Ellesmere 5979, fo. 11; ST 983
90 Amos, 137; ST 977
91 ST 983
92 CUL Ee 4 12, fo. 8; for example see Bod. Ashmolean 824, fo. 30
93 ST 985; SP 14/82/30, fo. 40
94 Amos, 145; HMC Downshire V, 509
95 ST 986
96 ST 985–86; Huntington Library Ellesmere 5979, fo. 9; ST 987; ST 978
97 ST 987; HMC Downshire V, 509
98 Spedding XII, 317
99 Amos, 141–42
100 SP 14/83/39, fo. 62v; ST 988
101 ST 989; Amos, 144–45
102 ST 991
103 Amos, 148–49
104 Amos, 151; ST 992

105   ST 992; Amos, 151
106   Amos, 151
107   ST 993; CUL Ee 4 12, fo. 7v
108   Amos, 152; ST 993
109   ST 993
110   ST 994
111   Ibid
112   CUL Ee 4 12, fo. 8; Amos, 154
113   CUL Ee 4 12, fo. 8; HMC Downshire V, 510; CUL Ee 4 12, fo. 8
114   Amos, 154; ST 995
115   CUL Ee 4 12, fo. 8; ST 995–6
116   ST 996
117   CUL Ee 4 12, fo. 8; Bod. Smith 17, fo. 31; HMC Downshire V, 509
118   Amos, 153
119   CUL Ee 4 12, fo. 8v; Bod. Smith 17, fo. 31
120   ST 995; HMC Downshire V, 510; Bod. Smith 17, fo. 31
121   ST 995; Amos, 155
122   HMC Downshire V, 510; CUL Ee 4 12, fo. 7v; ST 996
123   Bod. Smith 17, fo. 32; Holles I, 128; Gardiner, *Certain Letters of Gondomar*, 185; HMC Downshire V, 515; SP 14/87/29, fo. 68v
124   ST 996; Gardiner, *Certain Letters of Gondomar*, 185
125   HMC Downshire V, 510; Crino, 283
126   HMC Downshire V, 510; ST 997
127   HMC Downshire V, 511; ST 997
128   ST 997
129   Gardiner, *Certain Letters of Gondomar*, 185

CHAPTER EIGHT

1   SP 14/87/40, fo. 86
2   Weldon in Scott I, 424; Gardiner, *Certain Letters of Gondomar*, 181
3   Holles I, 128; SP 14/87/40, fo. 86; Gardiner, *Certain Letters of Gondomar*, 185–86
4   SP 14/87/29, fo. 68; Gardiner, *Certain Letters of Gondomar*, 185; Crino, 284–85
5   Holles I, 128; SP 14/87/57, fo. 117
6   SP 14/87/57, fo. 117; McClure II, 6; SP 14/87/24, fo. 34; Holles I, 131–32
7   ST 1007–1010
8   Spedding XII, 276–77
9   SP 14/87/34, fo. 75v; Molyneux, 76
10   D'Ewes in Halliwell I, 87; James L. Sanderson, 60
11   McClure II, 17

12   SP 16/172/2, fo. 3v
13   The original inventory is in the Folger Shakespeare Library, Washington. The reference is L.b 638 and copies are obtainable. Extracts in Kempe, 408–09; see also Braunmuller in Peck, *Mental World*, 231
14   McClure I, 480; *Truth Brought to Light*, 262
15   McClure II, 6
16   ST 1004
17   ST 998–1004, reprinted from Cabala I, 1
18   *Truth Brought to Light*, 360–61; SP 16/310/89, fo. 127
19   Holles III, 487; SP 16/310/89, fo. 127
20   SP 16/310/89, fo. 127
21   Holles I, 128; Carew, 44
22   SP 14/87/57, fo. 117; d'Ewes in Halliwell I, 80
23   McClure II, 14; SP 14/87/57, fo. 117
24   Wilson, 89
25   SP 14/88/30, fo. 57; Kempe, 399–400; Carew, 44, 60; Birch I, 440; McClure II, 43
26   Clifford, 47, 96; McClure II, 19
27   *Truth Brought to Light*, 362–63; SP 16/310/89, fo. 127
28   *Truth Brought to Light*, 360–61; Nichols III, 475
29   HMC Downshire VI, 31; Birch I, 431; Gardiner, *History of England* III, 98; Lockyer, 33
30   See McClure II, 151
31   SP 14/96/24, fo. 46; McClure II, 144; it is Weldon in Scott I, 376 who names Lady Suffolk as beautifying young men for the King's delectation.
32   McClure II, 156; Lockyer, 122
33   McClure II, 158, 79, 77, 85
34   McClure II, 170–71
35   Braunmuller in Peck, *Mental World*, 238; Braunmuller cites two inventories of Somerset's possessions, one dated 1619 and the other 1637. He viewed these at the Bedford Estate office in London but they have since been transferred to Woburn Abbey and cannot at present be located; Holles II, 288–89
36   SP 14/172/2, fo. 3v; Holles II, 292
37   Braunmuller in Peck, *Mental World*, 244, 247; Akrigg, *Jacobean Pageant*, 247
38   Holles III, 390
39   Holles II, 302; *Truth Brought to Light*, 360–61
40   Holles II, 364–5; ibid III, 387
41   HMC Cowper II, 11
42   Holles III, 415
43   Holles III, 510–11
44   Molyneux, 77
45   Wilson, 83; BL Add. 25348, fo. 5

46 D'Ewes in Halliwell I, 90
47 Wilson, 83
48 BL Add. 46189, fo. 29; Snow, 191
49 Knowler I, 359; ibid II, 58
50 Scott Thomson, 30; CSPD Charles I, VIII, 45, 244; Knowler I, 446
51 *Truth Brought to Light*, 362–63; ibid 361
52 Scott Thomson, 54, 71
53 Weldon in Scott I, 403, 385
54 Bod. Tanner 299, fo. 199v
55 ST 1003
56 SP 14/86/6, fo. 13; Birch I, 379; ibid I, 381
57 SP 14/82/37, fo. 49; Holles I, 128
58 ST 1003; BL Add. 15476, fo. 94v
59 SP 14/90/62, fo. 111–111v
60 SP 14/90/62, fo. 111–12
61 CUL Ee 4 12, fo. 4v; BL Add. 15476, fo. 93v; Holles I, 91; d'Ewes in Halliwell I, 72
62 Molyneux, 76
63 CUL Ee 4 12, fo. 9; ST 1002; Holles II, 292
64 McClure II, 6; SP 14/87/34, fo. 75v
65 BL Add. 25348, fo. 4; Weldon in Scott I, 426
66 Wilson, 83; Weldon in Scott I, 391, 426
67 Weldon in Scott I, 447; Lockyer, 27; Bowen, 433
68 D'Ewes in Halliwell I, 81
69 Gardiner, *Certain Letters of Gondomar*, 182
70 SP 14/87/27, fo. 56v; BL Add. 35832, fo. 5
71 Roger Coke, 67; Halliwell II, 333; Weldon in Scott I, 388–89
72 D'Ewes in Halliwell I, 74
73 Lindley, 69; SP 14/83/21, printed Amos, 220; HMC Downshire V, 510; CUL Ee 4 12, fo. 8
74 D'Ewes in Halliwell I, 88
75 Crino, 283
76 McClure II, 268; Sanderson, 419
77 Bowen, 316; HMC de l'Isle and Dudley V, 331; Spedding XIII, 124
78 BL Add. 15476, fo. 92v
79 Chester City Record Office, CR 62 2 19, fo. 11–11v
80 Spedding XII, 313
81 From 1616 edition of *The Wife*
82 Weldon in Scott I, 427

BIBLIOGRAPHY

Note: unless otherwise stated, London is the place of publication.

A., D.B., *The Court of the Most Illustrious and Magnificent James I*, 1619

Akrigg, G.P.V., *Jacobean Pageant*, 1962

—— (ed.), *Letters of King James VI and I*, University of California Press, 1984

Amos, Andrew, *The Great Oyer of Poisoning*, 1846

Anthony, Francis, *Aurum Potabile, or the Receipt of Dr F. Antonie showing his way and method, how he made that most excellent medicine for the body of man* in Collectanea Chymica, 1684

—— *The Apology or Defence of a Verity ... Concerning a Medicine called Aurum Potabile*, 1616

Ashley, Maurice, *The Stuarts in Love*, 1963

Ashton, Robert (ed.), *James I, by his contemporaries*, 1969

Aubrey, John, *Brief Lives*, ed. Oliver Lawson Dick, 1978

Aulicus Coquinariae in *Secret History of the Court of James I*, ed. W. Scott, 1811

Ayliffe, John, *Pa ·rgon Juris Canonici Anglicani or A Commentary by way of Supplement to the Canons and Contributions of the Church of England*, 1726

Baines, Barbara J., *Three Pamphlets on the Jacobean Anti-Feminist Controversy*, New York, 1978

Bald, R.C., *John Donne, A life*, Oxford, 1970

Bingham, Caroline, *James VI of Scotland*, 1979

—— *James I of England*, 1981

Birch, Thomas, *The Court and Times of James I*, 1848

Blyth, Meredith Wynter, *Poisons: their Effects and Detection*, 1920

Bourcier, Elisabeth (ed.), *The Diary of Sir Simonds d'Ewes, 1622–24*, Paris, 1974

Bowen, Catherine Drinker, *The Lion and the Throne. Life and Times of Sir Edward Coke*, 1957

Bray, Alan, *Homosexuality in Renaissance England*, 1982

Bruce, John (ed.), *Correspondence of King James VI of Scotland with Sir Robert Cecil and Others in England During the Reign of Queen Elizabeth*, Camden Society, LXXVIII, 1861

Burg, B.R., *Sodomy and the Perception of Evil: English Sea Rovers in the Seventeenth Century Caribbean*, New York, 1983

Calendar of State Papers, Domestic Series, James I, ed. M.A.E. Green, 1857–1859

Calendar of State Papers and Manuscripts Relating to English Affairs Existing in the Archives and Collections of Venice, ed. Rawdon Brown et al., 1864–98

Camden, William, 'Annals of King James I' in *A Complete History of England*, ed. W. Kennett, Vol. II, 1706

Campbell, John, *Lives of the Chief Justices of England*, 1849

Carew, George, Lord, *Letters from George Lord Carew to Sir Thomas Roe, 1615–17*, ed. John Maclean, Camden Society, 1860

Carleton Williams, Ethel, *Anne of Denmark*, 1970

Carter, Charles Howard, *The Secret Diplomacy of the Habsburgs*, New York, 1964

The Case of Insufficiency Discussed, Touching the Divorce Between the Lady Frances Howard and Robert Earl of Essex, 1711

Castiglioni, Arturo, *A History of Medicine*, 1947

Cecil, Algernon, *A life of Robert Cecil First Earl of Salisbury*, 1915

Chapman, George, *Works*, ed. A. Swinburne, 1875

Christison, Robert, *A Treatise on Poison*, Edinburgh, 1835

Clarendon, Edward, Earl of, *History of the Rebellion and Civil Wars in England*, ed. W.D. Macray, Oxford, 1888

Clark, George, *A History of the Royal College of Physicians of London*, Oxford, 1964

Clay, John (ed.), *Visitation of Cambridge in 1575 and 1619*, Publications of the Harleian Society, XLI, 1897

Clifford, Anne, *The Diary of Lady Anne Clifford*, ed. Vita Sackville-West, 1923

Coke, Edward, *Third Part of the Institutes of the Law of England*, 1644

Coke, Roger, *A Detection of the Court and State of England*, 1719

Complete Peerage by G.E. Cockayne, ed. H.A. Doubleday and Lord Howard de Walden, revised by Vicary Gibbs, 1929

Cornwallis, Jane, *Private Correspondence*, 1842

Cotta, John, *Cotta Contra Antonium*, 1623

Craigie, James, and Law, Alexander (eds.), *Minor Prose Works of King James VI and I*, Edinburgh, 1982

Crino, Anna Maria, 'Il Processo a Lord e Lady Somerset per l'assassinio di Sir

Thomas Overbury nelle relazioni de Francesco Quaratesi e di Pompilio Gaetani' in *English Miscellany*, 1951

Cuddy, Neil, 'The Revival of the Entourage: the Bedchamber of James I 1603–1625' in David Starkey (ed.), *The English Court from the Wars of the Roses to the Civil War*, 1987

—— 'Anglo-Scottish Union and the Court of James I' in *Transactions of the Royal Historical Society*, 5th Series, XXXIX, 1989

—— 'The Conflicting loyalties of a "Vulgar Counsellor": the third Earl of Southampton 1597–1624' in John Morrill, Paul Slack and Daniel Woolf (eds.), *Public Duty and Private Conscience in Seventeenth Century England: Essays presented to G.E. Aylmer*

Dalrymple, David, Lord Hailes (ed.), *Secret Correspondence of Sir Robert Cecil with James VI King of Scotland*, Edinburgh, 1766

Darmon, Pierre, *Trial by Impotence. Virility and Marriage in pre-revolutionary France*, 1985

Davenant, William, *The Tragedy of Albovine, King of the Lombards*, 1629

Deford, Miriam Allen, *The Overbury Affair*, Philadelphia, 1960

Dent, Arthur, *The Plain Man's Pathway to Heaven*, 1601

Devereux, Walter Bourchier, *Lives and Letters of the Devereux Earls of Essex*, 1853

d'Ewes, Sir Simonds, *Autobiography and Correspondence*, ed. James Orchard Halliwell, 1845

Dibdin, Lewis, *English Church Law and Divorce*, 1912

Dietz, F.C., *English Public Finance*, 1964

—— *Receipts and Issues of the Exchequer during the reigns of James I and Charles I*, Massachusetts, 1928

Donne, John, *Complete Poetry and Selected Prose*, ed. John Hayward, 1962

—— *Letters to Several Persons of Honour*, 1651

Drury, P.J., 'No Other Palace in the Kingdom will Compare with it: the Evolution of Audley End, 1605–1745' in *Architectural History*, XXIII, 1980

Edwards, E., *Life of Sir Walter Ralegh*, 1868

Egerton Papers, ed. J. Payne Collier, Camden Society XII, 1840

Foster, Elizabeth Read (ed.), *Proceedings in Parliament 1610*, 1966

Fraser, Antonia, *The Weaker Vessel*, 1984

Freedman, Sylvia, '*The White Devil and the Fair Woman with a Black Soul*' in Clive Bloom (ed.), *Jacobean Poetry and Prose*, 1988

Gardiner, Samuel R., *History of England from the Accession of James I to the Outbreak of the Civil War*, 1900

—— (ed.), *Parliamentary Debates in 1610*, Camden Society, 1862

—— 'Certain Letters of Diego Sarmiento de Acuna, Count of Gondomar, giving an account of the affair of the Earl of Somerset, with remarks on the career of Somerset as a public man' in *Archaelogia* XLI, 1867

——(ed.), *Narrative of the Spanish Marriage Treaty*, Camden Society CI, 1869

Garrison, Fielding H., *An Introduction to the History of Medicine*, Philadelphia, 1929

Glaister, John, and Rentoul, Edgar, *Medical Jurisprudence and Toxicology*, 1966

Goodman, Godfrey, *The Court of King James I*, ed. J.S. Brewer, 1839

Gough, Charles Edward, *Life and Characters of Sir Thomas Overbury*, Norwich, 1909

Halliwell, James Orchard (ed.), *Secret History of the Reign of King James I*, 1845

Harington, John, *Nugae Antiquae*, selected by Henry Harington, ed. Thomas Park, 1804

Harris, William, *Account of the Life and Writings of James I*, 1753

Hervey, Mary F.S., *Life, Correspondence and Collections of Thomas Howard Earl of Arundel*, Cambridge, 1921

Historical Manuscripts Commission, *Report on the Manuscripts of the Duke of Buccleuch and Queensberry*, Vol. I, 1899

Historical Manuscripts Commission, *Reports on the Manuscripts of Viscount de l'Isle and Dudley*, Vol. V, 1962

Historical Manuscripts Commission, *Report on the Manuscripts of the Marquess of Downshire*, Vols II–VI, 1936–1995

Historical Manuscripts Commission, *Supplementary Report on the Manuscripts of the Earl of Mar and Kellie*, 1930

Historical Manuscripts Commission, *Report on the Manuscripts of the Duke of Portland*, Vol. IX, 1923

Historical Manuscripts Commission, *Calendar of Manuscripts of the Marquess of Salisbury at Hatfield House*, 1883–1923

Holles, John, *Letters of John Holles*, ed. P.R. Seddon, Thoroton Society Record Series, Nottingham, 1975–86

Jonson, Ben, *Masques and Entertainments*, ed. Henry Morley, 1890

Just Downfall of Ambition, Adultery and Murder, 1616

Kelly, Henry Ansgar, *Matrimonial Trials of Henry VIII*, Stanford, 1976

Kempe, Alfred John (ed.), *The Loseley Manuscripts*, 1835

Knowler, William (ed.), *The Earl of Strafford's Letters and Despatches*, 1739

Le Comte, Edward, *The Notorious Lady Essex*, 1970

Lee, Maurice (ed.), *Dudley Carleton to John Chamberlain*, New Jersey, 1972

Leininger, Lorie Jerrell, 'Exploding the Myth of the Lustful Murderess: a Reinterpretation of Frances Howard's Role in the Death of Sir Thomas

Overbury' in *Topic*, XXXVI, 1982

Lilly, William, *Mr William Lilly's History of his Life and Times*, 1715

Lilly, William, *True History of King James I and King Charles I*, 1715

Lindley, David, *The Trials of Frances Howard. Fact and Fiction at the Court of King James*, 1993

Lindquist, Eric, 'The Failure of the Great Contract' in *Journal of Modern History*, LVII, 4 December 1985

Lockyer, Roger, *Buckingham*, 1984

Lodge, Edmund (ed.), *Illustrations of British History*, 1838

Loomie, A.J., *Spain and the Jacobean Catholics 1603–1612*, Vols I & II, Catholic Record Society Publications, LXIV and LXVIII, 1973–1978

—— 'Toleration and Diplomacy: the Religious Issue in Anglo-Spanish Negotiations 1603–5' in *Transactions of American Philosophical Society*, LIII part vi, 1963

McClure, Norman Egbert (ed.), *The Letters of John Chamberlain*. American Philosophical Society, Philadelphia, 1939

McElwee, William, *The Murder of Sir Thomas Overbury*, 1952

Macfarlane, Alan, *Marriage and Love in England 1300–1840*, 1986

McIlwain, C.H. (ed.), *The Political Works of James I*, Harvard, 1918

Marotti, Arthur F., *John Donne and Patronage* in G.F. Lytle and Stephen Orgel (eds.), *Patronage in the Renaissance*, 1981

Mathew, David, *James I*, 1967

—— *The Jacobean Age*, 1938

Mattingly, Garret, *Renaissance Diplomacy*, 1955

Mayerne, Theodore Turquet de, *Medicinal Counsels or Advices*, 1677

Moir, Thomas L., *The Addled Parliament of 1614*, Oxford, 1958

Molyneux, James More, 'Message from King James I to the Earl of Somerset in the case of Sir Thomas Overbury, sent on the 29th December 1615, through Sir George More, Lieutenant of the Tower' in *Archaelogia*, XLI, 1867

Nagy, Doreen, *Popular Medicine in Seventeenth Century England*, Ohio, 1988

Niccholes, Alexander, *A Discourse of Marriage and Wiving*, 1620

Nichols, John, *The Progresses, Processions and Magnificent Festivities of King James I*, 1828

Notestein, Wallace, *The House of Commons 1604–1610*, 1971

Oglander, Sir John, *A Royalist's Notebook*, ed. Francis Bamford, 1936

Orell, John, 'The Agent of Savoy at the Somerset Masque' in *Review of English Studies*, New Series, Vol. XXVIII, 1977

Orgel, Stephen, *The Jonsonian Masque*, Cambridge, Massachusetts, 1965

Overbury, Sir Thomas, *Miscellaneous Works in Prose and Verse*, ed. E.F. Rimbault, 1856

Patterson, R.F. (ed.), *Ben Jonson's Conversations with William Drummond of Hawthornden*, 1923

Peck, Linda Levy, *Northampton: Patronage and Policy at the Court of James I*, 1982

—— (ed.), *The Mental World of the Jacobean Court*, 1991

—— 'Corruption at the Court of James I: the Undermining of Legitimacy', in *After the Reformation: Essays in Honour of J.H. Hexter*, ed. Barbara C. Malament, Manchester, 1980

—— *Court Patronage and Corruption in Early Stuart England*, Boston, 1990

Phillips, Roderick, *Putting Asunder. A History of Divorce in Western Society*, Cambridge, 1988

Prestwich, Menna, *Cranfield. Politics and Profits under the Early Stuarts*, Oxford, 1966

Reformatio Legum, ed. John Foxe, 1571

Roberts, Clayton, and Duncan, Owen, 'The Parliamentary Undertaking of 1614' in *English Historical Review*, XCIII, 1978

Robinson, John Martin, *The Dukes of Norfolk*, Oxford, 1982

Rowse, Alfred Leslie, *Homosexuals in History*, 1977

—— *Simon Forman. Sex and Society in Shakespeare's Age*, 1974

Rushworth, John, *Historical Collections of Private Passages of State*, 1659

Sanderson, James L., 'Poems on an affair of State' in *Review of English Studies*, New Series XVII, 1966

Sanderson, William, *A Complete History of the Lives and Reigns of Mary Queen of Scotland and of her son and successor James VI King of Scotland and after King of Great Britain, Frances and Ireland*, 1656

Saslow, James M., *Ganymede in the Renaissance: Homosexuality in Art and Society*, New Haven, 1986

Schreiber, Roy E., 'The First Carlisle. James Hay, first Earl of Carlisle as Courtier, Diplomat and Entrepreneur' in *Transactions of the American Philosophical Society*, LXXIV, part vii, 1984

Scott, Sir Walter (ed.), *Secret History of the Court of James I*, Edinburgh, 1811

Scott Thomson, Gladys, *Life in a Noble Household*, 1937

Seddon, P.R., 'Robert Carr, Earl of Somerset' in *Renaissance and Modern Studies*, XIV, 1970

Sharpe, Kevin, 'Faction at the Early Stuart Court', in *History Today*, XXXIII, October 1983

—— *Sir Robert Cotton*, Oxford, 1979

—— (ed.), *Faction and Parliament*, 1985

Simpson, Keith, *Forensic Medicine*, 1950

Smith, Bruce R., *Homosexual Desire in Shakespeare's England. A Cultural*

Poetics, Chicago, 1991

Smuts, R. Malcolm, *Court Culture and the Origins of a Royalist Tradition in Early Stuart England*, Philadelphia, 1987

Snow, Vernon F., *Essex the Rebel. A life of Robert Deverux, Third Earl of Essex*, Lincoln, Nebraska, 1970

Spedding, James (ed.), *The Works of Francis Bacon*, 1857–74

—— 'Review of the Evidence respecting the conduct of King James I in the case of Sir Thomas Overbury' in *Archaelogia*, XLI, part i, 1867

State Trials, *A Complete Collection of State Trials*, ed. William Cobbett, 1809

Stephen, Sir James Fitzjames, *History of the Criminal Law of England*, 1883

Stone, Lawrence, *The Family, Sex and Marriage in England 1500–1800*, 1977

—— *The Crisis of the Aristocracy*, Oxford, 1965

—— *The Road to Divorce, England 1530–1987*, Oxford, 1990

—— *Family and Fortune*, Oxford, 1973

Strong, Roy, *Henry, Prince of Wales and England's Lost Renaissance*, 1986

Strong, Roy, *Tudor and Jacobean Portraits*, 1969

Strong, Roy, and Orgel, Stephen, *The Theatre of the Stuart Court*, California, 1973

Tillières, Comte Leveneur de, *Mémoires* ed. M.C. Hippeau, Paris, 1863

Thomas, Keith, *Religion and the Decline of Magic*, 1971

Thompson, C.J.S., *Poisons and Poisoners*, 1931

Trevor-Roper, Hugh, 'Medicine at the Early Stuart Court' in *From Counter Reformation to Glorious Revolution*, 1992

Truth Brought to Light or Narrative History of King James for the First Fourteen Years, ed. Walter Scott in Somers Tracts, II, 1809

Upton, Anthony F., *Sir Arthur Ingram*, Oxford, 1961

Weldon, Sir Anthony, *The Court and Character of King James I* in W. Scott (ed.), *Secret History of the Court of James I*, 1811

Welsby, Paul A., *George Abbot, the Unwanted Archbishop*, 1962

—— *Lancelot Andrewes*

White, Beatrice, *Cast of Ravens. The Strange Case of Sir Thomas Overbury*, 1965

Wilbraham, Sir Roger, *Journal*, Camden Miscellany, X, 1902

Willson, David Harris, *The Privy Councillors in the House of Commons, 1604–29*, Minneapolis, 1940

—— *James VI and I*, 1956

Wilson, Arthur, *The History of Great Britain, being the Life and Reign of King James I*, 1653

Winnett, A. R., *Divorce and Remarriage in Anglicanism*, 1958

Winwood, Ralph, *Memorials of Affairs of State in the Reigns of Queen Elizabeth and King James I*, 1725

Wormald, Jenny, 'James VI and I: Two Kings or One?' in *History*, New Series, LXVII, 1983

Wotton, Sir Henry, *Life and Letters of Sir Henry Wotton*, ed. Logan Pearsall Smith, Oxford, 1907

Zagorin, Perez, *The Court and the Country*, 1969

INDEX